AN INVITATION TO COMPUTER SCIENCE

SECOND EDITION

G. Michael Schneider
Macalester College

Judith L. Gersting
University of Hawaii—Hilo

Contributing author:
Sara Baase
San Diego State University

PWS Publishing

An Imprint of Brooks/Cole Publishing Company

I(T)P® An International Thomson Publishing Company

Pacific Grove • Albany • Belmont • Bonn • Boston • Cincinnati • Detroit • Johannesburg • London •
Madrid • Melbourne • Mexico City • New York • Paris • Singapore • Tokyo • Toronto • Washington

Sponsoring Editor: *Mike Sugarman*
Marketing Team: *Nathan Wilbur, Michele Mootz*
Editorial Associate: *Kathryn Schooling*
Production Editor: *Marlene Thom*
Production: *Pre-Press Company, Inc.*
Manuscript Editor: *Connie Day*

Manufacturing Buyer: *Vena Dyer*
Interior Design: *Geri Davis*
Interior Illustration: *Pre-Press Company, Inc.*
Cover Design: *Roger Knox*
Typesetting: *Pre-Press Company, Inc.*
Printing and Binding: *The Courier Co., Inc./Kendallville*

For more information, contact PWS Publishing at BROOKS/COLE PUBLISHING COMPANY:

BROOKS/COLE PUBLISHING COMPANY
511 Forest Lodge Road
Pacific Grove, CA 93950, USA

International Thomson Editores
Seneca 53, Col. Polanco
11560 México, D.F., México

International Thomson Publishing Europe
Berkshire House 168-173
High Holborn
London WC1V 7AA, England

International Thomson Publishing GmbH
Königswinterer Strasse 418
53227 Bonn, Germany

Nelson ITP
102 Dodds Street
South Melbourne, 3205
Victoria, Australia

International Thomson Publishing Asia
#05-10 Henderson Building
Singapore 0315

Nelson Canada
1120 Birchmount Road
Scarborough, Ontario, Canada M1K 5G4

International Thomson Publishing Japan
Hirakawacho Kyowa Building, 3F
2-2-1 Hirakawacho
Chiyoda-ku, Tokyo 102, Japan

Library of Congress Cataloging-in-Publication Data

Schneider, G. Michael.
    An invitation to computer science / G. Michael Schneider, Judith
L. Gersting; contributing author, Sara Baase.—2nd ed.
        p.   cm.
    Includes bibliographical references and index.
    ISBN 0-534-95115-5
    1. Computer science.   I. Gersting, Judith L.   II. Baase, Sara.
III. Title.
QA76.S3594   1998
004—dc21   98-30006
                                                       CIP

To my wife, Ruthann, and my children, Benjamin and Rebecca

G.M.S

To my husband, John, and to our children, Adam and Jason

J.L.G.

BRIEF CONTENTS

CONTENTS

Level 3

The Virtual Machine   232

Level 5

Applications   516

We have been enormously pleased by the enthusiastic response to the first edition of *Invitation to Computer Science*. The book has been used in many different and interesting ways: in a service course for non-majors, in a breadth-first introductory course for computer science majors, as a supporting text for high school and community college courses, and even in a "computer science immersion course" jointly taught by all the members of the computer science department. We believe that in the years to come an introductory overview class will play an increasingly important role in the undergraduate computer science curriculum.

In the second edition of *Invitation to Computer Science*, we have maintained the fundamental six-layer hierarchical structure of the first edition. However, we have made modifications to reflect the changes that have taken place in the discipline in the last three to four years. The most significant of these changes are described in the following paragraphs.

1. In Chapter 7, the language used to teach the basic concepts of programming has been changed from Pascal to C++. Although we feel that Pascal is still an excellent teaching language, most departments have switched to a more modern object-oriented language, either C++ or Java. For schools that use the text in a first course for majors, this meant that students were exposed to a language (Pascal) that they would probably not see again. We changed to C++ so that students would learn a language they will use extensively in future courses. Chapter 7 introduces the basic "imperative language" subset of C++, including data types, declarations, functions, parameters, assignment, conditional, and iteration. To support this change to C++, we have modified our laboratory software to include a C++ compiler in place of the Pascal compiler that came with the first edition. This will allow students to write, compile, and execute simple C++ programs.

2. To make programming more fun, as well as to reflect the growing importance of visualization, we have added to Chapter 7 a new section called "Graphical Programming." It discusses how graphics are implemented in hardware and software, describes typical software routines used to produce screen images, and explains how to create visual metaphors such as buttons and windows. To support this new section, our C++ laboratory compiler has been extended to include a small but realistic graphics library that students can use to create various shapes and images. This library contains a typical set of graphical functions—drawing circles, lines, and rectangles and setting background and pen colors. In addition, the laboratory manual includes a new laboratory experience (Laboratory Experience 13: C++ Programming, Graphics) that gives students the opportunity to do interesting graphical programming.

3. Because we now use C++ to teach basic programming language concepts, we can exploit that change by using the advanced features of C++ to introduce important concepts in object-oriented programming (OOP). Chapter 8 introduces some interesting OOP features of the language, such as classes, objects, and member functions. Rather than focus on detailed syntactic and semantic issues, which are really not appropriate, the text concentrates on the *why* of object-oriented programming: Why is object-oriented programming such an important design tool, and why are so many installations using this type of language for software development? Chapter 8 also takes a brief look at three special-purpose languages that have become more important to the computer science community in the last few years, SQL, Perl, and HTML.

4. The single biggest change in this second edition is the inclusion of a new chapter entitled "Computer Networks." As we all know, the rapid growth of network technology—LANs, the Internet, the Web, wireless—has caused enormous changes in both the field of computer science and society at large. We felt we could reflect the magnitude of this change only with a totally new chapter that provides a comprehensive summary of this area. Chapter 12 contains a detailed introduction to network technology, including transmission media, communication techniques, classes of networks (LANs, WANs), and network protocols, including Ethernet and TCP/IP. There is also a comprehensive historical overview of both the Internet and the World Wide Web. Finally, to give students some hands-on practice, there is a new network-related laboratory experience (Laboratory Experience 20: HTML and FTP Downloading) that introduces HTML programming and file transfer across a network.

5. We have significantly expanded and updated the chapter entitled "Artificial Intelligence" (which was Chapter 12 in the first edition but is Chapter 13 in this edition). The chapter has extensive new material on neural networks and how they are used to implement recognition and machine learning. It also includes a new section on searching and intelligent agents. To give students experience with this material, the laboratory software has been expanded to include a neural network simulator and a new laboratory experience on character recognition and machine learning (Laboratory Experience 21: Neural Networks).

These are the major changes in this new edition of *An Invitation to Computer Science*. However, many important but smaller changes are also sprinkled throughout the text. These include

- A discussion of floating-point representations in Chapter 4
- New material on cache memories in Chapter 5
- An expanded discussion in Chapter 14 on social issues aggravated by the growth of the Internet and the Web, including encryption, privacy, and the security of electronic commerce
- New boxed sections throughout the text that present fascinating facts as well as interesting supplementary material
- New Challenge Work problems at the end of every chapter. These are larger assignments appropriate for written reports, course projects, or team assignments.
- A selected Bibliography (entitled For Further Reading) at the end of each chapter
- The inclusion throughout the text of interesting Web addresses where students can go for additional material. To ensure that all students know how to use the Web, Laboratory Experience 1 has been expanded to include a section on Web browsing.

We hope you will be pleased with the changes made to the text, the laboratory manual, and the accompanying software and that you will find them beneficial in teaching your course. We believe that these changes will give students a more comprehensive and up-to-date overview of computer science.

We would like to thank the following reviewers for their helpful comments:

Susan T. Dean
Samford University

Lenwood S. Heath
*Virginia Polytechnic Institute
and State University*

Alan R. Hevner
University of South Florida

Gretchen Lynn
West Virginia Wesleyan College

Ellen L. Walker
Hiram College

Robert Walker
Kent State University

G. Michael Schneider
Macalester College
schneider@macalester.edu

Judith L. Gersting
University of Hawaii—Hilo
gersting@hawaii.edu

This is a text for a one-semester introductory course in computer science. It assumes no prior background or experience, and it is appropriate for use by either nonmajors or majors who want a broad overview of the field.

Introductory computer science service courses for nonmajors have undergone a number of changes in the last few years. In the 1970s and early 1980s, they were usually programming courses in FORTRAN, Pascal, or BASIC. At that time, it was felt that programming in a high-level language was the most important computing skill that students (usually of science or engineering) could acquire. In the mid- and late 1980s, the rapid growth in the use of computing caused the course to evolve into something called "computer literacy," where students learned about new applications of computers in such fields as business, medicine, law, education, and the arts. Finally, with the increased availability of personal computers and useful software packages, a typical early-1990s version of the computer science service course spends a semester teaching students how to use word processors, databases, spreadsheets, bulletin boards, and electronic mail.

Many people feel that the time is right for the introductory course in computer science to undergo yet another change. There are two reasons for this. First, many students coming to college today are quite familiar with personal computers and productivity software. They have been writing with word processors since high school and have been using networks, e-mail, and bulletin boards for years. (In fact, it is not uncommon for students to know more about computer networks than faculty members.) A course that teaches how to use software packages will be of little interest. Second, a course that concentrates on only one aspect of computer science, be it programming or applications, can give students a highly misleading view of our discipline. It is not unusual for students completing a computer literacy course to view computer science as simply the study of programming or software packages, a notably incorrect perception.

The feeling of many teachers now is that the first course should provide a breadth-first overview that introduces students to a wide range of topics in computer science. The material covered in this course could include such important and interesting topics as algorithms, hardware design, computer organization, system software, language models, programming, compilation, theory of computation, artificial intelligence, and social issues of computing. Students would be introduced to the richness of ideas addressed by professionals in computer science. A breadth-first approach would also bring us into line with most other scientific disciplines with respect to their survey course for nonmajors. For example, a chemistry service course introduces fundamental concepts (atoms, molecules, reactions) in addition to the uses and applications of chemistry. Similarly, a beginning physics course for nonmajors spends much of its time on a broad range of important theoretical concepts, such as elementary particles, force, matter, and energy.

That is exactly how this book is organized. It is a one-semester, breadth-first introduction to the discipline of computer science. It assumes absolutely no background in computer science, programming, or mathematics. It is appropriate for use as a text for a service course for students not majoring in computer science. It would also be fully appropriate for use at schools where the first course for majors is an overview of the discipline rather than a programming course in Pascal, C/C++, Java, or Scheme.

The text introduces a wide range of subject matter. However, it is not enough simply to present a mass of material, a wealth of facts and details. The discussion must be woven into some fabric, an organized theme that can unite the many topics covered. The book must create a big picture of computer science. Our way of offering such an overview is to present the discipline of computer science as a six-layer hierarchy of abstractions, with each layer in the hierarchy building on ideas and concepts presented earlier. Just as the chemist builds from protons and electrons to molecules and then to compounds, so too does this text build from such elementary concepts as algorithms, gates and circuits to higher-level ideas such as computer systems, virtual machines, languages, applications, and the social, legal, and ethical problems of technology.

The six levels in our hierarchy are

Level 1. The Algorithmic Foundations of Computer Science

Level 2. The Hardware World

Level 3. The Virtual Machine

Level 4. The Software World

Level 5. Applications

Level 6. Social Issues

Following an introductory chapter, Level 1 introduces the algorithmic foundations of computer science, the bedrock on which all other aspects of the discipline are built. It presents such important ideas as the design of algorithms, algorithmic problem solving, abstraction, pseudocode, iteration, and efficiency.

It illustrates these ideas using such well-known examples as searching a list, finding the largest element, sorting a list, and pattern matching.

The discussion in Level 1 assumes that our algorithms are executed by something called a "computing agent," an abstract concept for anything that can carry out the instructions in our solution. Then in Level 2, we say that we would like these algorithms to be executed by "real" computers to produce "real" results. Thus begins our discussion of hardware and computer organization. The initial discussion presents the basic building blocks of computer systems—binary numbers, Boolean logic, gates, and circuits. It then shows how these elementary concepts are used to construct a real computer, and it introduces the classic Von Neumann model of computing. It also presents a typical machine language instruction set and discusses how algorithms from Level 1 can be represented in machine language and run on the hardware of Level 2. It ends with a discussion of new directions in hardware design—massively parallel processors.

By the end of Level 2, students have been introduced to the basic concepts of logic design and computer organization, and they can appreciate the complexity of these subjects. This complexity is the motivation for Level 3, the virtual machine environment. This section describes how system software produces a user-oriented problem-solving environment that hides many of the hardware details discussed earlier. It presents the same problem discussed in Level 2, encoding an algorithm and running it, and it shows how easy that is to do in a virtual environment that contains software tools such as text editors, assemblers, loaders, and an operating system. Level 3 also discusses the services and responsibilities of operating systems and introduces the different types of systems that can be created, such as real-time systems, embedded computers, time sharing, local-area networks, and distributed systems.

Now that we have a supportive problem-solving environment, what do we want to do? Most likely we want to write programs to solve interesting problems. This becomes the motivation for Level 4, the world of software. Although the book should not be seen as a programming text, it contains an introduction to procedural languages and some of their most important concepts—variables, data types, assignment, conditional, iteration, and procedures. This will give students an appreciation for the task of the programmer and the power of the problem-solving environment created by a modern high-level programming language. However, we also want students to know that there are many other high-level language models, so the text includes an overview of the functional, logic, parallel, and object-oriented paradigms. This section also describes the design and construction of a compiler and shows how the programming languages described earlier must be translated into machine language for execution. This material ties together many ideas introduced earlier as it shows how an algorithm (Level 1) is coded into a high-level language and compiled into machine language (Level 4) and executed on a typical Von Neumann machine (Level 2) using the system software tools of Level 3. These frequent references to earlier concepts help to reinforce those ideas, and the use of "recurring themes" is a common teaching method in this text. In the conclusion to Level 4, we introduce the idea of computability and unsolvability. It describes a formal model of computing (a Turing machine) and uses that model to show that there are problems for which no general algorithmic solution can be found.

We now have a supportive software environment in which it is possible to write programs to solve important problems. The question is, What problems should we solve? What are some of the most important applications of computers? In Level 5 we present a few important uses of computers, including spreadsheets and modeling, databases, numeric and symbolic computing, networks, electronic mail, and artificial intelligence. There is no way in one section to cover all the important applications of information technology or to cover specific applications in minute detail. Our goal is to show students that application software packages are not "magic boxes" but rather are the result of the intelligent use of the computer science concepts developed in earlier chapters. We hope that this introduction to a few key applications will encourage readers to seek out information on applications that are specific to their own interests.

Finally, we reach the highest level of study, Level 6, which addresses social, ethical, legal, and professional issues raised by the applications discussed in Level 5. This section (written by contributing author Sara Baase) talks about such thorny problems as privacy concerns aggravated by the growth of on-line databases and security problems caused by the use of networks and telecommunication. This section introduces students to important social issues and makes them aware of the enormous impact that computer science and computer technology is having on society.

This, then, is the hierarchical structure of the text. It begins with the algorithmic foundations of the discipline and works its way upward from low-level hardware concepts through virtual machine environments, languages, software, and applications programs to the social issues raised by computer technology. This organizational tool is one of the most important aspects of the book; it enables us to present computer science as a unified, integrated, and coherent discipline.

Another important development in our field is the realization that, like physics, chemistry, and biology, computer science is an empirical, laboratory-based discipline in which learning comes not only from listening but also from doing and trying. Many complex ideas in computer science cannot be truly understood until they are visualized, observed, and manipulated. Today, most computer science faculty view a laboratory component as an essential part of every introductory course. This important development is fully reflected in our approach to teaching computer science. Associated with the text are a laboratory manual and custom-designed laboratory software that enable students to experiment with the concepts presented in this text.

The manual contains 21 separate laboratory experiences. Each laboratory assignment includes software that visualizes an important concept and gives students the chance to observe, study, analyze, and modify. For example, associated with Level 1 (the algorithmic foundations of computer science) are labs that animate the algorithms presented in Chapters 2 and 3 and that analyze the running time of these algorithms for different-sized data sets. Associated with Level 2 (the hardware world) are experiments that allow students to design and analyze logic circuits and program a simulated Von Neumann machine identical to the one presented in the text. To support Level 4 there are a compiler and graphics library that allow students to write a range of interesting programs.

Similarly, there are laboratory projects for virtually all the concepts discussed in the text. Each of the laboratories includes an explanation of how to use the software, a description of how to conduct the experiment, and discussion questions and problems for students to complete. Students should be able to work on their own or in collaborative teams to run these lab experiments, in either a closed-lab or an open-lab setting. Lab Experience 1 serves as an introduction to the entire software suite and also provides the students with a useful glossary-building tool that they can use with the text (and with other courses as well).

Computer science is a young and exciting discipline, and we hope that the material in this text, along with the laboratory projects, will convey this feeling of newness and excitement. By presenting the field in all of its richness—algorithms, hardware, software, applications, social issues—we hope to give students a deeper appreciation for the many diverse and interesting areas of research and study within the discipline of computer science.

We would like to thank the following reviewers for their valuable comments:

Ernest C. Ackermann
Mary Washington College

Elizabeth S. Adams
Hood College

Virginia T. Anderson
University of North Dakota

William N. Anderson, Jr.
Fairleigh Dickinson University

James D. Arthur
Virgina Polytechnic Institute

Douglas Baldwin
SUNY—Geneseo

Adrienne G. Bloss
Roanoke College

Anselm Blumer
Tufts University

Kim B. Bruce
Williams College

Jim Carter
University of Saskatchewan

Lillian N. Cassel
Villanova University

Darrah Chavey
Beloit College

John Cigas
Rockhurst College

David Cordes
University of Alabama

Lee D. Cornell
Mankato State University

Michelle Wahl Craig
University of Toronto

Grace Anne Crowder
Towson State University

Fadi Pierre Deek
New Jersey Institute of Technology

Herbert L. Dershem
Hope College

Maurice L. Eggen
Trinity University

Henry A. Etlinger
Rochester Institute of Technology

Daniel J. Falabella
Albright College

John E. Howland
Trinity University

Mary Kolesar
Utah State University

Ken Lambert
Washington & Lee University

Rickard A. Lejk
University of North Carolina

Jimmie M. Purser
Millsaps College

Samuel A. Rebelsky
Dartmouth College

Jane M. Ritter
University of Oregon

Larry F. Sells
Oklahoma City University

Cliff Shaffer
Virgina Polytechnic Institute

Angela B. Shiflet
Wofford College

Ted Sjoerdsma
Washington & Lee University

Jeff Slomka
Southwest Texas State University

Gordon A. Stegink
Hope College

Paul Stephan
Case Western Reserve University

Bill Taffe
Plymouth State College

Robert J. Wernick
San Francisco State University

Tom Whaley
Washington & Lee University

Craig E. Wills
Worcester Polytechnic Institute

Carol W. Wilson
Western Kentucky University

AN INTRODUCTION TO COMPUTER SCIENCE

1.1   INTRODUCTION

This text is an invitation to learn about one of the youngest and most exciting of scientific disciplines—**computer science**. Almost every day our newspapers, magazines, and televisions carry reports of new advances in computing, such as virtual reality systems that generate amazingly realistic three-dimensional images; high-speed supercomputers that perform trillions of mathematical operations per second; computer networks that transmit text, sound, and pictures anywhere in the world in fractions of a second; and chess programs that defeat top-ranked grand masters. The next few years will see technological breakthroughs that, until a few years ago, existed only in the minds of dreamers and science fiction writers. These are exciting times in computing, and our goal in this text is to provide the reader with an understanding of computer science and an appreciation for the diverse areas of research and study within this important new field.

Despite its simple-sounding name, computer science is unusual in that many people do not have an intuitive feel for the types of problems that professionals in this area study. The average person can produce a reasonably accurate description of most scientific fields, even if he or she did not study the subject in school. For example, you probably know that biology is the study of living organisms and that chemistry deals with the structure and composition of matter. However, you might not have the same intuitive understanding for the type of work that goes on in computer science. Before we describe what computer science is, let's look at a few common misconceptions about this new field of study.

MISCONCEPTION 1:   *Computer science is the study of computers.*

This apparently obvious definition is actually incorrect or, to put it more precisely, incomplete. For example, some of the earliest and most fundamental theoretical work in computer science took place during the period 1920–1940, years before the development of the first computer system. (This pioneering work was initially considered a branch of logic and applied mathematics, not the emergence of a new discipline. Computer science did not come to be recognized as a separate and independent field of scientific study until the late 1950s or early 1960s.) Even today, there are branches of computer science quite distinct from a study of "real" machines. In *theoretical computer science*, for example, researchers study the logical and mathematical properties of problems and their solutions. Frequently, these researchers investigate problems not with actual computers but rather with *formal models* of computation, which are easier to study and analyze mathematically. Their work involves pencil and paper, not circuits and disks.

This distinction between computers and computer science was beautifully expressed by computer scientists Michael R. Fellows and Ian Parberry in an article in the journal *Computing Research News*:

> Computer science is no more about computers than astronomy is about telescopes, biology is about microscopes, or chemistry is about beakers and test tubes. Science is not about tools. It is about how we use them, and what we find out when we do.[1]

MISCONCEPTION 2:   *Computer science is the study of how to write computer programs.*

For many people, an introduction to computer science involves learning to write programs in a language such as Pascal, C++, Scheme, or Java. This almost

---

[1] M. R. Fellows and I. Parberry, "Getting Children Excited About Computer Science," *Computing Research News* 5, no. 1 (January 1993).

universal use of programming as the entry to the discipline can create the misunderstanding that computer science is equivalent to computer programming. Again, this is a misleading point of view.

Programming is extremely important to the field, but it is so primarily as a tool by which researchers can study new ideas and build and test new solutions. When a computer scientist has designed and analyzed a new approach to solving a problem or has created a new way to represent information, then he or she will implement that idea as a computer program in order to test it on an actual computer system. This permits the researcher to see how well these new ideas work and whether they perform better than previous methods.

For example, searching a list to locate a specific item is one of the most common applications of computers, and it is frequently applied to huge problems, such as finding one name among the approximately 20,000,000 listings in the New York City telephone directory. (We will solve this problem in the next chapter.) A more efficient look-up method would be quite useful to both the telephone company and its users by reducing the time that customers must wait for directory assistance. Assume that we have designed what we believe to be a "new, improved" search technique. After analyzing it theoretically, we would study it empirically. We would write a program to implement our new method, execute it on our computer, and measure its performance: how much memory is required to store the program and data, and how much time it takes to locate a particular name. These tests would demonstrate under what conditions our new method is or is not better than the directory search procedures currently in use.

In computer science, it is not only the construction of a high-quality program that is important but also the methods it embodies, the services it provides, and the results it produces. It is possible to become so enmeshed in writing code and getting it to run that we forget that a program is only a means to an end, not an end in itself.

MISCONCEPTION 3: *Computer science is the study of the uses and applications of computers and software.*

If one's introduction to computer science is not programming, then it may be a course on the application of computers and software. Such a course typically involves learning to use a number of popular software packages, such as word processors, spreadsheets, database systems, electronic mail, and a World Wide Web browser.

These packages are widely used by professionals in all fields. However, learning to use a software package is no more a part of computer science than driver's education is a branch of automotive engineering. A wide range of people *use* computer software, but the computer scientist is responsible for *specifying, designing, building,* and *testing* software packages as well as the computer systems on which they run.

Looking back at the previous discussion, we can see that these three views of computer science are not necessarily wrong; they are just woefully incomplete. Concepts such as computers, programming languages, software, and applications *are* part of the discipline of computer science, but individually they do not capture the richness and diversity of this new field.

We have spent a good deal of time saying what computer science is *not*. What, then, is it? What are its basic concepts? What are the fundamental questions studied by professionals in this field? Is it possible to capture the breadth and scope of the discipline in a single definition? We answer these fundamental questions in the next section and, indeed, in the remainder of the text.

1.2   THE DEFINITION OF COMPUTER SCIENCE

There are many definitions of computer science, but the one that we feel best captures the richness and breadth of ideas embodied in this new field was first proposed by Professors Norman Gibbs and Allen Tucker.[2] As we will see from their definition, the central concept in computer science is the **algorithm**, and it is not possible to understand the field without a thorough understanding of this critically important idea. The Gibbs and Tucker definition of computer science follows.

Definition

Computer science   the study of algorithms, including

1. Their formal and mathematical properties
2. Their hardware realizations
3. Their linguistic realizations
4. Their applications

This definition says that it is the task of the computer scientist to design and develop algorithms to solve a range of important problems. This process includes the following operations:

- Studying the behavior of algorithms to determine whether they are correct and efficient (their formal and mathematical properties)
- Designing and building computer systems that are able to execute algorithms (their hardware realizations)
- Designing programming languages and translating algorithms into these languages so that they can be executed by the hardware (their linguistic realizations)
- Identifying important problems and designing correct and efficient software packages to solve these problems (their applications)

[2] N. E. Gibbs and A. B. Tucker, "A Model Curriculum for a Liberal Arts Degree in Computer Science," *Comm. of the ACM* 29, no. 3 (March 1986).

Because it is impossible to appreciate this definition fully without knowing what an algorithm is, let's look more closely at this term. We will first describe it informally and then, in the next section, examine this term much more rigorously.

The dictionary defines the word *algorithm* as follows:

al • go • rithm   n. *A procedure for solving a mathematical problem in a finite number of steps that frequently involves repetition of an operation; broadly: a step-by-step method for accomplishing some task.*

Informally, an algorithm is an ordered sequence of instructions that is guaranteed to solve a specific problem. It is a list that looks something like this:

STEP 1   Do something

STEP 2   Do something

STEP 3   Do something

:
:

STEP N   Stop, you are finished

If you are handed this list and carefully follow its instructions in the order specified, then when you reach the end, you will have solved the task at hand.

The operations used to construct algorithms all belong to one of only three categories:

1. *Sequential operations* A sequential instruction carries out a single well-defined task. When that task is finished, the algorithm moves on to the next operation. Sequential operations are usually expressed as simple declarative sentences.
   - Add 1 cup of butter to the mixture in the bowl.
   - Subtract the amount of the check from the current account balance.
   - Set the value of x to 1.

2. *Conditional operations* These are the "question-asking" instructions of an algorithm. They ask a question and then select the next operation to be executed on the basis of the answer to that question.
   - If the mixture is too dry, then add ½ cup of water to the bowl.
   - If the amount of the check is less than or equal to the current account balance, then cash the check; otherwise, tell the person that the account is overdrawn.
   - If x is not equal to 0, then set y equal to $1/x$; otherwise, print an error message that says we cannot divide by 0.

3. *Iterative operations* These are the "looping" instructions of an algorithm. They tell us not to go on to the next instruction but, instead, to go back and repeat the execution of a previous block of instructions.
   - Repeat the previous two operations until the mixture has thickened.
   - Repeat the following five steps until there are no more checks to be processed.
   - Repeat steps 1, 2, and 3 until the value of y is equal to +1.

We use algorithms (although we don't use that word) all the time—whenever we follow a set of instructions to assemble a child's toy, bake a cake, balance a checkbook, or go through the college registration process. A good example of an algorithm used in everyday life is the set of instructions shown in Figure 1.1 for programming a VCR to record a sequence of television shows. Note the three types of instructions in this algorithm: sequential (steps 2, 4, 5, 6, and 8), conditional (steps 1 and 7), and iterative (step 3).

Mathematicians use algorithms all the time, and much of the work done by early Greek, Roman, Persian, and Indian mathematicians involved the discovery of algorithms for important problems in geometry and arithmetic; an example is *Euclid's algorithm* for finding the greatest common divisor of two positive integers. (Exercise 7 at the end of the chapter presents this 2300-year-old algorithm.) We also studied algorithms in elementary school, even if we didn't know it. For example, in the first grade we learned an algorithm for adding two numbers such as

$$
\begin{array}{r}
47 \\
+25 \\
\hline
72
\end{array}
$$

The instructions our teacher gave were as follows: First add the rightmost column of numbers (7 + 5), getting the value 12. Write down the 2 under the line and carry the 1 to the next column. Now move left to the next column, adding (4 + 2) and the previous carry value of 1 to get the value 7. Write this value under the line, producing the correct answer 72.

Although as children we learned this algorithm informally, it can, like the VCR instructions in Figure 1.1, be written formally as an explicit sequence of in-

---

FIGURE 1.1

Programming Your VCR.
Example of an Algorithm

Algorithm for Programming Your VCR

Step 1   If the clock and calendar are not correctly set, then go to page 9 of the instruction manual and follow the instructions there before proceeding.

Step 2   Place a blank tape into the VCR tape slot.

Step 3   Repeat steps 4 through 7 for each program that you wish to record, up to a maximum of 10 shows.

Step 4   Enter the channel number that you wish to record, and press the button labeled CHAN.

Step 5   Enter the time that you wish recording to start, and then press the button labeled TIME-START.

Step 6   Enter the time that you wish recording to stop, and then press the button labeled TIME-FINISH.

Step 7   This completes the programming of one show. If you do not wish to record anything else press the button labeled END-PROG.

Step 8   Press the button labeled TIMER. Your VCR is now ready to record.

Abu Ja'far Muhammad ibn-Musa Al-Khowarizmi
(A.D. 780–850)

The word *algorithm* is derived from the last name of Muhammad ibn-Musa Al-Khowarizmi, a famous Persian mathematician and author of the eighth and ninth centuries. Al-Khowarizmi was a teacher at the Mathematical Institute in Baghdad and the author of the book *Kitab al jabr w'al muqabala*, which in English means "Rules of Restoration and Reduction." It was one of the earliest mathematical textbooks, and its title gave us the word *algebra* (the Arabic word *al jabr* means "reduction").

In A.D. 825, Al-Khowarizmi wrote another book about the base-10 positional numbering system that had recently been developed in India. In this book he described formalized, step-by-step procedures for doing arithmetic operations, such as addition, subtraction, and multiplication, on numbers represented in this new decimal system. In the twelfth century this book was translated into Latin, introducing the base-10 Hindu-Arabic numbering system to Europe, and Al-Khowarizmi's name became closely associated with these formal numerical techniques. When written in Latin characters rather than Arabic, his last name became rendered as Algorismus, and eventually the formalized procedures that he pioneered and developed became known as *algorithms* in his honor.

structions. Figure 1.2 shows an algorithm for adding two positive m-digit numbers. It expresses formally the operations informally described above. Again, note the three types of instructions used to construct the algorithm: sequential (steps 1, 2, 4, 6, 7, 8, and 9), conditional (step 5), and iterative (step 3).

FIGURE 1.2

Algorithm for Adding Two m-Digit Numbers

Algorithm for Adding Two m-Digit Numbers

Given: $m \geq 1$ and two positive numbers each containing m digits, $a_{m-1}\,a_{m-2}\cdots a_0$ and $b_{m-1}\,b_{m-2}\cdots b_0$
Wanted: $c_m\,c_{m-1}\,c_{m-2}\cdots c_0$, where $c_m\,c_{m-1}\,c_{m-2}\cdots c_0 = (a_{m-1}\,a_{m-2}\cdots a_0) + (b_{m-1}\,b_{m-2}\cdots b_0)$
Algorithm:

Step 1   Set the value of *carry* to 0.

Step 2   Set the value of i equal to the value 0.

Step 3   Repeat the instructions in steps 4 through 6 until the value of i is greater than $m - 1$.

   Step 4.   Add the two digits a_i and b_i to the current value of *carry* to get c_i.

   Step 5.   If $c_i \geq 10$, then reset c_i to ($c_i - 10$) and reset the value of *carry* to 1; otherwise, set the new value of *carry* to 0.

   Step 6.   Add 1 to i, effectively moving one column to the left.

Step 7   Set c_m to the value of *carry*.

Step 8   Print out the final answer, $c_m\,c_{m-1}\,c_{m-2}\cdots c_0$.

Step 9   Stop.

Even though it may not look it, this is the same "decimal addition algorithm" that you learned in grade school; and if you follow it rigorously, it is guaranteed to produce the correct result. Let's watch it work.

Add   (47 + 25)

$$m = 2$$
$$a_1 = 4 \quad a_0 = 7$$ $\left.\right\}$ The input
$$b_1 = 2 \quad b_0 = 5$$

Step 1 $carry = 0.$

Step 2 $i = 0.$

Step 3   We are now going to repeat steps 4 through 6 until i is greater than 1.

First repetition of the loop   (i has the value 0)

   Step 4   Add ($a_0 + b_0 + carry$), which is $7 + 5 + 0$, so $c_0 = 12$.

   Step 5   Because $c_0 \geq 10$, we reset **c_0 to 2** and reset $carry$ to 1.

   Step 6   Reset i to $(0 + 1) = 1$. Because i is not greater than 1, go back to step 4.

Second repetition of the loop   (i has the value 1)

   Step 4   Add ($a_1 + b_1 + carry$), which is $4 + 2 + 1$, so **$c_1 = 7$**.

   Step 5   Because $c_1 < 10$, we reset $carry$ to 0.

   Step 6   Reset i to $(1 + 1) = 2$. Because i is greater than 1, do not repeat but go to step 7.

Step 7   Set **$c_2 = 0$**.

Step 8   Print out the answer $c_2 c_1 c_0 = 072$ (see the boldface values).

Step 9   Stop.

We have reached the end of the algorithm, and it has correctly produced the sum of the two numbers 47 and 25, the three-digit result 072. (A slightly more clever algorithm would omit the unnecessary leading zero at the beginning of the number if the last carry value were a zero. We leave that modification as an exercise.) Try working through the algorithm shown in Figure 1.2 with another pair of numbers to be sure that you understand exactly how it functions.

The addition algorithm shown in Figure 1.2 is a highly formalized representation of a technique that most people learned in the first or second grade and that virtually everyone knows how to do informally. Why would we take such a simple task as adding two numbers and express it in so complicated a fashion? Why are formal algorithms so important in computer science? The answer is because of the following fundamentally important point:

> *If we can specify an algorithm to solve a problem, then we can automate its solution.*

Once we have formally specified an algorithm, we can build a machine (or write a program or hire a person) to carry out the steps contained in the algorithm. The machine (or program or person) does not need to be smart enough to understand the concepts or ideas behind the solution. It merely has to do step 1, step 2, step 3, . . . exactly as written. In computer science terminology, the machine, robot, person, or thing carrying out the steps of the algorithm is called a **computing agent**.

Thus computer science can be viewed as "the science of algorithmic problem solving." Much of the research and development work in computer science involves discovering correct and efficient algorithms for a wide range of interesting problems, studying their properties, designing programming languages into which those algorithms can be encoded, and designing and building computer systems that can automatically execute these algorithms in an efficient manner.

At first glance, it may seem that every problem can be solved algorithmically. However, as we shall see, that is not true. Chapter 10 will present the startling result (first proved by the German logician Kurt Gödel in the early 1930s) that there are problems for which no generalized algorithmic solution can possibly exist. These problems are, in a sense, *unsolvable*. No matter how much time and effort is put into obtaining a solution, none will ever be found. Gödel's discovery, which staggered the mathematical world, effectively places a limit on the ultimate capabilities of computers and computer scientists.

There are also problems where it is possible to specify an algorithm, but it would take a computing agent so long to execute that the solution is essentially useless. For example, to get a computer to play winning chess, we could create a *brute force* algorithm. Given a board position as input, the computer would examine every legal move it could possibly make, then every legal response an opponent could make to each initial move, then every response it could select to that move, and so on. This analysis would continue until the game reached a win, lose, or draw position. With that information the computer would be able to choose its next move optimally. If, for simplicity's sake, we assume that there are 40 legal moves from any given position on a chessboard, and it takes about 30 moves to reach a final conclusion, then the total number of board positions that our brute force program would need to evaluate in deciding its first move is

$$\underbrace{40 \times 40 \times 40 \times \ldots \times 40}_{30 \text{ times}} = 40^{30} \approx 10^{48}$$

If we could build a computer that evaluates one trillion (10^{12}) board positions per second (which is much too high at current levels of technology), it would take about 30,000,000,000,000,000,000,000,000 years for the computer to make its first move! Obviously, a computer cannot use a brute force technique to play a real chess game.

In addition to problems that cannot be solved efficiently or that cannot be solved at all, there also exist problems that we do not yet know *how* to solve algorithmically. Many of these involve tasks that require a degree of what we

In the Beginning . . .

There is no single date that marks the beginning of computer science. Indeed, there are many "firsts" that could be used to mark this event. For example, some of the earliest theoretical work on the logical foundations of computer science occurred in the 1930s. The first general-purpose, electronic computers appeared during the period 1942–1946. (We will discuss the history of these early machines in Chapter 5.) These first computers were one-of-a-kind experimental systems that never moved outside the research laboratory and had little or no impact on society. The first commercial machine, the UNIVAC I, did not make its appearance until June 1951, a date that marks the real beginning of the computer industry. The first high-level (i.e., English-like) programming language was FORTRAN. Some people mark its debut in 1957 as the beginning of the "software" industry. The appearance of these new machines and languages created new occupations, such as programmer, numerical analyst, and computer engineer. To address the intellectual needs of these workers, the first professional society for people in the field of computing, the Association for Computing Machinery (ACM), was established in 1947. (The ACM is still the largest professional computer science society in the world. Its Web home page is located at http://acm.org.) To help meet the rapidly growing need for computer professionals, the first Department of Computer Science was established at Purdue University in October 1962. It awarded its first M.Sc. degree in 1964 and its first Ph.D. in computer science in 1966. An undergraduate program was begun in 1968.

Thus, depending on what you consider the most important "first," the field of computer science is somewhere between 30 and 60 years old. Compared to such classic scientific disciplines as mathematics, physics, chemistry, and biology, computer science is the new kid on the block.

would term "intelligence." For example, after only a few days a baby recognizes the face of its mother from among the many faces it sees. In a few months it begins to develop coordinated sensory and motor control skills and can efficiently plan how to use them—how to get from the playpen to the toy on the floor without bumping into either the chair or the desk that are in the way. After a few years the child begins to develop powerful language skills and abstract-reasoning capabilities.

We take these abilities for granted, but the operations just mentioned—sophisticated visual discrimination, high-level problem solving, abstract reasoning, natural language understanding—cannot be done well (or even at all) using the computer systems and software packages currently available. The primary reason is that researchers do not yet know how to specify these operations algorithmically. That is, they do not yet know how to specify a solution formally in a detailed step-by-step fashion. As humans, we are simply able to do them using the "algorithms" in our heads. To appreciate this problem, imagine trying to describe algorithmically exactly what steps you follow when you are painting a picture, composing a poem, or formulating a business plan.

Thus algorithmic problem solving has many variations. Sometimes solutions do not exist; sometimes a solution is too inefficient to be of any use; sometimes a solution is not yet known. However, discovering an algorithmic solution has enormously important consequences. As we noted earlier, if we can create a correct and efficient algorithm to solve a problem, and if we encode it into a programming language, then we can take advantage of the speed and power of a computer system to automate the solution and produce the desired result. That is what computer science is all about.

1.3 ALGORITHMS

1.3.1 THE FORMAL DEFINITION OF AN ALGORITHM

The previous section discussed the central role that algorithms (creating them, analyzing them, representing them, executing them, and using them) play in computer science, and it provided an informal definition of what they are. This section provides a more thorough and formal definition of this critically important term.

Definition

> **Algorithm**   a well-ordered collection of unambiguous and effectively computable operations that, when executed, produces a result and halts in a finite amount of time.

This is a rather imposing definition, and it contains a number of important ideas. Let's take it apart, piece by piece, and analyze each of its separate points.

> *. . . a well-ordered collection . . .*

An algorithm is a collection of operations, and there must be a clear and unambiguous *ordering* to these operations. Ordering means that we know which operation to do first and that when we finish performing any one operation, we always know exactly what to do next. After all, we cannot expect a computing agent to carry out our instructions correctly if it is confused about which instruction it should be carrying out.

As an example of a set of operations that violates this ordering condition, consider the following "algorithm" that was taken from the back of a shampoo bottle and was intended as instructions on how to use the product.

STEP 1   Wet hair

STEP 2   Lather

STEP 3   Rinse

STEP 4   Repeat

At step 4, what operations should be repeated? If we go back to step 1, we will be unnecessarily wetting our hair. (It is presumably still wet from the previous operations.) If we go back to step 3 instead, we will not be getting our hair any cleaner because we have not reused the shampoo. The Repeat instruction in step 4 is ambiguous in that it does not clearly specify what to do next. Therefore, it violates the well-ordered requirement of an algorithm. (It also has a second and even more serious problem—it never stops! We will have more to say about this second problem shortly.) Statements such as

- Go back and do it again.   (Do *what* again?)
- Start over.   (From *where*?)
- If you understand this material,   (How *far*?)
  you may skip ahead.
- Do either part 1 or part 2.   (How do I decide *which* one to do?)

are ambiguous and can leave us confused and unsure about what operation to do next.

When designing algorithms for a computer system, it is all too easy to violate this ordering constraint by assuming that the computer has "common sense" and will be able to figure out where to go and what to do. For example, when we write the instruction "If Question 5 was answered correctly, then skip to the beginning of the next section" we are assuming that the computer has some way of knowing where the next section begins. Although a human could probably figure that out, a computer would have a much more difficult time.

We must be extremely precise in specifying the order in which operations are to be carried out. One possible way is to number the steps of the algorithm and use these numbers to specify the order of execution. For example, the ambiguous operations shown above could be made more precise as follows:

- Go back to step 3 and begin execution from that point.
- Start over from step 1.
- If you understand this material, skip ahead to line 21.
- If you are 18 years of age or older, do part 1 beginning with step 9; otherwise, do part 2 beginning with step 40.
- If Question 5 was answered correctly, then skip to the beginning of the next section, which can be found on page 9, line 12.

. . . of unambiguous and effectively computable operations . . .

Algorithms are composed of things called "operations," but what do those operations look like? What types of building blocks can be used to construct an algorithm? The answer to these questions is that the operations used in an algorithm must meet two criteria—they must be *unambiguous*, and they must be *effectively computable*. Let's look at each of these two terms separately.

Here is a possible "algorithm" for making a cherry pie:

STEP 1   Make the crust

STEP 2   Make the cherry filling

STEP 3   Pour the filling into the crust

STEP 4   Bake at 350°F for 45 minutes

For a professional baker, this algorithm would be fine. He or she would understand clearly how to carry out each of the operations listed above. Novice cooks, like most of us, would probably understand the intent of steps 3 and 4. However, we would probably look at steps 1 and 2, throw up our hands in confusion, say we don't know what to do, and ask for clarification. We might then be given more detailed instructions.

STEP 1   Make the crust

   1.1   Take one and one-third cups flour

   1.2   Sift the flour

   1.3   Mix the sifted flour with one-half cup butter and one-fourth cup water

   1.4   Roll into two 9-inch pie crusts

STEP 2   Make the cherry filling

   2.1   Open a 16-ounce can of cherry pie filling and pour into bowl

   2.2   Add a dash of cinnamon and nutmeg, and stir

With this additional information most people, even inexperienced cooks, would understand what to do, and they could successfully carry out this baking algorithm. However, there may be some people, perhaps young children, who still do not fully understand each and every line. In that case, we must go through the simplification process again and describe the ambiguous steps in even more elementary terms.

For example, the computing agent executing the algorithm might not know the meaning of the instruction "Sift the flour" in step 1.2, and we would have to explain it further.

   1.2   Sift the flour

      1.2.1   Get out the sifter, which is the device shown on page A-9 of your cookbook, and place it directly on top of a two-quart bowl

      1.2.2   Pour the flour into the top of the sifter and turn the crank in a counterclockwise direction

      1.2.3   Let all the flour fall through the sifter into the bowl

Now, even a child should be able to carry out these operations. But if that were not the case, then we would go through the simplification process yet one more time, until every operation, every sentence, every word was clearly understood.

An **unambiguous** operation is one that can be understood and carried out directly by the computing agent without needing to be further simplified or explained. When an operation is unambiguous, we call it a **primitive operation**, or simply a **primitive**, of the computing agent carrying out the algorithm. An algorithm must be composed entirely of primitives. Naturally, the primitive operations of different individuals (or machines) vary depending on their sophistication, experience, and intelligence, as was the case with the cherry pie recipe, which varied with the baking experience of the person following the instructions. Hence, what is an algorithm with respect to one computing agent may not be an algorithm with respect to another.

One of the most important questions we will be answering in this text is "What are the primitive operations of a typical modern computer system?" What operations can a hardware processor "understand" in the sense of being able to carry them out directly, and what operations must be further refined and simplified? For example, which of the following operations can be understood and executed by a computer?

Add x and y to get the sum z.

See whether x is greater than, equal to, or less than y.

Sort a list of names into alphabetical order.

Factor an arbitrary integer into all of its prime factors.

Make a cherry pie.

We will answer that interesting question in detail in the upcoming chapters. (Although computers have come a long way in the past few years, they cannot yet do good desserts!)

However, it is not enough for an operation to be understandable. It must also be *doable* by the computing agent. If an algorithm tells me to flap my arms really quickly and fly, I understand perfectly well what it is asking me to do. However, I am incapable of doing it. "Doable" means there exists a computational process that allows the computing agent to complete that operation successfully. The formal term for "doable" is **effectively computable**.

For example, here is an incorrect technique for finding and printing the 100th prime number (a prime number is a whole number not evenly divisible by any numbers other than 1 and itself, such as 2, 3, 5, 7, 11, 13, . . .).

STEP 1   Generate a list L of all the prime numbers: $L_1, L_2, L_3, \ldots$

STEP 2   Sort the list L into ascending order

STEP 3   Print out the 100th element in the list, L_{100}

STEP 4   Stop

The problem with these instructions is in step 1: "Generate a list L of *all* the prime numbers . . . ." That operation cannot be completed. There are an infinite number of prime numbers, and it is not possible in a finite amount of time to generate the desired list L. No such computational process exists, and the operation described in step 1 is not effectively computable. Here are some other examples of operations that may not be effectively computable:

Write out the exact decimal value of π.	(π cannot be represented exactly.)
Set *average* to $\dfrac{sum}{number}$.	(If *number* = 0, the division will be undefined.)
Set the value of *result* to $\sqrt{N}$.	(If $N < 0$, then $\sqrt{N}$ is undefined if you are using real numbers.)
Add 1 to the current value of *x*.	(What if *x* currently has no value?)

This last example explains why we had to initialize the value of the variable called *carry* to 0 in step 1 of Figure 1.2. In step 4 the algorithm says "Add the two digits a_i and b_i to the current value of *carry* to get c_i." If *carry* has no current value, then when the computing agent tries to perform the instruction in step 4, it will not know what to do. This operation is not effectively computable. Using it would be like a teacher telling everyone in the class to get out their books and turn to page X, without telling anyone the value of X. He or she would see a lot of confused faces.

> *. . . that produces a result . . .*

Algorithms solve problems. In order to know whether a solution is correct, an algorithm must produce a result that is observable to a user, such as a numerical answer, a new object, or a change to its environment. This way the user can look at the result and determine whether it is indeed the desired one. Without some observable result, we would not be able to say whether the algorithm is right or wrong. In the case of the VCR algorithm (Figure 1.1), the result will be a tape containing recorded TV programs. The addition algorithm (Figure 1.2) produces an *m*-digit sum.

Note that we use the word *result* rather than *answer*. Sometimes it is not possible for an algorithm to produce the correct answer because for a given set of input, a correct answer does not exist. In those cases the algorithm may produce something else, such as an error message, a red warning light, or an approximation to the correct answer. Error messages, lights, and approximations, though they are not necessarily what we expected, are all observable results.

> *. . . and halts in a finite amount of time.*

Another important characteristic of algorithms is that the result must be produced after the execution of a finite number of operations, and we must guarantee that the algorithm eventually reaches a statement that says "Stop,

FIGURE 1.3(a)

A Correct Solution to the Shampooing Problem

Algorithm for Shampooing Your Hair

STEP	OPERATION
1	Wet your hair
2	Set the value of *WashCount* to 0
3	Repeat steps 4 through 6 until the value of *WashCount* equals 2
4	Lather your hair
5	Rinse your hair
6	Add 1 to the value of *WashCount*
7	Stop, you have finished shampooing your hair

you are done" or something equivalent. This was the second problem with the shampooing algorithm shown earlier. We have already pointed out that it was not well ordered because we did not know which statements to repeat in step 4. However, even if we knew which block of statements to repeat, the algorithm would still be incorrect because it makes no provision to terminate. It will essentially run forever, or until we run out of hot water, soap, or patience. This is called an **infinite loop**, and it is a common error in the designing of algorithms.

Figure 1.3(a) shows an algorithmic solution to the shampooing problem that meets all the criteria discussed in this section if we assume that we want to wash our hair twice. The algorithm of Figure 1.3(a) is well ordered. Each step is numbered, and the execution of the algorithm unfolds sequentially, beginning at step 1 and proceeding from instruction i to instruction $i + 1$ unless the operation specifies otherwise. (For example, the iterative instruction in step 3 says that after completing step 6, you should go back and start again at step 4 until the value of *WashCount* equals 2.) The intent of each operation is (we assume) clear, unambiguous, and doable by the person washing his or her hair. Finally, the algorithm will halt. This is confirmed by the observation that *WashCount* is initially set to 0 in step 2. Step 6 says to add 1 to *WashCount* each time we lather and rinse our hair, so it will take on the values 0, 1, 2, ... However, the iterative statement in step 3 says stop lathering and rinsing when the value of *WashCount* reaches 2. At that point, the algorithm goes to step 7 and terminates execution with the desired result: clean hair. (Although it is correct, do not expect to see this algorithm on the back of a shampoo bottle in the near future.)

We should also mention that, as is true for any recipe or set of instructions, there is always more than a single way to write a correct solution. For example, the algorithm of Figure 1.3(a) could also be written as shown in Figure 1.3(b). Both of these are correct solutions to the shampooing problem. (Although they

Figure 1.3(b)

Another Correct Solution to the Shampooing Problem

Another Algorithm for Shampooing Your Hair

Step	Operation
1	Wet your hair
2	Lather your hair
3	Rinse your hair
4	Lather your hair
5	Rinse your hair
6	Stop, you have finished shampooing your hair

are both correct, they are not necessarily equally elegant. This point is addressed in Exercise 6 at the end of the chapter.)

1.3.2 The Importance of Algorithmic Problem Solving

The instruction sequences in Figures 1.1, 1.2, 1.3(a), and 1.3(b) are examples of the types of algorithmic solutions designed, analyzed, implemented, and tested by computer scientists, although they are much shorter and simpler. The operations shown in Figures 1.1 to 1.3 could be encoded into some appropriate language and given to a computing agent (such as a personal computer or a robot) to execute. The device would mechanically follow these instructions and successfully complete the task specified. Our device could do this without having to understand the creative processes that went into the discovery of the solution and without knowing the principles and concepts that underlie the problem. The robot simply follows the steps in the specified order (a required characteristic of algorithms), successfully completing each operation (another required characteristic), and ultimately producing the desired result after a finite amount of time (also required).

Just as the industrial revolution of the nineteenth century allowed us to construct machines to take over the drudgery of repetitive physical tasks, the "computer revolution" of the twentieth century has enabled us to implement algorithms that mechanize and automate the drudgery of repetitive mental tasks, such as adding long columns of numbers, finding names in a telephone book, sorting student records by course number, and retrieving hotel reservations from a file containing hundreds of thousands of pieces of data. This mechanization process offers the prospect of enormous increases in productivity. It also frees people to do those things that humans do much better than computers, such as creating new ideas, setting policy, doing high-level planning, and determining the significance of the results produced by a computer. Certainly, these operations are a much more effective use of that unique computing agent called the human brain.

PRACTICE PROBLEMS

Get a copy of the instructions that describe how to

a) register for classes at the beginning of the semester

b) use the card catalog or on-line computer catalog to see what is available in the college library on a given subject

c) use the copying machine in your building

d) log on to the World Wide Web

Look over the instructions and decide whether they meet the definition of an algorithm given in this section. If not, explain why, and rewrite each set of instructions so that it constitutes a valid algorithm. Also state whether each instruction is a sequential, conditional, or iterative operation.

1.4   ORGANIZATION OF THE TEXT

The purpose of this chapter has been to introduce the field of computer science, define some key concepts, and lay the groundwork for understanding the topics covered in the remainder of the text.

Certainly, the most important idea is the primacy and centrality of algorithms and algorithmic problem solving within the discipline of computer science. If we look back at the definition of computer science in Section 1.2, we see that it is the study of algorithms from a number of different viewpoints. In fact, the definition that began the chapter describes quite well the organization of the remaining sections and chapters of this text. This book is divided into six separate sections, called **levels**, each of which addresses an aspect of the definition of computer science. Let's repeat the definition and see how it maps into the sequence of topics to be presented.

Definition

Computer science   the study of algorithms, including

1. Their formal and mathematical properties

2. Their hardware realizations

3. Their linguistic realizations

4. Their applications

Computer science is the study of algorithms, including

1. *Their formal and mathematical properties* Level 1 of the text (Chapters 2 and 3) is entitled "The Algorithmic Foundations of Computer Science." It continues our discussion of algorithmic problem solving by introducing important mathematical and logical properties of algorithms. Chapter 2 presents the development of a number of algorithms to solve important, real-world problems—certainly more "real-world" than shampooing your hair. It also looks at concepts related to the problem-solving process, such as how we discover and create good algorithms, what notation we can use to express our solutions, and how we can check to see whether our proposed algorithm correctly solves the desired problem.

Our brute force chess example showed that it is not enough simply to develop a correct algorithm; we also want a solution that is efficient and that produces the desired result in a reasonable amount of time. (After all, would you want to market a chess-playing program that takes 10^{28} years to make its first move?) Chapter 3 describes ways to compare the efficiency of different algorithms and select the best one to use to solve a given problem. The material in Level 1 provides the necessary foundation for a study of the discipline of computer science.

2. *Their hardware realizations* Although our initial look at computer science investigated how an algorithm behaved when executed by some abstract "computing agent," we ultimately want to execute our algorithms on "real" machines to get "real" answers. Level 2 of the text (Chapters 4 and 5) is entitled "The Hardware World," and it looks at how to design and construct computer systems. It approaches this topic from two quite different viewpoints, or **levels of abstraction**.

Chapter 4 presents a detailed discussion of the underlying hardware. It introduces the basic building blocks of computers—binary numbers, transistors, logic gates, and circuits—and shows how these elementary electronic devices can be used to construct components to perform arithmetic and logic functions such as addition, subtraction, comparison, and sequencing. Although it is both interesting and important, this perspective produces a rather low-level view of a computer, much like studying an automobile as a collection of steel, aluminum, rubber, and glass. It is difficult to gain an understanding of how a computer works by studying only these elementary components, just as it would be difficult to understand human behavior by investigating the behavior of individual cells.

Therefore, Chapter 5 takes a higher-level view of the study of computer hardware. It looks at computers not as a bunch of wires and circuits but as an integrated collection of subsystems called memory, processor, storage, input/output, and communications. This is analogous to studying automobiles not as a set of basic materials but as a collection of large-scale components, such as the engine, transmission, and brakes.

A study of computer systems can be done at an even higher level. To understand how a computer works, we do not need to examine the functioning of every one of the thousands of components inside a machine. Instead, we need only be aware of a few critical pieces that are essential to our work. From the user's perspective, everything else is superfluous. This "user-oriented" view of a computer system and its resources is called a **virtual machine** or a **virtual environment**. A virtual machine is composed only of the hardware resources that the user perceives rather than of all the hardware resources that actually exist.

This viewpoint is analogous to our level of understanding of what happens under the hood of our car. There may be thousands of mechanical components inside an automobile engine, but most of us concern ourselves only with the items reported on the dashboard—oil pressure, fuel level, engine temperature. This is our "virtual engine," and that is all we need or want to know. We are all too happy to leave the remaining details about engine design to our friendly neighborhood mechanic.

Level 3 (Chapter 6), entitled "The Virtual Machine," describes how a virtual environment can be created by a component called **system software**. It also takes a look at the single most important and widely used piece of system software on a modern computer system, the operating system.

3. Their linguistic realizations After studying hardware design, computer organization, and virtual machines, you will have a pretty good idea of the techniques used to design and build computers. In the next section of the text, we ask the question "How can this hardware be used to solve problems?" Level 4, entitled "The Software World" (Chapters 7–10), takes a look at what is involved in designing and implementing computer software. It investigates the programs and instruction sequences executed by the hardware, rather than the hardware itself.

Chapter 7 introduces some fundamental programming language concepts using the well-known and widely used language C++. This chapter is certainly not intended to make you a proficient programmer. That would require far more than a single chapter. Instead, its purpose is to illustrate some basic features of modern programming languages and give you an appreciation for the interesting and challenging task of the computer programmer. It also introduces techniques involved in an important new style of visual problem solving called **computer graphics**.

C++ is only one of many programming languages used to encode algorithms. Chapter 8 introduces a number of alternative languages and language models in use today, including the object-oriented, functional, and parallel models. Chapter 9 describes how a program written in a high-level programming language like C++ can be translated into the low-level machine language codes first described in Chapter 5. Finally, Chapter 10 shows that, even when we marshal all the powerful hardware and software ideas described in the first nine chapters, problems exist that cannot be solved algorithmically. Chapter 10 demonstrates that there are, indeed, limits to computing.

4. Their applications By this point we have seen how to write programs to solve problems and how to execute them on a computer. However, most people are not computer scientists. They are concerned not with *creating* programs but simply with *using* programs, just as there are few automotive engineers but many, many drivers. In Level 5, entitled "Applications" (Chapters 11–13), we no longer care about *how* to build a program to solve a problem but look instead at *what* these programs can do.

Chapters 11 through 13 explore a few of the many important and popular applications of computers in current use, including modeling and simulation, information retrieval, numerical problem solving, telecommunications, networking, the World Wide Web, and artificial intelligence. This section cannot possibly survey all the ways in which computers are being used today or will be used in the future. Indeed, there is hardly an area in our modern, complex society that information technology has not affected in some important way. Readers interested in other computer applications should search out readings specific to their own areas of interest.

Finally, there are individuals who are not concerned with building computers, creating programs, or using any of the applications just described. Instead, they are interested in the social and cultural impacts—both positive and negative—of this new and ever-changing technology. They do not care either how we build machines and programs or what problems we solve. They are interested in *why* we have chosen to implement this new technology and in *what* the implications are for society.

To address this important new perspective on computer science, we have added a sixth level to the structure of our text: the social implications of computer and information technology. This material was not part of the original definition of computer science but has become an important area of study. In Level 6, entitled "Social Issues" (Chapter 14), we move to the highest level of abstraction—the view furthest removed from the computer itself—to discuss social, ethical, legal, and professional issues related to computer and information technology. These ideas are of critical importance, because even individuals not directly involved in developing or using computers will be deeply affected by them, just as society has been drastically and permanently altered by such technological developments as the telephone, television, and automobile. This last chapter takes a look at such thorny and difficult topics as the invasion of privacy, computer crime, and issues of constitutional rights and civil liberties. In these matters there are not always easy answers or even any answers at all. Our intent is simply to raise your awareness of these issues so that you may reach your own conclusions.

The overall six-layer hierarchy of this text is summarized in Figure 1.4. The organizational structure diagrammed in Figure 1.4 is one of the most important aspects of this text. To describe a field of study, it is not enough to present a mass of facts or a huge amount of detail. For learners to absorb, understand, and integrate this information, there must be a theme, a relationship, a thread that ties together the various parts of the narrative—in essence, a "big picture." Our big picture is Figure 1.4.

We first lay out the basic foundations of computer science (Level 1). We then proceed upward through five distinct layers of abstraction, from extremely low-level machine details such as electronic circuits and computer hardware (Level 2), through intermediate levels that address virtual machines (Level 3) and programming languages and software development (Level 4), to

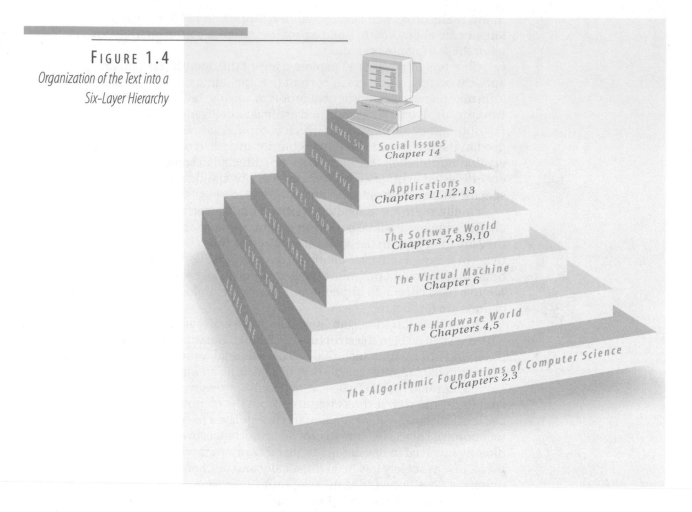

FIGURE 1.4

Organization of the Text into a Six-Layer Hierarchy

higher levels that investigate computer applications (Level 5) and address the use and misuse of information technology (Level 6). As the discussion of each level is completed, that material is used to help reveal the beauty and complexity of a higher and more abstract view of the discipline of computer science.

Just as a study of chemistry proceeds from protons, neutrons, and electrons to atoms, molecules, crystals, and, finally, chemical compounds, so too will we progress from transistors to circuits, components, computer systems, programs, applications, and, finally, social implications. We now begin that upward march and invite you to join us in our exploration of this fascinating new field. In the next chapter, we start with Level 1 of our hierarchy and begin a study of the algorithmic foundations of computer science.

Laboratory Experience 1

Associated with this text is a laboratory manual that includes software packages and a collection of 21 formal laboratory exercises. These laboratory experiences are designed to give you a chance to build, modify, play with, and experiment with ideas discussed in the text. You are strongly encouraged to carry out these laboratories in order to gain a deeper understanding of the concepts presented in the chapters. Learning computer science involves not just reading and listening but also doing and trying. Our laboratory exercises will give you that chance. (In addition, we hope that you will find them fun.)

Laboratory Experience 1, entitled "A Glossary and Web Browsing," is an introductory laboratory. Its purpose is to introduce fundamental operations that you will need in all future labs—operations such as using menus, buttons, and windows and accessing pages on the Web. (In the text, you will find a number of pointers to Web pages containing a wealth of information that complements our discussions.) In addition, the lab will provide a useful tool that you may use during your study of computer science and in other courses as well. You will learn how to use a computer to build a *glossary* of important technical terms along with their definitions and locations in the text. Please turn to Laboratory Experience 1 in the laboratory manual and try it now.

EXERCISES

1. Come up with some algorithms, apart from VCR instructions and cooking recipes, that you encounter in your everyday life. Write them out in any convenient notation, and show that they meet all of the criteria for algorithms that were presented in this chapter.

2. In the VCR instructions of Figure 1.1, step 4 says, "Enter the channel number that you wish to record and press the button labeled CHAN." In your opinion, is that an unambiguous and well-defined operation? Explain why or why not.

3. Trace through the decimal addition algorithm of Figure 1.2 using the following input values:

$$m = 3 \qquad a_2 = 1 \qquad a_1 = 4 \qquad a_0 = 9$$
$$b_2 = 0 \qquad b_1 = 2 \qquad b_0 = 9$$

At each step, show the values for c_3, c_2, c_1, c_0, and *carry*.

4. Modify the decimal addition algorithm of Figure 1.2 so that it does not print out nonsignificant leading zeroes. That is, the answer to question 3 would appear as 178 rather than 0178.

5. Under what conditions would the well-known quadratic formula

$$\text{Roots} = \left(-b \pm \sqrt{b^2 - 4ac}\,\right)/2a$$

not be effectively computable? (Assume that you are working with real numbers.)

6. Compare the two solutions to the shampooing algorithm shown in Figures 1.3(a) and 1.3(b). Which do you think is a better general-purpose solution? Why? (*Hint:* What if you wanted to wash your hair 1000 times?)

7. Here is Euclid's 2300-year-old algorithm for finding the greatest common divisor of two positive integers I and J.

Step	Operation
1	Get two positive integers as input. Call the larger value I and the smaller value J.
2	Divide I by J, and call the remainder R.
3	If R is *not* 0, then reset I to the value of J, reset J to the value of R, and go back to step 2.
4	Print out the answer, which is the value of J.
5	Stop.

a. Go through this algorithm using the input values 20 and 32. After each step of the algorithm is completed, give the values of *I*, *J*, and *R*. Determine the final output of the algorithm.

b. Does the algorithm work correctly when the two inputs are 0 and 32? Describe exactly what happens, and modify the algorithm so that it gives an appropriate error message.

8. A salesperson wants to visit 25 cities while minimizing the total number of miles she has to drive. Because she has studied computer science, she decides to design an algorithm to determine the optimal order in which to visit the cities to (1) keep her driving distance to a minimum, and (2) visit each city exactly once. The algorithm that she has devised is the following:

The computer would first list all possible ways to visit the 25 cities and then, for each one, determine the total mileage associated with that particular ordering. (Assume that the computer has access to a road map that provides the dis-

tances between all cities.) After determining the total mileage for each possible trip, the computer would search for the ordering with the minimum mileage and print out the list of cities on that optimal route. That is the order in which the salesperson should visit her destinations.

If a computer could analyze 10,000,000 separate paths per second, how long would it take the computer to determine the optimal route for visiting these 25 cities? On the basis of your answer, do you think this is a feasible algorithm? If it is not, can you think of a way to get a reasonable solution to this problem?

9. One way to do multiplication is by repeated addition. For example, 47×25 can be evaluated as $47 + 47 + 47 + \ldots + 47$ (25 times). Sketch out an algorithm for multiplying two positive numbers *a* and *b* by using this technique.

CHALLENGE WORK

1. Assume we have a "computing agent" that knows how to do one-digit subtraction where the first digit is at least as large as the second. (That is, we do not end up with a negative number.) Thus our computing agent can do such operations as $7 - 3 = 4$, $9 - 1 = 8$, and $5 - 5 = 0$. It can also subtract a one-digit value from a two-digit value in the range 10–18 as long as the final result has only a single digit. This capability enables it to do such operations as $13 - 7 = 6$, $10 - 2 = 8$, and $18 - 9 = 9$.

Using these primitive capabilities, design an algorithm to do *decimal subtraction* on two *m*-digit numbers, where $m \geq 1$. You will be given two unsigned whole numbers $a_{m-1} \ldots a_0$ and $b_{m-1} \ldots b_0$. Your algorithm must compute the value $c_{m-1} \ldots c_0$, the difference of these two values.

$$
\begin{array}{cccc}
a_{m-1} & a_{m-2} & \cdots & a_0 \\
- \ b_{m-1} & b_{m-2} & \cdots & b_0 \\
\hline
c_{m-1} & c_{m-2} & \cdots & c_0
\end{array}
$$

You may assume that the top number ($a_{m-1} \ldots a_0$) is greater than or equal to the bottom number ($b_{m-1} \ldots b_0$) so that the result will not be a negative value. However, do not assume that each individual

digit a_i is greater than or equal to b_i. If the digit on the bottom is larger than the digit on the top, then you will have to implement a *borrowing scheme* to allow the subtraction to continue. (*Caution*: It may have been easy to learn subtraction as a first-grader, but it is devilishly difficult to tell a computer how to do it!)

2. Our definition of the field of computer science is just one of many that have been proposed. Because it is so young, people working in the field are still debating how best to define exactly what they do. Review the literature of computer science (perhaps some of the books listed below) and browse the World Wide Web to locate other definitions of computer science. Compare these definitions with the one presented in this chapter and discuss the differences among them. Discuss how different definitions may give you a vastly different perspective on the field and what people in this field do. [*Note:* A very well-known and widely used definition of our field was presented in "Report of the ACM Task Force on the Core of Computer Science," reprinted in the journal *Communications of the ACM*, Vol. 32, No. 1 (January 1989).]

FOR FURTHER READING

Here are some books that will give you a good introduction to and overview of the field of computer science. Like this text, they survey many different aspects of the discipline.

Bierman, A. W. *Great Ideas in Computer Science*, 2nd ed. Cambridge, MA: MIT Press, 1997.

Brookshear, J. G. *Computer Science: An Overview*, 5th ed. Reading, MA: Addison Wesley Longman, 1997.

Decker, R., and Hirshfield, S. *The Analytical Engine: An Introduction to Computer Science*, 3rd ed. Boston, MA: PWS, 1998.

Dewdney, A. K. *The New Turing Omnibus*. New York: Freeman, 1993.

Dewdney, A. K. *Introductory Computer Science*. Boston, MA: Computer Science Press, 1996.

THE
ALGORITHMIC
FOUNDATIONS OF
COMPUTER
SCIENCE

LEVEL SIX — Social Issues
Chapter 14

LEVEL FIVE — Applications
Chapters 11,12,13

LEVEL FOUR — The Software World
Chapters 7,8,9,10

LEVEL THREE — The Virtual Machine
Chapter 6

LEVEL TWO — The Hardware World
Chapters 4,5

LEVEL ONE — The Algorithmic Foundations of Computer Science
Chapters 2,3

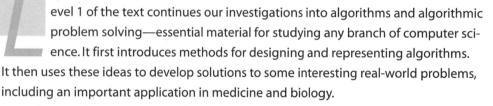

*L*evel 1 of the text continues our investigations into algorithms and algorithmic problem solving—essential material for studying any branch of computer science. It first introduces methods for designing and representing algorithms. It then uses these ideas to develop solutions to some interesting real-world problems, including an important application in medicine and biology.

When judging the quality of an essay or book report, we do not look only at such things as sentence structure, spelling, and punctuation. Although grammatical issues are important, we also evaluate the work's style, for it is a combination of correctness and expressiveness that produces a written document of high quality. So too for algorithms—correctness is not the only measure of "goodness." This section will present criteria for evaluating the quality and elegance of the algorithmic solutions that you develop.

ALGORITHM DISCOVERY AND DESIGN

2.1   INTRODUCTION

Chapter 1 introduced algorithms and algorithmic problem solving, two of the most fundamental concepts in computer science. Our introduction used examples drawn from everyday life, such as programming a VCR (Figure 1.1) and washing your hair (Figure 1.3). These are perfectly valid examples of algorithms, but as fascinating as they may be to shampoo makers and VCR manufacturers, they are not of immense interest to computer scientists. This chapter develops more fully the notions of algorithms and algorithmic problem solving and applies these ideas to problems that *are* of interest to computer scientists: searching lists, finding maxima and minima, and matching patterns. As we will see, these problems occur in many important applications.

2.2   REPRESENTING ALGORITHMS

2.2.1 PSEUDOCODE

Before presenting any algorithms, we must first make an important decision. How should we represent them? What notation should we use to express our algorithms so that they are clear, precise, and unambiguous?

One possibility would be **natural language**, the language we speak and write in our everyday lives. (In our case it is English, but it could be Spanish, Arabic, Japanese, Swahili, or any one of a thousand other languages.) This is an obvious choice because our own spoken and written language is the one with which we are most familiar. If we used natural language, then our algorithms would be written in much the same way as a term paper or an essay—a collection of pages divided into paragraphs and sentences. For example, when expressed in natural language, the addition algorithm of Figure 1.2 might look something like the paragraph given in Figure 2.1.

Comparing Figure 1.2 with Figure 2.1 illustrates the problems of using natural language to represent algorithms. Natural language can be extremely verbose, with the resulting algorithms ending up as rambling, unstructured paragraphs that are hard to follow. (Imagine reading 5, 10, or even 100 pages of text like Figure 2.1.) An unstructured, "free-flowing" writing style may be wonderful for essays, but it is horrible for algorithms. The lack of structure makes it difficult for the reader to locate specific sections of the algorithm, because they are buried deep inside the text. For example, on the eighth and ninth lines of Figure 2.1 there is a phrase that says, ". . . and begin the loop all over again." To what part of the algorithm does this refer? Without any clues to guide us, such as

FIGURE 2.1

The Addition Algorithm of Figure 1.2 Expressed in Natural Language

Initially, set the value of the variable *carry* to 0 and the value of the variable i to 0. When these initializations have been completed, begin looping until the value of the variable i becomes greater than $m - 1$. First, add together the values of the two digits a_i and b_i and the current value of the carry digit to get the result called c_i. Now check the value of c_i to see whether it is greater than or equal to 10. If c_i is greater than or equal to 10, then reset the value of *carry* to 1 and reduce the value of c_i by 10; otherwise, set the value of *carry* to zero. When you are done with that operation, add 1 to i and begin the loop all over again. When the loop has completed execution, set the leftmost digit of the result c_m to the value of *carry* and print out the final result, which consists of the digits $c_m c_{m-1} \ldots c_0$. After printing the result, the algorithm is finished, and it terminates.

indentation, line numbering, or highlighting, locating the beginning of that loop can be a daunting and time-consuming task. (For the record, the beginning of the loop corresponds to the sentence on the second line that starts "When these initializations have been completed . . . ." It is certainly not easy to determine this from a casual reading of the text.)

A second problem is that natural language is too "rich" in interpretation and meaning. Natural language frequently relies on either context or a reader's experiences to give precise meaning to a word or phrase. This permits different readers to interpret the same sentence in totally different ways. This may be acceptable, even desirable, when writing poetry or fiction, but it is again disastrous when writing algorithms that should always execute in the same way and produce identical results. We can see an example of this problem in the sentence on line 8 of Figure 2.1 that starts with "When you are done with that operation . . . ." When we are done with which operation? It is not at all clear from the text, and individuals may interpret the phrase *that operation* in different ways, producing radically different behavior. Given all of these problems, it is easy to see that natural languages do not provide the accuracy and precision needed to represent algorithms.

In place of natural languages we might be tempted to go to the other extreme. If we are ultimately going to execute our algorithm on a computer, why not write it out immediately as a computer program using a **formal programming language** such as Pascal, C++, or Java? If we adopt that approach, the addition algorithm of Figure 1.2 might start out looking like the C++ program fragment shown in Figure 2.2.

As an algorithmic design language, this notation is also seriously flawed. During the initial phases of design, we should be thinking and writing at a highly abstract level. However, using a programming language forces us to deal immediately with such low-level language issues as punctuation, grammar, and syntax. For example, the algorithm in Figure 1.2 contains an operation that says,

FIGURE 2.2

The Beginning of the Addition Algorithm of Figure 1.2 Expressed in C++

```
{ int i, m, Carry;
  int a[100], b[100], c[100];
  cin >> m;
  for (int j = 0; j <= m-1; j++)
     cin >> a[j] >> b[j];
  Carry = 0;
  i = 0;
  while (i < m)
  {
     c[i] = a[i] + b[i] + Carry;
     if c[i] >= 10
     {
        .
        .
        .
```

"Set the value of carry to 0." This is an easy statement to understand. However, when translated into C++, that statement becomes

```
Carry = 0;
```

Is this operation setting Carry to 0 or asking if Carry is equal to 0? Why does a semicolon appear at the end of the line? Was it necessary to capitalize the letter "C" in Carry? These picky technical details clutter our thoughts, and at this point in the solution process, they are totally out of place. When creating algorithms, a programmer should no more worry about semicolons and capitalization than a novelist should worry about type fonts and cover design when writing the first draft!

If the two extremes of natural languages and formal programming languages are both less than ideal, what notation should we use? What is the best way to represent the solutions shown in this chapter and the rest of the book?

Most computer scientists use a notation called **pseudocode** to design and represent algorithms. This is a special set of English language constructs modeled to look like the statements available in most programming languages. Pseudocode represents a good compromise between the two extremes of natural and formal languages. It is simple, highly readable, and has virtually no grammatical rules. (In fact, pseudocode is sometimes called a programming language without the details.) However, because it contains only statements that have a well-defined structure, it is easier to visualize the organization of a pseudocode algorithm than one represented as long, rambling natural-language paragraphs. In addition, because pseudocode closely resembles many popular programming languages, the subsequent translation of the algorithm into a computer program is relatively simple. The algorithms shown in Figures 1.1, 1.2, and 1.3(a) and (b) are all written in pseudocode.

We will need pseudocode constructs for the three classes of algorithmic operations introduced in Chapter 1: sequential, conditional, and iterative. We have chosen constructs that look something like the statements available in C++, because that is the language introduced later in the text (Chapter 7). However, keep in mind that pseudocode is *not* a formal language with rigidly standardized syntactic and semantic rules and regulations. On the contrary, it is an informal design notation used solely to express algorithms. If you do not like the specific constructs presented in the next two sections, feel free to modify them or select others that are more helpful to you in the design and development of algorithms.

2.2.2 SEQUENTIAL OPERATIONS

Our pseudocode must include instructions to carry out the three basic sequential operations called **computation**, **input**, and **output**.

The instruction for performing a **computation** and saving the result looks like the following. (Words and phrases inside quotation marks represent specific elements that you must insert when writing an algorithm.)

Set the value of "variable" to "arithmetic expression"

The meaning of this operation is first to evaluate the "arithmetic expression" and get a result. Then take that result and store it into the indicated "variable." A **variable** is simply a named storage location that can hold a data value. A commonly used analogy is that a variable is like a mailbox into which one can store a value and from which one can retrieve a value. Let's look at an example.

Set the value of *carry* to 0

First, evaluate the arithmetic expression, which in this case is just the constant value 0. Then store that result into the variable called *carry*. If *carry* had a previous value, say 1, it will be discarded and replaced by the new value 0. Pictorially, you can view this operation as producing the following state:

carry | 0 |

Here is another example:

Set the value of *Area* to (πr^2)

Assuming that the variable r has been given a value by a previous instruction in the algorithm, this statement evaluates the arithmetic expression πr^2 to produce a numerical result. This result is then stored in the variable called *Area*. If r does not have a value, an error condition occurs. This instruction is not effectively computable, and it cannot be completed.

We can see additional examples of computational operations in steps 4, 6, and 7 of the addition algorithm of Figure 1.2:

STEP 4   Add the two digits a_i and b_i to the current value of *carry* to get c_i

STEP 6   Add 1 to i, effectively moving one column to the left

STEP 7   Set c_m to the value of *carry*

Note that these three steps are not written in exactly the format just described. If we had used that notation, they would have looked like this:

STEP 4   Set the value of c_i to $(a_i + b_i + carry)$

STEP 6   Set the value of i to $(i + 1)$

STEP 7   Set the value of c_m to *carry*

However, in pseudocode it doesn't really matter exactly how you choose to write your instructions. At this point in the design of a solution, we do not care about the minor language differences between

Add *a* and *b* to get *c*

and

Set the value of *c* to $a + b$

As we noted earlier, pseudocode is not a precise set of notational rules to be memorized and rigidly followed. It is a flexible notation that can be adjusted to fit your own view about how best to express ideas and algorithms.

When writing arithmetic expressions, you may assume that the computing agent executing your algorithm has all the capabilities of a typical calculator. Therefore, it "knows" how to do all basic arithmetic operations such as $+$, $-$, $\times$, $\div$, $\sqrt{\ }$, absolute value, sine, cosine, and tangent. It also knows the value of important constants such as π.

The final two sequential operations enable our computing agent to communicate with "the outside world," which means everything other than the computing agent itself:

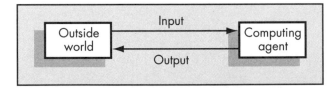

Input operations allow the computing agent to receive from the outside world data values that it may then use in later instructions. **Output** operations allow the computing agent to send results to the outside world for display. When the computing agent is a computer, communications with the outside world are done via the input/output equipment available on a typical computer system (e.g., keyboard, screen, mouse, and printer). However, when designing algorithms, we do not concern ourselves with such system details. We care only that data be given to us from somewhere (or somebody) when we request it and that results be sent to something (or someone) for presentation.

Our pseudocode instructions for input and output are expressed as follows:

Input: Get values for "variable", "variable", . . .

Output: Print the values of "variable", "variable", . . .

For example,

Get a value for *r*, the radius of the circle

When the algorithm reaches this input operation, it will wait until someone or something in the outside world provides it with a value for the variable *r*. (In a computer, this may be done by entering a value at the keyboard.) When the algorithm has received and stored a value for *r*, it will continue on to the next instruction. Here is an example of an output operation:

Print the value of *Area*

Assuming that the algorithm has already computed the area of the circle, this instruction says to display that value to the "outside world." This display may be shown on a screen or printed on a printer. However, as we have said, that level of detail is not important right now.

Sometimes we use an output instruction to display a message rather than the desired results. This could happen, for example, if we were unable to complete a computation because of an error condition. In that case we might execute something like the following operation. (To avoid confusion, we will use 'single quotes' to enclose messages. This will distinguish them from such pseudocode constructs as "variable" and "arithmetic expression", which are enclosed in double quotes.)

Print the message 'Sorry, no answers were computed'

Given the three sequential operations of computation, input, and output, we can now write some simple but useful algorithms. Figure 2.3 presents an algorithm to compute the average miles per gallon on a trip when given as input the number of gallons used and the starting and ending mileage readings on the odometer.

FIGURE 2.3
Algorithm for Computing Average Miles per Gallon

Average Miles per Gallon Algorithm (Version 1)

STEP	OPERATION
1	Get values for *gallons used, starting mileage, ending mileage*
2	Set the value of *distance driven* to (*ending mileage − starting mileage*)
3	Set the value of *average miles per gallon* to (*distance driven ÷ gallons used*)
4	Print the value of *average miles per gallon*
5	Stop

PRACTICE PROBLEMS   Write pseudocode versions of

1. An algorithm that gets three data values x, y, and z as input and outputs the *average* of those three values.

2. An algorithm that gets the radius r of a circle as input. Its output is both the circumference and the area of a circle of radius r. (We will examine this problem in detail in Chapter 7.)

3. An algorithm that gets the amount of electricity used in kilowatt-hours and the cost of electricity per kilowatt-hour. Its output is the total amount of the electric bill, including an 8% sales tax.

2.2.3 CONDITIONAL AND ITERATIVE OPERATIONS

The average miles per gallon algorithm in Figure 2.3 performs a set of operations once and then stops. It does not have the ability either to select among alternative operations or to perform a block of instructions more than once. A purely **sequential algorithm** of the type shown in Figure 2.3 is sometimes termed a **straight-line algorithm** because it executes its instructions in a straight line from top to bottom and then stops. Unfortunately, most real-world problems are not straight-line. They involve nonsequential operations such as branching and repetition.

To allow us to address these more interesting problems, our pseudocode needs two additional primitives to implement **conditional** and **iterative** operations. Together, these two types of operations are called **control operations**; they allow us to alter the normal sequential flow of control in an algorithm. As we saw in Chapter 1, control operations are an essential part of all but the very simplest of algorithms.

The **conditional statements** are the "question-asking" operations of an algorithm. They allow an algorithm to ask a question and, on the basis of the answer to that question, to select the next operation to perform. There are a number of ways to phrase a question, but the most common conditional primitive is the *if/then/else*, which has the following format:

if "a true/false condition" is true then

   first set of algorithmic operations

else (or otherwise)

   second set of algorithmic operations

The meaning of this algorithmic primitive is as follows:

1. Evaluate the true/false condition on the first line to see whether it is true or false.

2. If the condition is true, then do the first set of algorithmic operations and skip the second set entirely.

3. If the condition is false, then skip the first set of operations and do the second set.

4. In either case, once the appropriate set of operations has been completed, continue execution of the algorithm with the operation that follows the if/then/else instruction.

Basically, the if/then/else operation allows you to select exactly one of two alternatives—either/or, this or that. We saw an example of this primitive in step 5 of the addition algorithm of Figure 1.2. (The statement has been reformatted slightly to highlight the two alternatives clearly, but it has not been changed.)

If ($c_i \geq 10$) then

    Set the value of c_i to ($c_i - 10$)

    Set the value of *carry* to 1

Else

    Set the value of *carry* to 0

The condition ($c_i \geq 10$) can only be true or false. If it is true, then there is a carry into the next column, and we must do the first set of instructions—subtracting 10 from c_i and setting *carry* to 1. If the condition is false, then there is no carry, and we skip over these two operations. Instead we perform the second block of operations, which simply sets the value of *carry* to 0.

Figure 2.4 shows another example of the if/then/else primitive. It extends the miles per gallon algorithm of Figure 2.3 to include a second line of output

---

FIGURE 2.4

Second Version of the Average Miles per Gallon Algorithm

Average Miles per Gallon Algorithm (Version 2)

STEP	OPERATION
1	Get values for *gallons used, starting mileage, ending mileage*
2	Set the value of *distance driven* to (*ending mileage – starting mileage*)
3	Set the value of *average miles per gallon* to (*distance driven ÷ gallons used*)
4	Print the value of *average miles per gallon*
5	If *average miles per gallon* is greater than 25.0 then
6	Print the message 'You are getting good gas mileage.'
	Else
7	Print the message 'You are NOT getting good gas mileage.'
8	Stop

that says whether you are getting good gas mileage. Good gas mileage is defined as a value for average miles per gallon greater than 25.0 mpg.

The last algorithmic primitive to be introduced allows us to implement a **loop**—the repetition of a block of instructions. The real power of a computer comes not from doing a calculation once but from doing it many, many times. If, for example, we needed to compute a single value of average miles per gallon, we would be foolish to convert an algorithm like Figure 2.4 into a computer program and execute it on a computer. That would take from a few minutes to an hour. It would be far faster to use a calculator, which could complete the job in a few seconds. However, if we needed to do the same computation 1,000,000 times, the power of a computer to repetitively execute a block of statements becomes quite apparent. If each computation of average miles per gallon takes 5 seconds on a hand calculator, then one million of them would require about 2 months, not allowing for such luxuries as sleeping and eating. Once the algorithm was developed and the program written, a computer could carry out that same task in less than 1 second!

The algorithmic primitive that we will use to express the idea of **iteration**, also called **looping**, is

Repeat step i to step j until "a true/false condition" becomes true

    step i: operation

    step $i + 1$:   operation

    .

    .

    .

    step j: operation

What this instruction means is to perform all operations from step i to step j, inclusive. This block of operations is called the **loop body**. (These operations should be indented so that it is clear which operations belong inside the loop.) When the entire loop body has finished executing, evaluate the true/false condition at the beginning of the loop to see whether it has become true. This condition is called the **termination condition**, and its value is used to control execution of the loop. (This iterative primitive assumes the loop body will always be done at least once. The first test for termination is not done until after the completion of the first iteration.) If the termination condition is true, then the loop has finished, and the algorithm will go to the statement immediately following the loop. If the condition is false, then the loop has not finished. The algorithm must return to step i and execute the entire loop body again. This looping process continues until the loop body has completed execution and the termination condition is true. If it is possible for the termination condition never to become true, then we have violated one of the fundamental properties of an algorithm, and we have the error, first mentioned in Chapter 1, called an **infinite loop**.

Here is an example of a loop:

Step	Operation
1	Set the value of *count* to 1
2	Repeat step 3 to step 5 until (*count* > 100)
3	Set *square* to (*count* × *count*)
4	Print the values of *count* and *square*
5	Add 1 to *count*

We initialize the value of *count* to 1 in step 1 and begin the loop. We execute the loop body, which in this case includes the three statements in steps 3, 4, and 5. Those statements compute the value of *count* squared (step 3) and print out the value of both *count* and *square* (step 4). The last operation inside the loop body (step 5) adds 1 to *count* so that it now has the value 2. At this point we are at the end of the loop and must determine whether it should be executed again. Evaluate the termination condition, (*count* > 100), to see whether it is true or false. Because count is 2, the condition is false, and the algorithm must perform the loop body again. Looking at the entire loop, we can see that it will execute 100 times, producing the following output, which is a table of numbers and their squares from 1 to 100.

1	1
2	4
3	9
.	
.	
.	
100	10,000

At the end of the 100th pass through the loop, the value of count will be incremented in step 5 to 101. When the termination condition is evaluated, it will be true (because 101 is greater than 100), and the loop will terminate.

We can see additional examples of loop structures in steps 3 through 6 of Figure 1.2 and in steps 3 through 6 of Figure 1.3(a). Another example is shown in Figure 2.5, which is yet another variation of the average miles per gallon algorithm of Figures 2.3 and 2.4. In this modification, after finishing one computation, the algorithm asks the user whether he or she would like to do this calculation again. It waits until it gets a Yes or No response and repeats the entire algorithm until the response provided by the user is No.

We conclude our discussion on control instructions by saying that there are many variations of this particular looping construct. For example, some people use an "End of Loop" construct to mark the end of the loop rather than explicitly stating which steps are contained in the loop body. Using this approach, our loops would be written like this:

FIGURE 2.5

Third Version of the Average Miles per Gallon Algorithm

Average Miles per Gallon Algorithm (Version 3)

STEP	OPERATION
1	Repeat step 2 to step 10 until *Response* is No.
2	Get values for *gallons used, starting mileage, ending mileage*
3	Set the value of *distance driven* to (*ending mileage – starting mileage*)
4	Set the value of *average miles per gallon* to (*distance driven ÷ gallons used*)
5	Print the value of *average miles per gallon*
6	If *average miles per gallon* > 25.0 then
7	Print the message 'You are getting good gas mileage.'
	Else
8	Print the message 'You are NOT getting good gas mileage.'
9	Print the message 'Do you want to do this again, Yes or No?'
10	Get a value for *Response* from the user
11	Stop

FIGURE 2.5

Third Version of the Average Miles per Gallon Algorithm

    Repeat until "a true/false condition" becomes true

        operation

        .

        .

        .

        operation

    End of the loop

In this case, the loop body is delimited not by step numbers but by the two lines that read "Repeat until . . ." and "End of the loop".

It is also possible to think of a loop continuing to be done *while* a condition remains true rather than repeating *until* a condition becomes true. That is, think of the true/false condition as the criterion for *continuing* a loop rather than for *terminating* a loop. Thus the looping instruction

    Repeat until the sum is greater than 100 . . .

would be expressed as

    While the sum is not greater than 100 do . . .

or

    While the sum is less than or equal to 100 do . . .

When we use this "while alternative," our loops will be written something like the following:

While "a true/false condition" remains true do

    operation

    .

    .

    .

    operation

End of the loop

This iterative operation tells us first see whether the true/false condition, now called the *continuation condition*, is true or false. If it is initially false, then the loop will be skipped. If it is true, then the entire loop body will be executed, and when that is done, the continuation condition is checked again. When the condition becomes false, the loop is terminated, and the algorithm continues with the operation immediately following the loop. Note that in this variation, the loop condition is checked immediately rather than at the end of the first iteration. Therefore, a **while loop** can execute 0, 1, or more times, whereas a **repeat loop** must execute at least once.

Figure 2.6 summarizes the algorithmic operations introduced in this section. These operations represent the **primitives** of our computing agent. These are the instructions that we assume our computing agent understands and is capable of executing without further explanation or simplification. In the next section we will use these operations to design algorithms that solve some interesting and important problems.

From Little Primitives Mighty Algorithms Do Grow

Although the set of algorithmic primitives shown in Figure 2.6 may seem quite "puny," it is anything but! In fact, an important theorem in theoretical computer science proves that the operations shown in Figure 2.6 are sufficient to represent *any* valid algorithm. No matter how complicated it may be, if a problem can be solved algorithmically, it can be expressed using only the sequential, conditional, and iterative operations just discussed. This includes not only the simple addition algorithm of Figure 1.2 but also the monstrously complex algorithms needed to fly NASA's

space shuttles, run the international telephone switching system, and describe all the Internal Revenue Service's tax rules and regulations.

In many ways, building algorithms is akin to constructing essays or novels using only the 26 letters of the English alphabet, plus a few punctuation symbols. Expressive power does not always come from having a huge set of primitives. It can also arise from a small number of simple building blocks that can be combined in many interesting ways. That is the real secret of building algorithms.

FIGURE 2.6

Summary of Pseudocode Language Instructions

COMPUTATION:

Set the value of "variable" to "arithmetic expression"

INPUT/OUTPUT:

Get a value for "variable", "variable". . .
Print the value of "variable", "variable", . . .
Print the message 'message'

CONDITIONAL:

if "a true/false condition" is true then
    first set of algorithmic operations
else
    second set of algorithmic operations

ITERATIVE:

Repeat step *i* to step *j* until "a true/false condition" becomes true
    Step *i*: operation
    .
    .
    .
    Step *j*: operation

Repeat until "a true/false condition" becomes true
    operation
    .
    .
    .
    operation
End of the loop

While "a true/false condition" remains true do
    operation
    .
    .
    .
    operation
End of the loop

PRACTICE PROBLEMS

1. Write an if/then/else statement that sets the variable y to the value 1 if $x \geq 0$. If $x < 0$, then the statement should set y to the value 2. (Assume x already has a value.)

2. Write an algorithm that gets as input three data values x, y, and z and outputs the average of these values if the value of x is positive. If the value of x is either zero or negative, your algorithm should not compute the average but should print the error message 'Bad Data' instead.

3. Write an algorithm that gets as input a single data value x and outputs the three values x^2, $\sin x$, and $1/x$. This process is repeated until the input value for x is equal to 999, at which time the algorithm terminates.

2.3   EXAMPLES OF ALGORITHMIC PROBLEM SOLVING

2.3.1   EXAMPLE 1: LOOKING, LOOKING, LOOKING

The first problem we will solve was first mentioned in Chapter 1—searching for a particular person's name in a telephone book. This is just the type of simple and rather uninteresting repetitive mental task so well suited to computerization. (Many large telephone companies have implemented this application. Most of us have had the experience of dialing directory assistance and hearing the desired telephone number spoken in a computer-generated voice.)

Assume that we have a list of 10,000 names, called N_1, N_2, N_3, . . . , $N_{10,000}$, along with the 10,000 telephone numbers of those individuals, denoted as T_1, T_2, T_3, . . . , $T_{10,000}$. To simplify the problem, we will initially assume that all names in the book are unique and that the names need not be in alphabetical order. Essentially what we have described is a nonalphabetized telephone book of the following form:

Name	Telephone Number	
N_1	T_1	
N_2	T_2	
N_3	T_3	
.	.	10,000 (name, phone number) pairs
.	.	
.	.	
$N_{10,000}$	$T_{10,000}$	

Let's create an algorithm that allows us to input the name of any specific person, which we will denote as *NAME*. The algorithm will check to see if *NAME* is contained anywhere within the list of 10,000 names in our telephone book. If *NAME* is found, say, at position *j* (where *j* is some value between 1 and 10,000), then the output of our algorithm will be the telephone number of that person: the value T_j. If *NAME* is not in our telephone book, then the output of our algorithm will be the message "I am sorry but this name is not in the directory." This type of look-up algorithm has many uses in addition to the telephone directory application described here. For example, it could be used to locate the zip code of a particular city, the seat number of a specific airline passenger, or the room number of a hotel guest.

The process of finding a solution to a given problem, such as this telephone book look-up, is called **algorithm discovery**, and it is the most challenging and creative part of the overall problem-solving process. Discovering a correct and efficient algorithm to solve a complicated problem can be difficult, and it can involve equal parts of intelligence, hard work, past experience, artistic skill, and plain good luck. In this text we will develop solutions to a range of problems to give you experience in working with algorithms. Studying these examples, together with lots of practice, is by far the best way to learn how to do creative problem solving, just as experience and practice are the best way to learn how to write essays, hit a golf ball, or repair cars.

For this particular problem, the names are not in alphabetical order, so there is no clever way to speed up the search. With a random collection of names, we cannot come up with any method that is more efficient than looking at all the names in the list, one at a time, until we either find what we are looking for or come to the end of the list. This rather simple and straightforward technique is called **sequential search**, and it is the standard algorithm for searching an *unordered* list of values. For example, this is how we would search a telephone book to see who lives at 123 Elm Street, because a telephone book is not sorted by address. It is also the way that we look through a shuffled deck of cards trying to locate one particular card. A first attempt at designing a sequential search algorithm to solve our search problem might look something like Figure 2.7.

FIGURE 2.7	STEP OPERATION
First Attempt at Designing a Sequential Search Algorithm	

STEP	OPERATION
1	Get values for *NAME*, N_1, . . . , $N_{10,000}$, and T_1, . . . , $T_{10,000}$
2	If *NAME* = N_1 then print the value of T_1
3	If *NAME* = N_2 then print the value of T_2
4	IF *NAME* = N_3 then print the value of T_3
.	.
.	.
.	.
10,000	If *NAME* = $N_{9,999}$ then print the value of $T_{9,999}$
10,001	If *NAME* = $N_{10,000}$ then print the value of $T_{10,000}$
10,002	Stop

The solution shown in Figure 2.7 is extremely long. At 66 lines per page, it would require about 150 pages to write out the 10,002 steps in the completed solution. The algorithm of Figure 2.7 would also be unnecessarily slow. If we are lucky enough to find *NAME* in the very first position of the telephone book, N_1, then we get the answer T_1 almost immediately at step 2. However, the algorithm does not stop at that point. Instead, even though it has already found the correct answer, it foolishly asks 9,999 more questions looking for *NAME* in positions N_2, $N_3, \ldots, N_{10,000}$. Of course, humans have enough "common sense" to know that when they find an answer they have been searching for, they can stop. However, we cannot (and should not) assume common sense in a computer system. On the contrary, a computer will mechanically execute the entire algorithm from the first step to the last.

Not only is the algorithm excessively long and inefficient, it is also wrong. If the desired *NAME* is not in the list, this algorithm will simply stop (at step 10,002) rather than providing the desired result, a message that the name you requested is not in the directory. An algorithm is deemed correct only when it produces the correct result for *all* possible cases.

The problem with the attempt shown in Figure 2.7 is that we are not using **iteration**. Instead of writing an instruction 10,000 separate times, it is far better to write it only once and indicate that it is to be repetitively *executed* 10,000 times, or however many times it takes to obtain the answer. As we noted in the previous section, much of the power of a computer comes from being able to perform a loop—the repetitive execution of a block of statements a large number of times. Virtually every algorithm developed in this text contains at least one loop and usually many. (This is the difference between the two shampooing algorithms shown in Figures 1.3(a) and (b). The algorithm in the former contains a loop; that in the latter does not.)

The algorithm in Figure 2.8 shows how we might use a loop to implement the sequential search technique. It uses a variable called *i* as an **index**, or **pointer**, to the list of all names. That is, N_i refers to the ith name in the list. The algorithm then repeatedly executes a group of statements using different values of *i*. The variable *i* can be thought of as a "moving finger" scanning the list of names and pointing to the one on which we are currently working.

FIGURE 2.8

Second Attempt at Designing a Sequential Search Algorithm

STEP	OPERATION
1	Get values for *NAME*, $N_1, \ldots, N_{10,000}$ and for $T_1, \ldots, T_{10,000}$
2	Set the value of *i* to 1 and set the value of *Found* to NO
3	Repeat steps 4 through 7 until *Found* = YES
4	If *NAME* is equal to the ith name on the list N_i then
5	Print the telephone number of that person, T_i
6	Set the value of *Found* to YES
	Else (*NAME* is not equal to N_i)
7	Add 1 to the value of *i*
8	Stop

The first time through the loop the value of the index i is 1, so the algorithm checks to see whether *NAME* is equal to N_1, the first name on the list. If it is, then the algorithm writes out the result and sets *Found* to YES, which will cause the loop in steps 4–7 to terminate. If it is not the desired *NAME*, then i is incremented by 1 (in step 7) so that it now has the value 2, and the loop is executed again. The algorithm now checks (in step 4) to see whether *NAME* is equal to N_2, the second name on the list. In this way, the algorithm uses the single conditional statement "If *NAME* is equal to the ith name on the list . . ." to check up to 10,000 names. It executes that one line over and over, each time with a different value of i. This is the advantage of using iteration.

However, the attempt shown in Figure 2.8 is not yet a complete and correct algorithm because it still does not work when the desired *NAME* does not appear anywhere on the list. This final problem can be solved by checking the value of the index i. If i ever exceeds 10,000, then we have searched the entire list without finding the desired *NAME*. The loop should terminate, and the algorithm should produce the desired error message.

An iterative solution to the sequential search algorithm that incorporates this feature is shown in Figure 2.9. The sequential search algorithm shown in Figure 2.9 is a correct solution to our telephone book look-up problem. It meets all the requirements listed in Section 1.3.1: It is well ordered, each of the operations is clearly defined and effectively computable, and it is guaranteed to halt with the desired result after a finite number of operations. (In Exercise 12 at the end of this chapter you will develop an argument to prove that this algorithm will always halt.) Furthermore, this algorithm requires writing out only 9 steps to produce the answer, rather than the 10,002 steps of the first attempt in Figure 2.7. As you can see, not all algorithms are created equal.

FIGURE 2.9

The Sequential Search Algorithm

Sequential Search Algorithm

STEP	OPERATION
1	Get values for *NAME*, $N_1, \ldots, N_{10,000}$ and for $T_1, \ldots, T_{10,000}$
2	Set the value of i to 1 and set the value of *Found* to NO
3	Repeat steps 4 through 7 until either *Found* = YES or $i > 10,000$
4	If *NAME* is equal to the ith name on the list N_i then
5	Print the telephone number of that person, T_i
6	Set the value of *Found* to YES
	Else (*NAME* is not equal to N_i)
7	Add 1 to the value of i
8	If (*Found* = NO) then
	Print the message 'Sorry, but this name is not in the directory'
9	Stop

Looking back at the algorithm in Figure 2.9, our first thought may be that this is not at all how people search a telephone book by hand. When looking for a particular telephone number, we would never turn to page 1, column 1, and scan all names beginning with Aardvark, Alan—unless we happened to live in a *very* small community. Certainly, the New York City telephone company would not be satisfied with the performance of a directory search algorithm that always began on page 1 of its 1300-page telephone book.

The reason we solved the problem in this fashion is that our telephone book was not alphabetized. Given this lack of organization, we really had no choice in the design of a search algorithm. However, in real life we can do much better than sequential search, because telephone books *are* alphabetized, and we can exploit this fact during the search process. For example, we know that M is about halfway through the alphabet, so when looking for the name Middle, Michael, we would open the telephone book somewhere in the middle rather than to the first page. We would see exactly where we were by looking at the first letter of the names on the current page, and then we would move forward or backward toward names beginning with M. This approach allows us to find the desired name quickly.

This use of different search techniques points out a very important concept in the design of algorithms:

> *The selection of an algorithm to solve a problem is greatly influenced by the way the data are organized.*

An algorithm is a method for processing some data to produce a result, and the way the data are organized has an enormous influence both on the algorithm we select and on how speedily that algorithm can produce the desired result.

In Chapter 3 we will expand on the concept of the efficiency and goodness of algorithms, and we will present an algorithm for searching *alphabetized* telephone books that is far superior to the one shown in Figure 2.9.

2.3.2 EXAMPLE 2: BIG, BIGGER, BIGGEST

The second algorithm we will develop is similar to the sequential search in Figure 2.9 in that it also searches a list of values. However, this time the algorithm will be searching not for a particular value supplied by the user but for

Laboratory Experience 2

This laboratory experience will introduce the concept of *algorithm animation,* in which you can observe an algorithm being executed and actually watch as data values are transformed into final results. "Bringing an algorithm to life" in this way can help greatly in understanding what it does and how it works. The first animation that you will work with is the sequential search algorithm shown in Figure 2.9.

the numerically largest value in the entire list. This type of "find largest" algorithm could be used to answer a number of important questions. (With only a single trivial change, the same algorithm also finds the smallest value, so a better name for it might be "find extreme values.") For example, given a list of examinations, which student received the highest (or lowest) score? Given a list of annual salaries, which employee earns the most (or least) money? Given a list of grocery prices from different stores, where should I shop to find the lowest price? All these questions could be answered by executing the algorithm that we will design.

In addition to being important in its own right, this algorithm can also be used as a "building block" for the construction of solutions to other problems. For example, the Find Largest algorithm that we will develop could be used to implement a *sorting algorithm* that puts an unordered list of numbers in ascending order. (Find and remove the largest item in list A and move it to the first position of list B. Now repeat these operations, each time moving the largest remaining number in A to the next available slot of list B. We will develop and write this algorithm in Chapter 3.)

This is a very important idea. The examples in this chapter may lead you to believe that every algorithm must be built from only the most elementary and basic of primitives—the sequential, conditional, and iterative operations shown in Figure 2.6. That is not always the case. Once an algorithm has been developed, it may itself be used in the construction of other, more complex algorithms, just as we will use "find largest" in the design of a sorting algorithm. This is similar to what a builder does when constructing a home from prefabricated units rather than bricks and boards. Our problem-solving task need not always begin "at the beginning" but can instead build upon ideas and results that have come before. Every algorithm that we create becomes, in a sense, a primitive operation of our computing agent and can be used as part of the solution to other problems. That is why a collection of useful algorithms, called a **library**, is such an important tool in algorithm design and development.

Formally, the problem we will be solving in this section can be defined as follows:

Given a value $n \geq 2$ and a list containing exactly n unique numbers called $A_1, A_2, \ldots, A_n$, find and print out both the largest value in the list and the position in the list where that largest value occurred.

For example, if our list contained the five values

19, 41, 12, 63, 22   ($n = 5$)

then our algorithm should locate the largest value, 63, and say that it occurred in the fourth position of the list. (*Note:* Our definition of the problem states that all numbers in the list are unique, so there can be only a single occurrence of the largest number. Exercise 15 at the end of the chapter asks how our algorithm would behave if the numbers in the list were not unique and the largest number could occur two or more times.)

To design an algorithm to solve this problem, we might start out by asking ourselves how the same problem might be solved by hand. For example, what would we do if we were given a pile of papers each of which contained a single number and were asked to locate the largest number in the pile? (The following diagrams assume the papers contain the five values 19, 41, 12, 63, and 22.)

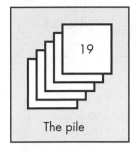

The pile

We might start off by saying that the first number in the pile (the top one) is the largest one that we have seen so far and then putting it off to the side where we are keeping the largest value.

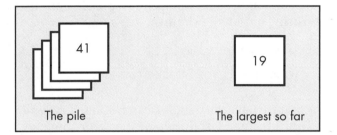

The pile   The largest so far

Now we might compare the top number in the pile with the one that we have called the largest one so far. In this case, the top number in the pile, 41, is larger than our current largest so far, 19, so we would want to make it the new largest so far. To do this, we would throw the value 19 into the wastebasket (or, better yet, into the recycle bin) and put the number 41 off to the side, because it is the largest value encountered so far.

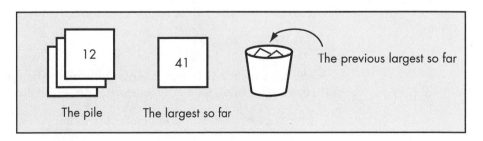

The pile   The largest so far   The previous largest so far

We now repeat this comparison operation, asking whether the number on top of the pile is larger than the largest value seen so far, now 41. This time the value on top of the pile, 12, is not larger, so we do not want to save it. We simply throw it away and move on to the next number in the pile.

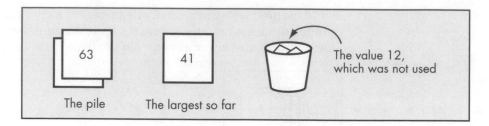

This compare-and-save-or-discard process continues until our original pile of numbers is empty, at which time the largest so far will be the largest value in the entire list.

Let's see how we can convert this informal, pictorial solution into a formal algorithm that is built from the primitive operations shown in Figure 2.6.

We certainly cannot begin to search a list for a largest value until we have a list to search. Therefore, our first operation must be to get a value for n, the size of the list, followed by values for the n-element list $A_1, A_2, \ldots, A_n$. This can be done using our input primitive:

> Get a value for n, the size of the list

> Get values for $A_1, A_2, \ldots, A_n$, the list to be searched

Now that we have the data, we can begin to implement a solution.

Our informal description of the algorithm stated that we should begin by calling the first item in the list, A_1, the largest value so far. We can express this formally as

> Set the value of *largest so far* to A_1

Our solution must also determine where that largest value occurred. To remember this value, let's create a variable called *location* to keep track of the position in the list where the largest value occurred. Because we have initialized *largest so far* to the first element in the list, we should initialize *location* to 1.

> Set the value of *location* to 1

We are now ready to begin looking through the remaining items in list A to find the largest one. However, if we write something like the following instruction:

> If the second item in the list is greater than *largest so far* then . . .

we will have made exactly the same mistake that occurred in the initial version of the sequential search algorithm shown in Figure 2.7. This instruction explicitly checks only the second item of the list. We would need to rewrite that statement to check the third item, the fourth item, and so on. Again, we are failing to use the idea of *iteration,* where we repetitively execute a loop as many times as it takes to produce the desired result.

To solve this problem let's use the same technique used in the sequential search algorithm. Let's not talk about the second, third, fourth, . . . item in the list but about the ith item in the list, where i is a variable that can take on different values during the execution of the algorithm. Using this idea, a statement such as

> If A_i > *largest so far* then . . .

can be executed with different values for i. This will allow us to check all n values in the list with a single statement. Initially, i should be given the value 2, because the first item in the list was automatically set to the largest value. Therefore, we want to begin our search with the second item in the list.

> .
>
> .
>
> .
>
> Set the value of i to 2
>
> .
>
> .
>
> .
>
> If A_i > *largest so far* then . . .

What operations should appear after the word "then"? When we find a new largest value, what should we do? A check of our earlier diagrams shows that we must reset the values of both *largest so far* and *location.*

> .
>
> .
>
> .
>
> Set the value of i to 2
>
> .
>
> .
>
> .
>
> If A_i > *largest so far* then
>
>   Set *largest so far* to A_i
>
>   Set *location* to i

If A_i is not larger than largest so far, then we do not want to do anything. To indicate this, our if-then instruction could include an else clause that looks something like

Else

   Don't do anything at all to *largest so far* and *location*

This is certainly correct, but instructions that tell us not to do anything are usually omitted from an algorithm because they do not carry any meaningful information.

Regardless of whether we do or do not reset the values of *largest so far* and *location*, we need to move on to the next item in the list. Our algorithm refers to A_i, the ith item in the list, so we can move to the next item by simply adding 1 to the value of i and repeating the if-then statement. The outline of this iteration can be sketched as follows:

.

.

.

Set the value of *i* to 2

.

.

.

If A_i > *largest so far* then
   Set *largest so far* to A_i
   Set *location* to *i*
Add 1 to the value of *i*
   .

.

.

However, we do not want to repeat the loop forever. (Remember that one of the properties of an algorithm is that it must eventually halt.) What stops this iterative process? When do we display our answer and terminate execution?

The conditional operation "If A_i > *largest so far* then . . ." is meaningful only if A_i represents an actual element of list A. Because A contains n elements numbered 1 to n, the value of i must be in the range 1 to n. If $i > n$, then the loop has searched the entire list, and it is finished. The algorithm can now print the values of both *largest so far* and *location*. Using our looping primitive, we can describe this iteration as follows:

FIGURE 2.10

Algorithm to Find the Largest Value in a List

Find Largest Algorithm

Get a value for n, the size of the list

Get values for $A_1, A_2, \ldots, A_n$, the list to be searched

Set the value of *largest so far* to A_1

Set the value of *location* to 1

Set the value of i to 2

Repeat until $i > n$

    If A_i > *largest so far* then

        Set *largest so far* to A_i

        Set *location* to i

    Add 1 to the value of i

End of the loop

Print out the values of *largest so far* and *location*

Stop

Set the value of i to 2

Repeat until $i > n$

    If A_i > *largest so far* then

        Set *largest so far* to A_i

        Set *location* to i

    Add 1 to the value of i

End of the loop

Print out the values of *largest so far* and *location*

We have now developed all the pieces of the algorithm and can finally put them together. Figure 2.10 shows the completed "find largest" algorithm. Figure 2.10 leaves out the numbering of the individual steps that was done in all previous examples. This omission is common, especially as algorithms get larger and more complex.

Laboratory Experience 3

This laboratory experience presents an animation of the "find largest" algorithm shown in Figure 2.10. Like the previous laboratory experience, it is intended to give you a deeper understanding of how this algorithm works by allowing you to observe its behavior during execution.

PRACTICE PROBLEM   Modify the algorithm of Figure 2.10 so that it finds the smallest value in a list
rather than the largest.

2.3.3 EXAMPLE 3: MEETING YOUR MATCH

The last algorithm to be developed in this chapter solves a common problem in computer science called **pattern matching**. As an example of this application, imagine that you have a collection of Civil War data files that you wish to use as resource material for an article on Abraham Lincoln. Your first step would probably be to search these files to locate every occurrence of the patterns "Abraham Lincoln," "A. Lincoln," and "Lincoln." The process of searching for a special pattern of symbols within a larger collection of information is called pattern matching. (Most good word processors provide this service as a menu item called FIND or something similar.)

Pattern matching need not be done with only characters and textual information. The same pattern-matching techniques that we will be discussing can be applied to almost any kind of information, including graphics, sound, and pictures. An important medical application of pattern matching is to input an X-ray or CT scan image into a computer and then have the computer search for special patterns, such as dark spots, which represent conditions that should be brought to the attention of a physician. This can help speed up the interpretation of X-rays and avoid the problem of human error caused by fatigue or oversight. (Computers do not get tired or bored!)

One of the most interesting and exciting uses of pattern matching is to assist microbiologists and geneticists in studying and mapping the *human genome*, the basis for all human life. The human genome is composed of a sequence of approximately three and a half billion *nucleotides*, each of which can be one of only four different chemical compounds. The names of these compounds are quite complex, so these nucleotides are usually referred to by the first letter of their chemical names: A, C, T, and G. Thus the basis for our existence turns out to be quite similar to a very large "text file" written in a four-letter alphabet.

...T C G G A C T A A C A T C G G G A T C G A G A T G...

Sequences of these nucleotides are called *genes*. There are about 100,000 genes in the human genome, and they determine virtually all of our physical characteristics—sex, race, eye color, hair color, and height, to name just a few. Genes are also an important factor in the occurrence of certain diseases. When a nucleotide is either missing or changed, it can result in one of a number of extremely serious genetic disorders, such as Down syndrome and Tay-Sachs disease. To help find a cure for these diseases, researchers are attempting to map the human genome—to locate individual genes that, when they exhibit a certain defect, cause a specific malady. A gene is typically composed of tens of thousands of nucleotides, and researchers generally do not know the entire sequence. However, they may know what a small portion of the gene—say, a few hundred nucleotides—looks like. Therefore, to search for one particular gene, they must match the sequence of nucleotides that they do know, called a *probe*, against the entire 3.5 billion-element genome to locate every occurrence of that probe. From this matching information, researchers hope to be able to isolate specific genes. For example,

Genome: ...T C A G G C T A A T C G T A G G...

Probe: T A A T C   *a match*

When a match is found, researchers can examine the nucleotides located before and after the probe to see whether they have located the desired gene and, if so, to see whether the gene is defective. If it is defective, physicians hope someday to be able to "clip out" the bad sequence and insert in its place a correct sequence, a process humorously referred to as creating "designer genes."

We have discussed this application at some length in order to dispel the notion that algorithms such as sequential search (Figure 2.9), "find largest" (Figure 2.10), and pattern matching are nothing more than academic exercises—useless algorithms that serve as examples for introductory classes but have absolutely no role in solving real-world problems. That is not true. The algorithms that we have presented (or will present) *are* important, either in their own right or as building blocks for algorithms to be used by physical scientists, mathematicians, engineers, and social scientists.

Let's formally define the pattern-matching problem as follows:

You will be given some text *composed of* n *characters that will be referred to as* $T_1 T_2 \ldots T_n$. *You will also be given a* pattern *of* m *characters,* m $\leq$ n, *that will be represented as* $P_1 P_2 \ldots P_m$. *The algorithm must locate every occurrence of the pattern within the text. The output of the algorithm is the location in the text where each match occurred. For this problem, the location of a match is defined to be the index position in the text where the match begins.*

For example, if our text is the phrase "to be or not to be, that is the question" and the pattern for which we are searching is the word "to", then our algorithm should produce the following output:

Text: *to* be or not to be, that is the question

Pattern: *to*

Output: Match starting at position 1.

Text: to be or not *to* be, that is the question

Pattern: *to*

Output: Match starting at position 14. (The t is in position 14, including blanks.)

Our pattern-matching algorithm is composed of two parts. In the first part, the pattern is aligned under a specific position of the text, and the algorithm sees whether there is a match at that given position. The second part of the algorithm "slides" the entire pattern ahead one character position. Assuming that we have not gone beyond the end of the text, the algorithm returns to the first part to check for a match at this new position. Pictorially, this algorithm can be represented as follows:

Repeat the following two steps.

Step 1. The matching process: $T_1\, T_2\, T_3\, T_4\, T_5 \ldots$
$P_1\, P_2\, P_3$

Step 2. The slide forward: $T_1\, T_2\, T_3\, T_4\, T_5 \ldots$
1-character slide $\rightarrow$ $P_1\, P_2\, P_3$

The algorithm involves repetition of these two steps beginning at position 1 of the text and continuing until the pattern has slid off the end of the text.

A first draft of an algorithm that implements these ideas is shown in Figure 2.11. Looking at Figure 2.11, we see that not all of the operations are expressed in terms of the basic algorithmic primitives of Figure 2.6. Whereas statements like "Set k, the starting location for the attempted match, to 1" and "Print the value of k, the starting location of the match" are just fine, the instruction that says, "Attempt to match every character in the pattern beginning at position k of the text" is certainly not a primitive. On the contrary, it is a high-level operation that, if written out using only the operations in Figure 2.6, would expand into many instructions.

Is it okay to use high-level statements like this in our algorithm? Wouldn't their use violate the requirement stated in Chapter 1 that algorithms be constructed only from unambiguous operations that can be directly executed by our computing agent?

The answer is that it is perfectly acceptable, and even quite useful, to use high-level statements like this during the *initial phase* of the algorithm design process. When starting to design an algorithm, we may not want to think only in terms of elementary operations such as input, computation, output, conditional, and iteration. Instead, we may first want to express our proposed solution in terms of high-level and broadly defined operations that may represent

FIGURE 2.11

First Draft of the Pattern-Matching Algorithm

Get values for n and m, the size of the text and the pattern, respectively
Get values for both the text $T_1\, T_2 \ldots T_n$ and the pattern $P_1\, P_2 \ldots P_m$
Set k, the starting location for the attempted match, to 1
Repeat until we have fallen off the end of the text
    Attempt to match every character in the pattern beginning at position k
        of the text (this is step 1 from above)
    If there was a match then
        Print the value of k, the starting location of the match
    Add 1 to k, which slides the pattern forward one position (this is step 2)
End of the loop
Stop

dozens or even hundreds of primitive instructions. Here are some examples of these higher-level constructs:

Sort the entire list into ascending order

Attempt to match the entire pattern against the text

Find a root of the equation

Using instructions like these in an algorithm allows us temporarily to postpone worrying about how to implement that operation and lets us focus instead on other aspects of the problem. Eventually, we will come back to these statements and express them in terms of our available primitives, but we can do this at our convenience.

The use of high-level instructions during the design process is an example of one of the most important intellectual tools in computer science—the concept of **abstraction**. Abstraction means the ability to separate the high-level view of an object from the low-level details of its implementation. It is abstraction that allows us to understand and intellectually manage any large, complex system, whether it is a mammoth corporation, a complex piece of machinery, or an intricate and very detailed algorithm. For example, the president of General Motors views the company in terms of its major corporate divisions and very high-level policy issues, not in terms of every worker, every supplier, and every car. Attempting to manage the company at that level of detail would drown him or her in a sea of detail.

In computer science we use abstraction a great deal because of the complexity of hardware and software. For example, abstraction allows us to view the hardware component called "memory" as a single, indivisible high-level entity without having to be aware of the 50,000,000 or more electronic devices that go into constructing a memory unit. (Chapter 4 examines how computer memories are built, and it makes extensive use of abstraction.) In the areas of algorithm design and software development, we use abstraction whenever we think of an operation at a high level, temporarily neglecting how we might actually implement that operation. This allows us to decide which details to address now and which to postpone. Viewing an operation at a high level of abstraction and fleshing out the details of its implementation at a later time constitute an important computer science problem-solving strategy called **top-down design**.

Ultimately, however, we have to describe how each of these high-level abstractions can be represented using the available algorithmic primitives. Let's do that now. The fifth line of the first draft of the pattern-matching algorithm shown in Figure 2.11 reads

Attempt to match every character in the pattern beginning at position k of the text.

When this statement is reached, the pattern is aligned under the text beginning with the kth character. Pictorially, we are in the following situation:

Text: $\quad T_1\ T_2 \ldots T_k\ T_{k+1}\ T_{k+2} \ldots T_{k+(m-1)} \cdots$

Pattern: $\qquad\qquad\quad P_1\ P_2 \quad P_3 \ldots P_m$

The algorithm must now perform the following comparisons:

Compare P_1 to T_k

Compare P_2 to T_{k+1}

Compare P_3 to T_{k+2}

.

.

.

Compare P_m to $T_{k+(m-1)}$

If the members of every single one of these pairs are equal, then there is a match. However, if even one pair is not equal, then there is not a match, and the algorithm can immediately cease all further comparisons at this location. Thus we must construct a loop that will execute until it has either completed m successful comparisons (i.e., until we have matched the entire pattern) or until it has detected a mismatch. Algorithmically, this iteration can be expressed in the following way. (Remember that k is the starting location in the text where we are attempting to find a match.)

Set the value of i to 1

Set the value of *Mismatch* to NO

Repeat until either ($i > m$) or (*Mismatch* = YES)

   If $P_i \neq T_{k+(i-1)}$ then

      Set *Mismatch* to YES

   Else

      Increment i by 1 (to move to the next character)

End of the loop

When the loop has finished, we can determine whether there has been a match by examining the current value of the variable *Mismatch*. If *Mismatch* is YES, then there was not a match because at least one of the characters was out of place. If *Mismatch* is NO, then every character in the pattern matched its corresponding character in the text, and there is a match.

If *Mismatch* = NO then

   Print the message 'There is a match at position'

   Print the value of k

Regardless of whether there was a match at position k, we must add one to k in order to begin searching the next position. This is the "sliding forward" step diagrammed earlier.

The final high-level statement in Figure 2.11 that needs to be expanded is the loop on line 4.

Repeat until we have fallen off the end of the text

What does it mean to "fall off the end of the text"? Where is the last possible place that a match can occur? To answer these questions, let's draw a diagram in which the last character of the pattern, P_m, lines up directly under T_n, the last character of the text.

Text: T_1 T_2 $\ldots$ T_{n-m+1} $\ldots$ T_{n-2} T_{n-1} T_n

Pattern: P_1 $\ldots$ P_{m-2} P_{m-1} P_m

We can determine from this diagram that the last possible place that a match could possibly occur is when the first character of the pattern is aligned under the character at position T_{n-m+1} of the text. We can see that by noting that P_m is aligned under T_n, P_{m-1} is under T_{n-1}, P_{m-2} is under T_{n-2}, etc. Thus, P_1, which can be written as $P_{m-(m-1)}$, will be aligned under $T_{n-(m-1)}$, which is T_{n-m+1}. If we tried to slide the pattern forward any further, we would truly "fall off" the end of the text. Therefore, our loop must terminate when k, the starting point for the match, exceeds the value $n-m+1$. We can express this as follows:

Repeat until $k > (n - m + 1)$

Again, we have all the pieces of our algorithm in place. We have expressed every statement in Figure 2.11 in terms of our basic algorithmic primitives and are ready to put it all together. The final draft of the pattern-matching algorithm is shown in Figure 2.12.

PRACTICE PROBLEMS

1. Consider the following "telephone book."

Name	Number
Smith	555-1212
Jones	834-6543
Adams	921-5281
Doe	327-8900

   Trace the sequential search algorithm of Figure 2.9 using each of the following *NAME*s and show the output produced.
   a. Adams
   b. Schneider

2. Consider the following list of seven data values.

   22, 18, 23, 17, 25, 30, 2

   Trace the "find largest" algorithm of Figure 2.10 and show the output produced.

3. Consider the following text.

   Text: A man and a woman

   Trace the pattern-matching algorithm of Figure 2.12 using the two-character pattern 'an' and show the output produced.

FIGURE 2.12

Final Draft of the Pattern-Matching Algorithm

Pattern-Matching Algorithm

Get values for n and m, the size of the text and pattern, respectively

Get values for the text $T_1 T_2 \ldots T_n$ and the pattern $P_1 P_2 \ldots P_m$

Set k, the starting location, to 1

Repeat until $k > (n - m + 1)$

    Set the value of i to 1

    Set the value of *Mismatch* to NO

    Repeat until either $(i > m)$ or $(Mismatch = \text{YES})$

        If $P_i \neq T_{k+(i-1)}$ then

            Set *Mismatch* to YES

        Else

            Increment i by 1 (move on to the next character)

    End of the loop

    If *Mismatch* = NO then

        Print the message 'There is a match at position'

        Print the value of k

    Increment k by 1

End of the loop

Stop, we are finished

2.4   CONCLUSION

You have now had a chance to see the step-by-step design and development of some interesting, nontrivial algorithms. You have also been introduced to a number of important concepts related to problem solving, including algorithm design, algorithm discovery, pseudocode, control statements, iteration, libraries, abstraction, and top-down design. However, by no means does this mark the end of our discussion about algorithms. On the contrary, the development of a correct solution to a problem marks only the first step in creating a useful solution.

Designing a technically correct algorithm to solve a given problem is only part of what computer scientists do. They also must ensure that they have created an *efficient* algorithm that generates results quickly enough for its intended users. Chapter 1 described a brute force chess algorithm that would, at least theoretically, play perfect chess but that would be of no earthly use to anyone because it would take centuries to make its first move. Similarly, a directory assistance program that takes 10 minutes to locate a telephone number would be of little or no use. A caller would surely hang up long before the answer was found. This practical concern for efficiency and usefulness is one of the hallmarks of computer science.

Therefore, after developing a correct algorithm, we must analyze it thoroughly and study its efficiency properties and operating characteristics. We must ask ourselves how quickly it will give us the desired results and whether it is better than other algorithms that solve the same problem. This analysis, which is the central topic of the next chapter, enables us to state that we have created not only a correct algorithm but an elegant, efficient, and useful one as well.

EXERCISES

1. Write pseudocode instructions to carry out each of the following computational operations.

   a. Determine the area of a triangle given values for the base b and the height h.

   b. Compute the interest earned in 1 year given the starting account balance B and the annual interest rate I and assuming simple interest—that is, no compounding. Also determine the final balance at the end of the year.

   c. Determine the flying time between two cities given the mileage M between them and the average speed of the airplane.

2. Using only the sequential operations described in Section 2.2.2, write an algorithm that gets values for the starting account balance B, annual interest rate I, and annual service charge S. Your algorithm should output the amount of interest earned during the year and the final account balance at the end of the year. Assume that interest is compounded monthly and the service charge is deducted once, at the end of the year.

3. Using only the sequential operations described in Section 2.2.2, write an algorithm that inputs four numbers corresponding to scores received on three semester tests and a final examination. Your algorithm should compute and display the average of all four tests, weighting the final exam twice as heavily as a regular test.

4. Write an algorithm that inputs the length and width of a carpet (in feet) as well as the cost in dollars (per square yard). The algorithm prints out the total cost of the carpeting, including a 6% sales tax.

5. Write an if-then-else primitive to do each of the following operations.

   a. Compute and display the value $(x \div y)$ if the value of y is not 0. If y does have the value 0, then display the message 'Unable to perform the division'.

   b. Compute the area and circumference of a circle given the radius r if the radius is greater than or equal to 1.0. Otherwise, your statement should compute only the circumference.

6. Modify the algorithm of Exercise 2 to include the annual service charge only if the starting account balance at the beginning of the year is less than $1000. If it is greater than or equal to $1000, then no annual service charge is included.

7. Write an algorithm that uses a loop to (1) read in 10 pairs of numbers, where each pair represents the score of a football game with the Computer State University (CSU) score listed first, and (2) for each pair of numbers, determine whether CSU won or lost. After reading in these 10 pairs of values, print out the won/lost/tie record of CSU. In addition, if this record is a perfect 10–0, then print out the message 'Congratulations on your undefeated season'.

8. Modify the test-averaging algorithm of Exercise 3 so that it inputs 15 test scores rather than 4. There are 14 regular tests and a final examination, which again counts twice as much as a regular test. Use a loop to input and sum the scores.

9. Modify the carpet computation algorithm of Exercise 4 so that after finishing the computation of one carpet, it starts on the computation of the next. This iterative process is repeated until we have located a carpet whose total cost is less than $1000.00.

10. Write an algorithm that is given your electric meter readings (in kilowatt-hours) at the beginning and end of each month of the year. The algorithm determines your annual cost of electricity on the basis of a charge of 6 cents per kilowatt-hour for the first 1000 kilowatt-hours of each month and

8 cents per kilowatt-hour beyond 1000. After printing out your total annual charge, the algorithm also determines whether you used less than 500 kilowatt-hours for the entire year, and if so, it prints out a message thanking you for conserving electricity.

11. Develop an algorithm to compute gross pay. The inputs to your algorithm will be the hours worked per week and the hourly pay rate. The rule for determining gross pay is to pay the regular pay rate for all hours worked up to 40.0, time-and-a-half for all hours over 40.0 up to 54.0, and double time for all hours over 54.0. Compute and display the value for gross pay using this rule. After displaying one value, ask the user whether he or she wants to do another computation. Repeat the entire set of operations until the user says no.

12. Develop a formal argument that "proves" that the sequential search algorithm shown in Figure 2.9 cannot have an infinite loop—that is, prove that it will always stop after a finite number of operations.

13. Modify the sequential search algorithm of Figure 2.9 so that it works correctly even if the names in the directory are not unique—that is, if the desired name may occur more than once. Your modified algorithm should find *every* occurrence of *NAME* in the directory and print out the telephone number corresponding to every match. In addition, after all the numbers have been displayed, your algorithm should print out how many occurrences of *NAME* were located. For example, if *NAME* occurred three times, the output of the algorithm might look something like this:

> 528-5638
>
> 922-7874
>
> 488-2020

A total of 3 occurrences were located.

14. Use the "find largest" algorithm of Figure 2.10 to help you develop an algorithm to find the median value in a list containing *N* unique numbers. The median of *N* numbers is defined as the value in the list in which approximately half the values are larger than it and half the values are smaller than it. For example, consider the following list of seven numbers.

> 26, 50, 83, 44, 91, 20, 55

The median value is 50 because three values (20, 26, and 44) are smaller and three values (55, 83, and 91) are larger. If *N* is an even value, then the number of values larger than the median will be one greater than the number of values smaller than the median.

15. With regard to the "find largest" algorithm of Figure 2.10, if the numbers in our list were not unique and therefore the largest number could occur more than once, would the algorithm find the first occurrence? the last occurrence? every occurrence? Explain precisely how this algorithm would behave when presented with this new condition.

16. On the sixth line of the "find largest" algorithm of Figure 2.10 there is an instruction that reads,

> Repeat until $i > n$

Explain exactly what would happen if we changed that instruction to read as follows:

a. Repeat until $i < n$
b. Repeat until $i = n$
c. Repeat until $i \geq n$

17. On the seventh line of the "find largest" algorithm of Figure 2.10 is an instruction that reads,

> If $A_i >$ largest so far then . . .

Explain exactly what would happen if we changed that instruction to read as follows:

a. If $A_i \geq$ largest so far then . . .
b. If $A_i <$ largest so far then . . .

Looking back over your answers to the previous two questions, what do they say about the importance of using the correct *relational operation:* $< = > \geq \leq \neq$?

18. Refer to the pattern-matching algorithm in Figure 2.12. What is the output of the algorithm if our text is

Text: We must band together and handle adversity

and we search for the word "and"? How can we have the algorithm find only the *word* "and" rather than any occurrence of the characters "a", "n", and "d"?

19. Refer to the pattern-matching algorithm in Figure 2.12. Explain how the algorithm would behave if we accidentally omitted the statement on line 16 that says,

> Increment k by 1

CHALLENGE WORK

1. Design an algorithm to find the *root* of a function $f(x)$, where the root is defined as a point x such that $f(x) = 0$. Pictorially, the root of a function is the point where the graph of that function crosses the x-axis.

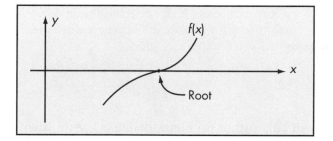

Your algorithm should operate as follows. Initially it will be given three values:

1. A starting point for the search
2. A step size
3. The accuracy desired

Your algorithm should begin at the specified starting point and begin to "walk up" the x-axis in units of step size. After taking a step, it should ask the question "Have I passed a root?" It can determine the answer to this question by seeing whether the sign of the function has changed from the previous point to the current point. (Note that below the axis the sign of $f(x)$ is negative; above the axis it is positive. If it crosses the x-axis, it must change sign.) If the algorithm has not passed a root, it should keep walking up the x-axis until it does. Pictorially,

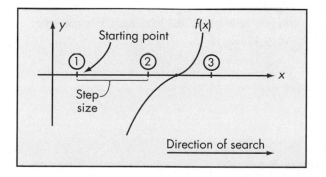

When the algorithm passes a root, it must do two things. First, it should change the sign of step size so that it will start walking in the reverse direction, because it is now past the root. Second, it is going to multiply step size by 0.1, so our steps are one-tenth as big as they were before. We now repeat the operation described above, walking down the x-axis until we pass the root.

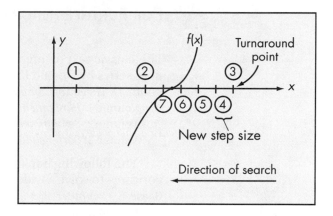

Again, the algorithm changes the sign of step size to reverse direction and reduces it to one-tenth of its previous size. As the diagrams show, we are slowly zeroing in on the root—going past it, turning around, going past it, turning around, and so forth. This iterative process stops when the algorithm passes a root and the step size is smaller than the desired accuracy. It has now bracketed the root within an interval that is smaller than the accuracy we want. At this point it should print out the midpoint of the interval and terminate.

There are many special cases that this algorithm must deal with, but in your solution you may disregard them. Assume that you will always encounter a root in your "travels" along the x-axis. After creating a solution, you may wish to look at some of these special cases, such as a function that has no real roots, a starting point that is to the right of all the roots, and two roots so close together that they fall within the same step.

2. Most people are familiar with the work of the great mathematicians of ancient Greece and Rome, such as Archimedes, Euclid, Pythagoras, and Plato. However, a great deal of important work in arithmetic, geometry, algebra, number theory, and logic was carried out by scholars working in Egypt, Persia, India, and China. For example, the concept of zero was first developed in India, and positional numbering systems (like our own decimal system) were developed and used in China, India, and the Middle East long before they made their way to Europe. Read about the work of mathematicians (such as Al-Khowarizmi) from these and other places, and write a paper describing their contributions to mathematics, logic, and (ultimately) computer science.

FOR FURTHER READING

The classic text on algorithms and algorithm problem solving is the multivolume series by Donald Knuth:

Knuth, D. *The Art of Computer Programming*. Reading, MA: Addison-Wesley.
    Volume 1: *Fundamental Algorithms*, 3rd ed., 1997.
    Volume 2: *Seminumerical Algorithms*, 3rd ed., 1998.
    Volume 3: *Sorting and Searching*, 2nd ed., 1998.

The following books provide additional information about the design of algorithms to solve a wide range of interesting problems.

Baase, S. *Computer Algorithms: Introduction to Design and Analysis*, 2nd ed. Reading, MA: Addison-Wesley, 1988. (Baase is also the author of Chapter 14 in this book, on social issues in computing.)

Cormen, T.; Leiserson, C.; and Rivest, R. *Introduction to Algorithms*. New York: McGraw-Hill, 1990.

Harel, D. *Algorithmics: The Spirit of Computing*, 2nd ed. Reading, MA: Addison-Wesley, 1992.

Sedgewick, R. *Algorithms in C++*. Reading, MA: Addison-Wesley, 1992. (*Note:* We will be looking at the programming language C++ in Chapters 7 and 8.)

The following is an excellent introduction to algorithm design using the control of the motions and actions of a "toy robot" as the basis for teaching problem solving.

Pattis, R.; Roberts, J.; and Stehlik, M. *Karel the Robot: A Gentle Introduction to the Art of Programming*, 2nd ed. New York: Wiley, 1995.

THE
EFFICIENCY OF
ALGORITHMS

3

3.1   INTRODUCTION

Finding algorithms to solve problems of interest is an important part of computer science. Algorithms to perform a variety of tasks were discussed in the previous chapter. Suppose an algorithm has been developed to solve a specific problem. By definition, this algorithm will have certain characteristics (an algorithm is a *well-ordered collection* . . . see Chapter 1). These are the necessary characteristics of any algorithm, but are there other, desirable characteristics? As an analogy, if we go to purchase an automobile, there are certain features that are part of the "definition" of an automobile, such as four wheels and an engine. These are the basics. However, we may also desire other things, such as ease of handling, style, and fuel efficiency. This analogy is not as superficial as it seems because we will find that very similar properties are desirable for algorithms as well.

3.2   ATTRIBUTES OF ALGORITHMS

First and foremost, we expect **correctness** from our algorithms. An algorithm intended to solve a problem must, by our formal definition of an algorithm in Chapter 1, give a result and then halt. But this is not enough; we also have every right to demand the result be a correct solution for the problem. One could consider this an inherent property of the definition of an algorithm (like the car being capable of transporting us where we want to go), but it bears emphasizing. An elegant and efficient algorithm that is an example of creative and intellectual genius, but that gives wrong results for the problem at hand, is worse than useless. It can lead to situations that are enormously expensive or even fatal. An important maxim in computer science is *First, make it correct!*

Determining that an algorithm gives correct results may not be as straightforward as it seems. For one thing, our algorithm may indeed be providing correct results—but to the wrong problem. This can happen when we design an algorithm without a thorough understanding of what the real problem is that we are trying to solve, and it is one of the most common causes of "incorrect" algorithms. Second, the algorithm must provide correct results for all possible input values for the problem, not just for those values that we expect are the most likely to occur. Do we know ahead of time what all those correct results are? (Probably not, or we would not be writing an algorithm to solve this problem.) But there may be a certain standard against which we can check the result for reasonableness, thus giving us a way to determine when a result is obviously incorrect. In some cases, as noted in Chapter 1, the correct result may be an error message saying that there is no correct answer. Third, there may be an issue of the accuracy of the result we are willing to accept as correct. If the "real" answer is π, for example, then we can only approximate its decimal value. Is 3.14159 close enough to be considered "correct"? Is 3.1416 close enough? What about 3.14?

If an algorithm to solve a problem exists and has been determined, after all the considerations of the previous paragraph, to give correct results, what more can we ask? To many mathematicians, this would be the end of the matter, for once a solution has been obtained and shown to be correct, it is no longer of interest (except possibly for use in obtaining solutions to other problems). This is where computer science differs significantly from theoretical disciplines such as pure mathematics and begins to take on an "applied" character more closely related to engineering or applied mathematics. The algorithms developed by computer scientists are not of merely academic interest. They are also intended to be *used*.

Suppose, for example, that a road is to be built to the top of a mountain. An algorithmic solution exists that gives a correct answer for this problem in the sense that a road is produced: Just build the road straight up the mountain. Problem solved. But the highway engineer knows that the road must be usable by real traffic and that this constraint limits the grade of the road. Existence and correctness of the algorithm are not enough; there are practical considerations as well.

The practical considerations for computer science arise because the algorithms developed will be executed in the form of computer programs running on real computers to solve problems of interest to real people. Let's consider the "people aspect" first. A computer program is seldom written to be used only once to solve a single instance of a problem. It is written to solve many instances of that problem with many different input values, just as the sequential search algorithm of Chapter 2 would be used many times with different lists of names and different target *NAME* values. Furthermore, the problem itself does not usually "stand still." If the program is successful, people will want to use it for slightly different versions of the problem, which means they will want the program slightly enhanced to do more things. After a program is written, it will therefore need to be maintained, both to fix any errors that are uncovered through repeated usage with different input values and to extend the program to meet new requirements. Much time and much money are devoted to **program maintenance**.

The person who has to modify a program, either to correct errors or to expand its functionality, often is not the person who wrote the original program. In order to make program maintenance as easy as possible, the algorithm the program uses should be easy to understand. **Ease of understanding**, clarity, "ease of handling"—whatever you want to call it—is a desirable characteristic for an algorithm.

On the other hand, there is a certain satisfaction in having an "elegant" solution to a problem. **Elegance** is the algorithmic equivalent of style. The classic example, in mathematical folklore, is the story of the German mathematician Karl

Frederick Gauss (1777–1855) who was asked as a schoolchild to add up the numbers from 1 to 100. The straightforward algorithm of adding $1 + 2 + 3 + 4 + \ldots + 100$ by adding one number at a time can be expressed in pseudocode as

1. Set the value of *sum* to 0

2. Set the value of *x* to 1

3. While *x* is less than or equal to 100 do steps 4 and 5

4.   Add *x* to *sum*

5.   Add 1 to the value of *x*

6. Print the value of *sum*

7. Stop

This algorithm can be executed to find that the sum has the value 5050. It is fairly easy to read through this pseudocode and understand how the algorithm works. It is also fairly clear that if we want to change this algorithm to one that adds the numbers from 1 to 1000, we only have to change the loop condition to

3. While *x* is less than or equal to 1000 do steps 4 and 5

However, Gauss noticed that the numbers from 1 to 100 could be grouped into 50 pairs of the form

$1 + 100 = 101$
$2 + 99 = 101$

.

.

.

$50 + 51 = 101$

so that the sum equals $50 \times 101 = 5050$. Now this is an elegant and clever solution algorithm. But is it easy to understand? If a computer program just said to multiply

$$\left(\frac{100}{2}\right)(100 + 1)$$

with no further explanation, we might guess how to modify the program to add up the first 1000 numbers, but would we really grasp what was happening enough to be sure the modification would work? (The Practice Problem at the end of this section discusses this.) Sometimes elegance and ease of understanding work at cross-purposes; the more elegant the solution, the more difficult it may be to understand. If an algorithm has both characteristics—ease of understanding and elegance—at the same time, that's a plus.

Now let's consider the real computers on which programs will run. Although these computers can execute instructions very rapidly and have some memory in which to store information, "time" and "space" are not unlimited resources. The computer scientist must be conscious of the resources consumed by a given algorithm, and if there is a choice between two (correct) algorithms that perform the same task, the one that uses fewer resources is preferable. **Efficiency** is the term used to describe an algorithm's careful use of resources. In addition to *correctness, ease of understanding*, and *elegance*, we look for *efficiency* as an extremely desirable attribute of an algorithm. In light of this list of attributes, the computer scientist's job involves much more than simply "coming up with" an algorithm.

Because of the rapid advances in computer technology, computers of today have much more memory capacity and execute instructions much more rapidly than computers of just a few years ago. Efficiency in algorithms may seem to be a moot point; we can just wait for the next generation of technology and it won't matter how much time or space is used. There is some truth to this, but as computer memory capacity and processing speed increase, people find ever more complex problems to be solved, so the boundaries of the computer's resources continue to be pushed. Furthermore, we will see in this chapter that there are algorithms that consume so many resources that they will never be practical, no matter what advances in computer technology occur.

How shall we measure the time and space consumed by an algorithm to determine whether it is efficient? Space efficiency can be judged by the amount of information the algorithm must store in the computer's memory in order to do its job, in addition to the initial data on which the algorithm is operating. If it uses only a few extra quantities while processing the input data, the algorithm is relatively space-efficient. If the algorithm requires almost as much additional storage as the input data itself takes up, or even more, then it is relatively space-inefficient.

How can we measure the time efficiency of an algorithm? Consider the sequential search algorithm shown in Figure 2.9 for looking up a name in the telephone directory where the names are not arranged in alphabetical order. How about running the algorithm on a real computer and timing it to see how many seconds (or maybe what small fraction of a second) it takes to find a name or announce that the name is not present? The difficulty with this approach is that there are three factors in this problem, each of which can affect the answer to such a degree as to make whatever number of seconds we come up with rather meaningless.

1. On what computer will we run the algorithm? Shall we use a modest portable machine or a huge supercomputer capable of doing many billions of calculations per second?

2. What telephone book (list of names) will we use, New York City or Mesquite, Nevada?

3. What name will we try to find? What if we pick a name that happens to be first in the list? What if it happens to be last in the list?

By just running our stopwatch, we are seeing the effects of variations in machine speed or variations due to input data rather than the efficiency (or lack thereof) inherent in the way the algorithm goes about solving the problem.

There is indeed a place for timing of the sort we have just described. For example, using the same input data (New York City and Karlenski, say) and timing the algorithm on different machines gives a comparison of machine speeds on identical tasks. Using the same machine and the same list of names but trying a variety of names to search for gives an indication of how the choice of *NAME* affects the algorithm's running time on that particular machine. These types of comparative timings are called **benchmarking**. They are useful for rating one machine against another with respect to one specific algorithm and for rating how sensitive a particular algorithm is with respect to variations in input on one particular machine.

However, what we mean by an algorithm's time efficiency is an indication of the amount of "work" required by the nature of the algorithm itself and the approach it uses. It is a measure of the inherent efficiency of the method, independent of the speed of the machine on which it is executing or the specific data on which it is working. Is the amount of work an algorithm does the same as the number of instructions it executes? Not all instructions do the same things, so perhaps they should not all be "counted" equally. Some instructions are carrying out work that is fundamental to the way the algorithm operates, whereas other instructions are carrying out peripheral tasks that must be done in support of the fundamental work. We will try to identify the fundamental unit or units of work of an algorithm. Once we have done this, it will be sufficient to count the number of instruction executions that do this work because the total number of instructions executed will be proportional to that count.

Suppose we find two algorithms, A and B, that both do the same task (processing n items in some way) using the same fundamental unit of work. Suppose also that A has to execute many more of these work units than B. On a particular machine, each work unit takes a certain amount of time, and A will require more time than B. This time differential will not disappear, no matter what the speed of the machine. If we run these two algorithms on a machine that runs much

---

PRACTICE PROBLEM   Use Gauss's approach to find a formula for the sum of the numbers from 1 to n,

$$1 + 2 + 3 + \ldots + n$$

where n is an even number. Your formula will be an expression involving n. Test your formula for the following sums.

    i. $1 + 2$

   ii. $1 + 2 + \ldots + 6$

  iii. $1 + 2 + \ldots + 10$

  iv. $1 + 2 + \ldots + 100$

   v. $1 + 2 + \ldots + 1000$

Now, to see whether the same formula works when n is odd, try it on

   a. $1 + 2 + 3$

   b. $1 + 2 + \ldots + 5$

   c. $1 + 2 + \ldots + 9$

faster than the previous machine, then the timing difference between algorithms A and B decreases. But if we use this faster machine to process a much larger quantity of input, the gap is just as bad as before. A faster machine can scale up the size of the input that produces the differential, but it cannot eliminate the differential. *It is the number of steps each algorithm requires, not the time the algorithm takes on a particular machine, that is important for comparing two algorithms that do the same task.*

3.3   A CHOICE OF ALGORITHMS

Algorithm efficiency appears to be an important attribute in comparing one algorithm with another for the same task. In this section we'll look at three different algorithms that solve the same problem and then examine their efficiency. We'll call this problem the "data cleanup" problem.

Suppose a survey has been taken that includes a question about the age of the person filling out the survey. Some people will choose not to answer this question. When data from the survey are entered in the computer, there must be a way to show "no response" to this question. An entry of 0 will be used to denote "no response," because a legitimate value for age would have to be a positive number. As an example, we'll assume that the age data from ten people who completed the survey are stored in the computer as the following ten-entry list, where the positions in the list range from 1 (far left) to 10 (far right).

0	24	16	0	36	42	23	21	0	27
1	*2*	*3*	*4*	*5*	*6*	*7*	*8*	*9*	*10*

In one use of the age data, the average age is to be computed. Because the 0 values are not legitimate data, including them in the average would produce too low a value. We want to perform a "data cleanup" and remove the 0 entries from the list before the average is computed. In our example, the cleaned-up data could consist of a ten-element list where the seven legitimate elements are the first seven entries of the list, and some quantity, let's call it *legit*, has the value 7 to indicate that only the first seven entries are legitimate. An alternative acceptable result would be a seven-element list consisting of the seven legitimate data items, in which case there is no need for a *legit* quantity.

3.3.1 THE SHUFFLE-LEFT ALGORITHM

Algorithm 1 to solve the data cleanup problem works as we might solve this problem using a pencil and paper (and an eraser) to modify the list. We could proceed through the list from left to right, pointing with a finger on the left hand to keep our place, and passing over nonzero values. Every time we encountered a 0 value, we would squeeze it out of the list by taking each remaining data item in the list and copying it over one cell to the left. We could use a finger on the right hand to move along the list and point at what to copy next. The value of *legit*, originally set to the length of the list, would be reduced by 1 every time a 0 was encountered. (Sounds complicated, but you'll see that it is easy.)

The original configuration is

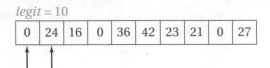

Finger of left   Finger of right
hand points   hand points
to cell 1.   to cell 2.

Because the first cell on the left contains a 0, the value of *legit* is reduced by 1, and all of the items to the right of the 0 must be copied one cell left. After the first such copy (of the 24), the situation looks like

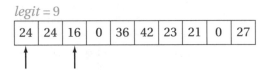

After the second copy (of the 16), we get

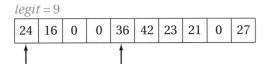

and after the third copy of (of the 0),

Proceeding in this fashion, we find that after we copy the last item (the 27), the result is

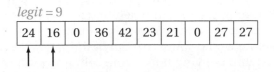

Because the right-hand finger has moved past the end of the list, one complete shuffle-left process has been completed. It required copying nine items. We reset the right-hand finger to start again.

legit = 9

| 24 | 16 | 0 | 36 | 42 | 23 | 21 | 0 | 27 | 27 |

We must again examine position 1 for a 0 value, because if the original list contained 0 in position 2, it would have been copied into position 1. If the value is not 0, as is the case here, both the left-hand finger and the right-hand finger move forward.

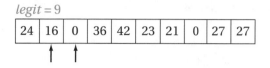

Moving along, we pass over the 16.

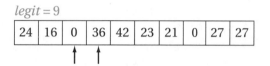

Another cycle of seven copies takes place to squeeze out the 0; the result is

legit = 8

| 24 | 16 | 36 | 42 | 23 | 21 | 0 | 27 | 27 | 27 |

The 36, 42, 23, and 21 are passed over, which results in

legit = 8

| 24 | 16 | 36 | 42 | 23 | 21 | 0 | 27 | 27 | 27 |

and then squeezing out the final 0 gives

legit = 7

| 24 | 16 | 36 | 42 | 23 | 21 | 27 | 27 | 27 | 27 |

after copying three items. The left-hand finger is pointing at a nonzero element, so another advance of both fingers gives

At this point we can stop because the left-hand finger is past the number of legitimate data items (*legit* = 7). In total, this algorithm (on this list) required examining all 10 data items, to see which ones were 0, and copying 9 + 7 + 3 = 19 items.

A pseudocode version of the shuffle-left algorithm to act on a list of *n* items appears in Figure 3.1. The quantities *left* and *right* correspond to the positions

FIGURE 3.1

The Shuffle-Left Algorithm
for Data Cleanup

1. Get values for n and the n data items
2. Set the value of *legit* to n
3. Set the value of *left* to 1
4. Set the value of *right* to 2
5. While *left* is less than or equal to *legit* do steps 6 through 14
6.   If the item at position *left* is not 0 then do steps 7 and 8
7.   Increase *left* by 1
8.   Increase *right* by 1
9.   Else (the item at position *left* is 0) do steps 10 through 14
10.   Reduce *legit* by 1
11.   While *right* is less than or equal to n do steps 12 and 13
12.   Copy the item at position *right* into position (*right* − 1)
13.   Increase *right* by 1
14.   Set the value of *right* to (*left* + 1)
15. Stop

where the left-hand and right-hand fingers point, respectively. You should trace through this algorithm for the preceding example to see that it does what we described.

In addition to the memory required to store the list itself, the shuffle-left algorithm requires four memory locations to store the quantities n, *legit*, *left*, and *right*.

3.3.2 THE COPY-OVER ALGORITHM

Algorithm 2 to solve the data cleanup problem works as we might using a pencil and paper if we decided to write a new list. It also proceeds by scanning the list from left to right. Every legitimate value is copied into a new list that is being built. Zero values are not copied into the new list. After this algorithm is finished, the original list still exists, but so does a new list in the desired form. For our example, the result would be

0	24	16	0	36	42	23	21	0	27

24	16	36	42	23	21	27

Every list entry gets examined to see whether it is 0 (as in the shuffle-left algorithm), and every nonzero list entry gets copied once (into the new list), so a total of seven copies are done for this example. This is fewer copies than the shuffle-left algorithm required, but a lot of extra memory space is required because an almost complete second copy of the list is stored. Figure 3.2 shows the pseudocode for this copy-over algorithm.

FIGURE 3.2

The Copy-Over Algorithm for Data Cleanup

1. Get values for *n* and the *n* data items
2. Set the value of *left* to 1
3. Set the value of *newposition* to 1
4. While *left* is less than or equal to *n* do steps 5 through 9
5.   If the item at position *left* is not 0 then do steps 6 through 8
6.   Copy the item at position *left* into position *newposition* in new list
7.   Increase *left* by 1
8.   Increase *newposition* by 1
9.   Else (the item at position *left* is 0) increase *left* by 1
10. Stop

3.3.3 THE CONVERGING-POINTERS ALGORITHM

For the third algorithm, imagine that we move one finger along the list from left to right and another finger from right to left. The left finger slides to the right over nonzero values. Whenever the left finger encounters a 0 item, we reduce the value of *legit* by 1, copy whatever item is at the right finger into the left-finger position, and slide the right finger one cell left. Initially in our example,

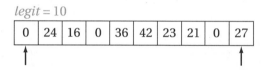

and because a 0 is encountered at position *left,* the item at position *right* is copied into its place, and both *legit* and *right* are reduced by 1. This results in

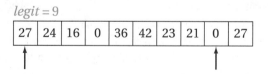

The value of *left* increases until the next 0 is reached.

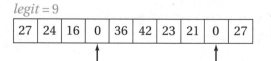

Again, the item at position *right* is copied into position *left,* and *legit* and *right* are reduced by 1.

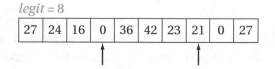

The item at position left is still 0, so another copy takes place.

legit = 7

| 27 | 24 | 16 | 21 | 36 | 42 | 23 | 21 | 0 | 27 |

From here on, the left finger advances until it meets the right finger, which is pointing to a nonzero element, and the algorithm stops. Once again, each element was examined to see whether it equaled 0. A total of only three copies were done—fewer even than for algorithm 2 but requiring no more memory space than algorithm 1. The pseudocode version of this converging-pointers algorithm is given in Figure 3.3.

3.3.4 Comparisons

We now have three different algorithms to do the data cleanup task. Judging by our example, algorithm 3, the converging-pointers algorithm, appears to require fewer copies and less memory space than either of the other two. Hence it would seem to be the most time- and space-efficient. However, we can't draw a conclusion on the basis of just one example, because the particular data sample we used may have some peculiarities that influenced the results. We need to be able to do a more general analysis of these, as well as other, algorithms. We will learn how to do this in the next section.

FIGURE 3.3

The Converging-Pointers Algorithm for Data Cleanup

1. Get values for *n* and the *n* data items
2. Set the value of *legit* to *n*
3. Set the value of *left* to 1
4. Set the value of *right* to *n*
5. While *left* is less than *right* do steps 6 through 10
6.   If the item at position *left* is not 0 then increase *left* by 1
7.   Else (the item at position *left* is 0) do steps 8 through 10
8.   Reduce *legit* by 1
9.   Copy the item at position *right* into position *left*
10.   Reduce *right* by 1
11. If the item at position *left* is 0, then reduce *legit* by 1
12. Stop

Laboratory Experience 4

In this laboratory experience, you will be able to run animations of the shuffle-left algorithm and the converging-pointers algorithm for the data cleanup problem. You'll be able to see the left and right pointers take on different values, which represent changing positions in the data list. As the algorithms run on various lists, you can count the number of copies of data elements that are required.

PRACTICE PROBLEMS   In the data cleanup problem, suppose the original data are

1. Write the data list after completion of algorithm 1, the shuffle-left algorithm.
2. Write the two data lists after completion of algorithm 2, the copy-over algorithm.
3. Write the data list after completion of algorithm 3, the converging-pointers algorithm.
4. Make up a data list such that step 11 of the converging-pointers algorithm (Figure 3.3) is needed.

3.4   MEASURING EFFICIENCY

The study of the efficiency of various algorithms is called the **analysis of algorithms**, and it is an important part of computer science. Later we will analyze the data cleanup algorithms just presented, but as a first example of the general analysis of an algorithm, we'll look at the sequential search algorithm.

3.4.1 SEQUENTIAL SEARCH

The pseudocode description of the sequential search algorithm from Chapter 2 appears in Figure 3.4, where we have assumed that the list contains *n* entries instead of 10,000 entries.

The central unit of work seems to be the comparison of the *NAME* being searched for against a name in the list. The essence of the algorithm is the repetition of this task against successive names in the list until *NAME* is found or the list is exhausted. The comparison takes place at step 4, within the loop composed of steps 4 through 7. Peripheral tasks include setting the initial value of the index *i*, writing the output, adjusting *Found*, and moving the index forward in the list of names. Why can these be considered peripheral tasks?

Setting the initial value of the index requires execution of only a single instruction, done at step 2. Writing output requires executing only a single instruction, either at step 5 if *NAME* was in the list or at step 8 if *NAME* was not in the list. Note that instruction 5, although it is part of the loop, writes output at most once (if *NAME* equals N_i). Similarly, setting *Found* to YES occurs at most once (if *NAME* equals N_i) at step 6. The initial setting of *Found* occurs as a single instruction in step 2. We can ignore the small contribution of these single-instruction executions to the total work done by the algorithm.

FIGURE 3.4
Sequential Search Algorithm

1. Get values for *NAME*, n, N_1, . . . , N_n and T_1, . . . , T_n
2. Set the value of i to 1 and set the value of *Found* to NO
3. Repeat steps 4 through 7 until either *Found* = YES or i is greater than n
4.   If *NAME* is equal to the ith name on the list, N_i, then do steps 5 and 6
5.   Print the telephone number of that person, T_i
6.   Set the value of *Found* to YES
7.   Else (*NAME* is not equal to N_i) add 1 to the value of i
8. If (*Found* = NO) then print the message 'I am sorry, but that name is not in the directory'
9. Stop

Moving the index forward is done once for each comparison, at step 7. We can get a good idea of the total amount of work the algorithm does by simply counting the number of comparisons and then multiplying by some constant factor to take care of the index-moving task. Perhaps the constant factor should be 2 because we do one index move for each comparison, so we would double the work. Perhaps it should be less because it is less work to add 1 to i than it is to compare *NAME* letter by letter against N_i. We will see in the next section why we don't have to pay too much attention to the value of this constant factor.

Therefore, we will take the basic unit of work to be comparison of *NAME* against a list element. One comparison is done at each pass through the loop in steps 4 through 7, so we must ask how many times the loop is executed. Of course, this depends on when, or whether, we find *NAME* in the list.

The minimum amount of work is done if *NAME* is the very first name in the list. This will require only one comparison, because *NAME* has then been found and the algorithm exits the loop after only one pass. This would be called the **best case**. The **worst case**, requiring the maximum amount of work, occurs if *NAME* is the very last name in the list, because *NAME* must be compared against all n names in the list before the loop terminates. If *NAME* is not in the list at all, the algorithm also compares *NAME* against all n names in the list before exiting the loop because the value of the index i exceeds n. Thus there are two conditions, each of which produces the worst-case behavior of the sequential search algorithm.

When *NAME* occurs somewhere in the middle of the list, it requires somewhere between 1 (the best case) and n (the worst case) comparisons. If we were to run the sequential search algorithm many times with random *NAME*s occurring at various places in the list and count the number of comparisons done each time, we would find that the average number of comparisons done is about $n/2$. (The exact average is actually slightly higher than $n/2$; see Exercise 7 at the end of the chapter.) It is not hard to explain why an average of approximately $n/2$ comparisons are done (or the loop is executed approximately $n/2$ times) when *NAME* is in the list. If *NAME* occurs halfway down the list, then roughly $n/2$ comparisons are required; random *NAME*s in the list will occur before the halfway point about half the time and after the halfway point about half the time, and these cases of less work and more work balance out.

This means that the average number of comparisons needed to find a *NAME* that occurs in a 10-element list is about 5, in a 100-element list about 50, and in a 1000-element list about 500. On small values of n — say, a few hundred or a few thousand names—the values of $n/2$ (the average case) or n (the worst case) are small enough that a computer could execute the algorithm quickly and get the desired answer in a fraction of a second. However, computers are generally used to solve not tiny problems but very large ones. Therefore, we are usually interested not in the behavior of an algorithm on little problems but in its behavior as the size of a problem(n) gets very, very large. For example, in the New York City telephone directory, n may be as large as 20,000,000. If the sequential search algorithm were executed on a computer that could do 50,000 comparisons per second, it would require on the average about

$$\frac{20,000,000}{2} \text{ comparisons} \times \frac{1}{50,000} \text{ seconds/comparison} = 200 \text{ seconds}$$

or $3\frac{1}{3}$ minutes, just to do the comparisons necessary to locate a specific name. Including the constant factor for advancing the index, the actual time needed would be even greater. It would require almost 7 minutes just to do the comparisons required to determine that a name was not in the directory! Sequential search does not seem to be sufficiently time-efficient for large values of n to be useful as a telephone directory look-up algorithm. Later in this chapter, we'll see a more efficient search algorithm that makes use of the fact that the names in the telephone directory are arranged in alphabetical order.

Information about the number of comparisons required to perform the sequential search algorithm on a list of n names is summarized in Figure 3.5. Note that the values for both the worst case and the average case in Figure 3.5 depend on n, the number of names in the list. The bigger the list, the more work must be done to search it. Few algorithms do the same amount of work on large inputs as on small inputs, simply because most algorithms require some sort of processing of the input data, and more data to process means more work to be done. The work an algorithm does is usually given in terms of a formula that depends on the size of the appropriate problem input. In the case of searching a list of names, the input size is the length of the list. For other tasks with other kinds of input, the size of the problem input may mean something different.

Finally, let's say a word about the space efficiency of sequential search. The algorithm stores the list of names and the target *NAME* as part of the input. The only additional memory required is storage for the index value i. A single additional memory location is insignificant compared to the size of the list of names, just as executing a single instruction to initialize the value of the index is insignificant beside the repetitive comparison task. Therefore, sequential search

FIGURE 3.5

Number of Comparisons to Find NAME *in a List of* n *Names Using Sequential Search*

Best Case	Worst Case	Average Case
1	n	$n/2$

uses essentially no more memory storage than the original input requires, so it is very space-efficient, partly because it makes no changes to the original list.

3.4.2 ORDER OF MAGNITUDE

When we analyzed the time efficiency of the sequential search algorithm, we glossed over the contribution of the constant factor for the peripheral work. As it turns out, we will be taking such a large-scale view that we can often ignore it! To see why this is the case, we need to understand a concept called *order of magntude*.

The worst-case behavior of the sequential search algorithm on a list of n names requires n comparisons, or if c is a constant factor representing the peripheral work, it requires cn total work. Suppose that c has the value 2. Then the values of n and $2n$ are

n	$2n$
1	2
2	4
3	6

and so on

These values are shown in Figure 3.6, which illustrates how the value of $2n$, which is the total work, changes as n changes.

We can add to this graph to show how the value of cn changes as n changes, where $c = 1$ or $c = \frac{1}{2}$ as well as $c = 2$ (Figure 3.7). These values of c are completely arbitrary.

Figure 3.8 presents a different view of the growth rate of cn as n changes for these three values of c.

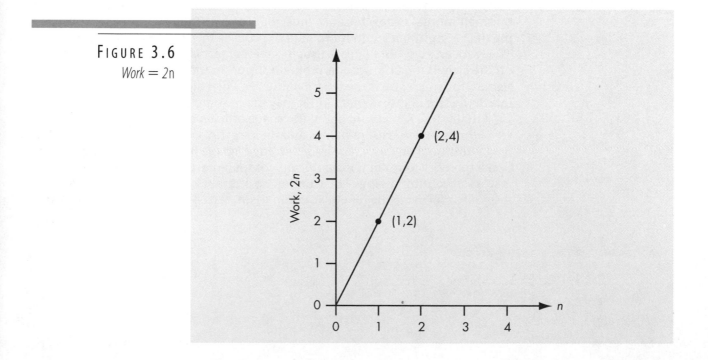

FIGURE 3.6
Work = 2n

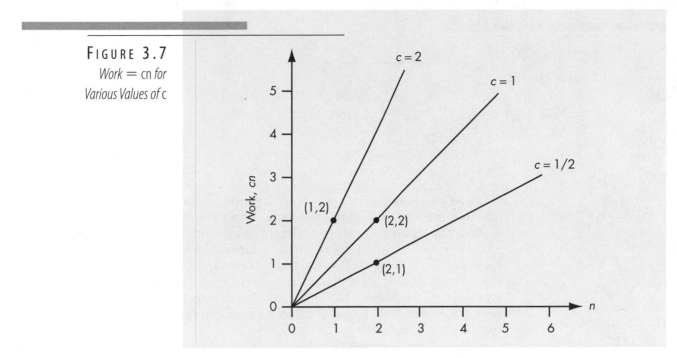

FIGURE 3.7

Work = cn for Various Values of c

Both Figure 3.7 and Figure 3.8 show that the amount of work *cn* increases as *n* increases, but at different rates. The work grows at the same rate as *n* when *c* = 1, at twice the rate of *n* when *c* = 2, and at half the rate of *n* when *c* = ½. However, Figure 3.7 also shows that all of these graphs follow the same basic straight-line shape of *n*. Anything that varies as a constant times *n* (and whose graph follows the basic shape of *n*) is said to be of **order of magnitude *n*,** written $\Theta(n)$. Sequential search is therefore an $\Theta(n)$ algorithm (an order-*n* algorithm) in both the worst case and the average case.

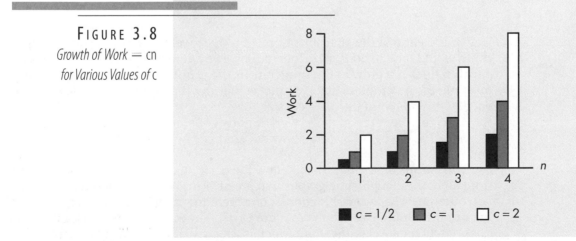

FIGURE 3.8

Growth of Work = cn for Various Values of c

FIGURE 3.9

Table of Calling Information

	1	2	3	4
1	243	187	314	244
2	215	420	345	172
3	197	352	385	261
4	340	135	217	344

Now let's look at another problem. Suppose a metropolitan area is divided into four telephone calling districts 1, 2, 3, and 4. The telephone company keeps track of the number of calls placed from one district to another and the number of calls placed within a district. This information is recorded per month in a table as shown in Figure 3.9. The entry in row 1, column 3, for example, shows the number of calls (314) placed from district 1 to district 3 for the month. The entry in row 3, column 1 shows the number of calls (197) placed from district 3 to district 1. The entry in row 1, column 1 shows the number of calls (243) placed from district 1 to district 1.

Now suppose we want to write an algorithm to process this information in some way, perhaps to write it out. The algorithm must look at each entry in the table, a total of 16 entries. The pseudocode form of the algorithm would be

> For each of rows 1 through 4 do the following
>
> > For each of columns 1 through 4 do the following
> >
> > > Write the entry in this row and column

This would say that for row 1, the algorithm moves through columns 1, 2, 3, and 4, writing each entry. Next the algorithm moves to row 2 and writes the entry in each of the four columns. Then it does the same thing with rows 3 and 4. Each of four rows requires writing the entry in each of four columns. The number of write operations done is thus

$$4 \times 4 = 16$$

Here it is clear that the 16 results from 4^2. If there were n districts, such an algorithm would have to do n^2 write operations. The amount of work done by this algorithm does not grow at the same rate as the problem size (or some constant multiple of the problem size), as the sequential search did. It grows at a rate equal to the *square* of the problem size.

An algorithm that does cn^2 work for any constant c is **order of magnitude n^2**, or $\Theta(n^2)$. Figure 3.10 shows how cn^2 changes as n changes, where $c = 1, 2,$ and ½.

The graphs of Figure 3.10 all follow the basic shape of n^2, which is different from all of the straight-line graphs that are of $\Theta(n)$. Thus we have come up with two different "shape classifications": one including all graphs that are $\Theta(n)$ and the other including all graphs that are $\Theta(n^2)$. The value of the constant factor does not affect the classification, which is why we can generally ignore it.

FIGURE 3.10
*Work = cn² for
Various Values of c*

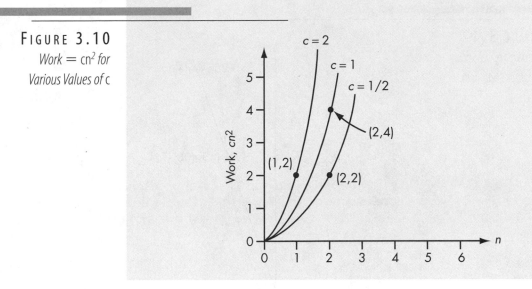

FIGURE 3.10

Work = cn^2 *for
Various Values of* c

If it is not important to distinguish among the various graphs that make up a given order of magnitude, why is it important to distinguish between the two different orders of magnitude n and n^2? We can find the answer by comparing the two basic shapes n and n^2, as is done in Figure 3.11.

Figure 3.11 indicates that n^2 grows at a much faster rate than n. The two curves cross at the point (1,1), and for any value of n larger than 1, n^2 has a value increasingly greater than n. Furthermore, anything that is order of magnitude n^2 will eventually have larger values than anything that is of order n, no matter what the constant factors are. For example, Figure 3.12 shows that if we choose a graph that is $\Theta(n^2)$ but has a small constant factor to keep the values down, say

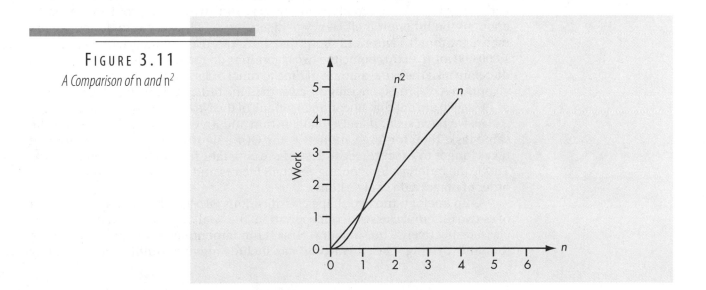

FIGURE 3.11

A Comparison of n *and* n²

FIGURE 3.12
For Large Enough n, 0.25n²
Has Larger Values Than 10n

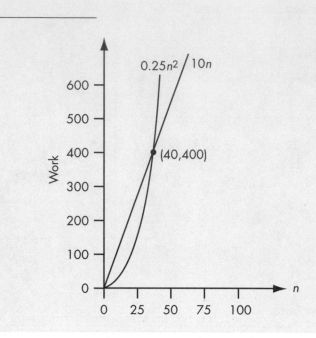

$0.25n^2$, and a graph that is $\Theta(n)$ but has a larger constant factor to pump the values up, say $10n$, it is still true that the $\Theta(n^2)$ graph eventually has larger values. (Note that the vertical scale and the horizontal scale are different.)

As a more extreme example, suppose that algorithm A does $0.0001n^2$ units of work to solve a problem with input size n and that algorithm B does $100n$ of the same units of work to solve the same problem. Here the factor of 100 that occurs with algorithm B is *one million times larger* than the factor of 0.0001 that occurs with algorithm A. Nonetheless, in the long run (when the problem gets large enough) the inherent inefficiency of algorithm A will cause it to do more work than algorithm B. Figure 3.13 shows that the "cross-over" point occurs at a value of 1,000,000 for n. At this point, the two algorithms do the same amount of work and therefore take the same amount of time to run. For larger values of n, the order-n^2 algorithm A will run increasingly slower than the order-n algorithm B. (Input sizes of 1,000,000 are not that uncommon—think of the New York City telephone list.)

As we have seen, if an $\Theta(n^2)$ algorithm and an $\Theta(n)$ algorithm exist for the same task, then for large enough n, the $\Theta(n^2)$ algorithm does more work and takes longer to execute, regardless of the constant factors for peripheral work. This is the rationale for ignoring constant factors and concentrating on the basic order of magnitude of algorithms.

As an analogy, the two shape classifications $\Theta(n^2)$ and $\Theta(n)$ may be thought of as two different classes of transportation, the "walking" class and the "driving" class, respectively. The "walking" class is fundamentally more time-consuming than the "driving" class. "Walking" can include jogging, running, and leisurely

FIGURE 3.13

A Comparison of Two Extreme $\Theta(n^2)$ and $\Theta(n)$ Algorithms

| | Number of Work Units Required | |
| | Algorithm A | Algorithm B |
n	$0.0001n^2$	$100n$
1,000	100	100,000
10,000	10,000	1,000,000
100,000	1,000,000	10,000,000
1,000,000	100,000,000	100,000,000
10,000,000	10,000,000,000	1,000,000,000

The Tortoise and the Hare

One way to compare performance among different makes of automobiles is to give the number of seconds it takes each car to go from 0 to 60 miles per hour. One way to compare performance among different makes of computers is to give the number of arithmetic operations, such as additions or subtractions of real numbers, that each one can do in 1 second. These operations are called "floating-point operations," and computers are advertised in terms of the number of **flops** (floating-point operations per second) they can crank out.

As a comparison, a personal computer based on the Pentium Pro 200 processor runs at about 75 megaflops (75 million floating-point operations per second). It sells for around $2000. The Cray T3E-900, a "parallel processor computing system" with 1320 processors, can achieve 670 gigaflops (670 billion floating-point operations per second). It is about 9000 times faster than the Pentium machine. The Cray sells for around $31 million, roughly 15,500 times the cost of the Pentium Pro. The stage is set for the race between the tortoise and the hare.

Not fair, you say? We'll see. Let's suppose the Pentium machine is assigned to run an $\Theta(n)$ algorithm, whereas the unfortunate Cray gets an $\Theta(n^2)$ algorithm for the same task. The work units are floating-point operations, and for simplicity, we'll take the constant factor to be 1 in each case. Here are the timing results:

n	PENTIUM PRO $\Theta(n)$	CRAY $\Theta(n^2)$
750	0.00001 sec	0.00000084 sec
7,500	0.0001 sec	0.000084 sec
75,000	0.001 sec	0.0084 sec
750,000	0.01 sec	0.84 sec
7,500,000	0.1 sec	84 sec
75,000,000	1 sec	8400 sec $=$ 2.3 hr
750,000,000	10 sec	840,000 sec $=$ 9.7 days

"Out of the gate"—that is, for small values of n—the Cray has a head start and takes less time. When $n = 75,000$, the Pentium machine is already slightly faster than the Cray. And by the time $n = 750,000,000$, it has left the Cray in the dust. The difference in order of magnitude between the algorithms was enough to slow down the mighty Cray and let the Pentium machine creep past, chugging along doing its more efficient $\Theta(n)$ algorithm.

The point of this little tale is obviously not to say that everyone who has bought a powerful computer system should have bought a PC instead! It is to note that the order of magnitude of the algorithm being executed can play a more important role than the raw speed of the computer.

strolling (which correspond to different values for c), but compared to any form of driving, these all proceed at roughly the same speed. The "driving" class can include driving a Geo and driving a Ferrari (which correspond to different values for c), but compared to any form of walking, these proceed at roughly the same speed. In other words, varying c can make modest changes within a class, but changing to a different class is a quantum leap.

Given two algorithms for the same task, we should usually choose the algorithm of the lesser order of magnitude, because for large enough n it will always "win out." It is for large values of n that we need to be concerned about the time resources being used, and as we noted earlier, it is often for large values of n that we are seeking a computerized solution in the first place.

We should note, however, that for smaller values of n, the size of the constant factor is significant. In Figure 3.12, the $10n$ line stayed above the $0.25n^2$ curve up to the cross-over point of $n = 40$, because it had a large constant factor relative to the factor for n^2. Varying the factors would change the cross-over point. If $10n$ and $0.25n^2$ represented the work of two different algorithms for the same task, and if we could be sure that the size of the input was never going to exceed 40, then the $0.25n^2$ algorithm would be preferable in terms of time resources used. (To continue the transportation analogy, for traveling short distances—say, to the end of the driveway—walking will be faster than driving because of the "overhead" of getting the car started, and so on. But for long distances, driving is faster.) However, making assumptions about the size of the input can be dangerous. A successful and efficient program designed to operate on small input size may be selected (perhaps because it seemed efficient) to solve instances of the problem with large input size, at which point the efficiency may go down the drain! Sequential search may serve for directory assistance in Mesquite, Nevada, but it won't translate satisfactorily to New York City. Part of

PRACTICE PROBLEMS

1. Using the information in Figure 3.5, fill in the following table for the number of comparisons required in the sequential search algorithm.

n	Best Case	Worst Case	Average Case
10			
50			
100			
1,000			
10,000			
100,000			

2. An algorithm does $14n^2 + 5n - 1$ units of work on input of size n. Explain why this is considered an $\Theta(n^2)$ algorithm even though there is a term that involves just n.

the job of **program documentation** is to make clear any assumptions or restrictions about the input size the program was designed to handle.

3.5 ANALYSIS OF ALGORITHMS

In Section 3.3, we found three different algorithms for the data cleanup problem, which requires removing 0 values from a list of positive numbers. On the basis of one example, it appeared that algorithm 1, the shuffle-left algorithm, was relatively space-efficient; that algorithm 2, the copy-over algorithm, was relatively time-efficient; and that algorithm 3, the converging-pointers algorithm, was efficient in its use of both space and time. Now that we can use order of magnitude to help classify the time efficiency of algorithms, we can do a formal analysis of these three algorithms to see whether this conclusion is correct. That will be our first task in this section.

We have already done an analysis of the sequential search algorithm and have learned that it is an $\Theta(n)$ algorithm in both the worst case and the average case. This algorithm solves a very common problem: **searching** a list of items (such as the names in a telephone directory) for a particular item. Another very common problem is that of **sorting** a list of items into order—either alphabetical order or numerical order. Later in this section we'll examine a sorting algorithm and analyze its efficiency. We'll also describe a new searching algorithm and compare its efficiency with that of the sequential search algorithm. Finally, we will analyze the pattern-matching algorithm from Chapter 2.

3.5.1 DATA CLEANUP

An analysis of the time efficiency of an algorithm must begin with identifying the units of work we are measuring. For the data cleanup problem, some amount of work is done in examining numbers in the list to see whether they are 0. All three algorithms must examine each of the n elements in the list, so this measure of work does nothing to distinguish one algorithm from the other, but it does give a base of at least $\Theta(n)$ work units for each algorithm. The other unit of work is that of copying numbers.

The copy-over algorithm, algorithm 2, is the easiest to analyze. The best case for this algorithm occurs if all elements are 0; no copies are done, and no extra space is used. The worst case occurs if there are no 0 values in the list. The algorithm copies all n nonzero elements into the new list. Combining the two types of work units, we find that the copy-over algorithm is only $\Theta(n)$ in time efficiency even in the worst case, because $\Theta(n)$ examinations and $\Theta(n)$ copies still equal $\Theta(n)$ steps. However, in the worst case this algorithm doubles the space required. Our conclusion that algorithm 2 is time-efficient and space-inefficient seems to have been correct.

Neither algorithm 1 (shuffle-left) nor algorithm 3 (converging-pointers) requires significant extra space, so both are space-efficient. As for time efficiency, a list with no 0 values, the worst case for algorithm 2, is the best case for algorithms 1 and 3. No copying is required. Conversely, a list with all 0 values, the best case for algorithm 2, is the worst case for algorithms 1 and 3. For algorithm 1, the first element is 0, which requires the remaining $n - 1$ elements to be copied one cell left and reduces *legit* from n to $n - 1$. After the 0 in position 2 gets copied into position 1, the first element is again 0, which again requires $n - 1$ copies and reduces *legit* from $n - 1$ to $n - 2$. This repeats until *legit* is reduced to 0, a total of n times. Thus there are n passes, during each of which $n - 1$ copies are done. The algorithm does

$$n(n - 1) = n^2 - n$$

copies. If we were to draw a graph of $n^2 - n$, we would see that for large n, the curve follows the shape of n^2. The second term can be disregarded, because as n increases, the n^2 term grows much larger than the n term; the n^2 term dominates and determines the shape of the curve. In general, any expression of the form $an^2 + bn + c$ is $\Theta(n^2)$. Algorithm 1 is thus an $\Theta(n^2)$ algorithm in the worst case.

When algorithm 3 faces a list of all 0 entries, it repeatedly copies the element at position *right* into the first position, each time reducing the value of *right*. *Right* goes from n to 1, with one copy done at each step, resulting in $n - 1$ copies. Algorithm 3 is $\Theta(n)$ in the worst case.

It is hard to define what an "average" case might be for any of these algorithms; the amount of work done depends on how many 0 values there are in the list and perhaps on where in the list they occur. If we assume, however, that the number of 0 values is some percentage of n and that these values are scattered throughout the list, then it can be shown that algorithm 1 will still do $\Theta(n^2)$ work, whereas algorithm 3 will do $\Theta(n)$. Figure 3.14 summarizes our analysis.

Let's emphasize again the difference between an algorithm that is $\Theta(n)$ in the amount of work it does and one that is $\Theta(n^2)$. In an $\Theta(n)$ algorithm, the work is proportional to n. Hence if you double n, you double the amount of work; if you multiply n by 10, you multiply the work by 10. But in an $\Theta(n^2)$ algorithm, the work is proportional to the *square* of n. Hence if you double n, you multiply the amount of work by 4; if you multiply n by 10, you multiply the work by 100.

This is probably a good place to explain why we worry about the difference between n and $2n$ when we are talking about space but simply classify n and $8000n$ as $\Theta(n)$ when we are talking about units of work. Units of work translate into time when the algorithm is executed, and time is a much more elastic resource than space. We want an algorithm to run in the shortest possible time,

	1. Shuffle-Left		2. Copy-Over		3. Converging-Pointers	
	Time	Space	Time	Space	Time	Space
Best case	$\Theta(n)$	n	$\Theta(n)$	n	$\Theta(n)$	n
Worst case	$\Theta(n^2)$	n	$\Theta(n)$	$2n$	$\Theta(n)$	n
Average case	$\Theta(n^2)$	n	$\Theta(n)$	$n \leq x \leq 2n$	$\Theta(n)$	n

FIGURE 3.14
Analysis of Three Data Cleanup Algorithms

but in many cases we don't have a fixed deadline for the exact time that can be expended. (In **real-time programming**, where a program is analyzing or controlling the results of an ongoing activity—such as landing the space shuttle—there is a fixed window of time within which the algorithm must complete its task. This constraint is the reason why real-time programming is difficult.) There is, however, a fixed upper bound on the amount of memory that the computer has available to use while executing an algorithm, so we track space consumption more closely. To be really picky, we note that the space usage in Figure 3.14 doesn't show the three or four extra memory cells needed to store other quantities used in the algorithms, such as *legit*, *left*, and *right*.

In summary, algorithm 3, the converging-pointers algorithm, is as space-efficient as algorithm 1 and as time-efficient as algorithm 2. It is often possible to modify an algorithm to make it more time-efficient at the expense of making it less space-efficient, or vice versa. This choice is called the **time-space tradeoff**. There is a time-space tradeoff between algorithms 1 and 2. Seldom is one fortunate enough to obtain improvement in both dimensions at once, as we have with algorithm 3. Here we seem to have been able to beat the time-space tradeoff and obtain the best of both worlds. This was possible in part because the data cleanup problem puts no requirements on the order of the nonzero elements in the "clean" list; algorithm 3 moves these elements out of their original ordering.

3.5.2 SELECTION SORT

As we have said, sorting a list of items into alphabetical or numerical order is a very common task. The registrar at your institution sorts students in a class by name, a mail-order business sorts its customer list by name, and the IRS sorts its tax records by Social Security number. In this section we'll look at an algorithm for sorting.

Suppose we have a list of numbers to sort into increasing order—for example,

5, 7, 2, 8, 3

The result of sorting this list would be the new list

2, 3, 5, 7, 8

We'll examine the **selection sort algorithm** to solve this task. The selection sort "grows" a sorted subsection of the list from the back to the front. We can look at "snapshots" of the progress of the algorithm on our example list, using a vertical line as the marker between the unsorted section at the front of the list and the sorted section at the back of the list in each case. At first the sorted subsection is empty; that is, the entire list is unsorted. This is how the list looks when the algorithm begins.

<u>5, 7, 2, 8, 3</u> |

Unsorted subsection (entire list)   Sorted subsection (empty)

Later, the sorted subsection of the list has grown from the back so that some of the list members are in the right place.

<u>5, 3, 2,</u> | <u>7, 8</u>

Unsorted subsection   Sorted subsection

FIGURE 3.15

Selection Sort Algorithm

1. Get values for *n* and the *n* list items
2. Set the marker for the unsorted section at the end of the list
3. Repeat steps 4 through 6 until the unsorted section of the list is empty
4.   Select the largest number in the unsorted section of the list
5.   Exchange this number with the last number in the unsorted section of the list
6.   Move the marker for the unsorted section forward one position.
7. Stop

Finally, the sorted subsection of the list has grown to be the whole list; there are no unsorted numbers, and the algorithm stops.

| 2,3,5,7,8

Unsorted subsection (empty)   Sorted subsection (entire list)

At any point, then, there are both a sorted and an unsorted section of the list. A pseudocode version of the algorithm is shown in Figure 3.15.

Before we illustrate this algorithm at work, take a look at step 4. It consists of finding the largest number in some list of numbers. We developed an algorithm for this task in Chapter 2 (Figure 2.10). When we get to step 4 in Figure 3.15, we can just insert the pertinent instructions from that algorithm. New algorithms can be built up from "parts" consisting of previous algorithms. As an analogy, a recipe for pumpkin pie might begin with the instruction "Prepare crust for a one-crust pie." The recipe for pie crust is a previous algorithm that is now being used as one of the steps in the pumpkin pie algorithm.

Let's follow the selection sort algorithm. Initially, the unsorted section is the entire list, so step 2 sets the marker at the end of the list.

5, 7, 2, 8, 3 |

Step 4 says to select the largest number in the unsorted section—that is, in the entire list. This number is 8. Step 5 says to exchange 8 with the last number in the unsorted section (the whole list). In order to accomplish this exchange, it is necessary not only to know that 8 is the largest value but also to know the location in the list where 8 is located. The "find largest" algorithm from Chapter 2 also provides this information. The exchange to be done is

5, 7, 2, 8, 3 |

After this exchange and after the marker is moved forward as instructed in step 6, the list looks like

5, 7, 2, 3 | 8

The number 8 is now in its correct position at the end of the list. It becomes the sorted section of the list, and the first four numbers are the unsorted section.

The unsorted section is not empty, so we repeat step 4 (find the largest number in the unsorted section); it is 7. Step 5 is to exchange 7 with the last number in the unsorted section, which is 3.

5, 7, 2, 3 | 8

After the marker is moved, the result is

5, 3, 2 | 7, 8

The sorted section is now 7, 8 and the unsorted section is 5, 3, 2.

Repeating the loop of steps 4–6 again, we find that the largest number in the unsorted section is 5. We exchange it with 2, the last number in the unsorted section

5, 3, 2 | 7, 8

and we move the marker, which yields

2, 3 | 5, 7, 8

Now the unsorted section (as far as the algorithm knows) is 2, 3. The largest number here is 3. Exchanging 3 with the last number of the unsorted section (which is also 3) produces no visible change. The marker is moved, giving

2 | 3, 5, 7, 8

When the only part of the list that is unsorted is the single number 2, there is also no visible change produced by carrying out the exchange. The marker is moved, giving

| 2, 3, 5, 7, 8

The unsorted section of the list is empty, and the algorithm terminates.

In order to analyze the amount of work the selection sort algorithm does, we must first decide on the unit of work to count. When we analyzed sequential search, the unit of work that we measured was a comparison between the name being searched for and the names in the list. At first glance there seem to be no comparisons of any kind going on in the selection sort. Ah, but remember that there is a subtask being done within the selection sort: the task of finding the largest number in the list. The algorithm from Chapter 2 for finding the largest value in a list begins by taking the first number in the list as the largest so far. The largest-so-far value is compared against successive numbers in the list; if a larger value is found, it becomes the largest so far.

When the selection sort algorithm begins, the largest-so-far value, initially the first number, must be compared to all the other numbers in the list. If there are n numbers in the list, $n - 1$ comparisons must be done. The next time through the loop, the last number is already in its proper place, so it is never involved in a comparison. The largest-so-far value, again initially the first number, must be compared to all the other numbers in the unsorted part of the list, which will require $n - 2$ comparisons. The number of comparisons keeps going down as the length of the unsorted section of the list gets smaller, until finally only one comparison is needed. The total number of comparisons is

$$(n - 1) + (n - 2) + (n - 3) + \ldots + 3 + 2 + 1$$

Reviewing our example problem, we can see that the following comparisons are done:

- To put 8 in place in the list 5, 7, 2, 8, 3 |
  Compare 5 (largest so far) to 7
    7 becomes largest so far
  Compare 7 (largest so far) to 2
  Compare 7 (largest so far) to 8
    8 becomes largest so far
  Compare 8 to 3
  8 is the largest
  Total number of comparisons: 4 (which is 5 − 1)
- To put 7 in place in the list 5, 7, 2, 3 | 8
  Compare 5 (largest so far) to 7
    7 becomes largest so far
  Compare 7 to 2
  Compare 7 to 3
  7 is the largest
  Total number of comparisons: 3 (which is 5 − 2)
- To put 5 in place in the list 5, 3, 2 | 7, 8
  Compare 5 (largest so far) to 3
  Compare 5 to 2
  5 is the largest
  Total number of comparisons: 2 (which is 5 − 3)
- To put 3 in place in the list 2, 3 | 5, 7, 8
  Compare 2 (largest so far) to 3
  3 is the largest
  Total number of comparisons: 1 (which is 5 − 4)

To put 2 in place requires no comparisons; there is only one number in the unsorted section of the list, so it is of course the largest number. It gets exchanged with itself, which produces no effect. The total number of comparisons is $4 + 3 + 2 + 1 = 10$.

The sum

$$(n − 1) + (n − 2) + (n − 3) + \ldots + 3 + 2 + 1$$

turns out to be equal to

$$\left(\frac{n − 1}{2}\right) n = \frac{1}{2} n^2 − \frac{1}{2} n$$

(You will recall from earlier in this chapter how Gauss computed a similar sum.) For our example with five numbers, this formula says that the total number of comparisons is (using the first version of the formula)

Length n of List to Sort	n²	Number of Comparisons Required
10	100	45
100	10,000	4,950
1,000	1,000,000	499,500

FIGURE 3.16

Comparisons Required by Selection Sort

$$\left(\frac{5-1}{2}\right)5 = \left(\frac{4}{2}\right)5 = (2)5 = 10$$

which is the number of comparisons we had counted.

The expression

$$\frac{1}{2}n^2 - \frac{1}{2}n$$

is $\Theta(n^2)$. The selection sort therefore does $\Theta(n^2)$ comparisons. It also does some additional work to exchange numbers in the list, but this additional work does not change the fact that the algorithm is order of magnitude n^2.

Remember that n is the size of the list we are sorting. As this list size increases, the amount of work required goes up in proportion to the square of n. If the list is 10 times longer, the work increases by much more than a factor of 10, as shown in Figure 3.16.

We haven't talked here about a best case, a worst case, or an average case for the selection sort. This algorithm does the same amount of work no matter how the numbers are initially arranged. It has no way to recognize, for example, that the list might already be sorted at the beginning.

Because selection sort is an $\Theta(n^2)$ algorithm (in all cases) and sequential search is an $\Theta(n)$ algorithm (in the worst case), we might conclude that sorting a list requires more work than searching a list. This is true, even though there are algorithms for sorting that do less work than the selection sort algorithm. There are also algorithms for searching that do less work than the sequential search algorithm. We'll see such an algorithm in the next section.

A word about the space efficiency of the selection sort is in order. The original list occupies n memory locations, and this is the major space requirement. Some storage is needed for the marker between the unsorted and sorted sections and for keeping track of the largest-so-far value and its location in the list, used in step 4. Surprisingly, the process of exchanging two values at step 5 also requires an extra storage location. Here's why. If the two numbers to be exchanged are at position X and position Y in the list, we might think the following two steps will exchange these values:

1. Copy the current value at position Y into position X

2. Copy the current value at position X into position Y

FIGURE 3.17

*An Attempt to Exchange
the Values at X and Y*

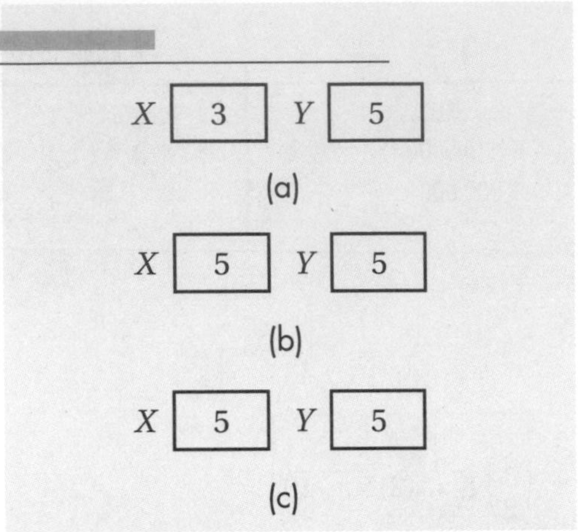

X [3]   Y [5]

(a)

X [5]   Y [5]

(b)

X [5]   Y [5]

(c)

The problem is that after step 1, the value at position X is the same as that at position Y. Step 2 does not put the original value of X into position Y. In fact, we don't even have the original value of position X any more. In Figure 3.17(a) we see the original X and Y values. At Figure 3.17(b), after execution of step 1, the current value of position Y has been copied into position X, writing over what was there originally. At Figure 3.17(c), after execution of step 2, the current value at position X (which is the original Y value) has been copied into position Y, but the picture looks the same as Figure 3.17(b).

Here's the correct algorithm, which makes use of one extra temporary storage location that we'll call T.

1. Copy the current value at position X into location T

2. Copy the current value at position Y into position X

3. Copy the current value at location T into position Y

Figure 3.18 illustrates that this algorithm does the job. In Figure 3.18(a), the temporary location contains an unknown value. After execution of step 1 (Figure

---

Laboratory Experience 5

Because sorting a list is such a common task, a lot of research has gone into finding good sorting algorithms. Selection sort is one sorting algorithm, but there are many others. One is the bubble sort, described in Exercises 14–16 at the end of this chapter. Others, such as insertion sort and quicksort, are described in the laboratory manual. This laboratory experience allows you to step through animations of these various sorting algorithms in order to understand how they work.

You may wonder why people don't simply use the one "best" sorting algorithm. It's not that simple. Some algorithms (unlike the selection sort) are sensitive to what the original input looks like. One algorithm may work well if the input is already close to being sorted, whereas another algorithm would work better if the input is rather random. An algorithm like selection sort has the advantage of being relatively easy to understand. If the size of the list, n, is fairly small, then an easy-to-understand algorithm may be preferable to one that is more efficient but more obscure.

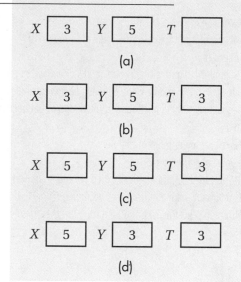

FIGURE 3.18

Exchanging the Values at X and Y

3.18b), it holds the current value of X. When Y's current value is put into X at step 2 (Figure 3.18c), T still holds the original X value. After step 3 (Figure 3.18d), the current value of T goes into position Y, and the original values of X and Y have been exchanged. (Step 5 of the selection sort algorithm thus stands for another algorithm, just as step 4 does.)

All in all, the extra storage required for the selection sort, over and above that required to store the original list, is slight. Selection sort is space-efficient.

3.5.3 BINARY SEARCH

Our second search algorithm, the **binary search algorithm**, works only when the list being searched is already sorted. To understand how binary search operates, let us go back to the problem of searching for *NAME* in a telephone directory.

When you go to look up the name Miranda in the telephone book, you do not do a sequential search beginning with the very first name in the directory and looking at each name in succession until you come to Miranda or the end of the directory! Instead you make use of the fact that the names in the directory have already been sorted into increasing (alphabetical) order. You open the phone book in a random place somewhere near the middle. If the name you see is Miranda, your search is over. If the name you see begins with P, you look farther toward the front of the book; if the name you see begins with L, you look farther toward the back of the book.

The binary search algorithm works in a similar fashion. It first looks for *NAME* at roughly the halfway point in the list. If the name there equals *NAME*, the search is over. If *NAME* comes alphabetically before the name at the halfway point, then the search is narrowed to the front half of the list, and the process begins again on this smaller list. If *NAME* comes alphabetically after the name at the halfway point, then the search is narrowed to the back half of the list, and the

FIGURE 3.19
Binary Search Algorithm
(list must be sorted)

1. Get values for *NAME*, n, $N_1, \ldots, N_n$ and $T_1, \ldots, T_n$
2. Set the value of *beginning* to 1 and set the value of *Found* to NO
3. Set the value of *end* to n
4. Repeat steps 5 through 10 until either *Found* = YES or *end* is less than *beginning*
5.   Set the value of m to the middle value between *beginning* and *end*.
6.   If *NAME* is equal to N_m, the name found at the midpoint between *beginning* and *end*, then do steps 7 and 8
7.   Print the telephone number of that person, T_m
8.   Set the value of *Found* to YES
9.   Else if *NAME* precedes N_m alphabetically, then set *end* = $m - 1$
10.   Else (*NAME* follows N_m alphabetically) set *beginning* = $m + 1$
11. If (*Found* = NO) then print the message 'I am sorry but that name is not in the directory'
12. Stop

process begins again on *this* smaller list. The algorithm halts when *NAME* is found or when the sublist becomes empty.

Figure 3.19 gives a pseudocode version of the binary search algorithm on an n-element list. Here *beginning* and *end* mark the beginning and end of the section of the list under consideration. Initially the whole list is considered, so at first *beginning* is 1 and *end* is n. If *NAME* is not found at the midpoint m of the current section of the list, then setting *end* equal to one less than the midpoint (step 9) means that at the next pass through the loop, the front half of the current section will be considered. Setting *beginning* equal to one more than the midpoint (step 10) means that at the next pass through the loop, the back half of the current section will be considered. Thus as the algorithm proceeds, the *beginning* marker can move toward the back of the list, and the *end* marker can move toward the front of the list. Should it ever happen that the *beginning* marker and the *end* marker cross over—that is, *end* becomes less than *beginning*—then the current section of the list is empty and the search terminates

Let's do an example, using seven names sorted into increasing (alphabetical) order. The following list shows not only the names in the list but also their locations in the list.

Ann	Bob	Cora	Devi	Grant	Nathan	Sue
1	2	3	4	5	6	7

Suppose we are searching this list for the name Cora. We set *beginning* to 1 and *end* to 7; the midpoint between 1 and 7 is 4. We compare the name at position number 4, Devi, with Cora. Cora precedes Devi alphabetically, so the algorithm sets *end* to $4 - 1 = 3$ (step 9) in order to continue the search on the front half of the list,

Ann	Bob	Cora
1	2	3

The midpoint between *beginning* = 1 and *end* = 3 is 2, so we compare the name at position number 2, Bob, with Cora. Cora follows Bob alphabetically, so the algorithm sets *beginning* to 2 + 1 = 3 (step 10) in order to continue the search on the back half of this list, namely

Cora

   3

At the next pass through the loop, the midpoint between *beginning* = 3 and *end* = 3 is 3, so we compare the name at position number 3, Cora, with Cora. We have found the name; the appropriate telephone number can be printed and *Found* changed to YES. Next the loop terminates, and then the algorithm terminates.

   Now suppose we search this same list for the name Maria. As before, the first midpoint is 4, so Devi is compared with Maria. Maria follows Devi, so the search continues with *beginning* = 5, *end* = 7 on the back half:

Grant   Nathan   Sue

   5   6   7

The midpoint is 6, so Nathan is compared with Maria. Maria precedes Nathan, so the search continues with *beginning* = 5, *end* = 5 on the front half:

Grant

   5

The midpoint is 5, so Grant is compared with Maria. Maria follows Grant, so *beginning* is set to 6 in order to continue the search on the "back half" of this list. The algorithm checks the condition at step 4 to see whether to repeat the loop again and finds that *end* is less than *beginning* (*end* = 5, *beginning* = 6). The loop is abandoned, and the algorithm moves on to step 11 and notes that Maria is not in the list.

   It is easier to see how the binary search algorithm operates if we list the locations of the names checked in a "tree-like" structure. The tree in Figure 3.20 shows the possible locations that will be searched for a seven-element list. The search starts at the top of the tree, at location 4, the middle of the original list. If the name at location 4 is *NAME*, the search halts. If *NAME* comes after the name at location 4 (as in our example with Maria), the right branch is taken and the next location searched is location 6. If *NAME* comes before the name at location 4 (as in our example with Cora), the left branch is taken and the next location searched is location 2. If *NAME* is not found at location 2, the next location searched will be either 1 or 3. Similarly, if *NAME* is not found at location 6, the next location searched will be either 5 or 7.

   In Figure 3.19, the binary search algorithm, we assumed in step 5 that there is a middle position between *beginning* and *end*. This happens only when there is an odd number of elements in the list. Let us agree to define the "middle" of an even number of entries as the end of the first half of the list. With eight elements, for example, the midpoint position would be location 4.

   1 2 3 <u>4</u> 5 6 7 8

FIGURE 3.20

Binary Search Tree for a Seven-Element List

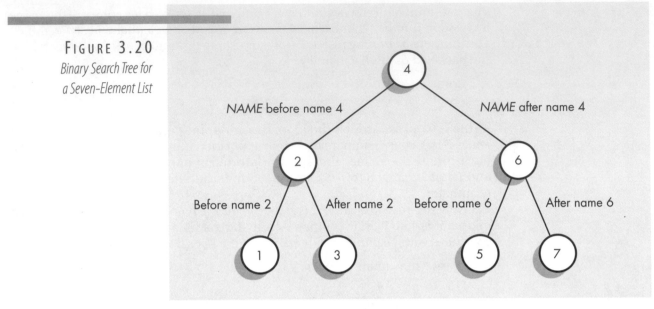

With this understanding, the binary search algorithm can be used on lists of any size.

Like the sequential search algorithm, the binary search algorithm relies on comparisons, so we will count the number of comparisons as an indication of the work done. The best case, as in sequential search, requires only one comparison—*NAME* is located on the first try. The worst case, as in sequential search, occurs when *NAME* is not in the list. However, we learn this much sooner in binary search than in sequential search. In our example of seven names, only three comparisons were needed to determine that Maria is not in the list. The number of comparisons needed is the number of circles in some branch from the top to the bottom of the tree in Figure 3.20. These circles represent searches at the midpoints of the whole list, half the list, one quarter of the list, and so on. This process continues as long as the sublists can be cut in half.

Let's do a minor mathematical digression here. The number of times a number *n* can be cut in half and not go below 1 is called the **logarithm of *n* to the base 2**, which is abbreviated lg *n* (also written in some texts as $\log_2 n$). For example, if *n* is 16, then we can do four such divisions by 2:

$$^{16}\!/_2 = 8$$

$$^8\!/_2 = 4$$

$$^4\!/_2 = 2$$

$$^2\!/_2 = 1$$

so lg 16 = 4. This is another way of saying that $2^4 = 16$. In general,

$$\lg n = m \quad \text{is equivalent to} \quad 2^m = n$$

Figure 3.21 shows a few values of *n* and lg *n*. From these, we can see that as *n* doubles, lg *n* increases by only 1, so lg *n* grows much more slowly than *n*. Figure

FIGURE 3.21

Values for n *and lg* n

n	lg n
8	3
16	4
32	5
64	6
128	7

FIGURE 3.22

A Comparison of n *and lg* n

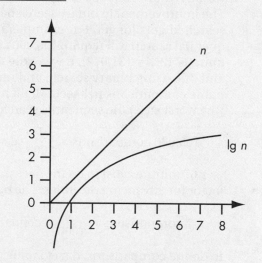

3.22 shows the two basic shapes of *n* and lg *n* and again conveys that lg *n* grows much more slowly than *n*.

Remember the analogy we suggested earlier about the difference in time consumed between $\Theta(n^2)$ algorithms—equivalent to various forms of walking—and $\Theta(n)$ algorithms—equivalent to various forms of driving? We carry that analogy further by saying that algorithms of $\Theta(\lg n)$ are equivalent to various forms of flying. Changing the coefficients of lg *n* may mean that we go from a Piper cub to an F-14, but flying, in any form, is still a fundamentally different—and faster—category from driving or walking.

Now suppose we are doing a binary search on *n* names. In the worst case, as we have seen, the number of comparisons is related to the number of times the list of length *n* can be halved. Binary search does $\Theta(\lg n)$ comparisons in the worst case (see Exercise 23 at the end of the chapter for an exact formula for the worst case). As a matter of fact, it also does $\Theta(\lg n)$ comparisons in the average case to find a name that is in the list (although the exact value is a smaller number than in the worst case). This is because most of the names in the list occur at or near the bottom of the tree, where the maximum amount of work must be done; recall that it also took three comparisons to find that Cora was in the list. As Figure 3.20 shows, relatively few locations (where *NAME* might be found and the algorithm terminate sooner) are higher in the tree.

Both binary search and sequential search solve the telephone book search problem, but these algorithms differ in the order of magnitude of the work they do. Binary search is an $\Theta(\lg n)$ algorithm, whereas sequential search is an $\Theta(n)$ algorithm, in both the worst case and the average case. To compare the binary search algorithm with the sequential search algorithm, suppose there are 100 elements in the list. In the worst case, sequential search would require 100 comparisons, binary search 7 ($2^7 = 128$). In the average case, sequential search would require about 50 comparisons, binary search 6 or 7 (still much less work). The improvement in binary search becomes even more apparent as the list to be searched gets longer. For example, if $n = 100,000$, then in the worst case, sequential search will require 100,000 comparisons, whereas binary search will require 17 ($2^{17} = 131,072$). If we wrote two programs, one using sequential search and one using binary search, and ran them on a computer that could do 1000 name comparisons per second, then to determine that a name is not in the list (the worst case) the sequential search program would use

$$100,000 \text{ comparisons} \times \frac{1}{1000} \text{ seconds/comparison} = 100 \text{ seconds}$$

or 1.67 minutes, just to do the necessary comparisons, disregarding the constant factor for advancing the index. The binary search program would use

$$17 \text{ comparisons} \times \frac{1}{1000} \text{ seconds/comparison} = 0.017 \text{ seconds}$$

to do the comparisons, disregarding a constant factor for updating the values of *beginning* and *end*. This is quite a difference.

Suppose our two programs are used with the 20,000,000 names we are assuming in the New York City phone book. On the average, the sequential search program would need about

$$\frac{20,000,000}{2} \text{ comparisons} \times \frac{1}{1000} \text{ seconds/comparison} = 10,000 \text{ seconds}$$

(about 2.78 hours!) just to do the comparisons to find a name in the list, whereas the binary search program would need (because $2^{25} \approx 33,000,000$) about

$$25 \text{ comparisons} \times \frac{1}{1000} \text{ seconds/comparison} = 0.025 \text{ second}$$

This is an even more impressive difference. Furthermore, it's a difference due to the inherent inefficiency of an $\Theta(n)$ algorithm compared to an $\Theta(\lg n)$ algorithm, which can be moderated but not solved by simply using a faster computer. If our computer does 50,000 comparisons per second, then the average times become about

$$\frac{20,000,000}{2} \text{ comparisons} \times \frac{1}{50,000} \text{ seconds/comparison} = 200 \text{ seconds}$$

or 3.33 minutes, for sequential search and about

$$25 \text{ comparisons} \times \frac{1}{50,000} \text{ seconds/comparison} = 0.0005 \text{ second}$$

for binary search. The sequential search alternative is simply not acceptable. That is why analyzing algorithms, and choosing the best one, can be so important. We also see, as we noted in Chapter 2, that the way the problem data are organized can greatly affect the best choice of algorithm to solve the problem.

The binary search algorithm works only on a list that has already been sorted. If the list is not sorted, it could first be sorted and binary search then used, but sorting also takes a lot of work, as we have seen. If a list is to be searched only a few times for a few particular names, then it is more efficient to do sequential search on the unsorted list (a few $\Theta(n)$ tasks). But if the list is to be searched repeatedly—as in the daily use of an automated telephone directory for the foreseeable future—it is more efficient to sort it and then use binary search: one $\Theta(n^2)$ task and many $\Theta(\lg n)$ tasks, as opposed to many $\Theta(n)$ tasks.

As to space efficiency, binary search, like sequential search, requires only a small amount of additional storage to keep track of beginning, end, and midpoint positions in the list. Thus it is space-efficient; in this case, we did not have to sacrifice space efficiency to gain time efficiency.

3.5.4 PATTERN MATCHING

The pattern-matching algorithm from Chapter 2 involves finding all occurrences of a pattern of the form $P_1 P_2 \ldots P_m$ within text of the form $T_1 T_2 \ldots T_n$. Recall that the algorithm simply does a "forward march" through the text, at each position beginning an attempt to match each pattern character against the text characters. The process stops only after text position $n - m + 1$, when the remaining text is not as long as the pattern so that there could not possibly be a match. This algorithm is interesting to analyze because it involves two measures of input size: n, the length of the text string, and m, the length of the pattern string. The unit of work is comparison of a pattern character with a text character.

Surprisingly, both the best case and the worst case of this algorithm can occur when the pattern is not in the text at all. The difference hinges on exactly *how* the pattern fails to be in the text. The best case occurs if the first character of the pattern is nowhere in the text, as in

Text: KLMNPQRSTX

Pattern: ABC

In this case, $n - m + 1$ comparisons are required, trying (unsuccessfully) to match P_1 with $T_1 T_2 \ldots T_{n-m+1}$ in turn. Each comparison fails, and the algorithm slides the pattern forward to try again at the next position in the text.

The maximum amount of work is done if the pattern *almost* occurs everywhere in the text. Consider, for example, the following case:

Text: AAAAAAAAAA

Pattern: AAAB

Starting with T_1, the first text character, the match with the first pattern character is successful. The match with the second text character and the second pattern character is also successful. Indeed $m - 1$ characters of the pattern match with the text before the mth comparison proves a failure. The process starts over from the second text character, T_2. Once again, m comparisons are required to find a mismatch. Altogether, m comparisons are required for each of the $n - m + 1$ starting positions in the text.

Another version of the worst case occurs when the pattern is found at each location in the text, as in

Text: AAAAAAAAA

Pattern: AAAA

This results in the same comparisons as are done as for the other worst case, the only difference being that the comparison of the last pattern character is successful.

Unlike our simple examples, pattern matching is usually of interest only when the pattern length is short compared to the text length—that is, when m is much less than n. In such cases, $n - m + 1$ is essentially n. The pattern-matching algorithm is therefore $\Theta(n)$ in the best case and $\Theta(m \times n)$ in the worst case.

It required somewhat pathological situations to create the worst cases we described above. In general, the forward-march algorithm performs quite well on text and patterns consisting of ordinary words. Other pattern-matching algorithms exist that are conceptually more complex but require less work in the worst case.

3.5.5 SUMMARY

Figure 3.23 shows an order-of-magnitude summary of the time efficiency for the algorithms we have analyzed.

Problem	Unit of Work	Algorithm	Best Case	Worst Case	Average Case
Searching	Comparisons	Sequential Search	1	$\Theta(n)$	$\Theta(n)$
		Binary Search	1	$\Theta(\lg n)$	$\Theta(\lg n)$
Sorting	Comparisons and Exchanges	Selection Sort	$\Theta(n^2)$	$\Theta(n^2)$	$\Theta(n^2)$
Data Cleanup	Examinations and Copies	Shuffle Left	$\Theta(n)$	$\Theta(n^2)$	$\Theta(n^2)$
		Copy Over	$\Theta(n)$	$\Theta(n)$	$\Theta(n)$
		Converging Pointers	$\Theta(n)$	$\Theta(n)$	$\Theta(n)$
Pattern Matching	Character Comparisons	Forward March	$\Theta(n)$	$\Theta(m \times n)$	

FIGURE 3.23

Order-of-Magnitude Time Efficiency Summary

PRACTICE PROBLEMS

1. For each of the following lists, perform a selection sort, and show the list after each exchange that has a visible effect.
   a. 4, 8, 2, 6
   b. 12, 3, 6, 8, 2, 5, 7
   c. D, B, G, F, A, C, E

2. Suppose that, using the list of seven names from this section, we try binary search to decide whether Grant is in the list. What names would be compared to Grant?

3. Use the first example pattern and text given in Section 3.5.4 for the worst case of the pattern-matching algorithm. What is m? What is n? What is $m \times n$? This algorithm is $\Theta(m \times n)$ in the worst case, but what is the exact number of comparisons done?

3.6 WHEN THINGS GET OUT OF HAND

We have so far found examples of algorithms that are $\Theta(\lg n)$, $\Theta(n)$, and $\Theta(n^2)$ in time efficiency. Order of magnitude, as we know, determines how quickly the values grow as n increases. An algorithm of order $\lg n$ does less work as n increases than does an algorithm of order n, which in turn does less work than one of order n^2. The work done by any of these algorithms is no worse than a constant multiple of n^2, which is a polynomial in n. Therefore, these algorithms are **polynomially bounded** in the amount of work they do as n increases.

There are some algorithms that must do work that is not polynomially bounded. Suppose we consider four cities, A, B, C, and D, that are connected as shown in Figure 3.24 and ask the following question: Is it possible to start at city A, go through every other city exactly once, and end up at A? Of course, we as humans can immediately see in this small problem that the answer is "yes" and that there are two such paths: A-B-D-C-A and A-C-D-B-A. However, an

FIGURE 3.24
Four Connected Cities

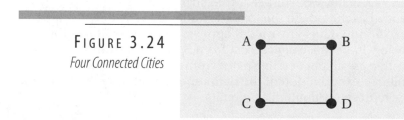

FIGURE 3.25

*Hamiltonian Circuits Among
All Paths from A in Figure 3.24
with Four Links*

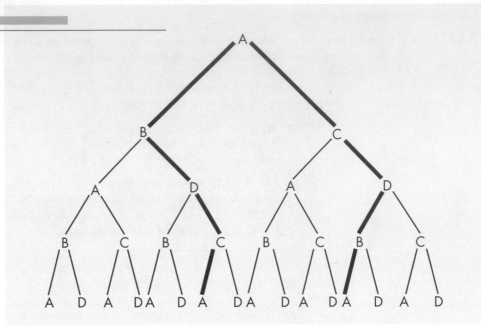

FIGURE 3.25

*Hamiltonian Circuits Among
All Paths from A in Figure 3.24
with Four Links*

algorithm doesn't get to "see" the entire picture at once, as we can; it has available to it only isolated facts such as "A is connected to B and to C," "B is connected to A and to D," and so on. If the number of *nodes* and connecting *edges* were large, even humans might not "see" the solution immediately. A collection of nodes and connecting edges is called a **graph**. A path through a graph that begins and ends at the same node and goes through all other nodes exactly once is called a **Hamiltonian circuit**, named for the Irish mathematician William Rowan Hamilton (1805–1865). If there are *n* nodes in the graph, then a Hamiltonian circuit, if it exists, must have exactly *n* links. In the case of the four cities, for instance, if the path must go through exactly A, B, C, D, and A (in some order), then there are five nodes on the path (counting A twice), and four links.

Our problem is to decide whether an arbitrary graph has a Hamiltonian circuit. An algorithm to solve this problem is to examine all possible paths through the graph that are the appropriate length to see whether any of them are Hamiltonian circuits. The algorithm can trace all paths by beginning at the starting node and choosing at each node where to go next. Without going into the details of such an algorithm, let's represent the possible paths with four links in the graph of Figure 3.24. Again, we will use a tree structure. In Figure 3.25, A is the tree "root," and at each node in the tree, the nodes directly below it are the choices for the next node. Thus any time B appears in the tree, it has the two nodes A and D below it, because edges exist from B to A and from B to D. The "branches" of the tree are all the possible paths from A with four links. Once the tree has been built, an examination of the paths shows that only the two dark paths in the figure represent Hamiltonian circuits.

The number of paths that must be examined is the number of nodes at the bottom level of the tree. There is one node at the top of the tree; we'll call the top of the tree level 0. The number of nodes is multiplied by 2 for each level down in the tree. At level 1 there are 2 nodes, at level 2 there are 2^2 nodes, at level 3 there are 2^3 nodes, and at level 4, the bottom of the tree, there are $2^4 = 16$ nodes.

Suppose we were looking for a Hamiltonian circuit in a graph with n nodes and two choices at each node. The bottom of the corresponding tree would be at level n, and there would be 2^n paths to examine. If we take the examination of a single path as a unit of work, then this algorithm must do 2^n units of work. This is more work than any polynomial in n. An $\Theta(2^n)$ algorithm is called an **exponential algorithm**. Hence the trial-and-error approach to solving the Hamiltonian circuit problem is an exponential algorithm. (We could improve on this algorithm by letting it stop tracing a path whenever a repeated node different from the starting node is encountered, but it will still be exponential. If there were more than two choices at a node, the amount of work would be even greater.)

Figure 3.26(a) shows the four curves lg n, n, n^2, and 2^n. The rapid growth of 2^n is not really apparent here, however, because that curve is "off the scale" for

FIGURE **3.26(a)**

Comparisons of lg n, n, n², and 2ⁿ

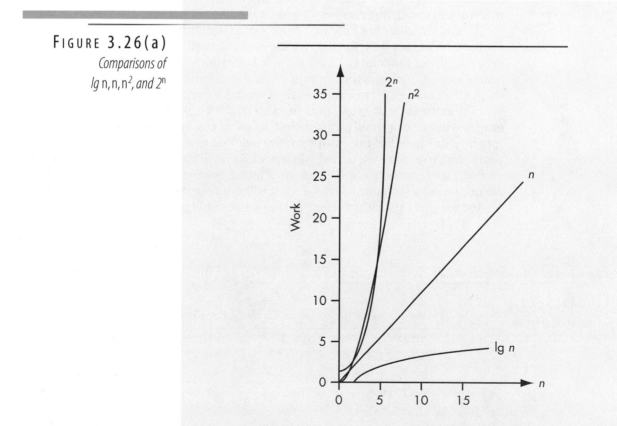

FIGURE 3.26(b)

Comparisons of lg n, n, n², and 2ⁿ

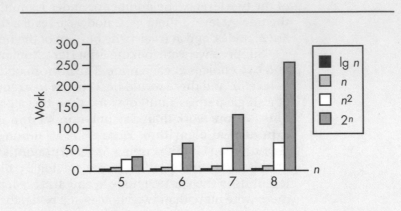

values of n above 5. Figure 3.26(b) compares these four curves for values of n that are still small, but even so, 2^n is already far outdistancing the other values.

To appreciate more fully why the order of magnitude of an algorithm is important, let's again imagine that we are running various algorithms as programs on a computer that can perform a single operation (unit of work) in 0.0001 second. Figure 3.27 shows the amount of time it will take for algorithms of $\Theta(\lg n)$, $\Theta(n)$, $\Theta(n^2)$, and $\Theta(2^n)$ to complete their work for various values of n.

The expression 2^n grows unbelievably fast. An algorithm of $\Theta(2^n)$ can take so long to solve even a small problem that it is of no practical value. Even if we greatly increase the speed of the computer, the results are much the same. We now see more than ever why we added *efficiency* as a desirable feature for an algorithm and why such an issue is independent of future advances in computer technology. No matter how fast computers get, they will not be able to solve a problem of size $n \geq 100$ using an algorithm of $\Theta(2^n)$ in any reasonable period of time.

FIGURE 3.27

A Comparison of Four Orders of Magnitude

		n		
Order	10	50	100	1000
$\lg n$	0.0003 sec	0.0006 sec	0.0007 sec	0.001 sec
n	0.001 sec	0.005 sec	0.01 sec	0.1 sec
n^2	0.01 sec	0.25 sec	1 sec	1.67 min
2^n	0.1024 sec	3570 years	4×10^{16} centuries	*Too big to compute*

The algorithm we have described here for testing an arbitrary graph for Hamiltonian circuits is an example of a **brute force algorithm**—one that beats the problem into submission by trying all possibilities. In Chapter 1 we described a brute force algorithm for winning a chess game; it consisted of looking at all possible game scenarios from any given point on and then picking a winning one. This is also an exponential algorithm. Some very practical problems have exponential solution algorithms. For example, the telephone company is interested in routing its calls along the shortest possible path from one telephone to another through all the various switching points in the telephone network. An exponential algorithm to solve this problem would be to examine all possible paths and then use the shortest one. As you can imagine, the telephone company uses a better (more efficient) algorithm than this one!

For some problems, however, no polynomially bounded algorithm to solve the problem exists. Such problems are called **intractable**; they are solvable, but the solution algorithms all require so much work as to be virtually useless. The Hamiltonian circuit problem is suspected to be such a problem, but we don't really know for sure! No one has yet found a solution algorithm that works in polynomial time, but neither has anyone yet proved that such an algorithm does not exist. This is a problem of great interest in computer science. A surprising number of problems fall into this "suspected intractable" category. Here's another one, called the **bin-packing problem**: Given an unlimited number of bins of volume 1 unit, and given n objects, all of volume between 0.0 and 1.0, find the minimum number of bins needed to store the n objects. A solution algorithm for this problem would be of interest to any manufacturer who ships sets of various items in standard-sized cartons and to someone who wants to record songs onto audio tapes in the most efficient way.

Problems for which no known polynomial solution algorithm exists are sometimes attacked by **approximation algorithms**. These algorithms don't solve the original problem, but they provide a close approximation to the solution. For example, an approximation algorithm to solve the bin-packing problem is to take the objects in order, put the first one into bin 1, and stuff each remaining object into the first bin that can hold it. This (reasonable) approach may not give the absolute minimum number of bins needed, but it gives a first cut at the answer. (Anyone who has watched passengers stowing carry-on baggage in an airplane has seen this approximation algorithm at work.)

As an example, suppose a sequence of four objects with volumes of 0.3, 0.4, 0.5, and 0.6 are stored using the "first-fit" algorithm described above. The result

Laboratory Experience 6

The various sorting algorithms examined in Laboratory Experience 5 (selection sort, quicksort, etc.) do different amounts of work on the same data sets. In this laboratory experience, you can run these sorting algorithms and clock the time they take. This will enable you to make some comparisons of time efficiency on different sizes of input.

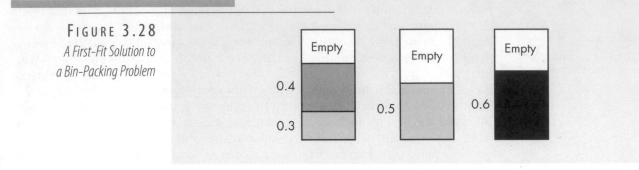

FIGURE 3.28

A First-Fit Solution to a Bin-Packing Problem

would require three bins, which would be packed as shown in Figure 3.28. However, this is not the optimal solution (see Exercise 29 at the end of the chapter).

In this last section we've wandered rather far afield into the realm of problems that have algorithmic solutions but no known "fast" (polynomial) solution algorithms. In Chapter 10, we will learn that there are problems with no algorithm at all to solve them, even if we are willing to accept an incredibly inefficient solution.

PRACTICE PROBLEMS

1. Consider the following graph:

Draw a tree similar to Figure 3.25 showing all paths from A and highlighting those that are Hamiltonian circuits (these are the same two circuits as before). How many paths have to be examined?

2. The following tree shows all paths with two links that begin at node A in some graph. Draw the graph.

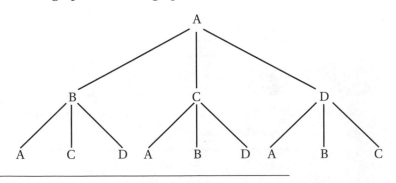

EXERCISES

1. a. Use Gauss's approach to find the sum

    $$2 + 4 + 6 + \ldots + 100$$

   b. Use Gauss's approach to find a formula for the sum of the even numbers from 2 to $2n$,

    $$2 + 4 + 6 + \ldots + 2n$$

   Your formula will be an expression involving n.

2. The **Fibonacci sequence** of numbers is defined as follows: The first and second numbers are both 1. After that, each number in the sequence is the sum of the two preceding numbers. Thus the Fibonacci sequence is

    $$1, 1, 2, 3, 5, 8, 13, 21, \ldots$$

   If $F(n)$ stands for the nth value in the sequence, then this definition can be expressed as

    $$F(1) = 1$$
    $$F(2) = 1$$
    $$F(n) = F(n - 1) + F(n - 2) \quad \text{for } n > 2$$

   a. Using the definition of the Fibonacci sequence, compute the value of $F(20)$.

   b. A formula for $F(n)$ is

    $$F(n) = \frac{\sqrt{5}}{5}\left(\frac{1 + \sqrt{5}}{2}\right)^n - \frac{\sqrt{5}}{5}\left(\frac{1 - \sqrt{5}}{2}\right)^n$$

   Using the formula (and a calculator), compute the value of $F(20)$.

   c. What are your opinions on the relative clarity, elegance, and efficiency of the two algorithms (using the definition and using the formula) to compute $F(20)$? Would your answer change if you considered $F(100)$?

3. A tennis tournament has 342 players. A single match involves 2 players. The winner of a match will play the winner of a match in the next round, whereas losers are eliminated from the tournament. The 2 players who have won all previous rounds play in the final game, and the winner wins the tournament. What is the total number of matches needed to determine the winner?

   a. Here is one algorithm to solve this question. Compute $342/2 = 171$ to get the number of pairs (matches) in the first round, which results in 171

   winners to go on to the second round. Compute $171/2 = 85$ with 1 left over, which results in 85 matches in the second round and 85 winners, plus the 1 left over, to go on to the third round. For the third round compute $86/2 = 43$, so the third round has 43 matches, etc. The total number of matches is $171 + 85 + 43 + \ldots$. Finish this process in order to find the total number of matches.

   b. Here is another algorithm to solve this question. Each match results in exactly one loser, so there must be the same number of matches as losers in the tournament. Compute the total number of losers in the entire tournament. (*Hint:* This isn't really a computation; it is a one-sentence argument.)

   c. What are your opinions on the relative clarity, elegance, and efficiency of the two algorithms?

4. Write the data list that results from running the shuffle-left algorithm to clean up the following data. Find the exact number of copies done.

3	0	0	2	6	7	0	0	5	1

5. Write the resulting data list and find the exact number of copies done by the converging-pointers algorithm when it is executed on the data of Exercise 4.

6. Explain in words how to modify the shuffle-left data cleanup algorithm to reduce slightly the number of copies it makes. (*Hint:* Must item n always be copied?) If this modified algorithm is run on the data list of Exercise 4, exactly how many copies are done?

7. We have said that the average number of comparisons needed to find a name in an n-element list using sequential search is "slightly higher than $n/2$." In this problem we will find an exact expression for this average.

   a. Suppose a random list of names has an odd number of names, say 15. At what position is the middle name? Using sequential search, how many comparisons are required to find the middle name? Repeat this exercise with a few more odd numbers until you can answer the following question: If there are n names in the list and n is an odd number, write an expression for the number of comparisons required to find the middle name.

b. Suppose a random list of names has an even number of names, say 16. At what positions are the two "middle" names? Using sequential search, how many comparisons are required to find each of these? What is the average of these two numbers? Repeat this exercise with a few more even numbers until you can answer the following question: If there are n names in the list and n is an even number, write an expression for the average number of comparisons required to find the two middle names.

c. Noting that half the names in a list fall before the midpoint and half after the midpoint, use your answer to parts (a) and (b) to write an exact expression for the average number of comparisons done using sequential search to find a name that occurs in an n-element list.

8. Here is a list of seven names:

   Sherman, Jane, Ted, Elise, Raul, Maki, John

   Search this list for each name in turn, using sequential search and counting the number of comparisons for each name. Now take the seven comparison counts and find their average. Did you get a number that you expected? Why?

9. Suppose the telephone company keeps a table like Figure 3.9 but with n telephone districts.

   a. Write a pseudocode algorithm to write out the table—that is, to write each of the entries in the table. As mentioned earlier, this will result in n^2 write operations being executed.

   b. Write a pseudocode algorithm to write out n copies of the table, one to give to each of the n district managers. Write an expression for the number of write statements the algorithm executes.

   c. What is the order of magnitude of the work done by the algorithm of part (b) if the unit of work is writing a table element?

10. Algorithms A and B perform the same task. On input of size n, algorithm A executes $0.003n^2$ instructions, and algorithm B executes $243n$ instructions. Find

the approximate value of n above which algorithm B is more efficient. (You may use a calculator.)

11. The shuffle-left algorithm for data cleanup is supposed to perform $n(n-1)$ copies on a list consisting of n 0s. Confirm this result for the list

   0   0   0   0   0   0

12. Perform a selection sort on the list

   7, 4, 2, 9, 6

   Show the list after each exchange that has a visible effect.

13. The selection sort algorithm could be modified to stop when the unsorted section of the list contains only one number, because that one number must be in the correct position. Show that this modification would have no effect on the number of comparisons required to sort an n-element list.

   Exercises 14–16 refer to another algorithm, called **bubble sort**, to sort an n-element list. Bubble sort makes multiple passes through the list from front to back, each time exchanging pairs of entries that are out of order. Here is a pseudocode version:

   1. Get values for n and the n list items
   2. Set the marker U for the unsorted section at the end of the list
   3. Repeat steps 4 through 8 until the unsorted section has just one element
   4.   Set the current element marker C at the second element of the list
   5.   Repeat steps 6 and 7 until C is to the right of U
   6.   If the item at position C is less than the item to its left then exchange these two items
   7.   Move C to the right one position
   8.   Move the marker for the unsorted section forward one position
   9. Stop

14. For each of the following lists, perform a bubble sort, and show the list after each exchange. Compare the number of exchanges done here and in Practice Problem 1 at the end of Section 3.5.

   a. 4, 8, 2, 6
   b. 12, 3, 6, 8, 2, 5, 7
   c. D, B, G, F, A, C, E

15. Explain why the bubble sort algorithm above does $\Theta(n^2)$ comparisons on an n-element list.

16. Suppose selection sort and bubble sort are both performed on a list that is already sorted. Does bubble sort do fewer exchanges than selection sort? Explain.

17. Consider the following list of names.

    Arturo, Elsa, JoAnn, John, Jose, Lee, Snyder, Tracy

    a. Use binary search to decide whether Elsa is in this list. What names will be compared to Elsa?
    b. Use binary search to decide whether Tracy is in this list. What names will be compared to Tracy?
    c. Use binary search to decide whether Emile is in this list. What names will be compared to Emile?

18. Use the binary search algorithm to decide whether 35 is in the following list.

    3, 6, 7, 9, 12, 14, 18, 21, 22, 31, 43

    What numbers will be compared to 35?

19. If a list is already sorted in increasing order, a modified sequential search algorithm can be used that compares against each element in turn, stopping if a list element exceeds the target value. Write a pseudocode version of this **short sequential search**.

20. This exercise refers to short sequential search (see Exercise 19).

    a. What is the worst-case number of comparisons of short sequential search on a sorted n-element list?
    b. What is the approximate average number of comparisons to find an element that is in a sorted list using short sequential search?
    c. Is short sequential search ever more efficient than regular sequential search? Explain.

21. For the eight-element list of Exercise 17, draw the tree structure that describes binary search on this list. What is the number of comparisons in the worst case? Give an example of a name to search for that would require that many comparisons.

22. Draw the tree structure that describes binary search on a list with 16 elements. What is the number of comparisons in the worst case?

23. We want to find an exact formula for the number of comparisons that binary search requires in the worst case on an n-element list. [We already know the formula is $\Theta(\lg n)$.]

    a. If x is a number that is not an integer, then $\lfloor x \rfloor$, called the **floor function** of x, is defined to be the largest integer less than or equal to x. For example, $\lfloor 3.7 \rfloor = 3$ and $\lfloor 5 \rfloor = 5$. Find the following values: $\lfloor 1.2 \rfloor, \lfloor 23 \rfloor, \lfloor 8.9 \rfloor, \lfloor -4.6 \rfloor$.

    b. If n is not a power of 2, then $\lg n$ will not be an integer. If n is between 8 and 16, for example, then $\lg n$ will be between 3 and 4 (because $\lg 8 = 3$ and $\lg 16 = 4$). Complete the following table of values.

n	$\lfloor \lg n \rfloor$
2	1
3	
4	2
5	
6	
7	
8	3

    c. For $n = 2, 3, 4, 5, 6, 7, 8$, draw a tree structure similar to Figure 3.20 to describe the positions searched by binary search. For each value of n, use the tree structure to find the number of comparisons in the worst case, and complete the following table:

n	Number of Comparisons, Worst Case
2	
3	
4	3
5	
6	
7	3
8	

    d. Comparing the tables of parts (b) and (c), find a formula involving $\lfloor \lg n \rfloor$ for the number of comparisons binary search requires in the worst case on an n-element list. Test your formula by drawing trees for other values of n.

24. Using the tree of Figure 3.20, find the number of comparisons to find each of items 1–7 in a seven-element list using binary search. Then find the average. Compare this with the worst case.

25. At the end of Section 3.5.3, we talked about the tradeoff between using sequential search on an unsorted list and sorting the list and then using binary search. If the size of the list $n = 100,000$, about how many worst-case searches must be done before the second alternative is better in terms of number of comparisons? (Hint: Let p represent the number of searches done.)

26. Suppose the pattern-matching problem is changed to require locating only the first instance, if any, of the pattern within the text.

   a. Describe the worst case, give an example, and give the exact number of comparisons (of a pattern character with a text character) required.

   b. Describe the best case, give an example, and give the exact number of comparisons required.

27. At about what value of n does an algorithm that does $100n^2$ instructions become more efficient than one that does $0.01(2^n)$ instructions? (Use a calculator.)

28. a. An algorithm that is $\Theta(n)$ takes 10 seconds to execute on a particular computer when $n = 100$. How long would you expect it to take when $n = 500$?

   b. An algorithm that is $\Theta(n^2)$ takes 10 seconds to execute on a particular computer when $n = 100$. How long would you expect it to take when $n = 500$?

29. Find an optimal solution to the bin-packing problem described in Section 3.6.

30. In the data cleanup problem, we assumed that the items were stored in a list with a fixed number of positions. Each item could be examined by giving its position in the list. This arrangement of data is called an **array**. Here is an array of four items.

43	13	55	39
1	2	3	4

Another way to arrange items is to have a way to locate the first item and then have each item "point to" the next item. This arrangement of data is called a **linked list**. Here are the same four items in a linked list arrangement:

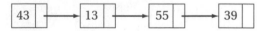

To examine any item in a linked list, one must start with the first item and follow the pointers to the desired item.

Unlike arrays, which are fixed in size, linked lists can shrink and grow. An item can be eliminated from a linked list by changing the pointer to that item so that it points to the next item instead.

   a. Draw the linked list that results when item 13 is eliminated from the foregoing linked list.

   b. Draw the linked list that results when data cleanup is performed on the following linked list.

19		0		53		28		0		33

   c. Describe (informally) an algorithm to do data cleanup on a linked list. You may assume that neither the first item nor the last item will have a value of 0, and you may assume the existence of operations such as "follow pointer" and "change pointer." If these operations are the unit of work used, show that your algorithm is an $\Theta(n)$ algorithm, where n is the number of items in the list.

CHALLENGE WORK

1. You are probably familiar with the children's song "Old MacDonald Had a Farm." The first verse is

   Old MacDonald had a farm, eee-eye, eee-eye, oh.
   And on that farm he had a cow, eee-eye, eee-eye, oh.
   *   With a moo-moo here and a moo-moo there,*
   *   Here a moo, there a moo,*
   *   Everywhere a moo-moo,*
   Old MacDonald had a farm, eee-eye, eee-eye, oh.

   In successive verses, more animals are added, and the middle refrain gets longer and longer. For example, the second verse is

   Old MacDonald had a farm, eee-eye, eee-eye, oh.
   And on that farm he had a pig, eee-eye, eee-eye, oh.
   *   With an oink-oink here and an oink-oink there,*
   *   Here an oink, there an oink,*
   *   Everywhere an oink-oink,*
   *   With a moo-moo here and a moo-moo there,*

Here a moo, there a moo,
Everywhere a moo-moo,
Old MacDonald had a farm, eee-eye, eee-eye, oh.

a. Show that after n verses of this song have been sung, the total number of syllables sung would be given by the expression

$22n(n + 1)/2 + 37n$

(You may assume that all animal names consist of one syllable, as in horse, dog, cat, goat, and so on.)

b. If singing this song is the algorithm, and the work unit is singing one syllable, what is the order of magnitude of the algorithm?[1]

2. **Linear programming** involves selecting values for a large number of quantities so that they satisfy a set of inequalities (such as $x + y + z \leq 100$) while at the same time maximizing (or minimizing) some particular function of these variables. Linear programming has many applications in communications and manufacturing. A trial-and-error approach to a linear programming problem would involve guessing at values for these variables until all of the inequalities are satisfied, but this may not produce the desired maximum (or minimum) value. In addition, real-world problems may involve hundreds or thousands of variables. A common algorithm to solve linear programming problems is called the **simplex method**. Although the simplex method works well for many common applications, including those that involve thousands of variables, its worst-case order of magnitude is exponential. Find information on the work of N. Karmarkar of Bell Labs, who discovered another algorithm for linear programming that is of polynomial order in the worst case and is faster than the simplex method in average cases.

For Further Reading

The first organized collection of algorithms was published as the following three-volume series, which is still quoted in computer science literature.

Knuth, D. *Fundamental Algorithms.* Vol. 1 of *The Art of Computer Programming,* 3rd ed. Reading, MA: Addison-Wesley, 1997.

Knuth, D. *Seminumerical Algorithms.* Vol. 2 of *The Art of Computer Programming,* 3rd ed. Reading, MA: Addison-Wesley, 1998.

Knuth, D. *Sorting and Searching.* Vol. 3 of *The Art of Computer Programming,* 2nd ed. Reading, MA: Addison-Wesley, 1998.

Other works on algorithms, their design, and their analysis include

Baase, S. *Computer Algorithms: Introduction to Design and Analysis,* 2nd ed. Reading, MA: Addison-Wesley, 1988.

Cormen, T. H.; Leiserson, C. E.; and Rivest, R. L. *Introduction to Algorithms.* New York: McGraw-Hill, 1990.

Neapolitan, R., and Naimipour, K. *Foundations of Algorithms.* Sudbury, MA: Jones and Bartlett, 1997.

Rawlins, G. *Compared to What? An Introduction to the Analysis of Algorithms.* New York: Freeman, 1992.

---

[1] This exercise is based on work found in Darrah Chavey, "Songs and the Analysis of Algorithms," *Proceedings of the Twenty-Seventh SIGCSE Technical Symposium* (1996), 4–8.

The following book offers a complete discussion on intractable or thought-to-be-intractable problems as of the date of its publication.

Garey, M. R., and Johnson, D. S. *Computers and Intractability, A Guide to the Theory of NP-Completeness.* New York: Freeman, 1979.

3.7   SUMMARY OF LEVEL 1

We defined computer science as the study of algorithms, so it is appropriate that Level 1 was devoted to exploring algorithms in more detail. In Chapter 2 we discussed how to represent algorithms using pseudocode. Pseudocode provides us with a flexible language in which to express the building blocks from which algorithms can be constructed. These building blocks include assigning a particular value to a quantity, choosing one of two next steps on the basis of some condition, or repeating steps in a loop.

We developed algorithmic solutions to three very practical problems: searching for a name in a list of names, finding the largest number in a list of numbers, and searching for a particular pattern of characters within a segment of text. In Chapter 3 we noted that computer scientists develop algorithms to be *used* and that this leads to a set of desirable properties for algorithms, such as ease of understanding, elegance, and efficiency, in addition to correctness. Of these, efficiency—which may be either time efficiency or space efficiency—is the most easily quantifiable. We analyzed the time efficiency of the sequential search algorithm and discovered that to search a list of n names requires n comparisons in the worst case and $n/2$ comparisons in the average case.

A convenient way to classify the time efficiency of algorithms is by examining the order of magnitude of the work they do. Algorithms that are of differing orders of magnitude do fundamentally different amounts of work. No matter what the constant factor that reflects peripheral work, and no matter how fast the computer on which these algorithms execute, for problems with sufficiently large input, the algorithm of the lowest order of magnitude will require the least time.

Through examining the data cleanup problem, we learned that algorithms that solve the same task can indeed differ in the order of magnitude of the work they do, sometimes by employing a time-space tradeoff. We found a selection sort algorithm that is $\Theta(n^2)$, we found a binary search algorithm that is $\Theta(\lg n)$, and we did an analysis of the pattern-matching algorithm from Chapter 2. We also learned that there are algorithms that require more than polynomially bounded time to complete their work and that such algorithms may take so long, regardless of the speed of the computer on which they are run, that they provide no practical solution method. Some important and practical problems may be intractable, having no polynomially bounded solution algorithms at all.

Some computer scientists work on deciding whether a particular problem is intractable. Some work on finding more efficient algorithms for problems—such as searching and sorting—that are such common tasks that a more efficient algorithm would greatly improve productivity. Still others seek to discover algorithms for new problems. Thus, as we said, the study of algorithms underlies much of computer science. But everything we have done so far has been a pencil and paper exercise. In terms of the definition of computer science that we gave in Chapter 1, we have been looking at the formal and mathematical properties of algorithms. It is time to move on to the next part of that definition: the hardware realizations of algorithms. When we execute real algorithms on real computers, those computers are electronic devices. How does an electronic device "understand" an algorithm and carry out its instructions? We begin to explore these questions in Chapter 4 as we enter the hardware world.

THE
HARDWARE
WORLD

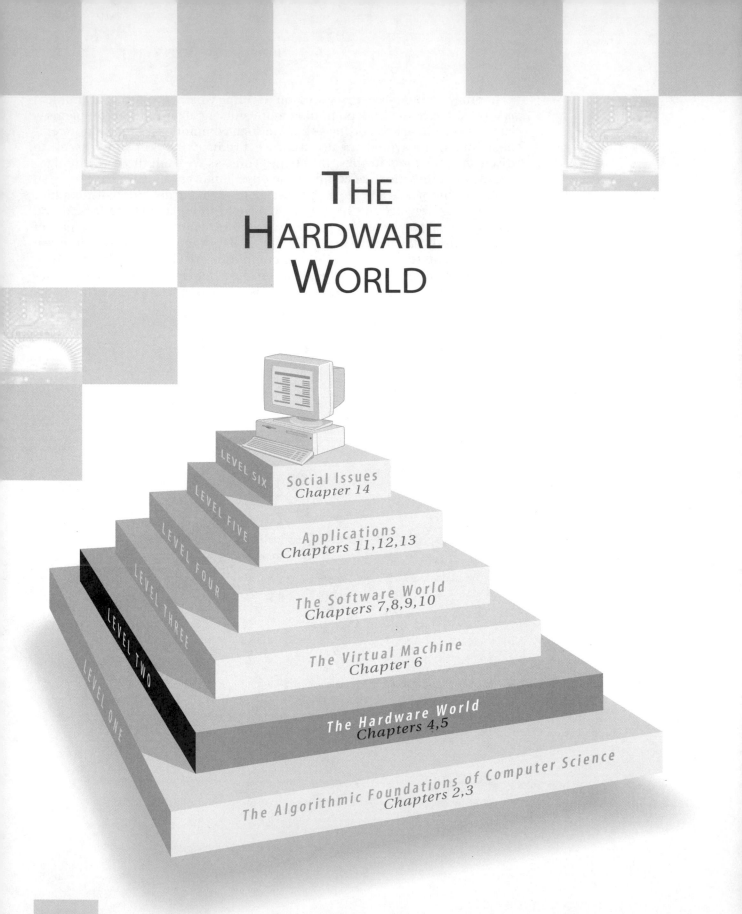

LEVEL SIX — Social Issues
Chapter 14

LEVEL FIVE — Applications
Chapters 11,12,13

LEVEL FOUR — The Software World
Chapters 7,8,9,10

LEVEL THREE — The Virtual Machine
Chapter 6

LEVEL TWO — The Hardware World
Chapters 4,5

LEVEL ONE — The Algorithmic Foundations of Computer Science
Chapters 2,3

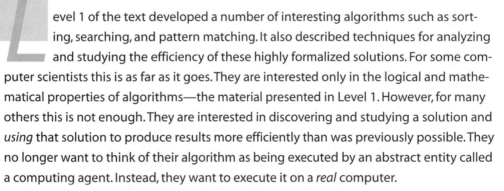

LEVEL

2

*L*evel 1 of the text developed a number of interesting algorithms such as sorting, searching, and pattern matching. It also described techniques for analyzing and studying the efficiency of these highly formalized solutions. For some computer scientists this is as far as it goes. They are interested only in the logical and mathematical properties of algorithms—the material presented in Level 1. However, for many others this is not enough. They are interested in discovering and studying a solution and *using* that solution to produce results more efficiently than was previously possible. They no longer want to think of their algorithm as being executed by an abstract entity called a computing agent. Instead, they want to execute it on a *real* computer.

Level 2 of the text launches our study of how to design and build computer systems, and it takes us into a fascinating new region of computer science, "the hardware world."

CHAPTER

4

THE BUILDING BLOCKS: BINARY NUMBERS, BOOLEAN LOGIC, AND GATES

4.1   INTRODUCTION

Level 1 of the text investigated the algorithmic foundations of computer science. It developed algorithms for searching tables, finding largest and smallest values, locating patterns, sorting lists, and cleaning up bad data. It also showed how to analyze and evaluate algorithms to demonstrate that they are not only correct but efficient and useful as well.

Our discussion assumed that these algorithms would be executed by something called a **computing agent**, an abstract concept representing any object capable of understanding and executing our instructions. We didn't care what that computing agent was—person, mathematical model, computer, or robot. In Level 1 we focused only on the creation of correct and efficient solutions to problems. However, in this section of the text we *do* care what our computing agent looks like and how it is able to execute instructions and produce results. In Level 2, "The Hardware World," we look at what is involved in designing and building real computers to solve "real-life" problems.

Level 2 is composed of two chapters, each of which takes a very different approach to this material. Chapter 4 begins our study of the hardware world by examining the fundamental building blocks used to construct computers. It discusses how to represent and store information inside a computer, how to use the principles of symbolic logic to design *gates*, and how to use gates to construct *circuits* that perform operations such as adding numbers, comparing numbers, and fetching instructions. These ideas are part of the branch of computer science known as **hardware design**, also called **logic design**.

The second part of Level 2, Chapter 5, investigates computer hardware from a higher-level perspective called **computer organization**. This chapter introduces the four major subsystems of a modern computer (memory, input/output, arithmetic/logic unit, control unit), demonstrates how they are built from the elementary building blocks described in Chapter 4, and shows how these subsystems can be organized into a complete, functioning computer system. By way of analogy with the human body, Chapter 4 can be considered equivalent to a study of such elementary material as DNA, genes, cells, and tissues. Chapter 5 then demonstrates how our organs (heart, lungs) and bodily systems (circulatory, respiratory) are built from these basic biological units.

4.2   THE BINARY NUMBERING SYSTEM

Our first concern with learning how to build computers is how computers represent information. Their internal storage techniques are quite different from the way you and I represent information in our notebooks, desks, and filing cabinets.

4.2.1 BINARY REPRESENTATION OF INFORMATION

Human beings (or at least those who live in English-speaking countries) represent information by using the following notational conventions:

a. Decimal representation for numerical values using the 10 digits 0, 1, 2, 3, 4, 5, 6, 7, 8, 9

b. The 26 letters A, B, C, . . . , X, Y, Z for textual information (as well as lowercase letters and a few special symbols for punctuation)

c. *Sign/magnitude notation* for signed numbers—that is, a + or − sign placed immediately to the left of the digits; −31 and +789 are examples

d. *Decimal notation* for real numbers, with a decimal point separating the whole-number part from the fractional part; an example is 12.34

These are the conventions for writing numbers and text to be read and understood by other persons. Therefore, it is tempting to believe that these well-known schemes are the same conventions that computers use to store information in memory. Surprisingly, this is not true.

When discussing the representation of information, we must distinguish between two types: The **external representation** of information is the way information is represented by humans and the way it is entered at a keyboard or displayed on a printer or screen. The **internal representation** of information is the way it is stored in the memory of a computer. This difference is diagrammed in Figure 4.1.

Externally, computers do use decimal digits, sign/magnitude notation, and the familiar 26-character alphabet. However, virtually every computer ever built stores data—numbers, letters, graphics—internally using the **binary numbering system.**

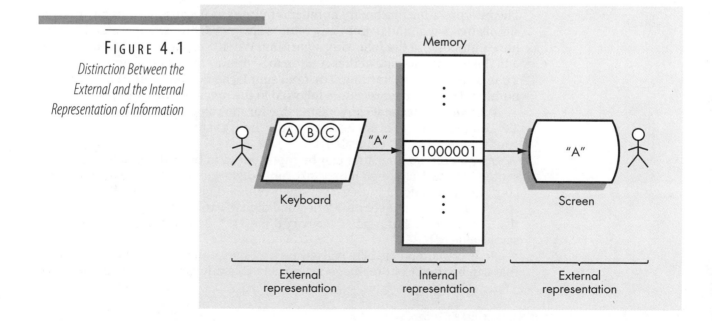

FIGURE 4.1

Distinction Between the External and the Internal Representation of Information

Memory

"A"

01000001

"A"

Keyboard

Screen

External representation

Internal representation

External representation

Binary is a **base-2 positional numbering system** not unlike the more familiar decimal, or base-10, system used in everyday life. In these systems the value or "worth" of a digit depends not only on its absolute value but also on its specific position within a number. In the decimal system there are 10 unique digits (0, 1, 2, 3, 4, 5, 6, 7, 8, and 9), and the value of the positions in a decimal number is based on powers of 10. Moving from right to left in a number, the positions represent ones (10^0), tens (10^1), hundreds (10^2), thousands (10^3), and so on. Therefore, the decimal number 2,359 is evaluated as follows:

$$(2 \times 10^3) + (3 \times 10^2) + (5 \times 10^1) + (9 \times 10^0)$$
$$= 2,000 + 300 + 50 + 9$$
$$= 2,359$$

The same concepts apply to binary numbers except that there are only two digits, 0 and 1, and the value of the positions in a binary number is based on powers of 2. Again, moving from right to left, the positions represent ones (2^0), twos (2^1), fours (2^2), eights (2^3), sixteens (2^4), etc. The two digits, 0 and 1, are frequently referred to as **bits**, a contraction of the words *b*inary dig*its*.

For example, the 6-digit binary number 111001 is evaluated as follows:

$$111001 = (1 \times 2^5) + (1 \times 2^4) + (1 \times 2^3) + (0 \times 2^2) + (0 \times 2^1) + (1 \times 2^0)$$
$$= 32 + 16 + 8 + 0 + 0 + 1$$
$$= 57$$

As a second example, the 5-digit binary quantity 10111 is evaluated in the following manner:

$$10111 = (1 \times 2^4) + (0 \times 2^3) + (1 \times 2^2) + (1 \times 2^1) + (1 \times 2^0)$$
$$= 16 + 0 + 4 + 2 + 1$$
$$= 23$$

The interpretation of a binary number is quite easy, because 1 times any value is simply that value, and 0 times any value is always 0. Thus, when evaluating a binary number, use the following algorithm: Whenever there is a 1 in a column, add the positional value of that column to a running sum, and whenever there is a 0 in a column, add nothing. The final sum is the decimal value of this binary number. This was the procedure followed in the previous two examples.

A binary-to-decimal conversion table for the values 0–31 is shown in Figure 4.2. You may want to evaluate a few of the binary values using this algorithm to confirm their decimal equivalents.

Any whole number that can be represented in base 10 can also be represented in base 2, although it may take more digits because a single decimal digit contains more information than a single binary digit. Note in the first example shown above that it takes only 2 decimal digits (5 and 7) to represent the quantity 57 in base 10, but it takes 6 binary digits (1, 1, 1, 0, 0, and 1) to express the same value in base 2.

In every computer there will always be a maximum number of binary digits that can be used to store integers. Typically, this value is 16, 24, or 32 bits. Once

FIGURE 4.2

Binary-to-Decimal Conversion Table

BINARY	DECIMAL	BINARY	DECIMAL
0	0	10000	16
1	1	10001	17
10	2	10010	18
11	3	10011	19
100	4	10100	20
101	5	10101	21
110	6	10110	22
111	7	10111	23
1000	8	11000	24
1001	9	11001	25
1010	10	11010	26
1011	11	11011	27
1100	12	11100	28
1101	13	11101	29
1110	14	11110	30
1111	15	11111	31

we have fixed this maximum number of bits (as part of the design of the computer), we also have fixed the largest integer value that can be represented in this computer. For example, if there are a maximum of 16 bits available to represent integer quantities, then the largest integer that can be represented is

1 1 1 1 1 1 1 1 1 1 1 1 1 1 1 1

(not unlike the number 99999, which is the maximum mileage value that can be represented on a 5-digit decimal odometer). This quantity is $2^{15} + 2^{14} + \ldots + 2^2 + 2^1 + 2^0 = 65,535$. Integers larger than this cannot be represented with 16 binary digits. Any operation on this computer that produces an integer value greater than 65,535 will result in the error condition called **arithmetic overflow**. This is an attempt to represent an integer that exceeds the maximum allowable value. If this could be a problem, then the computer could be designed to allow more than 16 bits to represent integers. However, no matter how many bits are ultimately used, there will always be a maximum value beyond which the computer cannot correctly represent any integer. This characteristic is one of the major differences between the disciplines of mathematics and computer science. In mathematics a quantity may usually take on any value, no matter how large. Computer science must deal with a finite—and sometimes quite limited—set of possible representations, and it must handle the errors that occur when those limits are exceeded.

Binary digits can be used to represent not only whole numbers but also other forms of data, including signed integers, decimal numbers, and characters. For example, to represent signed integers, we can use the leftmost bit of a number to represent the sign, with 0 meaning + and 1 meaning –. The remaining bits are used to represent the magnitude of the value. This form of integer representation is termed **sign/magnitude notation**, and it is one of a number of different techniques for representing positive and negative whole numbers. For example, to represent the quantity –49 in sign/magnitude, we could use seven binary digits with one bit for the sign and six bits for the magnitude:

1    $\underbrace{1\,1\,0\,0\,0\,1}$

–   49 $(2^5 + 2^4 + 2^0 = 32 + 16 + 1 = 49)$

The value +3 would be stored like this:

0    $\underbrace{0\,0\,0\,0\,1\,1}$

+   3 $(2^1 + 2^0 = 2 + 1 = 3)$

You may wonder how a computer knows that the 7-digit binary number 1110001 represents the signed integer value –49 rather than the unsigned whole number 113.

$$1110001 = (1 \times 2^6) + (1 \times 2^5) + (1 \times 2^4) + (1 \times 2^0)$$
$$= 64 + 32 + 16 + 1$$
$$= 113$$

The answer to this question is that a computer does *not* know. A sequence of binary digits can have many different interpretations, and there is no fixed, predetermined interpretation given to any binary value. A binary number stored in the memory of a computer takes on meaning only because it is used in a certain way. If we use the value 1110001 as though it were a signed integer, then it will be interpreted that way and will take on the value –49. If it is used as an unsigned whole number instead, then that is what it will become, and it will be interpreted as the unsigned whole number 113. The meaning of a binary number stored in memory is based solely on the context in which it is used.

Initially this may seem strange, but we deal with this type of ambiguity all the time in natural languages. For example, in the Hebrew language, letters of the alphabet are also used as numbers. Thus the Hebrew character א can stand for either the letter A or the number 1. The only way one can tell which meaning is appropriate is to consider the context in which the character is used. Similarly, in English the word *ball* can mean either a round object used to play games or an elegant formal party. Which interpretation is correct? We cannot say without knowing the context in which the word is used. The same is true for values stored in the memory of a computer system. It is the context that determines the meaning of a binary string.

Sign/magnitude notation is quite easy for people to work with and understand, but, surprisingly, it is used rather infrequently in real computer systems. The reason is the existence of a very "messy" and unwanted number: 10000 . . . 0000. Because the leftmost bit is a 1, this value is negative. The magnitude is 0000 . . . 0000. Thus this bit pattern represents the numerical quantity "negative zero," a value that has no real mathematical meaning and should not be distinguished from the other representation for zero, 00000 . . . 0000. The existence of two distinct bit patterns for a single numerical quantity causes headaches for computer designers (e.g., does 10000 . . . 000 = 00000 . . . 000?). Therefore, they tend to favor integer representations that do not suffer from this problem. (A Challenge Work problem at the end of this chapter invites you to investigate one of these alternative representation techniques called **two's complement** notation.)

Decimal numbers, such as 12.34 and -0.001275, can also be represented in binary by using the signed-integer techniques we have described. To do that, however, we must first convert the number to **scientific notation**:

$$\pm M \times B^{\pm E}$$

where M is the **mantissa**, B is the base of the exponent (usually 2), and E is the **exponent**. Let's work an example to illustrate these ideas. Assume we want to represent the decimal quantity $+5.75$. In addition, assume that we use 16 bits to represent the number, with 10 bits for the mantissa and 6 bits for the exponent. (The base B is assumed to be 2 and is not explicitly stored.) Both the mantissa and the exponent are signed numbers, so we can use the sign/magnitude notation that we just learned to represent each of them. In each of the two fields, we will use the leftmost bit to represent the sign and the remaining bits to encode the magnitude.

In binary, the value 5 is 101. To represent the fractional quantity 0.75, we need to remember that the bits to the right of the decimal point (or binary point in our case) have the positional values r^{-1}, r^{-2}, r^{-3}, and so on, where r is the base. Because $r = 2$ in our case, the positional values of the digits to the right of the binary point are halves (2^{-1}), quarters (2^{-2}), eighths (2^{-3}), sixteenths (2^{-4}), and so on. Thus

$$0.75 = \tfrac{1}{2} + \tfrac{1}{4} = 2^{-1} + 2^{-2} \quad \text{which in binary is } 0.11$$

Therefore, in binary $5.75 = 101.11$. Using scientific notation (and $B = 2$), we write this as

$$5.75 = 101.11 \times 2^0$$

Next, we must *normalize* the number so that its first significant digit is immediately to the right of the binary point. As we move the binary point, we adjust the value of the exponent so that the overall value of the number remains unchanged. If we move the binary point to the left one place (which makes the value smaller by a factor of 2), then we add 1 to the exponent (which makes it larger by a factor of 2). We do the reverse when we move the binary point to the right.

$$5.75 = 101.11 \times 2^0$$
$$= 10.111 \times 2^1$$
$$= 1.0111 \times 2^2$$
$$= .10111 \times 2^3 \quad \text{which is } (\tfrac{1}{2} + \tfrac{1}{8} + \tfrac{1}{16} + \tfrac{1}{32}) \times 8 = 5.75$$

We now have the number in the desired format and can put all the pieces together. We separately store the mantissa (excluding the binary point) and the exponent, both of which are signed integers and can be represented in sign/magnitude notation. The mantissa is stored with its sign—0, because it is a positive quantity—followed by the assumed binary point, followed by the magnitude of the mantissa, which in this case is 10111. Next we store the exponent, which is +3, or 000011 in sign/magnitude. The overall representation is

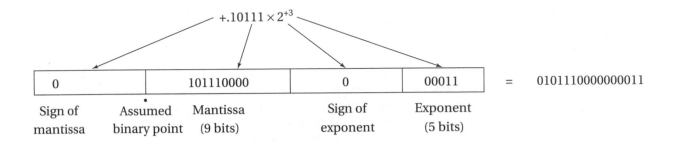

As a second example, let's determine the internal representation of the fraction $-\frac{5}{16}$.

$$-\frac{5}{16} = -(\frac{1}{4} + \frac{1}{16})$$

$$= -.0101 \times 2^0 \quad \text{(the value } -\frac{5}{16} \text{ in scientific notation)}$$

$$= -.101 \times 2^{-1} \quad \text{(after normalization)}$$

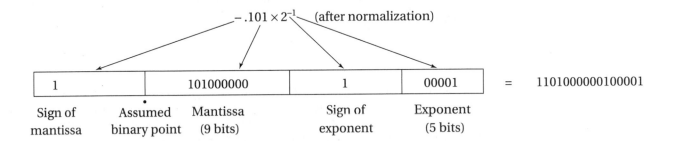

As our final example of the internal representation of information, let's look at how a computer is able to store *text*. To represent textual material in binary, the system assigns to each printable letter or symbol in our alphabet a unique number (this assignment is called a **code mapping**), and then it stores that symbol internally using the binary equivalent of that number. For example, here is one possible mapping of characters to numbers, which uses eight bits to represent each character.

Symbol	Decimal Value	Binary Value (Using Eight Binary Digits)
A	1	00000001
B	2	00000010
C	3	00000011
D	4	00000100
.	.	.
.	.	.
.	.	.
Z	26	00011010
.	.	.
.	.	.
.	.	.
@	128	10000000
!	129	10000001
.	.	.
.	.	.
.	.	.

To store the 4-character string "BAD!" in memory, the computer stores the binary representation of each individual character using the above 8-bit code.

BAD! = $\underbrace{00000010}_{B}$ $\underbrace{00000001}_{A}$ $\underbrace{00000100}_{D}$ $\underbrace{10000001}_{!}$

To facilitate the exchange of textual information, such as word processing documents and electronic mail, between computer systems, it would be helpful if everyone used the same code mapping. Fortunately, this is pretty much the case. The most widely used code for representing characters internally in a computer system is called **ASCII**, an acronym for the *A*merican *S*tandard *C*ode for *I*nformation *I*nterchange. ASCII is an international standard for representing textual information in the overwhelming majority of computers. It uses 8 bits to represent each character, so it is able to encode a total of $2^8 = 256$ different characters. These are assigned the integer values 0 to 255. However, only the numbers 32 to 126 have so far been assigned to printable characters. The remainder either are unassigned or are used for nonprinting control characters such as form feed and carriage return. Figure 4.3 shows the ASCII conversion table for the numerical values 32–126.

As we mentioned earlier, the only way a computer knows that the 8-bit value 01000001 represents the letter A and not the integer value 65 (1 + 64) is by the context in which it is used. If these 8 bits are sent to a display screen that expects characters, then this value will be interpreted as an A. If, on the other hand, this 8-bit value is sent to an arithmetic unit that adds unsigned numbers, then it will be interpreted as a 65 in order to make the addition operation meaningful.

FIGURE 4.3

ASCII Conversion Table

Keyboard Character	Binary ASCII Code	Integer Equivalent	Keyboard Character	Binary ASCII Code	Integer Equivalent
(blank)	00100000	32	P	01010000	80
!	00100001	33	Q	01010001	81
"	00100010	34	R	01010010	82
#	00100011	35	S	01010011	83
$	00100100	36	T	01010100	84
%	00100101	37	U	01010101	85
&	00100110	38	V	01010110	86
'	00100111	39	W	01010111	87
(	00101000	40	X	01011000	88
)	00101001	41	Y	01011001	89
*	00101010	42	Z	01011010	90
+	00101011	43	[	01011011	91
,	00101100	44	\	01011100	92
−	00101101	45	]	01011101	93
.	00101110	46	^	01011110	94
/	00101111	47	_	01011111	95
0	00110000	48	`	01100000	96
1	00110001	49	a	01100001	97
2	00110010	50	b	01100010	98
3	00110011	51	c	01100011	99
4	00110100	52	d	01100100	100
5	00110101	53	e	01100101	101
6	00110110	54	f	01100110	102
7	00110111	55	g	01100111	103
8	00111000	56	h	01101000	104
9	00111001	57	i	01101001	105
:	00111010	58	j	01101010	106
;	00111011	59	k	01101011	107
<	00111100	60	l	01101100	108
=	00111101	61	m	01101101	109
>	00111110	62	n	01101110	110
?	00111111	63	o	01101111	111
@	01000000	64	p	01110000	112
A	01000001	65	q	01110001	113
B	01000010	66	r	01110010	114
C	01000011	67	s	01110011	115
D	01000100	68	t	01110100	116
E	01000101	69	u	01110101	117
F	01000110	70	v	01110110	118
G	01000111	71	w	01110111	119
H	01001000	72	x	01111000	120
I	01001001	73	y	01111001	121
J	01001010	74	z	01111010	122
K	01001011	75	{	01111011	123
L	01001100	76	:	01111100	124
M	01001101	77	}	01111101	125
N	01001110	78	~	01111110	126
O	01001111	79			

PRACTICE PROBLEMS

1. What is the value of the 8-bit binary quantity 10101000 if it is interpreted a) as an unsigned integer, b) as a signed integer represented in sign/magnitude notation?

2. What would the unsigned decimal value 99 look like in binary using 8 bits?

3. What would the signed integers −300 and +254 look like in binary using 10 bits?

4. What would the 3-character string ABC look like internally using the ASCII code?

5. Using 10 bits to represent the mantissa (sign/magnitude) and 6 bits to represent the exponent (also sign/magnitude), show the internal representation of the following two values:
   a. + 0.25
   b. − 32$\frac{1}{16}$

4.2.2 THE RELIABILITY OF BINARY REPRESENTATION

At this point there is a fundamental question that must be answered: "Why are we bothering to use binary numbers?" Because people use decimal numbers to do their work, wouldn't it be more convenient to use a base-10 representation for both the external and the internal representation of information? If we did, then there would be no need to go through the time-consuming conversions diagrammed in Figure 4.1 and no need to learn the binary representation techniques discussed in the previous section.

There is absolutely no theoretical reason why one could not build a "decimal" computer or, indeed, a computer that stored numbers using base 3 (**ternary**), base 8 (**octal**) or base 16 (**hexadecimal**). The techniques described in the previous section apply to information represented in *any* base of a positional numbering system, including base 10.

Binary representation is used exclusively not for theoretical reasons but for **reliability**. As we shall see shortly, computers store information using electronic devices, and the internal representation of information must be implemented in terms of electronic quantities such as currents and voltage levels. Building a base-10 "decimal computer" requires finding a device with 10 distinct and stable energy states that can be used to represent the 10 unique digits (0, 1, . . . , 9) of the decimal system. For example, assume there exists a device that can store electrical charges in the range 0 to +45 volts. We could use it to build a decimal computer by letting certain voltage levels correspond to specific decimal digits:

Voltage Level	Corresponds to This Decimal Digit
0	0
+5	1
+10	2
+15	3
+20	4
+25	5
+30	6
+35	7
+40	8
+45	9

Storing the 2-digit decimal number 28 requires two of these devices, one for each of the digits in the number. The first device would be set to +10 volts to represent the digit 2, and the second would be set to +40 volts to represent the digit 8.

However, although this is theoretically feasible, it is certainly not recommended. As electrical devices age they become unreliable, and they may slowly *drift,* or change their energy state, over time. What if the device representing the value 8 (the one set to +40 volts) lost about 6% of its voltage, not a huge amount for an old well-used piece of equipment? The voltage would drop from +40 volts to about +37.5 volts. The question is whether the value +37.5 represents the digit 7 (+35) or the digit 8 (+40). It is impossible to say. If that same device lost another 6% of its voltage, it would drop from +37.5 volts to about +35 volts. Our 8 has now become a 7, and the original value of 28 has unexpectedly changed to 27. Building a reliable decimal machine can be an engineering nightmare.

The problem with a base-10 representation is that it needs to store 10 unique symbols, and therefore it needs devices that have 10 stable states. Such devices are extremely rare. Electrical systems tend to operate best in what is called a **bistable environment,** in which there are only two (rather than 10) stable states separated by a huge energy barrier. Examples of these bistable states include

- full on/full off
- fully charged/fully discharged
- charged positively/charged negatively
- magnetized/nonmagnetized
- magnetized clockwise/magnetized counterclockwise

In the binary numbering system there are only two symbols (0 and 1), so we can let one of the two stable states of our bistable device represent a 0 and the other a 1. This is a much more reliable way to represent information inside a computer.

For example, let's go back to our hypothetical electronic device that stored voltages in the range 0 to +45 volts. If we use binary rather than decimal to store the data, the representational scheme becomes much simpler:

$$0 \text{ volts} = 0 \quad \text{(full off)}$$
$$+45 \text{ volts} = 1 \quad \text{(full on)}$$

Now a 6% or even a 12% drift causes no problem in interpreting the value being represented. In fact, it takes an almost 50% change in voltage level to create a problem in interpreting a stored value. The use of binary for the internal representation of data significantly increases the inherent reliability of a computer. This single advantage is worth all the time it takes to convert from decimal to binary for internal storage and from binary to decimal for the external display of results.

4.2.3 BINARY STORAGE DEVICES

As we saw in the previous section, binary computers can be built out of any bistable device. This idea can be expressed more formally by saying that it is possible to construct a binary computer and its internal components using any hardware device that meets the following four criteria:

1. It has two stable energy states (one for a 0, one for a 1).
2. These two states are separated by a large energy barrier (so that a 0 does not accidentally become a 1, or vice versa).
3. It is possible to sense what state the device is in (to see whether it is storing a 0 or a 1) without permanently destroying the stored value.
4. It is possible to switch the state from a 0 to a 1, or vice versa, by applying a sufficient amount of energy.

There are many devices that meet these conditions, including some unexpected ones such as the familiar ON–OFF light switch. A light switch has two stable states (ON and OFF). These two states are separated by a large energy barrier so that a switch that is in one state will not accidentally change to the other. We can sense what state the switch is in by looking to see whether the label says ON or OFF (or just by looking at the lights), and we can change the state of the switch by applying a sufficient amount of energy via our fingertips. Thus it would be possible to build a reliable (albeit very slow and bulky) binary computing device out of ordinary light switches.

As you might imagine, computer systems are not built from light switches, but they have been built using a wide range of devices. This section reviews two of the most popular as examples of hardware technologies underlying the internal construction of computer systems. The first approach, magnetic cores, is no longer in use, but it is historically important. The second, transistors, is widely used and is a good example of the current state of computer technology.

Magnetic cores were used to construct computer memories for about twenty years. From roughly 1955 to 1975, this was by far the most popular storage technology, and it is not uncommon today to hear the memory unit of a computer referred to as **core memory** even though it has been decades since magnetic cores have been used.

A **core** is a small, magnetizable, iron oxide-coated "doughnut" about 1/50 of an inch in inner diameter with wires strung through its center hole. The two states used to represent the binary values 0 and 1 are based on the *direction* of the magnetic field of the core. When electric current is sent through the wire in one specific

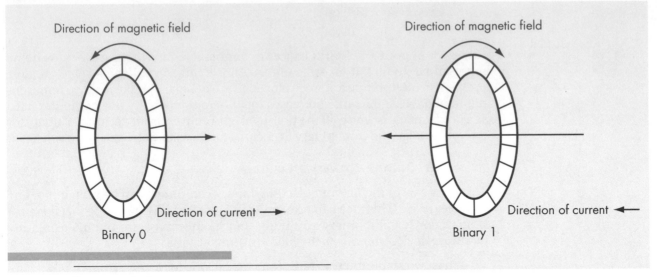

FIGURE 4.4

Using Magnetic Cores to Represent Binary Values

direction, say left to right, the core becomes magnetized in a counterclockwise direction.[1] This state could represent the binary value 0. Current sent in the opposite direction produces a clockwise magnetic field that could represent the binary value 1. These situations are diagrammed in Figure 4.4. Because magnetic fields do not change much over time, these two states are highly stable, and they formed the basis for the construction of memory devices to store binary numbers.

In the early 1970s core memories began to be replaced by other technologies that were smaller and cheaper, required less power, and were easier to manufacture. One-fiftieth of an inch in diameter and a few grams of weight per core may not seem like much but can produce a bulky and unworkable mess when memory units are constructed containing 100 million or more bits of storage. For example, a typical core memory unit from the 1950s or 1960s was a square about 2 or 3 inches on a side. It contained approximately 2,000–3,000 bits of storage. Two thousand bits of information packed into 4 square inches produces an information density of about 500 bits/in^2. That density would be totally inappropriate for today's compact personal computers and laptop systems, whose memory systems contain hundreds of millions of bits of information. At a density of 500 bits/in^2, a memory containing 100,000,000 bits would need a core unit of 200,000 in^2, which is a square about 450 inches, or 37.5 feet, on a side. Built from cores, our memory unit would stand three stories high!

Today, the elementary building block for all modern computer systems is no longer the core but the transistor. A **transistor** is much like the light switch mentioned earlier. It can be in an OFF state, which does not allow electricity to flow, or in an ON state, in which electricity can pass unimpeded. However, unlike the light switch, a transistor is a solid-state device that has no mechanical or mov-

---

[1]The "right-hand rule" of physics says that if the thumb of your right hand is pointing in the direction of the electric current, then the fingers will be curled in the direction of the magnetic field.

ing parts. The switching of a transistor from the OFF to the ON state, and vice versa, is done electronically rather than mechanically. This allows it to be fast as well as extremely small. Typically a transistor can switch states in about 2 to 10 billionths of a second, and at current technology levels, approximately 3 to 10 million transistors can fit in a space 1 cm^2. (Furthermore, hardware technology is changing so rapidly that both these numbers may be out of date by the time you read these words.)

Transistors are constructed from special materials called **semiconductors,** such as silicon and gallium arsenide. A large number of transistors, as well as the electrical conducting paths that connect them, can be printed photographically on a wafer of silicon to produce a device known as an **integrated circuit** or, more commonly, a **chip**. The chip is sometimes mounted inside a ceramic housing called a **dual in-line package** (DIP), which contains the input-output connectors called *pins* that allow one chip to communicate and exchange information with other chips. The DIP itself is mounted on a **circuit board,** which interconnects the different chips (e.g., memory, processor, communications) needed to build a complete computer system. The relationships among transistors, chips, DIPs, and circuit boards are diagrammed in Figure 4.5.

The use of photographic rather than mechanical production techniques has numerous advantages. Because light can be focused very sharply, these integrated circuits can be manufactured in very high densities (i.e., high numbers of transistors per square centimeter) and with a very high degree of accuracy. For example, modern chip manufacturing techniques can produce densities of about 3 to 10 million transistors/cm^2. This level of integration is termed **VLSI**, for *Very Large Scale Integration*. Engineers are working on new manufacturing techniques, termed **ULSI**, *Ultra Large Scale Integration*, that would eventually produce chips containing hundreds of millions or billions of transistors/cm^2. The more transistors that can be packed into a fixed amount of space, the greater the processing power of the computer and the greater the amount of information that can be stored in memory.

Another advantage of photographic production techniques is that it is possible to make a standard template, called a **mask**, that describes the circuit. This mask can be used to produce a virtually unlimited number of copies of that chip, much as a photographic negative can be used to produce an unlimited number of prints.

Together, these characteristics can result in very small and very inexpensive high-speed circuits. Whereas the first computers produced in the early 1940s filled huge rooms and cost millions of dollars, the processor inside a modern workstation is printed on a single chip of about 1–3 cm^2, contains millions of transistors, costs about $100, and is thousands of times more powerful than those early machines.

The theoretical concepts underlying the physical behavior of semiconductors and transistors, as well as the details of chip manufacture, are well beyond the scope of this book. They are usually discussed in courses in physics or electrical engineering. Instead, we will visualize a transistor in terms of the simplified model shown in Figure 4.6 and then use this model to explain its behavior. (Here is an example of the importance of abstraction in computer science.)

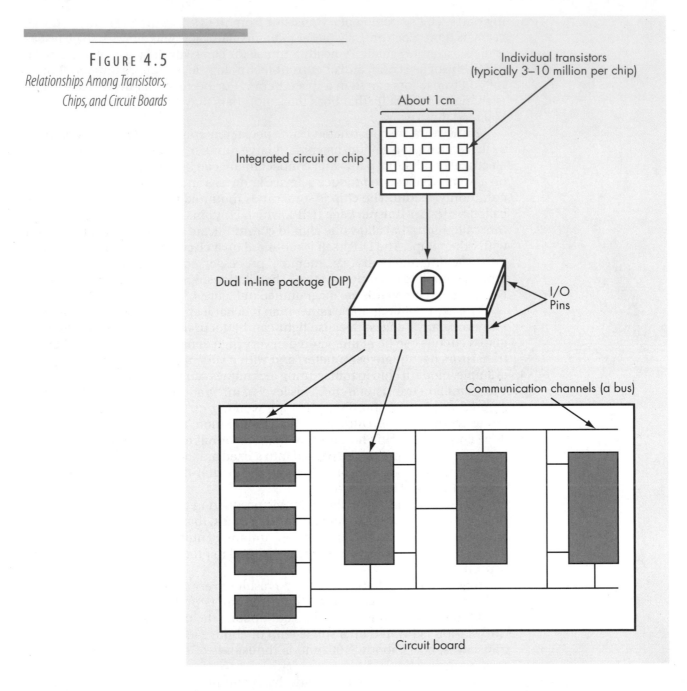

FIGURE 4.5

Relationships Among Transistors, Chips, and Circuit Boards

FIGURE 4.6

Simplified Model of a Transistor

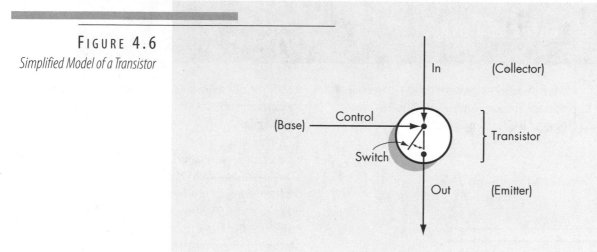

Dr. William Shockley (1910–1989)

Dr. William Shockley was the inventor (along with John Bardeen and Walter Brattain) of the transistor. His discovery has probably done as much to shape our modern world as any scientific advancement of the twentieth century. He received the 1956 Nobel Prize in Physics and, at his death, was a Distinguished Professor at Stanford University.

Shockley and his team developed the transistor in 1947 while working at Bell Laboratories. He left there in 1954 to set up the Shockley Semiconductor Laboratory in California—a company that was instrumental in the birth of the high-technology region called Silicon Valley. The employees of this company eventually went on to develop other fundamental advances in computing, such as the integrated circuit and the microprocessor.

However, although Shockley's work has been compared to that of Pasteur, Salk, and Einstein in importance, his reputation and place in history have forever been tarnished by his outrageous and controversial racial theories. His education and training were in physics and electrical engineering, but Shockley spent the last years of his life trying to convince people of the genetic inferiority of blacks. He became obsessed with these ideas, even though he was ridiculed and shunned by colleagues who abandoned all contact with him. Even though his work on the design of the transistor was of seminal importance, Shockley himself felt that his genetic theory on race and intelligence would ultimately be viewed as his most important contribution to science. By the time of his death in 1989, his intense racial bigotry prevented him from receiving the recognition that would otherwise have been his for monumental contributions in physics, engineering, and computer science.

Chips and DIP

When we describe a computer chip in terms of densities like 5 million, 10 million, or 100 million transistors/cm², it is hard to grasp what those numbers mean. These dimensions are on a scale totally different from the dimensions we work with every day—units such as inches, feet, and miles.

A chip containing 10 million transistors/cm² would be laid out in a two-dimensional grid with approximately 3,200 transistors in each dimension (3,200 × 3,200 = 10,240,000). In this layout, the distance between each transistor on the chip would be about 0.0003 cm, about 1/8000 of an inch. This is less than $\frac{1}{20}$ the diameter of the smallest grain of sand. To give you a better idea of how small this is, if the transistors in a typical chip were located 1 inch apart instead of 0.0003 cm apart (still reasonably small by human standards), the chip would be larger than a football field.

Thus the manufacturers of integrated circuits for computer systems must position, without a single error, millions of electrical devices on a chip the size of your fingernail, each component being located to an accuracy of a few ten-thousandths of a centimeter. Now you can begin to see why they call it *high technology*!

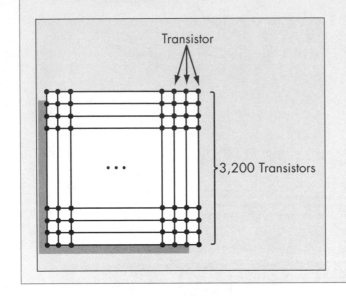

Transistor

3,200 Transistors

In this model (Figure 4.6), each transistor contains three lines—two input lines and one output line. The first input line, called the **control line** and also referred to as the **base**, is used to open or close the switch inside the transistor. If we set the input value on the control line to a 1 by applying a sufficient amount of voltage, the switch closes and the transistor enters the ON state. In this state, voltage coming from the **In** line, called the **collector**, goes directly to the **Out** line, called the **emitter**, and this voltage can be detected by a measuring device. This ON state could be used to represent the binary 1. If instead we set the input value of the control line to a 0 by not applying voltage, the switch opens and the transistor enters the OFF state. In this state no voltage can get through the transistor, so none is detected on the Out line. The OFF state could be used to represent the binary value 0.

This solid-state switching device forms the basis for the construction of virtually all computers built today, and it is the fundamental building block for all high-level components described in the upcoming chapters. Remember, however, that there is no theoretical reason why we must use transistors as our "elementary particles" when designing computer systems. Just as cores were replaced by transistors, transistors may ultimately be replaced by some newer technology (perhaps optical or biological) that is faster, smaller, and cheaper.

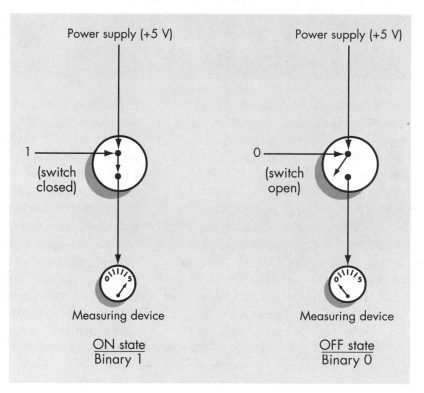

The only requirements for our building blocks are those given in the beginning of this section—that they be able to represent reliably the two binary values 0 and 1. That's the beauty of the binary numbering system.

4.3   BOOLEAN LOGIC AND GATES

4.3.1 BOOLEAN LOGIC

The construction of computer circuits is based on the branch of mathematics and symbolic logic called **Boolean logic**. This is the area of mathematics that deals with rules for manipulating the two logical values **true** and **false**.

It is easy to see the relationship between Boolean logic and computer design when we realize that the truth value *true* could represent the binary value 1 and the truth value *false* could represent the binary value 0. Thus anything stored internally as a sequence of binary digits (which, as we saw in an earlier section, is everything stored inside a computer) can also be viewed as a sequence of the logical values true and false, and these values can be manipulated by the operations of Boolean logic.

George Boole (1815–1864)

George Boole was an English mathematician and logician of the mid-nineteenth century. He was the son of a poor shoemaker and had virtually no formal education, having dropped out of school in the third grade. He taught himself mathematics and logic and mastered French, German, Italian, Latin, and Greek. He avidly studied the works of the great Greek and Roman philosophers such as Aristotle, Plato, and Euclid. He built upon their work in logic, argumentation, and reasoning and, in 1854, produced a book entitled *Introduction to the Laws of Thought*. This seminal work attempted to apply the formal laws of algebra and arithmetic to the principles of logic. That is, it treated reasoning as simply another branch of mathematics containing operators, variables, and transformation rules. He created a new form of logic containing the values *true* and *false* and the operators AND, OR, and NOT.

He also developed a set of rules describing how to interpret and manipulate expressions that contain these values.

At the time of its development, the importance of this work was not apparent, and it languished in relative obscurity. However, 100 years later, Boole's ideas became the theoretical framework underlying the design of all computer systems. In his honor, these true/false expressions became known as **Boolean expressions**, and this branch of mathematics is called **Boolean logic** or **Boolean algebra**.

Even though he had no formal schooling, Boole was eventually appointed Professor of Mathematics at Queens College in Cork, Ireland, and he received a gold medal from the Royal Mathematical Society. He is now universally recognized as one of the greatest mathematicians of the nineteenth century.

Let us define a **Boolean expression** as any expression that evaluates to either true or false. For example, the expression $(x = 1)$ is a Boolean expression because it is true if x is 1, and it is false if x has any other value. Similarly, both $(a \neq b)$ and $(c > 5.23)$ are Boolean expressions.

In "regular" mathematics (the mathematics of real numbers), the operations used to construct arithmetic expressions are $+$, $-$, $\times$, $\div$, and a^b, which map real numbers into real numbers. In Boolean logic, the operations used to construct Boolean expressions are AND, OR, and NOT, and they map a set of (true, false) values into a single (true, false) result.

The rule for performing the AND operation is as follows: If a and b are Boolean expressions, then the value of the expression (a AND b), also written as ($a \cdot b$), is *true* if and only if both a and b have the value *true*; otherwise, the expression (a AND b) has the value *false*. Informally, this rule says that the AND operation produces the value *true* if and only if both of its components are true. This idea can be expressed using a structure called a **truth table**, shown in Figure 4.7.

The two columns labeled Inputs in the truth table of Figure 4.7 list the four possible combinations of true/false values of a and b. The column labeled Output specifies the value of the expression (a AND b) for the corresponding values of a and b.

As an example of the use of the AND operation, imagine that we want to check whether a test score S is in the range 90 to 100 inclusive. We wish to develop a Boolean expression that is true if the score is in the desired range and is false otherwise. We cannot do this with a single comparison. If we test only that $(S \geq 90)$, then a score of 105, which is greater than or equal to 90, will produce the

FIGURE 4.7

Truth Table for the AND Operation

Inputs		Output
		a AND b
a	b	(also written a · b)
False	False	False
False	True	False
True	False	False
True	True	True

result *true*, even though it is out of range. Similarly, if we test only that ($S \le 100$), then a score of 85, which is less than or equal to 100, will also produce a *true*, even though it too is not in the range 90 to 100.

Instead, we need to determine whether the score S is greater than or equal to 90 *and* whether it is less than or equal to 100. Only if both conditions are true can we say that S is in the desired range. We can express this idea using the following Boolean expression:

$$(S \ge 90) \text{ AND } (S \le 100)$$

Each of the two expressions in parentheses can be either true or false depending on the value of S. However, only if both conditions are true will the expression evaluate to *true*. For example, a score of $S = 70$ would cause the first expression to be false (70 is not greater than or equal to 90), whereas the second expression would be true (70 is less than or equal to 100). The truth table in Figure 4.7 shows that the result of evaluating (*false* AND *true*) is *false*. Thus the expression will be false, telling us (as expected) that 70 is not in the range 90 to 100. You might wish to check the value of the above expression for $S = 135$ and $S = 95$ to confirm that it does indeed produce the correct results in all cases.

The second Boolean operation is OR. The rule for evaluating the OR operation is as follows: If a and b are Boolean expressions, then the value of the Boolean expression (a OR b), also written as ($a + b$), is *true* if a is *true*, if b is *true*, or if both are *true*. Otherwise, (a OR b) has the value *false*. The truth table for OR is shown in Figure 4.8.

FIGURE 4.8

Truth Table for the OR Operation

Inputs		Output
		a OR b
a	b	(also written a + b)
False	False	False
False	True	True
True	False	True
True	True	True

As an example of the use of the OR operation, imagine that we have a variable called *major* that specifies a student's college major. If we want to know whether a student is majoring in either math or computer science, we cannot accomplish this with a single comparison. The test (*major* = math) omits computer science majors, whereas the test (*major* = computer science) leaves out the mathematicians. Instead, we need to determine whether the student is majoring in *either* math or computer science (or perhaps in both). This can be expressed as follows:

(*major* = math) OR (*major* = computer science)

Now, if the student is majoring in either one or both of the two disciplines, then one or both of the two terms in the expression will be true. Referring to the truth table in Figure 4.8, we see that (*true* OR *false*), (*false* OR *true*), and (*true* OR *true*) all produce the value *true*, which lets us know that the student is indeed majoring in at least one of these two fields. However, if the student were majoring in English, both conditions would be false. Looking at Figure 4.8, we see that the value of the expression (*false* OR *false*) is *false*, which tells us that the student is not majoring in either math or computer science.

The last Boolean operator that we will introduce is NOT. Unlike AND and OR, which require two operands and are therefore called **binary operators**, NOT requires only one operand and is called a **unary operator**, like the square root operation in arithmetic. The rule for evaluating the NOT operation is as follows: If *a* is a Boolean expression, then the value of the expression (NOT *a*), also written as $\overline{a}$, is *true* if *a* has the value *false*, and it is *false* if *a* has the value *true*. The truth table for NOT is shown in Figure 4.9.

Informally, we say that the NOT operation reverses, or **complements**, the value of a Boolean expression, making it true if currently false, and vice versa. For example, the expression (gpa > 3.5) is true if your grade point average is greater then 3.5, and the expression NOT (gpa > 3.5) is true only under the reverse conditions. That is, it is true only when your grade point average is less than or equal to 3.5.

AND, OR, and NOT are the three operations of Boolean logic that we use in this chapter. Why have we introduced these Boolean operations in the first place? The previous section talked about hardware concepts such as energy states, electrical currents, transistors, and integrated circuits. Now it appears that we have changed directions and are discussing highly abstract ideas drawn from the disci-

FIGURE 4.9
Truth Table for the NOT Operation

Input	Output
	NOT a
a	(also written $\overline{a}$)
False	True
True	False

PRACTICE PROBLEMS

1. Assuming that $x = 1$ and $y = 2$, find the value of each of the following Boolean expressions:
   a. $(x = 1)$ AND $(y = 3)$
   b. $(x < y)$ OR $(x > 1)$
   c. NOT $[(x = 1)$ AND $(y = 2)]$

2. What is the value of the following Boolean expression if $x = 5$, $y = 10$, and $z = 15$?

   $(x = 5)$ AND $(y = 11)$ OR $([x + y] = z)$

   Did you have to make some assumptions when you evaluated this expression?

---

pline of symbolic logic. However, as we shall see in the next section, there is a very close relationship between the hardware concepts of Section 4.2.3 and the operations of Boolean logic. In fact, the fundamental building blocks of a modern computer system (the objects with which engineers actually design) are not the transistors introduced in Section 4.2.3 but the gates that implement the Boolean operations AND, OR, and NOT. Surprisingly, it is the rules of logic—a discipline developed by the Greeks 2,300 years ago and expanded by Boole 150 years ago—that provide the theoretical foundation for constructing modern computer hardware.

4.3.2 GATES

A **gate** is an electronic device that operates on a collection of binary inputs to produce a binary output. That is, it transforms a set of (0,1) input values into a single (0,1) output value according to a specific transformation rule. Although gates can implement a wide range of different transformation rules, the only ones we will be concerned with here are those that implement the three Boolean operations AND, OR, and NOT introduced in the previous section. These gates can be represented symbolically as shown, along with the truth tables that define their transformation rules, in Figure 4.10.

Comparing Figures 4.7 through 4.9 with Figure 4.10 shows that if we consider the value 1 equivalent to *true* and the value 0 equivalent to *false*, then these three electronic gates directly implement the corresponding Boolean operation. For example, an AND gate will have its output line set to 1 (set to some level of current or voltage that represents a binary 1) if and only if both of its inputs are 1. Otherwise, the output line will be set to 0 (set to some level of current or voltage that represents a binary 0). This is functionally identical to the rule that says the result of (*a* AND *b*) is *true* if and only if both *a* and *b* are *true*; otherwise, (*a* AND *b*) is *false*.

To construct an AND gate, we must use two transistors connected **in series**, as shown in Figure 4.11. The only way that the value 1 can appear on the output line is if both control lines, called Input-1 and Input-2 in Figure 4.11, are set to 1. This will put both of the transistors into the ON state, allowing voltage from the

FIGURE 4.10

The Three Basic Gates

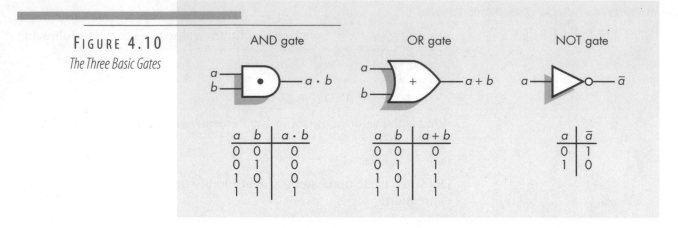

a	b	a · b
0	0	0
0	1	0
1	0	0
1	1	1

a	b	a + b
0	0	0
0	1	1
1	0	1
1	1	1

a	$\bar{a}$
0	1
1	0

power supply to pass unimpeded to the output line. If either Input-1 or Input-2 is a 0, then the corresponding transistor will be in the OFF state, and it will not allow voltage to pass. Thus the output of the gate shown in Figure 4.11 will be a 1 if and only if both inputs are a 1. This is the exact definition of the AND gate given in Figure 4.10.

To construct an OR gate, we again must use two transistors. However, this time they are connected **in parallel** rather than in series, as shown in Figure 4.12.

FIGURE 4.11

Construction of an AND Gate from Two Transistors

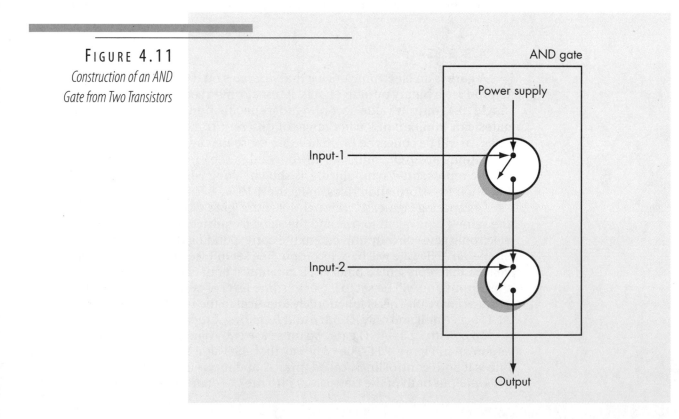

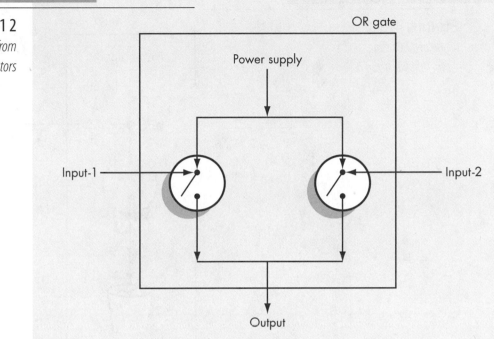

FIGURE 4.12

Construction of an OR Gate from Two Transistors

In Figure 4.12 we can see that if either, or both, of the control lines Input-1 and Input-2 are set to 1, then the corresponding transistor will be in the ON state, and voltage can pass from the power supply to the output line, producing an output of 1. Only if both control lines are 0, effectively shutting off both transistors, will the output be a 0. This is identical to the definition of the OR gate given in Figure 4.10.

A NOT gate requires only a single transistor. A diagram is shown in Figure 4.13. If the input line is a 1, then the transistor will pass the current through, and it will be discarded, producing an output of 0. (Note that a resistor must be placed on the output line so current will travel through the transistor instead of the output line. Electricity, like all fluids, follows the path of least resistance.) If the input line is a 0, the transistor blocks passage of current to the discard area, and it is transmitted to the output line, producing an output value of 1.

Gates of the type shown in Figures 4.10 to 4.13 are not "abstract entities" that exist only in textbooks and classroom discussions. They are actual electronic devices that are the building blocks used in the design and construction of modern computer systems. The reason for using gates rather than transistors is that a transistor is too elementary a device to act as the fundamental design component. It requires a designer to deal with such low-level issues as currents, voltages, and the laws of physics. Instead, transistors, grouped together to form more powerful building blocks called gates, allow us to think and design at a higher level. Instead of dealing with the complex physical rules associated with discrete electrical devices, we can use the power and expressiveness of mathematics and logic to build computers.

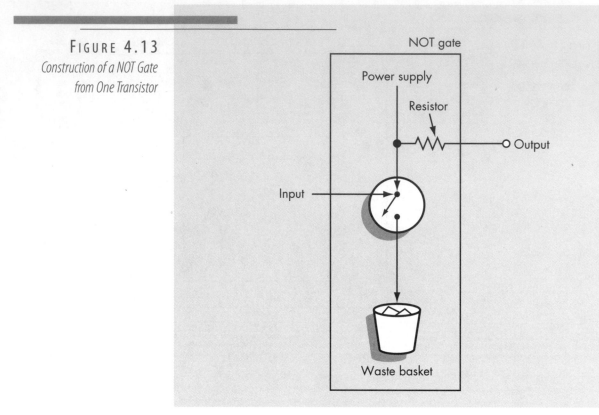

This seemingly minor change in viewpoint (from transistors to gates) has a profound effect on how computer hardware is designed and built. From this point on in our discussion of hardware design, we no longer need deal with anything "electrical." We no longer require a knowledge of transistors, resistors, or capacitors. No longer must we deal with voltages, currents, and resistance, nor need we be physicists or electrical engineers. Instead, our building blocks will be the three gates AND, OR, and NOT, and our circuit construction rules will be the rules of Boolean logic. Here is another example of the use of abstraction in computer science.

4.4   BUILDING COMPUTER CIRCUITS

4.4.1 INTRODUCTION

A **circuit** is a collection of logic gates 1) that transforms a set of binary inputs into a set of binary outputs, and 2) where the values of the outputs depend only on the current values of the inputs. (Actually, this type of circuit is more properly

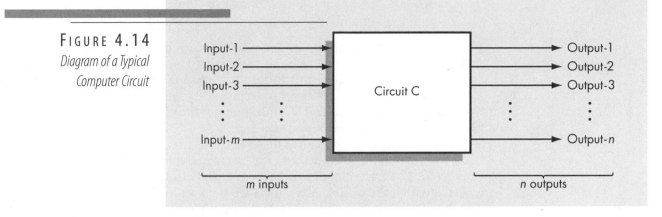

FIGURE 4.14

Diagram of a Typical Computer Circuit

called a **combinational circuit**. We will use the simpler term *circuit* in this discussion.) A circuit C with m binary inputs and n binary outputs is represented as shown in Figure 4.14.

Internally, the circuit shown in Figure 4.14 is constructed from the AND, OR, and NOT gates introduced in the previous section. These gates can be interconnected in any way so long as the connections do not violate the constraints on the proper number of inputs and outputs for each gate. Each AND and OR gate must have exactly two inputs and one output. Each NOT gate must have exactly one input and one output. For example, the following is the diagram of a circuit with two inputs labeled a and b and two outputs labeled c and d. It contains one AND gate, one OR gate, and two NOT gates.

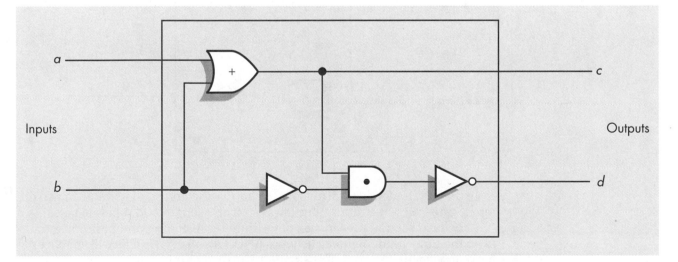

There is a direct relationship between Boolean expressions and **circuit diagrams** of this type. Every Boolean expression can be represented pictorially as a circuit diagram, and every output value in a circuit diagram can be written as a Boolean expression. For example, in the above diagram, the two output values labeled c and d are equivalent to the following two Boolean expressions:

$$c = (a \text{ OR } b)$$

$$d = \text{NOT} ((a \text{ OR } b) \text{ AND } (\text{NOT } b))$$

The choice of which representation to use depends on what we want to do. The pictorial view is better at allowing us to visualize the overall structure of the circuit, and it is often used during the design stage. A Boolean expression may be a more convenient representation for performing mathematical or logical operations, such as verification and optimization, on the circuit. We will use both representations in the following sections.

The value appearing on any output line of a circuit can be determined if we know the current input values and the transformations produced by each logic gate. (*Note:* There are circuits, called **sequential circuits**, that contain **feedback loops** in which the output of a gate is fed back as input to an earlier gate. The output of these circuits depends not only on the current input values but also on *previous* inputs. These circuits are typically used to build memory units because, in a sense, they can "remember" inputs. We will not discuss sequential circuits here.)

In the previous example, if $a = 1$ and $b = 0$, then the value on the c output line is 1, and the value on the d output line is 0. These values can be determined as follows:

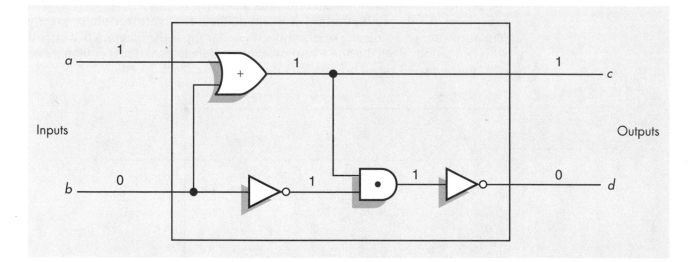

Note that it is perfectly legal to "split" or "tap" a line and send its value to two different gates. Here the input value b was split and sent to two separate gates.

The next section presents an algorithm for designing and building circuits from the three fundamental gate types AND, OR, and NOT. This will enable us to move to yet a higher level of abstraction. Instead of thinking in terms of transistors and electrical voltages (as in Section 4.2.3) or in terms of logic gates and truth values (Section 4.3.2), we can think and design in terms of circuits for high-level operations such as addition and comparison. This will make the task of understanding computer hardware much more manageable.

4.4.2 A Circuit Construction Algorithm

The circuit shown at the end of the previous section was simply an example, and it was not meant to carry out any meaningful operation. However, the circuits we want to build and study will perform useful arithmetic and logical functions. To create these important circuits, we need a way to take a description of a circuit's desired behavior and convert that description into a circuit diagram, composed of AND, OR, and NOT gates, that does exactly what we want it to do.

There are a number of **circuit construction algorithms** to accomplish this task, and the remainder of this section describes one such technique, called the **sum-of-products algorithm**, that will allow us to design circuits. The next section demonstrates how this algorithm works by constructing actual circuits that all computer systems need.

The four-step sum-of-products circuit construction algorithm operates as follows:

STEP 1: TRUTH TABLE CONSTRUCTION. First determine how the circuit should behave under all possible circumstances. That is, determine the binary value that should appear on each output line of the circuit for every possible combination of inputs. This information can be organized as a **truth table**. If a circuit has N input lines, and if each input line can be either a 0 or a 1, then there are 2^N combinations of input values, and the truth table will have 2^N rows. For each output of the circuit, we must specify the desired output value for every row in the truth table.

For example, if a circuit has three inputs and two outputs, then a truth table for that circuit will have $2^3 = 8$ input combinations and may look something like the following. (In this example, the output values are completely arbitrary.)

Inputs			Outputs	
a	b	c	Output-1	Output-2
0	0	0	0	1
0	0	1	0	0
0	1	0	1	1
0	1	1	0	1
1	0	0	0	0
1	0	1	0	0
1	1	0	1	1
1	1	1	0	0

$2^3 = 8$ input combinations

This circuit has two outputs labeled Output-1 and Output-2. The truth table specifies the value of each of these two output lines for every one of the eight possible combinations of inputs. We will use the preceding example to illustrate the subsequent steps in the algorithm.

STEP 2: SUBEXPRESSION CONSTRUCTION USING AND AND NOT GATES.   Choose any one output column of the truth table built in step 1 and scan down that column. Every place that you find a 1 in that output column, you will build a *subexpression* that produces the value 1 (i.e., is true) for exactly that combination of input values and no other. The way you build this subexpression is to examine the value of each input for this specific case. If the input is a 1, use that input value directly in your subexpression. If the input is a 0, first take the NOT of that input, changing it from a 0 to a 1, and then use that **complemented** input value in your subexpression. You now have an input sequence containing all 1s, and if all of these modified inputs are ANDed together (two at a time, of course), then the output value will be a 1. For example, let's look at the output column labeled Output-1 from the previous truth table.

Inputs				
a	*b*	*c*	Output-1	
0	0	0	0	
0	0	1	0	
0	1	0	1	← case 1
0	1	1	0	
1	0	0	0	
1	0	1	0	
1	1	0	1	← case 2
1	1	1	0	

There are two 1s in the column labeled Output-1; they are referred to as case 1 and case 2. We thus need to construct two subexpressions, one for each of these two cases.

In case 1, the inputs a and c have the value 0 and the input b has the value 1. Thus we apply the NOT operator to both a and c, changing them from 0 to 1. Because the value of b is 1, we can use b directly. We now have three modified input values, all of which have the value 1. ANDing these three values together yields the Boolean expression $(\overline{a} \cdot b \cdot \overline{c})$. This expression produces a 1 only when the input is exactly $a = 0$, $b = 1$, $c = 0$. In any other case, at least one of the three terms in the expression will be a 0, and when the AND operation is carried out, it produces a 0. (Check this yourself by trying some other input values and seeing what is produced.) Thus the desired subexpression for case 1 is

$$(\overline{a} \cdot b \cdot \overline{c})$$

The subexpression for case 2 is developed in an identical manner, and it results in

$$(a \cdot b \cdot \overline{c})$$

This subexpression produces a 1 only when the input is exactly $a = 1$, $b = 1$, $c = 0$.

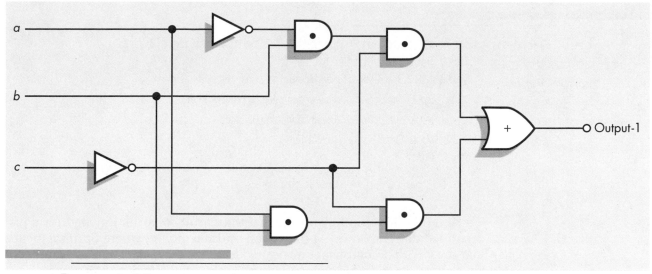

FIGURE 4.15

*Circuit Diagram for the
Output Labeled Output-1*

STEP 3: SUBEXPRESSION COMBINATION USING OR GATES.   Take each of the subexpressions produced in step 2 and combine them, two at a time, using OR gates. Each of the individual subexpressions produces a 1 for exactly one particular case where the truth table output is a 1, so the OR of the output of all of them will produce a 1 in *all* cases where the truth table has a 1 and in no other case. Consequently, the Boolean expression produced in step 3 implements exactly the function described in the output column of the truth table on which we are working. In the example above, the final Boolean expression produced during step 3 is

$$(\overline{a} \cdot b \cdot \overline{c}) + (a \cdot b \cdot \overline{c})$$

STEP 4: CIRCUIT DIAGRAM PRODUCTION.   Construct the final circuit diagram. To do this, convert the Boolean expression produced at the end of step 3 into a circuit diagram, using AND, OR, and NOT gates to implement the AND, OR, and NOT operators appearing in the Boolean expression. This circuit diagram will produce the output described in the corresponding column of the truth table created in step 1. The circuit diagram for the Boolean expression developed in step 3 is shown in figure 4.15.

We have successfully built the part of the circuit that produces the output for the column labeled Output-1 in the truth table shown in step 1. We now repeat steps 2, 3, and 4 for any additional output columns contained in the truth table. (In this example there is a second column labeled Output-2. We leave the construction of that circuit as a practice exercise.) When we have constructed a circuit diagram for every output of the circuit, we are finished. The sum-of-products algorithm is shown in Figure 4.16.

This has been a formal introduction to one particular circuit construction algorithm. The algorithm is not easy to comprehend in an abstract sense. The next section clarifies this technique by using it to design two circuits that perform the operations of comparison and addition. Seeing it used to design actual circuits will make the steps of the algorithm easier to understand and follow.

FIGURE 4.16

*The Sum-of-Products Circuit
Construction Algorithm*

Sum-of-Products Algorithm for Constructing Circuits

Step 1: Truth table construction

Repeat steps 2, 3, and 4 once for each output column in the truth table

    Step 2: Subexpression construction using AND and NOT gates

    Step 3: Subexpression combination using OR gates

    Step 4: Circuit diagram production

Step 5: Done

We end this section by noting that the circuit construction algorithm just described does not always produce an **optimal** circuit, where *optimal* means that the circuit accomplishes its desired function using the smallest number of logic gates. For example, using the truth table shown on page 148, our sum-of-products algorithm produced the seven-gate circuit shown in Figure 4.15. This is a correct answer in the sense that the circuit does produce the correct values for Output-1 for all combinations of inputs. However, it is possible to do much better. The circuit

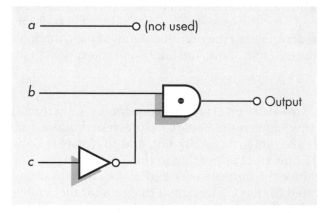

also produces the correct result using only two gates instead of seven. This difference is very important because each AND, OR, and NOT gate is a physical entity that costs real money, takes up space on the chip, requires power to operate, and generates heat that must be dissipated. Eliminating five unnecessary gates produces a real savings. The fewer gates we use, the cheaper, more efficient, and more compact will be our circuits—and hence the resulting computer. Algorithms for **circuit optimization**—that is, for reducing the number of gates needed to implement a circuit—are an important part of hardware design. A Challenge Work problem at the end of the chapter invites you to investigate this topic in more detail.

Laboratory Experience 7	To give you hands-on experience working with logic circuits, the first laboratory experience in this chapter introduces a software package called a **circuit simulator**. This is a program that enables you to construct logic circuits from the AND, OR, and NOT gates just described. After you have constructed a circuit, this program allows you to test your circuit design by observing the outputs of the circuit with any desired inputs.

PRACTICE PROBLEMS

1. Design the circuit to implement the output described in the column labeled Output-2 in the truth table on page 147.

2. Design a circuit using AND, OR, and NOT gates to implement the following truth table.

a	b	Output
0	0	0
0	1	1
1	0	1
1	1	0

   This is called the **exclusive-OR** operation. It is true if and only if a is 1 or b is 1, but not both.

3. Build a circuit using AND, OR, and NOT gates to implement the following truth table.

a	b	c	Output
0	0	0	1
0	0	1	0
0	1	0	0
0	1	1	0
1	0	0	0
1	0	1	0
1	1	0	0
1	1	1	1

   This is called a **full-ON/full-OFF** circuit. It is true if and only if all three of its inputs are OFF (0) or all three are ON (1).

4.4.3 EXAMPLES OF CIRCUIT DESIGN AND CONSTRUCTION

Let's use the algorithm described in Section 4.4.2 to construct two circuits important to the operation of any real-world computer, a compare-for-equality circuit and an addition circuit.

A COMPARE-FOR-EQUALITY CIRCUIT.   The first circuit we will construct is a **compare-for-equality circuit**, or CE circuit, which tests two unsigned binary numbers for exact equality. The circuit produces the value 1 (*true*) if the two numbers are equal and the value 0 (*false*) if they are not. Such a circuit could be used in many situations. For example, in the shampooing algorithm in Figure 1.3(a), there is an instruction that says

Repeat steps 4 through 6 until the value of *WashCount* is equal to 2

Our CE circuit could accomplish the comparison between *WashCount* and 2 and return a true or false, depending on whether these two values were equal.

Let's start by using the algorithm in Figure 4.16 to construct a simpler circuit called 1-CE, short for *1*-bit *c*ompare for *e*quality. A 1-CE circuit compares two 1-bit values a and b for equality. That is, the circuit 1-CE produces a 1 as output if both its inputs are 0 or both its inputs are 1. Otherwise, 1-CE produces a 0. After designing 1-CE, we will use it to create a "full-blown" comparison circuit that can handle numbers of any size.

Step 1 of the algorithm says to construct the truth table that describes the behavior of the desired circuit. The truth table for the 1-CE circuit is

a	b	Output	
0	0	1	← case 1
0	1	0	
1	0	0	
1	1	1	← case 2

Scanning down the output column of the truth table, we see that there are two 1 values, labeled case 1 and case 2, so step 2 of the algorithm is to construct two subexpressions, one for each of these two cases. The subexpression for case 1 is $(\overline{a} \cdot \overline{b})$ because this produces the value 1 only when $a = 0$ and $b = 0$. The subexpression for case 2 is $(a \cdot b)$, which produces a 1 only when $a = 1$ and $b = 1$.

We now combine the outputs of these two subexpressions with an OR gate, as described in step 3, to produce the Boolean expression

$$(a \cdot b) + (\overline{a} \cdot \overline{b})$$

Finally, in step 4, we convert this expression to a circuit diagram, which is shown in Figure 4.17.

The circuit shown in Figure 4.17 correctly compares two 1-bit quantities and determines whether they are equal. If they are equal, it outputs a 1. If they are unequal, it outputs a 0.

FIGURE 4.17
One-Bit Compare-for-Equality Circuit

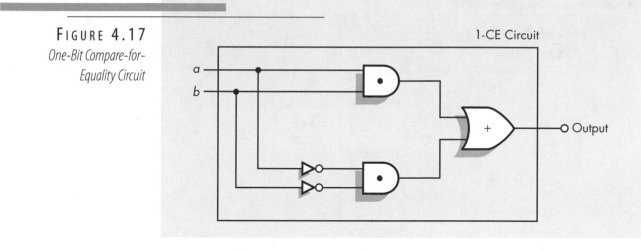

However, the numbers compared for equality by a computer are usually much larger than a single binary digit. We want a circuit that correctly compares two numbers that contain N binary digits. To build this "N-bit compare-for-equality" circuit, we will use N of the 1-CE circuits shown in Figure 4.17, one for each bit position in the numbers to be compared. Each 1-CE circuit produces a 1 if the two binary digits in its specific location are identical and produces a 0 if they are not. If every circuit produces a 1, then the two numbers are identical in every bit position, and they are equal. To check whether all our 1-CE circuits produce a 1, we simply AND together (two at a time) the outputs of all N 1-CE circuits. Remember that an AND gate produces a 1 if and only if both of its inputs are a 1. Thus the final output of the N-bit compare circuit is a 1 if and only if every pair of bits in the corresponding location of the two numbers is identical—that is, the two numbers are equal.

Figure 4.18 shows the design of a complete **N-bit compare-for-equality circuit** called CE. Each of the two numbers being compared, a and b, contains N bits, and they are labeled $a_{N-1} a_{N-2} \ldots a_0$ and $b_{N-1} b_{N-2} \ldots b_0$. The box labeled 1-CE in Figure 4.18 is the 1-bit compare-for-equality circuit shown in Figure 4.17.

Looking at Figures 4.17 and 4.18, you can see that we have designed a very complex electrical circuit without the specification of a single electrical device. The only "devices" in that diagram are gates to implement the logical operations AND, OR, and NOT, and the only "rules" we need to know in order to understand that diagram are the transformation rules of Boolean logic. George Boole's "not very important" work is the starting point for the design of every circuit found inside a modern computer.

An Addition Circuit. Our second example of circuit construction is an addition circuit called ADD that performs binary addition on two unsigned N-bit integers. Typically, this type of circuit is called a **full adder**. For example, assuming $N = 6$, our ADD circuit would be able to perform the following 6-bit addition operation:

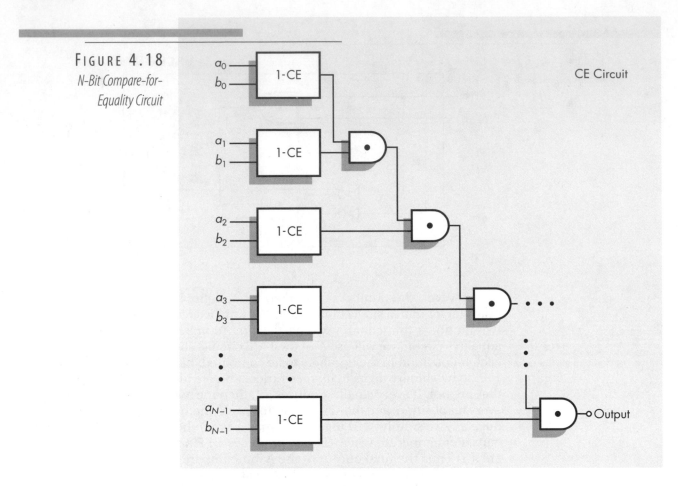

FIGURE 4.18
N-Bit Compare-for-Equality Circuit

CE Circuit

	1 1	(← the carry bit)
+	0 0 1 1 0 1	(the binary value 13)
	<u>0 0 1 1 1 0</u>	(the binary value 14)
	0 1 1 0 1 1	(the binary value 27, which is the correct sum)

Just as we did with the CE circuit of Section 4.4.3.1, we will carry out the design of the ADD circuit in two stages. First, we will use the circuit construction algorithm of Figure 4.16 to build a circuit called 1-ADD that adds a single pair of binary digits, with a carry digit. We can then interconnect N of these 1-ADD circuits to produce a complete N-bit full adder circuit called ADD.

Looking at the addition example shown above, we see that summing the values in column i will require us to add three binary values—the two binary digits in that column, a_i and b_i, and the carry digit from the previous column, called c_i. Furthermore, the circuit must produce two binary outputs: a sum digit s_i and a new carry digit c_{i+1} that propagates to the next column. The pictorial representation of the 1-bit adder circuit 1-ADD and its accompanying truth table are shown in Figure 4.19.

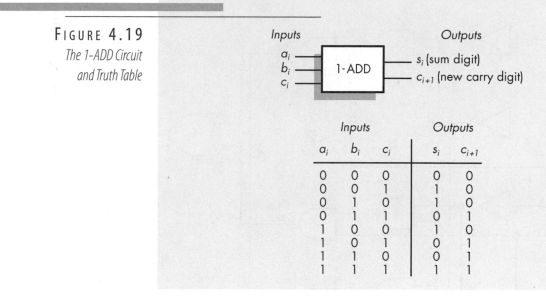

FIGURE 4.19

The 1-ADD Circuit and Truth Table

Inputs			Outputs	
a_i	b_i	c_i	s_i	c_{i+1}
0	0	0	0	0
0	0	1	1	0
0	1	0	1	0
0	1	1	0	1
1	0	0	1	0
1	0	1	0	1
1	1	0	0	1
1	1	1	1	1

Because the 1-ADD circuit being constructed has two outputs, s_i and c_{i+1}, we must repeat steps 2, 3, and 4 of the circuit construction algorithm twice, once for each output. Let's work on the sum output s_i first.

The s_i output column of Figure 4.19 contains four 1s, so we need to construct four subexpressions. In accordance with the guidelines given in step 2 of the construction algorithm, these four subexpressions are

Case 1 $\overline{a}_i \cdot \overline{b}_i \cdot c_i$
Case 2 $\overline{a}_i \cdot b_i \cdot \overline{c}_i$
Case 3 $a_i \cdot \overline{b}_i \cdot \overline{c}_i$
Case 4 $a_i \cdot b_i \cdot c_i$

Step 3 says to combine the outputs of these four subexpressions using three OR gates to produce the output labeled s_i in the truth table of Figure 4.19. The final Boolean expression for the sum output is

$$s_i = (\overline{a}_i \cdot \overline{b}_i \cdot c) + (\overline{a}_i \cdot b_i \cdot \overline{c}_i) + (a_i \cdot \overline{b}_i \cdot \overline{c}_i) + (a_i \cdot b_i \cdot c_i)$$

The logic circuit to produce the output whose expression is given above is shown in Figure 4.20. (This circuit diagram has been labeled to highlight the four separate subexpressions created during step 2 as well as the combining of the subexpressions in step 3 of the construction algorithm.)

We are not yet finished, because the 1-ADD circuit in Figure 4.19 has a second output—the carry into the next column. That means the circuit construction algorithm must be repeated for the second output column, labeled c_{i+1}.

The c_{i+1} column also contains four 1s, so we again need to build four separate subcircuits, just as for the sum output, and combine them using OR gates. The construction proceeds in a fashion similar to the first part, so we leave the

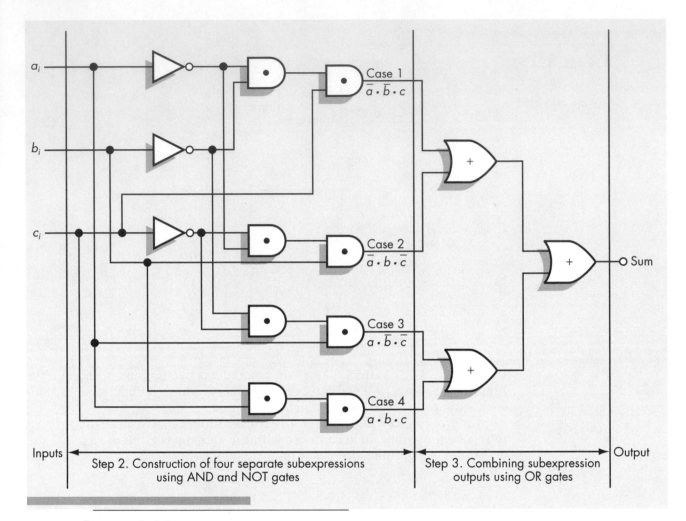

Inputs ← Step 2. Construction of four separate subexpressions using AND and NOT gates → Step 3. Combining subexpression outputs using OR gates → Output

FIGURE 4.20

Sum Output for the 1-ADD Circuit

details as an exercise for the reader. The Boolean expression describing the carry output c_{i+1} of the 1-ADD circuit is

$$c_{i+1} = (\overline{a}_i \cdot b_i \cdot c_i) + (a_i \cdot \overline{b}_i \cdot c_i) + (a_i \cdot b_i \cdot \overline{c}_i) + (a_i \cdot b_i \cdot c_i)$$

We have now built the two parts of the 1-ADD circuit that produce the sum and the carry outputs. The complete 1-ADD circuit is constructed by simply putting these two pieces together. Figure 4.21 shows the complete (and admittedly quite complex) 1-ADD circuit to implement 1-bit addition. To keep the diagram from becoming an incomprehensible tangle of lines, we have drawn it in a slightly different orientation from Figures 4.17 and 4.20. Everything else is exactly the same.

When looking at this rather imposing diagram, one should not become overly concerned with the details of every gate, every connection, every operation. The important concern reflected in Figure 4.21 is the *process* by which we were able to design such a complex and intricate circuit. We were able to transform the idea of

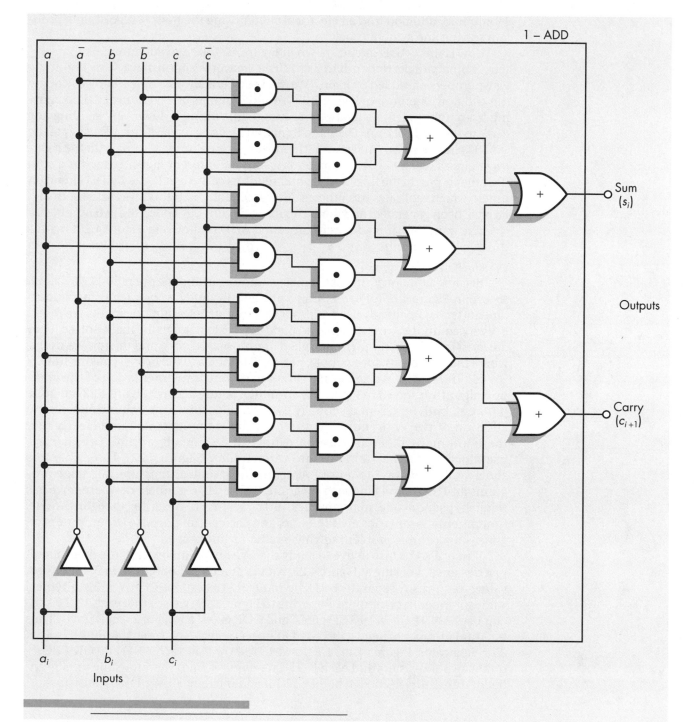

FIGURE 4.21

Complete 1-ADD Circuit
for 1-Bit Binary Addition

1-bit binary addition into an electrical circuit using the tools of algorithmic problem solving and symbolic logic.

How is the 1-ADD circuit shown in Figure 4.21 used to add numbers that contain N binary digits rather than just 1? The answer is simple if we think about the way numbers are added by hand. (We discussed exactly this topic when developing the addition algorithm of Figure 1.2.) We add numbers one column at a time, moving from right to left, generating the sum digit, writing it down, and sending any carry to the next column. The same thing can be done in hardware. We use N of the 1-ADD circuits shown in Figure 4.21, one for each column. Starting with the rightmost circuit, each 1-ADD circuit adds a single column of digits, generates a sum digit that is part of the final answer, and sends its carry digit to the 1-ADD circuit on its left, which replicates this process. After N repetitions of this process, all sum digits have been generated, and the N circuits have correctly added the two numbers.

The complete full adder circuit called ADD is shown in Figure 4.22. It adds the two N-bit numbers $a_{N-1} a_{N-2} \ldots a_0$ and $b_{N-1} b_{N-2} \ldots b_0$ to produce the sum $s_N s_{N-1} s_{N-2} \ldots s_0$.

Because addition is one of the most common arithmetic operations, the circuit shown in Figure 4.22 (or something equivalent) would be one of the most important and most frequently used arithmetic components. Addition circuits are found in every computer, workstation, and hand-held calculator in the marketplace. They are even found in computer-controlled thermostats, clocks, and microwave ovens, where they enable us, for example, to add 30 minutes to the overall cooking time.

Figure 4.22 is, in a sense, the direct hardware implementation of the addition algorithm shown in Figure 1.2. Although Figure 1.2 and Figure 4.22 are quite different, both represent essentially the same algorithm: the column-by-column addition of two N-bit numerical values. This demonstrates quite clearly that there are many different ways to express the same algorithm—in this case, pseudocode (Figure 1.2) and hardware circuits (Figure 4.22). Later chapters show additional ways to represent algorithms, such as machine language programs and high-level language programs. However, regardless of whether we use English, pseudocode, mathematics, or transistors to describe an algorithm, its fundamental properties are the same, and the central purpose of computer science—algorithmic problem solving—remains unchanged.

It may also be instructive to study the size and complexity of the ADD circuit just designed. Looking at Figure 4.22, we see that the addition of two N-bit integer values requires N separate 1-ADD circuits. Let's assume that $N = 32$, a typical value for modern computers. Referring to Figure 4.21, we see that each 1-ADD circuit uses 3 NOT gates, 16 AND gates, and 6 OR gates, a total of 25 logic gates. Thus the total number of logic gates used to implement 32-bit binary addition is $32 \times 25 = 800$ gates. Figures 4.11, 4.12, and 4.13 show that each AND and OR gate requires two transistors and each NOT gate requires one. Therefore, the total number of transistors needed to build a 32-bit adder circuit is over 1,500 transistors.

NOT:	$32 \times 3 = 96$ NOT gates $\times$ 1 transistor/gate	$=$	96
AND:	$32 \times 16 = 512$ AND gates $\times$ 2 transistors/gate	$=$	1,024
OR:	$32 \times 6 = 192$ OR gates $\times$ 2 transistors/gate	$=$	<u>384</u>
		Total	$= 1,504$ transistors

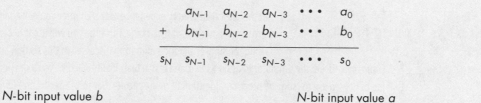

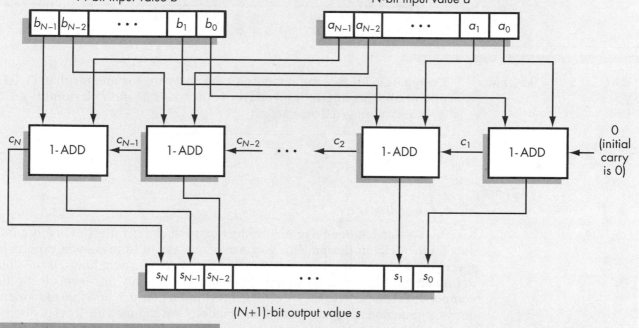

FIGURE 4.22

The Complete Full Adder ADD Circuit

(*Note:* Optimized 32-bit addition circuits can be constructed using as few as 500–600 transistors. However, this does not change the fact that it takes many, many transistors to accomplish this addition task.)

This computation emphasizes the importance of the continuing research into the miniaturization of electrical components. For example, if vacuum tubes were used instead of transistors, as was done in computers from about 1940 to 1950, the adder circuit shown in Figure 4.22 would be extraordinarily bulky; 1,504 vacuum tubes would occupy a space about the size of a large refrigerator. It would also generate huge amounts of heat, necessitating sophisticated cooling systems, and it would be very difficult to maintain. (Imagine the time it would take to locate one burned-out vacuum tube out of 1,504.) Using something on the scale of the magnetic core technology described in Section 4.2.3 and shown in Figure 4.4, the adder circuit would fit into an area a few inches square. However, modern VLSI circuit technology can achieve densities of 10,000,000 transistors/cm². At this level, the entire ADD circuit of Figure 4.22 would fit in an area smaller than the size of the period at the end of this sentence. That is why it is now possible to put powerful computer processing facilities not only in a room or on a desk but also inside a watch, inside a thermostat, or even inside the human body.

<table>
<tr><td>Laboratory Experience 8</td><td>In the second laboratory experience of this chapter, you will again be using the circuit simulator software package. This time you will use it to construct circuits using the sum-of-products algorithm discussed in this section and shown in Figure 4.16. Using the simulator to design, build, and test actual circuits will give you a deeper understanding of how to use the sum-of-products algorithm to create circuits that solve specific problems.</td></tr>
</table>

PRACTICE PROBLEM

Design a circuit that implements a 1-bit compare-for-greater-than (1-GT) operation. This circuit is given two 1-bit values, a and b. It outputs a 1 if $a > b$ and outputs a 0 otherwise.

4.4.4 SUMMARY

This section has been a brief introduction to the interesting but highly complex topic of circuit design. Our purpose here was not to make you experts in specifying and designing computer circuits but to demonstrate how it is possible to implement high-level arithmetic operations using only low-level electronic components like transistors. We also demonstrated how it is possible to reorient our viewpoint and raise our "level of abstraction." We changed the level of discussion from electricity to arithmetic, from hardware devices to mathematical behavior, from form to function. This is one of the first steps up the hierarchy of abstractions introduced in Figure 1.4. Succeeding chapters will take circuits like CE and ADD and use them as building blocks to construct yet higher-level abstractions such as functional units and complete computer systems.

4.5   CONTROL CIRCUITS

The previous section described the design of circuits for implementing arithmetic and logical operations. However, there are other, quite different, types of circuits that are also essential to the proper functioning of a computer system. This section briefly describes one of these other important circuit types, **control circuits**. These circuits are used not to implement arithmetic operations but to determine the order in which operations are carried out inside a computer and to select the correct data values to be processed. In a sense, they can be viewed as the sequencing and decision-making circuits inside a computer. These circuits are essential to the proper function of a computer because, as we noted in Chapter 1, algorithms and programs must be well ordered and must always know what operation to do next. The two major types of control circuits are called **multiplexors** and **decoders**, and, like everything else described in this chapter, they can be completely described in terms of gates and the rules of logic.

A **multiplexor** is a circuit that has 2^N **input lines** and 1 **output line**. Its function is to select exactly one of its 2^N input lines and copy the binary value on that input line onto its single output line. The way a multiplexor chooses one specific input is by using an additional set of N lines called **selector lines**. (Thus the total number of inputs to the multiplexor circuit is $2^N + N$.) The 2^N input lines of a multiplexor are numbered 0, 1, 2, 3, . . . , $2^N - 1$. Each of the N selector lines can be set to either a 0 or a 1, so we can use the N selector lines to represent all binary values from 000 . . . 0 (N zeroes) to 111 . . . 1 (N ones), which represent all integer values from 0 to $2^N - 1$. These numbers correspond exactly to the numbers of the input lines. Thus the binary number that appears on the selector lines can be interpreted as the identification number of the input line that is to be selected. Pictorially, a multiplexor looks like this:

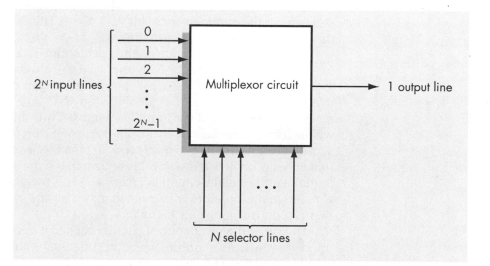

For example, if we had four (2^2) input lines (i.e., $N = 2$) coming into our multiplexor, numbered 0, 1, 2, and 3, then we would need two selector lines. The four binary combinations that can appear on this pair of selector lines are 00, 01, 10, and 11, which correspond to the decimal values 0, 1, 2, and 3, respectively (see Figure 4.2). The multiplexor selects the one input line whose identification number corresponds to the value appearing on the selector lines and copies the value on that input line to the output line. If, for example, the two selector lines were set to 1 and 0, then a multiplexor circuit would pick input line 2 because 10 in binary is 2 in decimal notation.

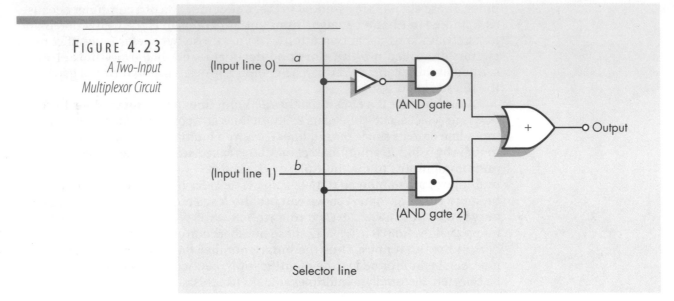

FIGURE 4.23

*A Two-Input
Multiplexor Circuit*

Implementing a multiplexor using logic gates is not difficult. Figure 4.23 shows a simple multiplexor circuit with $N = 1$. This is a multiplexor with two (2^1) input lines and a single selector line.

In Figure 4.23, if the value on the selector line is 0, then the bottom input line to AND gate 2 will always be 0, so its output will always be 0. Looking at AND gate 1, we see that the NOT gate will change its bottom input value to a 1. Because (1 AND a) is always a, the output of the top AND gate will be equal to the value of a, which is the value of the input from line 0. Thus the two inputs to the OR gate will be 0 and a. Because the value of the expression (0 OR a) is identical to a, by setting the selector line to 0 we have, in effect, selected as our output the value that appears on line 0. You should confirm that if the selector line has the value 1, then the output of the circuit in Figure 4.23 is b, the value appearing on line 1. We can design multiplexors with more than two inputs in a similar fashion, although they rapidly become more complex.

The second type of control circuit is called a **decoder** and it operates in the opposite way from a multiplexor. A decoder has N input lines numbered 0, 1, 2, ..., $N - 1$ and 2^N output lines numbered 0, 1, 2, 3, ..., $2^N - 1$.

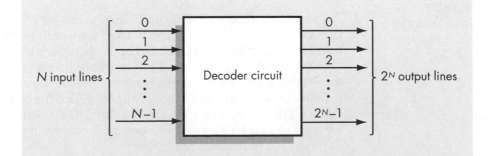

Each of the N input lines of the decoder can be set to either a 0 or a 1, and when these N values are interpreted as a single binary number, they can represent all integer values from 0 to $2^N - 1$. It is the job of the decoder to determine the value represented on its N input lines and then send a signal (i.e., a 1) on the single output line that has that identification number. All other output lines are set to 0.

For example, if our decoder has three input lines, it will have eight (2^3) output lines numbered 0 to 7. These three input lines can represent all binary values from 000 to 111, which is from 0 to 7 in decimal notation. If, for example, the binary values on the three input lines are 101, which is a 5, then a signal (a binary 1) would be sent out by the decoder on output line 5. All other output lines would contain a 0.

Figure 4.24 shows the design of a 2-to-4 decoder circuit with two input lines and four (2^2) output lines. These four output lines are labeled 0, 1, 2, and 3, and the only output line that will carry a signal value of 1 is the line whose identification number is identical to the value appearing on the two input lines. For example, if the two inputs are 11, then line 3 should be set to a 1 (11 in binary is 3 in decimal). This is, in fact, what happens because the AND gate connected to line 3 is the only one whose two inputs are equal to a 1. You should confirm that this circuit behaves properly when it receives the inputs 00, 01, and 10 as well.

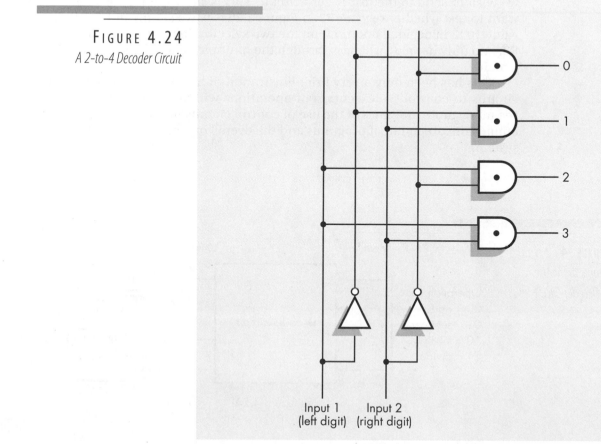

FIGURE 4.24
A 2-to-4 Decoder Circuit

Together, decoder and multiplexor circuits enable us to build computer systems that execute the correct instructions using the correct data values. As an example of their use, assume we have a computer that can carry out four different types of arithmetic operations—add, subtract, multiply and divide. Furthermore, assume that these four instructions have code numbers 0, 1, 2, and 3, respectively. We could use a decoder circuit to ensure that the computer performs the correct instruction. We need a decoder circuit with two input lines. It receives as input the 2-digit code number (in binary) of the instruction that we want to perform: 00 (add), 01 (subtract), 10 (multiply), or 11 (divide). The decoder interprets this value and sends out a signal on the correct output line. This signal is used to activate the proper arithmetic circuit and cause it to perform the desired operation. This behavior is diagrammed in Figure 4.25.

A decoder circuit can be used to select the correct instruction. A multiplexor can help ensure that the computer executes this instruction using the correct data. For example, suppose our computer has four special registers called R0, R1, R2, and R3. (For now, just consider a register to be a place to store a data value. We describe registers in more detail in the next chapter.) Assume that we have built a circuit called *test-if-zero* that can test whether any of these four registers contains the value 0. (This is actually quite similar to the CE circuit of Figure 4.18.) We can use a multiplexor circuit to select the register that we wish to send to the test-if-zero circuit. This is shown in Figure 4.26. If we want to test whether register R2 in Figure 4.26 is 0, we simply put the binary value 10 (2 in decimal notation) on the two selector lines. This selects register R2, and only its value will pass through the multiplexor and be sent to the test circuit.

This has been only a very brief illustration of how we can use electronic circuits to control the execution of operations within an algorithm. We will see many more examples of the use of control circuits in Chapter 5, which examines the execution of programs and the overall organization of a computer system.

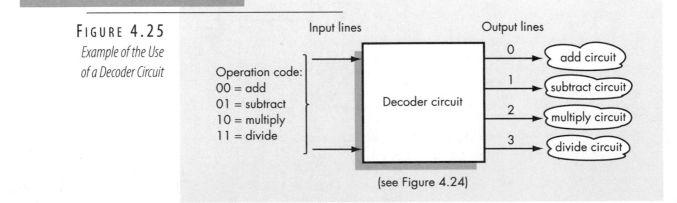

FIGURE 4.25

Example of the Use of a Decoder Circuit

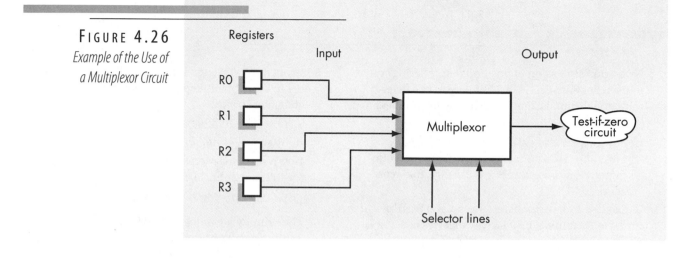

FIGURE 4.26

Example of the Use of a Multiplexor Circuit

4.6 CONCLUSION

This concludes our discussion on the representation of information and the design of computer circuits to process that information. We began with the most elementary component, bistable electronic devices such as transistors, and showed how they can be used to construct logic gates that in turn can be used to implement circuits to carry out useful functions. The next chapter continues this "upward climb" to higher levels of abstraction. It shows how arithmetic circuits such as compare for equality and addition (Section 4.4.3) and control circuits such as multiplexors and decoders (Section 4.5) can be used to construct entire computer systems.

After reading this chapter, you may have the feeling that although you understand the individual concepts that were covered, you don't understand, in the grand sense, what computers are or how they work. You may feel that you can follow the details but can't see the "big picture." One possible reason is that this chapter looked at computers from a very elementary viewpoint. Our investigation of computer systems in this chapter consisted of studying different types of specialized circuits. This is analogous to studying the human body as a collection of millions of cells of different types—blood cells, brain cells, skin cells, and so on. Cytology is certainly an important part of the field of biology, but understanding only the cellular structure of the human body provides no intuitive understanding of what people are and how we do such characteristic things as walk, eat, and breathe. Understanding these complex actions derives not from a study of molecules, genes, or cells, but from a study of higher-level organs, such as lungs, stomach, and muscles, and their interactions.

That is exactly what happens in the next chapter as we examine higher-level computer components such as processors, memory, and instructions and begin our study of the topic of computer organization.

EXERCISES

1. Given our discussion of positional numbering systems in Section 4.2.1, see whether you can determine the decimal value of the following numbers.

   a. 133 (base 4)
   b. 367 (base 8, also called *octal*)
   c. 1BA (base 16, also called *hexadecimal*. B is the digit that represents 11; A is the digit that represents 10.)

2. In Exercise 1(c), we used the letters A and B as digits of the base 16 number. Explain why that was necessary.

3. Determine the decimal value of the following unsigned binary numbers.

   a. 11000   c. 1111111
   b. 110001   d. 1000000000

4. If a computer uses 18 bits to represent integer values, what is the largest unsigned value that can be represented?

5. Assume that the following 10-bit numbers represent signed integers using sign/magnitude notation. The sign is the leftmost bit and the remaining 9 bits represent the magnitude. What is the decimal value of each?

   a. 1000110001   c. 1000000001
   b. 0110011000   d. 1000000000

6. a. What is "unusual" about the 10-bit value shown in Exercise 5(d)? Why could it cause problems on a computer system that used sign/magnitude notation? (*Hint:* Think about how it might affect the compare-for-equality circuit that we built.)

   b. Assume that we use 10 bits to represent signed integers, using sign/magnitude notation. What are the largest (in absolute value) positive and negative numbers that can be represented on our system?

7. Assume that our computer stores decimal numbers using 16 bits—10 bits for a sign/magnitude mantissa and 6 bits for a sign/magnitude base-2 exponent. (This is exactly the same representation used in the text.) Show the internal representation of the following decimal quantities.

   a. +7.5   b. −20.25   c. −1/64

8. Using the ASCII code set given in Figure 4.3, show the internal binary representation for the following character strings.

   a. AbC   c. $25.00
   b. Mike   d. (a+b)

9. How many binary digits would it take to represent the following phrase in ASCII code?

   Invitation to Computer Science

10. The primary advantage of using the binary numbering system rather than the decimal system to represent data is reliability, as we noted in Section 4.2.2. Describe two disadvantages of using binary rather than decimal notation for the internal representation of information.

11. Assume that $a = 1$, $b = 2$, and $c = 2$. What is the value of each of the following Boolean expressions?

    a. $(a > 1)$ OR $(b = c)$
    b. $[(a + b) > c]$ AND $(b \le c)$
    c. NOT $(a = 1)$
    d. NOT $[(a = b)$ OR $(b = c)]$

12. Assume that $a = 5$, $b = 2$, and $c = 3$. What is the problem with attempting to evaluate the following Boolean expression?

    $(a = 1)$ AND $(b = 2)$ OR $(c = 3)$

    How can we solve this problem?

13. Using the circuit construction algorithm of Section 4.4.2, design a circuit, using only AND, OR, and NOT gates, to implement the following truth table.

a	b	Output
0	0	1
0	1	1
1	0	1
1	1	0

    This operation is termed **NAND**, for *Not AND*, and it is frequently built as a single gate and used in the design of other computer circuits.

14. Using the circuit construction algorithm of Section 4.4.2, design a circuit, using only AND, OR, and NOT gates, to implement the following truth table.

a	b	Output
0	0	1
0	1	1
1	0	0
1	1	1

This operation is termed **logical implication**, and it is an important operator in symbolic logic.

15. Build a **majority-rules circuit**. This is a circuit that has three inputs and one output. The value of its output is 1 if and only if two or more of its inputs are 1; otherwise, the output of the circuit is 0. For example, if the three inputs are 0, 1, 1, your circuit should output a 1. If its three inputs are 0, 1, 0 it should output a 0. This circuit is frequently used in **fault-tolerant computing**—environments where a computer must keep working correctly no matter what. An example is a computer on a deep-space vehicle where repairs would be impossible. In these conditions, we might choose to put three computers on board and have all three do every computation. We would then say that if two or more of the systems produce the same answer, we would accept it. Thus one of the machines could fail and the system would still work properly.

16. Design an **odd-parity circuit**. This is a circuit that has three inputs and one output. The circuit outputs a 1 if and only if an even number (0 or 2) of its inputs are a 1. Otherwise, the circuit outputs a 0. Thus the sum of the number of 1 bits in the input and the output is always an odd number. (This circuit is used in error checking. By adding up the number of 1 bits, we can determine whether any single input bit was accidentally changed. If it was, the total number of 1s will be an even number when we know it should be an odd value.)

17. Design a **1-bit subtraction circuit**. This circuit takes three inputs—two binary digits a and b and a borrow digit from the previous column. The circuit has two outputs—the difference $(a - b)$, including the borrow, and a new borrow digit that propagates to the next column. Create the truth table and build the circuit. This circuit can be used to build N-bit subtraction circuits.

18. How many selector lines would be needed on a four-input multiplexor? On an eight-input multiplexor?

19. Design a **four-input multiplexor circuit**. Use the design of the two-input multiplexor shown in Figure 4.23 as a guide.

20. Design a **3-to-8 decoder circuit.** Use the design of the 2-to-4 decoder circuit shown in Figure 4.24 as a guide.

CHALLENGE WORK

1. *Circuit optimization* is a very important area of hardware design. As we mentioned earlier in the chapter, each gate in the circuit represents a real hardware device that takes up space on the chip, generates heat that must be dissipated, and increases costs. Therefore, the elimination of un-needed gates can represent a real savings. Circuit optimization investigates techniques to construct a new circuit that behaves identically to the original one but with fewer gates. The basis for circuit optimization is the transformation rules of symbolic logic. These rules allow you to transform one Boolean expression into an equivalent one that entails fewer operations. For example, the *distributive law* of logic says that

$$(a \cdot b) + (a \cdot c) = a \cdot (b + c)$$

The expressions on either side of the = sign are functionally identical, but the one on the right determines its value using one less gate (one AND gate and one OR gate instead of two AND gates and one OR gate).

Read about the transformation rules of binary logic and techniques of circuit optimization. Using these rules, improve the full adder circuit of Figure 4.22 so that it requires less than 1,504 transistors. Explain your improvements and determine exactly how many fewer transistors are required for your "new and improved" full adder circuit.

2. Although this chapter described a signed-integer representation method called sign/magnitude, most computer systems built today use another technique called **two's complement representation**. This popular method is based on the concepts of *modular arithmetic*, and it does not suffer from the problem of two different representations for the quantity 0. Read about this integer representation technique, learn how signed integers are represented, and write a report describing how this method works and the algorithms for adding and subtracting numbers represented in two's complement notation. In your report give the 16-bit, two's complement representation for the signed integer values +45, −68, −1, and 0. Then show how to carry out the arithmetic operations 45 + 45, 45 + (−68), and 45 + (−1).

FOR FURTHER READING

One of the most widely used texts in the field of hardware and logic design is

Patterson, D., and Hennessey, J. *Computer Organization and Design: The Hardware and Software Interface*, 2nd ed. San Francisco: Morgan Kaufman, 1997.

- Chapter 4: "Arithmetic for Computers." This is an excellent introduction to the representation of information inside a computer.
- Appendix B: "The Basics of Logic Design."

This book offers an excellent discussion of the major topics covered in this chapter—the representation of information, logic gates, and circuit design.

Among the other excellent books about gates, circuits, hardware, and logic design are

Forester, T. *The Microelectronics Revolution*. Cambridge, MA: M.I.T. Press, 1980.

Gajski, D. *Principles of Digital Design*. Englewood Cliffs, NJ: Prentice-Hall, 1996.

Katz, R. H. *Contemporary Logic Design*. New York: Benjamin Cummings, 1994.

Hayes, J. *Digital Logic Design*. Reading, MA: Addison-Wesley, 1993.

Mano, M., and Kime, C. *Logic and Computer Design Fundamentals*. Englewood Cliffs, NJ: Prentice-Hall, 1997.

Finally, a good reference text on the internal representation of numeric information and arithmetic algorithms is

Koren, I. *Computer Arithmetic Algorithms*. Englewood Cliffs, NJ: Prentice-Hall, 1993.

CHAPTER

5

COMPUTER SYSTEMS ORGANIZATION

5.1   INTRODUCTION

This chapter takes a second look at the design and organization of computers, but in quite a different way from the discussion in Chapter 4. That chapter introduced the elementary building blocks of computer systems—transistors, gates, and circuits. This information is essential to understanding computer hardware, just as a knowledge of atoms and molecules is necessary for any serious study of chemistry. However, as we noted at the end of the last chapter, it produces a very low-level view of computer systems, and even students who have mastered the material may still ask, "OK, but how do computers *really* work?"

Gates and circuits operate on the most elemental of data items, binary 0s and 1s, whereas people reason and work with more complex units of information, such as decimal numbers, character strings, and instructions. To understand how computers process this type of information, we must look at higher-level components than the gates and circuits of Chapter 4. We must study computers as collections of **functional units** or **subsystems** that perform tasks such as instruction processing, information storage, data transfer, input, and output. The branch of computer science that studies computers in terms of their major functional units and how they work is **computer organization**, and that is the subject of this chapter. This higher-level viewpoint will give us a much better understanding of how a computer really works.

All of the functional units introduced in this chapter are built from gates and circuits. However, those elementary components will no longer be visible because we are adopting a different viewpoint, a different perspective, a different **level of abstraction**. This is an extremely important point, and as we have said, the concept of abstraction is used throughout computer science. Without it, it would be virtually impossible to study computer design because of its enormous complexity. In fact, it would be difficult to study any complex technological system.

For example, suppose that system S is composed of a large number of elementary components a_1, a_2, a_3, . . . interconnected in very intricate ways, as shown in Figure 5.1(a). This is equivalent to viewing a computer system as thousands or millions of individual gates. Although this may be an important way to view system S, it can overwhelm us with detail. To deal with this problem, we can redefine the primitives of system S. We group together elementary components a_1, a_2, . . . , as in Figure 5.1(b), and call these larger units (A, B, C) the basic building blocks of system S. A, B, and C are treated as nondecomposable elements whose internal construction is hidden from view. We care only about what functions these components perform and how they interact. This leads to the higher-level system view shown in Figure 5.1(c), which is certainly a great deal simpler than the viewpoint of Figure 5.1(a), and that is how this chapter approaches the topic of computer hardware. Our primitives are much larger components, similar to A, B, and C, but internally they are still made up of the gates and circuits of Chapter 4.

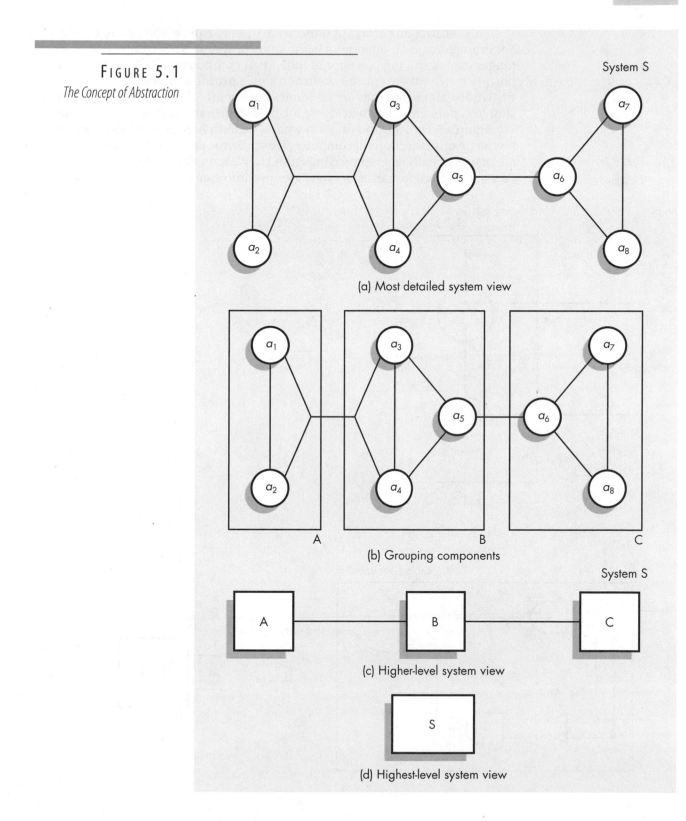

FIGURE 5.1
The Concept of Abstraction

(a) Most detailed system view

(b) Grouping components

(c) Higher-level system view

(d) Highest-level system view

This "abstracting away" of unnecessary detail can be done more than once. For example, at some later point in the study of system S of Figure 5.1, we may no longer care about the behavior of individual components A, B, and C. We may now wish to treat the entire system as a single primitive, nondecomposable entity whose inner workings are no longer important. This leads to the extremely simple system view shown in Figure 5.1(d), a view that we adopt in later chapters.

Figures 5.1(a), (c), and (d) form what is called a **hierarchy of abstractions**. A hierarchy of abstractions of computer science forms the central theme of this text, and it was initially diagrammed in Figure 1.4. We have already seen this idea in action in Chapter 4 as transistors were grouped into gates and gates into circuits:

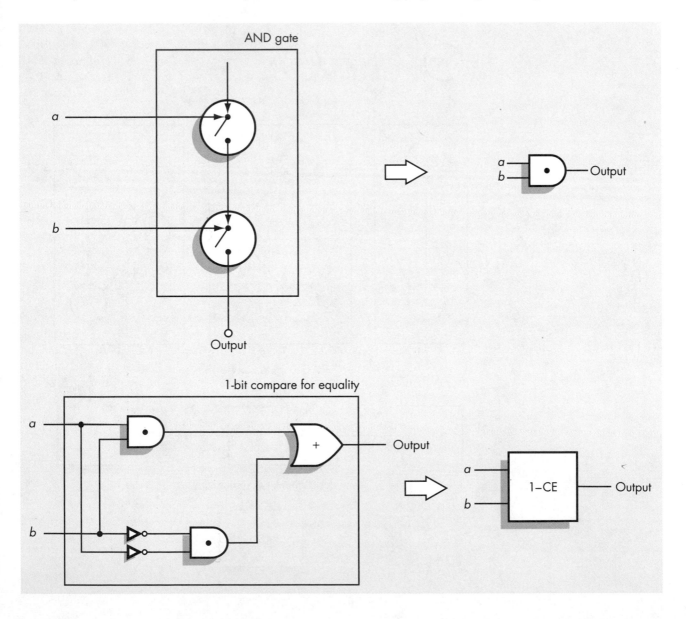

This process continues into Chapter 5, where we use the addition and comparison circuits of Section 4.4.3 to build an arithmetic unit and use the multiplexor and decoder circuits of Section 4.5 to construct a processor. These higher-level components then become our building blocks in all future discussions.

5.2 THE VON NEUMANN ARCHITECTURE

There are a huge number of computer systems on the market, manufactured by dozens of different vendors. There are $30-million supercomputers, million-dollar mainframes, minicomputers, workstations, laptops, and tiny hand-held "personal digital assistants" that cost only a few hundred dollars. In addition to size and cost, computers also differ in speed, memory capacity, input/output capabilities, and available software. The hardware marketplace is diverse, multifaceted, and ever-changing.

However, in spite of all these differences, virtually every computer in use today is based on a single design. Although a million-dollar mainframe and a thousand-dollar desktop computer may not seem to have much in common, they are based on the same fundamental principles.

An identical situation exists with automotive technology. Although a pickup truck, family sedan, and Ferrari racing car do not appear at all similar, "under the hood" they are all constructed using the same basic technology: a gasoline-powered internal combustion engine turning an axle that turns the wheels. Differences among various models of trucks and cars are not basic theoretical differences but simply variations on a theme, such as a bigger engine, a larger carrying capacity, or a more luxurious interior.

What appear to be huge differences among computer systems are also simply variations on the same theme. The structure and organization of virtually all modern computers are based on a single theoretical model of computer design called the **Von Neumann architecture**, named after the brilliant mathematician John Von Neumann, who first proposed it in 1946. (We will learn more about Von Neumann and his enormous contributions to computer science a little later in the chapter.)

The Von Neumann architecture is a model for designing and building computers that is based on the following three characteristics:

- A computer constructed from four major subsystems called **memory**, **input/output**, the **arithmetic/logic unit** (ALU), and the **control unit**. These four subsystems are diagrammed in Figure 5.2.
- The **stored program concept**, in which the instructions to be executed by the computer are represented as binary values and stored in memory.
- The **sequential** execution of instructions. One instruction at a time is fetched from memory to the control unit, where it is decoded and executed.

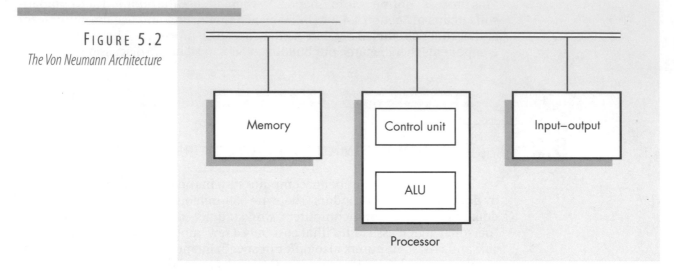

This section first looks individually at each of the four subsystems that make up the Von Neumann architecture and describes their design and operation. Then it puts these pieces together to show the operation of the overall Von Neumann model.

5.2.1 MEMORY AND CACHE

Memory is the functional unit of a computer that stores and retrieves the instructions and the data being executed. All information stored in memory is represented internally using the binary numbering system described in Section 4.2.

Computer memory uses an access technique called **random access**, and the acronym **RAM** (for *r*andom *a*ccess *m*emory) is frequently used to refer to the memory unit. A random access memory has the following three characteristics:

- Memory is divided into fixed-size units called **cells**, and each cell is associated with a unique identifier called an **address**. These addresses are unsigned integers 0, 1, 2, ...

- All accesses to memory are to a specified address, and we must always fetch or store a complete cell—that is, all the bits in that cell. The cell is the minimum unit of access.

- The time it takes to fetch or store a cell is the same for all cells in memory.

(*Note:* A **read-only memory**, abbreviated **ROM**, is simply a random access memory unit in which the ability to store information has been disabled. It is only possible to fetch information.) A model of a random access memory unit is shown in Figure 5.3.

As shown in Figure 5.3, the memory unit is made up of cells that contain a fixed number of binary digits. The number of bits per cell is called the **cell size** or the **memory width**, and it is usually denoted as W.

FIGURE 5.3

Structure of Random Access Memory

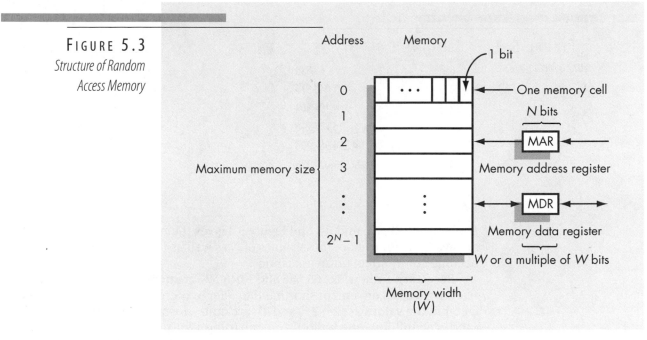

In earlier generations of computers there was no standardized value for cell size, and computers were built with values of $W = 6, 8, 12, 16, 24, 30, 32, 36, 48,$ and 60 bits. However, computer manufacturers have now agreed on a standard cell size of 8 bits, and this 8-bit unit is universally called a **byte**. Thus the generic term *cell* has become relatively obsolete, and it is more common now to refer to **memory bytes** as the basic unit. However, keep in mind that this is not a generic term but rather refers to a cell that contains exactly 8 binary digits.

With a cell size of 8 bits, the largest unsigned integer value that can be stored in a single cell is 11111111, which equals 255—not a very large number. Therefore, computers with a cell size of $W = 8$ use multiple memory cells to store a single data value. For example, many computers use 2 or 4 bytes (16 or 32 bits) to store one integer and either 4 or 8 bytes (32 or 64 bits) to store a single real number. This gives the range needed, but at a price. It may take several trips to memory, rather than one, to fetch a single data item.

Each memory cell in a RAM is identified by a unique unsigned integer address 0, 1, 2, 3, ... If there are N bits available to represent the address of a cell, then the smallest address is 0 and the largest address is a string of N 1s:

$$\underbrace{1111 \ldots 11}_{N \text{ digits}}$$

which is equal to the value $2^N - 1$. Thus the range of addresses available on a computer is $[0 \ldots (2^N - 1)]$, where N is the number of binary digits available to represent an address. This is a total of 2^N memory cells. The value 2^N is called the **maximum memory size** or the **address space** of the computer. Typical values of

FIGURE 5.4

Maximum Memory Sizes

N	MAXIMUM MEMORY SIZE (2^N)
16	65,536
20	1,048,576
22	4,194,304
24	16,777,216
32	4,294,967,296
40	1,099,511,627,776

N are 16, 20, 22, 24, and 32, and Figure 5.4 gives the maximum amount of memory available for each of these values of N as well as for $N = 40$, a value that may become common on future machines.

Because numbers like 65,536 and 1,048,576 are hard to remember, computer scientists use a convenient shorthand to refer to memory sizes. It is based on the fact that the values $2^{10}, 2^{20}, 2^{30}$, and 2^{40} are quite close in magnitude to one thousand, one million, one billion, and one trillion, respectively. Therefore, the letters K (kilo, or thousand), M (mega, or million), G (giga, or billion), and T (tera, or trillion) are used to refer to these units.

$2^{10} = 1K \ (= 1,024)$	$1\,KB = 1$ *kilobyte*
$2^{20} = 1M \ (= 1,048,576)$	$1\,MB = 1$ *megabyte*
$2^{30} = 1G \ (= 1,073,741,824)$	$1\,GB = 1$ *gigabyte*
$2^{40} = 1T \ (= 1,099,511,627,776)$	$1\,TB = 1$ *terabyte*

Thus a computer with $2^{16} = 65,536$ bytes of storage would be said to have 64 KB of memory, since $2^{16} = 2^6 \times 2^{10} = 64 \times 2^{10} = 64$ KB. This was a popular size for computers of the 1970s and early 1980s. Most computers today contain at least 16 MB of memory, and 32 MB to 128 MB is quite common, especially on larger machines. As memory technology advances and costs continue to drop, it will not be long before gigabyte memories become common. The 32-bit address, which allows an address space of 4 GB, barely supports that level of expansion, and it is quite likely that we will soon begin to see 40-bit addresses that will be able to address directly 2^{40}, or 1 trillion, bytes of memory.

When dealing with memory, it is important to keep in mind the distinction between an **address** and the **contents** of that address.

Address   *Contents*

42 | 1 |

The address of this memory cell is 42. The contents of cell 42 are the integer value 1. As we will soon see, some instructions operate on addresses, whereas others operate on the contents of an address. A failure to distinguish between these two values can cause confusion about how some instructions behave.

Powers of 10

When we talk about volumes of information such as megabytes, gigabytes, and terabytes, it is hard to fathom exactly what those massive numbers mean. Here are some rough approximations (say, to within an order of magnitude) of how much textual information corresponds to each of the storage quantities just introduced, as well as the next few on the scale.

Quantity	Amount in Bytes	Amount of Textual Information
1 byte	10^0	One character
1 kilobyte	10^3	One typed page
1 megabyte	10^6	Two or three novels
1 gigabyte	10^9	A departmental library or a large personal library
1 terabyte	10^{12}	The library of a major academic research university
1 petabyte	10^{15}	All printed material in all libraries in North America
1 exabyte	10^{18}	All words ever printed throughout human history
1 zettabyte	10^{21}	—

The two basic memory operations are **fetching** and **storing**, and they can be described formally as follows:

- *Fetch(address)*
  Meaning: Fetch a copy of the contents of the memory cell with the specified *address* and return those contents as the result of the operation. The original contents of the memory cell that was accessed are unchanged. This is termed a **nondestructive fetch**. In terms of the preceding diagram, the operation Fetch(42) would return the number 1. The value 1 would also still be in address 42.

- *Store(address, value)*
  Meaning: Store the specified *value* into the memory cell specified by *address*. The previous contents of the cell are lost. This is termed a **destructive store**. The operation Store(42, 2) would store a 2 in cell 42, overwriting the previous value of 1.

One of the characteristics of random access memory is that the time to carry out either a fetch or a store operation is the same for all 2^N addresses. At current levels of technology, this time, called the **memory access time**, is typically about 50–75 nsec (**nanosecond** = 1 nsec = 10^{-9} sec = 1 billionth of a second). Also note that fetching and storing are allowed only to an entire cell. If we wish, for example, to modify a single bit of memory, we first need to fetch the entire cell containing that bit, change the one bit, and then store the entire cell. The cell is the minimum accessible unit of memory.

There is one component of the memory unit shown in Figure 5.3 that we have not yet discussed, the **memory registers**. These two registers are used to implement the fetch and store operations. Both operations require two operands: the *address* of the cell being accessed and *value*, either the value stored by the store operation or the value returned by the fetch operation.

The memory unit contains two special registers whose purpose is to hold these two operands. The **Memory Address Register** (MAR) holds the address of the cell to be fetched or stored. Because the MAR must be capable of holding any address, it must be at least N bits wide, where 2^N is the address space of the computer.

The **Memory Data Register** (MDR) contains the data value being fetched or stored. We might be tempted to say that the MDR should be W bits wide, where W is the cell size. However, as mentioned earlier, on most computers the cell size is only 8 bits, and most data values occupy multiple cells. Thus the size of the MDR is usually a multiple of 8. Typical values of MDR width are 16, 32, and 64 bits.

Given these two registers, we can describe a little more formally what happens during the fetch and store operations in a random access memory.

- *Fetch(address)*
    1. Load the address into the MAR.
    2. Decode the address in the MAR.
    3. Copy the contents of that memory location into the MDR.

- *Store(address, value)*
    1. Load the address into the MAR.
    2. Load the value into the MDR.
    3. Decode the address in the MAR.
    4. Store the contents of the MDR into that memory location.

For example, to retrieve the contents of cell 123, we would initiate a fetch operation and (in binary, of course) load the value 123 into the MAR. When the operation is done, a copy of the contents of cell 123 will be in the MDR. To store the value 98 into cell 4, we initiate a store operation and load a 4 into the MAR and a 98 into the MDR.

The operation "Decode the address in the MAR" means that the memory unit must translate the N-bit address stored in the MAR into the set of signals needed to access that one specific memory cell. That is, the memory unit must be able to convert the integer value 4 in the MAR into the electronic signals needed to access *only* address 4 from all 2^N addresses in the memory unit. This may seem like magic, but it is actually a relatively easy task that applies ideas presented in the previous chapter. We can decode the address in the MAR using a **decoder circuit** of the type described in Section 4.5 and shown in Figure 4.24. (Remember that a decoder circuit has N inputs and 2^N outputs numbered $0, 1, 2, \ldots, 2^N - 1$. The circuit puts the signal 1 on the output line whose number equals the numeric value on the N input lines.) We simply copy the N bits in the MAR to the N input lines of a decoder circuit. Exactly one of its 2^N output lines will be ON, and this will be the line whose identification number corresponds to the address value in the MAR.

For example, if $N = 4$ (the MAR contains 4 bits), then we would have 16 addressable cells in our memory, numbered 0000 to 1111 (that is, 0 to 15). We could use a 4-to-16 decoder whose inputs are the 4 bits of the MAR. Each of the 16 out-

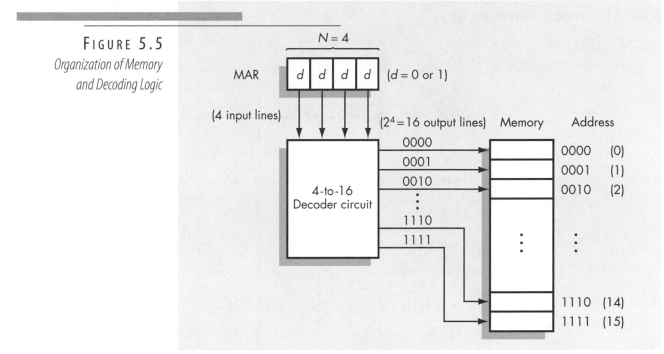

FIGURE 5.5

Organization of Memory and Decoding Logic

put lines would be associated with the one memory cell whose address is in the MAR and would enable us to fetch or store its contents. This situation is shown in Figure 5.5.

If the MAR contains the 4-bit address 0010 (decimal 2), then only the output line labeled 0010 in Figure 5.5 will be ON (that is, carry a value of 1). All others will be OFF. The output line 0010 is associated with the unique memory cell that has memory address 2, and the appearance of an ON signal on this line causes the memory hardware to copy the contents of location 2 to the MDR if it is doing a fetch, or to load its contents from the MDR if it is doing a store.

The only problem with the memory organization shown in Figure 5.5 is that it does not **scale** very well. That is, it could not be used to build a large memory unit. In modern computers a typical value for N, the number of bits used to represent an address, is at least 16 and is usually 20, 24, 32 or more. A decoder circuit with 16 input lines would have $2^{16} = 65,536$ output lines, which is quite unreasonable. Bigger ones become even more unreasonable to construct.

To solve this problem, memories are physically organized into a **two-dimensional**, rather than a one-dimensional, organization. In this structure, the 16-byte memory of Figure 5.5 would be organized into a two-dimensional 4×4 structure, rather than the one-dimensional 16×1 organization shown earlier. This two-dimensional layout is shown in Figure 5.6.

The memory locations are stored in **row major** order, with bytes 0–3 in row 0, bytes 4–7 in row 1 (01 in binary), bytes 8–11 in row 2 (10 in binary), and bytes 12–15 in row 3 (11 in binary). Each memory cell is connected to two selection lines, one called the **row selection line** and the other called the **column selection line**. When we send a signal down a single row selection line and a single

FIGURE 5.6

Two-Dimensional
Memory Organization

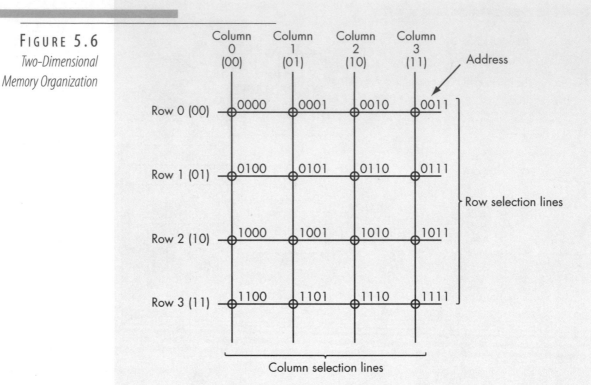

column selection line, only the memory cell located at the *intersection* of these two selection lines will carry out a memory fetch or a memory store operation.

How do we choose the correct row and column selection lines to access the proper memory cell? The answer is that instead of using one decoder circuit, we use two. Looking at the first two binary digits of the addresses in Figure 5.6, we see that they are identical to the row number. Similarly, looking at the last two binary digits of the address, we see that they are identical to the column number. Thus we should no longer view the MAR as being composed of a single 4-bit address, but as a 4-bit address made up of two distinct parts—the leftmost 2 bits, which specify the number of the row containing this cell, and the rightmost 2 bits, which specify the number of the column containing this cell. Each of these 2-bit fields is input to a separate decoder circuit that pulses the correct row and column lines to access the desired memory cell.

For example, if the MAR contains the 4-bit value 1101 (a decimal 13), then the two **high-order** (leftmost) bits 11 are sent to the row decoder, while the two **low-order** (rightmost) bits 01 are sent to the column decoder. The row decoder sends a signal on the line labeled 11 (row 3), and the column decoder sends a signal on the line labeled 01 (column 1). Only the single memory cell in row 3, column 1 becomes active and performs the fetch or store operation. Referring to Figure 5.6, we see that the memory cell in row 3, column 1 is the correct one— the cell with memory address 1101.

The two-dimensional organization of Figure 5.6 is far superior to the one-dimensional structure shown in Figure 5.5, because it can accommodate a much larger number of cells. A memory unit containing 64 KB (2^{16} bytes) would be organized into a 256×256 two-dimensional array. To select any one row or column requires a decoder with 8 input lines ($2^8 = 256$) and 256 output lines. This is a large number of output lines, but it is certainly more feasible to build two 8-to-256 decoders than the single 16-to-65,536 decoder required in a one-dimensional organization. Even memories of megabyte size can be managed using the two-dimensional memory organization just described.

To control whether memory does a fetch or a store operation, our memory unit needs one additional device called a **Fetch/Store Controller**. This unit determines whether we will put the contents of a memory cell into the MDR (a fetch operation) or put the contents of the MDR into a memory cell (a store operation). In a sense, the Fetch/Store Controller is like a traffic officer controlling the direction in which traffic can flow on a two-way street. This memory controller must determine in which direction information will flow on the two-way link connecting memory and the MDR. In order to know what to do, this controller receives a signal telling it whether it is to perform a fetch operation (an F signal) or a store operation (an S signal). On the basis of the value of that signal, the controller causes information to flow in the proper direction and the correct memory operation to take place.

Putting all of these discussions together leads to a complete model of the organization of a typical random access memory in a Von Neumann architecture. The model is shown in Figure 5.7.

Let's complete this discussion by seeing how complex it would be to study the memory unit of Figure 5.7 not at the abstraction level presented in that diagram, but at the gate and circuit level presented in Chapter 4. Let's assume that our memory unit contains 2^{24} cells (16 MB), each cell containing 8 bits. These are both typical values for a small system. There will be a total of about 128,000,000 bits of storage in this memory unit. A typical memory circuit used to store a single bit generally requires about 3 gates (1 AND, 1 OR, and 1 NOT) containing 5 transistors (2 per AND, 2 per OR, and 1 per NOT). Thus our 16-MB memory unit would contain about 384 million gates and 640 million transistors, and this does not even include the circuitry required to construct the decoder circuits, the controller, and the MAR and MDR registers! These numbers should help you appreciate the power and advantages of abstraction. Without it, studying a memory unit like the one in Figure 5.7 would be a much more formidable task.

CACHE MEMORY.   When Von Neumann created his idealized model of a computer, he included only a single type of memory. Whenever the processor needed an instruction or a piece of data, Von Neumann simply assumed it would get it from RAM using the fetch operation just described. However, as computers became faster, designers noticed that, more and more, the processor was sitting idle waiting for data or instructions to arrive. Processors were executing instructions so quickly that memory access was becoming a bottleneck. (It is hard to believe that a memory that can fetch a piece of data in 50 billionths of a second could slow anything down, but it does.) To solve this problem, designers needed to decrease memory access time to make it comparable with the time needed to execute an instruction. This could be done, but the size of RAM would make it horribly expensive; providing 16 or 32 MB of very-high-speed memory would price computers well beyond the reach of the ordinary person.

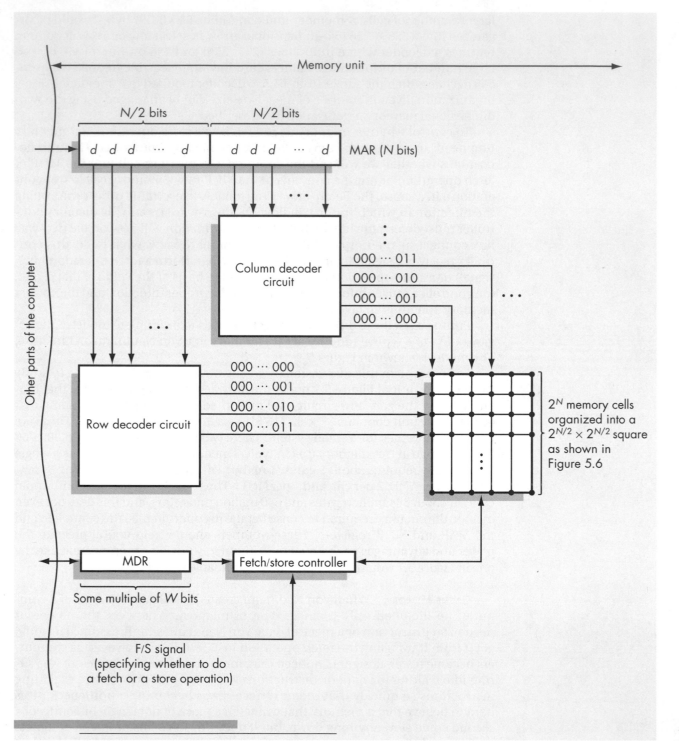

FIGURE 5.7
Overall RAM Organization

However, computer designers discovered that it really is not necessary to have *all* of memory be constructed from expensive, high-speed units in order to get a significant increase in speed. They observed that when a program fetches a piece of data or an instruction, there is a high likelihood that it will access that same instruction or piece of data in the very near future. Simply put, their observation, which is called the **Principle of Locality**, says that when the computer uses something, it will probably use it again very soon. (Think about a loop in an algorithm that keeps repeating the same instruction sequence over and over.) To exploit this observation, the first time that the computer references a piece of data, it should also move that data from "regular RAM memory" to a special, high-speed memory unit called **cache memory** (pronounced "cash," from the French word *cacher*, meaning "to hide"). A cache is typically 5 to 10 times faster than RAM but much smaller—on the order of kilobytes of storage rather than megabytes. However, this limited size is not a problem because the computer does not keep all of the data there, just those items that were accessed most recently and that, presumably, will be needed again immediately. The organization of the "two-level memory hierarchy" is as follows:

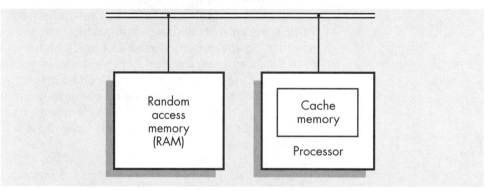

When the computer needs a piece of information, it does not immediately do the fetch operation described earlier. Instead, it carries out the following three steps:

1. Look first in cache memory to see whether the information needed is there. If it is, then the computer will be able to access it at the higher speed of the cache.

2. If it is not there, then access the desired information from RAM at the slower speed, using the fetch operation described above, and

3. Copy the data just fetched into the cache. If the cache is currently full, then discard one of the older items that has not recently been accessed. (The assumption is that we will not need it again for a while.)

This algorithm can significantly reduce the average time to access information. For example, assume that the access time of RAM is 50 nsec, whereas the average access time of the cache is 10 nsec, both fairly typical values. Furthermore, assume that the information we need is in the cache 60% of the time, a value called the **cache hit rate**. In this situation, 60% of the time we will get what we need in 10 nsec. Thus 40% of the time we will have wasted that 10 nsec because the information is not in the cache, and we will have to get the desired information from RAM. Our overall average access time will now be

$$(0.60 \times 10) + 0.40 \times (10 + 50) = 30 \text{ nsec}$$

PRACTICE PROBLEM

Assume that our memory unit was organized as a $1,024 \times 1,024$ two-dimensional array.

1. How big would the MAR register have to be?
2. How many bits of the MAR would have to be sent to the row decoder? To the column decoder?

---

which is a 40% reduction in access time. A higher cache hit rate can lead to even greater savings.

Surprisingly, a good analogy to cache memory is a home refrigerator. Without one we would have to go to the grocery store every time we needed an item; this corresponds to slow, regular memory access. Instead, when we go to the store we buy not only what we need now but also what we will need in the near future, and we put those items into our refrigerator. Now, when we need something, we do not immediately run to the store; instead we first check the refrigerator. If it is there, we can get it at a much higher rate of speed. We only need to go to the store when the food item we desire is not there.

Caches are found on every modern computer system today, and they are a significant contributor to the higher computational speeds achieved by new machines. Even though the formal Von Neumann model contained only a single memory unit, most computers built today have a multilevel hierarchy of random access memory.

5.2.2 INPUT/OUTPUT AND MASS STORAGE

The **input/output** (I/O) units are the devices that allow a computer system to communicate and interact with the outside world as well as store information. The random access memory described in the previous section is **volatile** memory—the information disappears when the power is turned off. Thus, without some type of long-term, **nonvolatile** archival storage, information could not be saved between shutdowns of the machine. This is the role of **mass storage devices** such as disks and tapes.

Of all the components of a Von Neumann machine, the I/O and mass storage subsystems are the most *ad hoc* and the most variable. Unlike the memory unit, I/O does not adhere to a single well-defined theoretical model. On the contrary, there are dozens of different I/O and mass storage devices manufactured by dozens of different companies and exhibiting many alternative organizations, so there is not a great deal that can be said in general. However, two important principles transcend the device-specific characteristics of particular vendors—**I/O access methods** and **I/O controllers**.

Input/output devices come in two basic types: those that represent information in *human-readable* form for human consumption, and those that store information in *machine-readable* form for access by a computer system. The former include such well-known I/O devices as keyboards, screens, and laser printers. The latter group of devices, usually referred to as **mass storage systems**, includes floppy disks, hard disks, optical disks, CD-ROMs, and tapes. Mass storage devices themselves come in two distinct forms, **direct access storage devices** (DASDs) and **sequential access storage devices** (SASDs).

Our discussion on random access memory in Section 5.2.1 described the fundamental characteristics of random access:

1. Every memory cell has a unique address.
2. It takes the same amount of time to access every cell.

A *direct access storage device* is one in which requirement number 2, equal access time, has been eliminated. That is, in a direct access storage device, every unit of information still has a unique address, but the time needed to access that unit depends on its physical location and the current state of the device.

The best examples of DASDs are the different types of disks listed earlier: hard disks, floppy disks, video disks, and so on. A disk stores information in units called **sectors**, each of which contains an address and a data block with a fixed number of characters:

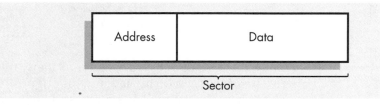

A fixed number of these sectors are placed on a concentric circle on the surface of the disk, called a **track**:

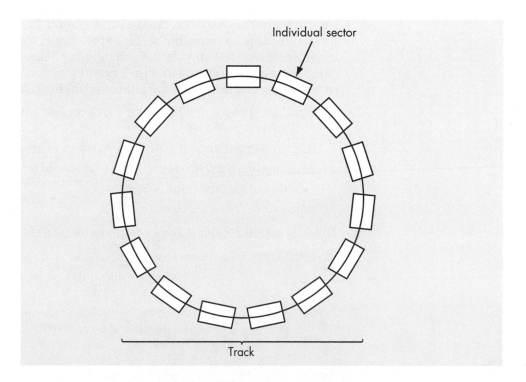

FIGURE 5.8
*Overall Organization of a
Typical Disk*

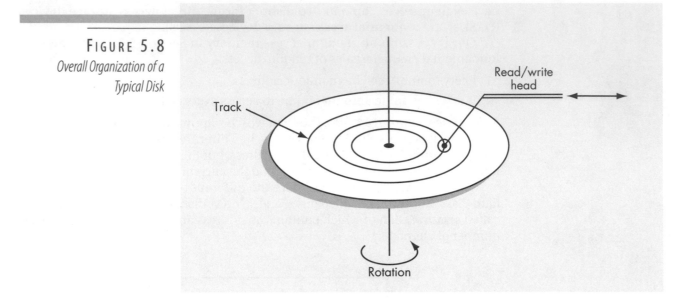

Finally, the surface of the disk contains many tracks, and there is a single **read/write head** that can be moved in or out to position itself over any track on the disk surface. The entire disk is rotating at high speed under the read/write head. This overall organization of a typical disk is shown in Figure 5.8.

The access time to any individual sector of the disk is made up of three components: seek time, latency, and transfer time. **Seek time** is the time needed to position the read/write head over the correct track; **latency** is the time for the beginning of the desired sector to rotate under the read/write head; **transfer time** is the time for the entire sector to pass under the read/write head and have its contents read into or written from memory. These values depend on the specific sector being accessed and the current position of the read/write head. Say we assume a disk drive with the following physical characteristics:

Rotation speed = 7200 rev/min = 120 rev/sec = 8.33 msec/rev
(1 **msec** = 0.001 sec)

Arm movement time = 0.02 msec to move to an adjacent track

Number of tracks/surface = 1,000 (numbered 0 to 999)

Number of sectors/track = 50

Number of characters/sector = 512

The access time for this disk can be determined as follows:

1. *Seek Time*   Best case = 0 msec (no arm movement necessary)

Worst case = 999 × 0.02 = 19.98 msec (must move from track 0 to track 999)

Average case = 300 × 0.02 = 6 msec (assume that on the average, the read/write head must move about 300 tracks)

2. *Latency*   Best case = 0 msec (sector is just about to come under the read/write head)

Worst case = 8.33 msec (we have just missed the sector and must wait one full revolution)

Average case = 4.17 msec (one-half a revolution)

3. *Transfer Time* $1/50 \times 8.33$ msec = 0.17 msec (the time for one sector, or 1/50 of a track, to pass under the read/write head)

The following table summarizes these computations (all values are in milliseconds).

	Best	Worst	Average
Seek Time	0	19.98	6
Latency	0	8.33	4.17
Transfer	0.17	0.17	0.17
Total	0.17	28.48	10.34

The best-case time and the worst-case time to fetch or store a sector on the disk differ by a factor of more than 150—0.17 msec versus 28.48 msec. The average access time is about 10 msec, a typical value for current disk drive technology. This table demonstrates the fundamental characteristic of all direct access storage devices, not just disks: They enable us to specify the address of the desired unit of data and go directly to that data item, but they cannot provide a uniform access time. Today, there are an enormous range of direct access storage devices in the marketplace, from tiny floppy disks that hold barely more than a megabyte, to hard disks and CDs that can store gigabytes, to massive on-line storage devices that are capable of recording and accessing 10–20 terabytes.

The second type of mass storage device uses an access technique called **sequential access.** With a sequential access storage device (SASD) we eliminate the requirement that all units of data be identifiable via unique address. Now, to find any given data item, we cannot simply fetch the contents of some specific sector address because that address no longer exists. Instead, we must search all data sequentially, repeatedly asking the question "Is this what I'm looking for?" If not, we move on to the next unit of data and ask the question again. Eventually we find what we are looking for or come to the end of the data.

A sequential access storage device behaves just like an audio cassette tape. To locate a specific song, we must run the tape for a while and then stop and listen. This process is repeated until we find the desired song or come to the end of the tape. A direct access storage device is like a compact disk (CD) that numbers all the songs and allows you to select any one. (The song number is the address.) Direct access storage devices are generally much faster at accessing individual pieces of information, and that is why they are much more widely used for mass storage. However, sequential access storage devices can be useful in specific situations, such as sequentially copying the entire contents of memory or of a disk drive. This type of **backup** operation fits the SASD model very well, and **tape backup units** are common storage devices on computer systems.

One of the fundamental characteristics of many (though not all) I/O devices is that they are very, very *slow* when compared to other components of a computer. For example, a typical memory access time is about 50 nsec. The time to complete the I/O operation "read one disk sector" was shown in the previous example to be about 10 msec.

Units such as nsec (billionths of a second), μsec (millionths of a second) and msec (thousandths of a second) are so small compared to human time scales that it is sometimes difficult to appreciate the immense difference between values like 50 nsec and 10 msec. The difference between these two quantities is a factor of 200,000—more than 5 orders of magnitude. To give a better indication of these values, consider that this is the same relative difference as that between 1 mile and eight complete revolutions of the earth's equator, or between a day and six centuries!

It is not uncommon for I/O operations such as reading a line on a terminal or printing a page on a laser printer to be 3, 4, 5, or 6 orders of magnitude slower than any other aspect of computer operation. If there isn't something in the design of a computer to account for this difference, components that operate on totally incompatible time scales will be trying to talk to each other, which will produce enormous inefficiencies. The high-speed components will sit idle for long stretches of time while they wait for the slow I/O unit to accept or deliver the desired character. It would be as though you could talk to someone at the normal human rate of 240 words/min (4 words/sec) but that person could respond only at the rate of 1 word every 8 hours—also a difference of 5 orders of magnitude. You wouldn't get much useful work done!

The solution to this problem is to use a device called an **I/O controller**. An I/O controller is like a special-purpose computer whose responsibility is to handle the details of input/output and to compensate for any speed differences between I/O devices and other parts of the computer. It has a small amount of memory, called an **I/O buffer**, and enough **I/O control and logic** processing capability to handle the mechanical functions of the I/O device, such as the read/write head, paper feed mechanism, and screen display. It is also able to transmit to the processor a special hardware signal, called an **interrupt signal**, when an I/O operation is done. The organization of a typical I/O controller is shown in Figure 5.9.

Let's assume that we want to display one line (80 characters) of text on a screen. First the 80 characters are transferred from their current location in memory to the I/O buffer storage within the I/O controller. This takes place at the high-speed data transfer rates of most computer components—millions or tens of millions of characters per second. Once this information is in the I/O buffer, the processor can instruct the I/O controller to begin the output operation. The control logic of the I/O controller handles the actual transfer of these 80 characters to the screen. This transfer may be at a much slower rate—perhaps only hundreds or thousands of characters per second. However, the processor does not sit idle during this output operation. It is free to do something else, perhaps to work on another program. The slowness of the I/O operation now affects *only* the I/O controller. The inefficiency and wasted time of all other components have been eliminated.

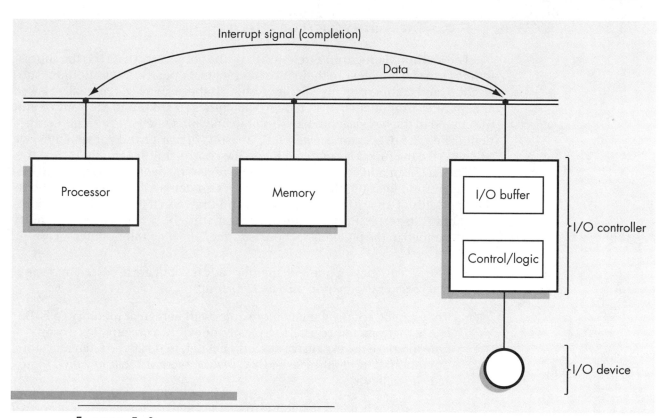

FIGURE 5.9

Organization of the I/O Controller

When all 80 characters have been displayed, the I/O controller sends out an *interrupt signal*. The appearance of this special signal indicates to the processor that the I/O operation is finished.

PRACTICE PROBLEM

Assume a disk with the following characteristics:
  Number of sectors per track = 20
  Number of tracks per surface = 50
  Number of surfaces = 2 (called a **double-sided** disk)
  Number of characters per sector = 1,024
  Arm movement time = 0.4 msec to move 1 track in any direction
  Rotation speed = 2,400 rev/min

1. How many characters can be stored on this disk?

2. What are the best-case, worst-case, and average-case access times for this disk? (Assume that the average seek operation must move 20 tracks.)

5.2.3 THE ARITHMETIC/LOGIC UNIT

The **arithmetic/logic unit** (referred to by the abbreviation ALU) is the subsystem that performs such mathematical and logical operations as addition, subtraction, and comparison for equality. Although they can be conceptually viewed as separate components, in all modern machines the ALU and the control unit (discussed in the next section) have become fully integrated into a single component called the **processor**. However, for reasons of clarity and convenience, we will describe the functions of the ALU and the control unit separately.

The ALU is made up of three parts: the registers, the interconnections between components, and the ALU circuitry. A **register** is a storage cell that holds the operands of an arithmetic operation and that, when the operation is complete, holds its result. Registers are quite similar to the random access memory cells described in the previous section, with the following minor differences:

- They do not have a numeric memory address but are accessed by a special **register designator** such as A, X, or R0.

- They can be accessed much more quickly than regular memory cells. Because there are few registers (typically, one or two dozen), it is reasonable to utilize the expensive circuitry needed to make the fetch and store operations 2 to 10 times faster than regular memory cells of which there may be millions.

- They are not used for general-purpose storage but for specific purposes such as holding the operands for an upcoming arithmetic computation.

For example, an ALU might have three special registers called A, B, and C. Registers A and B would hold the two input operands, and register C would hold the result. This organization is diagrammed in Figure 5.10.

In most cases, however, three registers would not be nearly enough to hold all the values that we might need. Therefore, a typical ALU might have 16 to 32 registers. To see why this many ALU registers are needed, let's take a look at what happens during the evaluation of the expression

$$(a + b) \times (c - d)$$

After we compute the expression $(a + b)$, it would be nice to keep this sum temporarily in a high-speed ALU register while evaluating the second expression $(c - d)$. Of course, we could always store the result of $(a + b)$ in a memory cell, but keeping it in a register allows the computer to fetch it more quickly when it is ready to complete the computation. In general, the more registers available in the ALU, the faster programs run.

A more typical ALU organization is illustrated in Figure 5.11, which shows an ALU with 16 registers designated R0 to R15. Any of the 16 ALU registers in Figure 5.11 could be used to hold the operands of the computation, and any register could be used to store the result.

FIGURE 5.10
Three-Register ALU Organization

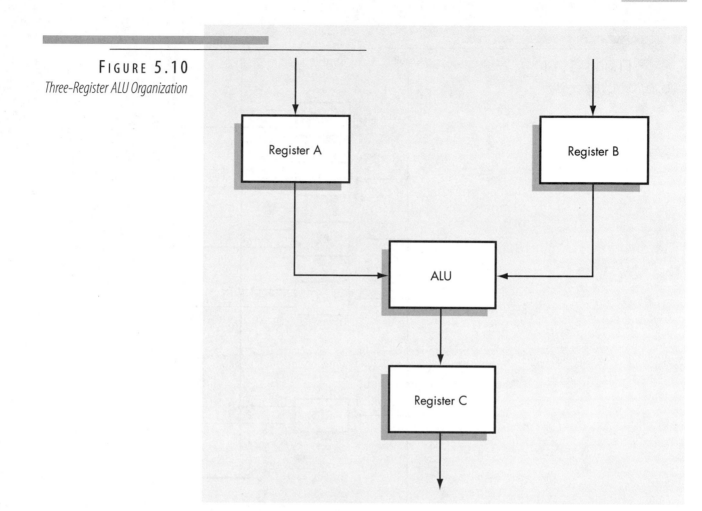

To perform an arithmetic operation with the ALU of Figure 5.11, we first move the operands from memory to the ALU registers. Then we specify which register holds the left operand by connecting that register to the data path called "Left." In computer science terminology, a data path for electrical signals (think of this as a wire) is termed a **bus**. We then specify which register to use for the right operand by connecting it to the bus labeled "Right." (Like RAM, registers also use nondestructive fetch, so, when it is needed, the value is only copied to the ALU. It is still in the register.) The ALU is enabled to perform the desired operation, and the answer is sent to any of the 16 registers along the bus labeled "Result." (The destructive store principle says that the previous contents of the destination register will be lost.) If desired, the result can be moved from an ALU register back into memory for longer-term storage.

FIGURE 5.11

Multiregister ALU Organization

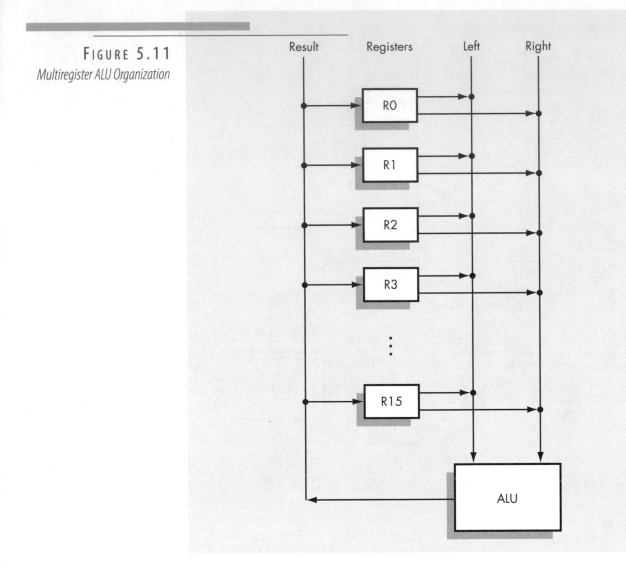

The final component of the ALU to be described is the **ALU circuitry** itself. These are the circuits that carry out such operations as

$a + b$ (Figure 4.22) $a = b$ (Figure 4.18)

$a - b$ $a < b$

$a \times b$ $a > b$

$a \div b$ $a \cdot b$ ($\cdot$ = AND)

Chapter 4 showed how circuits for these operations can be constructed from the three basic logic gates AND, OR, and NOT. The primary issue now is how to select the desired operation from among all the possibilities for a given ALU. For example, how do we tell an ALU that can perform the preceding eight operations that we want only the results of the one operation $a - b$?

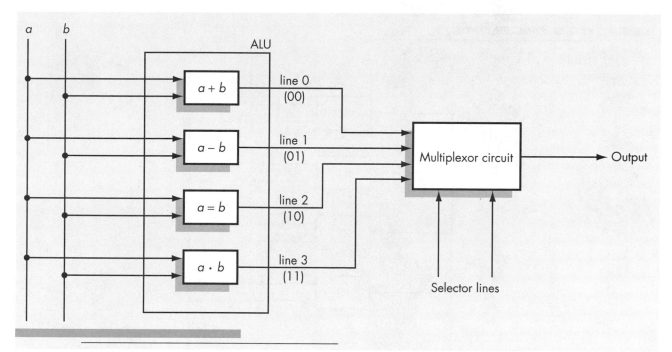

FIGURE 5.12

Using a Multiplexor Circuit to
Select the Proper ALU Result

One possible approach is to use the **multiplexor** control circuit introduced in Chapter 4 and shown in Figure 4.23. Remember that a multiplexor is a circuit with 2^N input lines numbered 0 to $2^N - 1$, N selector lines, and 1 output line. The selector lines are interpreted as a single binary number from 0 to $2^N - 1$, and the input line corresponding to this number has its value placed on the single output line.

Let's imagine for simplicity that we have an ALU that can perform four functions instead of eight. The four functions are $a + b$, $a - b$, $a = b$, and $a \cdot b$, and these operations are numbered 0, 1, 2, and 3, respectively (00, 01, 10, and 11 in binary). Finally, let's assume that every time the ALU is enabled and given values for a and b, it automatically performs all four possible operations rather than just the desired one. These four outputs can be input to a multiplexor circuit as shown in Figure 5.12.

Now place on the selector lines the identification number of the one operation whose output we want to keep. The result of the desired operation appears on the output line, and the other three answers are discarded. Thus, for example, to select the output of the subtraction operation, we input the binary value 01 (decimal 1) on the selector lines. This puts the output of the subtraction circuit on the output line of the multiplexor. The outputs of the addition, comparison, and AND circuits are discarded.

The design philosophy in building an ALU is not to figure out how to perform only the correct operation. It is to have *every* circuit "do its thing" and then select only the desired answer.

Putting Figures 5.11 and 5.12 together produces the overall organization of the ALU of the Von Neumann architecture. This model is shown in Figure 5.13.

FIGURE 5.13

Overall ALU Organization

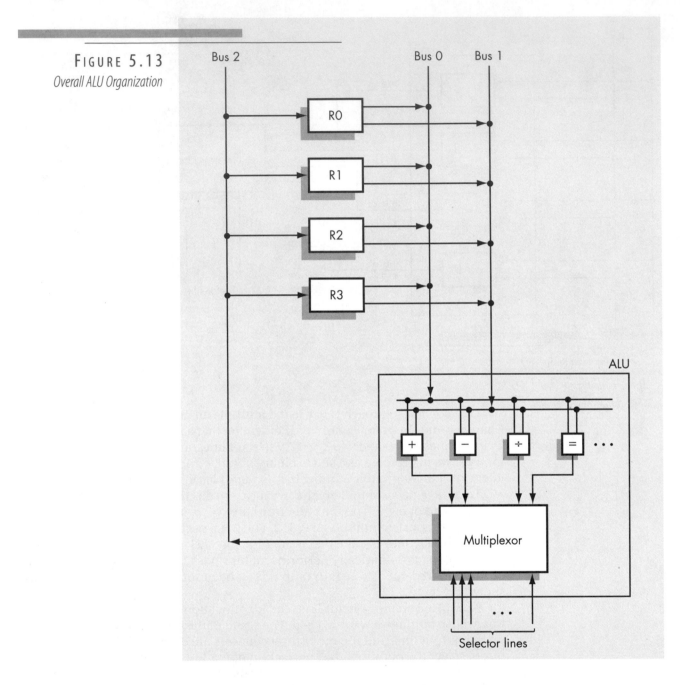

5.2.4 THE CONTROL UNIT

The most fundamental characteristic of the Von Neumann architecture is the idea of a **stored program**—a sequence of machine language instructions stored as binary values in memory. It is the task of the **control unit** to 1) **fetch** from memory the next instruction to be executed, 2) **decode** it—that is, deter-

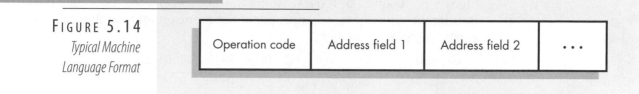

FIGURE 5.14
Typical Machine Language Format

Operation code	Address field 1	Address field 2	. . .

mine what is to be done, and 3) **execute** it by issuing the appropriate command to the ALU, memory, and I/O controllers. These three steps are repeated over and over until we reach the last instruction in the program, typically something called HALT, STOP, or QUIT.

Thus to understand the behavior of the control unit, we must first investigate the characteristics of machine language instructions.

MACHINE LANGUAGE INSTRUCTIONS.   The instructions that can be decoded and executed by the control unit of a computer are in a representation called **machine language**. Instructions in this language are expressed in binary, and a typical format is shown in Figure 5.14.

The **operation code** field (referred to by the shorthand phrase **op code**) is a unique unsigned-integer code assigned to each machine language operation recognized by the hardware. For example, 0 could be an ADD, 1 could be a COMPARE, and so on. If the operation code field contains k bits, then the maximum number of machine language operation codes is 2^k.

The **address field(s)** are the memory addresses of the values on which this operation will work. If our computer has a maximum of 2^N memory cells, then each address field must be N bits wide to enable us to address every cell. That is because it takes N binary digits to represent all addresses in the range 0 to $2^N - 1$. The number of address fields in an instruction typically varies from 0 to 3, depending on what the operation is and how many operands it needs to do its work. For instance, an instruction to add the contents of memory cell X to memory cell Y requires at least two addresses, X and Y. It could require three if the result were stored in a location different from either operand. In contrast, an instruction that tests the contents of memory cell X to see whether it is negative needs only a single address field, the location of cell X.

To see what this might produce in terms of machine language instructions, let's see what the following hypothetical instruction would actually look like when stored in memory.

ADD X,Y   Add the contents of addresses X and Y and put the sum back into cell Y

Let's assume that the op code for ADD is a decimal 9, cells X and Y correspond to addresses 99 and 100 (decimal), and the format of instructions is

op code	address 1	address 2
8	16	16

bits →

A decimal 9, in 8-bit binary, is 00001001. Address 99, when converted to 16-bit binary, is 0000000001100011. Address 100 is 1 greater: 0000000001100100. Putting these values together produces the representation of the instruction as it would appear in memory:

$$\underbrace{00001001}_{op\ code}\ \underbrace{0000000001100011}_{address\ 1}\ \underbrace{0000000001100100}_{address\ 2}$$

Somewhat cryptic to a person, but easily understood by a control unit.

The set of all operations that can be executed by a processor is called its **instruction set**, and the choice of exactly what operations to include or exclude from the instruction set is one of the most important and difficult decisions in the design of a new computer. There is no universal agreement on this issue, and the instruction sets of processors from different vendors are completely different. This is one reason why a computer that uses a Macintosh G3 processor cannot execute programs written for a system that contains an Intel Pentium II. The operation codes and address fields that these two processors recognize, understand, and carry out are different and completely incompatible.

The machine language operations on most machines are quite elementary, and each one typically performs a very small and simple task. The power of a processor comes not from the sophistication of operations in its instruction set but from the fact that it can execute each instruction very quickly, typically in a few billionths of a second.

In fact, the trend in newer processors is to make the instruction sets as small and as simple as possible. These machines are called **reduced instruction set computers** or **RISC machines**. This approach minimizes the amount of hardware circuitry (gates and transistors) needed to build a processor. The extra space on the chip can be used for devices to make the remaining instructions execute more quickly. A program for a RISC machine may require more instructions to solve a problem (because each one does only a small step), but this is more than compensated for by the fact that each instruction operates much faster so the overall running time is less. In the 1970s and 1980s a typical processor might have 200–400 machine language instructions in its instruction set. These processors are called **complex instruction set computers**, or **CISC machines**. Today, a modern RISC processor (such as the PowerPC or the DEC Alpha) may have as few as 30–50 unique instructions, but it is likely to run a program 1½ to 2 times faster than the CISC design. It appears that in the case of instruction sets, "small is beautiful."

A little later in this chapter we will present an instruction set for a hypothetical computer in order to examine how machine language instructions are executed by a control unit. To maximize the clarity of our discussion, we will not display these instructions in binary, as we did earlier. Instead, we will write out the operation code in English (for example, ADD, COMPARE, MOVE), use the capital letters X, Y, and Z to symbolically represent binary memory addresses, and use the letter R to represent an ALU register. Remember, however, that this notation is just for convenience. All machine language instructions are stored internally using binary representation.

Machine language instructions can be grouped into four basic classes called data transfer, arithmetic, compare, and branch.

1. **Data Transfer.** These are operations that move information between or within the different components of the computer—for example,

> Memory cell $\rightarrow$ ALU register
>
> ALU register $\rightarrow$ memory cell
>
> One memory cell $\rightarrow$ another memory cell
>
> One ALU register $\rightarrow$ another ALU register

All data transfer instructions follow the nondestructive fetch/destructive store principle described earlier. That is, the contents of the **source cell** (where it now is) are never destroyed, only copied. The contents of the **destination cell** (where it is going) are overwritten, and its previous contents are lost.

Examples of data transfer operations include

Operation		Meaning
LOAD	X	Load register R with the contents of memory cell X.
STORE	X	Store the contents of register R into memory cell X.
MOVE	X, Y	Copy the contents of memory cell X into memory cell Y.

2. **Arithmetic.** These are operations that cause the arithmetic/logic unit to perform a computation. Typically, they include arithmetic operations like $+$, $-$, $\times$, and $/$, as well as logical operations such as AND, OR, and NOT. Depending on the instruction set, the operands may reside in memory or they may be in an ALU register.

Examples of possible formats for arithmetic operations include the following. (*Note:* The notation CON(X) means the contents of memory address X.)

Operation		Meaning
ADD	X, Y, Z	Add the contents of memory cell X to the contents of memory cell Y and put the result into memory cell Z. This is called a **three-address instruction**, and it performs the operation $$CON(Z) = CON(X) + CON(Y)$$
ADD	X, Y	Add the contents of memory cell X to the contents of memory cell Y. Put the result into memory cell Y. This is called a **two-address instruction**, and it performs the operation $$CON(Y) = CON(X) + CON(Y)$$
ADD	X	Add the contents of memory cell X to the contents of register R. Put the result into register R. This is called a **one-address instruction**, and it performs the operation $$R = CON(X) + R$$ (Of course, R must be loaded with the proper value before executing the instruction).

Other arithmetic operations such as SUBTRACT, MULTIPLY, DIVIDE, AND, and OR could be structured in a similar fashion.

3. **Compare.** These operations compare two values and set an indicator on the basis of the results of the compare. Most Von Neumann machines have a special set of bits (or a special register) inside the processor called **condition codes**, and it is these bits that are set by the compare operations. For example, let's assume there are three 1-bit condition codes called GT, EQ, and LT that stand for greater than, equal to, and less than, respectively. The operation

COMPARE   X, Y   Compare the contents of memory cell X to the contents of memory cell Y and set the condition codes accordingly.

would set the condition codes in the following way:

Condition	How the Condition Codes Are Set		
CON (X) > CON (Y)	GT = 1	EQ = 0	LT = 0
CON (X) = CON (Y)	GT = 0	EQ = 1	LT = 0
CON (X) < CON (Y)	GT = 0	EQ = 0	LT = 1

4. **Branch.** The normal mode of operation of a Von Neumann machine is *sequential*. After completing the instruction in address i, the control unit executes the instruction in address $i + 1$. (*Note:* If each instruction occupies k memory cells rather than 1, then after finishing the instruction starting in address i, the control unit executes the instruction starting in address $i + k$. In the following discussions, we assume for simplicity that each instruction occupies one memory cell.) The **branch instructions** alter this normal sequential flow of control. Typically, the decision whether to branch is based on the current settings of the condition codes. Thus a branch instruction is almost always preceded by either a compare instruction or some other instruction that sets the condition codes. Typical branch instructions include

Operation		Meaning
JUMP	X	Take the next instruction unconditionally from memory cell X.
JUMPGT	X	If the GT indicator is a 1, take the next instruction from memory cell X. Otherwise, take the next instruction from the next sequential location.

(JUMPEQ and JUMPLT work similarly on the other two condition codes.)

| JUMPGE | X | If *either* the GT or the EQ indicator is a 1, take the next instruction from memory location X. Otherwise, take the next instruction from the next sequential location. |

(JUMPLE and JUMPNEQ work in a similar fashion.)

| HALT | | Stop program execution. Don't go on to the next instruction. |

These are some of the typical instructions that a Von Neumann computer can decode and execute. (One of the challenge questions at the end of this chapter asks you to investigate the instruction set of a real processor found inside a modern computer and compare it with what we have described here.)

The instructions that we have presented are quite simple and easy to understand. The power of a Von Neumann computer comes not from having thousands of complex built-in instructions but from the ability to combine a great

FIGURE 5.15

Examples of Simple Machine Language Instruction Sequences

Address	Contents
100	value of *a*
101	value of *b*
102	value of *c*

Algorithmic Notation   Machine Language Instruction Sequences

Address	Contents	(Commentary)
	⋮	

1. Set *a* to the value *b* + *c*

Address	Contents	Commentary
50	LOAD 101	Put the value of *b* into register R.
51	ADD 102	Add *c* to register R. It now holds *b* + *c*.
52	STORE 100	Store the contents of register R into *a*.

2. If *a* > *b* then

    set *c* to the value *a*

Else

    set *c* to the value *b*

Address	Contents	Commentary
50	COMPARE 100, 101	Compare *a* and *b* and set condition codes.
51	JUMPGT 54	Go to location 54 if *a* > *b*.
52	MOVE 101, 102	Get here if *a* ≤ *b*, so move *b* into *c*
53	JUMP 55	and skip the next instruction.
54	MOVE 100, 102	Move *a* into *c*.
55	• • •	Next statement begins here.

number of simple instructions into large, complex programs that can be executed extremely fast. Figure 5.15 shows examples of how these simple machine language instructions can be combined to carry out some of the high-level algorithmic operations first introduced in Level 1 and shown in Figure 2.6. (The examples assume that the variables *a*, *b*, and *c* are stored in memory locations 100, 101, and 102, respectively, and that the instructions occupy one cell each and are located in memory locations 50, 51, 52, ...)

PRACTICE PROBLEMS

Assume that the variables a, b, c, and d are stored in memory locations 100, 101, 102, and 103, respectively. Using any of the sample machine language instructions given in this section, translate the following pseudocode operations into machine language instruction sequences. Have your instruction sequences begin in memory location 50.

1. Set a to the value $b + c + d$

2. If $(a = b)$ then set c to the value of d

3. If $(a \leq b)$ then set c to the value of d
   Else
        set c to the value of $2d$ (that is, $d + d$)

4. Initialize a to the value d
   Repeat until $a > c$
        Set a to the value $(a + b)$
   End of the loop

Don't worry if these "mini-programs" are a little confusing. We treat the topic of machine language programming in more detail in the next chapter. For now, we simply want you to know what machine language instructions look like so that we can see how to build a control unit to carry out their functions.

CONTROL UNIT REGISTERS AND CIRCUITS.   It is the task of the control unit to fetch and execute instructions of the type shown in Figures 5.14 and 5.15. To accomplish this task, the control unit relies on two special registers called the **Program Counter (PC)** and the **Instruction Register (IR)** and on an **instruction decoder circuit**. The organization of these three components is shown in Figure 5.16.

The program counter holds the address of the *next* instruction to be executed. It is like a "pointer" specifying which address in memory the control unit must go to in order to get the next instruction. To get that instruction, the control unit sends the contents of the PC to the MAR in memory and executes the Fetch(address) operation described in Section 5.2.1. For example, if the PC holds the value 73 (in binary, of course), then when the current instruction is finished, the control unit will send the value 73 to the MAR and fetch the instruction contained in cell 73. The PC gets incremented by 1 after each fetch, because the normal mode of execution in a Von Neumann machine is sequential. (Again, we are assuming that each instruction occupies one cell. If an instruction occupied k cells, then the PC would be incremented by k.) Therefore, the PC frequently has its own incrementor (+1) circuit to allow this operation to be done quickly and efficiently.

The **instruction register (IR)** holds a copy of the instruction fetched from memory. The IR holds both the op code portion of the instruction, abbreviated IR_{op}, and the address(es), abbreviated IR_{addr}.

To determine what instruction is in the IR, the op code portion of the IR must be decoded using an **instruction decoder**. This is exactly the same type of

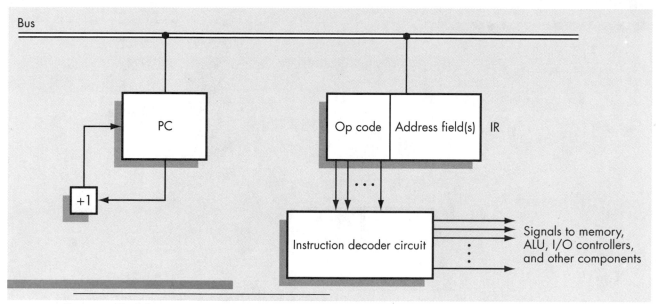

Bus

PC

+1

Op code | Address field(s) | IR

• • •

Instruction decoder circuit

Signals to memory, ALU, I/O controllers, and other components

FIGURE 5.16

Organization of the Control Unit Registers and Circuits

decoder circuit discussed in Section 4.5 and used in the construction of the memory unit (Figure 5.7). The k bits of the op code field of the IR are sent to the instruction decoder, which interprets them as a numerical value between 0 and $2^k - 1$. Exactly one of the 2^k output lines of the decoder will be set to a 1—specifically, the output line whose identification number matches the operation code of this instruction. Figure 5.17 shows a decoder that accepts a 3-bit op code field and has $2^3 = 8$ output lines, one for each of the eight possible machine language operations.

The three bits of the IR_{op} are fed into the instruction decoder, and they are interpreted as a value from 000 (0) to 111 (7). If the bits are, for example, 000, then line 000 in Figure 5.17 will be set to a 1. This line enables the circuitry that will carry out the ADD operation because the operation code for ADD is 000. The appearance of a 1 on this line will cause the following four things to happen: 1) fetch the two operands of the add and send them to the ALU, 2) have the ALU perform all of its possible operations, 3) select the output of the adder circuit, discarding all others, and 4) move the result of the add to the correct location. These are the four steps needed to carry out the ADD operation.

If the op code bits are 001 instead, then line 001 in Figure 5.17 will be set to a 1. This time the LOAD circuitry will be enabled, because the operation code for LOAD is the binary value 001. Instead of performing the previous four steps, the hardware will carry out the following three operations: 1) send the value of IR_{addr} to the memory unit, 2) fetch the contents of that address and put it in the MDR, and 3) copy the contents of the MDR into ALU register R. This is what is needed to perform a LOAD operation correctly.

For every one of the 2^k machine language operations in our instruction set, there will exist the circuitry needed to carry out, step by step, the function of that operation. The instruction decoder has 2^k output lines, and each output line enables the circuitry that performs the desired operation.

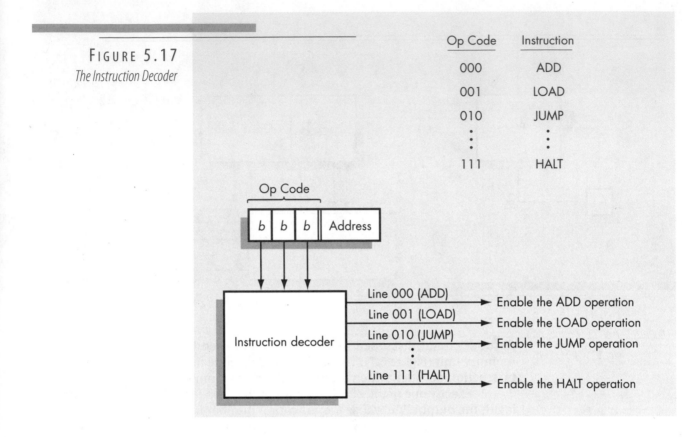

FIGURE 5.17
The Instruction Decoder

5.2.5 PUTTING ALL THE PIECES TOGETHER

We have now described each of the components of the Von Neumann architecture:

- Memory (Figure 5.7)
- Input/output (Figure 5.9)
- ALU (Figure 5.13)
- Control unit (Figures 5.16, 5.17)

This section puts all these pieces together and shows how the entire model functions. The overall organization of a Von Neumann computer is shown in Figure 5.18. Although highly simplified, this diagram is quite similar in structure to virtually every computer ever built! (A summary of the technical characteristics and performance measures of just about every processor in the marketplace is maintained by the "Chip Information Center" at the University of California–Berkeley. Its Web address is http://infopad.EECS.Berkeley.Edu/CIC.)

In order to see how the Von Neumann machine of Figure 5.18 would execute instructions, let's pick a hypothetical instruction set for our system. The instruction set that we will use is shown in Figure 5.19. We will use the same instruction

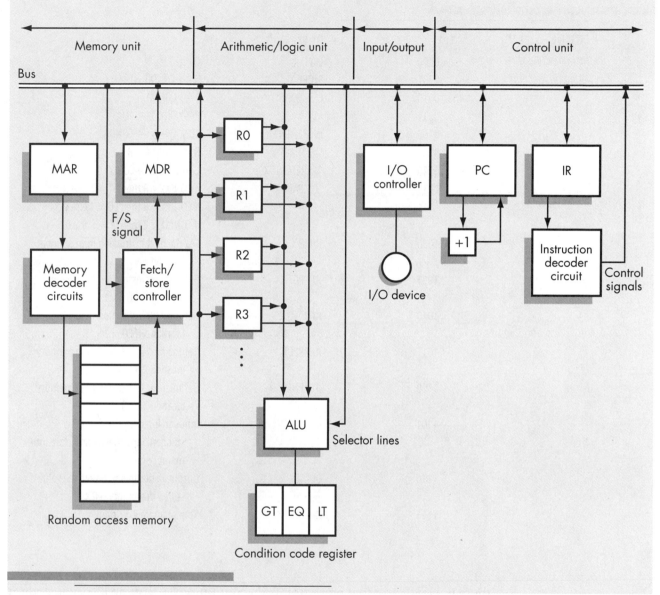

FIGURE 5.18

The Organization of a Von Neumann Computer

set in the laboratory experiences for this chapter and again in Chapter 6 when we introduce and study assembly languages. (Reminder: CON(X) means the contents of memory cell X, R stands for an ALU register, and GT, EQ, and LT are condition codes that have the value of 1 for ON and 0 for OFF.)

The execution of a program on the computer shown in Figure 5.18 proceeds in three phases called **fetch**, **decode**, and **execute**. These three steps are repeated for every instruction until either the computer executes a HALT instruction or

FIGURE 5.19

Instruction Set for Our
Von Neumann Machine

BINARY OP CODE	OPERATION	MEANING
0000	LOAD X	CON(X) → R
0001	STORE X	R → CON(X)
0010	CLEAR X	0 → CON(X)
0011	ADD X	R + CON(X) → R
0100	INCREMENT X	CON(X) + 1 → CON(X)
0101	SUBTRACT X	R − CON(X) → R
0110	DECREMENT X	CON(X) − 1 → CON(X)
0111	COMPARE X	if CON(X) > R then GT = 1 else 0
		if CON(X) = R then EQ = 1 else 0
		if CON(X) < R then LT = 1 else 0
1000	JUMP X	Get the next instruction from memory location X.
1001	JUMPGT X	Get the next instruction from memory location X if GT = 1.
1010	JUMPEQ X	Get the next instruction from memory location X if EQ = 1.
1011	JUMPLT X	Get the next instruction from memory location X if LT = 1.
1100	JUMPNEQ X	Get the next instruction from memory location X if EQ = 0.
1101	IN X	Input an integer value from the standard input device and store into memory cell X.
1110	OUT X	Output, in decimal notation, the value stored in memory cell X.
1111	HALT	Stop program execution.

there is a fatal error that prevents it from continuing (such as an illegal op code, a nonexistent memory address, or division by zero). Algorithmically the process can be described as follows:

Repeat until either a HALT instruction or a fatal error

Fetch phase

Decode phase

Execute phase

End of the loop

To describe the behavior of our Von Neumann computer during each of these three phases, we use the following notation:

CON(A)   The *con*tents of memory cell A. An instruction occupies 1 cell.

$A \rightarrow B$ Send the value stored in register A to register B. The following abbreviations refer to the special registers and functional units of the Von Neumann architecture introduced in this chapter:

PC   The program counter

MAR   The memory address register

MDR   The memory data register

IR   The instruction register, which is further divided into IR_{op} and IR_{addr}

ALU   The arithmetic/logic unit

R   Any ALU register

GT, EQ, LT The condition codes of the ALU

$+1$ A special increment unit attached to the PC

FETCH   Initiate a memory fetch operation (that is, send an F signal on the F/S control line of Figure 5.18).

STORE   Initiate a memory store operation (that is, send an S signal on the F/S control line of Figure 5.18).

ADD   Instruct the ALU to select the output of the adder circuit (that is, place the code for ADD on the ALU selector lines shown in Figure 5.18).

SUBTRACT Instruct the ALU to select the output of the subtract circuit (that is, place the code for SUBTRACT on the ALU selector lines shown in Figure 5.18).

A. *Fetch Phase.* During the fetch phase, the control unit gets the next instruction from memory and moves it into the IR. The fetch phase is the same for every instruction and consists of the following four steps.

1. $PC \rightarrow MAR$ Send the address in the PC to the MAR register.

2. FETCH   Initiate a fetch operation using the address in the MAR. The contents of that cell are placed in the MDR.

3. $MDR \rightarrow IR$ Move the instruction in the MDR to the instruction register so that we are ready to decode it during the next phase.

4. $PC + 1 \rightarrow PC$ Send the contents of the PC to the incrementor and put it back. This points the PC to the next instruction.

The control unit now has the current instruction in the IR and has updated the program counter so that it will correctly fetch the next instruction when the execution of this instruction is completed. It is ready to begin decoding and executing the current instruction.

B. *Decode Phase.* First it must decode the instruction. This is simple because all that needs to be done is to send the op code portion of the IR to the instruction decoder, which determines its type. The op code is the 4-bit binary value in the first column of Figure 5.19.

    1. $IR_{op} \rightarrow$ instruction decoder

The instruction decoder will generate the proper control signals to activate the circuitry to carry out this particular instruction.

C. *Execution Phase.* The actions that occur during the execution phase are obviously different for each instruction in the instruction set. The control unit circuitry generates the necessary sequence of control signals and data transfer signals to the other units (ALU, memory, and I/O) to accomplish the purpose of the instruction. The following are examples of what signals and transfers would take place during the execution phase of some of the instructions in Figure 5.19 using the Von Neumann model shown in Figure 5.18.

a) *LOAD X*   *Load register R from memory cell X.*
   1. $IR_{addr} \rightarrow$ MAR   Send address X (currently in IR_{addr}) to the MAR.
   2. FETCH   Fetch the contents of cell X and place that value in the MDR.
   3. MDR $\rightarrow$ R   Copy the contents of the MDR into register R.

b) *STORE X*   *Store register R into memory cell X.*
   1. $IR_{addr} \rightarrow$ MAR   Send address X (currently in IR_{addr}) to the MAR.
   2. R $\rightarrow$ MDR   Send the contents of register R to the MDR.
   3. STORE   Store the value in the MDR into memory cell X.

c) *ADD X*   *Add the contents of cell X and register R and put the result back into register R.*
   1. $IR_{addr} \rightarrow$ MAR   Send address X (currently in IR_{addr}) to the MAR.
   2. FETCH   Fetch the contents of cell X and place it in the MDR.
   3. MDR $\rightarrow$ ALU   Send the two operands of the ADD to the ALU.
   4. R $\rightarrow$ ALU
   5. ADD   Activate the ALU and select the output of the add circuit as the desired result.
   6. ALU $\rightarrow$ R   Copy the selected result into the R register.

d) *JUMP X*   *Jump to the instruction located in memory location X.*
   1. $IR_{addr} \rightarrow$ PC   Send address X to the PC so the instruction stored there will be fetched during the next fetch phase.

e) *COMPARE X*   *Compare to see whether CON(X) > R, CON(X) = R, or CON(X) < R, and set condition codes to GT, EQ, and LT, respectively. (Assume all codes are initially 0.)*
   1. $IR_{addr} \rightarrow$ MAR   Send address X to the MAR.
   2. FETCH   Fetch the contents of cell X and place it in the MDR.
   3. MDR $\rightarrow$ ALU   Send the contents of address X and register R to
   4. R $\rightarrow$ ALU   the ALU.
   5. SUBTRACT   Evaluate CON(X) − R. Don't save the result. Do it only so that the condition codes are set. If CON(X) − R > 0, then CON(X) > R and set GT to 1. If CON(X) − R = 0, then they are equal and set EQ to 1. If CON(X) − R < 0, then CON(X) < R and set LT to 1.

f) *JUMPGT   X*   *If GT condition code is 1, jump to the instruction in location X. Otherwise, continue to the next instruction.*

　　　1. IF GT = 1   Send the address X to the PC only if the GT condition code is set to 1. Other-
　　　　　THEN $IR_{addr} \rightarrow PC$ wise, nothing happens.

These are six examples of the sequence of signals and transfers that occur during the execution phase of the fetch/decode/execute cycle. There will be a unique sequence of actions for each of the 16 instructions in the sample instruction set of Figure 5.19 and for the 30–300 instructions in the instruction set of a typical Von Neumann computer. When the execution of one instruction is done, the control unit fetches the next instruction, starting the cycle all over again. That is the fundamental sequential behavior of the Von Neumann architecture.

These six examples again illustrate the concept of abstraction at work. In Chapter 4 we built complex arithmetic/logic circuits to do operations like addition and comparison. Using these circuits, Chapter 5 described a computer that can execute machine language instructions such as ADD X and COMPARE X,Y. A machine language instruction such as ADD X is a complicated concept, but it is quite a bit easier to understand than the enormously detailed full adder circuit shown in Figure 4.22, which contains 800 gates and 1,504 transistors. Abstraction has allowed us to replace a complex sequence of gate-level manipulations with the single machine language command ADD, which does addition without our having to know how—the very essence of abstraction.

Well, why should we stop here? Machine language commands, though better than hardware, are hardly user-friendly. (Some might even call them "user-intimidating.") Programming in binary and writing sequences of instructions such as

010110100001111010100001

is cumbersome, confusing, and very error-prone. Why not take these machine language instructions and make them more user-oriented and user-friendly? Why not give them features that allow us to write correct, reliable, and efficient programs more easily? Why not develop **user-oriented programming languages** designed for people, not machines? This is the next level of abstraction in our hierarchy, and we introduce that important concept in Level 3 of the text.

Laboratory Experience 9

The next laboratory experience introduces a software package that simulates the behavior of a Von Neumann computer. It will give you a chance to work with and observe the behavior of a Von Neumann machine quite similar to the one shown in Figure 5.18. Our simulated computer contains the same functional units introduced in this section, including memory, registers, arithmetic/logic unit, and control unit, and it uses the instruction set shown in Figure 5.19. The simulator will allow you to observe the step-by-step execution of machine language instructions and watch the flow of information that occurs during the fetch, decode, and execute phases. It will also allow you to write and execute your own machine language programs.

5.3   HISTORICAL OVERVIEW OF COMPUTER SYSTEMS DEVELOPMENT

This section takes a look back at the historical development of the Von Neumann architecture and discusses what the future might hold for computer systems. The appearance of some technologies, such as the telephone, the light bulb, and the first heavier-than-air flight, can be traced directly to a single place, a specific individual, and an exact instant in time. Examples include the flight of Orville and Wilbur Wright on December 17, 1903 in Kitty Hawk, North Carolina, and the famous phrase "Mr. Watson, come here, I need you" uttered by Alexander Graham Bell over the first telephone on June 2, 1875.

Computers were not like that. They did not appear in a specific room on a given day as the creation of some individual genius. Quite the contrary, the ideas that became part of the design of the first computers evolved over a period of hundreds of years, with contributions coming from many people, each building on and extending the work of earlier discoverers. This first section highlights some of the major events that led to the development of the modern computer system.

5.3.1 THE EARLY PERIOD: UP TO 1940

If this were a discussion of the history of mathematics and arithmetic instead of computer science, it would begin 3,000 years ago with the early work of the Greeks, Egyptians, Babylonians, and Persians. All these cultures were interested in and made important contributions to the fields of mathematics, logic, and numerical computation. For example, the Greeks developed the fields of geometry and logic; the Babylonians and Egyptians developed numerical methods for generating square roots, multiplication tables, and trigonometric tables used by early sailors; and in the ninth century the Persians developed the concept of algorithmic problem solving.

The first half of the seventeenth century saw a number of important developments related to automating and simplifying the drudgery of arithmetic computation. (The motivation for this work appears to be the sudden increase in scientific research during the sixteenth and seventeenth centuries in the areas of astronomy, chemistry, and medicine. This work required the solution of larger and more complex mathematical problems.) In 1614 the Scotsman John Napier invented **logarithms** as a way to simplify difficult mathematical computations. The early seventeenth century also witnessed the development of a number of new and quite powerful mechanical devices designed to help reduce the burden of arithmetic. The first **slide rule** appeared around 1622. In 1642 the French philosopher and mathematician Blaise Pascal designed and built one of the first **mechanical calculators** (named **Pascaline**) that could do addition and subtraction. A model of this early calculating device is shown in Figure 5.20.

The famous German mathematician Gottfried Leibnitz (who, along with Isaac Newton, was one of the inventors of the calculus) was also excited by the idea of automatic computation. He studied the work of Pascal and others, and in 1694 he constructed a mechanical calculator called **Leibnitz's Wheel** that

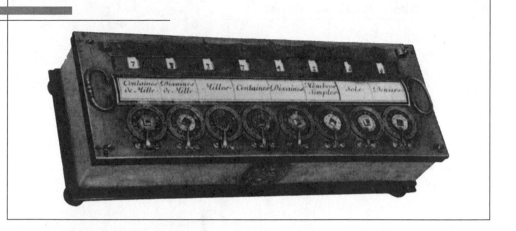

FIGURE 5.20

Pascaline. One of the Earliest Mechanical Calculators

could do not only addition and subtraction but multiplication and division as well. Both Pascal's and Leibnitz's machines used interlocking mechanical cogs and gears to store numbers and perform basic arithmetic operations. Considering the state of technology available to Pascal, Leibnitz, and others in the seventeenth century, these first calculating machines were truly mechanical wonders.

These early developments in mathematics and arithmetic were important milestones because they demonstrated how mechanization could simplify and speed up numerical computation. For example, Leibnitz's Wheel enabled seventeenth-century mathematicians to generate tables of mathematical functions many times faster than had previously been possible by hand. (It is hard to believe in this modern high-tech society, but in the seventeenth century the generation of a table of logarithms could represent a *lifetime's* effort of one person!) However, these early machines were not part of computer science, and the slide rule and mechanical calculators of Pascal and Leibnitz, though certainly impressive devices, were not computers. Specifically, they lacked two fundamental characteristics:

- They did not have a *memory* where information could be stored in machine-readable form.

- They were not *programmable.* A person could not provide *in advance* a sequence of instructions that could be executed by the device without manual intervention.

The first actual "computing device" to include both of these features was, surprisingly, not created for the purposes of mathematical computations. Rather, it was a *loom* used for the manufacture of rugs and clothing. It was developed in 1801 by the Frenchman Joseph Jacquard. Jacquard wanted to automate the weaving process, at the time a painfully slow and cumbersome task in which each separate row of the pattern had to be set up by the weaver and an apprentice. Because of this, anything but the most basic items of clothing was beyond the means of the average person.

Jacquard designed an automated loom that used **punched cards** to create the desired pattern. If there was a hole in the card in a particular location, then a hook could pass through the card, grasp a warp thread, and raise it to allow a

FIGURE 5.21
Drawing of the Jacquard Loom

second thread to pass underneath. If there was no hole in the card, then the hook could not pass through, and the thread would pass over the warp. Depending on whether the thread passed above or below the warp, a specific design would be created. Each punched card described one row of the pattern. Jacquard connected the cards and fed them through his loom, and it automatically sequenced from card to card, weaving the desired pattern. A drawing of the **Jacquard loom** is shown in Figure 5.21.

Jacquard's loom represented an enormously important stage in the development of computers. Not only was it the first programmable device, but it also showed how the knowledge of a human expert (in this case a master weaver) could be captured in machine-readable form and used to control a machine that accomplished the same task automatically. Once the program was created, the expert was no longer needed. The lowliest apprentice could load the cards into the loom, turn it on, and produce a finished, high-quality product, over and over again.

This development was so frightening to the craft guilds of the early nineteenth century that in 1811 it led to the formation of a group called the **Luddites**. The Luddites were violently opposed to this new manufacturing technology, and they burned down factories that attempted to use it. The movement lasted only a few years and its leaders were all jailed, but the name lives on today as a pejorative term for any group that is frightened and angered by the latest developments in any branch of science and technology, including computers.

One of the major contributions of these computing pioneers was the enormous influence they had on designers and inventors who came after them. One person strongly influenced by this early work was a mathematics professor at Cambridge University named Charles Babbage. Babbage was much interested in automatic computation. In 1823 he extended the ideas of Pascal and Leibnitz and constructed a working model of the largest and most sophisticated mechanical calculator of its time. This machine, called the **Difference Engine**, could do addition, subtraction, multiplication, and division to 6 significant digits, and it could solve polynomial equations and other complex mathematical problems as well. Babbage tried to construct a larger model of the Difference Engine that would be capable of working to an accuracy of 20 significant digits, but after 12 years of work he had to give up his quest. The technology available in the 1820s and 1830s was not sufficiently advanced to manufacture cogs and gears to the precise tolerances his design required. Like Galileo's helicopter or Jules Verne's atomic submarine, Babbage's ideas were fundamentally sound but years ahead of their time. (Interestingly, in 1991 the London Museum of Science, using Babbage's original plans, built an actual working model of the Difference Engine. It was 7 feet high, was 11 feet wide, weighed 3 tons, and had 4,000 moving parts. It worked exactly as Babbage had planned.)

However, Babbage did not stop his investigations with the Difference Engine. In the 1830s he designed a more powerful and general-purpose computational machine that could be configured to solve a much wider range of numerical problems. His machine had four basic components: a **mill** to perform the arithmetic manipulation of data, a **store** to hold the data, an **operator** to process automatically the instructions on punched cards (Babbage was familiar with the work of Jacquard), and an **output unit** to put the results onto punched cards. Although it would be about 110 years before a "real" computer would be built, Babbage's proposed machine, called the **Analytic Engine**, is amazingly similar in design to a modern computer. The four components of the Analytic Engine are virtually identical in function to the four major components of today's computer systems:

Babbage's Term	*Modern Terminology*
mill	arithmetic/logic unit (ALU)
store	memory
operator	control unit
output	input/output

Babbage died before a working steam-powered model of his Analytic Engine could be completed. Although he did not live to see it become a reality, his ideas lived on to influence others, and many computer scientists consider the Analytic Engine the first "true" computer system, even if it existed only on paper and in Babbage's dreams.

Another person influenced by the work of Pascal, Jacquard, and Babbage was a young statistician at the U.S. Census Bureau named Herman Hollerith.

Charles Babbage (1791–1871)
Ada Augusta Byron, Countess of Lovelace (1815–1852)

Charles Babbage, the son of a banker, was born into a life of wealth and comfort in eighteenth-century England. He attended Cambridge University and displayed an aptitude for mathematics and science. He was also an inventor and "tinkerer" who loved to build all sorts of devices—sort of a nineteenth-century hacker. Among the devices he constructed were unpickable locks, skeleton keys, speedometers, and even the first cow catcher for trains. His first and greatest love, though, was mathematics, and he spent the better part of his life creating machines to do automatic computation. Babbage was enormously impressed by the work of Jacquard in France. (In fact, Babbage had on the wall of his home a woven portrait of Jacquard that required the use of 24,000 punched cards.) He spent the last 30–40 years of his life trying to build a computing device, the Analytic Engine, based on Jacquard's ideas.

In that quest, he was helped by Countess Ada Augusta Byron, daughter of the famous English poet, Lord Byron. The countess was introduced to Babbage and was enormously impressed by his ideas about the Analytic Engine. As she put it, "We may say most aptly that the Analytic Engine weaves algebraic patterns just as the Jacquard Loom weaves flowers and leaves." Lady Lovelace worked closely with Babbage on specifying how instructions for the Analytic Engine would have to be organized to solve a particular mathematical problem. Because of that pioneering work, she is generally regarded as history's first computer programmer.

Babbage died in 1871 without being able to realize his dream. He also died quite poor, because the Analytic Engine ate up virtually all of his personal fortune. His work was generally forgotten until the twentieth century when it became instrumental in moving the world into the computer age.

Because of the rapid increase in immigration to America at the end of the nineteenth century, officials estimated that doing the 1890 enumeration manually would take from 10 to 12 years. The 1900 census would begin before the previous one was finished. Something had to be done.

What Hollerith did was design and build programmable card processing machines that could automatically read, tally, and sort data entered on punched cards. (Like Babbage, Hollerith knew about the earlier work of Jacquard.) Census data were coded onto cards using a machine called a **keypunch**. The cards were taken either to a **tabulator** for counting and tallying or to a **sorter** for ordering alphabetically or numerically. Both of these machines were programmable (via wires and plugs) so that the user could specify in advance such things as which card columns should be tallied and in what order the cards should be sorted. In addition, the machines had a small amount of memory to store results. Thus they had all four components described in Babbage's design of the Analytic Engine.

Hollerith's machines were enormously successful, and they were one of the first examples of the use of automated information processing to solve large-scale "real-world" problems. Whereas the 1880 census required 8 years to be completed, the 1890 census was finished in about 2 years, even though there was a 20% increase in the U.S. population during that decade.

Although they were not really general-purpose computers, Hollerith's card machines were a very clear and very successful demonstration of the enormous advantages to be gained from automated information processing. This fact was not lost on Hollerith, who left the Census Bureau in 1902 to found the Computing-Tabulating-Recording Company to build and sell these machines. He planned to market his new product to a country that was just entering the Industrial Revolution and that, like the Census Bureau, would be generating and processing enormous volumes of inventory, production, accounting, and sales data. He was right—spectacularly so—and his punched card machines became the dominant form of data processing equipment during the first half of the twentieth century, well into the 1950s and 1960s. During this period, virtually every major U.S. corporation had data processing rooms filled with keypunches, sorters, and tabulators, as well as drawer upon drawer of punched cards. Hollerith's tabulating machine company eventually evolved into the largest computing company in the world, IBM.

We have come a long way from the 1640s and Pascaline, the early adding machine constructed by Pascal. We have seen the development of more powerful mechanical calculators (Leibnitz), automated programmable manufacturing devices (Jacquard), a design for the first computing device (Babbage), and the initial applications of information processing on a massive scale (Hollerith). However, we have still not yet entered the "computer age." That did not happen until about 1940, and it was motivated by an event that, unfortunately, has fueled many of the important technological advances in human history—the outbreak of war.

5.3.2 THE BIRTH OF COMPUTERS: 1940–1950

The beginning of World War II created another, quite different set of information-based problems. Instead of inventory, sales, and payroll, the concerns of the 1940s became ballistics tables, troop deployment data, and secret codes. A number of research projects were started, funded largely by the military, to build automatic computing machines to perform these tasks and assist the Allies in the war effort.

Beginning in 1931, the U.S. Navy and IBM jointly funded a project at Harvard University under Professor Howard Aiken to build a computing device called Mark I. This was a general-purpose electromechanical programmable computer that used a mix of relays, magnets, and gears to process and store data. The Mark I used vacuum tubes and electric current to represent binary values, off for 0, on for 1. Until then most computing machines had used decimal representation, typically by having a 10-toothed gear, each tooth representing a digit from 0 to 9. The Mark I was completed in 1944 and is generally considered one of the first working general-purpose computers, about 110 years after Babbage's dream of the Analytic Engine. The Mark I had a memory capacity of 72 numbers, and it could be programmed to perform a 23-digit multiplication in the lightninglike time of 4 seconds. Though laughably slow by modern standards, the Mark I was operational for almost 15 years and produced a good deal of important and useful mathematical results.

At about the same time, a much more powerful machine was taking shape at the University of Pennsylvania in conjunction with the U.S. Army. During the early days of World War II, the Army was producing many new artillery pieces, but it found that it could not produce the firing tables equally fast. These tables told the gunner how to aim the gun on the basis of such input as distance to the

FIGURE 5.22

*Photograph of the
ENIAC Computer*

target and current values of temperature, wind, and elevation. Because of the enormous number of variables and the complexity of the computations (which use both trigonometry and calculus), these firing tables were taking more time to construct than the gun itself.

To help solve this problem, in 1943 the Army initiated a research project with J. Presper Eckert and John Mauchly of the University of Pennsylvania to build a completely electronic computing device. The machine, dubbed the ENIAC (*E*lectronic *N*umerical *I*ntegrator *a*nd *C*alculator), was completed in 1946 and was the first fully electronic general-purpose programmable computer. This pioneering machine is shown in Figure 5.22.

ENIAC contained 18,000 vacuum tubes and nearly filled a building; it was 100 feet long, was 10 feet high, and weighed 30 tons. Because it was fully electronic, it did not contain any of the slow mechanical components found in Mark I. Consequently, it executed instructions much faster. The ENIAC could add two 10-digit numbers in about 1/5000 of a second and could multiply two numbers in 1/300 of a second, a thousand times faster than the Mark I.

The Mark I and ENIAC are two well-known examples of early computers, but they are by no means the only ones of that era. For example, the ABC system (*A*tanasoff-*B*erry *C*omputer), designed and built by Professor John Atanasoff and his graduate student Clifford Berry at Iowa State University, was actually the first electronic computer, constructed during the period 1939–1942. However, it never received the recognition it deserved because it was a more specialized computer than ENIAC. It was useful for only one task, solving systems of simultaneous linear equations. In England, a computer called Colossus was built in 1943 under the direction of Alan Turing, a famous mathematician and computer scientist whom we will meet again in Chapter 10. This machine, one of the first computers built outside the United States, was used to crack the famous German Enigma code that the Nazis believed to be unbreakable. Colossus has also not received as much recognition as ENIAC, this time because of the secrecy that shrouded the Enigma project. Its very existence was not known until many years after the end of the war.

Interestingly enough, at about the same time that Colossus was taking form in England, a German engineer named Konrad Zuse was working on a computing device for the German Army. The machine, code named Z1, was similar in design to the ENIAC—a programmable, general-purpose, fully electronic computing device. Fortunately for the allied forces, the Z1 project was not successfully completed before the end of World War II.

Although the machines just described—ABC, Mark I, ENIAC, Colossus, and Z1—were computers in the fullest sense of the word (they had memory and were programmable), they did not yet look quite like modern computer systems. One more step was necessary, and that step was taken in 1946 by the individual who was most instrumental in creating the computer as we know it today, John Von Neumann.

Von Neumann was not only one of the most brilliant mathematicians who ever lived, but he was a genius in many other areas as well, such as experimental physics, chemistry, and computer science. Von Neumann, who taught at Princeton University, had worked with Eckert and Mauchly on the ENIAC project at the University of Pennsylvania. Even though that project was completed successfully, he recognized a number of fundamental shortcomings in ENIAC. In 1946 he proposed a radically different computer design based on a model called the **stored program computer**. Until then, all computers were programmed *externally* using wires, connectors, and plugboards. The memory unit stored only data, not instructions. To solve a different problem on these computers, a user had to rewire virtually the entire machine. For example, the plugboards on the ENIAC contained 6,000 separate switches, and reprogramming the ENIAC involved specifying the new settings for all these switches—not a trivial task.

Von Neumann proposed that the instructions that control the operation of the computer be encoded as binary values and stored internally in the memory unit along with the data. To solve a different problem, you do not rewire the machine. Instead you rewrite the sequence of instructions—that is, create a new program. Von Neumann had invented programming as it is known today.

The model of computing proposed by Von Neumann included many other important features introduced in the beginning of the chapter, and to honor him, this model of computation has come to be known as the **Von Neumann architecture**.

Von Neumann's research group at the University of Pennsylvania implemented his ideas, and they built one of the first stored program computers, called EDVAC, in 1950. At about the same time, a stored program computer called EDSAC was built at Cambridge University in England under the direction of Prof. Maurice Wilkes. The appearance of these machines, and others like them, really marks the beginning of the modern computer age. Even though they were much slower, bulkier, and less powerful than current machines, EDVAC and EDSAC executed programs in a fashion surprisingly similar to the miniaturized and immensely more powerful computers of the 1990s. A commercial model of the EDVAC, called UNIVAC I, was built by Eckert and Mauchly in 1951 and delivered to the U.S. Bureau of the Census—the first computer actually

And the Verdict Is . . .

Our discussion of what was happening in computing from 1939 to 1945 showed that many groups were involved in designing and building the first computers—at places like Harvard, Pennsylvania, Iowa, and Princeton in the United States and England and Germany overseas. Therefore, it would seem that no one individual can be credited with the title "Inventor of the Electronic Digital Computer."

Surprisingly, that is not true. In February 1964, the Sperry Rand Corp. (now UNISYS) was granted a U.S. patent on the ENIAC computer as the first fully electronic computing device, J. Presper Eckert and John Mauchly being its designers and builders. However, in 1967 a suit was filed in United States District Court in Minneapolis, Minnesota, to overturn that patent. The suit, *Honeywell v. Sperry Rand*, was heard before U.S. Federal Judge Earl Larson, and on October 19, 1973, his verdict was handed down. (Interestingly enough, this enormously important verdict was never given the media coverage it deserved because it hap-

pened in the middle of the Watergate hearings and on the very day that Vice President Spiro Agnew resigned in disgrace for tax fraud.) Judge Larson overturned the ENIAC patent on the basis that Eckert and Mauchly had been significantly influenced in their 1943–1944 work on ENIAC by earlier research and development work by John Atanasoff at Iowa State University during the period 1939–1943. (Mauchly had communicated extensively with Atanasoff and had even traveled to Iowa to see the ABC machine in person.) In a sense, the verdict declared that Atanasoff is really the inventor of the first computer. This decision was never appealed. Therefore, the official honor of having designed and built the first electronic computer, at least in U.S. District Court, goes to Prof. John Vincent Atanasoff.

On November 13, 1990, in a formal ceremony at the White House, Prof. Atanasoff was awarded the National Medal of Technology by President George Bush for his pioneering contributions to the development of the computer.

---

sold. (Interestingly enough, it ran for 12 years before it was retired, shut off for the last time, and moved to the Smithsonian Institute.)

The importance of Von Neumann's contributions to computer systems development cannot be overstated. Although his original proposals are over 50 years old, virtually every computer built today is a Von Neumann machine in its basic design. A lot has changed in computing, and a powerful graphics workstation and the EDVAC would appear to have little in common. However, the basic principles on which these disparate machines are constructed are virtually identical, and the same theoretical model underlies their operation. There is an old saying in computer science that "There is nothing new since Von Neumann!" This saying is certainly not true (much *has* happened), but it demonstrates the importance and amazing staying power of Von Neumann's original design.

5.3.3 THE MODERN ERA: 1950 TO THE PRESENT

From the point of view of this chapter and the ideas it will present, our historical review is complete. We have reached the modern era of computing, and the stored program model on which the EDVAC and EDSAC are based, the Von Neumann architecture, is precisely the model we studied in the beginning of this chapter. The last 50 years of computer development have involved taking this basic model and improving it in terms of both hardware and software. Since 1950, computer organization has been primarily an *evolutionary* process, not a revolutionary one. The enormous number of changes in computers in the last

John Von Neumann (1903–1957)

John Von Neumann was born in Budapest, Hungary. He was a genius in virtually every field that he studied, including physics, economics, engineering, and mathematics. At 18 he received an award as the best mathematician in Hungary (a country known for excellence in the field), and he received his Ph.D, *summa cum laude*, at the age of 21. He came to the United States in 1930 as a guest lecturer at Princeton University and taught there for 3 years. Then, in 1933, he became one of the founding members (along with Albert Einstein) of the Institute for Advanced Studies, where he worked for the next 20 years.

He was one of the most brilliant minds of the twentieth century, a true genius in every sense, both good and bad. He could do prodigious mental feats in his head, and his thought processes usually raced way ahead of "ordinary" mortals who found him quite difficult to work with. One of his colleagues joked that "Johnny wasn't really human, but after living among them for so long, he learned to do a remarkably good imitation of one."

Von Neumann was a brilliant theoretician who did pioneering work in pure mathematics, operations research, game theory, and theoretical physics. He was also an engineer who was concerned about practicalities and real-world problems, and it was this interest in applied issues that led Von Neumann into the design and construction of the first stored program computer. One of the first computers built using his stored program design principles (at Princeton University about a year after EDVAC) was affectionately called "Johnniac" in his honor, although Von Neumann detested that name. Like the UNIVAC I, it also has a place of honor at the Smithsonian Institute.

50 years have made them faster, smaller, cheaper, more reliable, and easier to use but have not drastically altered the basic ideas inherent in the Von Neumann architecture. However, the changes that have occurred are interesting, and this section briefly highlights some of these major developments.

The period 1950–1959 represents the **first generation** of computing. (These dates are only rough approximations, and they should not be taken too literally.) This era saw the appearance of UNIVAC I, the first computer built for sale, and the IBM 701, the first computer built by that huge company that would soon become a leader in this new field. These early systems were similar in design to EDVAC, and they were bulky, expensive, slow, and unreliable. They demanded very special care and had to be placed in "clean rooms" with special wiring and air conditioning. They used vacuum tubes for processing and storage, and they were horribly difficult to maintain. Just the process of turning the machine on could blow out a dozen tubes! For this reason, first-generation machines were used only by trained personnel and only in specialized locations such as large corporations, government and university research labs, and military installations where this type of expensive support environment could be provided. The first-generation machines did not have much of an impact on the average person.

The **second generation** of computing, roughly 1959–1965, heralded a major change in the size and complexity of computers. In 1959 the bulky vacuum tube was replaced by a single transistor only a few millimeters in size (Figure 4.6), and memory was now constructed using magnetic cores (Figure 4.4). These technologies not only dramatically reduced the size of computers but also increased

Good Evening, This Is Walter Cronkite

In the earliest days of computing (1951–1952), few people knew what a computer was, and even fewer had seen or worked with one. Computers were the tool of a very small group of highly trained technical specialists in such fields as mathematics, physics, and engineering. In those days, the general public's knowledge of computer science was limited to the robots and alien computers of science fiction movies.

This all changed in November 1952, when millions of Americans turned on the television set (itself a relatively new technology) to watch returns from the 1952 presidential election between Dwight D. Eisenhower and Adlai Stevenson. In addition to seeing Walter Cronkite and TV reporters and analysts, viewers were treated to an unexpected member of the news staff—a UNIVAC I. CBS executives had rented a computer and installed it in the very center of their set, where it sat, lights blinking and tape drives spinning. They planned to use UNIVAC to produce election predictions quickly and scoop rival stations that did their analyses by hand. Ironically, UNIVAC correctly predicted early that evening, on the basis of well-known statistical sampling techniques, that Eisenhower would win the election, but nervous CBS executives were so skeptical about this new technology that they did not go on the air with the computer's prediction until it had been confirmed by old-fashioned manual methods.

It was the first time that millions of TV viewers had actually seen this thing called an electronic digital computer. The CBS staff, who were also quite inexperienced in computer technology, treated the computer as though it were human. They would turn toward the computer console and utter phrases like "UNIVAC, can you tell me who is currently ahead in Ohio?" or "UNIVAC, do you have any prediction on the final electoral vote total?" In actuality, the statistical algorithms had been programmed in, days earlier, by the Remington Rand staff, but it looked great on TV! This first public appearance of a computer was so well received that computers were used many more times in the early days of TV, primarily on quiz shows, where they reinforced the public's image of the computer as a "giant electronic brain."

reliability and reduced costs. Suddenly, buying and using a computer became a real possibility for some small and medium-size businesses, colleges, and government agencies that could not have considered it before. This was also the era of the appearance of FORTRAN and COBOL, the first **high-level** ("English-like") **programming languages**. (We will study programming languages in Chapters 7 and 8.) Suddenly, it was no longer necessary to be an electrical engineer to solve a problem on a computer. One simply needed to learn how to write commands in a high-level language. The occupation called **programmer** was born.

This miniaturization process continued into the **third generation** of computing, which lasted from about 1965 to 1975. This was the era of the **integrated circuit** first described in Chapter 4. Rather than using discrete electronic components, integrated circuits with transistors, resistors, and capacitors were photographically etched onto a piece of silicon, which further reduced the size and cost of computers. From building-sized to room-sized, computers became desk-sized, and this period saw the birth of the first **minicomputer**—the PDP-1 manufactured by the Digital Equipment Corp. in 1963. It also saw the birth of a **software industry**, as companies sprang up to provide programs such as accounting packages and statistical programs to the ever-increasing numbers of computer users. By the mid-1970s, computers were no longer a rarity. They were being widely used throughout business, government, the military, and education.

FIGURE 5.23
The Altair 8800, the World's First Microcomputer

The **fourth generation**, 1975–1985, saw the appearance of the first **microcomputer**. Integrated circuits technology had advanced to the point where a complete computer system could be contained on a single circuit board (see Figure 4.5). The desk-sized machine of the early 1970s became a desktop machine, shrinking to the size of a typewriter. Figure 5.23 shows the Altair 8800, the world's first microcomputer, which appeared in January 1975.

It soon became unusual *not* to see a computer on someone's desk. The software industry exploded with all types of new packages—spreadsheets, databases, and drawing programs—to meet the needs of the burgeoning user population. This era saw the appearance of the first **computer networks**, as users realized that much of the power of computers derives not just from the numerical results of some program but also from an enhanced ability to communicate with other users. (We will look at networking in great detail in Chapter 12.) **Electronic mail** became an important application. Because so many users were novices who had never used a computer before, the concept of **user-friendly systems** evolved. This included new **graphical user interfaces** with pull-down menus, icons, and other visual aids to make computing easier and more fun. **Embedded systems** first appeared during this generation; these are systems that contain a computer inside them to control their operation. Computers were becoming small enough to be placed inside cars, thermostats, microwave ovens, and wrist watches.

The **fifth generation**, 1985–?, is where we are today. However, so much is changing so fast that many computer scientists believe that the concept of distinct generations of change has outlived its usefulness. In computer science, change is now a constant companion. Some of the recent developments in computer science include

- Massively parallel processors capable of trillions of computations per second
- Artificial intelligence and robotics
- Miniature laptop and palmtop computers

The World's First Microcomputer

The Altair 8800, shown in Figure 5.23, was the first microcomputer when it made its debut on the cover of *Popular Electronics* in January 1975. Its developer, Ed Roberts, owned a tiny electonics store in Albuquerque, New Mexico. His company was in desperate financial shape when he read about a new microprocessor from Intel, the Intel 8080. Roberts reasoned that this new chip could be used to sell a complete personal computer in kit form. He bought these new chips from Intel at the bargain basement price of $75 each and packaged them in a kit called the Altair 8800 (named after a character in the TV series Star Trek), which he offered to hobbyists for $397. Roberts figured he might sell a few hundred kits a year, enough to keep his company afloat temporarily. He ended up selling hundreds of them a day! The Altair microcomputer kits were so popular that he could not keep them in stock, and legend has it that people even drove to New Mexico and camped out in the parking lot to buy their computers.

This is particularly amazing in view of the fact that the original Altair was difficult to assemble and had only 256 bytes of memory, no I/O devices, and no software support. To program it, the user had to enter binary machine language instructions directly from the console switches. But even though it could do very little, people loved it because it was a real computer, and it was theirs.

The Intel 8080 chip did have the capability of running programs written in the language called BASIC that had been developed at Dartmouth in the early 1960s. A small software company located in the state of Washington wrote Ed Roberts a letter telling him that it had a BASIC compiler that could run on his Altair, making it much more easy to use. That company was called Microsoft—and the rest, as they say, is history.

- High-resolution graphical simulations, called **virtual reality**
- Powerful **multimedia user interfaces** incorporating sound, voice recognition, touch, photography, video, and television
- Integrated global telecommunications incorporating data, TV, telephone, FAX, the Internet, and the World Wide Web
- Wireless data communications
- Massive direct-access storage devices capable of storing and retrieving terabytes of data

In only 50 or so years, computers have progressed from the UNIVAC I, which cost millions of dollars, had a few thousand words of memory, and was capable of only a few thousand operations per second, to today's high-powered desktop workstation with 128 million memory cells, external storage for hundreds of billions of characters, and enough processing power to execute 300 million instructions per second, all for under $10,000. Changes of this magnitude have never occurred so quickly in any other technology. If the same rate of change had occurred in the auto industry, beginning with the 1909 Model-T, today's cars would be capable of traveling at a speed of 20,000 miles per hour, would get about a million miles per gallon, and would cost about $1.00!

Figure 5.24 lists some of the major events that occurred during each of the five generations discussed in this section. However, as we have said before, underlying all of these amazing improvements, the model describing the organization and construction of computers has not changed significantly in the last 50 years.

FIGURE 5.24

*Some of the Major
Advancements in Computing*

GENERATION	APPROXIMATE DATES	MAJOR ADVANCES
First	1950–1959	First commercial computers First symbolic programming languages Use of binary arithmetic, vacuum tubes for storage Punched card input/output
Second	1959–1965	Transistors and core memories First disks for mass storage Size reduction, increased reliability, lower costs First high-level programming languages and programmers First operating systems
Third	1965–1975	Integrated circuits Further reduction in size and cost, increased reliability First minicomputers Time-shared operating systems Appearance of the software industry First set of computing standards for compatibility between systems

Fourth	1975–1985	Large-scale and very-large-scale integrated circuits
		   (LSI, VLSI)
		Further reduction in size and cost, increased
		   reliability
		First microcomputer
		Growth of new types of software and of the
		   software industry
		Computer networks
		Graphical user interfaces

Fifth	1985–?	Ultra-large-scale integrated circuits (ULSI) Supercomputers and parallel processors Laptop workstations and hand-held computers Wireless computing On-line terabyte storage devices Global networks and distributed systems Artificial intelligence High-resolution graphics, visualization, virtual reality Multimedia user interfaces

5.3.4 THE FUTURE: NON–VON NEUMANN ARCHITECTURES

There is one final point we need to mention concerning computer organization. The Von Neumann architecture, which has been the central theme of this chapter, has served the field well for almost 50 years, but many computer scientists believe it may be reaching the end of its useful life.

The problems that computers are being asked to solve have grown significantly in size and complexity since the appearance of the first-generation machines in the late 1940s and early 1950s. Designers have been able to "keep up" with these larger and larger problems by building faster and faster Von Neumann machines. Through advances in hardware design, manufacturing methods, and circuit technology, computer designers have been able to take the basic sequential architecture described by Von Neumann in 1946 and improve its performance by 3 or 4 orders of magnitude. First-generation machines were able to execute about 10,000 machine language instructions per second. By the second generation, that had grown to about 1 *million instructions per second* (1 MIPS for short). Today, even a tiny desktop PC can perform about 10–30 million instructions per second (10–30 MIPS), and large workstations can execute instructions at the rate of 300–500 MIPS. Figure 5.25 shows the changes in computer speeds from the mid-1940s to the present. (*Note:* This graph is logarithmic. Each unit on the vertical axis is 10 times the previous one.)

Note that the period from about 1945 to about 1970 or 1980 was characterized by exponential increases in computation speed. However, as Figure 5.25 shows, the rate of improvement appears to be slowing down.

This slowdown is due to many things. One important limit on increased processor speed is the inability to place gates closer and closer together on a chip. Today's high-density VLSI chips have gates separated by less than 0.0003 cm., and it is becoming difficult to place components accurately any closer together. However, if we cannot get them any closer, then the time it takes to send data between two devices, such as the memory and the ALU, will become a limiting factor in the ultimate speed of our computer, because electronic signals cannot travel faster than the speed of light.

Even though the rate of increase in the performance of newer machines is slowing down, the size of the problems that researchers are attempting to solve is increasing dramatically. New applications in such areas as artificial intelligence, virtual reality, and simulation are rapidly increasing the demands placed on new computer systems. For example, to create a computer-generated animated movie, an important new application, a computer must generate 24 new images each second. Each image contains about $1,000 \times 1,000$ picture points whose position, color, and intensity must be recomputed for each new image. This means that 24,000,000 picture point computations need to be completed every second. Each of those computations may require the execution of a few dozen instructions. (Where does this point move to in the next frame? How bright is it? Is it visible or hidden behind something else?) Thus, to handle this application may require a computer capable of executing 1,000 MIPS, 10,000 MIPS, or more. This is well beyond the abilities of current systems. The inability of the sequential one-instruction-at-a-time Von Neumann model to handle today's large-scale problems is called the **Von Neumann bottleneck**, and it is a major problem in computer organization.

To solve this problem, computer engineers are rethinking many of the fundamental ideas presented in this chapter, and they are studying nontraditional approaches to computer organization called **non–Von Neumann architectures**. They are asking the question "Is there a different way to design and build computers that can solve problems 10 or 100 or 1,000 times larger than what can be handled by today's computers?" The answer is a resounding "Yes!"

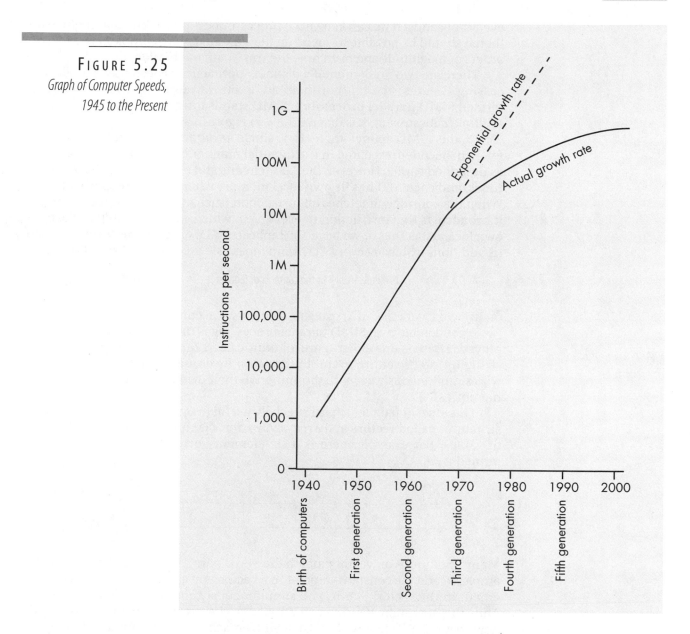

FIGURE 5.25

Graph of Computer Speeds, 1945 to the Present

One of the most important areas of research in these non–Von Neumann architectures is based on the following fairly obvious principle:

> *If you cannot build something to work twice as fast, do two things at once. The results will be identical.*

From this truism comes the principle of **parallel processing**, building computers not with one processor as shown in Figure 5.18, but with tens, hundreds, or even thousands. If we can keep each processor occupied with meaningful work, then it should be possible to speed up the solution to large problems by 1, 2, or 3 orders of magnitude and overcome the Von Neumann bottleneck.

There are two fundamentally distinct approaches to designing parallel processing systems, and both of them are in current use. The first technique is termed **SIMD parallel processing** (SIMD stands for *s*ingle *i*nstruction stream/ *m*ultiple *d*ata stream). It is diagrammed in Figure 5.26.

In the SIMD model there is a single program whose instructions are fetched/decoded/executed in a sequential manner by one control unit, exactly as described earlier. However, the ALU (circuits and registers) is replicated many times, and each ALU has its own local memory where it may keep private data. When the control unit fetches an instruction (such as a LOAD, ADD, or STORE), it **broadcasts** that instruction to every ALU, which executes it in parallel on its own local data. Thus, if we have 100 replicated ALUs, we can perform 100 parallel additions by having every ALU simultaneously execute the instruction

ADD X   Add memory cell X to the contents of register R

on its own local value of X, using its own personal copy of register R.

A good analogy to SIMD parallel processing is the way the game of Bingo is played. There is one caller (control unit) calling out a single number (the instruction) to the entire room. In the room listening are many people (ALUs) who simultaneously cover that number on their own private Bingo cards (local memories).

This style of parallelism is especially useful in operations on mathematical structures called **vectors** and **arrays**. A vector *V* is simply an ordered collection of values. For example, here is a six-element vector *V*, whose elements are termed $v_1, v_2, \ldots, v_6$.

	v_1	v_2	v_3	v_4	v_5	v_6
V	1	8	−13	70	9	0

Many operations on vectors match the SIMD parallel model quite well. For example, to add the constant value +1 to a vector, you add it to every individual element in the vector; that is, you simultaneously compute $v_1 + 1, v_2 + 1, \ldots$. Thus the operation $V + 1$, when applied to the previous vector, produces the new vector 2, 9, −12, 71, 10, 1. On a SIMD machine, this vector addition operation can be implemented in a single step by distributing one element of the vector to each separate ALU. Then in parallel, each arithmetic unit executes the following instruction:

INC   *v*   *v* is an element of the vector *V*. This instruction increments the contents of that location by +1.

In one time unit, we will update all six elements of the vector *V*. In the traditional Von Neumann machine, we would have to increment each element separately in a sequential fashion, so it would take six instructions:

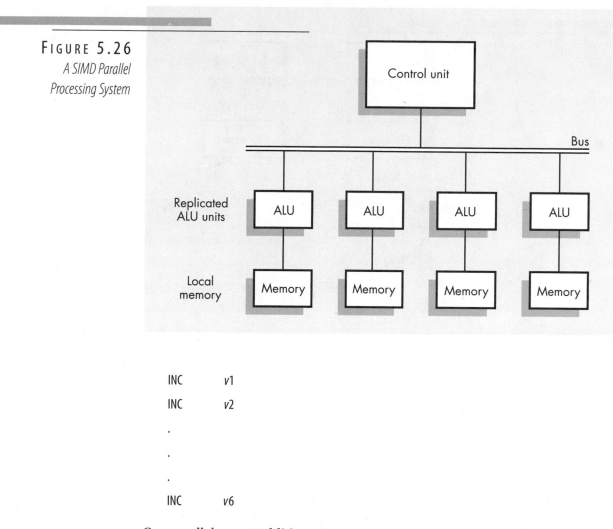

FIGURE 5.26

A SIMD Parallel Processing System

```
INC          v1
INC          v2
  .
  .
  .
INC          v6
```

Our parallel vector addition operator runs six times as fast. Similar speedups are possible with other vector and array manipulations.

SIMD parallelism was the first type of parallel processing put into widespread commercial use. It was the technique used to achieve breakthroughs in computational speeds on the first **supercomputers** of the early 1980s.

A more interesting and potentially more profitable form of parallelism is called **MIMD parallel processing** (*m*ultiple *i*nstruction stream/*m*ultiple *d*ata stream). In MIMD parallelism we replicate entire processors rather than just the ALU, and every processor is capable of executing its own separate program in its own private memory at its own rate. This model of parallel processing is diagrammed in Figure 5.27.

Each processor/memory pair in Figure 5.27 is a Von Neumann machine of the type described in this chapter. Each one is executing its own program in its own local memory at its own rate. However, rather than each having to solve the entire problem by itself, the problem is solved in a parallel fashion by all processors simultaneously. Each of the processors tackles a small part of the overall

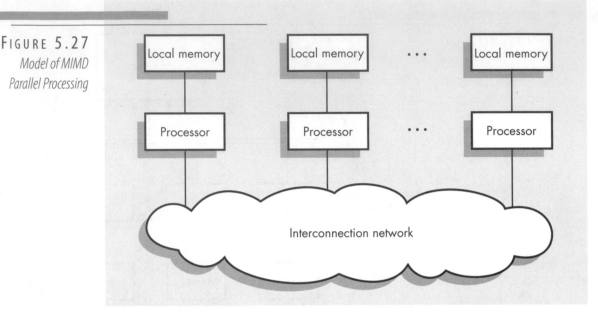

FIGURE 5.27
*Model of MIMD
Parallel Processing*

problem and then communicates its result to the other processors via the **inter-connection network** that allows processors to exchange messages and data.

A MIMD parallel processor would be an excellent system to help us speed up the New York Telephone Directory look-up problem discussed in Chapter 2. In the sequential approach that we described, the single processor doing the work had to search all 20,000,000 entries from beginning to end (or until the desired name was found). The analysis in Chapter 3 showed that using the sequential search algorithms and a computer that can examine 50,000 names per second, this look-up operation takes an average of about 3.5 minutes to find a particular name—much too long for the average person to wait.

If we use 100 processors instead of 1, however, the problem is easily solved. We just divide the 20,000,000 names into 100 equal-sized pieces and assign each piece to a different processor. Now each processor searches *in parallel* to see whether the desired name is in its own section. If it finds the name, it broadcasts that information to the other 99 processors so that they can stop searching. Each processor needs only to look through a list of 200,000 names, which is 1/100 the amount of work it had to do previously. Instead of requiring an average of about 3.5 minutes, we will now get our answer in 1/100 the time—about 2 seconds. Parallel processing has elegantly solved our problem.

MIMD parallelism is an exciting computational model because in addition to making possible massive speedups it is also a scaleable architecture. **Scaleability** means that, at least theoretically, it is possible to match the number of processors to the size of the problem. If 100 processors are not enough to solve the telephone book look-up problem, then 200 or 500 can be used instead, assuming the interconnect network can provide the necessary communications. (Communications can become a serious bottleneck in a parallel system.) In short, the resources applied to a problem can be in direct propor-

Chasing the Elusive Teraflop

This section introduced a unit called **MIPS**, for *millions of instructions per second*, as a measure of the speed of a computer. However, that is not a particularly useful measure. Our computer might be executing lots of instructions but not getting any useful work done. A more widely used measure of computer speed and power is **flops**, which stands for *floating-point operations per second*. A **floating point** is simply a real number, such as 12.446, −99.0, or +0.000001. Flops measure how fast a computer can do arithmetic operations on these numbers, such as (1.23 + 4.56) or (8.03 ÷ 0.222).

The first computer to achieve a speed of 1 million floating-point operations per second, which is written 1 Mflop and pronounced 1 **megaflop**, was the Control Data 6600 in the mid-1960s. Modern microprocessors, such as the Pentium Pro, PowerPC, and UltraSPARC, perform computations at rates of about 40–80 megaflops. The first machine to achieve 1 billion floating-point operations per second (1 Gflop or 1 **gigaflop**), was the Cray X-MP in the early 1980s. Today's largest supercomputers, such as the Cray T3E, Thinking Machines CM-5, and the Fujitsu VPP500, have computing speeds in the range of 50–600 gigaflops.

What was the next speed goal for computer designers? It was the **teraflop**, a sustained computing speed of 1 trillion arithmetic operations per second. This "holy grail" of computing speed was felt by some to be an almost unimaginable goal that would not be achieved for many years. However, in 1996 the Intel Corporation announced that its ULTRA computer had successfully become the world's first teraflop machine. This $55

million computer contains 9,072 Pentium Pro processors, and on December 16, 1996 it achieved a sustained computational speed of 1 trillion computations per second. In June 1997 that value was further increased to 1.34 trillion computations per second. To get an idea of how fast this is, consider that if all 6 billion human beings on the face of the earth worked together on a single problem, each person would have to carry out 220 calculations per second to match the rate achieved by the Intel ULTRA!

Why would we ever need a teraflop machine? The answer to this question has to do with the enormity of the problems generated by new areas of research and development. The federal government has described a set of important problems called "The Grand Challenges of Computing." These are fundamental problems in science and engineering whose solution would be made possible by the development of high-performance computing technology such as a teraflop machine. These problems include simulating the medical effect of new drugs; accurately modeling and analyzing earth science phenomena, such as severe weather and earthquakes; and mapping the human genome. Solving these problems will require the almost unimaginable speeds of a teraflop machine.

And just so you don't think computer designers are now sitting around and relaxing, there have already been preliminary discussions about what will be required to design and build the first **petaflop** machine, a computer capable of 10^{15} computations every second.

tion to the amount of work that needs to be done. **Massively parallel** MIMD machines containing over 9,000 independent processors have achieved solutions to large problems thousands of times faster than was possible using a single processor. (For an up-to-date listing of the fastest parallel computers, take a look at the home page of the *Performance Database*, a list of the most powerful computers in the world according to a set of standardized benchmarks. Its URL is www.netlib.org/performance/html/PDStop.html.

The real key to using massively parallel processors is to design solution methods that effectively utilize the large number of available processors. It does no good to have 1,000 processors available if only 1 or 2 are doing useful work while 998 or 999 are sitting idle, waiting for something to do. That would be equivalent to having a large construction crew at a building site but having the roofers, painters, and plumbers sitting around waiting for one person to put up the walls. The field of **parallel algorithms**, the study of techniques that make efficient use of parallel architectures, is an important branch of research in computer science. Advances in this area will go a long way toward speeding the development and use of large-scale parallel systems of the type shown in Figures 5.26 and 5.27.

In order to solve the complex problems of the twenty-first century, the computers of the twenty-first century will probably be organized much more like the parallel processing systems of Figures 5.26 and 5.27 than like the 50-year-old Von Neumann model of Figure 5.18.

EXERCISES

1. Go to the library and gather more detailed information about one of the early pioneers mentioned in this chapter—Pascal, Liebnitz, Jacquard, Babbage, Lovelace, Hollerith, Eckert, Mauchly, Aiken, Zuse, Atanasoff, Turing, or Von Neumann. Write a paper describing in detail that person's contribution to computing and computer science.

2. Get the technical specifications of the computer on which you are working (either from a technical manual or from your computer center staff). Determine its cost, its processing speed in MIPS, its ALU computation speed in Mflops (millions of floating point operations per second), the size and width of its primary memory, and the number of ALU registers. Compare those values with what was typically available on first-, second-, and third-generation computer systems.

3. What would be the advantages and disadvantages of using a very large memory cell size, say $W = 64$ instead of the standard size, $W = 8$? If each integer occupies *one* 8-bit memory cell and was stored using sign/magnitude notation, what are the largest (in terms of absolute value) positive and negative integers that could be stored? What if *two* cells are used to store integers?

4. At a minimum, how many bits would be needed in the MAR with each of the following memory sizes?

   a. 1 million bytes
   b. 10 million bytes
   c. 100 million bytes

5. A memory unit that was said to be 640 KB would actually contain how many memory cells? What about a memory of 16 MB?

6. Explain what use a read-only memory (ROM) could possibly serve in the design of a computer system. What type of information might be kept in a ROM, and how could that information originally get into the memory?

7. Assuming the square two-dimensional memory organization shown in Figure 5.6, what are the dimensions of a memory containing 1 MB (2^{20}) bytes of storage? How large would the MAR be? How many bits would be sent to the row and column decoders? How many output lines would these decoders have?

8. Assume a MAR that is organized as follows:

row select lines	column select lines
12 bits	12 bits

   What is the maximum size of the memory unit on this machine? What are the dimensions of the memory, assuming a square two-dimensional organization?

9. Assume that our MAR contains 20 bits, enabling us to access up to 2^{20} memory cells, which is 1 MB. However, our computer has 4 MB of memory. Explain how it might be possible to address all 4 MB memory cells using a MAR that contains only 20 bits.

10. Do you think that our human memory unit, the brain, does or does not follow the random access model described in Section 5.2.1? If you think not,

state why and explain in what ways the brain differs from RAM.

11. Assume that we have an arithmetic/logic unit that can carry out 20 distinct operations. Describe exactly what kind of multiplexor circuit would be needed to select exactly one of those 20 operations.

12. A typical floppy disk on a PC has the following characteristics:

    Rotation speed = 7200 rev/min

    Arm movement time = 1 msec fixed startup time + 0.1 msec for each track crossed (The 1 msec time is a constant no matter how far the arm moves.)

    Number of surfaces = 2 (a **double-sided** floppy disk. A single read/write arm holds both read/write heads.)

    Number of tracks per surface = 100

    Number of sectors per track = 20

    Number of characters per sector = 512

    a. How many characters can be stored on a single floppy disk?

    b. What are the best-case, worst-case, and average-case access times for this disk?

13. In general, information is stored on a disk not at random but in specific locations that help to minimize the time it takes to retrieve that information. Using the specifications given in Exercise 12, where would you place the information in a 15,000-byte file on the disk to speed up subsequent access to that information?

14. Assume that our disk unit had one read/write head per *track* instead of only one per surface. (A **head-per-track disk** is sometimes referred to as a **drum**.) Using the specifications given in Exercise 12, what are now the best-case, worst-case, and average-case access times? How much have the additional read/write heads helped reduce access times?

15. Discuss some situations wherein a sequential access storage device such as a tape could be a useful form of mass storage.

16. Assume that we are displaying information on a video display screen at the rate of 19,200 bits per second, which is typically the highest speed available. Furthermore, assume that we are working on a workstation with an instruction rate of 50 MIPS. How many instructions can the processor execute while it is waiting for the screen controller to output a single character?

17. Consider the following structure of the instruction register.

op code	address-1	address-2
6 bits	18 bits	18 bits

    a. What is the maximum number of distinct operation codes that can be recognized and executed by the processor on this machine?

    b. What is the maximum memory size on this machine?

18. Assume that the variables v, w, x, y, and z are stored in memory locations 200, 201, 202, 203, and 204, respectively. Using any of the machine language instructions in Section 5.2.4, translate the following algorithmic operations into their machine language equivalents.

    a. Set v to the value of $x - y + z$. (Assume the existence of the machine language command SUBTRACT X,Y,Z that computes CON(Z) = CON(X) − CON(Y).)

    b. Set v to the value $(w + x) - (y + z)$

    c. If $(v \geq w)$ then set x to y
       Else
          set x to z

    d. While $y < z$ do
          Set y to the value $(y + w + z)$
          Set z to the value $(z + v)$
       End of the loop

19. Explain why it would be cumbersome to translate the following algorithmic operation into machine language, given only the instructions introduced in this chapter.

    Set x to the value of $y + 19$

    Can you think of a way to solve this problem?

20. Describe the sequence of operations that might go on inside the computer during the execution phase of the following machine language instructions. Use the notation shown in Section 5.2.5.

    a. MOVE X, Y   Move the contents of memory cell X to memory cell Y.

    b. ADD X, Y   Add together the contents of memory cells X and Y. Put the result back into memory cell Y.

CHALLENGE WORK

1. It is easy to write a sequential algorithm that sums up a 100-element vector:

$$Sum = a_1 + a_2 + a_3 + \ldots + a_{100}$$

It would look something like

Set I to 1

Set Sum to 0

While I < 101 do the following

   Sum = Sum + a_I

   I = I + 1

End of the loop

Write out the value of Sum

Stop

It is pretty obvious that this algorithm will take about 100 units of time, where a unit of time is equivalent to the time needed to execute one iteration of the loop. However, it is not so easy to see how we might exploit the existence of *multiple* processors to speed up the solution to this problem.

Assume that instead of having only a single processor, you have 100. Design a parallel algorithm that utilizes these additional resources to speed up the solution to the previous computation. Exactly how much faster would your **parallel summation algorithm** execute than the sequential one? Did you need all 100 processors? Could you have used more than 100?

2. In this chapter we described the Von Neumann architecture in broad, general terms. However, "real" Von Neumann processors, such as the Pentium Pro, DEC Alpha, PA-RISC, PowerPC, and UltraSPARC, are much more complex than the simple model shown in Figure 5.18. Pick one of these processors (perhaps the processor inside the computer you are using for this class) and take an in-depth look at its design. Specifically, examine such issues as

   - Its instruction set and how it compares with the instruction set shown in Figure 5.19

   - The collection of available registers

   - The existence of cache memory

   - Its computing speed in MIPS and Mflops

   - How much primary memory it has and how memory is addressed in the instructions

   - Memory access time

   - In what size "chunks" can memory be accessed

   Write a report describing the real-world characteristics of the processor you selected.

FOR FURTHER READING

In the area of computer organization and machine architecture:

Hamacher, V.; Vranesic, Z.; and Zaky, S. *Computer Organization*, 4th ed. New York: McGraw-Hill, 1996.

Patterson, D., and Hennessey, J. *Computer Organization and Design: The Hardware/Software Interface*, 2nd ed. San Francisco: Morgan Kaufmann, 1998.

Stallings, W. *Computer Organization and Architecture*, 4th ed. Englewood Cliffs, NJ: Prentice-Hall, 1996.

Tanenbaum, A. *Structured Computer Organization*, 3rd ed. Englewood Cliffs, NJ: Prentice-Hall, 1991.

In the area of the historical development of computer systems:

Goldstine, H. *The Computer from Pascal to Von Neumann.* Princeton, NJ: Princeton
    University Press, 1972.

Randell B. *The Origins of Digital Computers.* New York: Springer-Verlag, 1977.

See also the home page of the Charles Babbage Institute, a center devoted to the study of the history of information technology. Its Web address is http://www.cbi.umn.edu.

In the area of parallel processing:

Almasi, G., and Gottlieb, A. *Highly Parallel Computing,* 2nd ed. New York: Benjamin
    Cummings, 1994.

Golub, G., and Ortega, J. *Scientific Computing: An Introduction with Parallel Computing.*
    New York: Academic Press, 1993.

5.4   SUMMARY OF LEVEL 2

We have now seen the basic principles underlying the design of a modern computer system. In Chapter 4 we looked at the basic building blocks of computers: binary codes, transistors, gates, and circuits. This chapter examined the standard model for computer design, called the Von Neumann architecture, and traced its historical development. It also discussed some of the shortcomings of that sequential model of computation and described briefly how parallel computers may be designed and built as we move into the next century.

At this point in our hierarchy of abstractions, we have created a fully functional computer system capable of executing an algorithm encoded as sequences of machine language instructions. The only problem is that the machine we have created, like that first Altair 8800, is enormously difficult to use and about as unfriendly and unforgiving as it could be. It has been designed and engineered from a machine's perspective, not a person's. Sequences of binary encoded machine language instructions such as

    1011010000001011   1001101100010111   0000101101011001

give a computer no difficulty, but they cause people to throw up their hands in despair. We need to create a more friendly environment—to make the computer and its hardware resources less intimidating and more accessible. Such an environment would be more conducive to developing correct solutions to problems and satisfying a user's computational needs.

The component that creates this kind of friendly problem-solving environment is called **system software**. It is an intermediary between the user and the hardware components of the Von Neumann machine. Without it, a Von Neumann machine would be virtually unusable by anyone but the most technically knowledgeable computer experts. We examine these ideas in the next level of our investigation of computer science.

THE
VIRTUAL
MACHINE

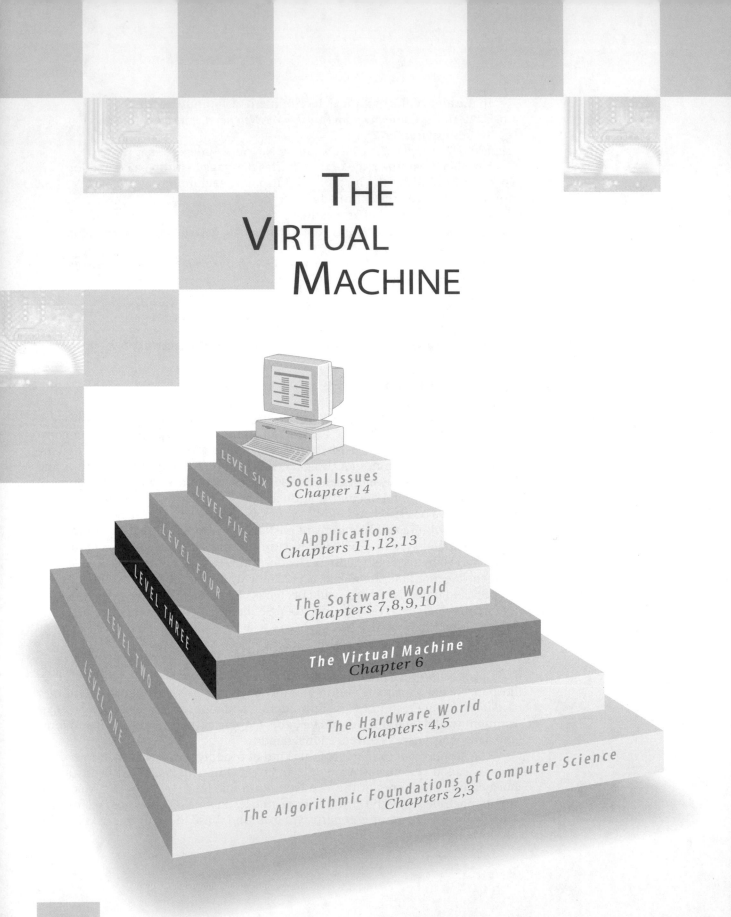

LEVEL SIX

Social Issues
Chapter 14

LEVEL FIVE

Applications
Chapters 11,12,13

LEVEL FOUR

The Software World
Chapters 7,8,9,10

LEVEL THREE

The Virtual Machine
Chapter 6

LEVEL TWO

The Hardware World
Chapters 4,5

LEVEL ONE

The Algorithmic Foundations of Computer Science
Chapters 2,3

I t has often been said that computer science is "the science of building pretend worlds." What that rather unusual comment means is that the underlying hardware structure of a computer can be so difficult to work with that we must create more friendly and more usable "virtual worlds" in which to work and solve problems. Without that layer of abstraction between us and the machine, we would be relegated to solving problems by applying only the ideas and capabilities studied in Level 2—binary numbers, digital circuits, absolute memory addresses, and machine language instructions. That is not a very comforting thought.

In this part of the text we will learn how to create these user-friendly "microworlds" and produce an environment in which efficient and productive problem solving is possible.

CHAPTER

6

AN INTRODUCTION TO SYSTEM SOFTWARE AND VIRTUAL MACHINES

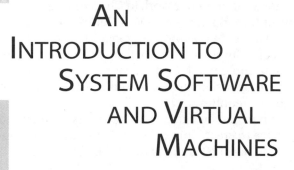

chapter outline

6.1   INTRODUCTION

Let's review for a moment our work in Chapters 4 and 5. Those two chapters described a computer model, called a Von Neumann machine, capable of executing programs written in machine language. This computer has all the hardware needed to solve important real-world problems, but it has no "support tools" to make that problem-solving task easy. The computer described in Chapter 5 is what is humorously called a **naked machine**: hardware bereft of any helpful user-oriented features.

Imagine what it would be like to work on a naked machine. To solve a problem, you would have to create hundreds or thousands of cryptic and highly confusing machine language instructions that looked like this:

10110100110100011100111100001000

and you would have to do that without making a single mistake. To execute properly, a program must be error-free, for even one minor mistake can cause it to behave incorrectly. Imagine the likelihood of writing a perfectly correct program containing thousands of instructions like the one shown above. Even worse, imagine trying to locate an error buried deep inside that incomprehensible mass of 0s and 1s. That is a truly depressing thought.

On a naked machine the data as well as the instructions must be represented in binary. For example, a program cannot refer to the decimal integer +9 directly but must express it as

0000000000001001   (the binary representation of +9 using 16 bits)

You cannot use the symbol A to refer to the first letter of the alphabet but must represent it using its 8-bit ASCII code value, which is decimal 65:

01000001   (the 8-bit ASCII code for "A". See Figure 4.3.)

As you can imagine, writing programs for a naked machine is no joy.

Even if you are lucky enough to get the program written correctly, your work is still not done. A program for a Von Neumann computer must be stored in memory prior to execution. Therefore, you must now take the program and store its instructions into sequential cells in memory. On a naked machine there is no assistance provided for this task, so the programmer must do it, one instruction at a time. Assuming that each instruction occupies one memory cell, the programmer would load the first instruction into address 0, the second instruction into address 1, the third instruction into address 2, . . ., until all have been stored.

Finally, what starts the program running? A naked machine does not do this automatically. (As you are probably coming to realize, a naked machine does not do *anything* automatically, except fetch, decode, and execute machine language instructions.) The programmer must initiate execution by storing a 0, the address of the first instruction of the program, into the program counter (PC) and pressing the START button. This begins the fetch/decode/execute cycle described in Chapter 5. The control unit fetches from memory the contents of the address in the PC, currently 0, and executes that instruction. The program continues sequentially from that point while the user prays that everything works, because he or she cannot bear to face a naked machine again!

We have painted a bleak picture but an honest one. Working directly with the hardware is a virtually impossible task. The functional units described in Chapter 5 were built from the standpoint of what is easy for hardware to do, not what is easy for people to do.

To make a Von Neumann computer usable, we must create a **user interface** between user and hardware. This interface would do many things:

- Hide from the user the messy and unnecessary details of the underlying hardware.
- Present information about what is happening in a way that does not require in-depth knowledge of the internal structure of the system.
- Allow easy user access to the resources available on this computer.
- Prevent accidental or intentional damage to hardware, programs, and data.

By way of analogy, let's look at how people use another common tool—the automobile. The internal combustion engine is a complex piece of technology, and very few people really understand how it works. For most of us, the functions of carburetors, distributors, and cam shafts are a total mystery. However, most people find driving a car quite easy. This is because the driver does not have to lift the hood and interact directly with the hardware in order to operate a car; that is, he or she does not have to drive a "naked automobile." Instead, there is an interface, the **dashboard**, that simplifies things considerably. The dashboard hides the details of engine operation that a driver does not need to know. What *is* important—things such as oil pressure, fuel levels, and vehicle speed— are presented in a simple, "people-oriented" way: oil indicator warning light on or off, fuel gauge empty or full, speed in miles per hour. Access to the engine and transmission is achieved in terms of a few simple operations: a key to start and stop, pedals to speed up or slow down, a shift lever to go forward and backward.

We need a similar interface for our Von Neumann machine. This "computer dashboard" should eliminate most of the hassles of working on a naked machine and let us view the hardware resources of Chapter 5 in a much friendlier way. Such an interface does exist, and it is called **system software**. That is our focal point in Level 3.

6.2 SYSTEM SOFTWARE

6.2.1 THE VIRTUAL MACHINE

System software is a collection of computer programs that manage the resources of a computer and facilitate access to those resources. It is important to remember that we are describing software, not hardware. There are no black boxes wired to a computer and labeled "system software." Software consists of

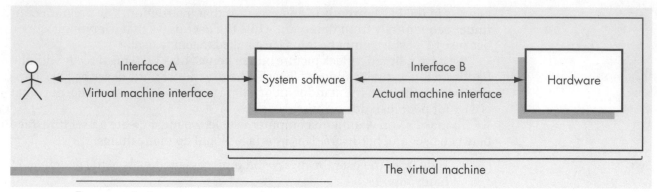

The virtual machine

FIGURE 6.1

The Role of System Software

sequences of instructions—programs—that solve a problem. However, instead of solving *user* problems, such as looking up names in a telephone book, system software has the responsibility of making a computer and its many resources easier to access and use.

System software acts as an *intermediary* between the users and the hardware, as shown in Figure 6.1. System software presents the user with a set of services and resources across the interface labeled A in Figure 6.1. These resources may actually exist, or they may be simulated by the software to give the user the illusion that they exist. The set of services and resources created by the software and seen by the user is called a *virtual machine* or a *virtual environment*. The system software, not the user, interacts with the actual hardware (that is, the naked machine) across the interface labeled B in Figure 6.1.

The system software has responsibilities similar to those of the dashboard of an automobile:

* Hide from the user details of the internal structure of the Von Neumann architecture.
* Present important information in a way that is easy to understand.
* Allow the user to access hardware resources in a simple and efficient way.
* Provide a secure and safe environment in which to operate.

For example, to add two numbers, it is much easier to use simple notation such as $a = b + c$ than to worry about 1) loading ALU registers from memory cells b and c, 2) activating the ALU, 3) selecting the output of the addition circuit, and 4) sending the result to memory cell a. The programmer should not have to know about registers, addition circuits, and memory addresses but instead should see a virtual machine that "understands" the symbols + and =.

After the program is written, it should be loaded into memory without the programmer having to specify where it should be placed. Instead, he or she should issue one command to the virtual machine that says, "Load my program and then execute it."

Finally, when the program is running and generating results, the programmer should be able to instruct the virtual machine to "Place the output of my

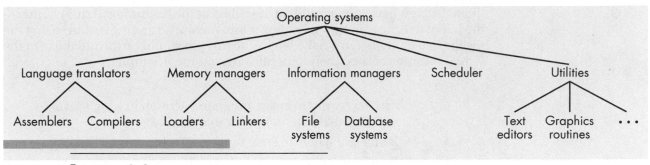

FIGURE 6.2

Types of System Software

program in a file on the disk." Messy I/O details such as sector addresses and I/O controllers should be the farthest thing from his or her mind.

All the useful services just described *are* provided by the system software available on any modern computer system, and it is much easier to do problem solving on a virtual machine than on a real one. The following sections show how this friendly user-oriented environment is created.

6.2.2 TYPES OF SYSTEM SOFTWARE

System software is not a single monolithic entity but a collection of many different programs. The types found on a typical computer are shown in Figure 6.2.

The program that controls the overall operation of the computer is the **operating system**, and it is the most important piece of system software on a computer. It is the operating system that communicates with the user, determines what he or she wants, and activates other system programs, applications packages, or user programs to carry out that request. The software packages that might handle these requests include

- **Language translators.** These programs, called **assemblers** and **compilers**, allow you to write in a user-oriented language rather than the machine language of Chapter 5.

- **Memory managers.** These routines allocate memory space for programs and data and load programs into memory prior to execution.

- **File systems.** These routines handle the storage and retrieval of information on mass storage devices such as the disks, CD-ROMs, and tapes described in Section 5.2.2.

- **Scheduler.** This system program keeps a list of programs ready to run on the processor and selects the one that will execute next. Typically, it keeps the list in priority order so that programs with higher priority run first.

- **Utilities.** These are collections of library routines that provide useful services either to a user or to other system routines. Text editors, graphics routines, and windowing packages are examples of utility routines. Sometimes these utilities are organized into collections called **program libraries**.

These system routines are used during every phase of problem solving on a computer, and it would be virtually impossible to get anything done without them. Let's go back to the problem described at the beginning of this chapter—the job of writing a program, loading it into memory, running it, and saving the results in a data file. On a naked machine this job would be formidable. On the virtual machine created by system software, it is much simpler:

Step	Task
1	Use a *text editor* to create program P written in a high-level, English-like notation rather than binary.
2	Use the *file system* to store program P on your hard disk.
3	Use a *language translator* to translate program P from a high-level language into a machine language program M.
4	Use a *loader* to allocate sufficient memory to hold program M and load its instructions into memory from the file where it is stored.
5	Use the *scheduler* to schedule and run program M.
6	Use the *file system* to store the output of the program into data file D.
7	If the program did not complete successfully, use a *debugger* to help locate the error.

On a virtual machine, the messy details of machine operation are no longer visible, and a user can concentrate on higher-level issues: writing the program, executing the program, and saving and analyzing results.

There are many types of system software, and it would be impossible to cover them all in a single chapter. Instead, we will study two types as representatives of the entire group. Section 6.3 treats assemblers, and Section 6.4 looks at the design and construction of operating systems. Together, these discussions offer a good overview of the virtual machine concept and the issues involved in building and using system software.

6.3   ASSEMBLERS AND ASSEMBLY LANGUAGE

6.3.1 ASSEMBLY LANGUAGE

One of the first places where we need a more friendly virtual environment is in our choice of programming language. Being designed from a machine's point of view, not a person's, machine language is complicated and difficult to understand. What specifically is wrong with machine language, and what needs to be changed? Many things.

- It uses binary. There are no English-like words, mathematical symbols, or other convenient mnemonics to make the language more readable.

- It allows only numeric memory addresses. A programmer cannot name an instruction or a piece of data and refer to it by name.

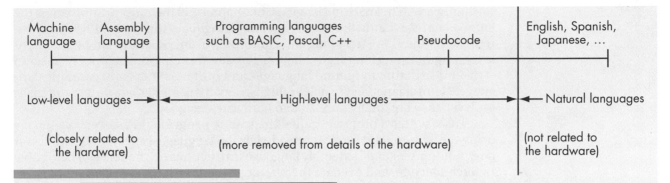

FIGURE 6.3

The Continuum of
Programming Languages

- It is difficult to change. If we insert or delete an instruction, all memory addresses following that instruction will change. For example, if we place a new instruction into memory location 503, then the instruction previously in location 503 is now in 504. All references to address 503 must be updated to point to 504. There may be hundreds of such references.

- It is difficult to create data. If a user wishes to store a piece of data in memory, he or she must compute the internal binary representation for that data item. These conversion algorithms are complicated and time-consuming.

The individuals who programmed on those early first-generation computers quickly realized the shortcomings of machine language. They developed a new language, called **assembly language**, designed for people as well as computers. Assembly languages created a more productive, user-oriented environment, and assemblers were one of the first pieces of system software to be widely used. When assembly languages first appeared in the early 1950s, they were one of the most important new developments in programming—so important, in fact, that they were considered an entirely new generation of language, analogous to the new generations of hardware described in Section 5.3. Assembly languages were termed **second-generation languages** to distinguish them from machine languages, which were viewed as **first-generation languages**.

Today, assembly languages are more properly viewed as **low-level programming languages**, which means they are closely related to the machine language of Chapter 5. Each symbolic assembly language instruction is translated into exactly *one* binary machine language instruction.

This contrasts with languages like BASIC, Pascal, C++, and Java, which are **high-level programming languages**. High-level languages are more user-oriented, they are not machine-specific, and they use both natural language and mathematical notation in their design. A single high-level language instruction is typically translated into *many* machine language instructions, and the virtual environment created by a high-level language is much more powerful than the one produced by an assembly language. We discuss high-level languages in detail in Chapters 7 and 8.

Figure 6.3 shows a "continuum of programming languages," from the lowest level (closest to the hardware) to the highest level (most abstract, farthest from the hardware). The machine language of Chapter 5 is the most primitive; it is the language of the hardware itself. Assembly language, the topic of this chapter, represents the first step along the continuum from machine language. High-level programming languages, the topic of the next chapter, are much closer in style and structure to natural languages and quite distinct from assembly language. Natural languages, such as English, Spanish, and Japanese, are the highest level; they are totally unrelated to hardware design.

A user writes a program, called the **source program**, in assembly language using the features and services provided by the language. However, the processor does not "understand" assembly language instructions, in the sense of being able to fetch, decode, and execute them as described in Chapter 5. The source program must be translated into a machine language program, called the **object program**. This translation is carried out by a piece of system software called an **assembler**. (Translators for high-level languages are called **compilers**. They are discussed separately in Chapter 9.) Once the object program has been produced, its instructions can be loaded into memory and executed by the processor exactly as described in Section 5.2.5. The complete translation/loading/execution process is diagrammed in Figure 6.4.

What are the services that an assembler provides? What are the advantages of writing in assembly language rather than machine language? There are three major advantages:

- Use of symbolic operation codes rather than numeric ones
- Use of symbolic memory addresses rather than numeric ones
- Pseudo-operations that provide useful user-oriented services such as data generation

This section describes a simple, but nonetheless realistic, assembly language that demonstrates these three advantages.

Our hypothetical assembly language is composed of instructions in the following format:

label: op code mnemonic   address field   --comment

The **comment** field, preceded in our notation by a double dash, --, is not really part of the instruction. It is a helpful explanation added to the instruction by a programmer and intended for someone reading the program. It is ignored during translation and execution.

Assembly languages allow the programmer to refer to op codes using a symbolic name, called the **op code mnemonic**, rather than by a number. We can write op codes using meaningful words like LOAD, ADD, and STORE rather than obscure binary codes like 0000, 0011, and 0001. Figure 6.5 shows an assembly language instruction set for a Von Neumann machine that has a single ALU register R and three condition codes GT, EQ, and LT. That figure lists each numeric op code, its assembly language mnemonic, and its meaning. This table is identical to Figure 5.19, the language used in Chapter 5 to introduce the Von Neumann architecture and explain how instructions are executed. (However, Chapter 5 was describing binary machine language and used symbolic names only for convenience. In this chapter we are describing assembly language where symbolic names, such as LOAD and ADD are actually part of the language.)

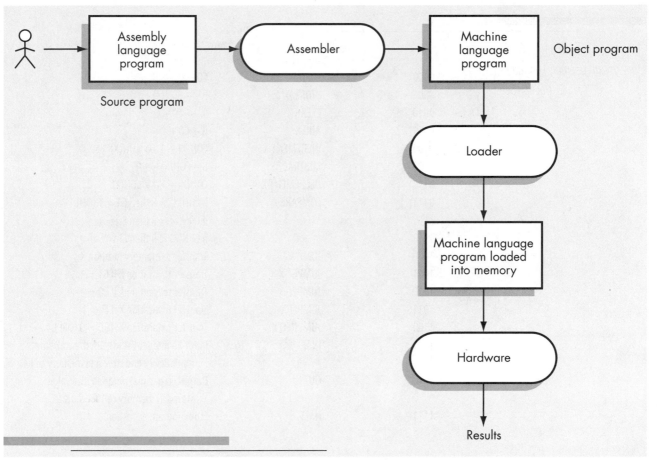

FIGURE 6.4

The Translation/Loading/Execution Process

Another advantage of assembly language is that it lets programmers use **symbolic addresses** in addition to numeric addresses. In machine language, to jump to the instruction in location 17, you must refer directly to address 17; that is, you must write JUMP 17 (in binary, of course). This is cumbersome, because if a new instruction is inserted anywhere within the first 17 lines of the program, the location where you wish to jump will change to 18. The old reference to 17 is incorrect, and the address field must be fixed. This makes modifying programs very difficult, and even small changes become big efforts. It is not unlike identifying yourself in a waiting line by position—as, say, the tenth person in line. As soon as someone in front of you leaves (or someone cuts into line ahead of you), that number is incorrect. It is far better to identify yourself using a characteristic that does not change as people enter or exit the line. For example, you are the person wearing the green suit with the orange and pink shirt. Those characteristics won't change (though maybe they should).

In assembly language we do exactly the same thing. We can attach a symbolic **label** to any instruction or piece of data in the program. The label becomes a permanent identification for this instruction or data, regardless of where it appears in the program or where it may be moved in memory. A label is a name

FIGURE 6.5

Typical Assembly Language
Instruction Set

BINARY OP CODE	OP CODE MNEMONIC	MEANING
0000	LOAD X	CON(X) → R
0001	STORE X	R → CON(X)
0010	CLEAR X	0 → CON(X)
0011	ADD X	R + CON(X) → R
0100	INCREMENT X	CON(X) + 1 → CON(X)
0101	SUBTRACT X	R − CON(X) → R
0110	DECREMENT X	CON(X) − 1 → CON(X)
0111	COMPARE X	if CON(X) > R then GT = 1 (ON)
		if CON(X) = R then EQ = 1
		if CON(X) < R then LT = 1
1000	JUMP X	Transfer to memory location X.
1001	JUMPGT X	Transfer to location X if GT = 1.
1010	JUMPEQ X	Transfer to location X if EQ = 1.
1011	JUMPLT X	Transfer to location X if LT = 1.
1100	JUMPNEQ X	Transfer to location X if EQ = 0 (OFF).
1101	IN X	Input an integer value from the standard input device and store it in memory cell X.
1110	OUT X	Output, in decimal notation, the value stored in memory cell X.
1111	HALT	Stop program execution.

(followed by a colon to identify it as a label) placed at the beginning of an instruction.

        BEGIN: LOAD X

The label BEGIN has been attached to the instruction LOAD X. This means that the name BEGIN is *equivalent to* the address of the memory cell that holds the instruction LOAD X. If, for example, the LOAD X instruction ends up being stored in memory cell 62, then the name BEGIN is equivalent to address 62. Any use of the name BEGIN in the address field of an instruction is treated in exactly the same way as though the user had written the numeric address 62. For example, to jump to the load instruction shown above, we do not need to know that it is stored in location 62. Instead, we need only write the instruction

        JUMP   BEGIN

Symbolic labels have two advantages over numeric addresses. The first is **program clarity**. As with the use of mnemonics for op codes, the use of meaningful symbolic names can make a program much more readable. Names like BEGIN, LOOP, COUNT, and ERROR carry a good deal of meaning and help people to understand what the code is doing. Memory addresses such as 73, 147, and 2001 do not. A second advantage of symbolic labels is **maintainability**. When we refer to an instruction via a symbolic label rather than an address, we no longer need to modify the address field when instructions are added to or removed from the program. Consider the following example:

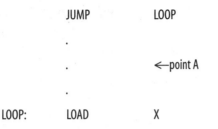

```
        JUMP        LOOP

          .

          .         ←point A

          .

LOOP:   LOAD        X
```

Say a new instruction is added to the program at point A. When the modified program is translated into machine language, all instructions following point A are placed in a memory cell whose address is 1 higher than it was before (assuming that each instruction occupies one memory cell). However, the JUMP refers to the LOAD instruction only by the name LOOP, not by the address where it is stored. Therefore, neither the JUMP nor the LOAD instruction needs to be changed. We need only retranslate the modified program. The assembler determines the new address of the LOAD X instruction, makes the label LOOP equivalent to this new address, and places this new address into the address field of the JUMP LOOP instruction. The assembler does all the messy bookkeeping previously done by the machine language programmer. That is the beauty of system software and the virtual machine environment that it creates.

The final advantage of assembly language programming is **data generation**. In Section 4.2.1 we showed the algorithms used to represent unsigned numbers, signed integers, floating point values, and characters. When writing machine language, the programmer must do these conversions. In assembly language, however, the programmer can ask the assembler to do them.

To make this request, we use a special type of assembly language op code called a **pseudo-op**. A pseudo-op (preceded in our notation by a period to indicate its type) does not generate a machine language instruction like other operation codes. Instead, it invokes a service of the assembler. One of these services is generating data in the proper binary representation for this system. There are typically assembly language pseudo-ops to generate integer, character, and (if the hardware supports it) real data values. In our example language, we will limit ourselves to one data generation pseudo-op called .DATA that builds signed integers. This pseudo-op converts the signed decimal integer in the address field to the proper binary representation. For example, the pseudo-op

```
FIVE:      .DATA      +5
```

tells the assembler to generate the binary representation for the integer +5, put it into memory, and make the label "FIVE" equivalent to the address of that cell.

If a memory cell contained 16 bits, and the next available memory cell was address 53, then this pseudo-op would produce

address   contents

53 | 0000000000000101 |

and the name FIVE would be equivalent to memory address 53. Similarly, the pseudo-op

NEGSEVEN: .DATA   −7

might produce the following 16-bit quantity, assuming sign/magnitude representation:

address   contents

54 | 1000000000000111 |

and the symbol NEGSEVEN would be equivalent to memory address 54.

We can now refer to these data items by their attached label. For example, to load the value +5 into register R, we can say

LOAD   FIVE

This is equivalent to saying LOAD 53, which would load register R with the contents of memory cell 53—that is, the integer +5. Note that if we had incorrectly said

LOAD   5

the contents of memory cell 5 would be loaded into register R. This is not what we intended, and the program would be wrong. Here is a good example of why it is so important to distinguish between the address of a cell and its contents.

To add the value −7 to the current contents of register R, we would write

ADD   NEGSEVEN

The contents of R (currently +5) and the contents of address NEGSEVEN (address 54, whose contents are −7) are added together, producing −2. This becomes the new contents of register R.

When generating data values, we must be careful not to place them in memory locations where they could be misinterpreted as instructions. In Chapter 4 we said that the only way a computer can tell that the binary value 01000001 is the letter A rather than the decimal value 65 is by the context in which it appears. The same is true for instructions and data. They are indistinguishable from each other, and the only way a Von Neumann machine can determine whether a sequence of 0s and 1s is an instruction or a piece of data is by how we use that sequence. If we attempt to execute a value stored in memory, then that value *becomes* an instruction whether we meant it to be or not.

For example, if we incorrectly write the sequence

LOAD   X

.DATA   +1

FIGURE 6.6

Structure of a Typical Assembly Language Program

```
.BEGIN              -- This must be the first line of the program.
   .                -- Here are assembly language instructions
   .                -- of the type shown in Figure 6.5.
   .
HALT
   .
   .                -- Data generation pseudo-ops such as
   .                -- .DATA are placed here, after the HALT.
.END                -- This must be the last line of the program.
```

then, after executing the LOAD X command, the processor will fetch, decode, and attempt to execute the "instruction" +1. This may sound meaningless, but to a processor, it is not. The representation of +1, using 16 bits, is

0000000000000001

Because this value is being used as an instruction, some of the bits will be interpreted as the op code and some as the address field. If we assume a 16-bit one-address instruction format, with the first four bits being the op code and the last 12 bits being the address field, then these 16 bits will be interpreted as follows:

$$\underbrace{0000}_{op\ code}\quad \underbrace{000000000001}_{address}$$

The "op code" is 0, which is a LOAD on our hypothetical machine (see Figure 6.5), and the "address field" contains a 1. Thus the data value +1 has accidentally turned into the following instruction:

LOAD   1   --Load register R with the contents of memory cell 1

This is obviously incorrect, but how is the problem solved? The easiest way is to remember to place all data in a section of the program where they cannot possibly be executed. One convenient place that meets this criterion is after the HALT instruction at the end of the program, because the HALT prevents any further execution. The data values can be referenced; they just cannot be executed.

A second service provided by pseudo-ops is **program construction**. Pseudo-ops that mark the beginning (.BEGIN) and end (.END) of the assembly language program specify where to start and stop the translation process, and they do not generate any instructions or data. Remember that it is the HALT instruction, not the .END pseudo-op, that terminates execution of the program. The .END pseudo-op ends the translation process. Figure 6.6, which shows the organization of a typical assembly language program, helps explain this distinction.

PRACTICE PROBLEMS

1. Assume that register R and memory cells 80 and 81 contain the following values:

   R: 20   memory cell 80: 43   memory cell 81: 97

   Using the instruction set shown in Figure 6.5, determine what value will end up in register R and memory cells 80 and 81 after each of the following instructions is executed. Assume that each question begins with the values shown above.

   a. LOAD 80   d. ADD 81
   b. STORE 81   e. IN 80
   c. COMPARE 80   f. OUT 81

2. Assume that memory cell 50 contains a 4 and that label L is equivalent to memory location 50. What value would each of the following LOAD instructions load into register R?

   a. LOAD 50   c. LOAD L
   b. LOAD 4   d. LOAD L+1   (Assume that this is legal.)

6.3.2 EXAMPLES OF ASSEMBLY LANGUAGE CODE

This section looks at how to use assembly language to translate algorithms into programs that can be executed on a Von Neumann computer. Today, few people do large-scale software development in assembly language; most prefer to use one of the higher-level languages mentioned in Figure 6.3 and described in succeeding chapters. Our purpose in offering these examples is to demonstrate how system software, in this case an assembler, can create a user-oriented virtual environment that supports effective and productive problem solving. The use of symbolic operation codes, symbolic addresses, and convenient data representations makes problem solving a far simpler task than it would be in the naked machine environment described at the beginning of this chapter.

One of the most common operations in any algorithm is the evaluation of arithmetic expressions. For example, the sequential search algorithm of Figure 2.9 contained the following arithmetic operations:

Set the value of i to 1   (line 2)

　　.

　　.

　　.

Add 1 to the value of i (line 7)

These algorithmic operations can be translated quite easily into assembly language as follows:

```
LOAD        ONE        --Put a 1 into register R.
STORE       I          --Store the constant 1 into i.
```

```
        .
        .
        .
      INCREMENT    I          --Add 1 to memory location i.
        .
        .
        .
  I:    .DATA      0          --The index value. Initially it is 0.
  ONE:  .DATA      1          --The constant 1.
```

Note how readable this code is, compared to machine language, because of such op code mnemonics as LOAD and STORE and the use of descriptive labels such as I and ONE.

As a second example, here is the assembly language translation of the arithmetic expression $A = B + C - 7$. (Assume that B and C have already been assigned values.)

```
      LOAD       B          --Put the value B into register R.
      ADD        C          --R now holds the sum (B + C).
      SUBTRACT   SEVEN      --R now holds the expression (B + C − 7).
      STORE      A          --Store the result into A.
        .
        .                   --These data should be placed after the HALT.
        .
  A:    .DATA     0
  B:    .DATA     0
  C:    .DATA     0
  SEVEN: .DATA    7          --The constant 7.
```

Another important algorithmic operation involves testing and comparing values. The comparison of values and the subsequent use of the outcome to decide what to do next are termed a **conditional** operation, which we first saw in Section 2.2.3. Here is a conditional that outputs the larger of two values x and y. Algorithmically, it is expressed as follows:

Input the value of x

Input the value of y

If $x \geq y$ then

   Output the value of x

Else

   Output the value of y

In assembly language, this conditional operation could be translated as follows:

	IN	X	--Read the first data value
	IN	Y	--and now the second.
	LOAD	Y	--Load the value of Y into register R.
	COMPARE	X	--Compare X to Y and set condition codes.
	JUMPLT	PRINTY	--If X is less than Y, jump to PRINTY.
	OUT	X	--We get here only if X ≥ Y, so print X.
	JUMP	DONE	--skip over the next instruction and continue.
PRINTY:	OUT	Y	--We get here if X < Y, so print Y.
DONE:	.		
	.		--The program continues here.
	.		
	.		--The following data go after the HALT.
	.		
X:	.DATA	0	--Space for the two data values.
Y:	.DATA	0	
	.		
	.		
	.		

Another important algorithmic primitive is **looping**, which was also introduced in Section 2.2.3. The following algorithmic example contains a repeat loop that executes 10,000 times.

Step	Operation	Explanation
1	Set i to 0	Start the loop counter at 0.
2	While the value of $i < 10,000$ do lines 3–9.	
	.	
3–8	.	Here is the loop body that is to be done 10,000 times.
	.	
9	Add 1 to the value of i	Increment the loop counter.
10	End of the loop	
11	Stop	

This looping construct is easily translated into assembly language.

```
                LOAD      ZERO        --Initialize the loop counter to 0.
                STORE     I           --This is step 1 of the algorithm.
    LOOP:       LOAD      MAXVALUE    --Put 10,000 into register R.
                COMPARE   I           --Compare I against 10,000.
                JUMPEQ    DONE        --If I = 10,000 we are done. (step 2)
                .         .

                .         .           --Here is the loop body. (steps 3–8)

                .         .
                INCREMENT I           --Add 1 to I. (step 9)
                JUMP      LOOP        --End of the loop body. (step 10)
    DONE:       HALT                  --Stop execution. (step 11)
    ZERO:       .DATA     0           --This is the constant 0.
    I:          .DATA     0           --The loop counter. It goes to 10,000.
    MAXVALUE:   .DATA     10000       --Maximum number of loop executions.
                .

                .
```

As a final example, we will show a complete assembly language program (including all necessary pseudo-ops) to solve the following problem:

Read in a sequence of non-negative numbers, one number at a time, and compute a running sum. When you encounter a negative number, print out the sum of the non-negative values and stop.

Thus, if the input is

8
31
7
5
−1

then the program should output the value 51, which is the sum (8 + 31 + 7 + 5).

An algorithm to solve this problem is shown in Figure 6.7, using the pseudocode notation of Chapter 2. Our next task is to convert the algorithmic primitives of Figure 6.7 into assembly language instructions. A program that does this is shown in Figure 6.8.

Of all the examples in this chapter, the program in Figure 6.8 demonstrates best what is meant by the phrase *user-oriented virtual environment.* Though it is not as clear as English or the pseudocode of Chapter 2, this program can be read and understood by humans as well as computers. Tasks such as modifying the program and locating an error are significantly easier on the code of Figure 6.8 than on its machine language equivalent.

The program in Figure 6.8 is an important "milestone" in that it represents a culmination of the algorithmic problem-solving process. Earlier chapters

FIGURE 6.7

*Algorithm to Compute
the Sum of Numbers*

Step	Operation
1	Set the value of *Sum* to 0
2	Input the first number *N*
3	While *N* is not negative, execute lines 4 and 5
4	Add the value of *N* to *Sum*
5	Input the next data value *N*
6	End of the loop
7	Print out *Sum*
8	Stop

introduced algorithms and problem solving (Chapters 1, 2, 3), discussed how to build computers to execute algorithms (Chapters 4, 5), and introduced system software that enables us to code algorithms into a language that computers can translate and execute (Chapter 6). The program in Figure 6.8 is the final result of this discussion. That program can be input to an assembler, translated into machine language, loaded into a Von Neumann computer, and executed to produce answers to our problem. This **algorithmic problem-solving cycle** is one of the central themes of computer science.

6.3.3 TRANSLATION AND LOADING

What happens to the assembly language program in Figure 6.8? What must be done so that it can be executed on a processor? Figure 6.4 shows that before our source program can be run, we must invoke two system software packages called an **assembler** and a **loader**.

The job of an **assembler** is to translate a symbolic assembly language program, such as the one in Figure 6.8, into machine language. We usually think of translation as an extremely difficult task. In fact, if two languages differ greatly in vocabulary, grammar, and syntax, it can be quite formidable. (This is why a translator for a high-level programming language is a very complex piece of software.) However, machine language and assembly language are very similar, and an assembler is a relatively simple piece of system software.

Laboratory Experience 10

This section of Chapter 6 has introduced assembly language instructions and programming techniques. However, as mentioned before, one does not learn programming and problem solving by reading and watching, but rather by doing and trying. In this laboratory experience you will be programming in an assembly language that is virtually identical to the one shown in Figure 6.5. You will be able to design and write programs like the one shown in Figure 6.8 and execute them on a simulated Von Neumann computer. You will observe the effect of individual instructions on the functional units of this machine and produce results. This experience should give you a deeper understanding of the concepts of assembly language programming and the Von Neumann architecture.

FIGURE 6.8

Assembly Language Program to Compute the Sum of Non-Negative Numbers

```
              .BEGIN                    --This marks the start of the program.
              CLEAR        SUM          --Set the running sum to 0 (line 1).
              IN           N            --Input the first number N (line 2).
--The next three instructions test whether N is a negative number (line 3).
AGAIN:        LOAD         ZERO         --Put 0 into register R.
              COMPARE      N            --Compare N and 0.
              JUMPLT       NEG          --Go to NEG if N < 0.
--We get here if N ≥ 0. We add N to the running sum (line 4).
              LOAD         SUM          --Put SUM into R.
              ADD          N            --Add N. R now holds (N + SUM).
              STORE        SUM          --Put the result back into SUM.
--Get the next input value (line 5).
              IN           N
--Now go back and repeat the loop (line 6).
              JUMP         AGAIN
--We get to this section of the program only when we encounter a negative value.
NEG:          OUT          SUM          --Print the sum (line 7)
              HALT                      --and stop (line 8).
--Here are the data generation pseudo-ops
SUM:          .DATA        0            --The running sum goes here.
  N:          .DATA        0            --The input data are placed here.
ZERO:         .DATA        0            --The constant 0
--Now we mark the end of the entire program.
              .END
```

PRACTICE PROBLEMS

1. Using the instruction set in Figure 6.5, translate the following algorithmic operations into assembly code. Show all necessary .DATA pseudo-ops.
   a. Add 1 to the value of x
   b. Add 50 to the value of x
   c. Set x to the value $y + z - 2$
   d. If $x > 50$ then output the value of x, otherwise input a new value of x

2. Using the instruction set in Figure 6.5, write a complete assembly language program (including all necessary pseudo-ops) that reads in numbers and counts how many inputs it reads until it encounters the first negative value. The program then prints out that count and stops. For example, if the input data were 42, 108, 99, 60, 1, 42, 3, −27, then your program would output the value 7 because there are seven non-negative values before the appearance of the negative value −27.

FIGURE 6.9
Structure of the Op Code Table

OPERATION	BINARY VALUE
ADD	0011
CLEAR	0010
COMPARE	0111
DECREMENT	0110
HALT	1111
.	.
.	.
.	.
STORE	0001
SUBTRACT	0101

An assembler must perform the following four tasks, none of which is particularly difficult.

- Convert symbolic op codes to binary.
- Convert symbolic addresses to binary.
- Perform the assembler services requested by the pseudo-ops.
- Put the translated instructions into a file for future use.

Let's see how these operations would be carried out using the hypothetical assembly language of Figure 6.5.

The conversion of symbolic op codes such as LOAD, ADD, and SUBTRACT to binary makes use of a structure called the **op code table**. This is an alphabetized list of all legal assembly language op codes and their binary equivalents. An op code table for the instruction set of Figure 6.5 is shown in Figure 6.9. (The table assumes that the op code field is 4 bits wide.)

The assembler looks up the operation code mnemonic in column 1 of the table and, when it has been found, replaces the characters with the 4-bit binary value in column 2. (If the mnemonic is not found, then the user has written an illegal op code, which will result in an error message.) Thus, for example, if we use the mnemonic SUBTRACT in our program, the assembler will convert it to the binary value 0101.

An interesting question is what algorithm to use to look up the op code in the op code table. We could select the sequential search algorithm introduced in Chapter 2 and shown in Figure 2.9. However, if we choose this algorithm, translation of our program may be slowed down significantly. The analysis of the sequential search algorithm in Chapter 3 showed that locating a single item in a list of N items takes, on the average, $N/2$ comparisons if the item is in the table and N comparisons if it is not. In Chapter 5 we stated that modern computers may have as many as 300 machine language instructions in their instruction set, so the size of the op code table of Figure 6.9 could be as large as $N = 300$. This means that using sequential search, we will perform an average of $N/2$, about 150, comparisons for every op code in our program. If our assembly language program contains

10,000 instructions (not an unreasonably large number), the op code translation task will require a total of 10,000 instructions × 150 comparisons/instruction = 1.5 million comparisons. That is a lot of searching, even for a computer.

We can do much better by realizing that the op code table of Figure 6.9 is sorted alphabetically. This enables us to use the more efficient **binary search** algorithm discussed in Section 3.5.3 and shown in Figure 3.19. On the average, the time it takes to find any element using binary search is not $N/2$ but $(\lg N)$, the logarithm of N to the base 2. [*Note:* $(\lg N)$ is the value k such that $2^k = N$]. For a table of size $N = 300$, $N/2$ is 150 whereas $(\lg N)$ is approximately 8 ($2^8 = 256$). This says that on the average, we will be able to find an op code in the table in about 8 comparisons rather than 150. If our assembly language program contains 10,000 instructions, then the op code translation task requires only about 10,000 × 8 = 80,000 comparisons rather than 1.5 million, a reduction of 1,420,000. By selecting a better algorithm, we have achieved a speed-up of

$$1,420,000 \div 1,500,000 \approx 95\%$$

To see what this has gained us, imagine that our computer can examine 100,000 symbolic op codes per second. Using sequential search, the computer will spend a total of

$$1,500,000 \div 100,000 = 15 \text{ seconds}$$

searching the op code table. That will add a great deal of time to the translation. However, using binary search, the assembler will spend only

$$80,000 \div 100,000 = 0.8 \text{ second}$$

doing op code look-up. A significant reduction!

This example demonstrates why algorithm analysis, introduced in Chapter 3, is such a critically important part of the design and implementation of system software. The clever replacement of a slow algorithm by a faster one can turn an "insoluble" problem into a solvable one, and a worthless solution into a highly worthwhile one. Remember that, in computer science, we are looking not just for correct solutions but for efficient ones as well.

After the op code has been converted into binary, the assembler must perform a similar task on the address field. It must convert the address from a symbolic value, such as X or LOOP, into the correct binary address. This task is more difficult than converting the op code, because the assembler itself must determine the correct numeric value of all symbols used in the label field. There is no "built-in" address conversion table equivalent to the op code table of Figure 6.9.

In assembly language a symbol is defined by appearing in the label field of an instruction or data pseudo-op. Specifically, the symbol is given the value of the address of the instruction to which it is attached. Assemblers usually make two passes over the source code, where a **pass** is defined as the process of examining and processing every assembly language instruction in the program, one instruction at a time. During the **first pass** over the source code, the assembler looks at every instruction, keeping track of the memory address where this instruction will be stored when it is translated. It does this by knowing where the program begins in memory and knowing how many memory cells are required to store each machine language instruction or piece of data. It also determines whether there is a symbol in the label field of the instruction. If there is, it enters

FIGURE 6.10

Generation of the Symbol Table

LABEL	CODE		LOCATION COUNTER
LOOP:	IN	X	0
	IN	Y	1
	LOAD	X	2
	COMPARE	Y	3
	JUMPGT	DONE	4
	OUT	X	5
	JUMP	LOOP	6
DONE:	OUT	Y	7
	HALT		8
X:	.DATA	0	9
Y:	.DATA	0	10

(a)

SYMBOL TABLE	
SYMBOL	ADDRESS VALUE
LOOP	0
DONE	7
X	9
Y	10

(b)

the symbol and the address of this instruction into a special table that it is building called a **symbol table**.

We can see this process more clearly in Figure 6.10(a). The figure assumes that each instruction and data value occupies one memory cell and that the first instruction of the program will be placed into address 0.

The assembler looks at the first instruction in the program, IN X, and determines that when this instruction is translated, it will go into memory cell 0. Because the label LOOP is attached to that instruction, the name LOOP is made equivalent to address 0. The assembler enters the (name, value) pair (LOOP, 0) into the symbol table. This process of associating a symbolic name with a physical memory address is called **binding**, and the two primary purposes of the first pass of an assembler are 1) to bind all symbolic names to address values and 2) to enter those bindings into the symbol table. Now, any time the programmer uses the name LOOP in the address field, the assembler can look up that symbol in column 1 of the symbol table and replace it with the address value in column 2, in this case address 0. (If it is not found, the programmer has used an undefined symbol, which will produce an error message.)

The next six instructions of Figure 6.10(a), from IN Y to JUMP LOOP, do not contain labels, so they do not add new entries to the symbol table. However, the assembler must still update the counter it is using to determine the address where each instruction will ultimately be stored. The variable used to determine the address of a given instruction or piece of data is called the **location counter**. The location counter values are shown in the third column of Figure 6.10(a). Using the location counter, the assembler can determine that the address values of the labels DONE, X, and Y are 7, 9, and 10 respectively. It will bind these symbolic names and addresses and enter them in the symbol table, as shown in Figure 6.10(b). When the first pass is done, the assembler will have constructed a symbol table that it can use during pass 2. The algorithm for pass 1 of a typical assembler is shown (using an alternative form of algorithmic notation called a **flowchart**) in Figure 6.11.

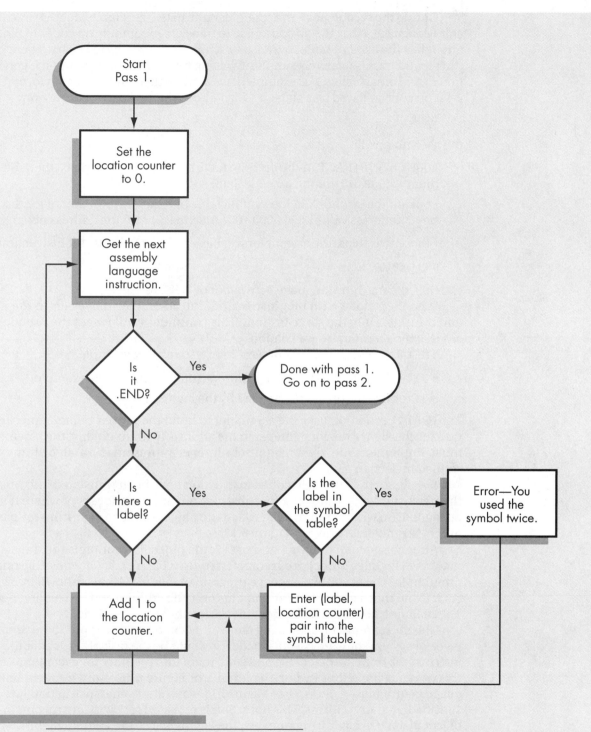

FIGURE 6.11

Outline of Pass 1 of
the Assembler

During the **second pass**, the assembler translates the source program into machine language. It has the op code table to translate mnemonic op codes to binary, and it has the symbol table to translate symbolic addresses to binary. Therefore, the second pass is relatively simple, involving two table look-ups and the generation of two binary fields. For example, if we assume that our instruction format is a 4-bit op code followed by a single 12-bit address, then given the instruction

```
SUBTRACT      X
```

the assembler will

1. Look up SUBTRACT in the op code table of Figure 6.9 and place the 4-bit binary value 0101 in the op code field.
2. Look up the symbol X in the symbol table of Figure 6.10(b) and place the binary address value 0000 0000 1001 (decimal 9) into the address field.

After these two steps, the assembler will have produced the 16-bit instruction

```
0101 0000 0000 1001
```

which is the machine language equivalent of SUBTRACT X.

When it is done with one instruction, the assembler moves on to the next and translates it in the same fashion. This continues until it sees the pseudo-op .END, which terminates translation.

The other responsibilities of pass 2 are also relatively simple.

- Handle data generation pseudo-ops (only .DATA in our example).
- Produce the object file needed by the loader.

The .DATA pseudo-op asks the assembler to build the proper binary representation for the signed decimal integer in the address field. To do this, the assembler must implement the sign/magnitude integer representation algorithms described in Section 4.2.

Finally, after all the fields of an instruction have been translated into binary, the newly built machine language instruction and the address of where it is to be loaded are written out to a file called the **object file**. The algorithm for pass 2 of the assembler is shown in Figure 6.12.

After completion of pass 1 and pass 2, the object file contains the translated machine language **object program** referred to in Figure 6.4. One possible object program for the assembly language program of Figure 6.10(a) is shown in Figure 6.13. (Note that a real object file contains only the address and instruction fields. The meaning field is included here for clarity only.)

The object program shown in Figure 6.13 would become input to yet another piece of system software called a **loader**. It would be the task of the loader to read instructions from the object file and store them into memory for execution. To do this, it reads an address value—column 1 of Figure 6.13—and a machine language instruction—column 2 of Figure 6.13—and stores that instruction into the specified memory address. This operation is repeated for every instruction in the object file. When loading is complete, the loader places the address of the first instruction (0 in this example) into the program counter (PC) to initiate execution. The hardware, as we learned in Chapter 5, then begins the fetch, decode, and execute cycle starting with the instruction whose address is located in the PC, namely the beginning of this program.

FIGURE 6.12

Outline of Pass 2 of the Assembler

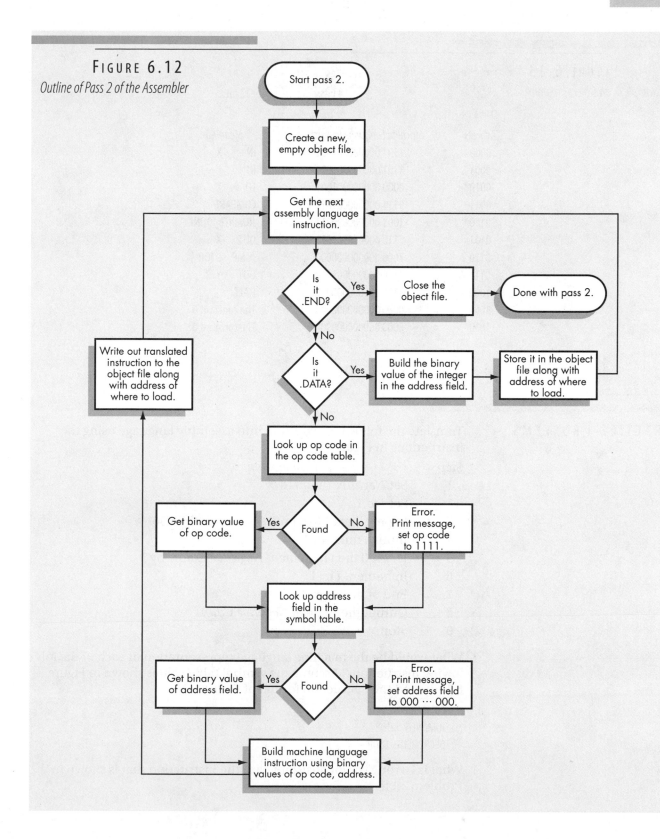

FIGURE 6.13

Example of an Object Program

INSTRUCTION FORMAT: OP CODE   ADDRESS

4 bits   12 bits

OBJECT PROGRAM:

Address	Machine Language Instruction	Meaning
0000	1101 000000001001	IN X
0001	1101 000000001010	IN Y
0010	0000 000000001001	LOAD X
0011	0111 000000001010	COMPARE Y
0100	1001 000000000111	JUMPGT DONE
0101	1110 000000001001	OUT X
0110	1000 000000000000	JUMP LOOP
0111	1110 000000001010	OUT Y
1000	1111 000000000000	HALT
1001	0000 000000000000	The constant 0
1010	0000 000000000000	The constant 0

PRACTICE PROBLEMS

1. Translate the following algorithm into assembly language using the instructions in Figure 6.5.

Step	Operation
1	Set *Negative Count* to 0
2	Set *i* to 1
3	Repeat lines 4 to 6 until *i* is greater than 50
4	Input a number *N*
5	If $N < 0$ then increment *Negative Count* by 1
6	Increment *i* by 1
7	End of the loop
8	Output the value of *Negative Count*
9	Stop

2. What would be the machine language representation of each of the following instructions? Assume the symbol table values shown in Figure 6.10(b) and the instruction format of Figure 6.13.

a. COMPARE Y

b. JUMPNEQ DONE

c. DECREMENT LOOP

3. What is "wrong" or inconsistent with the instruction that is shown in Problem 2(c)?

4. Take the assembly language program that you developed in Problem 1 and determine the physical memory address associated with each label in the symbol table. (Assume the first instruction is loaded into address 0.)

6.4   OPERATING SYSTEMS

To carry out the services just described (translate a program, load a program, and run a program), a user must issue **system commands**. These commands may be lines of text typed at a terminal, such as

>assemble MyProg   (Invoke the assembler to translate the program called MyProg.)

>run MyProg   (Load the translated MyProg into memory and start execution.)

or they may be menu items displayed on a screen and selected with a mouse and a button, using a technique called **point-and-click**.

Regardless of how it is done, the important question is what program examines these commands? What piece of system software waits for requests and activates other system programs like an assembler or loader to service these requests? The answer is the **operating system**, and, as shown in Figure 6.2, it is the "top-level" system software component on a computer. This section takes a look at the services provided by an operating system and traces how these services have evolved over the last 40 years.

6.4.1 FUNCTIONS OF AN OPERATING SYSTEM

An operating system is an enormously large and complex piece of software that has many responsibilities within a computer system. This section examines five of the most important tasks that it performs.

THE USER INTERFACE.   The operating system is executing whenever no other piece of user or system software is using the processor. Its most important task is to wait for a user command delivered via the keyboard, mouse, or other input device. If the command is legal, the operating system activates and schedules the appropriate software package to process the request. In this sense, the operating system acts like the computer's *receptionist* and *dispatcher*.

Operating system commands usually request access to hardware resources (processor, printer, communication lines), software services (translator, loader, text editor, application program), or information (data files, date, time). Examples of typical operating system commands are shown in Figure 6.14. Dozens or even hundreds of different commands are available on a modern operating system.

After a command is entered, it is analyzed to see which software package needs to be loaded and put on the schedule for execution. When that package has completed execution, control returns to the operating system, which waits

FIGURE 6.14

*Some Typical Operating
System Commands*

- Translate a program
- Load a translated program into memory
- Link together separate pieces of software to build a single program
- Run a program
- Save information in a file
- Retrieve a file previously stored
- List all the files for this user
- Print a file
- Copy a file from one I/O device to another
- Establish a network connection
- Tell me the current time and date

for a user to enter the next command. This **user interface** algorithm is diagrammed in Figure 6.15.

The user interfaces on the operating systems of the 1950s, 1960s, and 1970s were text-oriented. The system would display a **prompt character** on the screen to indicate that it was waiting for input, and then it would wait for something to happen. The user could then enter a command in a special, and sometimes quite complicated, **command language**. For example, on the UNIX operating system, widely used on personal computers and workstations, the following command asks the system to list the names and access privileges of the files contained in the Home directory of a user called Mike.

> ls −al /usr/Mike/Home .   (">" is the prompt character)

As you can see, commands were not always easy to understand, and learning the command language of the operating system was a major stumbling block for new users. Unfortunately, until you learned some basic commands, no useful work could be done.

Because users found text-oriented command languages very cumbersome, virtually all modern operating systems have a **graphical user interface**, abbreviated GUI. To communicate with a user, a GUI supports visual aids and point-and-click operations requiring a mouse, rather than textual commands. The interface uses **icons**, **pull-down menus**, **scrolling windows**, and other visualizations and graphical metaphors that make it much easier for a user to formulate requests.

For example, in Figure 6.16 we see a window listing the folders on the hard disk called Mike. One of these is a folder called Home. To list all the files contained in this folder, a user "points-and-clicks" on it, and the list of its files appears in a new window. Compare the clarity of that operation with the preceding UNIX command that does virtually the same thing.

Graphical interfaces are a good example of the high-level virtual machine created by the operating system. A GUI hides a great deal of the underlying hardware and software, and it makes the computer appear very easy to use. In reality,

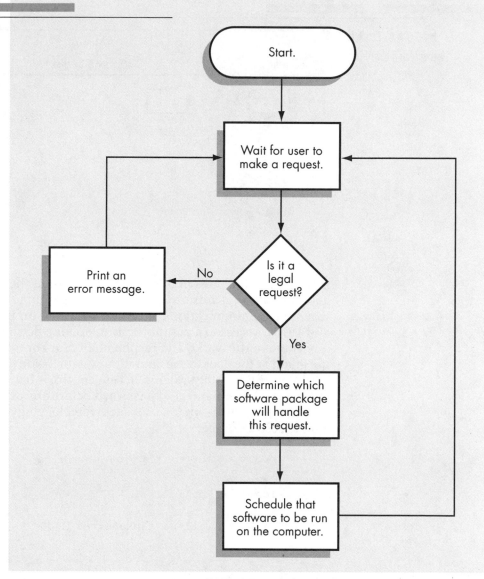

FIGURE 6.15
*User Interface Responsibility
of the Operating System*

the computer that produces the elegant windowing environment shown in Figure 6.16 is the same Von Neumann machine described in Chapters 4 and 5.

SYSTEM SECURITY AND PROTECTION.   In addition to being a receptionist, the operating system also has the responsibilities of a *security guard*—controlling access to the computer and its resources. It must prevent unauthorized users from accessing the system and prevent authorized users from doing unauthorized things.

At a minimum, the operating system must not allow people to log on to the computer if they have not been granted permission. In the "olden days" of computing (the 1950s and 1960s), security was implemented by physical

FIGURE 6.16
*Example of a Graphical
User Interface*

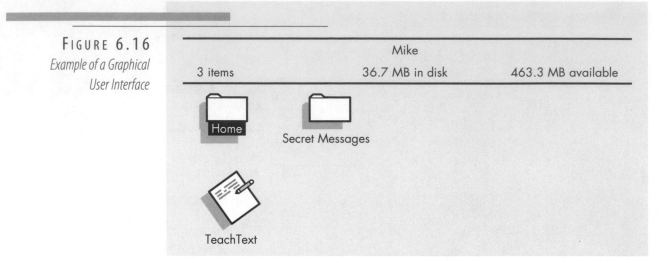

means—putting walls and locked doors around the computer and stationing actual security guards at the door to prevent unauthorized access. However, when telecommunications networks appeared on the scene in the late 1960s and 1970s, access to a computer by telephone became possible from virtually anywhere in the world, and responsibility for control of access migrated from the guard at the door to the operating system inside the machine.

In most operating systems, access control is handled by requiring a user to enter a legal **user name** and **password** before any other requests are accepted. For example, here is what a user sees when logging on to the central computer at Macalester College:

```
* * * * * * * * * * * * * * * * * * * * * * *
*                                           *
*                                           *
*  Welcome to Apollo ...                    *
*                                           *
*  Macalester College AlphaServer 2000      *
*                                           *
*                                           *
* * * * * * * * * * * * * * * * * * * * * * *

User Name:  Schneider
Password:  XXXXX      (Blocked out for security reasons)
$        ($ is the prompt. The system is now waiting for a user request.)
```

If an incorrect user name or password is entered, the operating system will not allow access to the computer. Similar security measures are implemented on Windows-95 , Macintosh, and UNIX machines.

It is also the operating system's responsibility to safeguard the **password file** that stores all valid user name/password combinations. It must prevent this file from being accessed by any unauthorized users, because that would compromise the security of the entire system. This is analogous to putting a lock on your door and also making sure you don't lose the key. (Of course, some privileged

A Machine for the Rest of Us

In January 1984, Apple Computer launched its new line of Macintosh computers with a great deal of showmanship: a TV commercial at the 1984 NFL Superbowl Game. The company described the Macintosh as a computer that anyone could understand and use—"a machine for the rest of us." People who saw and used it quickly agreed, and in the early days, its major selling point was that "a Macintosh is much easier to use than an IBM-PC."

However, the Macintosh and IBM-PC were extremely similar in terms of hardware, and they both looked a great deal like the architecture of Figure 5.18. Both systems used Von Neumann-type processors: the Intel 8086 in the PC and the Motorola 68000 in the Mac. These processors executed similar sets of machine language instructions exactly as described in Chapter 5. It certainly was not the underlying hardware that created these differences in ease of use.

What made the Macintosh appear to be easier to use was its radically new graphical user interface, created by two system software packages called the **Finder** and the **System**. They produced a sophisticated visual environment that most users found much easier to understand than the text-oriented interface of **MS-DOS**, the most popular PC-based operating system of the 1980s and early 1990s. IBM users quickly realized the importance of having a powerful user interface and in the early and mid-1990s began to switch to Microsoft **Windows**, which provided a windowing environment similar to the Macintosh. **Windows-95** and **Windows-98** were attempts at improving the ease of use of the Intel processor via even more powerful graphical interfaces.

We can see now that it was wrong for those early Macintosh users to say that "a Macintosh is easier to use than a PC." What they should have said is that "the virtual machine environment created by the Macintosh operating system is easier to use than the virtual machine environment created by the IBM-PC operating system." Maybe that was just too wordy!

users, called **superusers**, must be able to access and maintain this file. They are usually computer center employees.)

To provide this security, an operating system may **encrypt** the password file using an encoding algorithm that is extremely difficult to crack. We learned in Section 4.2.1 that textual information is stored using the 8-bit ASCII code. Because no *a priori* meaning is given to any sequence of binary digits, every ASCII text string also has a numeric interpretation. For example, the three-character password ABC is represented internally as the following 24 bits:

01000001	01000010	01000011
A	B	C

However, the system can treat these three characters as a single 24-bit signed-integer value. Using this numeric interpretation, the system can perform some sequence of mathematical operations on these 24 bits, such as left-shifting the bits by 6 positions circularly and then adding 15. When applied to the original text, these two operations produce the **encrypted text**

010100001001000011011111

This encrypted string of digits is what is stored in the password file.

If this encoded string is stolen and used as a password without first being decoded, it will not be correct, and the person using it will be denied access.

A thief must steal not only the encrypted text but also the algorithm to change the encrypted text back to the original characters. Without this information the stolen password is useless. Operating systems use encryption algorithms whenever they must provide a high degree of security for sensitive information.

Encryption is an active area of research in computer science. Password files are only one example of sensitive data whose security is critical. Corporate secrets, sensitive medical records, military data, and financial information also must be carefully protected against unauthorized access and change. Frequently, data are encrypted as they are transmitted across a network to foil anyone who taps into the communication line. Encryption specialists are the computer equivalent of locksmiths and safe builders.

Even when valid users gain access to the system, there are things they should not be allowed to do. The most obvious is that they should access only their own personal information. They should not look at the files or records of other users. Therefore, when the operating system sees a request such as

> open filename   (Open up a file and allow this user to access it.)

(Or the user clicks on Open in the File menu.)

it must check to see who is the owner of the file—that is, who created it. If the individual accessing the file is not the owner, then it must reject the request. Most operating systems allow the owner of a file to provide a list of additional authorized users or a class of authorized users, such as all students or all faculty. Like the password file, these **authorization lists** are highly sensitive files, and an operating system would probably store them in encrypted format.

Most modern operating systems not only determine whether you are allowed to access a file, they even check what type of operations you are permitted to do on that file. The following hierarchically ordered list shows the different levels of operations that various users may be permitted to do on a file.

- Read the information in the file but not change it
- Append new information to the end of the file but not change existing information
- Change existing information in the file
- Delete the entire file from the system

For example, the grade file GRADES of a student named Smith could have the authorization list shown in Figure 6.17

FIGURE 6.17
Authorization List for the File GRADES

File: GRADES

NAME	PERMITTED OPERATIONS	
Smith	R	(R = Read only)
Jones	RA	(A = Append)
Adams	RAC	(C = Change)
Doe	RACD	(D = Delete)

Hackers

Every new technology develops its own set of abusers and "undesirables"—those who see a new technology in terms not of potential benefits but of increased opportunities for misuse, just as automobiles brought wonderful benefits but also car thieves and drunk drivers. In computer science our abusive subculture goes by the name **hackers**.

Originally, the word *hacker* did not have a negative connotation. It was a mildly complimentary term for people who knew how to get things done on a computer—those somewhat strange and quirky individuals who seemed to know all the incomprehensible details about how computers worked. They were the "tinkerers" and "fixers" who could enter some weird sequence of commands that miraculously cured whatever was wrong with our system.

However, as computers became more and more important to the functioning of society, and as computer networks increased the number of machines that could be accessed by individuals, the term *hacker* took on a far different meaning. It became associated with individuals who *abuse* information technology for purposes of profit, revenge, or just plain fun; the computer equivalent of joyriding in a stolen automobile. Some hackers are especially fond of figuring out how to override security measures to gain unauthorized access to other computers—perhaps an extremely powerful machine at some university or research center. Once in the machine, they could make changes to data or steal valuable information. More often than not, they only do such things as write out anonymous messages or browse through files and randomly delete information: the technical equivalent of senseless vandalism. However, it can also become much more serious. Hackers sometimes plant a **virus**. This is a program that sits "incubating" inside a computer for a long time, perhaps months or years, until some external event (such as the occurrence of a particular date) causes it to wake up and do serious damage to the entire system.

Only recently has the legal system begun, through new laws and tougher enforcement, to deal with the issue of information abuse. Just as vandalism is not considered a harmless prank, the misuse of information technology is no longer viewed as the harmless intellectual play of "computer jockeys." It is seen for what it is—a serious crime with serious consequences and very severe penalties.

The authorization list of Figure 6.17 says that Smith, the student whose grades are in the file, has the right to access the file, but only to read the information. Jones, a clerk in the administration center, can read the file and can append new grades to the end of the file at the completion of the term. Adams, the school's registrar, can read and append information and is also allowed to change the student's grades if an error was made. Doe, the director of the computer center, can do all of these operations as well as delete the file and all its information.

Permission to look at information can be given to a number of people. However, changing information in a file is a sensitive operation (think about changing a payroll file), and permission to make such changes must be limited. Deleting information is the most powerful and potentially damaging operation of all, and its use must be restricted to people at the highest level. It is the operating system's responsibility to ensure that individuals are authorized to carry out the operation they request.

We close this section on security by saying that system software can prevent you not only from doing damage to others but also from harming *yourself*. This feature is perhaps most apparent when you unintentionally enter a command to erase your entire hard disk. Before carrying out this potentially catastrophic operation, the system prompts you to confirm that you indeed want to do it and, if not, lets you undo it, saving a great deal of frustration and heartache. This is certainly one of the best examples of a user-friendly virtual environment.

EFFICIENT ALLOCATION OF RESOURCES.   Section 5.2.2 described the enormous difference in speed between a processor and an I/O unit: up to 5 orders of magnitude. To handle that difference, we created a hardware device called an I/O controller (Figure 5.9) that frees the processor to do useful work while the I/O operation is being completed. What useful work can a processor do in this free time? What keeps it busy and ensures that this valuable resource is used efficiently? Again, it is the operating system's responsibility to see that the resources of a computer system are used efficiently as well as correctly.

To ensure that a processor does not sit idle if there is useful work to do, the operating system keeps a **queue** (a waiting line) of programs ready to run. Whenever the processor is idle, the operating system picks one of these ready jobs and assigns it to the processor. This guarantees that the processor always has something to do.

To see how this algorithm might work, let's define the following three classes of programs:

Running   The program currently executing on the processor (assume one)

Ready   Programs that are loaded in memory and ready to run but are not yet executing

Waiting   Programs that cannot run because they are waiting for an I/O operation (or some other time-consuming event) to complete

Here is how these three lists might look at some instant in time:

Waiting	*Ready*	*Running*
	B	A
	C	
	D	

There are four programs, called A, B, C, and D, loaded in memory. Program A is executing on the processor; B, C, and D are ready to run and are in line waiting their turn. Assume that A performs the I/O operation "read a sector from the disk." We saw in Section 5.2.2 that, relative to processing speeds, this operation takes a long time, about 10 msec or so. While it is waiting for this operation to complete, the processor has nothing to do, and system efficiency plummets.

To solve this problem, the operating system can do some shuffling. It first moves program A to the waiting list, because it must wait for its I/O operation to finish before it can continue. It then selects one of the ready programs (say B) and assigns it to the processor, which starts executing it. This leads to the following situation:

Waiting	*Ready*	*Running*
A	C	B
	D	

PRACTICE PROBLEM

Assume that programs spend about 25% of their time waiting for I/O operations to complete. If there are two programs loaded into memory, what is the likelihood that both programs will be blocked waiting for I/O and there will be nothing for the processor to do? What percentage of time will the processor be busy? (This value is called **processor utilization**.) By how much does processor utilization improve if we have four programs in memory instead of two?

Instead of sitting idle while A waits for I/O, the processor works on program B and gets something useful done. Perhaps B also does an I/O operation. The operating system repeats the same steps. It moves B to the waiting list, picks any ready program (say C) and starts executing it, producing the following situation:

Waiting	Ready	Running
A	D	C
B		

As long as there is one program that is ready to run, the processor will always have something useful to do.

At some point, the I/O operation that A started will be completed, and the "I/O completed interrupt signal" described in Section 5.2.2 will be generated. The appearance of that signal indicates that program A is now ready to run, but it cannot do so immediately because the processor is currently assigned to C. Instead, the operating system moves A to the ready list, producing the following situation:

Waiting	Ready	Running
B	D	C
	A	

Programs cycle from running to waiting to ready and back to running, each one using only a portion of the resources of the processor.

In Chapter 5 we stated that the execution of a program was an unbroken repetition of the fetch/decode/execute cycle from the first instruction of the program to the HALT. Now we see that this view may not be completely accurate. For reasons of efficiency, the history of a program may be a sequence of starts and stops—a cycle of execution, waits for I/O operations, waits for the processor, followed again by execution. By having many programs loaded in memory and sharing the processor, the operating system can use the processor to its fullest capability and run the overall system more efficiently.

THE SAFE USE OF RESOURCES. Not only must resources be used *efficiently*, they must also be used *safely*. That doesn't mean that an operating system must prevent a user from sticking his or her finger in the power supply and getting electrocuted! It means that it is the job of the operating system to prevent programs or users from attempting operations that could cause the computer system to enter a state where it is incapable of doing any further work—a "frozen" state where all useful work has come to a grinding halt.

To see how this could happen, imagine a computer system that has one laser printer, one tape drive, and two programs A and B. Program A wants to load a data file from a tape drive and print it on the laser printer. Program B wants to do the same things. Each of them makes the following requests to the operating system:

Program A	*Program B*
Get the tape drive.	Get the laser printer.
Get the laser printer.	Get the tape drive.
Print the file.	Print the file.

If the operating system satisfies the first request of each program, then A will "own" the tape drive and B will have the laser printer. When A now requests ownership of the laser printer, it will be told that the printer is being used by B, and it will have to wait. Similarly, B will be told that it will have to wait for the tape drive until A is finished. Each program will be waiting for a resource to become available that never will be free. This situation is called a **deadlock**. Programs A and B are in a permanent waiting state, and if there is no other program ready to run, all useful work on the system will cease.

More formally, deadlock means that there is a set of programs each of which is waiting for an event to occur before it may proceed, but that event can be caused only by another waiting program in the set. Everybody is waiting, and nothing happens.

As another example of deadlock, imagine a telecommunication system in which program A sends messages to program B, which acknowledges their correct receipt. Program A cannot send another message to B until it knows that the last one has been correctly received.

Program A	*Program B*
Message →	
	← Acknowledge
Message →	
	← Acknowledge
Message →	

At this point, B sends an acknowledgment, but let's say it gets lost. (Perhaps there was static on the line, or a lightning bolt jumbled the signal.) What happens? Program A is stopped, waiting for receipt of an acknowledgment from B. Program B is stopped, waiting for the next message from A. Deadlock! Neither side can proceed, and unless something is done, all communication between the two will cease.

How does an operating system solve these problems and handle deadlock conditions? There are two basic approaches, called **deadlock prevention** and **deadlock recovery**. In deadlock prevention, the operating system uses resource allocation algorithms that prevent deadlock from occurring in the first place. In the example of the two programs simultaneously requesting the laser printer and the tape drive, the problem was caused by the fact that each program had a portion of the resources needed to solve its problem, but neither had all that it had requested. To prevent this, the operating system could use the following algorithm:

> If a program cannot get all the resources that it needs, it must give up all the resources it currently owns and issue a completely new request.

Essentially, this resource allocation algorithm says, "If you cannot get everything you need, then you get nothing." If we had used this algorithm, then after program A acquired the laser printer but not the tape unit, it would have had to relinquish ownership of the printer. Now B could get everything it needed to execute, and no deadlock would occur. (It could also work in the reverse direction, with B relinquishing ownership of the tape unit and A getting the needed resources. Which scenario unfolds depends on the exact order in which requests are made.)

In the telecommunications example, one possible deadlock prevention algorithm is to insist that messages and acknowledgements never get garbled or lost. Unfortunately, that is impossible. Real-world communication systems (telephone, microwave, satellite) do make errors, so we are powerless to guarantee that deadlock conditions can never occur. Instead we must detect them and recover from them when they do occur. This is typical of the class of methods called **deadlock recovery algorithms**.

For example, here is a possible algorithmic solution to our telecommunications problem:

Sender: Number your messages with the non-negative integers 0, 1, 2, … and send them in numerical order. If you send message number i and have not received an acknowledgment for 30 seconds, send message i again.

Receiver: When you send an acknowledgment, include the number of the message you received. If you get a duplicate copy of message i, send another acknowledgment and discard the duplicate.

Using this algorithm, here is what might happen:

Program A	Program B
Message (1) →	
	← Acknowledge (1)
Message (2) →	
	← Acknowledge (2) (Assume this acknowledgment is lost.)

At this point we have exactly the same deadlock condition described earlier. However, this time we are able to recover in a relatively short period. For 30 seconds nothing happens. However, after 30 seconds A sends message (2) a second time. B acknowledges it and discards it (because it already has a copy), and communication continues:

(Wait 30 seconds.)

Message (2) →   (A second copy)

         ← Acknowledge (2)   (Discard this duplicate copy)

Message (3) →

.

.

.

We have successfully recovered from the deadlock, and the system is again up and running.

Regardless of whether we prevent deadlocks from occurring or recover from those that do occur, it is the responsibility of the operating system to create a virtual machine in which the user never sees deadlocks and does not worry about them. The operating system should create the illusion of a smoothly functioning, highly efficient, virtually error-free environment—even if, as we know from our glimpse behind the scene, that is not always the case.

SUMMARY.   In this section we have highlighted some of the major responsibilities of the critically important software package called the operating system:

- User interface management   (a receptionist)
- Program scheduling and activation   (a dispatcher)
- Control of access to system and files   (a security guard)
- Efficient resource allocation   (an efficiency expert)
- Deadlock detection, error detection   (a traffic officer)

These are by no means the operating system's only responsibilities, which can also include such areas as input/output processing, allocating priorities to programs, swapping programs in and out of memory, recovering from power failures, managing the system clock, and literally dozens of other tasks, large and small, essential to keeping the computer system running smoothly.

As you can imagine, given all these responsibilities, an operating system is an extraordinarily complex piece of software. An operating system for a large network of computers can require hundreds of thousands of lines of code, take hundreds of person-years to develop, and cost as much to develop as the hardware on which it runs. Even operating systems for personal computers and workstations (such as Windows-95, Windows-NT, UNIX, and the Macintosh System) are huge programs developed over periods of years by teams of dozens of computer scientists. Designing and creating a high-level virtual environment is a difficult job, but without it, computers would not be so widely used nor anywhere near as important as they are today.

6.4.2 HISTORICAL OVERVIEW OF OPERATING SYSTEMS DEVELOPMENT

Like the hardware on which it runs, system software has gone through a number of changes, or generations, since the earliest days of computing. The functions and capabilities of a modern operating system described in the previous section did not appear all at once but rather evolved over many years.

During the **first generation** of system software (roughly 1945–1955, but again these dates are approximate), there really were no operating systems and there was very little software support of any kind—typically just the assemblers and loaders described in Section 6.3. All machine operation was "hands-on." Programmers would sign up for a block of time and, at the appointed time, show up in the machine room carrying all the necessary programs, punched cards, and tapes. They had the entire computer to themselves, and they were responsible for all machine operation. They loaded their assembly language programs into memory along with the assembler and, by punching some buttons on the console, started the transla-

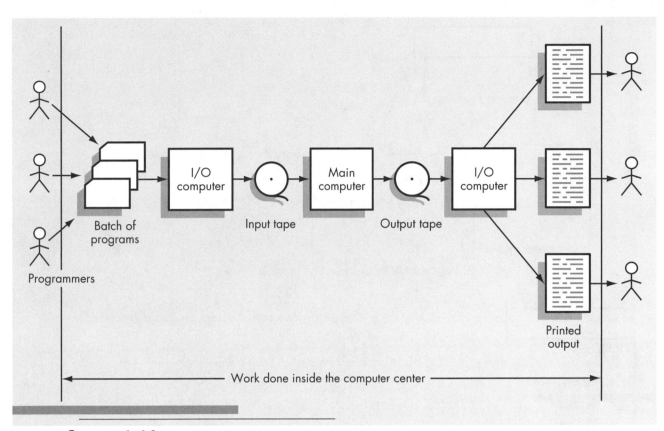

FIGURE 6.18

*Operation of a Batch
Computer System*

tion process. Next they loaded their program into memory and started it running. Working with first-generation software was a lot like working on the naked machine described at the beginning of the chapter. It was attempted only by highly trained professionals intimately familiar with the computer and its operation.

System administrators quickly realized that this was a horribly inefficient way to use a very expensive piece of equipment. (Remember that those early computers cost millions of dollars.) A programmer would sign up for an hour of computer time, but the majority of that time was spent analyzing results and trying to figure out what to do next. During this "thinking time," the system was idle. Eventually, the need to keep machines busy led to the development of a **second generation** of system software called **batch operating systems** (1955–1965).

In second-generation batch operating systems, rather than operate the machine directly, a programmer would hand the program, typically entered on punched cards, to a trained computer operator who grouped it into a "batch"— hence the name. After a few dozen programs were collected, the operator would carry this batch of cards to a small I/O computer that would put these programs on tape. This tape would be carried into the machine room and loaded onto the "big" computer that would actually run the users' programs, one at a time, writing the results to yet another tape. During the last stage, this output tape would be carried back to the I/O computer to be printed and handed to the programmer. The entire cycle is diagrammed in Figure 6.18.

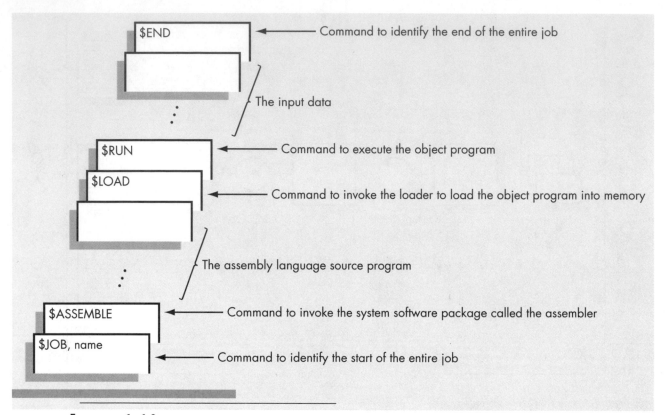

FIGURE 6.19

Structure of a Typical Batch Job

This cycle may seem cumbersome, and from the programmer's point of view, it was. (Every programmer who worked in the late 1950s or early 1960s has horror stories about waiting many hours—even days—for a program to be returned, only to find out that there was a missing comma.) From the computer's point of view, however, this new batch system worked wonderfully, and system utilization increased dramatically. No longer were there delays while a programmer was setting up to perform an operation. There were no long periods of idleness while someone was mulling over what to do next. As soon as one job was either completed normally or halted because of an error, the computer went to the input tape, loaded the next job, and started execution. As long as there was work to be done, the computer could be kept busy.

Because programmers no longer operated the machine, they needed a way to communicate to the operating system what had to be done, and these early batch operating systems were the first to include a **command language**, also called a **job control language**. This was a special-purpose language in which users wrote commands specifying to the operating system (or the human operator) what operations to perform on their programs. These commands were interpreted by the operating system, which initiated the proper action. The "receptionist/dispatcher" responsibility of the operating system had been born. A typical batch job was a mix of programs, data, and commands, as shown in Figure 6.19.

By the mid-1960s, the use of integrated circuits and other new technologies had boosted computational speeds enormously. The batch operating system just described kept only a single program in memory at any one time. If that job paused for a few milliseconds to complete an I/O operation (such as read a disk sector or print a file on the printer), the processor simply waited. As computers became faster, designers began to look for ways to use those idle milliseconds. The answer they came up with led to a **third generation** of operating systems called **multiprogramming operating systems** (1965–1985).

In a multiprogramming operating system, there are many user programs simultaneously loaded into memory, rather than just one:

Memory

Operating System
Program 1
Program 2
Program 3

If the currently executing program pauses for I/O, one of the other ready jobs is selected for execution so that no time is wasted. The cycle of running/waiting/ready states was described on pages 268–269, and it led to significantly higher processor utilization.

In order to make this all work properly, the operating system had the new responsibility of protecting user programs (and itself) from damage by other programs. When there was a single program in memory, the only user program that could be damaged was your own. Now, with many programs in memory, an erroneous instruction in one user's program could play havoc with any of the others. For example, the seemingly harmless instruction

STORE   1000   --Store the contents of register R into memory cell 1000.

should not be executed if the physical address 1000 is not located within the program. It could wipe out an instruction or piece of data in someone else's program, causing unexpected behavior and (probably) incorrect results.

The third-generation operating system would keep track of the upper and lower address bounds of each program in memory:

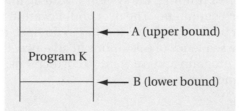

and insure that no program ever attempted a memory reference outside this range. If it did, then the system would cease execution of that program, produce an error message, remove that program from memory, and begin work on another ready program.

Similarly, the operating system could no longer permit any program to execute a HALT instruction, because that would shut down the processor and prevent it from finishing any other programs in memory. These third-generation systems developed the concept of **user operation codes** that could be included in any user program and **privileged operation codes** whose use was restricted to the operating system or other system software. The HALT instruction became a privileged op code that could be executed only by a system program, not by a user program.

These multiprogrammed operating systems were the first to have extensive protection and error detection capabilities, and the "traffic officer" responsibility began to take on much greater importance than in earlier systems.

During the 1960s and 1970s, computer networks and telecommunications systems developed and grew rapidly. Another form of third-generation operating system evolved to take advantage of this new technology. It was called a **time-sharing** system, and it is a variation of the multiprogrammed operating system just described.

As before, many programs can be stored in memory rather than just one. However, instead of requiring the programmer to load all system commands, programs, and data in advance, a time-sharing system allows them to be entered **on-line**—that is, entered dynamically by users sitting at terminals and communicating interactively with the operating system. This configuration is shown in Figure 6.20.

The terminals are connected to the central computer via communication links and can be located anywhere. This new system design freed users from the "tyranny of geography." No longer did they have to go to the computer to hand in their deck of cards; the services of the computer were delivered directly to them via their terminal. However, now that the walls and doors of the computer center no longer provided security and access control, the "security guard/watchman" responsibility became an extremely important part of operating system design.

In a time-sharing system, a user would sit down at a terminal, log in, and initiate a program or make a request by entering a command:

>run   MyJob

In this example, the program called MyJob would be loaded into memory and would compete for the processor with all other ready programs. When the program was finished running, the system would again display a prompt (">") and wait for the next command. The user could examine the results of the last program, think for a while, and decide what to do next, rather than having to determine the entire sequence of operations in advance. For example, say there was a mistake in the program and we want to correct it using a text editor. We can enter the command

>edit   MyJob

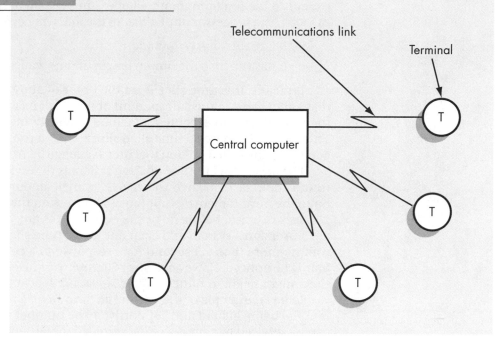

FIGURE 6.20

Configuration of a Time-Shared Operating System

which will load the text editor into memory, schedule it for execution, and cause the file system to load the file called MyJob.

However, one minor change was needed to make this new system work efficiently. In a "true" multiprogramming environment, the only event, other than termination, that causes a program to be **suspended** (taken off the processor) is the execution of a slow I/O operation. What if the program currently executing is heavily **compute-bound**? That is, it does mostly computation and little or no I/O (for example, computing the value of π to a million decimal places). It could run for minutes or even hours before it would be suspended and the processor given to another program. During that time, all other programs would have to sit patiently in the ready queue, waiting their turn. This is analogous to being in line at a bank behind someone depositing thousands of checks.

In a noninteractive environment this situation may be acceptable because no one is sitting at a terminal waiting for output. In fact, it may even be desirable, because a compute-bound job keeps the processor heavily utilized. In a time-sharing system, however, this waiting would be disastrous. There *are* users sitting at terminals communicating directly with the system and expecting an immediate response. If they do not get some type of response soon after entering a command, they may start banging on the keyboard and, eventually, hang up the phone. (Isn't that what you would do if the party at the other end of a telephone did not respond for several minutes?)

Therefore, to design a time-sharing system, we must make the following change to the multiprogrammed operating system described earlier. A program can keep the processor until *either* of the following events occurs:

- It initiates an I/O operation.
- It has run for a maximum length of time, called a **time slice**.

Typically, this time slice is on the order of about a tenth of a second. This may seem like a minuscule amount of time, but it isn't. As we saw in Chapter 5, the typical time to execute a machine language instruction is about 20 nsec. Thus, in the 0.1-second time slice allocated to a program, a modern processor could execute over 5 million machine language instructions.

The basic idea in a time-sharing system is to service many users in a circular, round-robin fashion, giving each user a small amount of time and then moving on to the next. If there are not too many users on the system, the processor can get back to a user before he or she even notices any delay. For example, if there are 5 users on a system and each one gets a time slice of 0.1 second, a user will wait no more than 0.5 second for a response to a command. This delay would hardly be noticed. However, if 40 or 50 users were actively working on the system, they might begin to notice a 4- or 5-second delay and become irritated. (This would be an example of the "virtual environment" created by the operating system *not* being helpful and supportive!) The number of simultaneous users that can be serviced by a time-sharing system depends on 1) the speed of the processor, 2) the time slice given to each user, and 3) the type of operation each user is doing (how many use the full time slice, and how many stop before that).

Time sharing was the dominant form of operating system during the 1970s and 1980s, and time-sharing terminals sprouted throughout government offices, businesses, and campuses.

The early 1980s saw the appearance of the first personal computers (PCs), and in many business and academic environments the "dumb" terminal began to be replaced by these newer PCs. Initially, the PC was viewed as simply another type of terminal, and during its early days it was used primarily to access a central time-sharing system. However, as PCs became faster and more powerful, people soon realized that much of the computing being done on the centralized machine could be done much more conveniently and at far less cost by the microcomputers sitting on their desktops.

During the late 1980s and the 1990s computing rapidly changed from the centralized environment typical of batch, multiprogramming, and time-sharing systems to a **distributed environment** in which much of the computing was done remotely in the office, in the laboratory, on the shop floor, and in the classroom. Computing moved out of the computer center to where the work was being done. Initially, the operating systems available for early personal computers were simple **single-user operating systems** that gave one user total access to the entire system. Because personal computers were so cheap, there was really no need for many users to share their resources, and the time-sharing and multiprogramming designs of the third generation became less important.

Although personal computers were relatively cheap (and were becoming cheaper all the time), many of the peripherals and supporting gear—laser

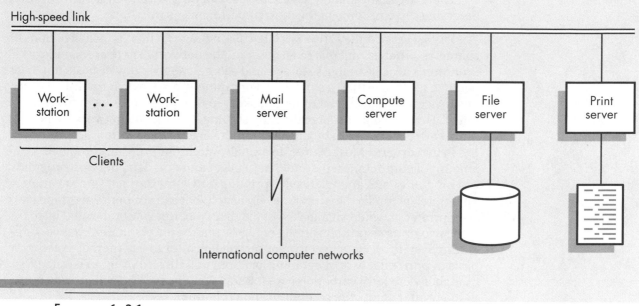

High-speed link

| Work-station | ... | Work-station | Mail server | Compute server | File server | Print server |

Clients

International computer networks

FIGURE 6.21
A Local Area Network

printers, large disk drives, tape back-up units, and specialized software packages—were not. In addition, electronic mail was growing in importance, and stand-alone PCs were unable to communicate easily with other users and partake in this important new application. The personal computer era required a new approach to operating system design. It needed a virtual environment that supported both *local computation* and *remote access* to other users and shared resources.

This led to the development of a **fourth-generation** operating system called a **network operating system** (1985–present). A network operating system manages not only the resources of a single computer but also the capabilities of a telecommunications system called a **local area network**, or **LAN** for short. (We will take a much closer look at networks in Chapter 12.) A LAN is a network that is located in a geographically contiguous area such as a room, a building, or a campus. It is composed of personal computers, high-powered workstations, and special shared resources called **servers**, all interconnected via a high-speed (tens or hundreds of millions of bits/second) **bus** that is usually made of **coaxial** or **fiber-optic cable**. A typical LAN configuration is shown in Figure 6.21.

The users of the individual computers in Figure 6.21, who are called **clients**, can perform local computations, oblivious to the existence of the network. In this mode, the operating system provides exactly the same services described earlier: loading and executing programs and managing the resources of this machine.

However, a user can also access any one of the shared network resources just as though it were local. The system software will do the work needed to access that resource, hiding the details of communication and contention for this shared resource with other nodes. These technical issues are of no concern to the network user who is working in a high-level virtual environment.

There are many shared resources that can be provided by a network and its operating system. Some of the most important are

File servers. A file server is a large disk storage facility (typically billions of characters) that is available to any user on the network. There are significant economies of scale in mass storage, and a large-capacity device costs much less per byte of storage than a small one. For example, a 4-Gbyte hard disk may cost only twice as much as a 500-Mbyte disk, even though it holds eight times as much. Thus buying one large disk and sharing it among all network users is more cost-effective than buying everyone a small storage unit.

Print servers. Most people do a small amount of printing compared to the amount of computation they do. They collect and edit data, develop programs, run programs, and analyze results, printing only after they get some answers. Therefore, it would be foolish for every user to have his or her own expensive laser printer. It would sit idle 95% of the time. A better solution would be to place two or three printers on the network as a shared resource. A network operating system allows a user to choose which printer to use (perhaps on the basis of print quality or geographic location) and then to print on it exactly as though it were local without regard for how the information will be transmitted to the printer across the communications channel.

Compute server. Personal computers are getting much faster, but there will always exist massive computations beyond the capabilities of the machine on your desktop. For these jobs (which include large numerical computations and big simulation models), the network could provide a single high-speed computing system available to everyone on the network. (It might, for example, be a parallel processor of the type discussed in Section 5.3.4). When the job you are running is too large for your desktop computer, the network operating system would allow you to execute it on the network compute server, using virtually the same command used to run it locally.

Mail server. A local area network allows us to communicate with anyone connected to our network, but what about national or international telecommunications? How do we communicate with people who are not in our building or on our campus? To support that service, we need a shared network service called a **mail server**. This is a computer system accessible to all LAN users and connected to an international wide-area telecommunications system. All **electronic mail** (usually abbreviated to **e-mail**) in the LAN is routed to the mail server. If it is for a local user, the mail server immediately directs it to the proper machine, and it never leaves the LAN. If it is for a remote user, the mail server sends it out on its remote telecommunications link.

Network operating systems create a virtual machine that extends beyond the boundaries of the local system on which the user is working. They hide the underlying details of telecommunications and let us see a huge pool of resources—computers, servers, users—all accessible exactly as though they were connected to our own computer. This fourth-generation virtual environment, which is exemplified by modern operating systems such as Windows-95, Windows-NT, Windows-98, Macintosh, and UNIX, is diagrammed in Figure 6.22.

One important variation of the network operating system is called a **real-time operating system**. During the 1980s computers became smaller and

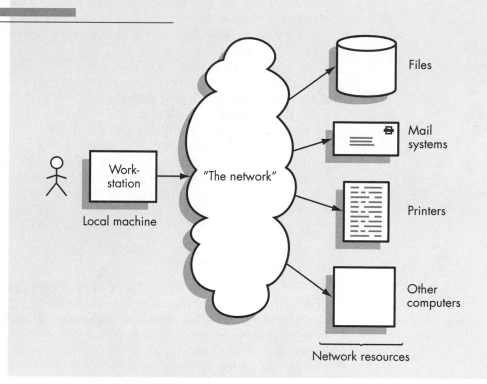

FIGURE 6.22

The Virtual Environment of a
Network Operating System

smaller, and it became common to place them inside other pieces of equipment to control their operation. These types of computers are called **embedded systems**; examples include computers placed inside automobile engines, microwave ovens, thermostats, assembly lines, airplanes, and watches.

One typical large mechanical system, a 747 jet plane, contains hundreds of embedded computer systems inside its engines, braking system, wings, landing gear, and cabin. The central computer controlling the overall operation of the airplane is connected by LAN to these embedded computers that are monitoring system functions and sending status information. Now imagine that the central computer receives two requests. The first request is from a cabin monitoring system, which says that it is too cool in the cabin and that it wants the central system to raise the temperature a little for passenger comfort. The second message says that another plane is approaching on the same flight path, and there is about to be a mid-air collision. It would like the central computer to take evasive action. Which request should be serviced next? Of course, the collision detection message, even though it arrived second. In all the operating systems described, we have implied that the system satisfies requests for services and resources in the order received. In some systems, however, certain requests are much more important than others, and when these important requests arrive, we must drop everything else to service them. Other examples include the need to attend immediately to a chemical reaction that is overheating and about to explode and the need for a microwave oven to shut off exactly when it is supposed to.

A real-time operating system manages the resources of embedded computers that are controlling ongoing physical processes and that have requests that must be serviced within fixed time constraints. This type of operating system guarantees that it can service these important requests within that fixed amount of time. For example, it may guarantee that if a collision detection message arrives, the software to implement collision avoidance will be activated and executed within 50 milliseconds regardless of what it is currently doing. The way that this is typically done is that all requests to a real-time operating system are **prioritized**. Instead of being handled in first-come, first-served order, they are handled in priority sequence, from most important to least important, where "importance" is defined in terms of the time-critical nature of the request. A real-time operating system lets passengers be uncomfortably cool for a few more seconds while it handles the problem of avoiding a crash.

6.4.3 THE FUTURE

The discussions in this chapter have shown that, just as there have been huge changes in hardware over the last 50 years, there have been equally huge changes in system software during the same period. We have progressed from a first-generation environment in which a user personally managed the computing hardware, using a complicated text-oriented command language, to current fourth-generation systems in which users request services from anywhere in a network, using enormously powerful and easy-to-use graphical user interfaces.

And just as hardware capabilities are continuing to improve, there is also no reason to believe that the evolution of software has ended. On the contrary, there is a good deal of computer science research directed at further improvements in the high-level virtual environment created by a modern fourth-generation operating system, and a "fifth-generation" operating system is not too far off.

These fifth-generation systems will have even more powerful user interfaces that incorporate not only text and graphics but photography, touch, sound, fax, video, and TV as well. These **multimedia user interfaces** will interact with users and solicit requests in a variety of ways. Instead of "point-and-click," a fifth generation might allow you to speak the command "Please display my meeting schedule for May 6." The visual display may include separate windows for a verbal reminder about an important event and a digitally encoded photograph of the person with whom you are meeting. Just as text-only systems are now viewed as outmoded, today's text and graphics system may be viewed as too limiting for high-quality user/system interaction.

A fifth-generation operating system will typically be a **parallel processing operating system** that will manage systems containing hundreds or even thousands of processors. Users do not want to be bothered with the technical details of MIMD or SIMD parallel processing described in Chapter 5. They simply want their programs to run faster; how that is accomplished is the task of the system, not the user. The operating system will need to recognize opportunities for parallel execution, send the separate tasks to the appropriate processor, and coordinate their concurrent execution, all in a transparent way. On this virtual

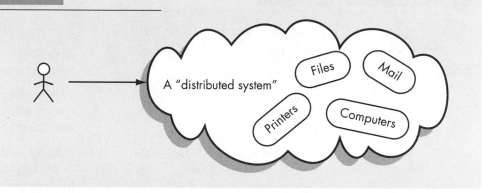

FIGURE 6.23

Structure of a Distributed System

machine, a user would be unaware that multiple processors even exist, except for the fact that programs run 10, 100, or 1,000 times faster. Without some type of software support, a massively parallel system would be a "naked parallel processor" just as difficult to work with as the "naked machine" discussed at the beginning of this chapter.

Finally, the new fifth-generation operating systems will create a truly **distributed computing environment** in which users do not need to know the location of a given resource within the network. In current network operating systems, the communication details are hidden, but not the existence of separate nodes in the network (Figure 6.22). The user is aware that there is a network and must specify the network node where the work is to be done. In a typical fourth-generation network operating system, a user issues the following types of commands:

- Access file F on file server S and copy it to my local system.
- Run program P on machine M.
- Save file F on file server T.
- Print file F on print server Q.

Compare these commands with how the manager of a business gives instructions to an assistant: "Get this job done. I don't care how or where. Just do it, and when you are done, give me the results." The details of how and where to get the job done are left to the underling. The manager does not want to be bothered with those details and is concerned only with results.

In a truly **distributed operating system**, the user is the manager and the operating system the assistant, and the user does not care where or how the system satisfies a request as long as it gets done correctly. The users of a distributed system would not see a network of distinct sites or "local" and "remote" nodes. Instead, they would see a single **distributed system** that provides resources and services. The individual nodes and the boundaries between them would no longer be visible to the user, who would think only in terms of *what* must be done, not *where* it will be done or *which* node will do it. This situation is diagrammed in Figure 6.23.

FIGURE 6.24

Some of the Major Advances in Operating Systems Development

GENERATION	APPROXIMATE DATES	MAJOR ADVANCES
First	1945–1955	No operating system available Programmers operated the machine themselves
Second	1955–1965	Batch operating systems Improved system utilization Development of the first command language
Third	1965–1985	Multiprogramming operating systems Time-sharing operating systems Increasing concern for protecting programs from damage by other programs Creation of privileged and user instructions Interactive use of computers Increasing concern for security and access control First personal computer operating systems
Fourth	1985–present	Network operating systems Local area networks File servers, print servers, compute servers Remote access, e-mail Graphical user interfaces Real-time operating systems Embedded systems
Fifth	??	Multimedia user interfaces Massively parallel operating systems Distributed computing environments

Now the very existence of both a telecommunication system and separate computer systems is hidden from view. In a distributed operating system, the commands shown earlier might be expressed as follows:

- Access file F wherever it may be.
- Run program P on any machine currently available.
- Save file F wherever there is sufficient room.
- Print file F on any laser printer with 400 dpi resolution that is not in use right now.

This is certainly the highest and most powerful virtual environment we have yet described, and an operating system that could create such an environment would significantly enhance the productivity of all its users. These "fifth-generation dashboards" would make using the most powerful and most complex computer system as easy as driving a car—perhaps even easier.

Figure 6.24 summarizes the historical evolution of operating systems, much as Figure 5.24 summarized the historical development of computer hardware.

EXERCISES

1. What serves the role of the user interface in other high-technology devices commonly found in the home or office, such as a VCR, stereo system, television, copier, or microwave oven? Pick one specific device and discuss how well its interface is designed and how easy it is to use. Does the device use techniques of computer system interfaces, such as menus and icons?

2. Can you think of situations where you might *want* to see the underlying hardware of the computer system? That is, you want to interact with the actual machine, not the virtual machine. How could you accomplish this? (Essentially, how could you bypass the operating system?)

3. Assume that you write a letter in English and have a friend translate it into Spanish. In this scenario, what is equivalent to the source program of Figure 6.4? the object program? the assembler?

4. Assume that memory cells 60 and 61 and register R currently have the following values:

   Register R: 13   60:   472
                               61:          −1

   Using the instruction set in Figure 6.5, what will be in register R and memory cells 60 and 61 after completion of each of the following operations? Assume that each instruction starts from the above conditions.

   a. LOAD   60   d. COMPARE   61
   b. STORE   60   e. IN   61 (Assume that the user enters a 50.)
   c. ADD   60   f. OUT   61

5. Assume that memory cell 79 contains the value +6. In addition, the symbol Z is equivalent to memory location 79. What would be placed in register R by each of the following load commands?

   a. LOAD   79   c. LOAD   Z
   b. LOAD   6   d. LOAD   Z+1 (Assume that this is allowed.)

6. Say we accidently execute the following piece of data:

   .DATA 16387

   Describe exactly what would happen. Assume that the format of machine language instructions on this system is the same format shown in Figure 6.13.

7. What is the assembly language equivalent of each of the following binary machine language instructions? Assume the format described in Figure 6.13 and the numeric op code values shown in Figure 6.5.

   a. 0101001100001100
   b. 0011000000000111

8. Is the following data generation pseudo-op legal or illegal? Why?

   THREE: .DATA   2

9. Using the instruction set shown in Figure 6.5, translate the following algorithmic primitives into assembly language code. Show all necessary .DATA pseudo-ops.

   a. Add 3 to the value of K
   b. Set K to (L + 1) − (M + N)
   c. If K > 10 then output the value of K
   d. If (K > L) then output the value of K and increment K by 1
           otherwise output the value of L and increment L by 1
   e. Set K to 1
       Repeat the next two lines until K >100
           Output the value of K
           Increment K by 1
       End of the loop

10. What, if anything, is the difference between the following two sets of instructions?

LOAD	X		INCREMENT	X
ADD	TWO		INCREMENT	X
.				
.				
.				
TWO:	.DATA 2			

11. Look at the assembly language program in Figure 6.8. Is the statement CLEAR SUM on line 2 necessary? Why or why not? Is the statement LOAD ZERO on line 4 necessary? Why or why not?

12. Modify the program in Figure 6.8 so that it separately computes and prints the sum of all positive numbers and all negative numbers and stops when it sees the value 0. For example, given the input

12, −2, 14, 1, −7, 0

your program should output the two values 27 (the sum of the three positive values 12, 14, and 1) and −9 (the sum of the two negative numbers −2 and −7) and then halt.

13. Write a complete assembly language program (including all necessary pseudo-ops) that reads in a series of integers, one at a time, and outputs the largest and smallest values. The input will consist of a list of integer values containing exactly 100 numbers.

14. Assume that we are using the 16 distinct op codes in Figure 6.5. If we write an assembly language program that contains 100 instructions and our processor can do about 50,000 comparisons per second, what is the maximum time spent doing operation code translation using:

   a. Sequential search (Figure 2.9)
   b. Binary search (Figure 3.19)

In this case, which one of these two algorithms would you recommend using? Would your conclusions be significantly different if we were programming in an assembly language with 300 op codes rather than 16? if our program contained 50,000 instructions rather than 100?

15. What value will be entered in the symbol table for the symbols AGAIN, ANS, X and ONE in the following program? (Assume that the program is loaded beginning with memory location 0.)

```
        .BEGIN
        --Here is the program.
        IN          X
        LOAD        X
AGAIN:  ADD         ANS
        SUBTRACT    ONE
        STORE       ANS
        OUT         ANS
        JUMP        AGAIN
        --Here are the data.
ANS:    .DATA       0
X:      .DATA       0
ONE:    .DATA       1
        .END
```

16. Look at the assembly language program in Figure 6.8. Determine the physical memory address associated with every label in the symbol table. (Assume that the program is loaded beginning with memory location 0.)

17. Is the following pair of statements legal or illegal? Explain why.

```
LABEL:    .DATA    3
LABEL:    .DATA    4
```

If it is illegal, will the error be detected during pass 1 or pass 2 of the assembly process? Explain why.

18. What are some drawbacks in using passwords to limit access to a computer system? Describe some other possible ways for an operating system to limit access. In what type of application might these alternative safeguards be appropriate?

19. Assume our 2-byte, 16-bit password is the character string MS. Determine what the encrypted representation of our password would be if the encryption algorithm were

NOT (password + 500)

What would be the "decryption" algorithm? That is, if we were given the encrypted password, how could we recover the original value?

20. Why are authorization lists so sensitive that they must be encrypted and protected from unauthorized change? What kind of damage is possible if these files are modified in unexpected or unplanned ways?

21. Assume that any individual program spends about 50% of its time waiting for I/O operations to be completed. What percentage of time is the processor doing useful work (called **processor utilization**) if there are three programs loaded into memory? How many programs should we keep in memory if we want processor utilization to be at least 95%?

22. Here is an algorithm for calling a friend on the telephone:

  1. Dial the phone and wait for either an answer or a busy signal
  2. If the line is not busy then do steps 3 and 4
  3.   Talk as long as you want
  4.   Hang up the phone, you are done
  5. Otherwise (the line is busy)
  6.   Wait exactly 1 minute
  7.   Go back to step 1 and try again

During execution this algorithm could get it into a situation where, as in the deadlock problem, no useful work can ever get done. Describe the problem, explain why it occurs, and suggest how it could be solved.

23. Explain why a batch operating system would be totally inadequate to handle such modern applications as airline reservations and automatic teller machines.

24. In a time-sharing operating system, why is system performance so sensitive to the value that is selected for the time slice? Explain what type of system behavior we would be likely to observe if the value selected for the time slice were too large? too small?

25. As hardware (processor/memory) costs became significantly cheaper during the 1980s and 1990s, time sharing became a much less attractive design for operating systems. Explain why this is the case.

26. See whether the computer system on which you are working is part of a local area network. If it is, determine what servers are available on the net and learn how they are used. Is there a significant difference between the ways you access local resources and remote resources?

27. The following four requests could come in to an operating system as it is running on a computer system.
    - The clock inside the computer has just "ticked," and we need to update the seconds counter.
    - The program running on processor 2 is trying to perform an illegal operation code.
    - Someone pulled the plug on the power supply, and the system will run out of power in 50 msec.
    - The disk has just read the character that passed under the read/write head, and it wants to store it in memory before the next one arrives.

In what order should the operating system handle these requests?

CHALLENGE WORK

1. In Chapter 2 we wrote a number of algorithms that assumed the ability to specify a list of values. That is, our algorithm contained statements such as

Get values for $A_1, A_2, \ldots A_N$, the list to be searched

Here we are thinking not only of individual data items such as A_1 and A_2 but also of a collection of such items, the list. A collection of related data items is called a **data structure**. High-level programming languages like Pascal and C++ provide users with a rich collection of data structures that go by such names as arrays, lists, structures, and unions. We can program with these structures just as though they were an inherent part of the hardware of the computer. However, the discussions in the previous two chapters have shown that data structures such as lists of numbers do *not* exist directly in hardware. There are no machine language instructions that could carry out the type of algorithmic command shown above. When you write an instruction that uses a structure such as a list, the language translator (that is, the compiler) must map it into what is available on the hardware—the machine language instruction set shown in Figure 5.19 and the sequential addresses in our memory. (This is another good example of the virtual environment created by a piece of system software.)

Write an assembly language program to sum up a list of 50 numbers that are read in and stored in memory. Here is the algorithm you are to translate:

Read in 50 numbers $A_1, A_2, \ldots, A_{50}$

Set *Sum* to 0

Set *I* to 1

Repeat until $I > 50$

    $Sum = Sum + A_I$

    $I = I + 1$

End of the loop

Write out the value of *Sum*

To implement this algorithm, you will have to simulate the concept of a list of numbers using the assembly language resources that are available. (Here is a hint on how to do it: Remember that in the Von Neumann architecture there is no distinction between an instruction and a piece of data. Therefore, an assembly language instruction such as LOAD A can be treated as data and modified by other instructions.)

FOR FURTHER READING

Here are some excellent introductory texts on the design and implementation of operating systems. Most of them also include a discussion of some specific modern operating system such as UNIX or Windows-95.

Flynn, I., and McIver, A. *Understanding Operating Systems*, 2nd ed. Boston: PWS, 1997.

Nutt, G. *Operating Systems: A Modern Perspective*. Reading, MA: Addison-Wesley, 1997.

Silbershatz, A., and Galvin, P. *The Design of Operating Systems*, 5th ed. Reading, MA: Addison-Wesley, 1998.

Stallings, W. *Operating Systems*, 3rd ed. Englewood Cliffs, NJ: Prentice-Hall, 1998.

Tanenbaum, A. S., and Woodhull, A. *Operating Systems: Design and Implementation*, 2nd ed. Englewood Cliffs, NJ: Prentice-Hall, 1997.

For a discussion of future directions in operating system design, especially network and distributed operating systems, here are a couple of excellent references:

Coulouris, G.; Dollimore, J.; and Kindberg, T. *Distributed Operating Systems: Concepts and Design*, 2nd ed. Reading, MA: Addison-Wesley, 1994.

Tanenbaum, A. *Distributed Operating Systems*. Englewood Cliffs, NJ: Prentice-Hall, 1995.

Finally, here is an excellent general reference on system software:

Clarke, D., and Merusi, D. *System Software: The Way Things Work*. Englewood Cliffs, NJ: Prentice-Hall, 1998.

6.5 SUMMARY OF LEVEL 3

We have seen that the hardware described in Chapters 4 and 5 is, by itself, unusable. Trying to work directly with the components of a Von Neumann machine—processors, memory, ALU—is impossible for any but the most technically knowledgeable users. To make the system accessible, the system software must create a people-oriented *virtual machine* that is easy to use and easy to understand. In addition to ease of use, this virtual machine provides a number of other beneficial services, including resource management, security, access control, and efficient use of resources. A great deal of work has been done trying to determine exactly what is an optimal virtual environment and how to create it. Operating systems have evolved from early batch systems through multiprogramming and time sharing to the current network and real-time operating system. Future designs will probably incorporate multimedia interfaces and massively parallel processors, and they will encase users in a distributed system in which the user deals only with what operations need to be done, not with where or how they can be done. The future of computer systems definitely lies in the direction of higher-level and more powerful virtual environments.

Now that we have created a powerful, user-friendly virtual hardware environment in which to work, what do we want to do with it? Well, we probably want to write programs that solve important problems. In the next level of the text, we leave the domain of hardware (real and virtual) as we begin our study of "the software world."

THE SOFTWARE WORLD

LEVEL SIX — Social Issues
Chapter 14

LEVEL FIVE — Applications
Chapters 11,12,13

LEVEL FOUR — The Software World
Chapters 7,8,9,10

LEVEL THREE — The Virtual Machine
Chapter 6

LEVEL TWO — The Hardware World
Chapters 4,5

LEVEL ONE — The Algorithmic Foundations of Computer Science
Chapters 2,3

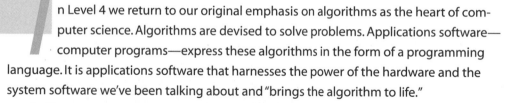

LEVEL

4

n Level 4 we return to our original emphasis on algorithms as the heart of computer science. Algorithms are devised to solve problems. Applications software—computer programs—express these algorithms in the form of a programming language. It is applications software that harnesses the power of the hardware and the system software we've been talking about and "brings the algorithm to life."

In Chapter 7 we see programming language ideas as implemented in one specific programming language, C++. Other examples of programming languages and different language design philosophies are introduced in Chapter 8. Chapter 9 explains how high-level programming language statements get translated into the low-level statements that can be executed on machine hardware. Yet in spite of all the power of modern hardware and software, and no matter how clever we may be in designing algorithms, problems exist that have no algorithmic solution. Chapter 10 demonstrates that the power of computing, as algorithmic problem solving, is limited.

INTRODUCTION TO HIGH-LEVEL LANGUAGE PROGRAMMING

7.1   WHERE DO WE STAND?

As of the end of the previous chapter, we have a complete and workable computer system. We have moved up from the ungainliness of machine language programming, which the computer is designed to understand, to assembly language programming. This level of abstraction creates a virtual environment in which we can pretend that we are communicating directly with the computer even though we are using a language more suited to human communication than (binary) machine language. We know about the system software needed to support this virtual environment. This includes the assembler that translates our assembly language program into machine language. It also includes the operating system that actually accepts our request to load and execute a program and coordinates and manages the other software tools needed to accomplish this task.

We've created a pretty nice little world here. In the "early days" of computing—say, the 1950s—this was quite a satisfactory programming environment, for two reasons. First, the people writing computer programs were for the most part very technically oriented folk. Many had backgrounds in engineering, they were familiar with the inner workings of a computer, and they were accustomed to dealing with difficult problems steeped in mathematical notation. Second, because assembly language is so closely tied to machine language, assembly language programmers could see the kinds of processor activity that the assembly language instructions would generate. By being sufficiently clever in their choice of instructions, they could often reduce this activity and shave a small amount off the execution time that their programs required. As an example, the sequence of assembly language instructions

```
          LOAD      X
          ADD       ONE
          STORE     X

            .           .

            .           .

            .           .

ONE:      .DATA     1
```

could be replaced by the single instruction

```
          INCREMENT  X
```

This is not the sort of performance improvement obtained by changing from a sequential search algorithm to a binary search algorithm. It is a "fine-tuning" improvement that may save a few millionths of a second, or even a few seconds if these instructions occur inside a loop that is executed many times. But remember that in this era, no one had a powerful personal computer sitting on his or her desk. Programmers were competing with one another to share the resources of a mainframe computer, and although these computers were physically large, they did not have the processing speed or memory capacity of today's personal computers. Conserving machine resources, even in tiny amounts, was important.

The next few decades, however, produced trends that negated both of these reasons. First, computer usage spread into more and more avenues of endeavor, permeating society to a degree that would probably not have been believed in the 1950s. "Nontechie" types needed to write programs too, and they demanded a more comfortable programming environment. This was provided through the use of high-level programming languages, which we talk about in this chapter and the next (and also through evolving operating systems and other system software, which were discussed in Chapter 6). Actually, this is a bit of a chicken-and-egg situation. New programmers demanded better languages, and better languages opened the door for new programmers. Each process fueled the other. Also during this period, incredible strides in technology made machines so powerful that conserving resources was generally not the issue it once was, and the overhead of execution time occasioned by the use of high-level programming languages became acceptable.

7.2 HIGH-LEVEL LANGUAGES

Let's review some of the aspects of assembly language programming that made people look for still better alternatives. Suppose our task is to add two integers. In the assembly language of Chapter 6, the following instructions would have to be included (assume that *B* and *C* have already been assigned values).

```
        LOAD     B
        ADD      C
        STORE    A
         .        .
         .        .
         .        .
A:      .DATA    0
B:      .DATA    0
C:.     .DATA    0
```

The three .DATA statements request storage for signed integers, generate the binary representation of the integer value 0 to occupy that storage initially, and ensure that the labels *A*, *B*, and *C* will be bound to those memory locations. The

LOAD statement copies the current contents of the memory location labeled *B* into the ALU register R, the ADD statement adds the current contents of the memory location labeled *C* to what is currently in register R, and the STORE instruction copies the contents of R (which is now *B* + *C*) into the memory location labeled A.

In order to perform a simple arithmetic task, we had to manage all the data movement of the numbers to be combined as well as the resulting answer. This is a microscopic view of a task—we'd like to be able to say something like "add *B* and *C*, and call the result *A*," or better yet, something like "*A* = *B* + *C*." But each assembly language statement corresponds to at most one machine language statement (you may recall from Chapter 6 that the pseudo-op .DATA statements do not generate any machine language statements). Therefore, individual assembly language statements, though easier to read, can be no more powerful than the underlying machine instructions. For the same reason, assembly language programs are machine-specific. An assembly language statement that runs on machine X is nothing but a slightly "humanized" machine language statement for X, and it will not execute on a machine Y that has a different instruction set. Indeed, machine Y's assembler won't know what to do with such a statement.

Finally, assembly language instructions are rather stilted. STORE A does not sound much like the sort of English we customarily speak, although STORE is certainly more expressive than its binary machine language counterpart.

To summarize, assembly language has the following disadvantages:

1. The programmer must "manually" manage the movement of data items between and among memory locations (although such data items can be assigned abbreviated names).

2. The programmer must take a microscopic view of a task, breaking it down into tiny subtasks at the level of what is going on in individual memory locations.

3. An assembly language program is machine-specific.

4. Statements are not English-language-like (although operations are given mnemonic code words as an improvement over a string of bits).

High-level programming languages were created to overcome these deficiencies. Thus we should have the following expectations of a program written in a high-level language:

1. The programmer need not manage the details of the movement of data items within memory or pay any attention to exactly where those items are stored.

2. The programmer can take a macroscopic view of tasks, thinking at a higher level of problem solving (add *B* and *C*, and call the result *A*). The "primitive operations" used as building blocks in algorithm construction (see Chapter 1) can be larger.

3. Programs written in a high-level language will be portable rather than machine-specific.

4. Programming statements in a high-level language will be closer to standard English and will use standard mathematical notation.

High-level programming languages are often called **third-generation languages**, reflecting the progression from machine language (first generation) to assembly language (second generation) to high-level language. They are another step along the continuum of Figure 6.3. This also suggests what by now you have suspected: We've reached another layer of abstraction, another virtual environment designed to distance the human still further from the low-level electronic components of the machine.

7.2.1 PROGRAM TRANSLATION

There is a price to pay for our higher level of abstraction. When we moved from machine language to assembly language, we needed a piece of system software—an assembler—to translate assembly language instructions into machine language (object code). This was necessary because the computer itself—that is, the collection of electronic devices—can respond only to binary machine language instructions. Now that we have moved up another layer in the language in which we choose to communicate with the computer, we will need another translator to convert our high-level language instructions into machine language instructions. Or perhaps we'll translate high-level language instructions only into assembly language instructions and then turn the job over to an assembler. At any rate, we need another piece of system software to do this translation task. Such a piece of software is called a **compiler**.

Sometimes a group of high-level language instructions performs a task so useful (sorting or searching, for example) that many other programs could employ this same task as part of whatever job they do. The code for this useful task can be written and thoroughly tested to be sure it is correct. Then the object code for the task can be stored in a **code library**. Another program can just "check out" a copy of this object code from the library and request that the copy be included along with its own object code. A piece of system software called a **linker** inserts requested object code from code libraries into the object code for the requesting program. Thus a high-level program might go through the transitions shown in Figure 7.1.

The work of the compiler is discussed in more detail in Chapter 9. Let us note here, however, that the compiler has a tougher job than the assembler. An assembler has a one-for-one translation task because each assembly language instruction corresponds to (must be translated into) at most one machine language instruction. A single high-level programming language instruction, on the other hand—precisely because a high-level language is more expressive than assembly language—can "explode" into many assembly language instructions.

7.2.2 WHICH LANGUAGE?

We will illustrate some of the concepts of a high-level programming language by using **C++**. The popular C++ language was developed in the early 1980s

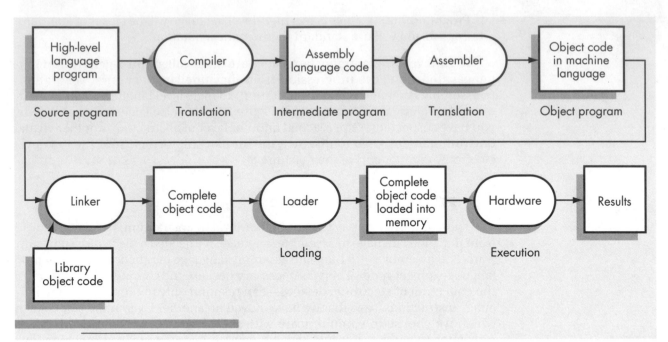

FIGURE 7.1

Transitions of a High-Level Language Program

by Bjarne Stroustrup at AT&T Bell Laboratories (now part of Lucent Technologies) and was first commercially released by AT&T in 1985. Our purpose here is not to make you an expert programmer—any more than our purpose in Chapter 4 was to make you an expert circuit designer. Indeed, there is much about the language that we will not even discuss. You will, however, get a sense of what programming in a high-level language is like, and perhaps you will see why some people think it is one of the most fascinating of human endeavors.

7.3   A SKELETON C++ PROGRAM

Figure 7.2 shows a very simple but complete C++ program. Even if you know nothing about the C++ language, it is not hard to get the general drift of what the program is doing.

Someone running this program (the "user") could have the following dialog with the program, where boldface indicates what the user types:

```
Please enter your favorite number: 13

Your favorite number is 13.
That is a nice number.
```

The general form of a typical C++ program is shown in Figure 7.3. In order to compare our simple example program with this form, we have reproduced the

A Remarkable History

Dr. Bjarne Stroustrup is a member of the Computer Science Research Center at Bell Labs in Murray Hill, New Jersey. In addition to his work in programming languages, his research interests include distributed systems, operating systems, and simulation.

Bell Laboratories was created as part of AT&T in 1925 and remained part of AT&T after the telephone restructuring agreement of 1982. But a further restructuring of AT&T in 1996 resulted in the creation of Lucent Technologies, of which Bell Labs is a part, providing leading-edge research and development support. In 1996 Bell Labs employed 24,000 people in the United States, operated in 16 other countries as well, and had a research and development budget of $2.53 billion.

Dr. Stroustrup's accomplishment as the designer and original implementor of a new programming language is remarkable, but it is only one of many remarkable accomplishments to have been achieved at Bell Labs. Through its long history of technological research and innovation, Bell Labs has become something of a national treasure.

- The first of seven Nobel Prizes to be awarded to Bell Labs scientists was won in 1937 by Dr. Clinton J. Davisson for his experimental confirmation of the wave nature of electrons.

- The transistor (see Chapter 4) was invented in 1947 by three Bell Lab scientists, John Bardeen, Walter Brattain, and William Shockley, who later shared the Nobel Prize for this work.

- Bell Labs was awarded its first patent in 1925, the year of its founding, for a "clamping and supporting device."

- In 1994 Bell Labs was awarded its 25,000th patent, this one for a "method of recognizing handwritten symbols," useful for handheld computers that do handwriting recognition. To appreciate fully the magnitude of 25,000 patents, we should note that this patent was awarded to Bell Labs on the 25,027th day of its existence. A patent a day was awarded over a period of nearly 70 years!

- This remarkable rate of technological achievement shows no sign of slowing down; in fact, it is accelerating. From March 1996 to the end of the year, Bell Labs averaged three patents per business day.

FIGURE 7.2

A Simple C++ Program

```
//program Numerology
//this program gets the user's favorite number
//and prints a greeting

#include <iostream.h>

void main()
{
  int your_number;  //stores the number entered by user

  cout << "Please enter your favorite number:";
  cin >> your_number;
  cout << endl;
  cout << "Your favorite number is " << your_number "."
    << endl;
  cout << "That is a nice number." << endl;
}
```

FIGURE 7.3

The Overall Form of a
Typical C++ Program

```
prologue comment          [optional]
include directives        [optional]
functions                 [optional]
main function
{
    declarations          [optional]
    main function body
}
```

example program in Figure 7.4 with a number in front of each line. The numbers are there for reference purposes only; they are *not* part of the program.

Lines 1–3 in the program of Figure 7.4 are C++ **comments**. Anything appearing on a line after the double slash symbol (//) is ignored by the compiler, just as anything following the double dash (--) was treated as a comment in the assembly language programs of Chapter 6. The computer pays no attention to comments; they are included in a program only to give information to the human readers of the code. Every high-level language has some facility for including comments, because understanding code that someone else has written (or understanding your own code after a period of time has passed) is very difficult without the additional notes and explanations that comments provide. Comments are one way to *document* a computer program to make it more understandable. The comments in the program of Figure 7.4 give the program a name (again, just for the benefit of human readers) and describe what the program does. These three comment lines together make up the **prologue comment** (the introductory comment that comes first) for the program. According to the general form of Figure 7.3, the prologue comment is optional, but providing it is always a good idea.

Line 4 is a directive to the compiler that refers to the iostream library. The eventual effect is that the linker includes some object code from the library. The C++ language itself, surprisingly, does not provide a way to get data into a program or for a program to display results. The iostream library contains code for these purposes. C++ has a large collection of code libraries, such as mathematical and graphics libraries, so many other **include directives** are possible. Include directives are also optional, but it would be a trivial program indeed that did not need input data or produce output results, so virtually every C++ program has at least the include directive shown in our example.

Our sample program has no functions other than the main function (note that such functions are optional). The purpose of additional functions is to do some calculation or perform some subtask for the main function, much as the "find largest" algorithm from Chapter 2 is used by the selection sort algorithm of Chapter 3.

Line 5 signals the beginning of the main function, the code for which occurs between the curly braces at lines 6 and 13. Line 7 of the sample program is a declaration. Declarations name and describe any items of data that will be used within the main function. Line 7 indicates that an integer quantity called

FIGURE 7.4

The Program of Figure 7.2 (numbers added for reference)

```
1.   //program Numerology
2.   //this program gets the user's favorite number
3.   //and prints a greeting

4.   #include <iostream.h>

5.   void main()
6.   {
7.     int your_number;  //stores the number entered by
                         //user

8.     cout << "Please enter your favorite number:";
9.     cin >> your_number;
10.    cout << endl;
11.    cout << "Your favorite number is "
            << your_number << "." << endl;
12.    cout << "That is a nice number." << endl;
13.  }
```

your_number will be used to store the value the user enters. Here a descriptive name has been used for this quantity as an aid in documenting its purpose in the program, and a comment provides further clarification. Declarations are also optional in the sense that if a program does not use any data, no declarations are needed, but here again, it would be unusual to find such a trivial program.

Lines 8–12 make up the main **function body**, where the real work of the program gets done. Messages to the user begin with "cout"; the single "cin" statement gets the value the user entered for his or her favorite number and stores it in *your_number*.

Blank lines in C++ programs are ignored and are used, like comments, to make the program more readable to humans. In our example program, we've used blank lines to isolate the include statement and to separate the declaration statement from the main function body.

Figure 7.3 is a rather simplified view of a C++ program (that's why our simple example program looked so much like it.) The rest of this chapter is devoted to filling in the details.

7.4 VIRTUAL DATA STORAGE

One of the improvements we seek in a high-level language is freedom from having to manage data movement within memory. Although assembly language does not require us to give the actual memory address of the storage location to be used for each item, as we must in machine language, we still have to move values one by one back and forth between memory and the ALU as simple modifications are made. We want the computer to let us use data values by name in any sort of appropriate computation without having to think about where they are stored or what is currently in some register in the ALU. In fact, we do not even want to know that there *is* such a thing as an ALU where data are moved to be operated on; instead, we want the virtual machine to manage the details when we request that a computation be performed. A high-level language allows this, and it also allows the names for data items to be more meaningful than in assembly language.

Names in a programming language are called **identifiers**. Each language has its own specific rules for what a legal identifier can look like. In C++, an identifier can be any combination of letters, digits, and the underscore symbol (_), as long as it does not begin with a digit. Identifiers beginning with underscore characters should be avoided, however; they are generally used for special purposes. An additional restriction is that an identifier cannot be one of the few **keywords** that have a special meaning in C++. (Keywords within programs will be shown in boldface.) The three integers *B*, *C*, and *A* in our assembly language program could therefore have more descriptive names, such as *Price*, *Tax*, and *Total_Cost*. The use of descriptive identifiers is one of the greatest aids to human understanding of a program. Because identifiers can be almost arbitrarily long, you should not hesitate to use an identifier such as *Temperature_at_the_Pipe_Opening* if this is the best way to describe something. C++ is a **case-sensitive** language, which means that upper-case letters are distinguished from lower-case letters. Thus *total_cost*, *Total_cost*, and *Total_Cost* are three different identifiers. Identifiers are used not only to name data items but also to name additional functions besides the main function. For now, however, we'll concentrate on data items.

Data that a program uses can come in two flavors. Some quantities are fixed throughout the duration of the program, and their values are known ahead of time. These quantities are called **constants**. An example of a constant is the integer value 2. Another is an approximation to π, say 3.1416. The integer 2 is a constant that we don't have to name by an identifier, nor do we have to build the value 2 in memory manually by the equivalent of a .DATA pseudo-op. We can just use the symbol "2" directly in any program statement. Likewise, we could use "3.1416" for the real number value 3.1416, but if we are really using this number as an approximation to π, it is more informative to use the identifier *PI*.

Some quantities used in a program have values that change as the program executes, or their values are not known ahead of time but must be obtained from the computer user (or from a data file previously prepared by the user) as the program runs. These quantities are called **variables**. For example, in a program doing computations with circles (where we might use the constant *PI*), we might also need to obtain from the user or a data file the radius of the circle of interest. This variable could be given the identifier *Radius*.

Identifiers for variables serve the same purpose in program statements as pronouns do in ordinary English statements. The English statement "He will be home today" has specific meaning only when we plug in the value for which "He" stands. Similarly, a program statement equivalent to the pseudocode

Set the value of *Circumference* to 2 $\times$ *PI* $\times$ *Radius*

FIGURE 7.5
Some of the C ++
Standard Data Types

int	a positive or negative integer quantity
double	a real number
char	a character (a single keyboard character, such as 'a')

becomes an actual computation only when a numeric value has been stored in the memory location referenced by the *Radius* identifier.

We know that all data are represented internally in binary form. In Chapter 4, we noted that any one sequence of binary digits could be interpreted as a whole number, a negative number, a real number (one containing a decimal point, such as 28.342 or −17.5), or a letter of the alphabet. C++ asks that we give information in the program about each item of data—what identifier we want to use for it and whether it represents an integer, a real number, or a letter of the alphabet. This tells the C++ compiler how many bytes are needed to store an item of data—that is, how many memory cells are to be considered as one **memory location** referenced by one identifier, and also how the string of bits in that memory location is to be interpreted. (We saw in Chapter 6 that it is actually the first pass of the assembler that makes use of this information.)

The way to give this information within a C++ program is to declare each data item. A **declaration** does three things:

1. It tells whether the data item is a constant or a variable.
2. It tells the identifier that will be used throughout the program to name the item.
3. It tells the **data type** for that item.

C++ provides several standard data types, as shown in Figure 7.5. To declare *Radius* as a real number variable, for example, we would write

```
double Radius;
```

A semicolon must appear at the end of every executable C++ instruction, which means pretty much everywhere except at the end of a comment, an include directive, or the beginning of a function such as

```
void main()
```

The semicolon requirement is kind of a pain in the neck, but the C++ compiler will generate one or more error messages if you omit the semicolon, so after the first few hundred times this happens, you tend to remember to put it in.

C++, along with every other programming language, has very specific rules of **syntax**—the correct form for each component of the language. Having a semicolon at the end of every executable statement is a C++ syntax rule, as is the rule for legal identifiers. The programmer must obey all syntax rules of the language. Any violation of. the syntax rules generates an error message from the compiler because the compiler does not recognize or know how to translate the offending code. The syntax rules for a programming language are often defined by a formal grammar, much as correct English is defined by rules of grammar.

If we are really going to compute the circumference of a circle, then we will also need to request storage for the value we compute, and (because the radius is to be a real number) that value should also be a real number. The declarations could read

```
double Radius;            //radius of a circle—given
double Circumference;     //circumference of a circle—
                          //computed
```

or, because both of these variables share the same data type, the identifiers can go in a list, and the declaration could look like this:

```
double Radius, Circumference;  //given radius and
                               //computed circumference
                               //of a circle
```

C++ is a **free-format language**, which means that it does not matter where things are placed on a line. For example, we could have written

```
double Radius,
                Circumference;
//given radius
//and computed         circumference
        //of a circle
```

though this is clearly harder to read. The free-format characteristic explains why a semicolon is needed to mark the end of an instruction.

What about the constant *PI*? We want to assign the fixed value 3.1416 to the *PI* identifier. Constant declarations are just like variable declarations, with the addition of the keyword **const** and the requirement to assign the fixed value.

```
const double PI = 3.1416;
```

Constant identifiers often use all upper-case letters, but the compiler pays attention only to the presence of **const** in the declaration. Once a quantity has been declared as a constant, then any attempt later in the program to change its value generates an error message from the compiler. Again, constants such as the 2 we would need in the circumference computation do not have to be declared; when "2" is first encountered in a program statement, the binary representation of the integer 2 is automatically generated and stored in a memory location, to be made use of as needed.

It is also possible to declare a whole collection of related variables at one time. Doing so makes it possible for storage to be set aside as needed to contain each of the values in this collection. For example, suppose we want to record the number of "hits" on our Web site for each month of the year. The value for each month would be a single integer. We want a collection of 12 such integers, or-

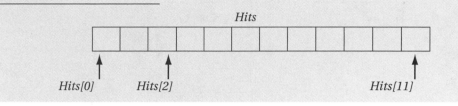

FIGURE 7.6

A 12-Element Array Hits

dered in a particular way. An **array** groups together a collection of memory locations that all store data of the same type. The following statement declares an array:

```
int Hits[12];
```

The 12 indicates that there are to be 12 memory locations set aside, each to hold a variable of type **int**. The collection as a whole is referred to as *Hits*, and the 12 individual array elements are numbered from *Hits[0]* to *Hits[11]*. (Note that a C++ array counts from 0 up to 11 instead of from 1 up to 12.) Thus we would use *Hits[0]* to refer to the first entry in *Hits*, which would represent the number of visits to the Web site during the first month of the year, January. *Hits[2]* would refer to the number of visits during March, and *Hits[11]* to the number of visits during December. In this way we have used one declaration to cause 12 separate (but related) **int** storage locations to be set up. Figure 7.6 shows how we can think of this array.

Here is an example of the power of a high-level language. In assembly language, we could name only individual memory locations—that is, individual items of data—but in C++ we can also assign a name to an entire collection of related data items. An array thus enables us to talk about an entire table of values or the individual elements making up that table. If we were writing C++ programs to implement the data clean-up algorithms of Chapter 3, we could use an array of integers to store the 10 data items.

The picture of an array in Figure 7.6 looks like a one-dimensional table of values. We can use arrays to represent two-dimensional tables also. Suppose, for example, that we wish to work with the following data, which represent two separate water meter readings at each of three distinct sites.

	SITE 1	SITE 2	SITE 3
FINAL READING	14.3	15.2	16.4
INITIAL READING	13.9	14.2	12.7

Even though these six real number values will be stored in sequential memory locations, we can think of them as displayed in a two-dimensional table with two rows and three columns. This is reflected in the following declaration:

```
double WaterReadings[2][3];
```

We can refer to any particular member of the array by giving numbers for its row location and its column location. If the water meter data above are actually

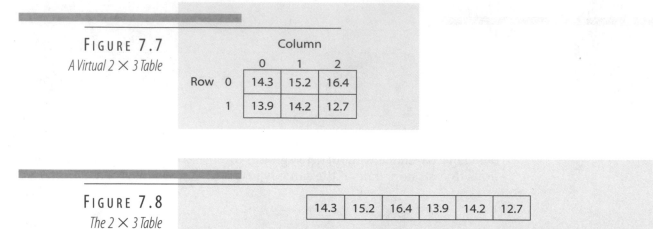

FIGURE 7.7
A Virtual 2 × 3 Table

FIGURE 7.8
*The 2 × 3 Table
Stored in Memory*

stored in the array *WaterReadings*, then the value of *WaterReadings*[1][2] is 12.7 because this is the entry in the second row, third column (remember that C++ counts up from 0). Figure 7.7 shows the virtual representation of this array in memory (that is, how our high-level virtual environment allows us to think about this array). Figure 7.8 shows its actual representation in memory, assuming that the first storage location has address 1001 and that each number that is type double uses 8 bytes of storage. It will be the job of the C++ compiler to convert between these two representations. The user will be totally unaware that *WaterReadings*[1][2] must be converted into the address for the sixth element in the one-dimensional array storage (address 1041) and may continue to think in terms of the 2 × 3 two-dimensional arrangement.

When the user has a mental model of a collection of data items that are related or "structured" in some way, that collection is called a **data structure**. This is a virtual arrangement; that is, the user thinks of these items as being arranged in some fashion that the user finds useful, such as a two-dimensional table. Then the features available in the programming language must be used to implement that virtual arrangement. In the case of a "two-dimensional table" data structure, the implementation is easily accomplished by using a C++ array.

As a final example of how we need to plan ahead for the data our program will use, suppose we want to write a program to convert a value in miles into the corresponding value in kilometers. These will be real number values, so we will need two type **double** variables: one to hold the value in miles and one to hold the corresponding computed value in kilometers. The program will need to use a conversion factor to change miles into kilometers; because this conversion factor does not change, we will declare it as a program constant. The following declarations would be suitable:

```
const double Miles_To_Kms = 1.609;  //conversion factor
double Miles;                        //distance in miles
double Kilometers;                   //equivalent
                                     //distance in kms
```

PRACTICE PROBLEMS

1. Which of the following are legitimate C++ identifiers?

   `MartinBradley    C3P_OH    amy3    3Right    const`

2. Write a declaration statement for a C++ program that will use one integer quantity called *Number*.

3. How many memory locations will be needed to store the array *Box* given the following declaration? Assuming that each integer requires 4 bytes, how many memory cells will be used?

   `int Box [4][3];`

4. How would you reference the item stored in the first row and first column (upper left corner) of the array *Box* declared in Problem 3?

7.5   STATEMENT TYPES

Now that we can reserve memory for data items by the simple expedient of giving the name of what we want to store and describing its data type, we need to examine additional kinds of programming instructions (statements) that C++ provides. These are the statements that will let us actually manipulate these data items and do something useful with them. The instructions in C++, or indeed in any high-level language, are designed as components for algorithmic problem solving rather than as one-to-one translations of the underlying machine language instruction set of the computer. Thus they allow the programmer to work at a higher level of abstraction. In this section we examine three types of high-level programming language statements. They are consistent with the pseudocode operations we described in Chapter 2 (see Figure 2.6).

One type of statement is *input/output statements*. An **input statement** collects a specific value from the user for a variable within the program. In our circle program that computes the circumference of a circle from its radius, we need an input statement to get the specific value of the radius that is to be used in the computation. An **output statement** writes a message or the value of a program variable to the user's screen (or to a file on some permanent storage medium such as a disk). Once the circle program has computed the value of the circumference, we need an output statement to display that value on the screen.

Another type of statement is an **assignment statement**, which assigns a value to a program variable. This sounds similar to what an input statement does, but the difference is that this value is not collected directly from the user but is computed within the program itself. Indeed, in pseudocode we called this a computation operation.

The third type of statement is a *control statement*. A program executes one instruction or program statement at a time. Without directions to the contrary, the instructions are executed sequentially, from first to last in the program. (In Chapter 2 we called this a straight-line algorithm.) If we imagined, beside each program statement, a little light bulb that lights up while that statement is being executed, we would see a ripple of lights from the top to the bottom of the program. Sometimes, however, we want to interrupt this sequential progression and jump around in the program (which was accomplished by the instructions JUMP, JUMPGT, and so on, in assembly language). The pattern of lights then would not be sequential. This progression of lights would illustrate the **flow of control** in the program—that is, the path through the program that is traced by following the currently executing statement. **Control statements** direct the flow of control and can cause it to deviate from the usual sequential flow.

7.5.1 INPUT/OUTPUT STATEMENTS

Remember that the job of an input statement is to collect, from the user, specific values for variables in the program. In pseudocode, to get the value for the radius of a circle, we would say something like

Get value for *Radius*

C++ can do this task using an input statement of the form

```
cin >> Radius;
```

Because all variables must be declared before they can be used, the declaration statement that says *Radius* is to be a variable (of data type double) precedes this input statement.

Let's say that we have written the entire circle program and it is now actually executing. When the preceding input statement is encountered, the program will stop and wait until the user enters a value for *Radius* (by typing it at the keyboard, followed by pressing the ENTER or RETURN key). For example, the user could type

13.5 <ENTER>

By this action, the user contributes a value to the **input stream**, the sequence of values entered at the keyboard. The input stream is named *cin* (pronounced "see-in"). The arrows (>>) in the input statement above stand for the **extraction operator** that removes the next value from the input stream and stores it in the memory location referenced by the identifier *Radius*. The *cin* stream and the extraction operator are supplied by the iostream library; that's why any C++ program that requires an input statement needs the include directive

```
#include <iostream.h>
```

Once the value of the circumference has been computed and stored in the memory location referenced by *Circumference*, a pseudocode operation for producing output would be something like

Print the value of *Circumference*

Output in C++ is handled as the opposite of input. A value stored in memory—in this case the value of the variable *Circumference*—is copied and inserted into the **output stream** by the **insertion operator** <<. The output stream is called *cout* (pronounced "see-out"). The appropriate statement is

```
cout << Circumference;
```

The output stream and the insertion operator are again provided as part of the iostream library.

It is easy to confuse the direction of the arrows for input and output. The extraction operator extracts a value from the input stream and puts it *into the variable to which it points*:

```
cin >> Radius;
```

The insertion operator takes a value from a variable and inserts it *into the output stream to which it points*:

```
cout << Circumference;
```

Depending on the size of the value, C++ may write out real number values in either **fixed-point format** or **scientific notation**. For a radius of 13.5, the circumference in fixed-point format is

```
84.8232
```

whereas in scientific notation (also called **floating-point format**), it is

```
8.482320e+001
```

which means 8.482320×10^1. (The "e" means "times 10 to the power of . . .") It may be convenient to specify one output format or the other, rather than leaving this up to the system to decide. To force all subsequent output into fixed-point notation, we put the following somewhat mysterious formatting statement in the program.

```
cout.setf(ios::fixed);
```

To force all subsequent output into scientific notation, we use the statement

```
cout.setf(ios::scientific);
```

It is also possible to control the number of places behind the decimal point that are displayed in the output. Inserting the statement

```
cout.precision(2);
```

before the output statement would result in a fixed-point output of

```
84.82
```

The corresponding result for scientific notation would be

```
8.48e+001
```

Each value is rounded to two digits behind the decimal point (picking up the 2 from the cout.precision statement), although the fixed-point value shows a total of four significant digits, and the scientific notation format shows only three. The ability to specify the number of decimal digits in fixed-point output is particularly handy for dealing with dollar-and-cent values, where we always expect to see two digits behind the decimal point.

As an additional control over the appearance of output, the programmer can also specify the total number of columns to be taken up by the next output value. Inserting into the output stream the "set width" expression

```
setw(n)
```

where n has some integer value, allots n columns for the next value that is output, including the decimal point. If n is too small, the entire value will be written out anyway, overriding the width specification. If n is too big, the value will be right-justified within the allotted space. The statement

```
cout << setw(8) << Circumference;
```

requests eight columns for the value of the circumference. Using *setw* helps to align columns of values but is generally less important when writing out single values. Unlike the fixed-point or floating-point format, which only needs to be set once, the *setw* expression must be used each time a value is to be written out. In addition, *setw* is available from a different set of library files, so another include statement is required in order to use it, namely

```
#include <iomanip.h>
```

If the user suddenly sees the number 84.82 on the screen, he or she may have no idea what it represents. Some additional output information in the form of text is needed to describe this value. Textual information can be inserted into the output stream by placing it within quotation marks. Information within quotation marks ("") is called a **literal string** and is printed out exactly as is. For example, we could use the output statement

```
cout << "The circumference that corresponds "
     << "to this radius is " << Circumference;
```

This is one C++ instruction (note the single terminating semicolon) that happens to take up two lines. It contributes two literal strings and the value of one variable to the output stream, each requiring an insertion operator. Assuming that we are using fixed-point format with precision set to 2, the output would be

```
The circumference that corresponds to this radius is 84.82
```

Note that in the program instruction we put a space between the word "is" and the closing quotation mark, so this space is part of the text to be written. Without this space, the output would be

```
The circumference that corresponds to this radius is84.82
```

Output formatting largely determines how attractive and easy to read the output is. We might want to design the output to look like

```
        The circumference that corresponds
to this radius is

        84.82
```

We can accomplish this with the four statements

```
cout << "      The circumference that corresponds" << endl;
cout << "to this radius is" << endl;
cout << endl;
cout << setw(16) << Circumference << endl;
```

Each statement produces one line of output because *endl* (an abbreviation for END Line) sends the cursor to the next line on the screen. The result is that the next value in the output stream begins on a new line. Using *endl* is another way to format output. In the first output statement above, the blank spaces in the literal string before the word "The" produce the indenting. The third output statement contains neither a literal string nor an identifier; its effect is to write a blank line. The *setw* expression in the final output statement positions the numerical value of *Circumference* right-justified within 16 columns.

At this point, let's back up a bit and note that we also need to print some text information before the input statement in order to alert the user that the program expects some input. A statement such as

```
cout << "Enter the value of the radius of a circle"
    << endl;
```

acts as a **user prompt**.

Assembling all of these bits and pieces, we can see that

```
cout << "Enter the value of the radius of a circle"
    << endl;
cin >> Radius;
    . . .
cout << "The circumference that corresponds "
    << "to this radius is " << Circumference << endl;
```

would serve to prompt the user for the input value, read that value into memory, and write out the computed value of the circumference along with an informative message. In the middle, marked above by . . . , we need a program statement

PRACTICE PROBLEMS

1. Write two statements that prompt the user to enter a value for a variable called *Quantity* and then collect that value.

2. A program has computed a value for the variable *Height*. Write an output statement that will print this variable using six columns and such that successive output will appear on the next line.

3. What will appear on the screen after execution of the following statement?

```
cout << "This is" << "goodbye" << endl;
```

to compute the value of the circumference. We will be able to do this with a single assignment statement.

7.5.2 THE ASSIGNMENT STATEMENT

As we said earlier, an assignment statement assigns a value to a program variable. This is accomplished by evaluating some expression and then writing the resulting value in the memory location referenced by the program variable. The general pseudocode operation

Set the value of "variable" to "arithmetic expression"

has as its C++ equivalent

variable = expression;

The expression on the right gets evaluated, and the result is then written into the memory location named on the left. As an example, suppose that *A*, *B*, and *C* have all been declared as integer variables in some program. The assignment statements

```
B = 2;
C = 5;
```

would result in *B* taking on the value 2 and *C* taking on the value 5. After execution of

```
A = B + C;
```

A has the value that is the sum of the current values of *B* and *C*. Assignment is a destructive operation, so whatever *A*'s previous value was, it is gone. Note that this one assignment statement says to add the values of *B* and *C* and assign the result to *A*. Here is the one-step, higher-level-of-thinking solution to the problem we discussed early in this chapter. This one high-level statement is equivalent to the three assembly language statements we needed to do this same task (LOAD B, ADD C, STORE A). A high-level language program thus packs more power per line than an assembly language program. To put it another way, whereas a single assembly language program instruction is equivalent to a single machine language instruction, a single C++ instruction is usually equivalent to many assembly language program instructions or machine language instructions.

In the assignment statement, the expression on the right is evaluated first. Only then is the value of the variable on the left changed. This means that an assignment statement like

```
A = A + 1;
```

makes sense. If A has the value 7 before this statement is executed, then the expression evaluates to

7 + 1, or 8

and 8 then becomes the new value of A. (Here it becomes obvious that the assignment instruction symbol = is not the same as the mathematical equals sign =, because $A = A + 1$ would not make sense mathematically.)

All four basic arithmetic operations can be done in C++, where they are denoted by

- \+   Addition
- –   Subtraction
- *   Multiplication
- /   Division

For the most part this is standard mathematical notation, rather than the somewhat verbose assembly language op code mnemonics such as SUBTRACT. The reason why a special symbol is used for multiplication is that $\times$ would be confused with x, an identifier, $\cdot$ (a multiplication dot) doesn't appear on the keyboard, and juxtaposition—writing AB for $A*B$—would look like a single identifier named AB.

We do have to pay some attention to data types. In particular, division has one peculiarity. If at least one of the two values being divided is a real number, then division behaves as we expect. Thus

7.0/2   7/2.0   7.0/2.0

all result in the value 3.5. However, if the two values being divided are both integers, then the result will be an integer value; if the division doesn't "come out even," the integer value is obtained by truncating the answer to an integer quotient. Thus

7/2

results in the value 3. Think of grade-school long division of integers:

$$\begin{array}{r} 3 \\ 2\overline{)7} \\ \underline{6} \\ 1 \end{array}$$

Here the quotient is 3 and the remainder is 1. C++ also provides an operation, with the symbol %, to obtain the integer remainder. Using this operation,

```
7 % 2
```

results in the value 1. If the values are stored in type **int** variables, the same thing happens. For example,

```cpp
int numerator;
int denominator;
numerator = 7;
denominator = 2;
cout << "The result of " << numerator << "/"
     << denominator << " is "
     << numerator/denominator << endl;
```

will produce the output

```
The result of 7/2 is 3
```

As soon as an arithmetic operation involves one or more real numbers, any integers are converted to their real number equivalent, and the calculations are done with real numbers.

Data types also play a role in assignment statements. Suppose the expression in an assignment statement evaluates to a real number and is then assigned to an identifier that has been declared as an integer. The real number will be truncated, and the digits behind the decimal point will be lost. Assigning an integer value to a type **double** identifier merely changes the integer to its real number equivalent. C++ does this **type casting** (changing of data type) automatically.

Assigning a numeric value to an identifier of type **char** can have very unpredictable results and is not a sensible thing to be doing at any rate. An expression that has a character value can be assigned to a variable that has been declared to be type **char**. Suppose that *Letter* is a variable of type **char**. Then

```cpp
Letter = 'm';
```

would be a legitimate assignment statement, giving *Letter* the value of the character 'm'. Note that single quotation marks are used here, as opposed to the double quotation marks used with a literal string.

Now we can compute the circumference of the circle. We use the assignment statement

```cpp
Circumference = 2*PI*Radius;
```

The main part of our circle program would thus look like

```cpp
cout << "Enter the value of the radius of a circle"
     << endl;
cin >> Radius;
Circumference = 2*PI*Radius;
cout << "The circumference that corresponds "
     << "to this radius is " << Circumference << endl;
```

PRACTICE PROBLEMS

1. *NewNumber* and *Next* are integer variables in a C++ program. Write a statement to assign the value of *NewNumber* to *Next*.

2. What will be the value of *Average* after the following statements are executed? (*Total* and *Number* are type **int**, and *Average* is type **double**.)

```
Total = 277;
Number = 5;
Average = Total/Number;
```

As another example, the program to convert miles to kilometers could contain the following statements. Here the output statement has two segments of text with the computed value inserted in the middle.

```
cout << "Enter the number of miles" << endl;
cin >> Miles;
Kilometers = Miles_To_Kms*Miles;
cout << "This number equals " << Kilometers
  << " kilometers." << endl;
```

As in the previous example, the program prompts the user for data, collects the data value that the user gives, does a computation, and writes the result. The program instructions are executed sequentially. Next we'll see how to use control statements to vary sequential flow.

7.5.3 CONTROL STATEMENTS

We mentioned earlier that sequential flow of control is the default; that is, a program executes instructions sequentially from first to last. The flowchart in Figure 7.9 illustrates this situation, where S1, S2, . . ., are program instructions (program statements).

As we stated in Chapter 2, no matter how complicated the task to be done, only three types of control mechanisms are needed:

1. **Sequential** (the default case, no action required)
2. **Conditional** (the choice of what instructions to execute next depends on some condition)
3. **Looping** (a group of instructions may be executed many times)

There is nothing to be done to achieve sequential flow of control; this is what occurs if the program does not contain any instances of the other two control structures. In the circle program, for instance, instructions are executed sequentially beginning with the input prompt, then the input statement, next the computation, and finally the output statement.

In this section, we look at the other two control mechanisms. In Chapter 2, we introduced pseudocode notation for conditional operations and looping. In Chapter 6, we saw how to write somewhat laborious assembly language code to implement conditional operations and looping. Now we'll see how C++

FIGURE 7.9
Sequential Flow of Control

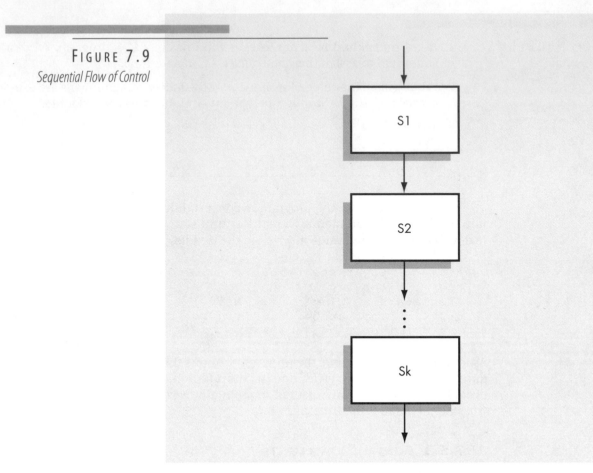

provides instructions that carry out these control structure mechanisms directly—more evidence of the power of high-level language instructions compared to assembly language instructions. We can think in a pseudocode algorithm design mode, as we did in Chapter 2, and then translate that pseudocode rather directly into C++ code.

Conditional flow of control begins with the evaluation of a **Boolean condition**, also called a **Boolean expression**, that can be either true or false. We discussed these "true/false conditions" in Chapter 2, and we also encountered Boolean expressions in Chapter 4, where they were used to design circuits. A Boolean condition often involves comparing the values of two expressions and determining whether they are equal, whether the first is greater than the second, and so on. Again assuming that A, B, and C are integer variables in a program, the following are legitimate Boolean conditions:

A == 0   (Does A currently have the value 0?)

B < (A + C)   (Is the current value of B less than the sum of the current values of A and C?)

A != B   (Does A currently have a different value from that of B?)

FIGURE 7.10

C++ Comparison Operators

COMPARISON	SYMBOL	EXAMPLE	EXAMPLE RESULT
the same value as	==	2 == 5	false
less than	<	2 < 5	true
less than or equal to	<=	5 <= 5	true
greater than	>	2 > 5	false
greater than or equal to	>=	2 >= 5	false
not the same value as	!=	2 != 5	true

If the current values of *A, B,* and *C* are 2, 5, and 7, respectively, then the first condition is false (*A* does not have the value zero), the second condition is true (5 is less than 2 plus 7), and the third condition is true (*A* and *B* do not have equal values).

Comparisons need not be numeric in nature. They can also be done between variables of type **char**, where the "ordering" is the usual alphabetic ordering. If *Initial* is a value of type **char** with a current value of 'D', then

```
Initial == 'F'
```

is false because *Initial* does not have the value 'F', and

```
Initial < 'P'
```

is true because 'D' precedes 'P' in the alphabet (or, more precisely, because the binary code for 'D' is numerically less than the binary code for 'P').

Figure 7.10 shows the comparison operations available in C++. Note the use of the two equality signs to test whether two expressions have the same value. The single equality sign is used in an assignment statement, the double equality sign in a comparison.

Boolean conditions can be built up using the Boolean operators of AND, OR, and NOT. Truth tables for these operators were given in Chapter 4 (Figures 4.7–4.9). The only new thing is the symbolism that C++ uses for these operators, shown in Figure 7.11.

A conditional statement relies on the value of a Boolean condition (true or false) to decide what programming statement to execute next. If the condition is true, one statement will be executed next, but if the condition is false, a different statement will be executed next. Control is therefore no longer in a straight-line (sequential) flow but hops to one place or to another. Figure 7.12 illustrates the

FIGURE 7.11

C++ Boolean Operators

OPERATOR	SYMBOL	EXAMPLE	EXAMPLE RESULT
AND	&&	(2 < 5) && (2 > 7)	false
OR	||	(2 < 5) || (2 > 7)	true
NOT	!	!(2 == 5)	true

FIGURE 7.12

*Conditional Flow
of Control (If-Else)*

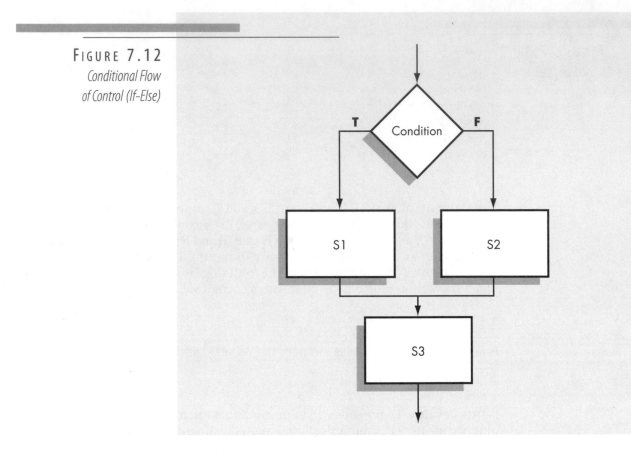

way we can think about this situation. If the condition is true, the statement S1 will be executed (and statement S2 will not); if the condition is false, the statement S2 will be executed (and statement S1 will not). In either case, the flow of control then continues on to statement S3.

The C++ instruction that carries out conditional flow of control is called an **if-else** statement. It has the following form (note that the words "if" and "else" are lower-case and that the Boolean condition must be in parentheses).

if (Boolean condition)

    S1;

else

    S2;

Below is a simple if-else statement, where we are again assuming that *A*, *B*, and *C* are integer variables.

```
if (B < (A + C))
        A = 2*A;
else
        A = 3*A;
```

FIGURE 7.13
If-Else with Empty Else

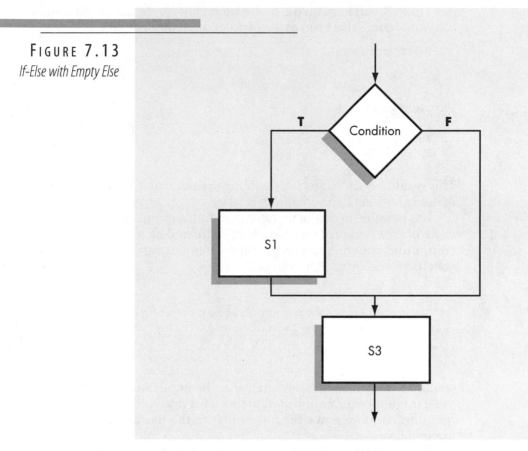

Suppose that when this statement is reached, the values of *A*, *B*, and *C* are 2, 5, and 7, respectively. As we noted before, the condition $B < (A + C)$ is then true, so the statement

```
A  =  2*A;
```

will be executed and the value of *A* will be changed to 4. However, suppose that when this statement is reached, the values of *A*, *B*, and *C* are 2, 10, and 7, respectively. Then the condition $B < (A + C)$ is false, the statement

```
A  =  3*A;
```

will be executed, and the value of *A* will be changed to 6.

A variation on the if-else statement is to allow an "empty else" case. Here we want to do something if the condition is true, but if the condition is false, we want to do nothing. Figure 7.13 shows how we can think about the empty else case. If the condition is true, statement S1 will be executed, and after that the flow of control will continue on to statement S3, but if the condition is false, nothing happens except to move the flow of control directly on to statement S3.

This "if" variation on the if-else statement can be accomplished by omitting the word "else." This form of the instruction therefore looks like

if (Boolean condition)

    S1;

We could write

```
if (B < (A + C))
    A = 2*A;
```

This would have the effect of doubling the value of *A* if the condition is true and of doing nothing if the condition is false.

It is possible to combine statements into a group by putting them within the curly braces { and }. The group is then treated as a single statement, called a **compound statement**. A compound statement can be used anywhere a single statement is allowed. For example,

```
{
  cout << "This is the first statement." << endl;
  cout << "This is the second statement." << endl;
  cout << "This is the third statement." << endl;
}
```

would be treated as a single statement. The implication is that in Figure 7.12, S1 or S2 might be compound statements. This possibility makes the if-else statement much more powerful and similar to the pseudocode conditional statement in Figure 2.6.

For example, let's expand on our circle program, which up to now has been used to compute the circumference of a circle from its radius. Suppose we give the user of the program a choice of computing either the circumference or the area of the circle. This situation is ideal for a conditional statement. Depending on what the user wants to do, the program should do one of two tasks. For either task, the program still needs information about the radius of the circle. The program must also collect information to indicate which task the user wishes to perform. We'll need an additional variable in the program to store this information. Let's use a variable called *Task_to_do* of type **char** to collect the user's choice of which task to perform. We'll also need another variable to represent the value of the area once it has been computed. The computed area will be a real number value; we'll use *Area* of type **double** as the identifier for this quantity. The program's declarations are now

```
const double PI = 3.1416; //value of pi
double Radius;            //radius of a circle—
                          //given
double Circumference;     //circumference of a
                          //circle—computed
double Area;              //area of a circle—
                          //computed
```

```
char Task_to_do;            //holds user choice to
                            //compute circumference
                            //or area
```

We have to add additional statements to the program (an input statement preceded by an appropriate prompt to the user) to collect the value for *Task_to_do*. Then we'll use an if-else statement to compute either the circumference or the radius. The main function body of our program can now be written as follows:

```
cout << "Enter the value of the radius of a circle"
     << endl;
cin >> Radius;
cout << endl;

//See what user wants to compute
cout << "Enter your choice of task." << endl;
cout << "C to compute circumference, A to compute "
     << "area: ";
cin >> Task_to_do;
cout << endl;
if (Task_to_do == 'C')  //compute circumference
{
    Circumference = 2*PI*Radius;
    cout << "The circumference that corresponds "
         << "to this radius is " << Circumference
         << endl;
}
else         //compute area
{
    Area = PI*Radius*Radius;
    cout << "The area that corresponds "
         << "to this radius is " << Area << endl;
}
cout << endl;
```

The condition evaluated at the beginning of the if-else statement tests whether *Task_to_do* has the value 'C'. If so, then the condition is true and the first group of statements is executed—that is, the circumference is computed and written out, along with an appropriate message. If *Task_to_do* does not have the value 'C', then the condition is false. In this event the second group of statements is executed—that is, the area is computed and written out, along with an appropriate message. Note that because of the way the condition is written, if *Task_to_do* does not have the value 'C', it is assumed that the user wants to compute the area, even though *Task_to_do* may have any other non-'C' value (including 'c') that the user may have typed in response to the prompt. Also, we had to use a compound statement for each "branch" of the conditional statement. Not only were the two computations distinct, but the resulting output message was also different in each case, so both the computation and the output were bundled together in a group.

The two statement groups were identified by the enclosing curly braces, but we also indented them to make them easier to pick out when one is looking at the program. Indenting helps make a program easier to read. Like comments, indentation is ignored by the computer but is valuable documentation to help people understand a program.

Let's modify the miles-to-kilometers program so that it either converts miles to kilometers or kilometers to miles, depending on the user's choice. We can use the same two variables as before, *Miles* and *Kilometers*. If the user chooses to convert miles to kilometers (this is what the current program allows), then *Miles* will contain the value input by the user, and *Kilometers* will contain a value computed as the program executes. If the user chooses to convert kilometers to miles, then the roles will be reversed: *Kilometers* will contain the value input by the user, and *Miles* will contain a value computed by the program. We do need one new variable to collect the user's choice (we'll call it *Task_to_do* again, but this time, just to be different, let's collect a number instead of a letter to signify the choice). We also need a new constant, the conversion factor to change kilometers into miles. The declarations for the new program are

```
const double Miles_To_Kms = 1.609; //conversion factor
const double Kms_To_Miles = 0.622; //conversion factor
double Miles;                      //distance in miles
double Kilometers;                 //equivalent
                                   //distance in kms
int Task_to_do;                    //user's choice on
                                   //which conversion
                                   //to do
```

Within the main function body of the program, we must prompt for and collect the user's choice. On the basis of that choice, the program prompts for and collects the appropriate input value (miles or kilometers) and computes and writes out the corresponding output value (kilometers or miles, respectively). Here's how the rest of this program might look:

```
cout << "Change miles to kilometers (enter 1)"
     << endl;
cout << "or kilometers to miles (enter 2): ";
cin >> Task_to_do;
cout << endl;

if (Task_to_do == 1)
{
     cout << "Enter the number of miles" << endl;
     cin >> Miles;
     Kilometers = Miles_To_Kms*Miles;
     cout << "This number equals " << Kilometers
          << " kilometers." << endl;
}
else
{
     cout << "Enter the number of kilometers: "
          << endl;
```

FIGURE 7.14
While Loop

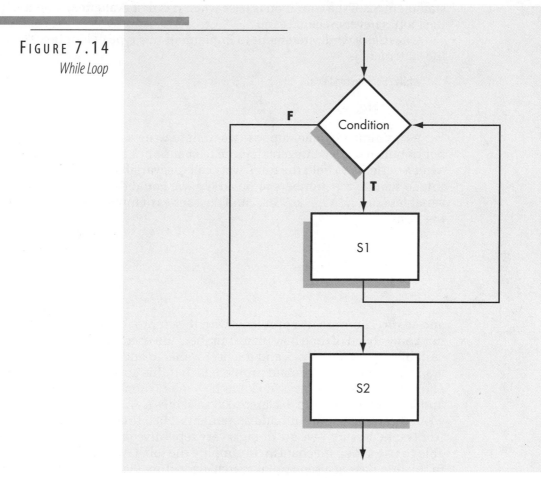

```
cin >> Kilometers;
Miles = Kms_To_Miles*Kilometers;
cout << "This number equals " << Miles
     << " miles." << endl;
}
```

Now let's look at the third variation on flow of control, namely looping (iteration). Here we want to execute the same group of statements (called the **loop body**) perhaps many times. Again a Boolean condition comes into play. In the while loop of our Chapter 2 pseudocode, the loop body is executed as long as (while) some condition remains true. The condition is tested before each execution of the loop body. When the condition finally becomes false, the loop body is not executed again, which is usually expressed by saying that the algorithm *exits* the loop. In order to ensure that the algorithm ultimately exits the loop, the condition must be such that its truth value can be affected by what happens when the loop body is executed. Figure 7.14 shows the situation. The loop body is statement S1 (which can be a compound statement), and S1 is executed while the condition is true. Once the condition is false, the flow of control moves on to statement S2. If the condition is false when it is first evaluated, then the body of the loop is never executed at all.

C++ uses a **while** statement to implement this type of looping. The form of the statement is

while (Boolean condition)

     S1;

As a simple example, suppose we want to write a program to add up a number of non-negative integers that the user supplies and write out the total. We need a variable to hold the total; we'll call this variable *Sum*, and it is data type **int**. To handle the numbers to be added, we could declare a bunch of integer variables such as *N1, N2, N3, . . .* and do a series of input-and-add statements of the form

```
cin >> N1;
Sum = Sum + N1;
cin >> N2;
Sum = Sum + N2;
```

and so on. There are two problems with this approach. The first is that we may not know ahead of time how many numbers the user wants to add. If we declare variables *N1, N2, . . . , N25*, and the user wants to add 26 numbers, the program won't do the job. The second problem is that this approach requires too much effort. Let's suppose that we do know how many numbers the user wants to add, and it is 2,000. We could declare 2,000 variables (*N1, . . . , N2000*), and we could write the above input-and-add statements 2,000 times, but it wouldn't be fun. Nor is it necessary—we are doing a very repetitive task here, and we should be able to use a loop mechanism to simplify the job. (We faced a similar situation in the first pass at a sequential search algorithm, Figure 2.7; our solution there was also to use iteration.)

One more minor problem should be mentioned. Even if we use a loop mechanism, we will still be adding a succession of values to *Sum*. Unless we are sure that the value of *Sum* is zero to begin with, we cannot be sure that the answer isn't nonsense. Remember that the identifier *Sum* is simply an indirect way to designate a memory location in the computer. That memory location will contain a pattern of bits, perhaps left over from whatever was stored there when some previous program was run. We cannot assume that just because this program hasn't used *Sum*, its value is zero. (In contrast, the assembly language statement SUM: .DATA 0 reserves a memory location filled with the value zero.) If we want the value of *Sum* to be zero to begin with, we had better use an assignment statement to guarantee this. **Initialization of variables** is the name given to the process of using assignment statements to be sure that we know the values of certain variables before any other use is made of them in the program.

Now on to the loop mechanism. First, let's note that once a number has been read in and added to *Sum*, the program doesn't need to know the value of the number any longer. We can declare just one integer variable called *Number* and use it repeatedly to hold the first numerical value, then the second, and so on. The general idea is then

```
Sum = 0; //initialize Sum
while ( there are more numbers to add)
{
        cin >> Number;
        Sum = Sum + Number;
}
cout << "The total is " << Sum << endl;
```

Now we have to figure out what the condition "there are more numbers to add" really means. Because we are adding non-negative integers, we could ask the user to enter one extra integer that is not part of the legitimate data but indeed is a signal that there *are* no more data. Such a value is called a **sentinel value**. For this problem, any negative number would be a good sentinel value. Because the numbers to be added are all non-negative, the appearance of a negative number signals the end of the legitimate data. We don't want to process the sentinel value (because it is not a legitimate data item); we only want to use it to terminate the looping process. This might suggest the following code:

```
Sum = 0;                    //initialize Sum
while (Number >= 0)         //but there is a problem here,
                            //see following discussion
{
        cin >> Number;
        Sum = Sum + Number;
}
cout << "The total is " << Sum << endl;
```

Here's the problem. How can we test whether *Number* is greater than or equal to 0 if we haven't read the value of *Number* yet? We need to do a preliminary input for the first value of *Number* outside of the loop and then test that value in the loop condition. If it is non-negative, we want to add it to *Sum* and then read the next value and test it. Whenever the value of *Number* is negative (including the first value), we want to do nothing with it—that is, we want to avoid executing the loop body. The following statements will do the job; we've also added instructions to the user.

```
Sum = 0;                    //initialize Sum
cout << "Please enter numbers to add; ";
cout << "terminate with a negative number." << endl;
cin >> Number;              //this will get the first value
while (Number >= 0)
{
        Sum = Sum + Number;
        cin >> Number;
}
cout << "The total is " << Sum << endl;
```

The value of *Number* gets changed within the loop body by reading in a new value. The new value is tested, and if it is non-negative, the loop body executes again, adding the data value to *Sum* and reading in a new value for *Number*. The loop will terminate when a negative value is read in. Remember our earlier requirement that something within the loop body must be able to affect the truth value of the condition. In this case, it is reading in a new value for *Number* that has the potential to change the value of the condition from true to false. Without this requirement, the condition, once true, would remain true forever, and the loop body would be endlessly executed. This results in what is called an **infinite loop**. A program that contains an infinite loop will execute forever (or until the programmer gets tired of waiting and interrupts the program, or until the program exceeds some preset time limit).

The problem we've solved here, adding nonnegative integers until a negative sentinel value occurs, is the same one solved using assembly language in Chapter 6. The preceding C++ code is almost identical to the pseudocode version of the algorithm shown in Figure 6.7. Thanks to the power of the language, the C++ code embodies the algorithm directly, at a high level of thinking, whereas in assembly language this same algorithm had to be translated into the lengthy and awkward code of Figure 6.8.

We could use a while loop to process data for a number of circles. During each pass through the loop, the program will compute the circumference or area of a circle for which the user has given the radius. The body of the loop is therefore exactly like our previous code. All we are adding here is the framework that provides looping. To terminate the loop, we could use a sentinel value, as we did for the program above. A negative value for *Radius*, for example, would not be a legitimate value and could serve as a sentinel value. Instead of that, let's allow the user to control loop termination by having the program ask the user whether he or she wishes to continue. We'll need a variable to hold the user's response to this question. Let's suppose that a variable *More* of type **char** has been declared. Then we can write the main body of the program as follows:

```
cout << "Do you want to process a circle? (Y or N): ";
cin >> More;
cout << endl;
while (More == 'Y') //more circles to process
{
   cout << "Enter the value of the radius of a "
      << "circle" << endl;
   cin >> Radius;
   cout << endl;

   //See what user wants to compute
   cout << "Enter your choice of task." << endl;
   cout << "C to compute circumference, "
      << "A to compute area: ";
   cin >> Task_to_do;
   cout << endl;
   if (Task_to_do == 'C') //compute circumference
   {
      Circumference = 2*PI*Radius;
      cout << "The circumference that corresponds "
         << "to this radius is " << Circumference
         << endl;
   }
   else                  //compute area
```

```
  {
    Area = PI*Radius*Radius;
    cout << "The area that corresponds "
      << "to this radius is " << Area << endl;
  }
  cout << endl;
  cout << "Do you want to process more circles? "
    << "(Y or N): ";
  cin >> More;
  cout << endl;
}
//finish up
cout << "Program will now terminate." << endl;
```

Of course, the user could answer "N" at the first query, and then the loop body would never execute at all, and the user would just see the termination message. A similar approach could be used to process a number of miles-to-kilometers conversions.

7.6 PUTTING THE PIECES TOGETHER

Let's review briefly the types of C++ programming statements we've learned. We can do input and output—reading values from the user into memory, writing values out of memory for the user to see, all done by using meaningful variable identifiers to reference memory locations. We can assign values to variables within the program. And we can direct the flow of control by using conditional statements or looping. Many other statement types are available in C++, but one can do just about everything using only the modest collection of statements we have described. The power lies in how these statements can be combined and nested within groups to produce ever more complex courses of action.

7.6.1 THE COMPLETE PROGRAM

Figure 7.3, which is reproduced in Figure 7.15, gives an outline for a simple C++ program. At this point, we have almost everything we need to write a complete circle-processing program. We need to assemble the code we've got in the right order and to fill in the missing pieces, which are

- A prologue comment to explain what the program does (optional but recommended for program documentation)
- An include directive for iostream.h (necessary because our program uses *cin* and *cout*)
- The start of the main function
- A declaration for the *More* variable
- Some output formatting to control the number of digits behind the decimal point

PRACTICE PROBLEMS

1. What is the output from the following section of code?

```
Number1 = 15;
Number2 = 7;
if (Number1 >= Number2)
    cout << 2*Number1 << endl;
else
    cout << 2*Number2 << endl;
```

2. What is the output from the following section of code?

```
Scores = 1;
while (Scores < 20)
{
    Scores = Scores + 2;
    cout << Scores << endl;
}
```

3. What is the output from the following section of code?

```
quota_this_month = 7;
quota_last_month = quota_this_month + 1;
if ((quota_this_month > quota_last_month) ||
    (quota_last_month >= 8))
{
    cout << "Yes";
    quota_last_month = quota_last_month + 1;
}
else
{
    cout << "No";
    quota_this_month = quota_this_month + 1;
}
```

4. How many times will the statement marked with * be executed in the following section of code?

```
left = 10;
right = 20;
while (left <= right)
{
 *  cout << left << endl;
    left = left + 2;
}
```

5. Write a C++ statement that outputs "Equal" if the values of *Night* and *Day* are the same but otherwise does nothing.

Our program uses no other functions besides the main function, so we can skip that (optional) section.

The complete program is shown in Figure 7.16. This is real computer code that would execute on any computer with a C++ compiler. Figure 7.17 shows what would actually appear on the screen when this program is executed with some sample data.

FIGURE 7.15
A C++ Program Outline

prologue comment	[optional]
include directives	[optional]
functions	[optional]
main function	
{	
declarations	[optional]
main function body	
}	

7.6.2 MEETING EXPECTATIONS

At the beginning of this chapter, we gave four expectations for programs written in a high-level programming language. Now that we know the essentials of writing programs in C++, it is time to see how well this particular language allows these expectations to be met.

1. *The programmer need not manage the details of the movement of data items within memory or pay any attention to exactly where those items are stored.* The programmer's only responsibilities are to declare all constants and variables the program will use. This involves selecting identifiers to represent the various data items and indicating the data type of each. The identifiers can be descriptive names that meaningfully relate the data to the problem being solved. Data values are moved as necessary within memory by program instructions that simply reference these identifiers, without the programmer having any idea which specific memory locations contain which values, or what value currently exists in an ALU register. The concepts of memory address and movement between memory and the ALU, along with the effort of generating constant data values, have disappeared.

2. *The programmer can take a macroscopic view of tasks, thinking at a higher level of problem solving.* Instead of the "micromanagement level" of moving data values here and there and carefully orchestrating the limited operations available at the machine language or assembly language level, the programmer can, for example, write the formula to compute the circumference of the circle given its radius. The details of how the instruction is carried out—how the data values are moved about and exactly how the multiplication of real number values is done—are handled elsewhere. Compare the power of conditional and looping instructions, which are tools for algorithmic problem solving and resemble the operations with which we constructed algorithms in pseudocode, with the assembly language instructions LOAD, STORE, JUMP, and so on, which are tools for data and memory management.

3. *Programs written in a high-level language will be portable rather than machine-specific.* As long as the machine you wish to use has a compiler for the language in which your program is written, you should be able to execute your program on that machine. (Actually, life is not quite that simple, as we'll see in a moment.) The details of that particular computer's assembly language or machine language must be known by the compiler, but not by your program.

FIGURE 7.16

*Complete Program
to Process Circles*

```
//program circle
//This program allows the user to compute the
//circumference or area, after giving the radius,
// of any number of circles.

#include <iostream.h>

void main()
{
  const double PI = 3.1416;//value of pi
  double Radius;             //radius of a circle - given
  double Circumference;      //circumference of a circle
                             //- computed
  double Area;               //area of a circle -
                             //computed
  char Task_to_do;           //holds user choice to
                             //compute circumference
                             //or area
  char More;                 //controls loop for
                             //processing more circles

  cout.setf(ios::fixed);
  cout.precision(2);

  cout << "Do you want to process a circle? (Y or N): ";
  cin >> More;
  cout << endl;
  while (More == 'Y')  //more circles to process
  {
    cout << "Enter the value of the radius of a "
      << "circle" << endl;
    cin >> Radius;
    cout << endl;

    //See what user wants to compute
    cout << "Enter your choice of task." << endl;
    cout << "C to compute circumference, "
      << "A to compute area: ";
    cin >> Task_to_do;
    cout << endl;
    if (Task_to_do == 'C') //compute circumference
    {
      Circumference = 2*PI*Radius;
      cout << "The circumference that corresponds "
        << "to this radius is " << Circumference
        << endl;
    }
    else               //compute area
    {
      Area = PI*Radius*Radius;
      cout << "The area that corresponds "
        << "to this radius is " << Area << endl;
    }
```

FIGURE 7.16
(continued)

```
            cout << endl;
            cout << "Do you want to process more circles? "
                 << "(Y or N): ";
            cin >> More;
            cout << endl;
        }

        //finish up
        cout << "Program will now terminate." << endl;
    }
```

```
Do you want to process a circle? (Y or N): Y

Enter the value of the radius of a circle
2.7

Enter your choice of task.
C to compute circumference, A to compute area: C

The circumference that corresponds to this radius is 16.96

Do you want to process more circles? (Y or N): Y

Enter the value of the radius of a circle
2.7

Enter your choice of task.
C to compute circumference, A to compute area: A

The area that corresponds to this radius is   22.90

Do you want to process more circles? (Y or N): Y

Enter the value of the radius of a circle
14.53

Enter your choice of task.
C to compute circumference, A to compute area: C

The circumference that corresponds to this radius is 91.29

Do you want to process more circles? (Y or N): N

Program will now terminate.
```

FIGURE 7.17

A Sample Session Using the Program of Figure 7.16

Hence there is a compiler for each (high-level-language, machine-type) pair. There are C++ compilers for PCs, C++ compilers for Macintoshes, C++ compilers for Digital Equipment Corporation VAX mainframes, and so on, and there are BASIC, C, Pascal, and other high-level programming language compilers for these same machines.

Now what's the catch we just referred to? Each programming language has a certain core of instructions that are considered standard. Any decent compiler for that language must support that core. In fact, national and international standards

FIGURE 7.18

*A Pseudocode Version
of the Circle Program*

Get value for user's choice about continuing
While the user wants to continue, do the following steps
    Get value for the radius
    Get value for the user's choice of task
    If task choice is circumference then compute and print circumference
        otherwise compute and print area
    Get value for user's choice for continuing

groups such as ANSI (American National Standards Institute) and ISO (International Standards Organization), which exist to develop standards for an incredible number of things, also develop standards for programming languages. Compilers will thus be built to support "ANSI-standard language X." However, there are often nice features or types of instructions that are not considered a standard part of the language and that some compilers will support, whereas others will not. If you have written your program to take advantage of some of these nice extra features—often referred to as "bells and whistles"—that are available on your particular compiler, the program may not work with a different compiler. The price for using nonstandard features is the possibility of sacrificing portability.

The standardization process for any entity is necessarily a slow one because it seeks to satisfy the interests of a number of parties, such as consumers, industry, and government. If official standardization comes too late, it must bow to what may have become a de facto standard by common usage. If standardization is imposed too early, it may thwart the development of new ideas or technology. At the time this book was written, the ANSI standard for C++ was nearing completion after more than eight years. In November, 1997, the combined C++ subcommittees of ANSI and ISO submitted their C++ standards draft, part of a document of some 800 pages, for final ISO approval. While waiting for an official standard, the "unofficial standard" has been the description of the language given in *The C++ Programming Language*, second edition, by Bjarne Stroustrup. Stroustrup, as noted earlier, was the original developer of the C++ language.

4. *Programming statements in a high-level language will be closer to standard English and will use standard mathematical notation.* If we were planning how to write the circle program, we might first outline it in pseudocode, as shown in Figure 7.18. Though somewhat stilted, pseudocode is still close to standard English. The actual code, Figure 7.16, is very similar to this. C++ provides us with statements that give natural implementations of "while condition do something . . ." or "if condition do something . . . ."

Indeed, even though we built up the circle program in bits and pieces, the usual way to write such a program is first to do a pseudocode version of what we want the program to accomplish, similar to Figure 7.18, and then, working from this outline, to write the code. Later in this chapter, we'll examine the entire process of producing a correct and usable program. The point here is that the more English-language-like the programming language, the easier it is to convert the outline into actual programming instructions. In addition, C++ allows us to use standard mathematical notation such as A + B.

C++, then, seems to have been rather successful in meeting our expectations for a high-level programming language. We've used C++ as a fairly typical language to illustrate one way in which these expectations might be satisfied, but it is far from the only language. In the next chapter, we look briefly at other high-level programming languages.

Laboratory Experience 11

In this laboratory experience, you will execute a number of complete C++ programs that have already been written. These programs make use of input, output, assignment, and control statements. You'll be asked to modify these programs to allow them to do something more or something different than before. In addition, you'll design, write, and execute a complete C++ program of your own.

PRACTICE **P**ROBLEMS

1. Write a complete C++ program to read in the user's first and last initials and write them out. (*Hint:* By using multiple extraction operators, you can use a single input statement to collect more than one value from the input stream.)

2. Write a complete C++ program that asks for the price of an item and the quantity purchased and writes out the total cost.

3. Write a complete C++ program that asks for a number. If the number is less than 5, it is written out, but if it is greater than or equal to 5, twice that number is written out.

4. Write a complete C++ program that asks the user for a positive integer n and then writes out all the numbers from 1 up to and including n.

7.7   KEEPING THE PIECES APART

The programs we have written have been relatively simple. As problems and their solutions become more complex, so do the programs written to solve those problems. Although it is fairly easy to understand what is happening in the 40 or so lines of the circle program, imagine trying to understand a program that is 50,000 lines long. Imagine trying to write such a program! It is not possible to understand—all at once—everything that goes on in a 50,000-line program.

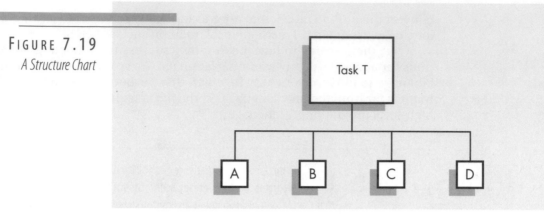

FIGURE 7.19
A Structure Chart

7.7.1 DIVIDE AND CONQUER

Writing large programs becomes an exercise in managing complexity. The solution is a problem-solving approach called **divide and conquer**. A program is to be written to do a certain task; let's call it task T. Suppose we can divide this task into smaller tasks, say A, B, C, and D, such that if we could just do those four tasks in the right order, we would be able to do task T. Then our high-level understanding of the problem needs to be concerned only with *what* A, B, C, and D do and how they must work together to accomplish T. We do not, at this stage of the game, need to understand *how* A, B, C, and D can be done. Figure 7.19, an example of a **structure chart** or **structure diagram**, represents this situation. Task T is composed in some way of subtasks A, B, C, and D. Later we can turn our attention to, say, subtask A, and see whether it also can be decomposed into smaller subtasks (see Figure 7.20). In this way, we continue to break the task down into smaller and smaller pieces, finally arriving at subtasks that are simple enough that it is easy to write the code to carry them out. By *dividing* the problem into small pieces, we can *conquer* the complexity that would be too overwhelming if we looked at the whole problem all at once.

Divide and conquer is, as we said, a problem-solving approach and not just a computer programming technique. Outlining a term paper into major and minor topics is a divide-and-conquer approach to writing the paper. Doing a Form 1040 Individual Tax Return for the Internal Revenue Service can involve the subtasks of completing Schedules A, B, C, D, and so on and then reassembling the results. Designing a house can be broken down into subtasks of designing floor plans, wiring, plumbing, and the like. Large companies organize their management responsibilities using a divide-and-conquer approach; what we have called structure charts become, in the business world, organization charts.

How is the divide-and-conquer problem-solving approach reflected in the resulting computer program? If we thought about how to solve the problem in terms of subtasks, then the program should show that same structure; that is, part of the code should do subtask A, part should do subtask B, and so on. We divide the code into *modules* or *subprograms*, each of which does some part of the overall task. Then we empower these modules to work together to solve the original problem.

FIGURE 7.20

A More Detailed Structure Chart

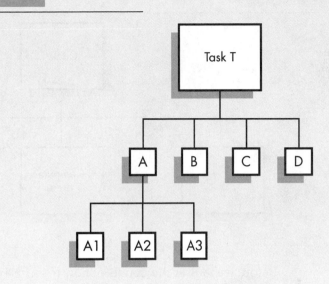

7.7.2 USING FUNCTIONS

In C++, modules of code are called **functions**. Each function in a program should do one and only one subtask. These "subtask functions" are the optional functions listed before the mandatory main function in the C++ program outline of Figure 7.15. When subtask functions are used, the main function consists primarily of invoking these subtasks in the correct order and allowing them to work together.

For example, we can think of the main function body of our circle program (Figure 7.16) in the following way. There is a loop that does some stuff as long as the user wants. What stuff gets done? Some input is obtained from the user (the radius of the circle, and the choice of computing circumference or area). Then the circumference gets computed or the area gets computed. We've identified three subtasks, as shown in the structure chart of Figure 7.21.

We can visualize the main function body of the program at a pseudocode level as shown in Figure 7.22. This divide-and-conquer approach to solving the problem can (and should) be planned first in pseudocode, without regard to the details of the programming language to be used to implement the solution. If the three subtasks (input, circumference, area) can all be done, then arranging them within the structure of Figure 7.22 will solve the problem. We can write a function for each of the subtasks. Although we now know what form the main function body will take, we have pushed the details of how to do each of the subtasks off into the other functions. Execution of the program begins with the main function. Every time the flow of control reaches the equivalent of a "do subtask" instruction, it will transfer to the appropriate function code and execute that code. When execution of the function code is complete, flow of control will transfer back to the main function and pick up where it left off.

FIGURE 7.21

Structure Chart for the Circle Task

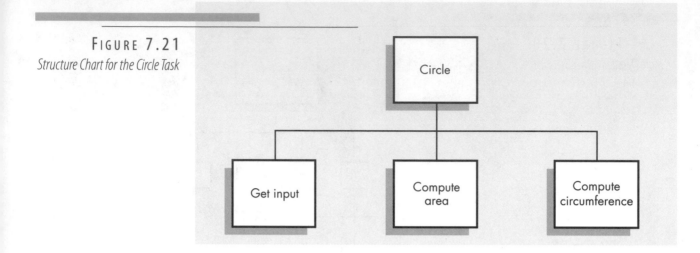

FIGURE 7.21

Structure Chart for the Circle Task

Before we look at the details of how to write a function, we need to examine the mechanism that allows the functions to work together with each other and with the main function. This mechanism consists of passing information about various quantities in the program back and forth between the other functions and the main function. The theory here is that because each function is doing only one subtask of the entire task, it does not need to know the values of all variables in the program. It only needs to know the values of the variables with which its particular subtask is concerned. Allowing a function access only to pertinent variables prevents that function from inadvertently changing a value it has no business changing.

When the main function wants a subtask function to be executed, it gives the name of the function (which is an ordinary C++ identifier) and also a list of the identifiers for variables that concern that function. This is called an **argument list**. In our circle example, let's name the three functions *Get_Input*, *Do_Circumference*, and *Do_Area* (names that are descriptive of the subtasks these functions carry out). The *Get_Input* function is supposed to collect the values for the variables *Radius* and *Task_to_do*. The main program invokes the *Get_Input* function with the statement

```
Get_Input(Radius, Task_to_do);
```

which takes the place of the "Do the input subtask" line in Figure 7.22. When this statement is reached, control passes to the *Get_Input* function. After execution of this function, control returns to the main function, and the variables *Radius* and *Task_to_do* have the values obtained for them within *Get_Input*.

The *Do_Circumference* function is supposed to compute and write out the value of the circumference, and in order to do that, it needs to know the radius. Therefore, the variable *Radius* is a legitimate argument for this function. The main function will contain the statement

```
Do_Circumference(Radius);
```

FIGURE 7.22

*A High-Level Modular
View of the Circle Program*

Get value for user's choice about continuing
While the user wants to continue
    Do the input subtask
    If (Task = 'C') then
        do the circumference subtask
    else
        do the area subtask
    Get value for user's choice about continuing

in place of the "do the circumference subtask" in Figure 7.22. When this statement is reached, the variable *Radius* will convey the value of the radius to the *Do_Circumference* function, and the function will compute and write out the circumference. It would appear, then, that *Circumference* is also a variable of interest to the *Do_Circumference* function. Yes it is, but it is of interest to this function alone in the sense that *Do_Circumference* does the computation and writes out the result. No other use is made of the circumference in the entire program, so neither any other function nor the main function has to have anything to do with *Circumference*. Any function can have its own constant and variable declarations, just like the main function. A constant or variable declared within a function is known, and can be used, only within that function; it is said to be **local** to that function (a **local variable** or a **local constant**). We will declare *Circumference* as a local variable in the *Do_Circumference* function.

In order to compute the circumference, the *Do_Circumference* function also needs to know the value of the constant *PI*. We could declare *PI* as a constant local to *Do_Circumference*, but *Do_Area* is going to need the same constant, and it is silly to declare it twice. Instead, we will declare *PI* right after the program #include directives, not within any function. This will make *PI* a **global constant** whose value is known everywhere. The value of a constant cannot be changed, so there is no reason to prevent any function from having access to its value.

The *Do_Area* function computes and writes out the area and needs to know the radius, so the line "do the area subtask" in Figure 7.22 will be replaced by

```
Do_Area(Radius);
```

Area will be a local variable within *Do_Area*.

Now we can write the main function of the modularized version of the circle program, shown in Figure 7.23. The main function body is a direct translation of Figure 7.22. If, in starting from scratch to write this program, we had taken a divide-and-conquer approach, broken the original problem down into three subtasks, and come up with the outline of Figure 7.22, it would have been easy to get from there to Figure 7.23. The only additional task would have been determining the variables needed.

FIGURE 7.23

The Main Function in a Modularized Version of the Circle Program

```cpp
void main()
{
  double Radius;        //radius of a circle - given
  char Task_to_do;      //holds user choice to
                        //compute circumference or area
  char More;            //controls loop for processing
                        //more circles

  cout.setf(ios::fixed);
  cout.precision(2);

  cout << "Do you want to process a circle? (Y or N): ";
  cin >> More;
  cout << endl;
  while (More == 'Y')   //more circles to process
  {
    Get_Input(Radius, Task_to_do);

    if (Task_to_do == 'C') //compute circumference
      Do_Circumference(Radius);
    else                   //compute area
      Do_Area(Radius);

    cout << endl;
    cout << "Do you want to process more circles? "
      << "(Y or N): ";
    cin >> More;
    cout << endl;
  }

  //finish up
  cout << "Program will now terminate." << endl;
}
```

7.7.3 WRITING FUNCTIONS

Now we know how the main function can invoke another function. (In fact, using the same process, any function can invoke another function. A function can even invoke itself.) It is time to see how to write the code for these other, non-main functions. The general outline for a C++ function is shown in Figure 7.24.

The function header consists of three parts:

A return indicator

The function identifier

A parameter list

The **return indicator** classifies a function as a "void" or a "nonvoid" function. We'll explain this distinction later, but the three functions we need for the circle

FIGURE 7.24

The Outline for a C ++ Function

```
function header
{
        local declarations        [optional]
        function body
}
```

program are all void functions, so the return indicator is the keyword **void**. (All of our main functions have been void functions as well.) The **function identifier** can be any legitimate C++ identifier. The parameters in the **parameter list** correspond to the arguments in the statement in the main function that invokes this function; that is, the first parameter in the list matches the first argument given in the statement that invokes the function, the second parameter matches the second argument, and so on. It is through this correspondence between parameters and arguments that information (data) flows from the main function to other functions, and vice versa. The data type of each parameter must be given as part of the parameter list, and it must match the data type of the corresponding argument. For example, because the *Get_Input* function is invoked with the two arguments *Radius* and *Task_to_do*, the parameter list for the *Get_Input* function header has two parameters, the first of type **double** and the second of type **char**. These parameters may or may not have the same identifiers as the corresponding arguments; for the *Get_Input* function, we'll let the parameter identifiers also be *Radius* and *Task_to_do*. Finally, no semicolon appears at the end of a function header.

One additional aspect of the parameter list in the function header concerns the use the function will make of each parameter. Consider the statement that invokes the function; an argument in the invoking statement carries a data value to the corresponding parameter in the function header. If the value is one that the function must know in order to do its job but should not change, then the argument is **passed by value**. The function receives a copy of the data value but never knows the memory location where the original value is stored. If the function changes the value of its copy, this change has no effect when control returns to the main function. If, however, the value passed to the function is one that the function should change, and the main function should know the new value, then the argument is **passed by reference**. The function receives access to the memory location where the value is stored, and any changes it makes to the value will be seen by the main function after control returns there. Included in this category are arguments whose values are unknown when the function is invoked (which really means that they are meaningless values of whatever happens to be in the memory location associated with that identifier) but the function will change those unknown values into meaningful values.

By default, arguments in C++ are passed by value, which protects them from change by the function. Explicit action must be taken by the programmer to pass an argument by reference; specifically, the symbol & must appear in front of the corresponding parameter in the function parameter list.

FIGURE 7.25

The Get_Input *Function*

```
void Get_Input(double &Radius, char &Task_to_do)
//gets radius and choice of task from the user
{
  cout << "Enter the value of the radius of a circle"
    << endl;
  cin >> Radius;
  cout << endl;

  //See what user wants to compute
  cout << "Enter your choice of task." << endl;
  cout << "C to compute circumference, "
    << "A to compute area: ";
  cin >> Task_to_do;
  cout << endl;
}
```

How do we decide whether to pass an argument by value or by reference? A general rule of thumb is that if the main function needs to obtain a new value back from a function when execution of that function terminates, then the argument must be passed by reference (by inserting the & into the parameter list). Otherwise, pass the argument by value, the default arrangement.

In the *Get_Input* function, both *Radius* and *Task_to_do* are values that *Get_Input* obtains from the user and that the main function will need to know when *Get_Input* terminates, so both of these will be passed by reference. The header for the *Get_Input* function is shown below, along with the invoking statement from the main function. Note that the parameters *Radius* and *Task_to_do* are in the right order, have been given the correct data types, and are both marked for passing by reference. Also remember that although the arguments are named *Radius* and *Task_to_do* because those are the variable identifiers declared in the main function, the parameters could have different identifiers, and it is the parameter identifiers that are used within the body of the function.

```
void Get_Input(double &Radius,  char &Task_to_do)
                                        //function header
Get_Input(Radius, Task_to_do);   //function invocation
```

The body of the *Get_Input* function comes from the corresponding part of Figure 7.16. If we hadn't already written this code, we could have done a pseudocode plan first. The complete function appears in Figure 7.25, where a comment has been added to document the purpose of the function.

The *Do_Circumference* function needs to know the value of *Radius* but will not change that value. Therefore, *Radius* is passed by value. Why all the fuss about distinguishing between arguments passed by value and those passed by reference? If functions are to effect any changes at all, then clearly reference pa-

FIGURE 7.26

The Do_Circumference *Function*

```
void Do_Circumference(double Radius)
//computes and writes out the circumference of
//a circle with radius Radius
{
   double Circumference;
   Circumference = 2*PI*Radius;
   cout<< "The circumference that corresponds "
       << "to this radius is " << Circumference << endl;
}
```

rameters are necessary, but why not just make everything a reference parameter? Suppose that in this example *Radius* is made a reference parameter. If an instruction within *Do_Circumference* were inadvertently to change the value of *Radius*, then that new value would be returned to the main function, and any subsequent calculations using this value (there are none in this example) would be in error. Making *Radius* a value parameter prevents this. Now, you may say, how could one possibly write a program statement that would change the value of a variable inadvertently? In something as short and simple as our example, this probably would not happen, but in a more complicated program, it might. Distinguishing between passing by value and passing by reference is just a further step in controlling a function's access to data values in order to limit the damage the function might do. The code for the *Do_Circumference* function appears in Figure 7.26.

The *Do_Area* function is very similar. Let's assemble everything back together and give the complete modularized version of the program. In Figure 7.27, only the main function needs to know the value of *More*; no other function needs access to this value, so that variable is never passed as an argument. The main function header

```
void main( )
```

also follows the form for any function header. In other words, the main function truly is a C++ function. It has an empty parameter list because it is the starting point for the program, and there's no other place that could pass argument values to it.

So there we have it, a complete modularized version of our circle program, where subtasks are done by separate functions. Because it seems to have been rather a lot of effort to have arrived at this second version (which, after all, does the same thing as the program in Figure 7.16), let's review what the new version does and why this effort is worthwhile.

The modularized version of the program is compartmentalized in two ways. First, it is compartmentalized with respect to task. The major task is accomplished by doing a series of subtasks, and the work for each subtask takes place within a separate function. This leaves the main function free of details and

FIGURE 7.27

*The Complete
Modularized
Circle Program*

```
//program circle2
//This program allows the user to compute
//the circumference or area, after giving the radius,
//of any number of circles.
//Illustrates functions

#include <iostream.h>

const double PI = 3.1416;    //value of pi

void Get_Input(double &Radius, char &Task_to_do)
//gets radius and choice of task from the user
{
  cout << "Enter the value of the radius of a circle"
    << endl;
  cin >> Radius;
  cout << endl;

  //See what user wants to compute
  cout << "Enter your choice of task." << endl;
  cout << "C to compute circumference, "
    << "A to compute area: ";
  cin >> Task_to_do;
  cout << endl;
}

void Do_Circumference(double Radius)
//computes and writes out the circumference of
//a circle with radius Radius
{
  double Circumference;
  Circumference = 2*PI*Radius;
  cout << "The circumference that corresponds "
    << "to this radius is " << Circumference << endl;
}

void Do_Area (double Radius)
//computes and writes out the area of
//a circle with radius Radius
{
  double Area;
  Area = PI*Radius*Radius;
  cout << "The area that corresponds "
    << "to this radius is " << Area << endl;
}
```

FIGURE 7.27

(continued)

```cpp
void main()
{
  double Radius;        //radius of a circle - given
  char Task_to_do;      //holds user choice to
                        //compute circumference or area
  char More;            //controls loop for processing
                        //more circles

  cout.setf(ios::fixed);
  cout.precision(2);

  cout << "Do you want to process a circle? (Y or N): ";
  cin >> More;
  cout << endl;
  while (More == 'Y')  //more circles to process
  {
    Get_Input(Radius, Task_to_do);

    if (Task_to_do == 'C') //compute circumference
      Do_Circumference(Radius);
    else                    //compute area
      Do_Area(Radius);

    cout << endl;
    cout << "Do you want to process more circles? "
      << "(Y or N): ";
    cin >> More;
    cout << endl;
  }

  //finish up
  cout << "Program will now terminate." << endl;
}
```

consisting primarily of invoking the appropriate function at the appropriate point. As an analogy, think of the president of a company calling on various assistants to carry out tasks as needed. The president does not need to know *how* a task is done, only the name of the person responsible for carrying it out. Second, the program is compartmentalized with respect to data in the sense that the data values known to the various functions are controlled through parameter lists, and through the use of value instead of reference parameters where appropriate. In our analogy, the president gives each assistant the information he or she needs to do the assigned task, and he expects relevant information to be returned, but not all assistants know all information.

This compartmentalization is useful in many ways. It is useful when we *plan the solution* to a problem, because it allows us to use a divide-and-conquer approach. We can think about the problem in terms of subtasks. This makes it easier for us to understand how to achieve a solution to a large and complex problem. It is also useful when we *code the solution* to a problem, because it allows us to concentrate on writing one section of the code at a time. We can write a function and then fit it into the program so that the program gradually expands rather than having to be written in total all at once. Developing a large software project is a team effort, and different parts of the team can be writing different functions at the same time. It is useful when we *test the program*, because we can test one new function at a time as the program grows, and any errors are localized to the function being added. (The main function can be tested early by writing appropriate headers but empty bodies for the remaining functions.) Compartmentalization is useful when we *modify the program*, because changes tend to be localized within certain subtasks and hence within certain functions in the code. And finally it is useful for anyone (including the programmer) who wants to *read* the resulting program. The overall idea of how the program works, without the details, can be gleaned from reading the main function; if and when the details become important, the appropriate code for the other functions can be consulted.

A special type of C++ function can be written to compute a single value rather than carry out a subtask. For example, *Do_Circumference* does everything connected with the circumference, both calculating the value and writing it out. We can write a function called *Circumference* that only computes the value of the circumference and then returns that value to the main function, which writes it out. (We can use the identifier *Circumference* for this function only because we will no longer need a program variable of that name.) A function that returns a single value to the section of the program that invoked it is a nonvoid function. Instead of using the word "void" as the return indicator in the function header, a nonvoid function uses the data type of the single returned value. In addition, a nonvoid function must contain a return statement, which consists of the keyword **return** followed by an expression for the value to be returned. (This explains why we have always written the main function as a void function; it is never invoked anywhere else in the program and does not return a value.)

The code for the *Circumference* function would be simply

```
double Circumference(double Radius)
{
       return 2*PI*Radius;
}
```

A nonvoid function is invoked wherever the returned value is to be used, rather than in a separate statement. The invocation

```
Circumference(Radius)
```

actually becomes the value returned by the *Circumference* function and is used as part of the output statement in the main function. Figure 7.28 shows a third version of the circle program using nonvoid *Circumference* and *Area* functions. Figure 7.29 summarizes several sets of terms introduced in this section.

FIGURE 7.28

A Circle Program Using Nonvoid Functions

```cpp
//program circle3
//This program allows the user to compute the
//circumference or area, after giving the radius,
//of any number of circles.
//Illustrates non-void functions

#include <iostream.h>

const double PI = 3.1416;   //value of pi

void Get_Input(double &Radius, char &Task_to_do)
//gets radius and choice of task from the user
{
  cout << "Enter the value of the radius of a circle"
    << endl;
  cin >> Radius;
  cout << endl;

  //See what user wants to compute
  cout << "Enter your choice of task." << endl;
  cout << "C to compute circumference, "
    << "A to compute area: ";
  cin >> Task_to_do;
  cout << endl;
}

double Circumference(double Radius)
{
  return  2*PI*Radius;
}

double Area(double Radius)
{
  return  PI*Radius*Radius;
}

void main()
{
  double Radius;       //radius of a circle - given
  char Task_to_do;     //holds user choice to
                       //compute circumference or area
  char More;           //controls loop for processing
                       //more circles

  cout.setf(ios::fixed);
  cout.precision(2);

  cout << "Do you want to process a circle? (Y or N): ";
  cin >> More;
  cout << endl;
  while (More == 'Y')  //more circles to process
  {
    Get_Input(Radius, Task_to_do);
```

FIGURE 7.28
(continued)

```cpp
if (Task_to_do == 'C') //compute circumference
{
  cout << "The circumference that corresponds "
    << "to this radius is "
    << Circumference(Radius) << endl;
}
else                //compute area
{
  cout << "The area that corresponds "
    << "to this radius is " << Area(Radius)
    << endl;
}
cout << endl;
cout << "Do you want to process more circles? "
  << "(Y or N): ";
cin >> More;
cout << endl;
}

//finish up
cout << "Program will now terminate." << endl;
}
```

FIGURE 7.29
Some C++ Terminology

TERM	MEANING	TERM	MEANING
Local variable	Declared and known only within a function	Global constant	Declared outside any function and known everywhere
Argument passed by value	Function receives a copy of the value and can make no permanent changes in the value	Argument passed by reference	Function gets access to memory location where the value is stored; changes it makes to the value persist after control returns to main function
Void function	Performs a task, function invocation is a complete C++ statement	Nonvoid function	Computes a value, must include a return statement, function invocation is used within another C++ statement

Laboratory Experience 12

This laboratory experience builds on the previous one, again using the C++ compiler. Here you will work with C++ programs that use functions and with some that use an array.

PRACTICE PROBLEMS

1. What will the output be after executing the following C++ program?

```cpp
#include <iostream.h>
void DoIt(int &number)
{
    number = number + 4;
}
void main()
{
    int number;

    number = 7;
    DoIt(number);
    cout << number << endl;
}
```

2. What will the output be after executing the following C++ program?

```cpp
#include <iostream.h>
void DoIt(int number)
{
    number = number + 4;
}
void main()
{
    int number;

    number = 7;
    DoIt(number);
    cout << number << endl;
}
```

3. Write a C++ function that performs an input task for the main program, collecting two integer values *One* and *Two* from the user.

4. Suppose a nonvoid function called *Tax* gets a value *Subtotal* from the main function, multiplies it by a constant tax rate called *Rate*, and returns the resulting tax value. All quantities are type **double**.
   a. Write the function header.
   b. Write the return statement in the function body.
   c. Write the statement in the main program that writes out the tax.

7.8

GRAPHICAL PROGRAMMING

7.8.1 THE IMPORTANCE OF VISUALIZATION

The programs that we have looked at so far all produce *textual output*—output composed of the characters {A . . . Z, a . . . z, 0 . . . 9} along with a few punctuation marks. For the first 30–35 years of software development, text was virtually the only method of displaying results in human-readable form, and in those early days it was quite common for programs to produce huge stacks of alphanumeric output. However, in the last 10 years an alternative form of output—*graphics*—has become much more widely used. With graphics, we are no longer limited to 100 or so printable characters; instead, programmers are free to construct whatever shapes and images they desire.

The intelligent and well-planned use of graphical output can produce some phenomenal improvements in software. For example, graphics can make it much easier to understand how to use a program. We discussed this issue in Chapter 6, where we described the move away from the text-oriented operating systems of the 1970s and 1980s, such as MS-DOS and VMS, to more powerful and user-friendly graphical user interfaces (GUIs), such as Windows 95, Windows 98, and the Macintosh System. Instead of having to learn dozens of complex text-oriented commands for such things as copying, editing, deleting, moving, and printing files, GUIs can present users with simple and easy-to-understand visual metaphors of these operations—for example,

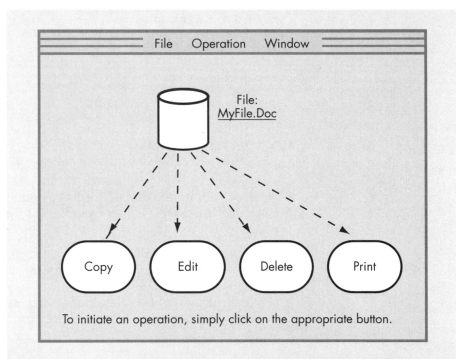

In addition to enhancing clarity and ease of understanding, graphical output can make massive amounts of output much easier to analyze. Some programs, especially large computer models, can produce millions of pieces of data. For example, a computer model of the wing of a jet aircraft might simulate airflow every few inches along the surface in order to produce an accurate model of wing behavior. This will generate thousands of pieces of data on air speed, lift, drag, and turbulence. Presenting these results as hundreds of printed pages would almost certainly overwhelm most users. Instead, graphics enables us to display this information in a visual format that is much easier to comprehend.

FIGURE 7.30

Visualization of a Three-Dimensional Surface

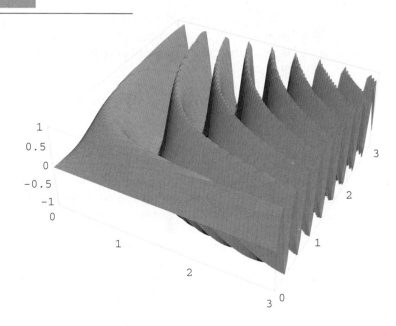

For example, Figure 7.30 is the visualization of the surface of the mathematical function $z = \text{Sin}(2x \times y)$, for x and y in the range $[0 \ldots 3]$. If this output were displayed as thousands of numerical coordinates rather than as a three-dimensional surface, the shape would be much more difficult to discern, and we would spend a great deal more time trying to analyze the results.

For another example, look ahead to Figure 14.5, which is the output of a program that models the behavior of an automobile during a 35-mph crash. Again, see how the use of graphics makes it easy to understand what is happening. Now imagine how difficult it would be to glean that same level of understanding from raw numerical output.

Computer graphics is an essential tool for programs that model complex physical, social, and mathematical systems. In fact, a new branch of computer science, called **scientific visualization**, studies the issue of how best to display large volumes of scientific data to make their significance and behavior more immediately understandable.

Finally, there are many applications of computers that would simply be impossible without the ability to display output visually. Applications such as virtual reality, computer-aided design/computer-aided manufacturing (CAD/CAM), games and entertainment, medical imaging, and computer mapping would not have become anywhere near as important as they are without the enormous improvements that have occurred in the areas of graphics and visualization.

We have spent a good deal of time describing the *why* of graphics—why it has become such an important software development technique. However, the question we now want to address is *how*—how do we do graphical programming? What features must be added to a programming language like C++ to produce screen images such as those in Figure 7.30? We answer that interesting question in the following section.

7.8.2 GRAPHIC PRIMITIVES

Modern computer terminals use what is called a **bit mapped display** in which the screen is made up of thousands of individual picture elements, called **pixels**, laid out in a two-dimensional grid. The number of pixels on the screen varies from system to system; typical values range from 512×340 up to 1560×1280. Naturally, the more pixels available, the sharper the visual image. Terminals with a large number of pixels are usually termed **high-resolution** terminals.

In a **black and white display**, each pixel takes on one of only two values—black and white—which can be represented by a single binary digit. A **gray scale display** might allocate 8 bits to each pixel to allow for $2^8 = 256$ shades of gray at each point. A **color display** would require 24 bits per pixel, with 8 bits used to represent the value of each of the three primary colors—red, blue, and yellow. The memory that stores the actual screen image is called a **frame buffer**. A high-resolution color display would need a frame buffer with (1560×1280) pixels $\times$ 24 bits/pixel $= 47,923,000$ bits or about 6 MB of memory for a single image. (One of the problems with graphics is that it requires many times the amount of memory needed for storing text.)

The individual pixels in the display are addressed using a two-dimensional coordinate grid system, the pixel in the upper left-hand corner being (0, 0). The overall pixel-numbering system is summarized in Figure 7.31.

The specific values for *maxX* and *maxY* in Figure 7.31 are, as mentioned earlier, system-dependent. (Note that this coordinate system is not the usual mathematical one. Here the origin is in the upper left corner, and *y* values are measured downward.)

The terminal hardware displays on the screen the frame buffer value of every individual pixel. For example, if we have a black and white monitor (0 = white, 1 = black), and if the frame buffer value in position (24, 47) is a 1, then the hardware will set the color of the pixel located at column 24, row 47 to black, as shown in Figure 7.32.

The operation diagramed in Figure 7.32 must be repeated for all of the 200,000 to 2 million pixels on the screen. However, the setting of a pixel is not permanent; on the contrary, its color and intensity fade quickly. Therefore, each pixel must be "repainted" often enough so that our eyes do not detect any "flicker," or change in intensity. This requires the screen to be completely updated, or refreshed, 30–50 times per second. By setting various sequences of pixels to black and white (or shades of gray or different colors), the user can have the screen display any desired shape or image. This is the fundamental way in which graphical output is achieved.

To control the setting and clearing of pixels, programmers use a collection of software routines that are part of a special package called a **graphics library**. Virtually all modern programming languages, including most implementations of C++, come with an extensive and powerful graphics library for creating different shapes and images. Typically, an "industrial strength" graphics library includes hundreds of routines for everything from drawing simple geometric shapes like lines and circles, to creating and selecting colors, to more complex operations such as displaying scrolling windows, pull-down menus, and buttons. Here we will restrict our discussion to the more modest set of functions

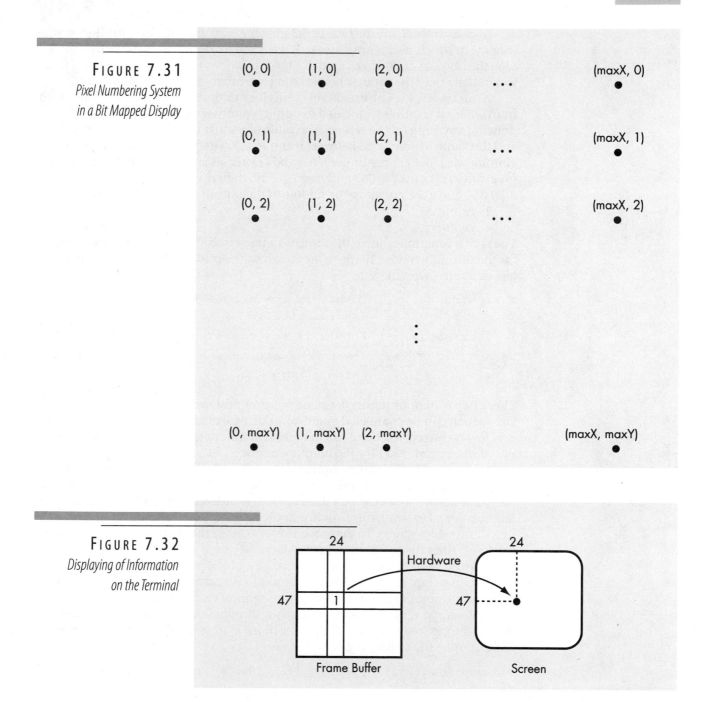

FIGURE 7.31
Pixel Numbering System in a Bit Mapped Display

FIGURE 7.32
Displaying of Information on the Terminal

available in the laboratory software package created for this book. Although the set is unrealistically small, the ten graphics routines in our graphics library will give you a good idea of what visual programming is like and will enable you to produce some interesting, nontrivial images on the screen. These routines are described in the following paragraphs.

1. *clearscreen(I)*. If the integer parameter $I <= 0$, then the output window (the window in which results are displayed) is cleared to a white background. If $I >= 1$, then the output window is cleared to a black background. It is recommended that you initially clear the window before doing any other graphical operations.

2. *moveto(x, y)*. The execution of this instruction causes the cursor to move from where it is currently located to output window position (x, y) *without* drawing anything on the screen. The value of x must be between 0 and *maxX*, and the value of y must be between 0 and *maxY*. The pixels are numbered beginning with $(0, 0)$ in the upper left-hand corner, as shown in Figure 7.31. Thus, for example, if $maxX = 600$ and $maxY = 800$, then the operation *moveto(300, 400)* will move the cursor to the middle of the output window.

3. *getmaxx( )*

4. *getmaxy( )*

These two functions return the integer value of maxX and maxY, respectively, for the output window. To move the cursor to the middle of the window, regardless of its size, we can write

```
X = getmaxx();     //this is the number of pixels
                   //horizontally

Y = getmaxy();     //this is the number of pixels vertically

moveto(X/2,Y/2);   //now move the cursor to the midpoint of
                   //the screen
```

These two functions return the value of *maxX* and *maxY* for the *current* window size, which can be changed dynamically during execution. That is, if the output window is resized, a second call to these two functions will return the new values of *maxX* and *maxY* for the output window.

5. *setcolor(I)*. This command sets the color of the pen that will be drawing lines and shapes on the screen. If you have a color display, then this routine typically allows you to set the pen to any one of hundreds or even thousands of different colors. However, our simple graphics package assumes that you have a black and white screen. In that case, if $I <= 0$, then the pen color is set to white; if $I >= 1$, then the pen color is set to black.

A white pen on a white background or a black pen on a black background will not show up. This feature can be used to do erasure. Simply reset the pen color to the color of the background and redraw your image. It will disappear.

6. *lineto(x, y)*. This operation draws a straight line from the current position of the cursor to output window position (x, y) using the current pen color. For example, the sequence of commands

```
clearscreen(0);        //clear the screen to white
setcolor(1);           //set the pen color to black
moveto(20, 20);        //move the cursor to screen
                       //position (20, 20)
lineto(100, 100);      //now draw a line from (20, 20)
                       //to (100, 100)
```

will draw a black line from cursor position (20, 20) to position (100, 100), producing something like this:

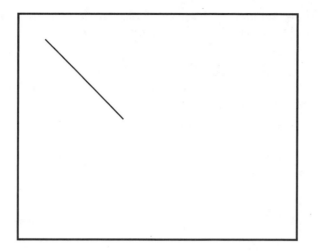

(On your system, the exact location and length of the line may be slightly different because of differences in screen resolution.)

What actually happens internally when you execute a *lineto* command? The answer is that the terminal hardware determines (using some simple geometry and trigonometry) exactly which pixels on the screen must be "turned on" (set to the current value of the pen color) to draw a straight line between the specified coordinates. For example, if the pen color is black (i.e., 1) then the two commands *moveto(1, 1)*; and *lineto(4, 4)*; will cause the hardware to set the following four pixels in the frame buffer to the value 1.

Now, when the hardware draws the frame buffer on the screen, these four pixels will be colored black. Because the pixels are approximately 1/100 of an inch apart, our eyes will perceive not four individual black dots but an unbroken line segment.

7. *rectangle(x1, y1, x2, y2)*. This function will draw a rectangle whose upper left and lower right corners are located at coordinates $(x1, y1)$ and $(x2, y2)$. The instruction

```
rectangle(25, 60, 75, 100);
```

will produce the following image:

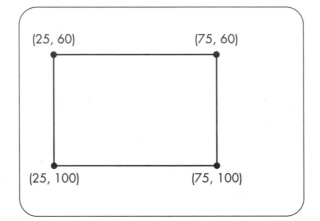

The same diagram will be produced from the instruction

```
rectangle(75, 100, 25, 60);
```

8. *circle(x, y, r)*. This routine will draw a circle whose center is located at position (x, y) and whose radius is r, the units being pixels. The instruction

```
circle(100, 150, 125);
```

will draw the figure

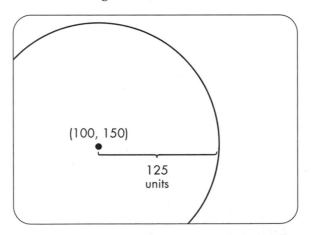

Note that portions of the circle beyond the edge of the window are discarded, a graphics operation called **clipping.** All functions in our graphics library clip those parts of the image that lie outside the window boundaries.

9. *writedraw(value, x, y)*. This operation will display the indicated value at the specific (x, y) window coordinates. The value can be either an integer (such as 234),

an individual character ('A'), or a string ("Press here"). The (x, y) coordinates represent the position of the bottom left pixel of the leftmost part of the value. For example, if we want to display the string "Hello" in the output window, we should enter as the (x, y) coordinate the exact position of the lower left pixel in the letter 'H'.

The inclusion of the "writedraw" operation allows us to mix both graphical and textual output on a single screen. For example, to produce a circular button containing the message "stop", we would do the following:

```
circle(200, 200, 40);        //first draw a circle
writedraw("Stop", 186, 200); //then put the label "Stop"
                             //inside the circle
```

This produces the following image:

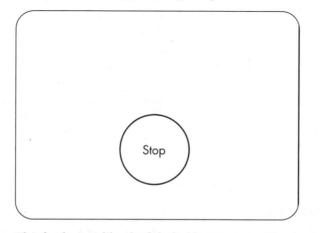

This looks just like the labeled buttons used in modern graphical interfaces. This example demonstrates how you can combine primitive operations such as "circle" and "writedraw" to generate more complex images such as a labeled button.

10. *getmouse(x, y).* Our last routine is used not for output but for input. The *getmouse* routine stores the (x, y) coordinates of the cursor at the instant the mouse button is clicked. This allows the user to input information via the mouse. For example, suppose we have the following rectangular stop button on the screen:

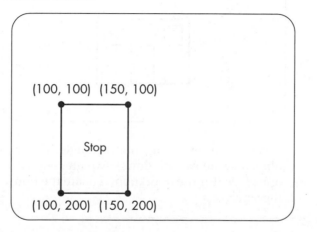

and we ask users to click inside the button if they wish to quit the program. We can use the *getmouse* function to obtain the cursor coordinates and determine whether they lie inside the button boundaries. Using the numbers shown above, we need to determine whether the cursor coordinates lie within a rectangle located at (100,100), (100,200), (150,200), (150,100).

```
getmouse(X, Y);
//see if the user clicked inside the
//rectangular bounds of the button

if  ((X >= 100) && (X <= 150)
   && (X >= 100) && (Y <= 200))
       { . . . //the user clicked inside the
                //button and wants to stop}
else
       { . . . //the user clicked outside the button}
```

These are the 10 graphics routines included in the C++ compiler component of our laboratory software. As we have said, the number of routines found in a production software development package is much larger. However, the routines described here will enable you to do some interesting graphics and, even more important, give you an appreciation for how visually oriented software is developed.

PRACTICE PROBLEM

1. Write the sequence of commands to draw the following "house" on the screen.

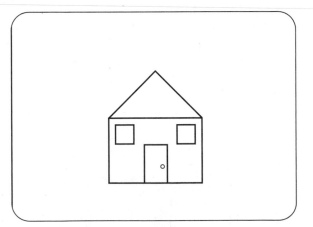

Create the house using four rectangles (for the base of the house, the door, and the two windows), two line segments (for the roof), and one circle (for the doorknob). Locate the house anywhere you want on the screen.

| Laboratory Experience 13 | The 10 drawing routines that we have described in this section are fully supported by the C++ compiler that comes with your laboratory software. In this laboratory assignment you will learn more about the graphics library included with the compiler, and you will write some actual graphics programs that display visual images on the screen. |

7.8.3 AN EXAMPLE OF GRAPHICS PROGRAMMING

We will finish this section with a somewhat larger and more "computer-oriented" example of the use of graphics. We will use the routines in our graphics library to create a *titled window*—a rectangular window with a second rectangle on top that contains a textual label. Here is an example of a titled window:

Titled windows are quite common; they are part of just about every graphical interface. If you have ever used a GUI, you have no doubt opened a window similar in form to this one. Now we will show how it can be drawn on the screen using our basic graphics functions.

Although you may view the diagram above as one large rectangle, in reality there are two separate rectangles positioned directly on top of one another.

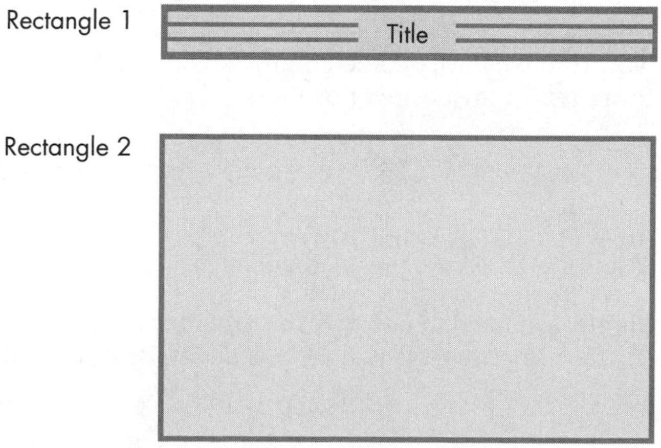

Therefore, we must first draw these two separate rectangles, making sure that their coordinates are set so that they are properly positioned on top of one another. For this example, we will make the size of the large bottom rectangle 300×220 and the size of the smaller top rectangle 300×30. Before doing this drawing, we clear the screen.

```
clearscreen(0);              //clear the screen to a
                             //white background
setcolor(1);                 //set the color to black
rectangle(50, 50, 350, 80);  //this produces the top
                             //rectangle
rectangle(50, 80, 350, 330); //and this produces the
                             //larger bottom one
```

After these four commands are executed, the screen will contain

We now must put the four horizontal lines inside the top rectangle. We will draw these lines so that they divide the upper rectangle into thirds both horizontally and vertically.

Now that we have decided on the layout, here are the commands to draw these four lines in the desired position:

```
moveto(50, 60); lineto(150, 60);    //these commands draw
                                    //4 horizontal lines
moveto(50, 70); lineto(150, 70);
moveto(250, 60); lineto(350, 60);
moveto(250, 70); lineto(350, 70);
```

Finally, we need to position the title in the middle of the white space created by the four lines that we just drew. This can be done with our writedraw routine:

```
writedraw("Title", 180, 70);   //write "Title" in the
                               //middle of the top rectangle
```

FIGURE 7.33

Commands to Produce a Titled Window

```
clearscreen(0);
setcolor(1);
rectangle(50, 50, 350, 80);
rectangle(50, 80, 350, 300);
moveto(50, 60);
lineto(150, 60);
moveto(50, 70);
lineto(150, 70);
moveto(250, 60);
lineto(350, 60);
moveto(250, 70);
lineto(350, 70);
writedraw("Title", 180, 70);
```

The complete sequence of commands needed to create our rectangular titled window is summarized in Figure 7.33. (However, because of differences in screen size and resolution, the parameters for these commands may have to be modified slightly to get your display positioned just right.) In the exercises at the end of the chapter, we ask you to add some other features to this window. These modifications can all be done using the basic drawing routines described in this section.

7.9   THE BIG PICTURE

Because any C++ program must ultimately be translated by a compiler, there are very stringent syntax rules about punctuation, use of keywords, and so on, for each program statement. If something about a program statement cannot be understood by the compiler, then the compiler cannot translate the program; if the compiler cannot translate a program, then its instructions cannot be executed. There is no way to work around this situation. This obstacle leads beginning programming students to conclude that the major effort should be devoted to implementation—that is, restating an algorithm in computer code and ridding that code of syntax errors to the point where it finally executes.

In reality, implementation represents a relatively small part of the **software life cycle**—the overall sequence of steps needed to complete a large-scale software project. Studies have shown that on big projects (system software such as operating systems or compilers, for example, or large applications such as writing a program to manage an investment company's portfolio), the initial implementation of the program may occupy only 10–20% of the total time spent by programmers and designers. About 25–40% of their time is spent on problem

FIGURE 7.34

*Steps in the Software
Development Life Cycle*

1. Before implementation
   - Feasibility study
   - Problem specification
   - Program design
   - Algorithm selection or development, and analysis
2. Implementation
   - Coding
   - Debugging
3. After implementation
   - Testing, verification, and benchmarking
   - Documentation
   - Maintenance

specification and program design—important planning steps that must be completed prior to implementation. Another 40–65% is spent on tasks that follow implementation—reviewing, modifying, fixing, and improving the original code and writing finished documentation. Although there is no universal agreement on the exact sequence of steps in the software life cycle, Figure 7.34 summarizes one possible breakdown. We'll discuss each of these steps shortly.

The major reason why a beginning programming student may not see or appreciate the entire software development life cycle has to do with the size of the programming assignments usually solved in introductory classes. The programs are extremely and unrealistically small (like our circle program), and that single difference can create a skewed and misleading view of the software development process. It is somewhat akin to a civil engineering student building a matchstick bridge that is 5 inches long; a multitude of new problems must be addressed when that task is scaled up to a full-sized, real-life bridge.

7.9.1 SCALING UP

The programs that students write in a first course may be 50–100 lines long. Even by the end of the course, programs are usually not longer than a few hundred lines. Real-world programs are 2, 3, or even 4 orders of magnitude larger. Operating systems or compilers contain tens or hundreds of thousands of lines. Truly large software systems, such as the NASA space-shuttle ground control system and the data management system of the U.S. Census Bureau, may require the development of more than a million lines of code. To give you an idea how monstrously large that is, a printed listing of a million-line C++ program would be 17,000 pages long—about the size of 50 books. The difference in complexity between a million-line software package and a 100-line homework assignment is the same as the difference between a 300-page novel and a single sentence!

Vital Statistics for Real Code

The Windows operating system for PCs was created by Microsoft Corporation. Development of this system (which was originally called the Interface Manager) began in 1981. Subsequently renamed Microsoft Windows, the system was not released until November 1985, after 55 person-years of effort. Since then, there have been a number of evolutions—various versions of Windows, Windows for Workgroups, Windows 95, and Windows 98. Microsoft also developed an operating system called Windows NT ("New Technology") designed to provide a more robust platform with better security for multi-user systems and networks. The first version of Windows NT was released in 1993, and it has also evolved since then.

The original Windows NT project began with a team of 10 or 12 people and expanded to include over 200 in both technical and support staff roles. Over the 4-year development effort for the first version, this translated into hundreds of person-years of labor merely to get the system out the door, to say nothing of maintenance work required to support this version and the efforts to upgrade it to new versions. The majority of the Windows NT system is written in C, a programming language we will mention again in the next chapter. The final system contains several hundred thousand lines of code. This is a "very large" project by the standard of Figure 7.35. Clearly, a project of this magnitude required careful design and management. Windows 95, released in August 1995, required about 8,000,000 lines of code, which clearly puts it into the "massive skyscraper" category of Figure 7.35.

Closer to home, the software for the laboratory component of this book was written by two people and required an effort of about 750 person-hours. The code is written in another programming language called Smalltalk, and consists of over 10,000 lines of code. Smalltalk is a very powerful, high-level language; the same tasks implemented in a C++ program might require about 50,000 lines of code and a great deal more development time.

Figure 7.35 categorizes software products in terms of size, the number of programmers needed for development, and the duration of the development effort. These numbers are very rough approximations, but they will give you an idea of the size of some widely used software packages. Analogous building construction projects are also listed.

Virtually all software products developed for the marketplace are neither trivial nor small but fall instead into either the "Medium" or the "Large" category of Figure 7.35. The "Very large" and "Extremely large" categories are enormous intellectual enterprises. It would be impossible to develop correct and maintainable software systems of that size without extensive planning and design, just as it is impossible to build a 50-story skyscraper without paying a great deal of attention to project planning and project management. Both endeavors would also be impossible for a single individual to carry out; a team development effort is essential in building software, just as in constructing buildings.

7.9.2 THE SOFTWARE LIFE CYCLE

Each step in the software development life cycle, as given in Figure 7.34, has its own purpose and activities. Each should also result in a written document

FIGURE 7.35

Size Categories of Software Products

CATEGORY	TYPICAL NUMBER OF PEOPLE	TYPICAL DURATION	PRODUCT SIZE IN LINES OF CODE	EXAMPLES	BUILDING ANALOGY
Trivial	1	1–2 weeks	< 500	Student homework assignments	Small home improvement
Small	1–3	A few weeks or months	500–2,000	Student team projects, advanced course assignments	Adding on a room
Medium	2–5	A few months to 1 year	2,000–10,000	Research projects, simple production software such as assemblers, editors, recreational and educational software	Single-family house
Large	5–25	1–3 years	10,000–100,000	Most current applications—word processors, spreadsheets, operating systems for small computers, compilers	Small shopping mall
Very large	25–100	3–5 years	100,000–1 M	Large-scale real-time operating systems, airline reservations systems, inventory control systems for multinational companies	Large office building
Extremely large	> 100	> 5 years	> 1 M	Advanced military work, international telecommunications networks	Massive skyscraper

that reflects past decisions and guides future actions. Keep in mind that every major software project is developed as a team effort, and these documents help keep various members of the team informed and working toward a common goal. We'll outline each step.

1. *The feasibility study.* The **feasibility study** is concerned with evaluating a proposed project and comparing the costs and benefits of using a computer system for the project. Even though the cost of computer hardware has dropped dramatically, computers are still not insignificant purchases. In addition to the costs of the machine itself, there may be costs for peripherals such as laser

printers and telecommunications links. The costs of software (purchased or produced in-house), equipment maintenance, and salary for developers or consultants, technical support people, and data entry clerks must all be factored in, as well as the costs incurred in training new users on the system. The overall cost of using a computer to solve a problem can be much higher than expected, and it *can* be more than the value of the information produced. Thus the following question should be asked:

> *Is it worth it for me (or whoever the user may be) to buy a computer (or get a newer, faster system) and write or buy software to solve my (or his or her) problem?*

At the end of the feasibility study, a **feasibility document** expresses the resulting recommendation: whether to proceed with the planned purchase of hardware and software. The creation of this document can be a very complex process that involves considerations well beyond computer science that are more the province of business, law, management, economics, psychology, and accounting. The purpose of the feasibility study is to make users realize that a computer is simply a tool and that the first thing to determine is whether it is the right tool for the job.

2. *Problem specification.* If it is determined that the project is feasible and will benefit from computer solution, we move on to the problem specification phase. **Problem specification** involves developing a clear, concise, and unambiguous statement of the exact problem to be solved. Because the original problem statement used in the feasibility study was no doubt written in a natural language, such as English, it may be unclear, incomplete, or even internally contradictory. During the problem specification phase, the software designers and the customer (the users) must hammer out each and every inconsistency, ambiguity, and gap. It is much easier and cheaper to make changes at this stage than to make changes in software months down the road. Consider how much more practical it is to change your mind when looking at the blueprints of your new home than after the foundation has been dug and the walls have started to go up. The rough initial problem statement must finally be transformed into a complete problem specification.

The **problem specification document** commits the final and complete problem specification to paper and serves to guide the software developers in all subsequent decisions. The specification document describes exactly how a program will behave in all circumstances—not only in the majority of cases but even under the most unusual conditions. It includes a description of the data expected to be input to the program, as well as what results should be computed and how these results are to be displayed as output. It may also include limitations on the time allotted to produce those computations or on the amount of memory the program requires.

This document, once agreed to by the developer and the customer, becomes essentially a legal contract describing what the developer promises to provide and what the customer agrees to accept. Like a contract, it usually includes a delivery schedule and a price, and it is signed by both the customer and the developer.

3. *Program design.* Now that it is clear *what* is to be done, it is time to plan *how* it is to be done. In this **program design phase**, the divide-and-conquer

strategy we mentioned earlier comes into play. The larger the project, the more crucial it is to think of it in terms of smaller building blocks that are created individually and then properly assembled to make a whole. Although problems that result in small programs of 50–100 lines can be thought of in one piece, problems that result in 100,000-line programs cannot. But such a problem could be broken down into 1000 small tasks, each taking on the order of 100 lines to implement. The overall solution is then much easier to complete. A good analogy is the way an encyclopedia is created. The task of writing a 20- to 30-volume encyclopedia is monumental, but it can be managed and completed in a reasonably efficient manner by treating it as thousands of individual articles, each one of which is small and relatively easy to write.

Since the **program design document** includes a breakdown of the overall problem into subtasks and sub-subtasks, many layers of refinement into successively smaller pieces may be required. These pieces will ultimately be translated into separate modules of code. The design may be illustrated by structure charts such as that shown in Figure 7.20. There must also be a complete specification of each module: what it is to do, what information it needs to know in order to do it, and what the other modules in the program need to know from it when it is done. This information must be sufficiently detailed that a programmer could take the description and write, for example, a C++ function with the appropriate parameters for passing information back and forth to and from the rest of the program.

The process of program design is one of the truly creative and interesting parts of the software development life cycle. It is related to coding in roughly the same way that designing an airplane is related to riveting a wing!

4. *Algorithm selection or development, and analysis.* Once the various subtasks have been identified, algorithms must be found to carry them out. For example, one subtask may be to search a list of numbers for some particular value. In Chapters 2 and 3 we encountered two different algorithms for searching: sequential search and binary search. If there is a choice of algorithms, they must be weighed to determine which is more suitable for this particular task, and perhaps they must be analyzed to see which is more efficient. It may also be the case that an algorithm has to be developed from scratch. This, too, is a very creative process. Documentation of this phase includes a description of the algorithms chosen or developed, perhaps in pseudocode, and the rationale for their use.

5. *Coding.* **Coding** is the process of translating the detailed module and algorithm designs into actual computer code. If the design has been carefully developed, this should be a relatively routine job. Perhaps reusable code can even be pulled from a program library.

This is the step that usually comes to mind when people think of software development. However, as we have shown, a great deal of important preparatory work must precede the actual production of code. Inexperienced programmers may think that they will save time by skipping the earlier phases and getting right to the coding. The opposite is usually true. In all but the most trivial of programs, tackling coding without first doing problem specification, program design, and algorithm selection or development will ultimately lead to more time being spent and a poorer outcome.

The coding phase also results in a written document, the listing of the program code itself.

6. *Debugging.* **Debugging** is the process of locating and correcting program errors, and it can be a slow and expensive operation that requires as much effort as writing the program in the first place. Errors can occur because a program statement fails to follow the correct rules of syntax, which makes the statement unrecognizable by the compiler and results in an error. Though irritating, these **syntax errors** are accompanied by messages from the compiler that help to pinpoint the problem. Another class of errors, called **run-time errors**, occur only when the program is run using certain sets of data that result in some illegal operation, such as dividing by zero. The system software also provides messages to help detect the cause of run-time errors. The third, and most subtle, class of errors is **logic errors**. These are errors in the algorithm used to solve the problem. Some incorrect steps are done that result in wrong answers, but there are no error messages to help pinpoint the problem. Indeed, the first step in debugging a logic error is to notice that the answers are wrong.

Debugging has always been one of the most frustrating, agonizing, and time-consuming steps in the programming process. The need for a great deal of debugging usually means that insufficient time was spent on carefully specifying, organizing, and structuring the solution. If the design is poorly done, then the resulting program is often a structural mess, with convoluted, hard-to-understand logic. On the other hand, devoting careful attention to the design phases can help reduce the amount of debugging that must be done.

Careful documentation of the debugging process includes notes on the problems found and on how the code was changed to solve them. This may prevent later changes from reintroducing old errors.

7. *Testing, verification, and benchmarking.* Even though a program produces correct answers for 1, 5, or even 1000 data sets, how can we be sure that it is indeed 100% correct and will work on all data? One approach, called **empirical testing**, is to design a special set of test cases and run the program using these test data. Test data that are carefully chosen to exercise all the different logic paths through a program can help uncover errors. In a conditional statement, for example, one set of data should make the Boolean expression true, so that one block of code is executed. Another set of data should make the same Boolean expression false, so that the other block of code is executed. The quantity of the test data does not matter; what matters is that the data cover all the various cases. Having said that, however, we should note that in all but the most trivial programs, it is not possible to "cover all the cases." The best that can be said is that the more thorough the testing, the higher the level of our confidence that the program is correct.

A second approach to confirming a program's reliability is to use mathematical logic to attempt to prove that a computer program is correct. **Program verification** can be used to prove that if the input data to a program satisfy certain conditions, then, after the program has been run on these data, the output data satisfy certain other conditions. This is not a magic wand that gives us blanket assurance that the program will absolutely behave as we wish. Furthermore, the program verification process is tedious and time-consuming. That's why program testing is used much more than formal program verification to increase the reliability of a program.

In addition to correctness, the problem specification may have required certain performance characteristics such as the amount of time to compute the results. **Benchmarking** the program means running it on many data sets to be sure its performance falls within those required limits. At the completion of testing (or verification) and benchmarking, we should have a correct and efficient program that is ready for delivery. Of course, all of the testing, verification, and benchmarking results are committed to paper as evidence that the program meets its specifications.

8. *Documentation.* Program documentation is all of the written material that makes a program understandable. This includes **internal documentation**, which is part of the program code itself. Good internal documentation consists of choosing meaningful names for program identifiers, using plenty of comments to explain the code, and separating the program into short modules, each of which does one specific subtask. **External documentation** consists of any materials assembled to help understand the program. Although we have put this step rather late in the software development process, you will note that each preceding step produced some form of documentation. Program documentation goes on throughout the software life cycle. The final, finished program documentation is written in two forms. **Technical documentation** is written so that programmers who later want to modify the program can understand the code. Such information as structure charts, descriptions of algorithms, and program listings fall in this category. **User documentation** is written to help someone run the program. Such documentation includes written user's manuals and any on-line tutorials or help systems that the user can bring up while the program is running.

9. *Maintenance.* Programs are not static entities that, once completed, never change. Because of the time and expense involved in developing software, successful programs are used for a very long time. It is not unusual for a program to be in use 5, 10, or 15 years after it was written. In fact, the typical life cycle for a medium-size to large software package is 1–3 years in development and 5–15 years in the marketplace. During this long period of use, errors may be uncovered, new hardware may be purchased on which the program has to run, user needs may change, and the whims of the marketplace will fluctuate. The original program must be modified and brought out in new versions to meet these changing needs. **Program maintenance**, the process of adapting an existing software product for any of the reasons just stated, may consume as much as 65% of the total software life cycle budget. If the program has been well planned, carefully designed, well coded, thoroughly tested, and well documented, then program maintenance will be a much easier task. Indeed, it is with an eye to program maintenance (and to reducing its cost) that we stressed the importance of these earlier steps.

Maintenance should not really be viewed as a separate step in the software life cycle. Rather, it involves repetition of some or all of the steps previously described, from a feasibility study through implementation, testing, and updated documentation. Maintenance, then, reflects the fact that the software life cycle is truly a *cycle*, in which it is necessary to redo earlier phases of development as our software changes, grows, and matures.

7.10 CONCLUSION

In this chapter we looked at one representative high-level programming language, C++. We saw how the use of a high-level language overcomes many of the disadvantages of assembly language programming, creating a more comfortable and useful environment for the programmer. In a high-level language, the programmer need not manage the storage or movement of data values in memory. The programmer can think about the problem at a higher level of problem solving, can use program instructions that are both more powerful and more English-language-like, and can write a program that is much more portable among various hardware platforms. We also saw how modularization, through the use of functions and parameters, allows the program to be more cleanly structured.

We discussed the entire software life cycle, noting that for large, real-world programs, software development must be a managed discipline. Coding is but a small part of the software development process.

As we have said, C++ is not the only high-level language. Other languages have different ways to do assignments, conditional statements, and looping statements. Still other languages take quite a different approach to problem solving. In the next chapter, we look at some other languages and language approaches and also address the question of why there are so many different programming languages.

EXERCISES

1. Write a C++ declaration for one real number quantity to be called *Rate*.

2. Write a C++ declaration for two integer quantities to be called *Order_One* and *Order_Two*.

3. Write a C++ declaration for a constant quantity to be called *EvaporationRate*, which is to have the value 6.15.

4. A C++ main function will need one constant *Stock_Time* with a value of 4, one integer variable *Inventory*, and one real number variable *Sales*. Write the necessary declarations.

5. You want to write a C++ program to compute the average of three quiz grades for a single student. Decide what variables your program will need and write the necessary declarations.

6. Given the declaration

   ```
   int List[10];
   ```

   how would you refer to the eighth number in the array?

7. Write a C++ declaration for a two-dimensional array *Box* with 5 rows and 7 columns to hold real number values.

8. Given the declaration

   ```
   int Table[5][3];
   ```

how would you refer to the marked cell below?

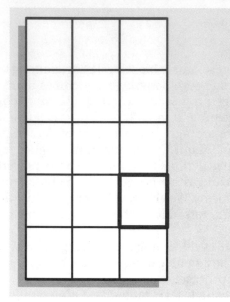

9. Can you think of a situation in which a three-dimensional table would be an appropriate data structure? Write a C++ declaration to implement such a data structure.

10. Write C++ statements to prompt for and collect values for the time in hours and minutes (two integer quantities).

11. An output statement may contain more than one variable identifier. Say a program computes two integer quantities *Inventory_Number* and *Number_Ordered*. Write a single output statement that prints these two quantities along with appropriate text information.

12. The integer quantities *A, B, C,* and *D* currently have the values 13, 4, 621, and 18, respectively. Write the exact output generated by the following statement, using b to denote a blank space.

```
cout << setw(5) << A << setw(3)
   << B << setw(3) << C << setw(4)
   << D << endl;
```

13. Write C++ formatting and output statements to generate the following output, assuming that *Density* is a type **double** variable with the value 63.78.

```
The current density is 63.8,
to within one decimal place.
```

14. What will be the output after the following sequence of statements is executed? (Assume that the integer variables *A* and *B* have been declared.)

```
A = 12;
B = 20;
B = B + 1;
A = A + B;
cout << 2*A << endl;
```

15. Write the body of a C++ main function that gets the length and width of a rectangle from the user and computes and writes out the area. Assume that the variables have all been declared.

16. a. In the circle program of Figure 7.16, the user must respond with "C" to choose the circumference task. In a situation like this, it is polite to accept either upper-case or lower-case letters. Rewrite the condition in the program to allow this.

    b. Again in the circle program, rewrite the condition for continuation of the program to allow either an upper-case or a lower-case response.

17. Write a C++ main function that gets a single character from the user and writes out a congratulatory message if the character is a vowel (a, e, i, o, or u), but otherwise writes out a "you lose, better luck next time" message.

18. Insert the missing line of code so that the following adds the integers from 1 to 10, inclusive.

```
value = 0;
top = 10;
score = 1;
while (score <= top)
{
    value = value + score;
    - - - - //the missing line
}
```

19. What will be the output after the following main function is executed?

```
void main()
{
    int low, high;
    low = 1;
    high = 20;
    while (low < high)
```

```
    {
            cout << low << " " << high
            << endl;
            low = low + 1;
            high = high - 1;
    }
}
```

20. Write a C++ main function that outputs the even integers from 2 through 30, one per line. Use a while loop.

21. In a while loop, the Boolean condition that tests for loop continuation is done at the top of the loop, before each iteration of the loop body. As a consequence, the loop body might not be executed at all. Our pseudocode language of Chapter 2 contains a repeat-until loop construction in which a test for loop termination occurs at the bottom of the loop rather than at the top, so that the loop body will always execute at least once. C++ contains a **do-while** statement that tests for loop continuation at the bottom of the loop. The form of the statement is

    do
            S1;
    while (Boolean condition);

    where, as usual, S1 can be a compound statement. Write a C++ main function to add up a number of non-negative integers that the user supplies and to write out the total. Assume that the first value is non-negative, and use a do-while statement.

22. Write a C++ program that asks for a duration of time in hours and minutes and writes out the duration only in minutes.

23. Write a C++ program that asks for the user's age in years. If the user is under 35, then quote an insurance rate of $2.23 per hundred for life insurance; otherwise, quote a rate of $4.32.

24. Write a C++ program that reads integer values until a 0 value is encountered and then writes out the sum of the positive values read and the sum of the negative values read.

25. Write a C++ program that reads in a series of positive integers and writes out the product of all the integers less than 25 and the sum of all the integers greater than or equal to 25. Use 0 as a sentinel value.

26. a. Write a C++ program that reads in 10 integer quiz grades and computes the average grade. (*Hint:* Remember the peculiarity of integer division.)
    b. Write a C++ program that asks the user for the number of quiz grades and computes the average grade.

27. Write a (void) C++ function that receives two integer arguments and writes out their sum and their product.

28. Write a (void) C++ function that receives an integer argument representing the number of videos rented so far this month and a real number argument representing the sales amount for videos sold so far this month. The function asks the user for the number of videos rented today and the sales amount for videos sold today and then returns the updated figures to the main function.

29. Write a (nonvoid) C++ function that receives three integer arguments and returns the maximum of the three values.

30. Write a C++ program to balance a checkbook. The program needs to get the initial balance, the amounts of deposits, and the amounts of checks. Allow the user to process as many transactions as desired; use separate functions to handle deposits and checks.

31. Write a C++ program to compute the cost of carpeting three rooms. Make the carpet cost a constant of $8.95 per square yard. Use four separate functions to collect the dimensions of a room in feet, convert feet into yards, compute the area, and compute the cost per room. The main function should use a loop to process each of the three rooms, add the three costs, and write out the total cost. (*Hint:* The function to convert feet into yards will have to be used twice for each room, with two different arguments. Hence it does not make sense to try to give the parameter the same name as the argument.)

32. Determine the resolution of the screen on your computer (perhaps from your instructor or the local computer center.) Using this information, determine how many bytes of memory are required for the frame buffer to store
    a. A black and white image (1 bit per pixel)
    b. A gray scale image (8 bits per pixel)
    c. A color image (24 bits per pixel)

33. Using the routines called *getmaxx* and *getmaxy*, determine the resolution of the laboratory software output window for your computer. After printing these values, resize the output window and print out the new values. What is the largest size you can get for your output window?

34. Using the *moveto* and *lineto* commands described in Section 7.8.2, draw an isosceles triangle with the following configuration:

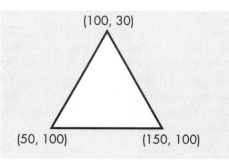

35. Discuss what problem the display hardware might encounter while attempting to execute the following operations, and explain how this problem could be solved.

```
moveto(1,1);
lineto(4,5);
```

36. Draw a square with sides 100 pixels in length. Then inscribe a circle of radius 50 inside the square. Position the square and the inscribed circle in the middle of the screen.

37. Create the following three labeled rectangular buttons in the output window.

Have the space between the Start and Stop buttons be the same as the space between the Stop and Pause buttons.

38. Create the following image of a "teeter-totter."

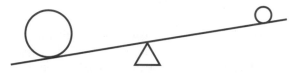

39. Add the three features shown in the following diagram to the titled window that was described in Section 7.8.3 and implemented by the code in Figure 7.33.

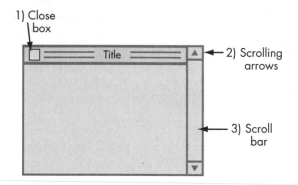

40. Write a program that inputs the coordinates of three mouse clicks from the user and then draws a triangle in the output window using those three points.

CHALLENGE WORK

1. **Cryptology** is the science of "secret codes." Messages are encoded before they are sent for the purpose of keeping their content secret if they are intercepted by the wrong parties, and they are decoded when they are received to retrieve the original information. The most famous instances of cryptology occur in military history, beginning with Julius Caesar of the Roman Empire, who developed the Caesar cypher, and certainly including the German Enigma code cracked by the Allies during World War II. Transmitting information securely has taken a modern turn with electronic

commerce on the Internet and concerns over protection of consumer credit card numbers and other personal data.

A **Caesar cypher**, also called a **shift cypher**, involves shifting each character in the message to another character some fixed distance farther along in the alphabet. Specifically, let s be some integer between 1 and 25 that represents the amount of shift. Each letter in the message is encoded as the letter that is s units farther along in the alphabet, with the last s letters of the alphabet shifted in a cycle to the first s letters. For example, if $s = 3$, then A is encoded as D, B is encoded as E, X is encoded as A, and Z is encoded as C. Decoding a message requires knowledge of s. For example, if $s = 3$, then the code word DUPB is decoded as ARMY.

a. Write a C++ main function that collects a message from the user and writes it out again. Assume for simplicity that the message consists of a single word no more than 10 characters in length and that only the 26 upper-case letters of the alphabet are used. Use an array of 10 elements of type **char** to store the message. Ask the user to enter no more than 10 characters and to terminate the message by entering some special character such as "%". Notify the user and exit the program if the message has more than 10 characters; otherwise, write out the message. Use a variable to keep track of the number of array elements actually used (which could be less than 10 if the message word is short) so that you do not write out meaningless characters stored at the end of the array.

b. Write a C++ function to modify the array to represent the encoded form of the message using a Caesar cypher. Have the main function ask for the shift amount. Pass the message array to the encoding function. A parameter corresponding to an array argument has the form

   identifier [ ]

   Array arguments are automatically passed by reference, so there is no need to use the & in front of the parameter. Additional arguments that the function needs are the number of array elements actually used and the value of the

shift amount. C++ stores character data as an integer, so to get the character s units along in the alphabet, you can simply add s to the original character. This will work for everything except the end of the alphabet; here you will have to be a bit more clever to cycle back to the beginning of the alphabet once the shift is applied.

Have the main program invoke the encoding function and then write out the encoded form of the message.

c. Write a C++ function to modify the array containing the encoded message back to its original form. This function will also need the number of array elements used and the value of the shift amount as arguments, as well as the array itself. The body of the function should accomplish the reverse of the encoding function.

   Have the main program invoke the decoding function and then write out the decoded form of the message, which should agree with the original message.

d. Be sure to test your program with different values for s and different word lengths.

2. The management of the entire software development process described in Section 7.9 is known as **software engineering**. The word *engineering* in *software engineering* is intended to convey the engineering aspects of software development: imposing engineering principles and discipline to produce, in a timely and cost-effective manner, a workable product to solve a problem.

   Read more about software engineering and write a short paper on one or more of the following topics:

   • Black-box and white-box testing
   • CASE tools
   • Configuration management
   • Data dictionary
   • JAD (Joint Application Development) sessions
   • Rapid prototyping
   • Requirements tracing
   • Software metrics
   • Stubs and drivers
   • Waterfall model

FOR FURTHER READING

There are many, many textbooks on C++ programming. Here are a few that are designed for beginning programmers.

Dale, N., Weems, C., and Headington, M. R. *Programming and Problem Solving with C++.* Sudbury, MA: Jones and Bartlett, 1997.

Deitel, H. M., and Deitel, P. J. *C++: How to Program,* 2nd ed. Englewood Cliffs, NJ: Prentice-Hall, 1998.

Lambert, K., and Nance, D. *Understanding Programming and Problem Solving with C++.* Boston: PWS, 1996.

Professor Lambert is one of the coauthors of the laboratory manual and software that accompany this text.

Savitch, W. *Problem Solving with C++: The Object of Programming.* Reading, MA: Addison-Wesley, 1996.

Here is the definitive C++ language reference by the designer of the language. It contains the "C++ Reference Manual," used as the basis for the ANSI draft C++ standard.

Stroustrup, B. *The C++ Programming Language,* 2nd ed. Reading, MA: Addison-Wesley, 1991.

For a discussion of the history of C++, see the first part of

Stroustrup, B. *The Design and Evolution of C++.* Reading, MA: Addison-Wesley, 1994.

The classic work on software engineering, first published in 1975, was republished 20 years later because the truths it contains are still relevant today. These essays on the management of software engineering projects are relevant to most managerial situations, and they are entertaining and easy to read.

Brooks, Jr., Frederick P. *The Mythical Man-Month: Essays on Software Engineering, Anniversary Edition.* Reading, MA: Addison-Wesley, 1995.

THE
TOWER OF BABEL

8.1   WHY BABEL?

The biblical story of the Tower of Babel takes place at a time when "the whole earth had one language and few words" and all could understand one another. The people began to build a city with a mighty tower, when suddenly all began speaking in various tongues and could no longer communicate. They became confused, abandoned the tower, and scattered "over the face of all the earth." A shared enterprise was difficult or impossible to pursue without the mutual understanding fostered by a common language, and (the message this allegory was intended to convey) the power of what people could do was thus forever limited. Similarly, in modern times it has been argued that if all peoples of the earth spoke a common language, the chances of war would be greatly reduced.

Although we can't address the problems of the political arena here, it might seem that having all computer programs written in the same programming language would have an appealing simplicity. In Chapter 7, we became familiar with one high-level programming language, C++. C++ is a powerful general-purpose programming language, and a great many C++ programs have been written to do a great many things. But as we noted in the last chapter, C++ isn't the only high-level programming language. Why aren't all programs written in C++? Are there some things that can't be done using a C++ program? If so, then why aren't all programs written in some other language that overcomes the deficiencies of C++?

There are multiple programming languages not so much because there are tasks that one programming language cannot do but because each programming language was designed to meet specific needs. Consequently, one language may be better suited than others for writing certain kinds of programs. The situation is somewhat analogous to the automobile market. The basic automotive needs of the country could probably be served by a single car model and a single truck model. So why do we have seemingly endless models from which to choose? The answer lies partly in competition: Various automotive companies are all trying to corner a share of the market. More than that, though, the answer lies in the variety of ways we use our automobiles. Although a luxury car could be used for off-roading, it is not designed well for that use; a four-wheel-drive vehicle does the job better, more safely, and more efficiently. Although a sports car could be used to haul Little Leaguers home from the ball game, it is not designed well for that use; a minivan serves this purpose better. The diversity of tasks for which we use our automobiles has promoted a variety of automotive models, each better designed than other models to handle some range of tasks.

The same thing applies to programming languages. As an example, we *could* use C++ to write programs for solving engineering problems (and it has indeed been so used). However, C++ was not designed with engineering applications in mind. Although C++ supports the basic arithmetic operations of addition, subtraction, multiplication, and division by providing simple operators

(+, −, *, /) to do these tasks, there is no operator for exponentiation—that is, raising a value to a power. Computing $(2.84)^{1.8}$ in a C++ program, for example, can certainly be done but it requires some effort.[1] Calculations involving exponents are performed hundreds of times in many engineering and other numerical-based applications, so why not use a language that provides an operator for exponentiation because that language was designed with such tasks in mind? We'll discuss such a language—FORTRAN—in the next section.

Similarly, suppose our program is to write out complicated sales reports with columns of figures and blocks of information strategically located on the page. Specifying the exact placement of output on the page is rather tedious in C++. Why not use a language that allows detailed output formatting because it was designed with such a purpose in mind? Again, we'll briefly discuss such a language—COBOL—in the next section.

What if we want a program to interact with a database, to manipulate graphics, or to act as a hyperlinked Web page? Any of these specialized tasks is probably best done with a specialized language designed for just that purpose.

A major reason, then, for the proliferation of programming languages is the proliferation of programming tasks to be done. Another reason is that different philosophies have developed about how people should think when they are writing programs. This has resulted in several families of programming languages that take quite different approaches from C++, and we'll look at some of these approaches in Section 8.5.

8.2   PROCEDURAL LANGUAGES

In this section, we briefly discuss five different programming languages that all follow the same "philosophy" as C++ in that they are **procedural languages** (also called **imperative languages**). A program written in a procedural language consists of sequences of statements that manipulate data items; that is, they change the contents of memory cells. It is the programmer's task to devise the appropriate step-by-step sequence of "imperative commands"—instructions in the programming language—that when carried out by the computer will accomplish the desired task.

Procedural languages follow directly from the Von Neumann architecture of a computer described in Chapter 5, an architecture characterized by sequential fetch-decode-execute cycles. A random access memory stores and fetches values to and from memory cells. Thus it makes sense to design a language whose most fundamental operations are storing and retrieving data values. For example,

---

[1] The C++ expression for $(2.84)^{1.8}$ is exp(1.8*log(2.84)), using functions available in the math library that are linked in with an #include <math.h> directive.

```
a = 1;        //store value 1 in location a
c = a + b;    //retrieve a and b, add, store result in location c
```

Even though we have seen that a high-level programming language allows the programmer to think of memory locations in abstract rather than physical terms, the programmer is still directing, via program instructions, every change in the value of a memory location.

The procedural languages we will discuss in this section are FORTRAN, COBOL, Pascal, C, and Ada. These languages differ in how the statements must be arranged on a line and in how variables can be named. They differ in the details of how a new value is assigned to a variable, in the mechanisms the language provides for directing the flow of control through conditional and looping statements, and in the statement forms that control input and output. They also differ in how programs can be broken down into modules to handle separate tasks and in how those modules share information. But once again, all are procedural languages that tell the computer in a step-by-step fashion how to manipulate the contents of memory locations. In a general sense, then, the languages are quite similar, just as French, Spanish, and Italian are all members of the family of romance languages. Rather than studying the syntactical differences among these programming languages, we'll concentrate on the history and "intent" of each one.

8.2.1 FORTRAN

The name FORTRAN derives from *FOR*mula *TRAN*slation. The very name indicates the affiliation of the language with "formulas" or engineering-type applications. Developed in the mid-1950s by a group at IBM headed by John Backus, in conjunction with some IBM computer users, the first commercial version of FORTRAN was released in 1957. This makes FORTRAN the first high-level programming language. Early computer users were often engineers who were solving problems with a heavy mathematics or computational flavor. FORTRAN has some features ideally suited to these applications, such as the exponentiation operator we mentioned earlier, the ability to carry out extended-precision arithmetic with many decimal places of accuracy, and the ability to work with the complex number system. Updated versions of FORTRAN (FORTRAN II, FORTRAN IV, FORTRAN 77, Fortran 90, and High Performance Fortran) have been introduced over the years, incorporating new data types and new statements to direct the flow of control.

Early versions of FORTRAN did not allow the use of mathematical symbols such as < to compare two quantities; the keypunches that were used to create the punched cards on which early FORTRAN programs were submitted to the computer had no such symbols. Thus the C++ condition

```
Number < 0
```

would have been expressed in FORTRAN as

```
NUMBER .LT. 0
```

(FORTRAN requires variable identifiers to be upper-case.) Early versions of FORTRAN also had no while loop mechanism. The effect of a while loop was obtained by using an IF statement together with GO TO statements. The C++

```
while (Number >= 0)
{
    .
    .
    .
    cin >> Number;
}
```

would have been accomplished by

```
10  IF (NUMBER .LT. 0) GO TO 20
        .
        .
        .
        READ(*,*) NUMBER
        GO TO 10
20...
```

If *NUMBER* is less than 0, the GO TO statement transfers control to statement 20. If *NUMBER* is greater than or equal to 0, something is done and then another value for *NUMBER* is obtained (READ is the equivalent of *cin*). Control is then redirected by the second GO TO statement back to statement 10 where the new value is tested.

Directing the flow of control by GO TO statements is similar to the use of the various JUMP statements in the assembly language of Chapter 6, and it reflects the fact that FORTRAN's developers were, after all, working from assembly language. In the absence of an equivalent to the C++ while statement, there is no choice but to use GO TO statements carefully to implement looping, as shown above. Excessive and careless use of GO TOs, however, can make a program very difficult to read. (Imagine reading a novel where in the middle of page 49 you are told to stop reading this page and to begin reading at the top of page 215. Then, when you reach page 218, you are told to stop, go back, and start reading page 125. You might wonder whether you were really following the plot.) Code filled with GO TO statements that send the flow of control all over the place can be a nightmare. Such "spaghetti code" tangled across hundreds of lines can be very difficult to unravel. Given that a GO TO statement is available, it is up to the programmer's individual discipline to avoid abusing it. The potential for such abuse prompted the well-known computer scientist E. W. Dijkstra to write a letter headed "Go To Statement Considered Harmful," which appeared in the *Communications of the ACM* (Association for Computing Machinery) in 1968. This sparked the "GO TO controversy" about the merits of programming language constructs, such as the while loop, that would remove this temptation for abuse. From our perspective 30 years later, this controversy seems rather quaint, but it provoked lively discussion at the time.

FORTRAN was designed to support numerical computations. This led to concise mathematical notation (aside from the early < dilemma just mentioned) and to the availability of a number of mathematical functions within the language.

Old Dog, New Tricks #1

FORTRAN was first introduced over 40 years ago, in 1957. In the history of computing, this is roughly the Jurassic Age. But FORTRAN is no extinct dinosaur. Instead, it is a chameleon, changing with the times. Thanks to the ever-increasing hardware capability, FORTRAN runs on PCs while still providing the power to tackle "number-crunching" problems. However, the programmer can now use an environment with a graphical user interface to develop code, and that code can present a graphical user interface to the ultimate user of the program.

As further proof of FORTRAN's continued usefulness, evolution has taken place at the other end of the computing spectrum as well. A standard for HPF (High Performance Fortran) has been developed. This version of FORTRAN is designed to run on massively parallel processors that can bring huge amounts of computer horsepower to bear on suitable problems. Parallelism is especially useful for speeding up the kinds of calculations on large arrays that often occur in scientific and engineering problems, FORTRAN's traditional domain.

FORTRAN can "talk with" many other modern programming languages, which allows mixed-language programs to be built that capture the best features of each language for the application at hand. Given these adaptations, FORTRAN, in one form or another, is likely to live on well into the next century.

Another design goal was to optimize the resulting object code—that is, to produce object code that took as little space and executed as efficiently as possible. (Remember that when FORTRAN was developed, machine resources were scarce and precious.) In the same spirit, FORTRAN allows **external libraries** of well-written, efficient, and thoroughly tested code modules that are separately compiled and then drawn on by any program that wishes to use their capabilities. Because of FORTRAN's extensive use as a programming language over the years, a large and well-tested FORTRAN library collection exists, so in many cases, programmers can use existing code instead of having to write all code from scratch. This feature is sometimes highly touted for newer languages such as C++, but FORTRAN designers got there first. FORTRAN was an extremely successful language; millions of lines of FORTRAN code are still in use, and thanks to its evolution over time, FORTRAN has remained an effective language for engineering applications.

8.2.2 COBOL

The name COBOL derives from *CO*mmon *B*usiness-*O*riented *L*anguage. COBOL was developed in 1959–1960 by a group headed by Grace Hopper of the U.S. Navy. FORTRAN and COBOL were the dominant high-level languages of the 1960s and 1970s. COBOL was designed to serve business needs such as managing inventories and payrolls. In such applications, summary reports are important out-

---

PRACTICE PROBLEM   Write a FORTRAN condition to test whether the value of *ITIME* is less than or equal to 7. Use early FORTRAN syntax.

put products. Much of the processing in the business world concerns updating "master files" with changes from "transaction files." For example, a master inventory file might contain names, manufacturers, and quantities available for various items in inventory; a transaction file would contain names and quantities of items sold out of inventory or delivered to inventory over some period of time. The master file would be updated from the transaction file on a daily or weekly basis to reflect the new quantities available, and a summary report would be printed. The user doesn't interact directly with the COBOL program; rather, the user prepares the master file (once) and the transaction file (regularly). As is consistent with this intended usage, COBOL is far more adept at handling file input than keyboard input.

In the design of COBOL, particular attention was paid to input formatting for data being read from files and to output formatting both for writing data to a file and for generating business reports with information precisely located on the page. Therefore, much of a COBOL program may be concerned with formatting, described by "PICTURE clauses" in the program.

Another design decision in developing COBOL was that programs should describe what they are doing in English-like phrases. As a result, COBOL programs are rather verbose. Instead of C++'s succinct and mathematical

```
sum = a + b;
```

COBOL would say

```
ADD A TO B GIVING SUM.
```

This compromise actually sacrifices one of the goals of high-level languages that we enumerated in the previous chapter, to use standard mathematical notation, but this was a deliberate decision on the part of the COBOL language designers to allow COBOL programs to be written by people who were less "formula-oriented."

COBOL programs are highly portable across many different COBOL compilers, are quite easy to read, and are very well suited to manipulating large data files. Because COBOL has been around for a long time, there are many existing COBOL applications programs. COBOL probably provides as much as 75% of the existing code, making it, even today, the most widely used language. Nonetheless, the continuing importance of COBOL as a commercial programming language had perhaps been overlooked by those outside the business world until the "Year 2000 problem" came into view (see the box on page 380). The magnitude of the Year 2000 problem, also known as the Y2K problem (K stands for *kilo*, or "thousand"), has refocused attention on COBOL. A large number of companies have come into existence whose sole purpose is to help other companies solve their Y2K problem. And many about-to-retire or already-retired COBOL programmers have found their services once again in high demand.

An updated international standard for COBOL, with changes incorporated as of March 1997, is now under review. Among the new features proposed are built-in functions to check that arguments passed to date functions fall within acceptable ranges; though this has always been an issue, the Year 2000 problem heightens awareness of such concerns. Information can be obtained at

http://www.cobol.org

The Year 2000 Problem

The Year 2000 problem deals with a lurking time bomb in **legacy code** (old but still-running programs). When these programs were written, their authors never imagined their longevity. In addition, computer memory was at a premium, so efficiency was the order of the day. Why store four digits of a date (1967, say) when two digits (67) would be sufficient (the 19 prefix was to be assumed) and would take less space?

Now comes the new millenium, however, when 02 should mean 2002, but in these programs will be interpreted as 1902. The consequences could be dire. As of the stroke of midnight, December 31, 1999, Social Security recipients may fail to receive payments because they haven't been born yet.

On the same theory, prison doors may fling open for those serving life sentences. Interest calculations on a loan taken out 6 months earlier will fail because the loan period has been *negative* 99.5 years. Bank vaults with computerized time locks may refuse to open until another century has gone by. What will happen to airline and hotel reservations? What will happen to life insurance policies? What will happen to employee records, the stock market, the Internal Revenue Service, and so forth? What happens to any information sorted by date when 2000 (00) will be treated as earlier than 1999 (99)? Computer programs not equipped to handle the year 2000 at best will crash and at worst will output bizarre information.

Making code Y2K-compliant is technically simple: Just change every date reference to four digits instead of two. It is the magnitude of this "simple" task—and the short time frame left to carry it out—that is staggering. It is necessary to locate each line of code where a date entry needs to be changed.

Estimates by industry analysts and computer consulting firms such as The Gartner Group include the following:

- There are approximately 150 *billion* lines of code to be found and corrected.
- The cost could run as much as 40 cents per line of code.
- The Social Security Administration will require an estimated 300 employee years to correct the 30 million lines of code in its systems. Similar estimates come from a Fortune 500 insurance company.
- The U.S. government alone will spend $30 billion on the Y2K problem.
- The United States as a whole will spend more than $70 billion on the Y2K problem.
- The worldwide cost to fix the Y2K problem may run up to $600 billion.
- Companies that fail to address the Y2K problem can expect up to 60% of their applications to fail at or before the turn of the century.

Practice Problem

The PICTURE clause in COBOL specifies the number of columns to use for output. For example, the COBOL statements

```
02 FILLER    PICTURE is X(18)
             VALUE IS "This is the output".
```

specify that the literal string be printed out using 18 columns. Write an equivalent C++ statement.

8.2.3 PASCAL

The programming language Pascal was named after Blaise Pascal, the inventor of the Pascaline calculator, whom we mentioned in Chapter 5. The language was designed by Professor Niklaus Wirth of Zurich, Switzerland, in the early 1970s.

Dr. Niklaus Wirth grew up in Switzerland but earned his Ph.D. at the University of California at Berkeley in 1963. He was one of the first computer science faculty members at Stanford before he returned to Switzerland to join the Swiss Federal Institute of Technology (ETH) in Zurich in 1967. Here at "Europe's M.I.T.," where Albert Einstein taught physics, Wirth has made a number of major contributions to computer science, including the design of the successors to Pascal, the programming languages Modula (1980) and Oberon (1988). Oberon is simpler yet more powerful than its predecessors. It was originally developed as an operating system and programming environment featuring a graphical user interface for the Ceres workstation computer, also designed by Wirth and his colleagues in 1986. Prof. Wirth has been awarded the Turing Award of the Association for Computing Machinery (ACM) and the Computer Pioneer Award of the Institute for Electrical and Electronic Engineers Computer Society (IEEE/CS). The ACM and the IEEE/CS are the two major professional computer science organizations.

In designing Pascal, Wirth wanted a language that would be easy to learn and would help enforce good programming techniques. (Remember the GO TO controversy that had erupted a short time earlier.) He intended Pascal to be primarily a language for teaching programming. As such it gained wide acceptance, and for many years it was the primary language taught to computer science majors at most universities across the country.

Pascal code looks very similar to our pseudocode of Chapter 2, so the code is easy to read and the syntax easy to learn. Unlike C++, Pascal is a relatively "small" language. It is quite possible to learn all of the different statements supported in Pascal, what they mean, and how they work, just as Wirth intended. Very few people would claim that level of knowledge in the C++ language.

Plain vanilla Pascal never gained much acceptance as an "industrial-strength" language for solving problems in the real world. But Pascal's usefulness as a commercial language soared with the development in the early 1990s of Delphi by Borland International, Inc. Delphi is a programming environment that uses Pascal as its language core but gives the programmer the ability to develop windows-based applications with modern graphical user interfaces.

PRACTICE PROBLEM

Describe what you suspect will be the output from the following section of Pascal code, given that *A* has the value 3 and *B* has the value 7.

```
if (A < 6) and (B > 10) then
        writeln('yes')
else
        writeln('no');
```

8.2.4 C

C was developed in the early 1970s by Dennis Ritchie at AT&T Bell Laboratories. It was originally designed for systems programming—in particular, for writing the operating system UNIX. UNIX had been developed at Bell Labs a short time before and was originally written primarily in assembly language. Ritchie sought a high-level language in which to rewrite the operating system in order to gain all the advantages of high-level languages: ease of programming, portability, and so on.

Since that time, C has become a popular general-purpose language for two major reasons. One is the relationship between C and UNIX itself. UNIX has been implemented on many different computers, and UNIX provides many "tools" that support C programming. A second reason for C's popularity is its efficiency—that is, the speed with which its operations can be executed. This efficiency derives from the fact that C programs can make use of low-level information such as knowledge of where data are stored in memory. In this respect, C is closer to assembly language than other high-level languages are, yet it still has the powerful statements and portability to many machines that high-level languages offer. One can imagine C humming along as a high-level language but then, every once in a while when efficiency is really important, slipping into a low-level, machine-dependent configuration. One of the goals of a high-level language is to provide a level of abstraction that shields the programmer from any knowledge of the actual hardware/memory cells used during program execution (Figure 8.1a). C provides this outlook, unless the programmer wishes to make use of the low-level constructs available in C that give him or her a direct view of the actual hardware (Figure 8.1b).

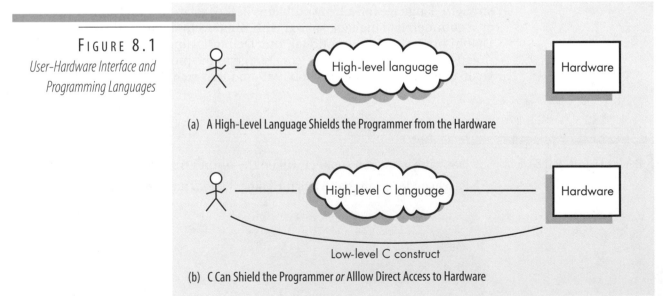

FIGURE 8.1

User–Hardware Interface and Programming Languages

(a) A High-Level Language Shields the Programmer from the Hardware

(b) C Can Shield the Programmer *or* Alllow Direct Access to Hardware

For example, suppose that *Number* is a variable in a C program. Then *&Number* in that same program refers to the memory address where the value of *Number* is stored. Note the distinction between the content of a memory cell and the address of that cell. Given that the value of *Number*, say 234, is stored in the memory cell with address 1000, then *Number* refers to the value 234, but *&Number* refers to 1000 (Figure 8.2). It is possible to write a C program statement that passes *&Number* as an argument to an output function so that the program would actually write out the memory address value (1000). The ability to print an actual memory address is not available in most other high-level languages.

C not only provides a way to see the actual memory address where a variable is stored but also gives the programmer some control over the address where information is stored. C includes a data type called **pointer**; variables of pointer type contain—instead of integers, real numbers, or characters—memory addresses. For example, the statement

```
int* intPointer;
```

declares *intPointer* as a pointer variable that will contain the address of a memory cell containing integer data. The assignment

```
intPointer = (int*) 800;
```

assigns the memory address 800 as the value of *intPointer*. Figure 8.3(a) illustrates this situation: The pointer variable *intPointer* is stored at some unknown memory address, but the content of *intPointer* is the memory address 800. The value stored at the address contained in *intPointer*, in this case stored at 800, is denoted by **intPointer*. In other words, **intPointer* is the value contained in the address to which *intPointer* points. We can find out what this value is by writing out **intPointer*. We can also assign an integer value, say 3, to be the content of memory address 800 by the statement

```
*intPointer = 3;
```

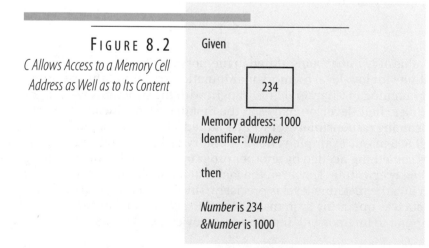

FIGURE 8.2

C Allows Access to a Memory Cell Address as Well as to Its Content

Given

234

Memory address: 1000
Identifier: *Number*

then

Number is 234
&Number is 1000

FIGURE 8.3

Storing a Value in a Specific Memory Location Using C

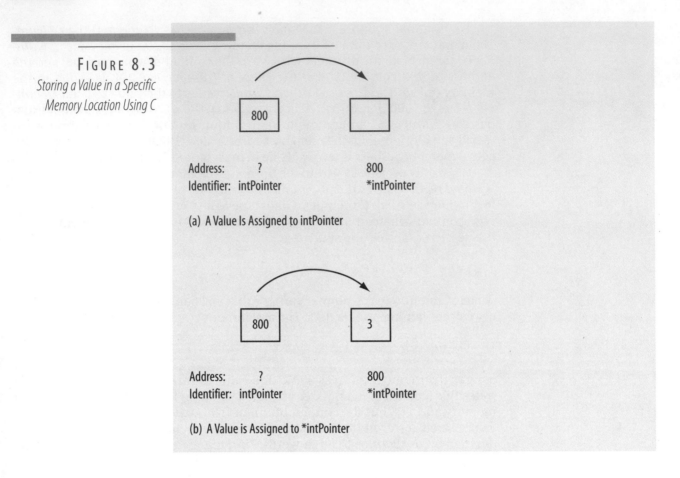

Address: ?   800
Identifier: intPointer   *intPointer

(a) A Value Is Assigned to intPointer

Address: ?   800
Identifier: intPointer   *intPointer

(b) A Value is Assigned to *intPointer

which results in Figure 8.3(b). We have controlled the content of a specific memory location, and now we know exactly what is stored in memory location 800. Similarly, if *Number* is an integer variable that has been stored somewhere in memory, then the statement

```
*intPointer = Number;
```

results in the value of *Number* being stored in memory cell 800.

This capability for low-level memory manipulation smacks of the assembly language programming of Chapter 6. It is fraught with the problems we sought to avoid by going to high-level languages in the first place; specifically, the programmer is assuming responsibility for what is stored where. For example, what if memory cell 800 in our example is not a memory cell allocated to this program? Perhaps something needed by another program, or even by the operating system, has been overwritten. However, the fact that it enables the programmer to reach down into the machine level is precisely why C is useful for writing system software such as operating systems, assemblers, compilers, programs that allow the computer to interact with input/output devices, and so on.

A program to interact with an I/O device is called a **device driver**. Consider, for example, the problem of writing a device driver for the mouse on a PC. The "serial port" of the computer, to which the mouse is connected, reads changes in the mouse position by changes in voltage levels. It stores the voltage levels in fixed locations in memory, as allocated by the operating system. The job of the mouse driver is to translate voltage levels to specific locations on the screen so that any application software that uses the mouse, such as a word processor, does not have to interact with low-level hardware information (abstraction again!). The mouse driver program would have to access the specific memory locations where voltage information is stored. A language like C provides such a capability.

C is the most widely used language for writing system software, again because of the versatility its design philosophy bestowed on it. It combines the power of a high-level language with the ability to circumvent that level of abstraction and work at the assembly-language-like level. But C is also used for a great deal of general-purpose computing.

C was developed, as we said, in the early 1970s at Bell Labs, whereas C++ was developed in the early 1980s, again at Bell Labs. Coincidence? No; C++ is a "superset" of C. What this means is that all of the C language is part of C++, so everything that can be done in C—including the ability to change the contents of specific memory locations—can be done in C++. But C++ adds many new features to C, giving it more sophistication and cleaner ways to do certain tasks. The biggest extension that C++ provides over C is the ability to do object-oriented programming, which we discuss in Section 8.3.

8.2.5 ADA

Probably more than any other language we have studied, Ada has a long and interesting development history. It all started in the mid 1970s when the various branches of the United States armed services set about trying to develop a common high-level programming language for use by defense contractors. They began with a process to specify not the constructs of a programming language but instead the requirements that any such language would have to meet, including such characteristics as efficiency, reliability, readability, and maintainability.

PRACTICE PROBLEMS

1. Suppose a C program uses a variable called *Rate*. Explain the distinction in the program between *Rate* and *&Rate*.

2. Suppose that *Rate* is an integer variable in a C program with the value 10 and that *intPointer* is a pointer variable for integer data. *Rate* is stored at memory address 500. After the statement

   ```
   intPointer = &Rate;
   ```

   what is the value of *intPointer?

The original set of requirements, first circulated for discussion in 1975, was known as "Strawman." Successively tighter and more thorough requirements bore the names "Woodenman" and "Tinman." The Tinman requirements were approved in 1976, and a large number of existing programming languages were evaluated in the light of these requirements. All were found wanting, and it became clear that a new language would have to be developed. The "Ironman" specification, issued in 1977, became the standard against which to measure a new language. A design competition was held, and the requirements were further specified in "Steelman."

The eventual language design winner was chosen in 1979, and the new language was christened Ada, after Ada Augusta Byron Lovelace, daughter of the poet Lord Byron and later the wife of Lord Lovelace. Ada was trained in mathematics and science at the wish of her mother, who sought to steer Ada away from the mental instability and moral lapses she despised in Lord Byron. Lady Ada Lovelace is regarded as the world's first programmer on the basis of her correspondence with Charles Babbage and her published notes on his work with the Analytic Engine (see the box on page 212).

An updated requirements document, less imaginatively named the Ada 9X Requirements and issued in December 1990, became the basis for the current international standard, the Ada 95 Reference Manual.

Ada, like C++, is a large language, and it has been accepted not only in the defense industry, where its use was mandated by the Department of Defense, but for other technological applications and as a general-purpose language as well. Ada is known for its multiprocessing capability—the ability to allow multiple tasks to execute independently and then synchronize and communicate when directed. It is also known as a strongly object-oriented language.

The Web site

http://www.adahome.com/

is a great source for information on the Ada programming language, including more details of its early history.

PRACTICE PROBLEM

What do you think is accomplished by the following Ada program?

```
with ada_io; use ada_io;
procedure simple is
begin
   for i in 1..10 loop
      put(i);
      put(' ');
   end loop;
   new_line;
end;
```

8.2.6 A Final Word

This concludes our brief look at five different high-level programming languages. Once again, we've only superficially touched on the differences among these languages. Suffice it to say that each language has strengths and weaknesses that reflect its design philosophy, and most have evolved over time in ways that reflect changes in thinking about the way to do programming.

One of these changes is the emphasis on object-oriented programming, or OOP. We mentioned that C++ is an extension of C that, among other things, supports OOP. Ada is an OO (object-oriented) language. But there is also an Object Pascal version of Pascal, and—surprise—even COBOL is moving toward OO. In the next section we take a look at object-oriented programming.

8.3   OBJECT-ORIENTED PROGRAMMING

Object-oriented programming can be traced to Alan Kay's work at Xerox Palo Alto Research Center in the early 1970s, which resulted in the development of Smalltalk, the original object-oriented programming language. The software used in the Laboratory Experiences for this book is written in the current version of Smalltalk.

8.3.1 What Is It?

The divide-and-conquer approach to programming that we advocated in Chapter 7 is a "traditional" approach. The focus is on the overall task to be done, how to break it down into subtasks, and how to write algorithms for the various subtasks that will be carried out by communicating modules. The program can be thought of as a giant statement executor designed to carry out the major task, even though the main program may simply call, in turn, on the various modules that do the subtask work.

Object-oriented programming (OOP) takes a somewhat different view. A program is considered to be a simulation of some part of the world that is the domain of interest. "Objects" populate this domain. Objects in a banking system, for example, might be savings accounts, checking accounts, and loans. Objects in a company personnel system might be employees. Objects in a medical office might be patients and doctors. Each object is an example drawn from a class of similar objects. The "savings account class" in the bank has certain properties associated with it, such as name, Social Security number, account type, and account balance. Each individual savings account at the bank is an example of (an object of) the savings account class, and each has specific values for these common properties; that is, each savings account has a specific value for the name of the account holder, a specific value for the account balance, and so forth.

Java

Another object-oriented language that has received a great deal of attention is Java, developed at Sun Microsystems, Inc. Unlike FORTRAN, COBOL, Pascal, C, C++, and Ada, which were carefully developed as programming languages, the Java language was almost an accident. In early 1991, Sun created a team of top-notch software developers and gave them free rein to do whatever creative thing they wanted to try. The somewhat secret "Green team" isolated itself and set to work mapping out a strategy. Its focus was on the consumer electronics market. Televisions, VCRs, stereo systems, laser disk players, and video game machines all operated on different CPUs. Over the next 18 months the team worked to develop the GUI, a programming language, an operating system, and a hardware architecture for a handheld remote-control device called the *7 that would allow various electronic devices to communicate over a network. In contrast to the high-end workstations that were a Sun hallmark, the *7 was designed to be small, inexpensive, easy-to-use, reliable, and equipped with software that could function over the multiple hardware platforms the consumer electronics market represented.

Armed with this technology, Sun went looking for a business market but found none. In 1993 Mosaic, the first graphical Internet browser, was created at the National Center for Supercomputing Applications, and the World Wide Web began to emerge. This development sent the Sun group in a new direction where their capabilities with platform-independence, reliability, security, and GUI paid off: They wrote a Web browser.

The programming language component of the *7 was named Oak, for a tree outside the window of language developer James Gosling. Later renamed Java, the language was used for the Web browser. Java is based on C++ but lacks many of the features that can make C++ programs error-prone. It is a smaller language designed to be platform independent. Like C++, it is an object-oriented language.

Java programs come in two flavors, applications and applets. Applications are complete, stand-alone programs of the type we've been looking at in C++. Applets are embedded in Web pages on central servers; when the user views a Web page with a Java-compatible browser, the applet's code is temporarily transferred to the user's system (whatever that system may be) and executed by the browser itself. Java applets bring audio, video, and real-time user interaction to Web pages, making them "come alive" and become much more than static, hyperlinked text. For example, a Java applet might show your computer system's time on an animated analog clock face on the screen, or display a streaming ticker tape of stock market quotes, or allow you to book an airline reservation on-line. The common Web browsers, such as Netscape Navigator from Netscape Communications Corporation and Microsoft's Internet Explorer, are Java-compatible.

To learn more about Java, go to

http://java.sun.com/

So far, this is similar to the idea of a data type in C++; in the circle program, *Radius*, *Circumference*, and *Area* were all examples (objects) from the data type (class) "double"; the class has one property (a numeric quantity), and each object has its own specific value for that property. However, in object-oriented programming, a class also has one or more subtasks associated with it, and all objects from that class can perform those subtasks. In carrying out its subtask, each object can be thought of as providing some service. A savings account, for example, can compute compound interest due on the balance. When an object-oriented program is executed, the program generates messages, in the form of requests for services, that are passed to the various objects. The objects respond by performing the requested service—that is, carrying out the subtask. Thus the main function in a C++ program, acting as a user of the savings account class, might request a particular savings account object to perform the service of computing interest due.

There are three terms often associated with object-oriented programming, as illustrated in Figure 8.4. The first term is **encapsulation**. Each class has its own little program module to perform each of its subtasks. Any user of the class (such as the main program) can request an object of that class to invoke the appropriate module and thereby perform the subtask service. What the class user sees is the **interface** of the class, which describes the services provided and explains how to request an object to perform that service. The details of the module code are known only to the class. (In the savings account example, the details of the algorithm used to compute interest due belong only to the class.) The advantage to this separation of powers is that a given class's modules may be modified in any way desired, as long as the interface remains unchanged. (If the bank wants to change how it computes interest, only the code for the savings account class needs to be modified; any programs that use the services of the savings account class can remain unchanged.) A class therefore consists of two components, its properties and its subtask modules, and both components are "encapsulated"—bundled—with the class.

A second term associated with object-oriented programming is **inheritance**. Once a class A of objects is defined, a class B of objects can be defined as a "subclass" of A. Every member of class B is also a member of class A; this is sometimes called an "is a" relationship. Objects in the B class "inherit" all of the properties of objects in class A (including the ability to do what those objects can do), but they may also be given some special property or ability. The benefit is that class B does not have to be built from the ground up but rather can take advantage of the fact that class A already exists. In the banking example, a Senior Citizens savings account would be a subclass of the savings account class. Any Senior Citizens savings account object is also a savings account object, but it may have special properties or be able to provide special services.

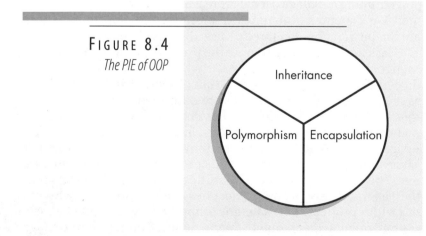

FIGURE 8.4
The PIE of OOP

The third term is **polymorphism**. *Poly* means "many." Objects may provide services that should logically have the same name because they do roughly the same thing, but the details differ. In the banking example, both savings account objects and checking account objects should provide a "compute interest" service, but the details of how interest is computed differ in these two cases. Thus one name, the name of the service to be performed, has several meanings, depending on the class of the object providing the service. It may even be the case that more than one service with the same name exists for the same class, although there must be some way to tell which service is meant when it is invoked by an object of that class.

Let's change analogies from the banking world to something more fanciful in the sports arena and consider a football team. Every member of the team's backfield is an "object" of the "backfield" class. The quarterback is the only "object" of the "quarterback" class. Each backfield object can perform the service of carrying the ball if he (or she) receives the ball from the quarterback; ball carrying is a subtask of the backfield class. The quarterback who hands the ball off to a backfield object is requesting that object to perform that subtask because it is "public knowledge" that the backfield class carries the ball and that this service is invoked by handing off the ball to a backfield object. The "program" to carry out this subtask is *encapsulated* within the backfield class in the sense that it may have evolved over the week's practice and may depend on specific knowledge of the opposing team, but at any rate, its details need not be known to other players. *Inheritance* can be illustrated by the halfback subclass within the backfield class. A halfback object can do everything a backfield object can but may also be a pass receiver. And *polymorphism* can be illustrated by the fact that the backfield may invoke a different "program" depending on where on the field the ball is handed off. Of course our analogy is imperfect, because not all human "objects" from the same class behave in precisely the same way, fullbacks sometimes receive passes, and so on.

8.3.2 A C++ EXAMPLE

How do these ideas get translated into real programs? The details, of course, vary with the programming language used. Figure 8.5 shows a C++ program that is object-oriented. We'll spend a little time explaining how it works. First, note that the program can be thought of in three pieces: the class interfaces, the main function, and the class implementations (note the program comments that help identify these sections.)

The domain of interest for this program is that of geometric shapes. In the class interfaces section, four different classes are described: *Circle, Rectangle, Square,* and *Square2*. Each class description consists of a public part and a private or protected part. The public part describes, in the form of C++ function headers, the services or subtasks that an object from the class can perform. For example, any circle object can set the value of its radius and can compute and write out its area. The private or protected part describes the properties that any object of the class possesses. A circle object has a radius property, whereas a rectangle has a width property and a height property. A square object has a side property, as one might expect, but a Square2 object doesn't seem to have

FIGURE 8.5
A C++ Program with
Classes and Objects

```cpp
#include <iostream.h>
const double PI = 3.1416;

//class interfaces
class Circle
{
public:
  void Set_Radius(double value);
  //sets radius of the circle equal to value

  void Do_Area();
  //computes and writes out area of circle
private:
  double Radius;
};

class Rectangle
{
public:
  void Set_Width(double value);
  //sets width of rectangle equal to value

  void Set_Height(double value);
  //sets height of rectangle equal to value

  void Do_Area();
  //computes and writes out area of rectangle
protected:
  double Width;
  double Height;
};

class Square
{
public:
  void Set_Side(double value);
  //sets the side of the square equal to value

  void Do_Area();
  //computes and writes out the area of the square
private: double Side;
};

class Square2: public Rectangle
//Square is derived class of Rectangle,
//uses only the inherited Height and Width
//properties and the inherited Do_Area function
{
public:
```

FIGURE 8.5

(continued)

```
void Set_Side(double value);
//sets the side of the square equal to value
};

//main function
void main()
{
  Circle Joe;
  Joe.Set_Radius(23.5);
  Joe.Do_Area();

  Rectangle Luis;
  Luis.Set_Width(12.4);
  Luis.Set_Height(18.1);
  Luis.Do_Area();

  Square Anastasia;
  Anastasia.Set_Side(3);
  Anastasia.Do_Area();

  Square2 Tyler;
  Tyler.Set_Side(4.2);
  Tyler.Do_Area();
}


//class implementations
void Circle::Set_Radius(double value)
{
  Radius = value;
}


void Circle::Do_Area()
{
  double Area;
  Area = PI*Radius*Radius;
  cout << "The area of a circle with "
     << "radius " << Radius << " is " << Area
     << endl;
}

void Rectangle::Set_Width(double value)
{
  Width = value;
}
```

FIGURE 8.5
(continued)

```cpp
void Rectangle::Set_Height(double value)
{
  Height = value;
}

void Rectangle::Do_Area()
{
  double Area;
  Area = Width*Height;
  cout << "The area of a rectangle with "
    << "dimensions " << Width << " and " << Height
    << " is " << Area << endl;
}

void Square::Set_Side(double value)
{
  Side = value;
}

void Square::Do_Area()
{
  double Area;
  Area = Side*Side;
  cout << "The area of a square with "
    << "side " << Side << " is " << Area << endl;
}

void Square2::Set_Side(double value)
{
  Height = value;
  Width = value;
}
```

any properties or, for that matter, any way to compute its area. We will have more to say about the difference between the *Square* class and the *Square2* class shortly.

The main function uses these classes. It creates objects from the various classes, much as any C++ program can create variables of the various data types. Just as

```cpp
int Number;
```

creates a variable named *Number* of data type **int**, the statement

```cpp
circle Joe;
```

creates an object named *Joe* of class *Circle*. After each object is created, the main program requests the object to set its dimensions, using the values given, and to compute and write out its area. For example, the statement

```
Joe.Set_Radius(23.5);
```

instructs the circle named *Joe* to invoke the *Set_Radius* function of *Joe*'s class, thereby setting *Joe*'s radius to 23.5. Figure 8.6 shows the output after the program in Figure 8.5 is run.

The class implementations section contains the actual code for the various functions "advertised" in the class interfaces. Each function begins with a modified form of the usual C++ function header. The modification consists of putting the class name and two colons in front of the function name so that the function code is associated with the proper class. Here we see polymorphism at work, because there are lots of *Do_Area* functions; when the program executes, the correct function is used on the basis of the class to which the object invoking the function belongs. After all, computing the area of a circle is quite different from computing the area of a rectangle. The algorithms themselves are straightforward; they employ assignment statements to set the dimensions and the usual formulas to compute the area of a circle, rectangle, and square. The functions can use properties of the object that invoke them without needing to have the values of those properties passed as arguments. For example, the *Do_Area* function for the circle knows the radius of the circle object that invoked it; hence, in contrast to our previous versions of this function, there are no parameters.

Square is a stand-alone class with a *Side* property and a *Do_Area* function. The *Square2* class, however, recognizes the fact that squares are special kinds of rectangles. The *Square2* class is a subclass of the *Rectangle* class, as is indicated by the reference to *Rectangle* in the class interface of *Square2*. It inherits the *Width* and *Height* properties from the "parent" *Rectangle* class; the "protected" status of these properties in the *Rectangle* class indicates that they can be extended to any subclass. *Square2* also inherits the *Set_Width*, *Set_Height*, and *Do_Area* functions. It addition, *Square2* has its own function, *Set_Side*, because setting the value of the "side" makes sense for a square but not for an arbitrary rectangle. What the user of the *Square2* class doesn't know is that there really isn't a "Side" property; the *Set_Side* function merely sets the inherited *Width* and *Height* properties to the same value. To compute the area, then,

FIGURE 8.6

Output from the Program of Figure 8.5

```
The area of a circle with radius 23.5 is 1734.95
The area of a rectangle with dimensions 12.4 and 18.1 is 224.44
The area of a square with side 3 is 9
The area of a rectangle with dimensions 4.2 and 4.2 is 17.64
```

the *Do_Area* function inherited from the *Rectangle* class can be used, and there's no need to redefine it or even to copy the existing code. Here we see inheritance at work.

Inheritance can be carried through multiple "generations." We might redesign the program so that there is one "superclass" that is a general *Shape* class, of which *Circle* and *Rectangle* are subclasses, *Square2* being a subclass of *Rectangle* (see Figure 8.7 for a possible class hierarchy).

Although the program of Figure 8.5 can be kept in one file, it can also be split into separate files, roughly in the three sections described. The class interfaces can be kept in a **header file**; a programmer wishing to use these classes in an application program could see this file, discover what properties and services are available, and learn how to use them. The main function—the application that the programmer is creating—is a separate program in a separate file. And the implementation of the classes is kept in a third file to be used as needed by the main function. In fact, the implementation of the classes may be compiled into object code, stored in a library, and linked with the main function when the program executes (see Figure 7.1). The programmer doesn't see the implementations; the object code gets included by the linker because the application program contains the proper include directives. Here we see encapsulation: the wrapping of implementation with the class and not with the class user. The class can change the implementation code, and as long as the class interface remains the same, the application code need not change. If the objects of the class perform the advertised services, the user of the class need not see the details.

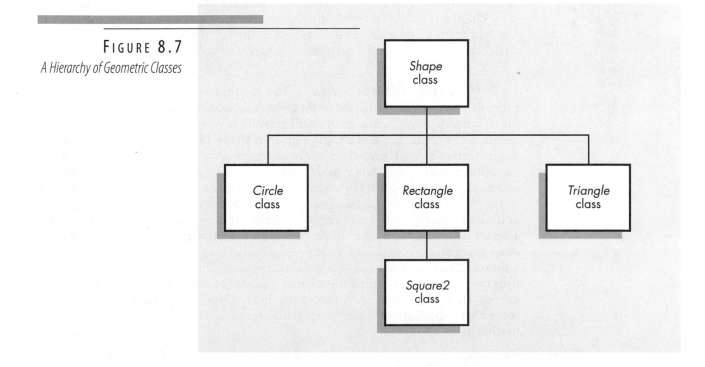

FIGURE 8.7

A Hierarchy of Geometric Classes

8.3.3 WHAT HAVE WE GAINED?

Now that we have some idea of the flavor of object-oriented programming, we should ask what we gain by this approach. There are two major reasons why OOP is becoming a popular way to program:

- Software reuse
- A more natural "world view"

SOFTWARE REUSE.   Manufacturing productivity took a great leap forward when Henry Ford invented the assembly line. Automobiles could be assembled using identical parts so that each car did not have to be treated as a unique creation. The goal is to make software development more of an assembly-line operation and less of a hand-crafted, start-over-each-time process. Object-oriented programming is a step toward this goal: A useful class that has been implemented and tested becomes a component available for use in future software development. Anyone who wants to write an application program involving circles, for example, can use the already written, tried-and-tested *Circle* class. As the "parts list" (the class library) grows, it becomes easier and easier to find a "part" that fits, and less and less time has to be devoted to writing original code. If the class doesn't quite fit, perhaps it can be modified to fit by creating a subclass; this is still less work than starting from scratch. Software reuse implies more than just more rapid code generation. It also means improvements in *reliability;* these classes have already been tested, and if properly used, they will work correctly. And it means improvements in *maintainability;* thanks to the encapsulation property of object-oriented programming, changes can be made in class implementations without affecting other code, although such change requires retesting the classes. Recall from Section 7.9.2 the importance of testing and maintenance as part of the software development life cycle; OOP can reduce the time (and money) that must be devoted to these activities.

A MORE NATURAL "WORLD VIEW."   The traditional view of programming is procedure-oriented, with a focus on tasks, subtasks, and algorithms. But wait—didn't we talk about subtasks in OOP? Haven't we said that computer science is all about algorithms? Does OOP abandon these ideas? Not at all. It is more a question of *when* these ideas come into play. Object-oriented programming recognizes that in the "real world," tasks are done by entities (objects). Object-oriented program design begins by identifying those objects that are important in the domain of the program because their actions contribute to the mix of activities present in the banking enterprise, the medical office, or wherever. Then it is determined what makes each object important—that is, what subtasks the object contributes to this mix. Finally, an algorithm to carry out each subtask must be designed. We saw in the modularized version of the circle program in Chapter 7 how the overall algorithm could be broken down into pieces that are isolated within functions. Object-oriented programming repackages those functions by encapsulating them within the appropriate class of objects.

Object-oriented programming is an approach that allows the programmer more closely to model or simulate the world as we see it, rather than mimic the sequential actions of the Von Neumann machine. It provides another buffer between the real world and the machine, another level of abstraction in which the programmer can create a virtual problem solution that will ultimately be translated into electronic signals on hardware circuitry.

Finally, we should mention graphical user interfaces, with their windows, icons, buttons, and menus. In Section 7.8, we saw a bit of the programming mechanics that can be used to draw the graphics items that make up a visual interface. But a functional GUI also provides an example of object-oriented programming at work. A general button class, for example, can have properties of height, width, location on the screen, text that may appear on the button, and so forth. Each individual button object has specific values for those properties. The button class can perform certain services by responding to messages; messages are generated by events (for example, the user clicking the mouse on a button triggers a "mouse-click" event). Each particular button object personalizes the code to respond to these messages in unique ways.

Old Dog, New Tricks #2

BASIC (*Beginner's Allpurpose Symbolic Instruction Code*) is a programming language that was developed by John Kemeny at Dartmouth College in 1963–1964. As the name suggests, it was intended to be a general language. It was also designed to be easy to learn and use. During the 1960s, programming was a rather difficult task relegated to technical professionals or, in the academic world, to advanced undergraduate engineering, math, and physics majors. BASIC was Kemeny's attempt to design a programming language easy enough for anyone to learn, including high school and elementary school students. This effort was very successful. BASIC was the programming language supplied with most microcomputers throughout the 1980s, and as such it introduced many people, in and out of school, to simple programming ideas. Although BASIC had come a long way from its simple beginnings, it was still not viewed as a very sophisticated language.

But recently BASIC has gotten a new lease on life and a whole new look. Visual Basic, a Microsoft product, is a version of BASIC that is object-oriented in that it supports classes, encapsulation, and polymorphism, as well as graphical user interfaces with objects that respond to messages. The programming environment allows a programmer to develop visually appealing, windows-based application programs using powerful tools built into the Visual Basic system, yet the language itself is still relatively easy to learn. A further step in the evolution of Visual Basic is its support of Active-X controls, which are similar to Web-based Java applets. Old languages that can evolve with the times need never die!

As evidence of the popularity of Visual Basic, consider the following estimates[1] of the number of worldwide developers (people writing programs) for various languages:

Total of C, C++, and Java	300,000 (a city about the size of Mesa, Arizona)
Visual Basic	3,000,000 (a city about the size of Chicago or Los Angeles)

[1]*Information Week,* April 28, 1997

PRACTICE PROBLEMS

1. What would be the output from execution of the following section of code if it were added to the main function of the C++ program in Figure 8.5?

```
Square One;
One.Set_Side(10);
One.Do_Area();
```

2. In the hierarchy of Figure 8.7, suppose that the *Triangle* class is able to perform a *Do_Area* function. What two properties should any triangle object have?

8.4   SPECIAL-PURPOSE LANGUAGES

Although each of the procedural languages we have mentioned has its own strong points, all are more or less general-purpose languages. In this section we visit three languages that were each designed for one specialized task. These three are merely representative; many other specialized languages exist.

8.4.1 SQL

Our first specialized language is SQL, which stands for *Structured Query Language*. SQL is designed to be used with databases, which are collections of related facts and information. We'll do some work with databases in Chapter 11, but here is the general idea. A database stores data; the user of the database must be able to add new data and to retrieve data already stored. For example, the database may contain information on vendors with which a retail store does business. For each vendor, it may contain the name, address, and phone number of the vendor, the name of the product line the vendor sells, and perhaps the amount of stock purchased from that vendor during the previous business quarter. The database user should be able to add information on a new vendor and to retrieve information on a vendor already in the database.

But if this is all that a database could do, it would simply be acting as an electronic filing cabinet. Databases can also be queried—that is, the user can pose questions to the database. Queries can furnish information that is more than the sum of its parts because they combine the individual data items in various ways. For example, the vendor database could be queried to reveal the names of all vendors with whom the store has done more than $40,000 worth of business in the past quarter or all vendors from a certain ZIP code. Such queries might be framed in SQL as

```
SELECT NAME
FROM VENDOR
WHERE PURCHASE > 40000;

SELECT NAME
FROM VENDOR
WHERE ZIP = 95082;
```

SQL is the language used to frame database queries. SQL was originally developed by IBM. In 1986 it was adopted by the American National Standards Institute (ANSI) as the standard query language in the United States, and it has since been adopted by the International Standards Organization (ISO) as an international standard. Even database systems that provide users with simpler—even graphical—ways to frame queries are simply using a front end that eventually translates the query into an equivalent SQL statement.

8.4.2 PERL

The next specialized language is Perl, which stands for *Practical Extraction and Report Language*. The name says it all. Perl is designed to scan arbitrary text files (of arbitrarily large size), extract various kinds of information that is contained within the text, and print reports based on the extracted information. The language syntax is somewhat based on C. Perl does a job that can be done by other languages or system commands but does it more efficiently, sometimes using sophisticated pattern-matching techniques to speed up the process of scanning large amounts of data for a particular text string. (We looked at a simple pattern-matching algorithm in Section 2.3.3.)

As an example of a case where the services of a Perl program would be useful, consider a Web page that asks the user to fill out a form with some information, perhaps to purchase something over the Internet. The form collects the information entered by the user as one long string of text. For example, the user may be asked to fill in his or her name and address by typing into text boxes on the form. When the user clicks a button to submit the form, the information from the form is delivered as one long text string such as

name = Betsy+Begonia&street=221+Main&city=Little+Rock&state=AR

This string needs to be split at the & and = signs into the components for name, street, city, and state. The + signs need to be replaced with blanks. This information can then be used to print out a report or update a database.

For further information about the Perl language, go to

http://perl.com/perl

8.4.3 HTML

Our third and final special-purpose language is HTML, which stands for *HyperText Markup Language*. This is the language used to create HTML documents that, when viewed with Web browser software, become Web pages. An HTML document consists of the text to be displayed on the Web page, together with a number of special characters called **tags** that achieve formatting, special effects, and references to other HTML documents. Tags are enclosed in angle brackets (< >) and often come in pairs. The end tag, the second tag in the pair, looks like the begin tag, the first tag in the pair, but with an additional / in front.

The overall format for an HTML document is

```
<html>
<head>
<title>  stuff to go in the title bar  </title>
</head>
<body>
          stuff to go on the page
</body>
</html>
```

Here we see the paired tags for the document as a whole (<html, </html>), the head (<head>, </head>), the title (<title>, /title>)—framing what will appear in the title bar of the page window—and the body (<body>, </body>)—framing what will be on the page itself.

Of course, other material needs to go between the beginning and ending "body" tags, or the page will be blank. Figure 8.8 shows the body of an HTML document, and Figure 8.9 shows what the body of the Web page actually looks

FIGURE 8.8
HTML Code for a Web Page

```
<html>
<head>
<title>First Page</title>
</head>

<body>
<h1>This is an H1 heading</h1>
<p>This text is <b>BOLD </b> and this text is
<i>italic</i></p>
<p>Below is a bulleted list:</p>
<ul>
<li>First item</li>
<li>Second item</li>
</ul>
<p>And here is a link to another document called
  <a href="second.htm">Second Page</a></p>
</body>

</html>
```

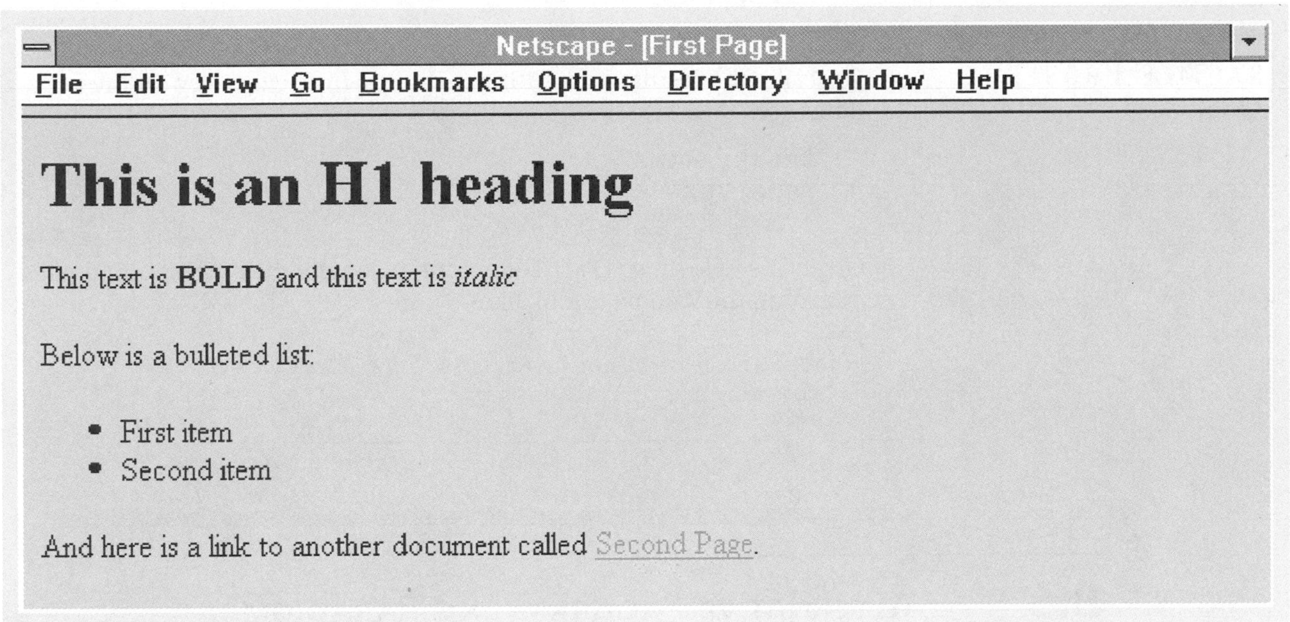

FIGURE 8.9

Body of the Web Page Generated by Figure 8.8

like when viewed with a Web browser. By comparing the two, you can probably understand the meaning of the tags used, as explained in Figure 8.10.

Early word processors required the user to type in various codes manually to mark text for boldface, italic, and so forth. Later, more sophisticated word processors with GUI interfaces reduced these tasks to point-and-click. Much the same situation is coming to pass with HTML code. HTML documents themselves are simply text files that one can create with any text editor by typing the appropriate tags. But Web editor software makes it possible to create HTML code by, for example, highlighting text and clicking a button to insert the tags for making the text boldface.

FIGURE 8.10

Some HTML Tags

HTML tag	Purpose
h1	Create H1 heading, the heading (bold) with largest font size
p	New paragraph
b	Bold
i	Italic
ul	Unordered list (bulleted list)
li	List item
a href ="..."	Provides hyperlink address

PRACTICE PROBLEMS

1. Describe the result of executing the following SQL query on the vendor database.

   ```
   SELECT NAME
   FROM VENDOR
   WHERE CITY = 'CHICAGO';
   ```

2. Given the following HTML statement, what will the corresponding line of text on the Web page look like?

   ```
   <p>These are the <i>times</i> that try
   <b>men's souls</b></p>
   ```

8.5   ALTERNATIVE PROGRAMMING PARADIGMS

Computer scientists are fond of the word *paradigm*. A **paradigm** is a model or mental framework for representing or thinking about something. The paradigm of procedural programming languages says that a sequence of detailed instructions is provided to the computer. Each instruction is concerned with accessing or modifying the contents of a memory location. If the computer carries out these instructions one at a time, then the final result of all the memory cell manipulations will be the solution to the problem at hand. This sounds suspiciously like our definition of an algorithm way back in Chapter 1 ("a well-ordered collection of unambiguous and effectively computable operations that when executed produces a result . . ."). In fact, programming in a procedural language consists of

1. Planning the algorithm
2. Capturing the "unambiguous and effectively computable operations" as program instructions

In a procedural programming language, then, we must pay attention to the details of exactly how the computer is going to accomplish the desired task in a step-by-step fashion. In object-oriented programming, the procedural paradigm still holds, but the step-by-step instructions may be split into multiple small sets that are encapsulated within classes.

In this section we look at programming languages designed as alternatives to the procedural approach—languages based on other paradigms. It is as though we have studied French, Spanish, and Italian (different but related languages) and are now about to embark on a study of Arabic, Japanese, or sign language—languages totally different in form, structure, and alphabet. Alternative paradigms for programming languages include viewing a program's actions as

- A combination of various transformations upon items (functional programming)

- A series of logical deductions from known facts (logic programming)
- Multiple copies of the same subtask or multiple subtasks of the same problem being performed simultaneously by different processors (parallel programming)

We'll look briefly at each of these alternative programming paradigms, focusing on the different conceptual views rather than on the details of a language's syntax. In short, this chapter won't make you an expert programmer, or even a novice programmer, in any of these languages, but you'll have a sense of some of the different approaches to programming languages that have been developed. Both LISP, mentioned in the next section, and Prolog, discussed in Section 8.5.2, are often used in artificial intelligence work; for more information on artificial intelligence, see Chapter 13.

8.5.1 Functional Programming

Functional programming had its start with the design of the LISP (*LISt Processing*) programming language by John McCarthy at M.I.T. in 1958. This makes LISP second only to FORTRAN in longevity. John Backus (who, you will recall, led the development of FORTRAN) argued for functional programming as opposed to "conventional Von Neumann languages" and introduced the language FP (for *Functional Programming*) in 1977. Other functional programming languages or dialects of LISP have been developed. We will look at examples using Scheme, which is a functional programming language derived from LISP in the late 1970s. More information on Scheme may be found at

http://www-swiss.ai.mit.edu/scheme-home.html

A **functional programming language** views every task in terms of (surprise!) functions. Unlike the more general usage of the word in C++, *function* in this context means something like a mathematical function—a recipe for taking an argument (or possibly several arguments) and doing something with them to compute a single value. More formally, when the arguments are given values, the function transforms those values, according to some specified rule, into a corresponding resulting value. Different values for the arguments can produce different resulting values. The doubling function $f(x) = 2x$ transforms the argument 3 into 6 because $f(3) = 2*3 = 6$, and it transforms the argument 6 into 12 because $f(6) = 2*6 = 12$. In the grand sense, we can think of a program as a function acting on input data (the arguments) and transforming them into the desired output.

In a functional programming language, certain functions, called **primitive functions** or just **primitives**, are defined as part of the language. Other functions can be defined and named by the programmer. To define the doubling function using Scheme, we could say

```
(define (double x)
      (* 2 x))
```

The keyword "define" indicates that we are defining a new function. The function name and its list of arguments follow in parentheses. The function name is *double*, and *x* is its single argument. The definition says that when this function is invoked, it is to multiply the argument value by 2. Having defined the function, we can now invoke it in a program by giving the function name, followed by a list of values for the arguments of the function. (For the *double* function, there is only one number in the list of argument values because there is only one argument.) Scheme responds immediately to a function invocation by displaying the result, so the following interaction could occur as the user invokes the *double* function with various argument values (boldface indicates what the user types).

(double 4)

```
8
```

(double 8)

```
16
```

Here's the definition of another function:

```
(define (square x)
   (* x x))
```

which says that the function named *square*, when invoked, is to multiply the single argument value by itself. Thus a dialog with Scheme could be

(square 3)

```
9
```

Functions, once defined, can be used in the definition of other functions. This can lead to nested tasks that must be performed. The function *polynomial*, defined by

```
(define (polynomial x)
   (double (square x)))
```

is the function that we would write mathematically as $g(x) = 2x^2$. Using this function, the dialog could be

(polynomial 3)

```
18
```

When the *polynomial* function is invoked with the argument 3, Scheme consults the function definition and sees that this is really

```
(double (square 3))
```

Thus the polynomial function must invoke the *double* function, and it is to invoke that function with an argument value of "(square 3)". Therefore, the first thing to do is to invoke the *square* function with an argument value of 3. The result is $3^2 = 9$. This 9 gets used as the argument value for the double function, resulting in 18. The total computation is equivalent to $g(3) = 2(3)^2 = 2(9) = 18$.

Here we've defined one function (*polynomial*) in terms of another function (*double*) acting on the result of applying a third function (*square*). In functional programming languages, we can build up complex combinations of functions that use the results of applying other functions, which use the results of applying still other functions, and so on. In fact, functional programming languages are sometimes called **applicative languages** because of this property of repeatedly applying functions.

As the name LISP suggests, LISP processes lists of things, and so does Scheme. The arguments to functions, then, are often lists. As a trivial case, "nothing" can be thought of as an empty list, which is called *nil*. We will use four primitive list-processing functions available in Scheme. The first function is called *list*. This function can have any number of arguments, and its action is to create a list out of those arguments. Therefore

(list 3 4 5)

evaluates to the list 3, 4, 5, which we will write as

(3 4 5)

Two other list-processing functions are called *car* (pronounced as when it means an automobile) and *cdr* (pronounced "could-er"). (The names have historical significance from the distant past. Car stands for "Contents of Address Register," and cdr stands for "Contents of Decrement Register." These registers were part of the architecture of the IBM 704 computer on which LISP was originally implemented.) The *car* function takes a nonempty list as its argument and produces as a result the first element in that list. Therefore a dialog with Scheme could consist of

(car (list 3 4 5))

3

The *cdr* function takes a nonempty list as its argument and produces as a result the list that remains after the first element has been removed. Therefore

(cdr (list 3 4 5))

evaluates to the list

(4 5)

As a special case, when the *cdr* function is applied to an argument consisting of a one-element list, the empty list is produced as the result. Thus

(cdr (list 5))

evaluates to the list *nil*. Note that the *car* function applied to a list evaluates to a list element, whereas the *cdr* function applied to a list evaluates to another, shorter list.

One final primitive list-processing function is *null?*, which has a single list as its argument and evaluates to true if the list is *nil* (empty) and to false if the list is nonempty. Armed with these primitives, we can at last write a little Scheme program (Figure 8.11) to add some non-negative integers.

FIGURE 8.11

*Scheme Program to Add
Non-Negative Integers*

```
(define (adder input-list)
  (cond ((null? input-list) 0)
    (else (+ (car input-list)
      (adder (cdr input-list)))))))
```

Dialog with the program in Figure 8.11 could result in

(adder (list 3 4 5))

```
12
```

Let's see how this works. Our function *adder* was defined to have one argument, symbolically denoted in the definition by *input-list*. Now we're invoking this function where the argument has the value of (*list* 3 4 5); that is to say, the function is to operate on (3 4 5). The *cond* function (short for "conditional") is acting like a C++ if-else statement: It's equivalent to

```
if (null? input-list)
   total = 0;
else
   total = (car input-list) + (adder(cdr input-list));
```

The condition "null? input-list" is evaluated and found to be false because *input-list* at this point is (*list* 3 4 5). The else clause is executed, and it says to add two quantities. The first of these two quantities is (*car input-list*), which is (*car* (*list* 3 4 5)), or 3. Thus 3 is to be added to the second quantity. The second quantity is the result of invoking the *adder* function on the argument (*cdr input-list*), which is (*cdr* (*list* 3 4 5)), or (4 5). The value, as constructed so far, is therefore

3 + (*adder* (*list* 4 5))

Now the program invokes the *adder* function again, this time with an argument of (*list* 4 5) instead of (*list* 3 4 5). Once again we test whether this list is *nil* (it isn't), so we add together

(*car* (*list* 4 5)) + (*adder* (*cdr* (*list* 4 5)))

or

4 + (*adder* (*list* 5))

The *adder* function is invoked again with an argument of (*list* 5). The list still is not *nil*, so we add together

(*car* (*list* 5)) + (*adder* (*cdr* (*list* 5)))

or

$5 + (adder\ nil)$

A final invocation of the *adder* function, this time with the *nil* list as its argument, takes the other branch of the *cond* statement, which results in 0. Altogether, then, we've done

$(adder\ (list\ 3\ 4\ 5))$

or

$$(adder\ (3\ 4\ 5)) =$$
$$3 + (adder\ (4\ 5)) =$$
$$3 + 4 + (adder\ (5)) =$$
$$3 + 4 + 5 + (adder\ nil) =$$
$$3 + 4 + 5 + 0 = 12$$

The definition of the *adder* function involves the *adder* function again, this time acting on a shorter list. Note in our example how we had to invoke the *adder* function repeatedly—first on (3 4 5), then on (4 5), next on (5), and finally on *nil*. Something that is defined in terms of "smaller versions" of itself is said to be **recursive**, so the *adder* function is a recursive function.

Recursion is one of the features of functional languages that makes possible short and elegant solutions to many problems. Although recursion is a dominant mode of operation in functional languages, many procedural languages also support recursion, so that's not the major argument for using a functional language. Then what is the benefit of going to a functional language?

A functional language allows for clarity of thought; data values are transformed by flowing, as it were, through a stream of mathematical functions. The programmer has no concern about where intermediate values are stored, nor indeed about how a "list" could occupy many memory cells. Another layer of abstraction has been offered to the programmer—the rarefied layer of pure mathematics. Because functions are described in a mathematical way by what they do to an item of data rather than by how they modify memory cells in the process of doing it, the possibility of side effects is eliminated. A **side effect** occurs when a function, in the course of acting on its argument values to produce a result value, also changes other values that it has no business changing. Implementing a function in a procedural language, where the major mode of operation is modification of memory cells, opens the door to potential side effects.

Laboratory Experience 14

If you have access to a LISP or Scheme interpreter, this laboratory experience will guide you through some functional programming exercises. You'll see that a higher level of problem solving is possible than in the C++ exercises, where you had to write step-by-step instructions to manipulate data values by way of specific memory locations.

Simplicity Is in the Eye of the Beholder

We used recursion to define the function to add a list, as follows: Add the first list element to the result of adding the rest of the list elements together. The recursive way of thinking takes a bit of getting used to. For example,

- Reading a book can be defined as reading the first page followed by reading the rest of the book.
- Climbing a ladder can be defined as climbing the first rung followed by climbing the rest of the ladder.
- Eating a six-course meal can be done by eating the first course followed by eating the rest of the meal.

Having learned to program in a procedural language, some people are initially uncomfortable with the recursive style of functional languages. However, this seems to be more a matter of what one is used to rather than any inherent "difficulty factor." Many people argue for using a functional language like Scheme as a *first* programming language because of its simplicity, clarity, and elegance.

The functional language Logo was developed by Seymour Papert at M.I.T. in 1980 specifically as an educational tool for young children, who seem to take to it readily. In Logo one can use "turtle graphics"—that is, a "turtle" can be programmed to move about on the screen, tracing lines as it travels, and thereby drawing various figures. (The original M.I.T. turtle was an actual mechanical model of a turtle that children could direct to move about on the floor, tracing lines on a sheet of paper.) For example, the turtle can be programmed to draw a square recursively by first drawing one side and then drawing the remaining three sides of the square. Here's the Logo (recursive) version of the sequential search algorithm, as expressed by one of the authors' children: "To find the elephant in the zoo, look in the first cage, and if it's not there, then look in the rest of the zoo!"

Does this seem like an easier way to think about sequential searching than the algorithm we developed in Chapter 2?

PRACTICE PROBLEMS

1. To what does each of the following evaluate?

   a. **(cdr (list 1 2 3 4))**

   b. **(car (cdr (list 4 5 6)))**

2. Define a function in Scheme that adds 3 to a number.

8.5.2 LOGIC PROGRAMMING

We saw that functional programming gets away from explicitly instructing the computer about the details of each step to be performed; instead, it specifies various transformations of data and then allows combinations of transformations to be performed. **Logic programming** goes a step further in the direction of not specifying exactly how a task is to be done. In logic programming, various facts are asserted to be true, and on the basis of these facts, a logic program can infer or deduce other facts. When a **query** (a question) is posed to the program, it begins with the storehouse of facts and attempts to apply logical deductions, in as efficient a manner as possible, to answer the query.

Logic programming languages are sometimes called **declarative languages** (as opposed to imperative languages) because their programs, instead of issuing commands to do certain things, make declarations or assertions that various facts are true.

A domain of interest is defined in which the declarations make sense (such as medicine, literature, or chemistry), and the queries are related to that domain. Logic programming has been used to write **expert systems**. In an expert system about a particular domain, a human "expert" in that domain contributes facts based on his or her knowledge and experience. A logic program using these facts as its declarations can then, presumably, make inferences that are close to those the human expert would make.

The best-known logic programming language is Prolog, which was developed in France at the University of Marseilles in 1972 by a group headed by A. Colmerauer. Prolog stands for *PRO*gramming in *LOG*ic; the language was originally intended as a tool for natural language processing. Interest in Prolog received a great boost when the Japanese announced their Fifth Generation Project in 1981. The goal of this effort, which later proved to be too ambitious, was to provide a knowledge-based society through the use of computers that make logical inferences and can interact with human beings in a "natural" way through both spoken and written language.

Prolog programs consist of *facts* and *rules*. A **fact** expresses a property about a single object or a relationship among several objects. As an example, let us write a Prolog program about the domain of American history. We are interested in which U.S. presidents were in office when certain events occurred and in the chronology of those presidents' terms in office. Here is a short list of facts (declarations):

```
president(lincoln, gettysburg_address).
president(lincoln, civil_war).
president(nixon, first_moon_landing).
president(jefferson, lewis_and_clark).
president(kennedy, cuban_missile_crisis).
president(fdr, world_war_II).

before(jefferson, lincoln).
before(lincoln, fdr).
before(fdr, kennedy).
before(kennedy, nixon).
```

The interpretation of these facts is fairly obvious. The declaration

```
president(jefferson, lewis_and_clark).
```

for example, asserts or declares that Jefferson was U.S. President during the Lewis and Clark expeditions. And

```
before(kennedy, nixon).
```

asserts that Kennedy was president before Nixon. (There are a number of versions of Prolog available; the version we used requires that identifiers for specific items begin with lower-case letters and have no internal blanks.)

This list of facts constitutes a Prolog program. We interact with the program by posing queries; this is the way Prolog programs are executed. For example, the user could make the following query (boldface indicates what the user types):

?-before(lincoln, fdr).

Prolog will respond

```
Yes.
```

because "before(lincoln, fdr)" is a fact in the program. After every response, Prolog will also ask

```
More?  (Y/N):
```

because there may be multiple responses to the query. If we wish to see further responses, we answer yes. If we answer yes when there are no further responses, as in this case, Prolog will simply respond

```
No.
```

Here's some further dialog with Prolog using this same program. We won't bother to write the "More? (Y/N):" that appears after each Prolog response.

?-president(lincoln, civil_war).

```
Yes.
```

?-president(truman, world_war_II)

```
No.
```

The first query corresponds to a declaration in the program, and the second does not.

More complicated queries can be phrased. A query of the form A, B is asking Prolog whether fact A and fact B are both in the program. Thus a query such as

?-president(lincoln, civil_war), before(lincoln, fdr)

will produce a "Yes" response because both facts are in the program. The interpretation is that Lincoln was president during the Civil War and that Lincoln was president before FDR.

So far, Prolog appears to be little more than some sort of retrieval system that does look-ups on a table of facts. But Prolog can do much more. Variables can be used within queries, and this is what gives Prolog its power. Variables must begin with upper-case letters. The query

?-president(lincoln, X).

is asking for a match against facts in the program of the form president(lincoln,"something")

In other words, X can stand for anything that is in the "president relation" with Lincoln. The responses are

```
X = gettysburg_address
X = civil_war
```

because both

```
president(lincoln, gettysburg_address).
president(lincoln, civil_war).
```

are facts in the program. (Remember that in order to see more than one response, we have to keep answering yes when asked "More? (Y/N): ".)

Let's describe what it means for one president to precede another in office. It may appear that the *before* relation already takes care of this. Certainly if "before(X,Y)" is true, then President X precedes President Y. However, in our example program,

```
before(lincoln, fdr).
before(fdr, kennedy).
```

are both true, but that does not tell us that Lincoln precedes Kennedy (which is also true). Of course, we could add another *before* fact to cover this case, but that is an *ad hoc* patch. Instead, let's add further declarations to the program to define the *precede* relation. We already know that two presidents in the *before* relation should also be in a *precede* relation. Furthermore, from the example above, it would appear that if X is before Z and Z is before Y, then "precede(X,Y)" should also be true. But we can say more than that: If X is before Z and Z precedes Y, then "precede(X,Y)" should be true. This extension means that Jefferson precedes Kennedy because

before(fdr, kennedy)

implies   precedes(fdr, kennedy)

before(lincoln, fdr)

precedes(fdr, kennedy)

implies   precedes(lincoln, kennedy)

and

before(jefferson, lincoln)

precedes(lincoln, kennedy)

implies   precedes(jefferson, kennedy)

Using this reasoning, we have derived three new "precedes" facts that were not in the original list of facts.

Thus we want to say that there are two ways in which X can precede Y:

precedes(X,Y) if before(X,Y)

precedes(X,Y) if before(X,Z) and precedes(Z,Y)

We can make declarations in our Prolog program that express the *precedes* relation, but this time the declarations are stated as rules rather than as facts. A Prolog **rule** is a declaration of an "if A then B" form, which means that if A is true (A is a fact), then B is also true (B is a fact). The actual Prolog declarations follow; think of the notation B :- A meaning "if A then B."

```
precedes(X,Y)  :- before(X,Y).
precedes(X,Y)  :- before(X,Z), precedes(Z,Y).
```

The rule for *precedes* includes *precedes* as part of its definition; it is therefore a recursive rule.

Our Prolog program now consists of the facts and rules shown in Figure 8.12. Here's some further dialog, using the new program. Be sure you understand why each query receives the response or responses it does.

?-precedes(fdr, kennedy).

```
Yes.
```

?-precedes(lincoln, nixon).

```
Yes.
```

precedes(lincoln, X).

```
X  =  fdr

X  =  kennedy

X  =  nixon
```

FIGURE 8.12

A Prolog Program

```
president(lincoln, gettysburg_address).
president(lincoln, civil_war).
president(nixon, first_moon_landing).
president(jefferson, lewis_and_clark).
president(kennedy, cuban_missile_crisis).
president(fdr, world_war_II).

before(jefferson, lincoln).
before(lincoln, fdr).
before(fdr, kennedy).
before(kennedy, nixon).

precedes(X,Y)  :- before(X,Y).
precedes(X,Y)  :- before(X,Z), precedes(Z,Y).
```

Let's add one final declaration to the program—a declaration that says that event X occurred earlier than event Y if X took place during president R's term in office, Y took place during president S's term in office, and president R precedes president S. (Do you agree with this definition of the *earlier* relation?) Here's the rule:

```
earlier(X,Y) :- president(R,X), president(S,Y), precedes(R,S).
```

Then a final query of

?-earlier(world_war_II, X)

produces the responses

```
X = first_moon_landing
X = cuban_missile_crisis
```

In this simple example, it is easy to check that the responses to our queries are correct, and it is also not difficult to do the necessary comparisons with the program declarations to see how Prolog was able to arrive at its responses. The interesting thing to note, however, is that the program consists solely of declaratives (facts and rules), not instructions about what steps to take in order to produce the answers. The program provides the raw material, and in the logic programming paradigm, this raw material is inspected more or less out of our sight, and without our detailed instructions, to deduce the answers to a query.

Figure 8.13 illustrates the situation. The programmer builds a **knowledge base** of facts and rules about a certain domain of interest; this knowledge base constitutes the program. Interaction with the program takes place by posing queries—sometimes rather complex queries—to an **inference engine** (also called a **query interpreter**). The inference engine is a piece of software that is supplied as part of the language itself; that is, it is part of the compiler or interpreter, not something the programmer has to write. The inference engine can

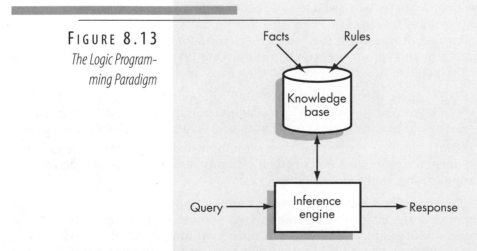

FIGURE 8.13
The Logic Program-
ming Paradigm

access the knowledge base, and it contains its own rules of deductive reasoning based on symbolic logic. For example, a Prolog inference engine processing the program in Figure 8.12 would conclude that

```
precedes(fdr, kennedy)
```

is true from the rule of the form

```
if before(X,Y) then precedes(X,Y)
```

together with the fact

```
before(fdr, kennedy)
```

because it is a rule of deductive reasoning (known as **modus ponens**) that "if A then B" together with "A" must result in "B." The programmer need not supply this rule or instruct the inference engine when it should be applied. Thus the inference engine can be thought of as providing still another layer of abstraction between the programmer and the machine. The programmer supplies the fundamental facts and rules about the domain but does not direct the computer's step-by-step processing of those facts and rules to answer a query.

This is a somewhat idealistic view of logic programming; in actuality, the idiosyncrasies of Prolog compilers mean that programmers do need to understand something about the order in which rules of logic will be applied. Yet Prolog still gives us a good sense of the logic programming paradigm, where the intent is to concentrate on the "what" [is true] rather than on the "how" [to find it] that is the hallmark of procedural programming.

8.5.3 PARALLEL PROGRAMMING

We mentioned in Chapter 5 that the computing problems of the 21st century are pushing the boundaries of the Von Neumann model of sequential processing. Figure 8.14 lists some of the "grand challenges" of the 1990s, identified by the government-sponsored High Performance Computing and Communications Initiative. Parallel processing, in one of its several forms, seems to hold promise of providing the necessary speed to solve problems of this type, which require great computational resources.

Parallel processing is really a catch-all term for a variety of computing architectures and approaches to algorithms. Let's review the two approaches to parallel architectures discussed in Chapter 5:

SIMD (single instruction stream/multiple data stream): a single control unit broadcasts a single program instruction to multiple ALUs, each of which carries out that instruction on its own local data stored in its local memory.

MIMD (multiple instruction stream/multiple data stream): numerous interconnected processors execute their own programs on their own data, communicating results as necessary.

The algorithms with which we are familiar operate sequentially (because they were designed for Von Neumann-type execution). To reap the benefits of parallel architecture, new algorithms must be found, which may involve new ways of thinking about problem solutions. In contrast to our approach in the other sections of this chapter, we're not going to talk about a specific "parallel

FIGURE 8.14
*"Grand Challenge"
Computing Problems*

- 48-hour weather prediction
- Modeling oil reservoirs
- Chemical dynamics
- Vehicle dynamics
- Fluid turbulence
- Human genome project
- Ocean circulation model

programming language." Instead we will discuss some of the general approaches to parallel programming.

An example (given in Chapter 5) of SIMD processing is adding a constant value *K* to each element in a 6-element vector *V*. There would be six ALUs, each with an ID number from 1 to 6. Each ALU would have its own local or "private" data consisting of one of the six vector components; that is, the ALU with ID 1 would have a private copy of *V* in its local memory which would actually consist of just *V*[1]. The ALU with ID 2 would have *V*[2] as its private copy of *V*. All ALUs would need access to the constant value *K*, which could be stored in a shared memory accessible by all. We can imagine that programming instructions for this operation in a language designed to support SIMD processing would look something like

```
V : private
K : public
   .
   .
   .
PARALLEL [1..6]
  V = V + K;
END PARALLEL
```

Here *V* has been declared as a "private" data item that is stored in the local memory of the appropriate ALU and that differs from one ALU to the next. *K* has been declared as a "public" data item stored in shared memory and identical to each ALU. The "PARALLEL" instruction says that all ALUs with ID numbers 1 to 6 are to do, in lockstep, the statement V = V + K.

PRACTICE PROBLEMS

Using the Prolog program of Figure 8.12, what will be the result of each of the following queries?

1. **?-before(jefferson, kennedy).**

2. **?-president(X, lewis_and_clark).**

3. **?-precedes(jefferson, X).**

The MIMD example from Chapter 5 has to do with the name search task. Here the 20,000,000-entry list to be searched is partitioned into 100 separate chunks of size 200,000 and parceled out to 100 processors. All of the processors execute simultaneously—but not necessarily in instruction-by-instruction lockstep—the search task on their portion of the data. In a language designed to support MIMD processing, we might see something like

```
YOURLIST = LIST[1..200000] : private
NAME : public
  .

  .

  .
PARALLEL[1..100]
  SEQSEARCH (YOURLIST, NAME, FOUND, INTERRUPT)
  IF FOUND, SEND INTERRUPT
END PARALLEL
```

Here a section of the overall list has been declared as private data (stored in the local memory of the appropriate processor), and NAME has been declared as "public" data (to be broadcast to all processors). The "PARALLEL" instruction says that all processors with ID numbers 1 to 100 are to initiate a sequential search for NAME on their 200,000-element portion of the list. If NAME is found, the processor is to broadcast this information to all other processors by sending an "INTERRUPT" signal. Each processor's sequential search algorithm is modified to halt if an "INTERRUPT" signal is received, because that means another processor has found NAME, and the search can be halted.

MIMD processing does not require that each processor be doing the same task. For example, an instruction like

```
PARALLEL
  PROC 1: A = 1
  PROC 2: READ(B)
  PROC 3: AVERAGE(X,Y,Z)
END PARALLEL
```

tells processor 1 to do an assignment, processor 2 to read a value, and processor 3 to execute an "average" function. These actions are to be done in parallel, but they may not be completed simultaneously because they are of different complexity. The PARALLEL statement as a whole will be completed when all of these actions are finished (see Figure 8.15).

A slightly more sophisticated level of MIMD parallel processing occurs when a divide-and-conquer approach can be used on a task. The task is successively partitioned into smaller and smaller parts and handed off to other processors, until a number of processors have a trivial case of the task to perform. They perform this task and give the results back to the processors that gave the task to them. These processors in turn do a little work and then give the results back to the processors that gave the task to them, and so on, back to the originating processor. For example, finding the largest element in a list of elements can be the task assigned to the highest-level processor, who partitions the list in two and hands each half to a processor. Each of these two processors hands off half of its list to one of two

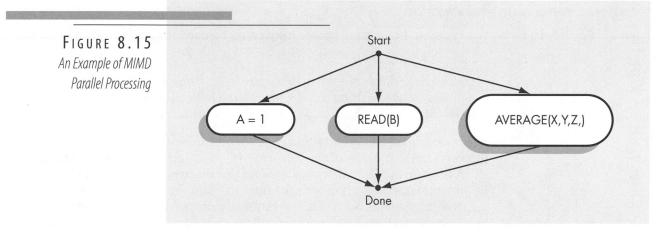

FIGURE 8.15

An Example of MIMD Parallel Processing

processors, and so on, creating the pyramid effect shown in Figure 8.16. At the bottom of the pyramid is a collection of processors that only have to find the largest element in a one-element or two-element list, a trivial task. They each pass their result up to their "parent" processor, who must select the larger of two numbers and pass that value up to its parent. All the way back up the pyramid, each processor has only to select the larger of two numbers. When the processor at the top of the pyramid completes this minor task, the entire major task of finding the overall largest number has been completed. Here not every processor is doing the same thing at exactly the same time, but each one (except for those at the bottom of the pyramid) must both move the data down and push results back up.

Still higher levels of parallelism involve careful identification of separate subtasks that may be executed concurrently. None of these subtasks can require any results from any of the other subtasks. For a large-scale problem—one that can

FIGURE 8.16

A Divide-and-Conquer Approach Using Multiple Processors

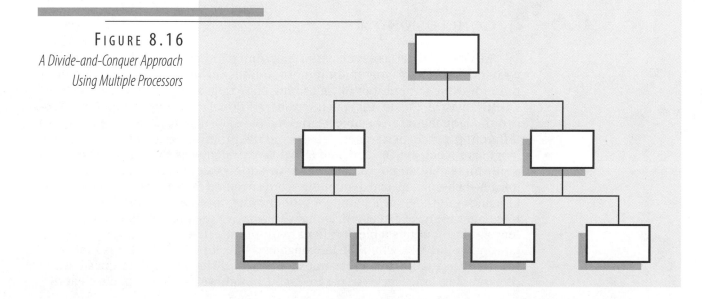

PRACTICE PROBLEM   Explain how parallel processing could be used to evaluate the expression

$$A + B + C + D$$

If each addition operation takes one "time slot," what is the savings that can be achieved by using parallel processing instead of sequential processing?

---

make use of a large number of processors—this can be a very difficult job. It requires thorough understanding of the flow of information from one subtask to another.

A final form of parallelism, a type we will discuss again in Chapter 13, is the neural network. Patterned after the human brain, **neural networks** can involve massive interconnections of many extremely simple devices. They are one of the most interesting areas of artificial intelligence today.

We expect the use of parallelism to speed up processing time because subtasks are being executed concurrently. But one potential drawback concerns the amount of communications traffic between the separate processors, both to distribute code and data and to share results. At some point, an increase in the number of processors can become more of a hindrance than a help in speeding up the overall processing time required for the task because of the increased data communication involved. This is analogous to having too many people on a committee. The work involved in keeping everyone informed slows down the real work, so it would have been more efficient to have fewer people doing the job.

One of the important aspects of work in parallel processing is the design of efficient algorithms that keep all the processors busy, cut down on the communications required, and significantly speed up execution time over that required for sequential processing.

8.6   CONCLUSION

We've seen that there is an entire spectrum of programming languages, each with its own features that make it more suitable for some types of applications than for others. A number of well-known languages (we looked at FORTRAN, COBOL, Pascal, C, and Ada) fall into the traditional, procedural paradigm. Procedural languages can be object-oriented (C++, Visual Basic, Java), leading to a different program design perspective and the promise of software reuse. Some languages (such as SQL, Perl, and HTML) are designed as special-purpose tools. Still others rely on combinations of function evaluations (a functional language—Scheme), logical deductions from specified facts (a logic programming language—Prolog), or a parallel programming approach. Figure 8.17 lists the languages we have discussed, along with some of the other major languages. A few words about this table: It is hard to pinpoint a date for a programming language. Should it be when the language was developed, when it was first commercially used, or when it became standardized? It is also sometimes hard to pigeonhole a language as to paradigm. Although we've tried to make clear distinctions in this chapter, some languages combine features drawn from several approaches. Finally, someone's favorite language may have been omitted. (By all means, add it to the table.) At any rate, it is certain that the programming language world has been, and continues to be, a "Tower of Babel."

The trend in programming language design is to develop still higher levels of abstraction in our programming languages. This allows the human programmer to think in "bigger pieces" and more novel or conceptual ways about solving the problem at hand. We would like eventually to be able to write programs that contain only the instruction "solve the problem." Yet we must remember that code written in any high-level programming languages is still of no use to the computer trying to execute that code. No matter how abstract and powerful the language for front-end communication with the computer, the machine itself is still toiling away at the bit level. The services of an appropriate translator must be employed to take the code down into the machine language of that computer. The workings of a translator are discussed in the next chapter.

FIGURE 8.17

Programming Languages at a Glance

Name	Date	Type
FORTRAN	1955–57	Procedural
ALGOL 60	1958–60	Procedural
COBOL	1959–60	Procedural
BASIC	1963–64	Procedural
PL/1	1964	Procedural
ALGOL-68	1968	Procedural
Pascal	1971	Procedural
C	1974	Procedural
Modula-2	1977	Procedural
Ada	1979	Procedural/Parallel
Oberon	1988	Procedural/Parallel
Smalltalk	1971–1980	Object-oriented
Flavors	1979	Object-oriented
C++	1983	Object-oriented
Visual Basic	1988	Object-oriented
Java	1995	Object-oriented
SQL	1986	Database queries
Perl	1987	Text extraction/reporting
HTML	1994	Hypertext authoring
LISP	1958	Functional
APL	1960	Functional
Scheme	1975	Functional
FP	1977	Functional
ML	1978	Functional
Prolog	1972	Logic
Occam II	1987	Parallel
Linda	1989	Parallel
High Performance Fortran	1993	Parallel

EXERCISES

1. What do you think the output from the following section of FORTRAN code will be?

```
    ISUM = 0
    I = 1
20  IF (I .GT. 4) GO TO 30
        ISUM = ISUM + I
        I = I + 1
        GO TO 20
30  WRITE(*,*) ISUM
```

2. Exponentiation is expressed in FORTRAN by **; that is, 3**2 means 3^2. If *I* has the value 7 and *J* has the value 3, what is the value of the FORTRAN expression

```
((I - J)**2)/2
```

3. What do you think is the value of RESULT after execution of the following COBOL code? Assume that *INITIAL* has the value 100.

```
MOVE INITIAL TO INDEX.
ADD 1 TO INDEX.
ADD INITIAL TO INDEX.
ADD INITIAL TO INDEX GIVING
  RESULT.
```

4. Given that the user enters the values

89

116

0

43

−99

what will the following Pascal program give as output? (*Hint:* The "input, output" in the first line is needed for Pascal I/O, and anything appearing within curly braces is treated as a comment.)

```
program Adder(input, output);
{adds non-negative integers
  supplied by the user,
terminates when a negative
  value is given}
```

```
var
   Number: integer; {current
                      number
                      being read}
   Sum: integer;    {running Sum}

begin
   writeln('Enter non-negative
     integers, terminate with
     negative integer');
   Sum := 0;   {initialize Sum}
   readln(Number);
   while (Number >= 0) do
   begin
       Sum := Sum + Number;
       readln(Number);
   end;
   writeln('The total of these
     integers is ', Sum);
end.
```

5. Convert the following Pascal code to C++. (*Hint:* The "input, output" in the first line is needed for Pascal I/O, and anything appearing within curly braces is treated as a comment.)

```
program stuff(input, output)
{reads and writes an integer}

var
   X : integer;
begin
   writeln('Enter number');
   readln(X);
   writeln('The number is ',X)
end.
```

6. What is true after the following statements in a C program have been executed?

```
int* intPointer;
intPointer = (int*) 500;
*intPointer = 10;
```

7. Write a section of C code that stores in memory location 1000 the integer value currently in SAM.

8. The following section of Ada code conveys the services that a "teller" object can perform. What are these services?

```
task type teller is
  -- Entries to do simple
    transactions and return status
    entry deposit ( id : cust_id;
      val : in money; stat : out
      status );
    entry withdraw( id : cust_id;
      val : in money; stat : out
      status );
    entry balance ( id : cust_id;
      val : out money; stat :
      out status );
end teller;
```

9. Which procedural language might be most appropriate for a program to do each of the following applications and why?
   a. Compute trajectories for a satellite launcher.
   b. Monitor an input device feeding data from an experiment to the computer.
   c. Process the day's transactions at an ATM (automated teller machine).

10. Write a C++ *Do_Circumference* function for the *Rectangle* class of Figure 8.5.

11. Draw a class hierarchy diagram similar to Figure 8.7 for the following classes:

    Student, Undergraduate_Student, Graduate_Student, Sophomore, Senior, PhD_Student

12. Imagine that you are writing a program using an object-oriented programming language. Your program will be used to maintain records for a real estate office. Decide on one class in your program, and cite a service that objects of that class might provide.

13. In the vendor database described in Section 8.4.1, the user wants to know all of the cities where there are vendors from whom the store bought more than $10,000 worth of stock the previous business quarter. Write an SQL query for this information.

14. A user submits a form via the World Wide Web. The text string received looks like this:

    name＝Evan＋Burke&card＝Visa&number＝
    8443261344895&order＝French＋perfume

    A Perl program is used to extract the information. What information has the user supplied?

15. Describe what you think the corresponding text on a Web page will look like if this is the HTML statement:

    ```
    <p><center> <font size =12 color
    = "green"> How Now Brown Cow
    </center></p>
    ```

16. What will be the result of the following Scheme expression?

    (car (cdr (cdr (list 16 19 21))))

17. Write a Scheme function that returns a list consisting of the first two values in the input list but in the opposite order.

18. Consider the following Scheme function:

    ```
    (define (mystery input-list)
      (cond ((null? input-list) 0)
        (else ( + 1 (mystery (cdr
          input-list))))))
    ```

    What is the result of invoking the function as follows?

    (mystery (list 3 4 5))

    Explain what this function does in general.

19. Consider the following Scheme function:

    ```
    (define (unknown n)
      (cond ((= n 1) 1)
        (else (* n (unknown
          (- n 1))))))
    ```

    The condition (= n 1) means "If $n = 1$ . . . ." What do you think will be the result of the following function invocation?

    (unknown 4)

20. After the rule
    ```
    earlier(X,Y) :- president(R,X),
      president(S,Y), precedes(R,S).
    ```

    is added to the Prolog program of Figure 8.12, what is the result of each of the following queries?

    a. ?- earlier(lewis_and_clark, civil_war).
    b. ?-earlier(world_war_II, first_moon_landing).
    c. ?-earlier(X, world_war_II).

21. Here is the beginning of a Prolog program about a family. The facts are

```
male(eli)
male(bill)
male(joe)
female(mary)
female(betty)
female(sarah)
parent-of(eli, bill)
parent-of(mary, bill)
parent-of(bill, joe
parent-of(bill, betty)
parent-of(bill, sarah)
```

The declaration

```
male(eli)
```

asserts that Eli is male, and

```
parent-of(eli, bill)
```

asserts that Eli is Bill's parent. Draw a "family tree" based on these facts.

22. Add to the Prolog program of Exercise 21 a rule to define "father-of".

23. Add to the Prolog program of Exercise 21 a rule to define "daughter-of".

24. a. Add to the Prolog program of Exercise 21 a rule to define "ancestor-of".
    b. After this rule is added, determine the result of the query

    ?-ancestor-of(X,sarah)

25. Suppose the symbolic arrangement of Figure 8.16 is used in a divide-and-conquer algorithm to compute the largest element in a list of eight elements. Assume that the time to partition a list in half and pass it to subprocessors is $0.003n$ μsec, where n is the size of the list to be partitioned. Assume that the time to compare two values and find the larger of the two is 1 μsec. Assume that the time to pass the larger value back to a parent processor is 0.001 μsec. Compute the time required to do this task compared with doing it on a sequential processor that uses the "find largest" algorithm of Chapter 2, which also involves a series of comparisons of two values and finding the larger of the two.

CHALLENGE WORK

1. An automobile leasing company has asked you to design an object-oriented program to manage its business. The company leases both cars and trucks and wants to keep track of information about vehicles it has available for lease. It also wants to be able to compute the terms of lease financing for any particular vehicle.

   You decide that the objects of interest in the company's business are the vehicles available for lease. Each vehicle has a number of properties, and each should be able to perform the service of computing its own lease terms on the basis of the value of one or more of these properties.

   a. List the properties you would use for a class called *Vehicle*. These might include, for example, the make, model, engine type (V6, V8), retail price, and so on.
   b. All trucks are vehicles, but trucks have some properties, such as towing weight, that don't apply to all vehicles. List the additional properties you would use for a *Truck* subclass of the *Vehicle* class.
   c. The terms of a car lease are based on the following formula:

For a short-term lease (2 years), the down payment is 20% of the retail price of the vehicle. The monthly lease fee includes a payment toward the retail price of the vehicle such that at the end of the lease, 20% of the retail price remains to be paid. In addition, the monthly lease fee includes interest at an annual rate of 12% computed on the "average balance due over the life of the lease," which is half of the purchase price minus the down payment.

For a long-term lease (5 years), the down payment is 20% of the retail price of the vehicle. The monthly lease fee includes a payment toward the retail price of the vehicle such that at the end of the lease, 10% of the retail price remains to be paid. In addition, the monthly lease fee includes interest on the payment at an annual rate of 8% computed on the "average balance due over the life of the lease," which is half of the purchase price minus the down payment..

Write a C++ function called *Lease_Terms* that will allow a vehicle object to compute and write out its lease down payment and monthly payment. Assume that information from the user on whether the lease is short-term or long-term is passed as an argument to this function.

d. Truck leases are always short-term leases, but they require a down payment of only 15%, and the annual interest rate is 10%. Write a C++ function for the *Truck* version of *Lease_Terms*.

2. Find information on one of the Grand Challenge problems of Figure 8.14. Write a report on

- What the problem involves
- The benefits to be obtained from solving it
- Why it is computationally challenging
- Why parallel processing may be able to, or has been able to, help solve it
- The current state of progress toward a solution

FOR FURTHER READING

As with C++, there are many books devoted to each of the programming languages we have discussed. Here are some samples:

Etter, D. M. *Structured FORTRAN 77 for Engineers and Scientists*, 5th ed. Reading, MA: Addison-Wesley, 1997.

Zirkel, G., and Berlinger, E. *Understanding FORTRAN 77 and 90.* Boston, MA: PWS, 1994.

Stern, N., and Stern, R. *Structured COBOL Programming*, 8th ed. New York: Wiley, 1997.

Leestma, S., and Nyhoff, L. *Pascal Programming and Problem Solving with Software*, 4th ed. Englewood Cliffs, NJ: Prentice-Hall, 1993.

Savitch, W. *Pascal, An Introduction to the Art and Science of Programming*, 4th ed. Reading, MA: Addison-Wesley, 1995.

Deitel, H. M., and Deitel, P. J. *C: How to Program*, 2nd ed. Englewood Cliffs, NJ: Prentice-Hall, 1994.

Hanly, J. R., and Koffman, E. *Problem Solving and Program Design in C*, 2nd ed. Reading, MA: Addison-Wesley, 1996.

Feldman, M., and Koffman, E., *Ada 95: Problem Solving and Program Design*, 2nd ed. Reading, MA: Addison-Wesley, 1997.

Bishop, J. *Java Gently.* Reading, MA: Addison-Wesley, 1997.

Lewis, J., and Loftus, W. *Java Software Solutions: Foundations of Program Design.* Reading, MA: Addison-Wesley, 1997.

Lambert, K., and Osborne, M. *Smalltalk in Brief: Introduction to Object-Oriented Software Development.* Boston: PWS, 1997.

Honeycutt, J. *Using HTML 4*, 4th ed., Special Edition. Indianapolis, IN: QUE Publishing, 1997.

Springer, G., and Friedman, D. P. *Scheme and the Art of Programming*. New York: McGraw-Hill, 1989.

Covington, M. A.; Nute, D.; and Vellino, A. *Prolog Programming in Depth*. Englewood Cliffs, NJ: Prentice-Hall, 1997.

For an easy introduction to programming from an object-oriented point of view, see

Bergin, J.; Stehlik, M.; Roberts, J.; and Pattis, R. *Karel++, A Gentle Introduction to the Art of Object-Oriented Programming*. New York: Wiley, 1997.

The following book is a standard on object-oriented design and the object-oriented approach:

Booch, G. *Object-Oriented Analysis and Design with Applications*, 2nd ed. Reading, MA: Addison-Wesley, 1994.

The following books offer more advanced discussions on the theory and issues behind programming language design and implementation:

Sethi, R. *Programming Languages: Concepts and Constructs*, 2nd ed. Reading, MA: Addison-Wesley, 1996.

Pratt, T. W., and Zelkowitz, M. *Programming Languages: Design and Implementation*, 3rd ed. Englewood Cliffs, NJ: Prentice-Hall, 1996.

COMPILERS AND LANGUAGE TRANSLATION

9.1 INTRODUCTION

The previous two chapters described a number of high-level languages that differ widely in structure and behavior. However, though they are quite different in design, they are all identical in one respect: No computer in the world can understand them. There are no "C++ computers" or "Pascal processors" that can execute programs directly in the high-level languages of Chapters 7 and 8. In Chapter 6 we learned that assembly language must be translated into machine language prior to execution. High-level languages must also be translated into machine language prior to execution—this time by a special piece of system software called a **compiler**. Compilers for languages like those discussed in Chapters 7 and 8 are very complex programs. They contain thousands of lines of code and require dozens of person-years to complete. Unlike the assemblers of Chapter 6, these translators are definitely *not* easy to design or implement.

There is a simple explanation for the vast difference in complexity between assemblers and compilers. Assembly language and machine language are related **1-to-1**; that is, one assembly language instruction produces exactly one machine language instruction. In this case, translation is really a replacement process in which the assembler looks up a symbolic value in a table (either the op code table or the symbol table) and replaces it by its numeric equivalent:

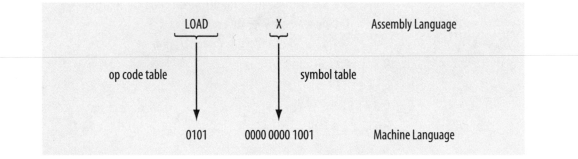

This is equivalent to translating English into Spanish by looking up each individual English word in an English/Spanish dictionary and replacing it by exactly one Spanish word:

This is a book.

Este es un libro.

This is a simple way to do translation, and this approach does work for assemblers. Unfortunately, for most English sentences it does not. Often, a single English word must be translated into a multiword Spanish phrase or vice versa. This same problem exists in the translation of high-level programming languages like C++.

The relationship between a high-level language and machine language is not 1-to-1 but **1-to-many**. That is, one high-level language statement, such as an assignment or conditional, usually produces *many* machine language or assembly language instructions. For example,

C++		Assembly Language	
a = b + c - d;	→	LOAD	B
		ADD	C
		SUBTRACT	D
		STORE	A

To determine which machine language instructions must be generated, a compiler cannot simply look up a name in a table. Instead, it must do a thorough linguistic analysis of the structure (syntax) and meaning (semantics) of each high-level language statement. This is far more difficult than table look-up, and writing a compiler can be a daunting task, not unlike building the operating systems discussed in Chapter 6. In fact, building a compiler for a modern high-level programming language can be one of the most difficult of system software projects.

When performing a translation, a compiler has two distinct goals. The first is **correctness**. The machine language code produced by the compiler must do exactly what the high-level language statement describes, and nothing else. For example, here is a typical C++ assignment statement:

```
A = (B + C) - (D + E);
```

Assume that a compiler translates this statement into the following assembly language code:

```
-- Compute the term (B + C)

         LOAD    B        -- Register R holds the value of B

         ADD     C        -- Now it holds the result (B + C)

         STORE   B        -- Let's store the result temporarily in B (See comments below)

-- Next compute the term (D + E)

         LOAD    D        -- Register R holds the value of D

         ADD     E        -- Now it holds the result (D + E)

         STORE   D        -- Let's store the result temporarily in D (See comments below)
```

-- Finally, subtract the two terms and store the result in A

LOAD	B	-- This loads (B + C)
SUBTRACT	D	-- This is (B + C) − (D + E)
STORE	A	-- Put the result in A. We are done translating the statement.

This translation is *wrong*. Although the code does evaluate $(B + C) − (D + E)$ and store the result into A, it does two things it should not do. The translated program destroys the original contents of the variables B and D when it does the first two STORE operations. This is *not* what the C++ assignment statement is supposed to do, and this compiler has produced an incorrect translation. All of its efforts to translate this statement into machine language have been for naught.

In addition to correctness, a compiler has a second goal. The code it produces should be reasonably **efficient** and **concise**. Even though memory costs have come down and processors are much faster, programmers will not accept gross inefficiencies in either execution speed or size of the compiled program. They may not care whether a compiler eliminates every wasted microsecond or every unnecessary memory cell, but they do want it to produce reasonably fast and efficient machine language code. For example, to compute the sum $2x_0 + 2x_1 + 2x_2 + \ldots + 2x_{50,000}$, an inexperienced programmer might write

```
sum = 0.0;
i = 0;
while (i <= 50000)
{
        sum = sum + (2.0 * x[i]);
        i = i + 1;
}
```

This loop includes the time-consuming multiplication operation (2.0 * x[i]). By the rules of arithmetic, this operation can be moved outside the loop and done just once. A "smart" compiler should recognize this and translate the previous fragment as though it had been written as follows:

```
sum = 0.0;
i = 0;
while (i <= 50000)
{
        sum = sum + x[i];
        i = i + 1;
};
sum = sum * 2.0;
```

By restructuring the loop, a smart compiler saves 50,000 unnecessary multiplications.

As you can see, we have our work cut out for us in this chapter. We want to describe how to construct a compiler that can read and interpret high-level language statements, understand what they are trying to do, correctly translate their intentions into machine language without errors or unexpected side effects, and do all of this cleverly and efficiently. Building a compiler is a major undertaking.

The remainder of this chapter gives an overview of the steps involved in building a compiler for a procedural, "C++-like" language. No single chapter could investigate the subtleties and complexities of this huge subject. We can, however, give you an appreciation for some of the issues and concepts involved in designing and implementing this important piece of system software.

9.2 THE COMPILATION PROCESS

The general structure of a compiler is shown in Figure 9.1. However, there is a good deal of variability in the design and organization of a compiler, so this diagram should be viewed more as an idealized model than as an exact description of how all compilers are structured. The four phases of compilation listed in Figure 9.1 are

- *Phase I: Lexical analysis.* Here is where the compiler examines the individual characters in the source program and groups them into syntactical units, called tokens, that will be analyzed in succeeding stages. This operation is analogous to grouping letters into words prior to analyzing text.

- *Phase II: Parsing.* During this stage the sequence of tokens formed by the scanner is checked to see whether it is syntactically correct according to the rules of the programming language. This phase is roughly equivalent to checking whether the words in the text form grammatically correct sentences.

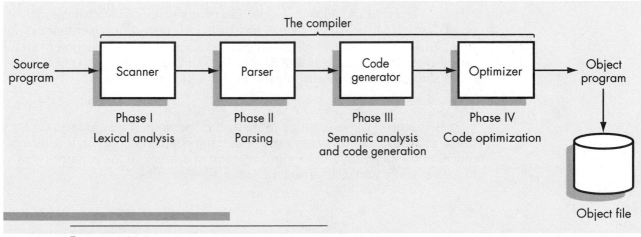

FIGURE 9.1

General Structure of a Compiler

- *Phase III: Semantic analysis and code generation.* If the high-level language statement is structurally correct, then the compiler analyzes its meaning and generates the proper sequence of machine language instructions to carry out these actions.
- *Phase IV: Code optimization.* During this phase the compiler takes the generated code and sees whether it can be made more efficient, either by making it run faster or having it occupy less memory.

When these four phases are complete, we will have a correct and efficient machine language translation of the original high-level language **source program**. In the final step this machine language code, called the **object program**, is written to an **object file**. We have reached the stage labeled "Machine language program" in Figure 6.4, and the resulting object program can be handled in exactly the fashion shown in that figure. That is, it can be loaded into memory by the loader and executed by the processor to produce the desired results.

The overall sequence of operations performed on a high-level language program is summarized in Figure 9.2. The following sections take a closer look at each of the four phases of the compilation process.

9.2.1 PHASE I: LEXICAL ANALYSIS

The first step in the compilation process is **lexical analysis**, and the program that performs it is called, appropriately enough, a **lexical analyzer**, although it is more commonly termed a **scanner**. Its job is to group input characters into units called **tokens**. These are syntactical units that are treated as single, indivisible entities for the purposes of translation. For example, take a look at the following assignment statement:

```
a = b + 319 − delta;
```

Your eyes probably saw an assignment statement containing some symbols (*a*, *b*, *delta*), a number (319), and some operators (=, +, −, ;). However, your eyes and your brain actually had to do a great deal of processing to create these objects, just as they have to do a great deal of processing to create words, sentences, and paragraphs from the individual characters on this page. In the assignment statement shown above, high-level linguistic objects such as symbols and numbers do not yet exist. Initially, there are only the following 21 characters:

tab, a, blank, =, blank, b, blank, +, blank, 3, 1, 9, blank, −, blank, d, e, l, t, a, ;

It is the task of the scanner to discard nonessential characters, such as blanks and tabs, and then group the remaining characters into high-level syntactical units such as symbols, numbers, and operators. In the example shown above, a scanner would construct the following eight tokens:

a

=

b

+

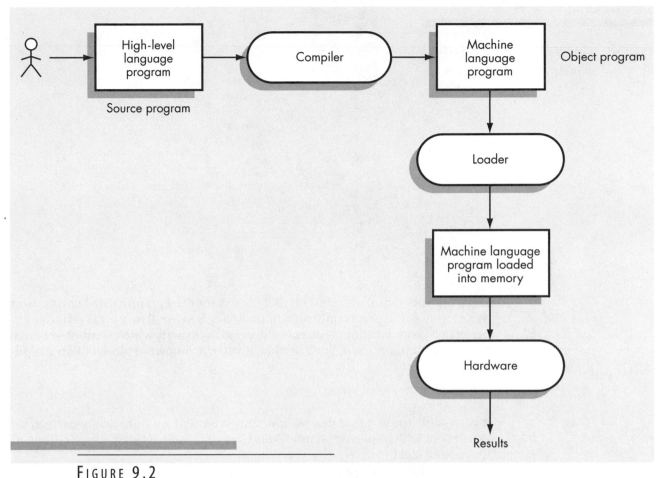

FIGURE 9.2

Overall Execution Sequence on a High-Level Language Program

319

—

delta

;

From now on, our compiler will no longer have to deal with individual characters. Instead, it can work at the level of symbols (such as *delta*), numbers (319), and operators (+, −).

In addition to building tokens, a scanner must classify tokens as to type—that is, is each a symbol, a number, an assignment operator? A powerful language like C++ may have 40 or 50 token types. Our simple examples are limited to the classifications listed in Figure 9.3.

The scanner assigns the classification number 1 to all legal symbols, such as *a*, *b*, and *delta*. Similarly, all numbers, regardless of their specific value, are assigned classification number 2. The reason why all symbols and all numbers

FIGURE 9.3

Typical Token Classifications

Token Type	Classification Number
symbol	1
number	2
=	3
+	4
–	5
;	6
==	7
if	8
else	9
(	10
)	11

can be grouped into a single classification is that the grammatical correctness of a statement depends only on whether a legal symbol or a legal number appears in a given location. It does not depend on exactly which symbol or which number is actually used. For example, given the following model of an assignment statement:

"symbol" = "symbol" + "number";

it is possible to state that this assignment statement is syntactically correct, regardless of which specific "symbol" and "number" are actually used (as long as they are all legal).

Using the token types and classification values shown in Figure 9.3, it is now possible to describe exactly what a scanner must do:

> *The input to a scanner is a high-level language statement from the source program. Its output is a list of all the tokens contained in that statement as well as the classification number of each token found.*

Here are some examples (using the classification values shown in Figure 9.3):

Input:	`a = b + 319 − delta;`	
Output:	Token	Classification
	a	1
	=	3
	b	1
	+	4
	319	2

—	5
delta	1
;	6

Input: **if** (*a* == *b*) *xx* = 13; **else** *xx* = 2;

Output: *Token*   *Classification*

Token	Classification
if	8
(	10
a	1
==	7
b	1
)	11
xx	1
=	3
13	2
;	6
else	9
xx	1
=	3
2	2
;	6

Regardless of which programming language is being analyzed, every scanner does virtually the same set of operations: (1) It discards blanks and other nonessential characters looking for the beginning of a token. (2) When it finds the beginning, it puts characters together until (3) it detects the end of the token, at which point it classifies the token and begins looking for the next one. This algorithm works properly regardless of what the tokens look like.

We can see this process more clearly by looking at an algorithm for grouping natural language characters into words:

This is English.
Este es Espanol.
Kore wa Nihongo desu.

Even though these three sentences are in different languages, the algorithm for constructing words is identical: (1) Discard blanks until you find a nonblank character. (2) Group characters together until (3) you encounter either a blank or the character ".". You have now built a word. Go back to step 1 and repeat the entire sequence to locate the next word. This is essentially the same algorithm that is used to build a lexical scanner for high-level programming languages.

PRACTICE PROBLEMS

Using the token types and classification numbers given in Figure 9.3, determine the output of a scanner given the following input statements.

a. `x = x + 1;`

b. `if (a + b42 == 0) a = zz - 12;`

9.2.2 PHASE II: PARSING

INTRODUCTION. During the **parsing** phase, a compiler determines whether the tokens recognized by the scanner during phase I fit together in a grammatically meaningful way. That is, it determines whether they are a syntactically legal statement of the programming language. This step is analogous to the operation of "diagramming a sentence" that is taught in elementary school. For example, to prove that the sequence of words

The man bit the dog

is a correctly formed sentence, we must show that the individual words can be grouped together structurally to form a proper English language sentence:

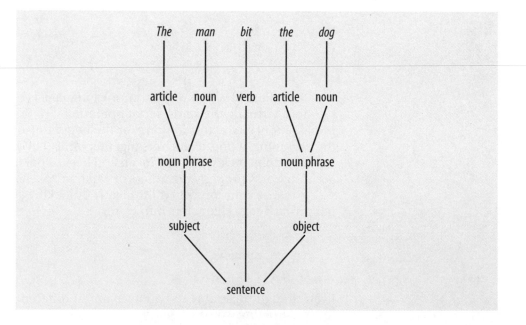

If we are unable to diagram the sentence, then it is not correctly formed. For example, when we try to analyze the sequence "The man bit the", here is what happens:

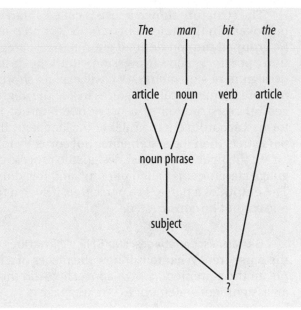

At this point in the analysis we are stuck, because there is no object for the verb "bit." We cannot diagram the sentence and must conclude that it is not properly formed.

The same thing happens with statements in a programming language, which are roughly analogous to sentences in a natural language. If a compiler is able to "diagram" a statement such as $a = b + c$, it concludes that the statement is structurally correct:

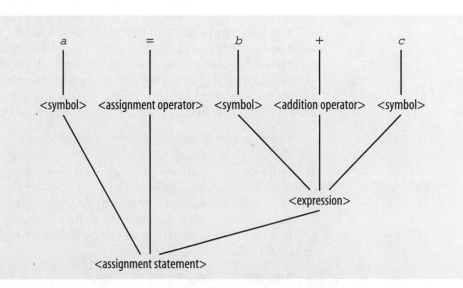

The structure shown above is called a **parse tree**. It starts from the individual tokens in the statement, a, $=$, b, $+$, and c, and shows how these tokens can be grouped into predefined grammatical categories such as <symbol>, <addition operator>, and <expression> until the desired goal is reached, in this case, <assignment statement>. (We will explain shortly why we are writing the names of these grammatical categories inside the angle brackets "<" and ">".) The successful construction of a parse tree is proof that this statement is correctly formed according to the rules of the language. If a parser cannot produce such a parse tree, then the statement is not correctly formed.

In the field of compiler design, the process of diagramming a high-level language statement is called **parsing**, and it is done by a program called a **parser**. The output of a parser is a parse tree, if such a tree exists, or an error message if one cannot be constructed.

GRAMMARS, LANGUAGES, AND BNF.   How does a parser know how to construct the parse tree? What tells it how the pieces of a language fit together? For example, in the statement shown above, how did the parser know that the format of an assignment statement in our language is

<symbol> = <expression>

The answer is that it does not know; we must tell it. The parser must be given a formal description of the **syntax**—the grammatical structure—of the language that it is going to analyze. The most widely used notation for representing the syntax of a programming language is called **BNF**, an acronym for **Backus-Naur Form**, named after its designers John Backus and Peter Naur.

In BNF, the syntax of a language is specified as a set of **rules**, also called **productions**. The entire collection of rules is called a **grammar**. Each individual BNF rule looks like this:

left-hand side ::= "definition"

The **left-hand side** of a BNF rule is the name of a single grammatical category, such as <symbol>, <expression>, or <assignment statement>. The BNF operator ::= means "is defined as," and "definition," which is also called the **right-hand side**, specifies the grammatical structure of the symbol appearing on the left-hand side of the rule. The definition may contain any number of objects. For example, here is a BNF rule that defines how an <assignment statement> is formed:

<assignment statement> ::= <symbol> = <expression>

This rule says that the syntactical construct called <assignment statement> is defined as a <symbol> followed by the token = followed by the syntactical construct called <expression>. In order to have a structurally correct assignment statement, these three objects must all be present in exactly that order.

Here is a BNF rule that gives one possible definition for the English language construct called <sentence>.

<sentence> ::= <subject> <verb> <object>

This rule says that a <sentence> is defined as a <subject> followed by a <verb> followed by an <object>. It is this rule that allowed us to parse "The man bit the dog."

Finally, the simple BNF rule

<addition operator> ::= +

says that the grammatical construct <addition operator> is defined as the single character +.

If a parser is analyzing a statement in a language, and it sees exactly the same sequence of objects that appears on the right-hand side of a BNF rule, it is allowed to replace them with the one grammatical object on the left-hand side of that rule. For example, given our BNF rule for <assignment statement>:

<assignment statement> ::= <symbol> = <expression>

if a parser encounters the three objects <symbol>, =, and <expression> next to each other in the input, it can replace them with the object appearing on the left-hand side of the rule—in this case, <assignment statement>. In a sense, the parser is constructing one branch of the parse tree, which looks like this:

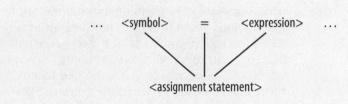

We say that the three objects, <symbol>, =, and <expression>, **produce** the grammatical category called <assignment statement>, and that is why a BNF rule is also called a **production**.

BNF rules use two different types of objects, called **terminals** and **nonterminals**, on the right-hand side of a production. **Terminals** are the actual tokens of the language recognized and returned by a scanner. The terminals of our language are the 11 tokens listed in Figure 9.3:

<symbol>	==
<number>	**if**
=	**else**
+	(
−	)
;	

The important characteristic of terminals is that they are not defined any further by other rules of the grammar. That is, there is no rule in the grammar that explains the "meaning" of such objects as <symbol>, =, +, and **if**. They are simply elements of the language, much like the words *man*, *bit*, and *dog* in our earlier example.

The second type of object used in a BNF rule is a **nonterminal**. A nonterminal is not an actual element of the language but an intermediate grammatical category used to help explain and organize the language. For example, in the analysis of the English sentence "The man bit the dog," we created grammatical categories called article, noun, verb, noun phrase, subject, and object. These categories help us to understand the structure of the sentence and show that it is correctly formed, but they are not actual words of the sentence being studied.

In every grammar, there is one special nonterminal called the **goal symbol**. This is the highest-level nonterminal, and it is the nonterminal object that the parser is trying to produce as it builds the parse tree. When the parser has produced the goal symbol, it has proved the syntactical correctness of the sentence or statement being analyzed. In our English language example, the goal symbol is <sentence>; in our assignment statement example, it is, naturally, <assignment statement>. When this nonterminal goal symbol has been produced, the parser has finished building the tree, and the statement has been successfully parsed. The collection of all statements that can be successfully parsed is called the **language** defined by a grammar.

All nonterminals are written inside angle brackets; examples include <expression> and <assignment statement>. Some terminals also are written in angle brackets when they do not represent actual characters of the language (such as +) but rather groups of characters constructed by the scanner, such as <symbol> or <number>. However, it is easy to tell the difference between the two. A terminal like <symbol> is not defined by any other rule of the language. That is, there is no rule anywhere in the grammar that looks like this:

<symbol> ::= "definition of a symbol"

Terminal symbols are like the words and punctuation marks of a language, and a parser does not have to know anything more about their syntactical structure in order to analyze a sentence.

However, nonterminals are constructed by the parser from more elementary syntactical units. Therefore, nonterminals such as <expression> and <assignment statement> must be further defined by one or more rules that specify exactly how this nonterminal is constructed. For example, there must exist at least one rule in our grammar that has the nonterminal <expression> as the left-hand side. This rule tells the parser how to form expressions from other terminals and nonterminals:

<expression> ::= "definition of expression"

Similarly, there must be at least one rule that specifies the structure of an assignment statement:

<assignment statement> ::= "definition of assignment statement"

We can summarize the difference between terminals and nonterminals by saying that terminals never appear on the left-hand side of a BNF rule, whereas nonterminals must appear on the left-hand side of one or more rules.

The three symbols <, >, and ::= used as part of BNF rules are termed **meta-symbols**. This means that they are symbols of one language (BNF) that are being used to describe the characteristics of another language. In addition to these three, there are two other metasymbols used in BNF definitions. The vertical bar, |, means OR, and it is used to separate two alternative definitions of a nonterminal. This could be done without the vertical bar by just writing two separate rules:

<nonterminal> ::= "definition 1"

<nonterminal> ::= "definition 2"

However, it is sometimes more convenient to use the | character and write a single rule:

<nonterminal> ::= "definition 1" | "definition 2"

For example, the rule

<arithmetic operator> ::= + | − | * | /

says that an arithmetic operator is defined as *either* a + *or* a − *or* a * *or* a /. Without the | operator, we would need to write four separate rules, which would make the grammar much larger. Here is a rule that defines the nonterminal <digit>:

<digit> ::= 0 | 1 | 2 | 3 | 4 | 5 | 6 | 7 | 8 | 9

We will see many more examples of the use of the OR operator.

The final metasymbol used in BNF definitions is the Greek character lambda, Λ, which represents the **null string**—nothing at all. It is possible that a nonterminal can be "empty," and the symbol Λ is used to indicate this. For example, the nonterminal <signed integer> can be defined as an optional sign preceding an integer value, such as +7 or −5 or 8. To define the idea of an optional sign in BNF, we could say:

<signed integer> ::= <sign> <number>

<sign>   ::= + | − | Λ

which says that <sign> may be either a + or a −, or it may be omitted entirely.

PARSING CONCEPTS AND TECHNIQUES.   Given this brief introduction to grammars, languages, and BNF, we can now explain how a parser works. A parser receives as input the BNF description of a high-level language and a sequence of tokens recognized by the scanner. The fundamental rule of parsing follows.

> *If, by repeated applications of the rules of the grammar, a parser can convert the sequence of input tokens into the goal symbol, then that sequence of tokens is a syntactically valid statement of the language. If it cannot convert the input tokens into the goal symbol, then this is* not *a syntactically valid statement of the language.*

PRACTICE PROBLEMS

1. Write a single BNF rule that defines the nonterminal <Boolean operator>. (Assume that the three possible Boolean operators are AND, OR, and NOT.)

2. Create a BNF grammar that describes all 1- or 2-character identifiers that begin with the letter *i* or *j*. The second character, if present, can be any letter or digit. What is the goal symbol of your grammar?

3. Write a BNF grammar that describes Boolean expressions of the form

   (var op var)

   where "var" can be one of the symbols *x*, *y*, and *z*, and "op" can be one of the three relational operators ==, >, and <. The parentheses are part of the expression.

4. Using the grammar created in Problem 3, show the parse tree for the expression $(x > y)$.

5. Using the grammar created in Problem 3, show what happens when you try to parse the illegal expression $(x ==)$.

6. Modify your grammar from Problem 3 so that the enclosing parentheses are optional. That is, Boolean expressions can be written as either (var op var) or var op var.

To illustrate this idea, here is a three-rule grammar:

Number	Rule
1	<sentence> ::= <noun> <verb> .
2	<noun> ::= bees | dogs
3	<verb> ::= buzz | bite

The grammar contains five terminals: bees, dogs, buzz, bite, and ".", and three nonterminals: <sentence>, <noun>, and <verb>. The goal symbol is <sentence>.

In addition to the grammar, we also provide a sequence of tokens such as "Dogs", "bite", and ".". The parser attempts to transform these tokens into the goal symbol <sentence> using the three BNF rules given above:

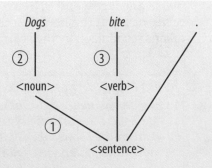

In this case the parse was successful. (The numbers in the diagram indicate which rule is being applied). Thus, "Dogs bite." is a syntactically valid sentence of the language defined by this three-rule grammar. However, the following sequence of tokens:

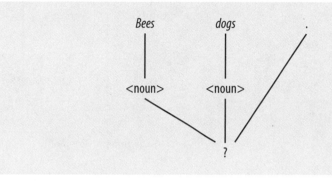

leads to a dead end. We have not yet produced the goal symbol <sentence>, but there is no rule in the grammar that can be applied to the sequence <noun> <noun> ".". That is, no sequence of terminals and nonterminals in the parse tree constructed so far matches the right-hand side of any rule. This means that "Bees dogs." is *not* a valid sentence of our language.

Grammars for "real" high-level languages like C++ are very large, containing hundreds of productions. Therefore, it is not feasible to use these grammars as examples. Even a grammar describing individual statements can be quite complex. For example, the BNF description of a C++ assignment statement, complete with variables, constants, operators, parentheses, and procedure calls, can easily require 20 or 30 rules. Therefore, the following examples all use highly simplified "toy" languages to keep the level of detail manageable and enable us to focus on important concepts.

Our first example is a grammar for a highly simplified assignment statement in which the only operator is $+$, numbers are not permitted, and the only allowable variable names are x, y, and z. A first attempt at designing a grammar for this simplified assignment statement is shown in Figure 9.4.

If the input statement is $x = y + z$, then the parser can determine that this statement is correctly formed because it can construct a parse tree (Figure 9.5). The parse tree of Figure 9.5 is the *output* of the parser, and it is the information that is passed on to the next stage in the compilation process.

FIGURE 9.4

First Attempt at a Grammar for a Simplified Assignment Statement

Number		Rule
1	<assignment statement>	::= <variable> = <expression>
2	<expression>	::= <variable> | <variable> + <variable>
3	<variable>	::= $x \mid y \mid z$

FIGURE 9.5

Parse Tree Produced by the Parser

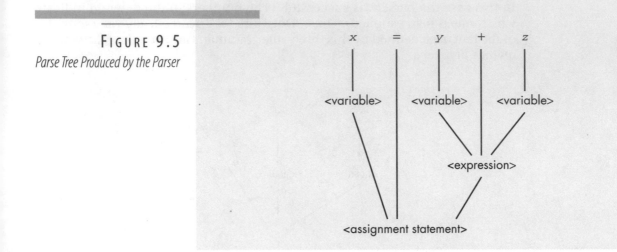

Building a parse tree like the one in Figure 9.5 is not as easy as it may appear. Often two or more rules of a grammar may be applied to the current input string, and the parser is not sure which one to choose. For example, assume that our grammar includes the following two rules:

Number	Rule
1	<t1> ::= A B
2	<t2> ::= B C

and that the statement being parsed contains the 3-character string . . . A B C . . . . We could apply either rule 1:

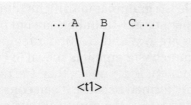

or rule 2:

One of these choices may be correct, whereas the other may lead down a grammatical dead end, and the parser has no idea which is which.

You were probably not aware that an identical situation occurred in the example shown in Figure 9.5. Assume that the parser has reached this position in building the parse tree for the statement $x = y + z$:

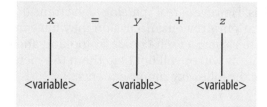

In Figure 9.5, the parser next grouped the three objects <variable>, +, and <variable> into an <expression> using rule 2. However, at this point the parser has other options. For example, it could choose to parse the nonterminal <variable> generated from the symbol y to <expression> using rule 2 and then parse the sequence <variable> = <expression> to <assignment statement> using rule 1. This produces the following parse tree:

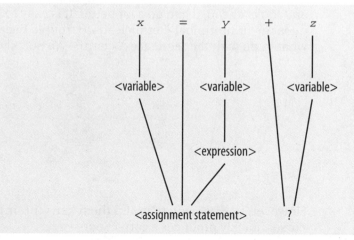

Unfortunately, this was the wrong choice. Although the parser did generate the goal symbol <assignment statement>, it did not use all the tokens. There are an extra plus sign and <variable> that were not used. (What it did was accidentally parse the assignment statement $x = y$ instead of $x = y + z$.) The parser went down the wrong path and has reached a point where it is unable to continue. It must now go back to the point where it made the incorrect choice and try something else. For example, it now might choose to parse the nonterminal <variable> generated from z to <expression> using rule 2. Unfortunately, this is also a dead end; it produces the sequence <variable> + <expression>, which does not match the right-hand side of any rule.

The process of parsing is a complex sequence of applying rules, building grammatical constructs, seeing whether things are moving toward the correct answer (the goal symbol), and, if not, "undoing" the rule just applied and trying another. It is much like finding one's way through a maze. You try one path, and if it works, fine. If not, you back up to where you made your last choice and try another, hoping that this time it will lead in the right direction.

This sounds like a haphazard and disorganized way to analyze statements, and in fact it is. However, "real" parsing algorithms don't rely on a random selection of rules, as our previous discussion may have implied. Instead, they try to be a little more clever in their choice by looking ahead to see whether the rule they plan to apply will or will not help them to reach the goal. For example, assume we have the following input sequence:

    A B C

and this grammar:

    <goal> ::= <term> C

    <term> ::= A B | B C

We have two choices on how to parse the input string. We can either group the two characters A B to form a <term>, or we can group B C instead. A totally random choice will cause us to be wrong about half the time, but if a parser is clever and looks ahead, it can do a lot better. It is easy to see that grouping B C to produce the nonterminal <term> leads to trouble because there is no rule telling us what to do with the sequence A <term>. We quickly come to a dead end:

However, by choosing to group the tokens A B into <term> instead of B C, the parser quickly produces a correct parse tree:

There are many well-known **look-ahead parsing algorithms** that use the ideas just described. These algorithms "look down the road" a few tokens to see what would happen if a certain choice were made. This helps keep the parse moving in the right direction, and it significantly reduces the number of false starts and dead ends. These algorithms can do very efficient parsing, even for large languages with hundreds of rules.

There is another important issue in the design of grammars. Let's assume we attempt to parse the following assignment statement:

$$x = x + y + z$$

using the grammar in Figure 9.4. No matter how hard we try to build a parse tree, it is just not possible:

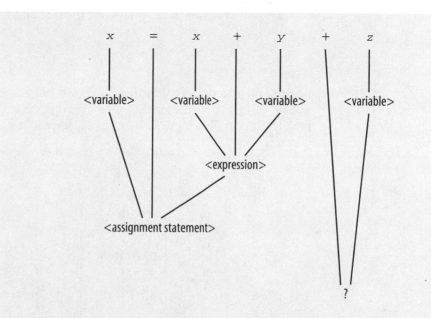

All other attempts lead to a similar fate.

The problem is that the grammar in Figure 9.4 does not correctly describe the desired language. We wanted a language that allowed expressions containing an *arbitrary number* of plus signs. However, the grammar of Figure 9.4 describes a language in which expressions may contain at most a single addition operator. More complicated expressions such as $x + y + z$ cannot be parsed, and they are incorrectly excluded from our language.

One of the biggest problems in building a compiler for a programming language is designing a grammar that

- Includes every valid statement that we want to be in the language
- Excludes every invalid statement that we do *not* want to be in the language

In this case, a statement that should be a part of our language ($x = x + y + z$) was excluded. If this statement were contained in a program, the parser would not recognize it and would not be able to translate it into machine language. The grammar in Figure 9.4 is wrong in the sense that it does not define the language that we wanted.

Rule Number	Rule
1	<assignment statement> ::= <variable> = <expression>
2	<expression> ::= <variable> | <expression> + <expression>
3	<variable> ::= x | y | z

Let's redo the grammar of Figure 9.4 so that it describes an assignment statement that allows expressions containing an arbitrary number of occurrences of the plus sign. That is, our language will include such statements as:

```
x = x + y + z
x = x + x + x + y + x + z + z
```

This second attempt at a grammar is shown in Figure 9.6.

The grammar in Figure 9.6 does recognize and accept expressions with more than one plus sign. For example, here is a parse tree for the statement $x = x + y + z$:

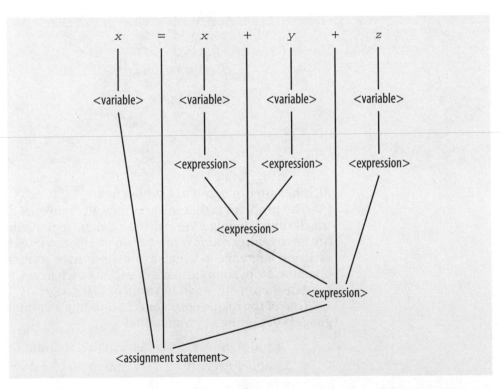

Note that rule 2 of Figure 9.6 uses the nonterminal <expression> on both the left-hand and the right-hand side of the same rule. In essence, the rule defines the nonterminal symbol <expression> in terms of itself. This is called a **recursive definition**, and its use is very common in BNF. (We saw another use of recursion when we discussed the Scheme functional programming language in Chapter 8.) It is recursion that allows us to describe an expression not just with one or two or three or . . . plus signs but with an *arbitrary* and *unbounded* number.

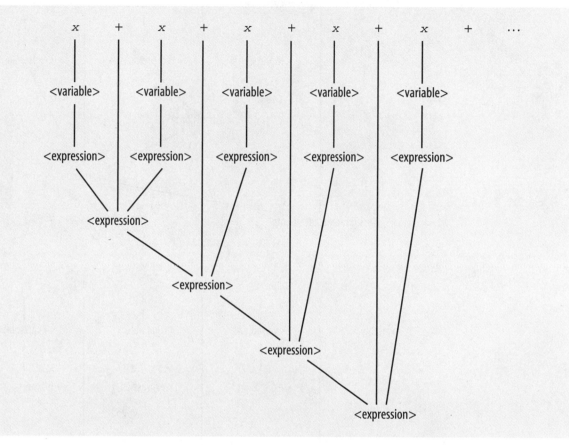

We have solved one problem, that of making sure our grammar defines a language that includes expressions with multiple addition operators. Unfortunately, though one problem has disappeared, another has unexpectedly popped up, and the grammar of Figure 9.6 is still not correct. To demonstrate the nature of this new problem, let's take the same statement that we have been analyzing:

    x = x + y + z

and construct another parse tree using the grammar of Figure 9.6. Both trees are shown in Figure 9.7.

Using this assignment statement and the grammar in Figure 9.6, it is possible to construct *two* parse trees. This may not seem to be a problem, because the construction of a parse tree has been used only to demonstrate that a statement is correctly formed. Building two parse trees would imply that the parser has demonstrated correctness in two different ways. This should be twice as good as demonstrating correctness in only one way.

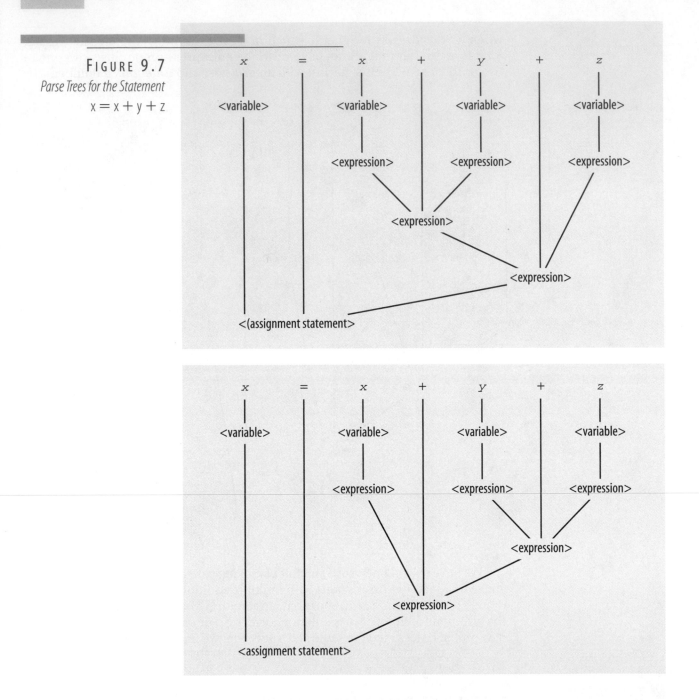

FIGURE 9.7
Parse Trees for the Statement
x = x + y + z

However, a parse tree not only serves to demonstrate that a statement is correct; it also assigns it a specific *meaning*, or *interpretation*. The next phase of compilation will use this parse tree to understand what a statement means, and it will generate code on the basis of that meaning. The existence of two different parse trees implies two different interpretations of the same statement, which is disastrous. A grammar that allows the construction of two or more distinct parse trees for the same statement is said to be **ambiguous**.

This problem can occur in natural languages as well as programming languages. Consider the following ambiguous sentence:

I saw the man in the store with the dogs.

This sentence has two distinct meanings depending on how we choose to parse it:

Interpretation 1: I saw the man in the *store* (with the dogs).

Meaning: The man I viewed was in a pet store that sells dogs.

Interpretation 2: I saw the *man* in the store (with the dogs).

Meaning: The man I viewed was walking his dogs and was inside some type of store.

These two interpretations say very different things, so the sentence can leave us confused about what the speaker meant. In the areas of languages and grammars, ambiguity is decidedly *not* a desirable property.

The two parse trees shown in Figure 9.7 correspond to the following two interpretations of the assignment statement $x = x + y + z$.

$x = (x + y) + z$ (Do the operation $x + y$ first.)

$x = x + (y + z)$ (Do the operation $y + z$ first.)

Because addition is associative [that is, $(a + b) + c = a + (b + c)$], in this case the ambiguity does not cause a serious problem. However, if the statement were changed slightly to

$x = x - y - z$

then these two different interpretations could lead to completely different results:

$x = (x - y) - z$ which evaluates to $x - y - z$

$x = x - (y - z)$ which evaluates to $x - y + z$

We now have a situation where a statement could mean one thing using compiler C on machine M and something totally different using compiler C' on machine M', depending on which parse tree it happens to construct. This contradicts the spirit of machine independence, which is a basic characteristic of all high-level languages.

To solve the problem, the assignment statement grammar must be rewritten a third time so that it is no longer ambiguous. This new grammar is shown in Figure 9.8. To see that the grammar of Figure 9.8 is not ambiguous, try parsing the statement $x = x + y + z$ in the two ways shown in Figure 9.7. You will see that one of these two parse trees cannot be built.

As a second example, Figure 9.9 shows the BNF grammar for a simplified version of the C++ **if-else** statement that allows only a single assignment state-

FIGURE 9.8	*Rule Number*	*Rule*
Third Attempt at a Grammar	1	<assignment statement> ::= <variable> = <expression>
for Assignment Statements	2	<expression> ::= <variable> | <expression> + <variable>
	3	<variable> ::= $x \mid y \mid z$

FIGURE 9.9	*Number*	*Rule*
Grammar for a Simplified	1	<if statement> ::= **if** (<Boolean expression>) <assignment statement> ;
Version of the C++		<else clause>
***if-else** Statement*	2	<Boolean expression> ::= <variable> | <variable> <relational> <variable>
	3	<relational> ::= == | < | >
	4	<variable> ::= $x \mid y \mid z$
	5	<else clause> ::= **else** <assignment statement> ; | Λ
	6	<assignment statement> ::= <variable> = <expression>
	7	<expression> ::= <variable> | <expression> + <variable>

PRACTICE PROBLEMS

1. Using the grammar of Figure 9.8, show the parse tree for the assignment statement

    ```
    x = x + y
    ```

2. Using the grammar of Figure 9.8, show the parse tree for the assignment statement

    ```
    x = x + y + z
    ```

3. Using the grammar of Figure 9.9, show the parse tree for the statement

    ```
    if (x > y) x = y;
    ```

4. Tell what language is described by the following pair of rules:

    <string> ::= <character> \| <character> <string>

    <character> ::= $a \mid b$

5. Write a BNF grammar that describes strings containing any number of repetitions of the character pair AB. That is, all of the following strings are part of the language: AB ABAB ABABAB ABABABABAB . . . .

ment in the two separate clauses and allows the **else** clause to be omitted. The <Boolean expression> can include at most a single use of the relational operators ==, <, and >. The nonterminal <assignment statement> is defined in the same way as in Figure 9.8. Figure 9.10 shows the parse tree for the statement

```
if (x == y) x = z; else x = y;
```

using the grammar of Figure 9.9.

Even though this **if-else** statement has been greatly simplified, its grammar still requires seven rules, and its parse trees have become quite "bushy." Grammars for real statements, not our toy ones, can rapidly become large and complicated, and BNF grammars for programming languages like C++, Java, or Pascal can contain many hundreds of productions.

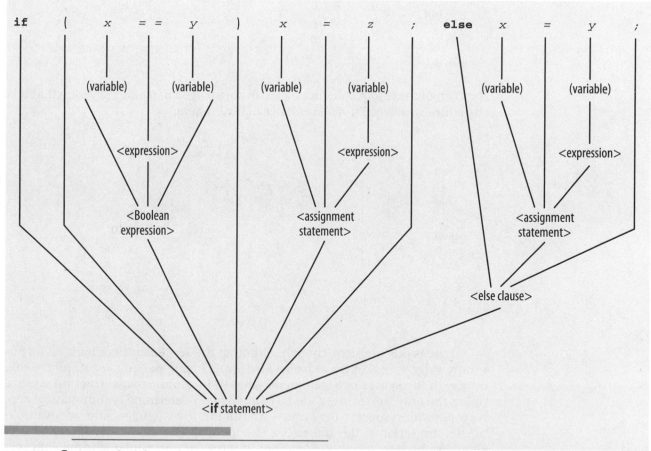

FIGURE 9.10

*Parse Tree for the Statement **if** (x == y) x = z; **else** x = y;*

We have progressed a long way from our original input file, which was simply a sequence of characters. Our compiler has produced a set of tokens and built a parse tree showing how these tokens form a grammatically correct statement. However, we are not yet finished, because we still do not have the necessary end product of compilation—the translated machine language program. That happens in the next stage.

9.2.3 PHASE III: SEMANTICS AND CODE GENERATION

Let's look back at one of the example grammars used in the previous section.

<sentence> ::= <noun> <verb> .

<noun> ::= dogs | bees

<verb> ::= bite | bark

The language defined by this grammar contains exactly four sentences:

dogs bite.

dogs bark.

bees bite.

bees bark.

For each of these four sentences, we can construct a parse tree showing that it is (structurally, at least) a valid sentence of the language:

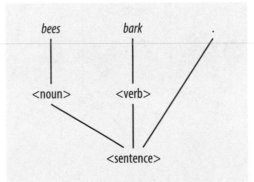

There is one problem, though. Although the sentence "Bees bark." is structurally valid, it makes no sense whatsoever! During parsing, a compiler deals only with the **syntax** of a statement—that is, its grammatical structure. At that point, the only "correctness" that a compiler can determine is grammatical correctness with respect to the syntactical rules of the language. Another example of this limitation is the sentence "The man bit the dog." This sentence was shown to be structurally correct, but in terms of meaning it is somewhat unusual! (It certainly would be news.)

This problem is dealt with during the next phase of translation. During this phase, a compiler examines the **semantics** of a programming language statement. It analyzes the *meaning* of the tokens and tries to understand the *actions* they perform. If the statement is meaningless, as "bees bark" is, then it is semantically rejected, even though it is syntactically correct. If the statement is meaningful, then the compiler translates it into machine language.

It is easy to give examples of English language sentences that are syntactically correct but semantically meaningless:

The orange artichoke flew to the elephant.

But what are semantically meaningless statements in high-level programming languages?

One possibility is the following C++ assignment statement:

```
sum = a + b;
```

This is obviously correct syntactically, but what if the variables *a* and *b* are declared as follows:

```
char a;
double b;
int sum;
```

What does it mean to add a character to a real number? What is the result of adding 'Q' + 3.1416? In most cases this operation has no meaning, and perhaps it should be rejected as semantically invalid. (Most C++ compilers *will* accept this statement and try to turn it into something meaningful, though that is usually a futile task.)

To check for this semantic error, a compiler must look at the parse tree to see whether there is a branch that looks something like this:

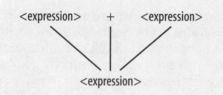

If there is such a branch, then the compiler must examine the data types of the two expressions being added to see whether they "make sense." That is, it must determine whether addition is defined for the data types of the two expressions.

The compiler does this by examining the **semantic records** associated with each nonterminal symbol in the grammar, such as <expression> and <variable>. A semantic record is a data structure that stores information about a nonterminal, such as the actual name of the object and its data type. For example, the nonterminal <variable> might have been constructed from the actual character variable named CH. This relationship would be represented by a link between the nonterminal <variable> and a semantic record containing the name CH and its data type, *char*. Pictorially, we would represent this link as follows:

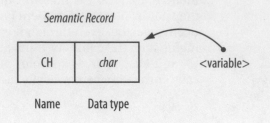

The initial semantic records in our parse tree would be built by the compiler when it saw the declarations of new objects. Additional semantic records would be constructed as the parse tree grew and new nonterminals were produced. Thus, a more realistic picture of the parse tree for the expression $a + b$ (assuming both are declared as integers) might look like this:

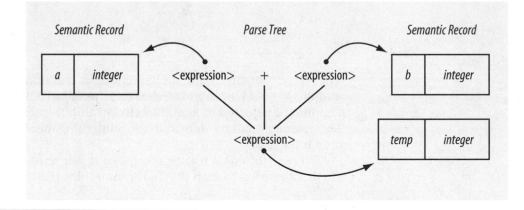

This parse tree says that we are adding two <expression>s that are integer variables named a and b. The result will be an <expression> stored in the integer variable *temp*, a name picked by the compiler. Because addition is well defined for integers, this operation makes perfectly good sense, and the compiler can generate machine language instructions to carry out this addition. If, however, the parse tree and its associated semantic records looked like this:

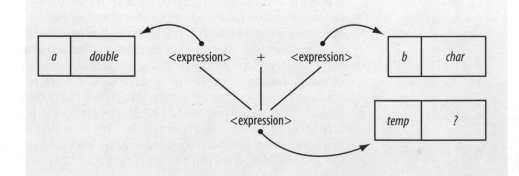

the compiler might determine that this is not a meaningful operation because addition is not defined between a real number and a character. The compiler could reject this parse tree for semantic, rather than syntactical, reasons.

Thus the first part of code generation involves a pass over the parse tree to determine whether all branches of the tree are semantically valid. If so, then the compiler can generate machine language instructions. If not, there is a semantic error, and generation of the machine language is suppressed because we do not want the processor to execute meaningless code. This step is called **semantic analysis**.

Following semantic analysis, the compiler makes a second pass over the parse tree, not to determine correctness but to produce the translated code. Each branch of the parse tree represents an action, a transformation of one or more grammatical objects into another. The compiler must determine how that transformation can be accomplished in machine language. This step is called **code generation**.

Let's work through the complete semantic analysis and code generation process using the parse tree for our old standby, the assignment statement $x = y + z$, where x, y, and z are all integers. The example uses the instruction set shown in Figure 6.5.

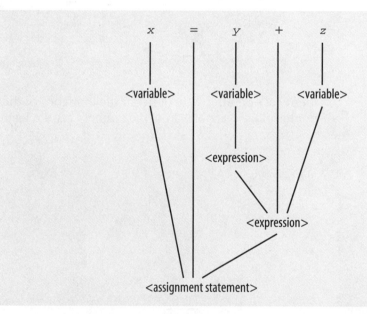

Typically, code generation begins at the productions in the tree that are nearest to the original input tokens. The compiler takes each production and, one branch at a time, translates that production into machine language operations or data generation pseudo-ops. For example, the following branch in the parse tree:

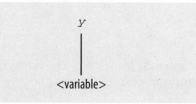

could be implemented by allocating space for the variable *y* using the .DATA pseudo-op

```
Y:    .DATA    0
```

In addition to generating this pseudo-op, the compiler must build the initial semantic record associated with the nonterminal <variable>. This semantic record will contain, at a minimum, the name of this <variable>, which is *y*, and its data type, which is *integer.* (The data type information comes from the C++ **int** declaration, which is not shown.) Here is what is produced after analyzing and translating the first branch of the parse tree:

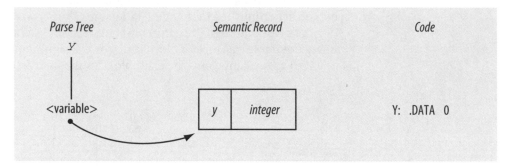

Identical operations are done for the branches of the parse tree that produce the nonterminal <variable> from the symbols *x* and *z*, leading to the following situation:

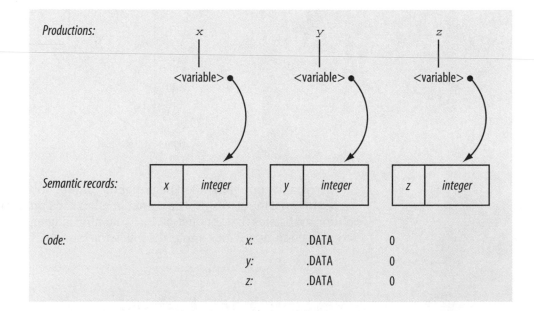

The production that transforms the nonterminal <variable> generated from *y* into the nonterminal <expression>:

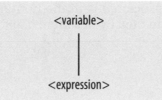

does not generate any machine language code. This branch of the tree is really just the renaming of a nonterminal to avoid the ambiguity problem discussed earlier. This demonstrates an important point: Although most branches of a parse tree produce code, some do not. However, even though no code is produced, the compiler must still create a semantic record for the new nonterminal <expression>. It is identical to the one built for the nonterminal <variable>.

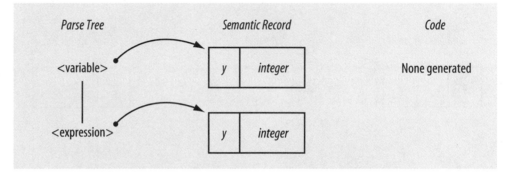

The branch of the parse tree that implements addition:

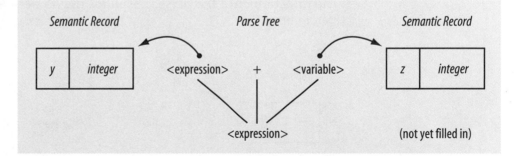

can be translated into machine language using the assembly language instruction set presented in Section 6.3.2. The compiler loads the value of <expression> into a register, adds the value of <variable>, and stores the resulting <expression> into a temporary memory location. This can be accomplished using the LOAD, ADD, and STORE operations in our instruction set. The names to use in the address field of the instructions can be determined by looking in the semantic records associated with the nonterminals <expression> and <variable> . The code generated by this branch of the parse tree is

    LOAD   Y

    ADD   Z

    STORE   TEMP

TEMP is the name of a memory cell picked by the compiler to hold the result (Y + Z). Whenever the compiler creates one of these temporary variables, it must also remember to generate memory space for it using the DATA pseudo-op

    TEMP: .DATA 0

In addition, the compiler records the name (TEMP) and the data type (*integer*) of the result in the semantic record associated with this new nonterminal called <expression>. Here is what is produced by this branch of the parse tree:

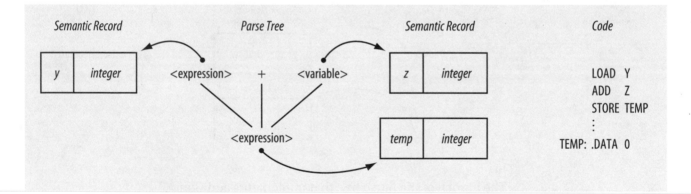

The final branch of the parse tree builds the nonterminal called <assignment statement>:

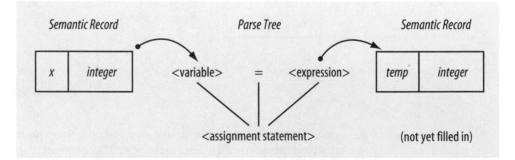

This production is translated into machine language by loading the value of the <expression> on the right-hand side of the assignment operator, using a LOAD instruction, and storing it, via a STORE operation, into the <variable> on

the left-hand side of the assignment operator. Again, the names to use in the address fields of the machine language instructions are obtained from the semantic records associated with <variable> and <expression>. The machine language code generated by this branch of the parse tree is

```
LOAD    TEMP
STORE   X
```

The compiler must also build the semantic record associated with the newly created nonterminal <assignment statement>. The name (*x*) and the data type (*integer*) of the variable on the left-hand side of the assignment operator are copied into that semantic record because the value stored in that variable is considered the value of the entire assignment statement.

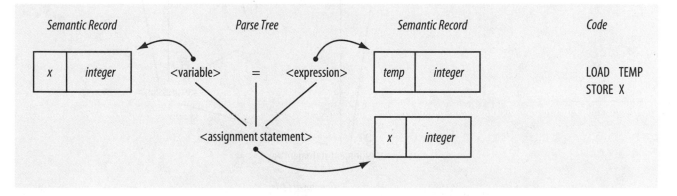

Our compiler has now analyzed every branch in the parse tree, and it has produced the following translation. (We have separated the pseudo-ops and executable instructions for clarity.)

```
        LOAD     Y
        ADD      Z
        STORE    TEMP
        LOAD     TEMP
        STORE    X
         . . .
    X:  .DATA    0
    Y:  .DATA    0
    Z:  .DATA    0
 TEMP:  .DATA    0
```

This is an exact translation of the assignment statement $x = y + z$. After many pages of discussion, we have achieved our original goal, the correct translation of a high-level programming language statement into machine language.

Figure 9.11 shows the code generation process for the slightly more complex assignment statement $x = x + y + z$. The branches of the parse tree are labeled and referenced by comments in the code. (The parse tree was constructed using the grammar shown in Figure 9.8.)

FIGURE **9.11**

*Code Generation for the
Assignment Statement*
$x = x + y + z$

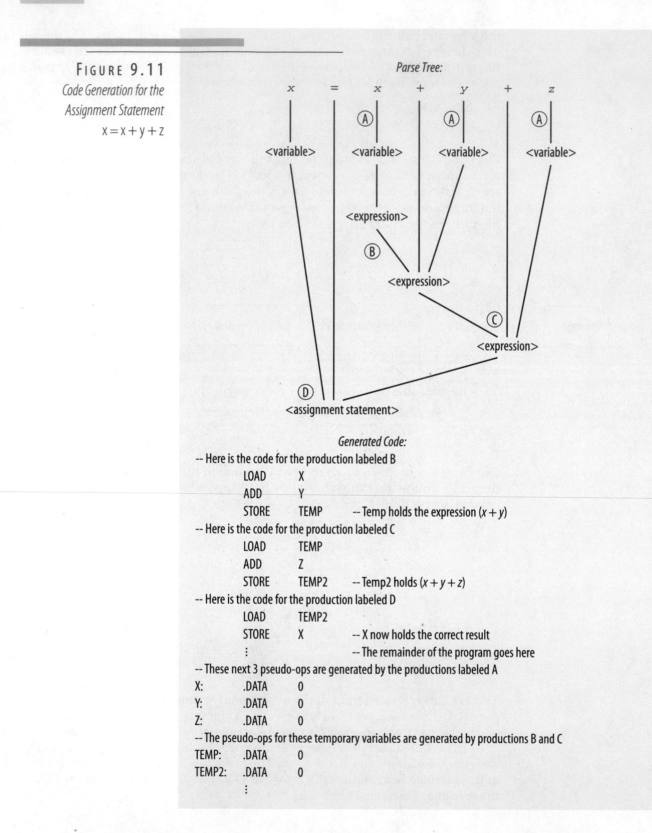

Parse Tree:

Generated Code:
```
-- Here is the code for the production labeled B
        LOAD     X
        ADD      Y
        STORE    TEMP       -- Temp holds the expression (x + y)
-- Here is the code for the production labeled C
        LOAD     TEMP
        ADD      Z
        STORE    TEMP2      -- Temp2 holds (x + y + z)
-- Here is the code for the production labeled D
        LOAD     TEMP2
        STORE    X          -- X now holds the correct result
        ⋮                   -- The remainder of the program goes here
-- These next 3 pseudo-ops are generated by the productions labeled A
X:      .DATA    0
Y:      .DATA    0
Z:      .DATA    0
-- The pseudo-ops for these temporary variables are generated by productions B and C
TEMP:   .DATA    0
TEMP2:  .DATA    0
        ⋮
```

The code of Figure 9.11 could represent the end of the compilation process because generating a correct machine language translation was our original goal. However, we are not quite finished. In the beginning of the chapter, we said that a compiler really has *two* goals: correctness and efficiency. The first goal has been achieved, but not necessarily the second. We have produced correct code, but not necessarily good code. Therefore, the next and final operation is **optimization**, where the compiler polishes and "fine-tunes" the translation so that it runs a little faster or occupies a little less memory.

Laboratory Experience 15

In the laboratory experience for Chapter 9, you will see how a compiler actually translates the high-level C++ statements you first learned in Chapter 7. You will observe as a compiler carries out each of the phases of translation described in the preceding sections. You will see how a compiler interprets each of the three basic statement types—sequential, conditional, and iterative—and better understand how it is able to produce a correct machine language translation.

PRACTICE PROBLEM

Go through the code generation process for the simple assignment statement $x = y$. The parse tree for this statement is

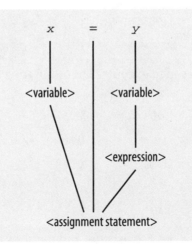

For each branch in the tree, show what semantic records are created and what code is generated.

9.2.4 Phase IV: Code Optimization

As we noted in Chapter 8, the first high-level language and compiler was FORTRAN, which appeared in 1957. (It was created by John Backus, the B of BNF.) At that time everyone programmed in assembly language because nothing else was available. Given all the shortcomings of assembly language, one would have expected programmers to flock to FORTRAN and thank their lucky stars that it was available. After all, it is certainly a lot easier to understand the statement $a = b + c$ than the rather cryptic sequence LOAD B, ADD C, STORE A.

Surprisingly, programmers did *not* accept this new language very quickly. The reason had nothing to do with the power and expressiveness of FORTRAN. Everyone admitted that it was far superior to assembly language in terms of clarity and ease of use. The problem had to do with **efficiency**—the ability to write highly optimized programs that contained no wasted microseconds or unnecessary memory cells.

In 1957 (early second-generation computing), computers were still enormously expensive; they typically cost millions of dollars. Therefore, programmers cared more about avoiding wasted computing resources than simplifying their job. No one worried about the productivity of programmers earning $2.00/hour compared to optimizing the use of a multimillion-dollar computer system. In 1957 the guiding principle was "Programmers are cheap, hardware is expensive!"

When programmers used assembly language, they were working on the actual machine, not the virtual machine created by the system software and described in Chapter 6. They were free to choose the instructions that ran most quickly or used the least amount of memory. For example, if the INCREMENT, LOAD, and STORE instructions execute in 1 μsec, whereas an ADD takes 2 μsec, then translating the assignment statement $x = x + 3$ as

INCREMENT	X	-- x + 1	1 μsec
INCREMENT	X	-- x + 2	1 μsec
INCREMENT	X	-- x + 3	1 μsec

requires 3 μsec to execute. This code runs 33% faster than if it had been translated as

LOAD	X		1 μsec
ADD	THREE	-- x + 3	2 μsec
STORE	X		1 μsec
	. . .		
THREE:	.DATA	3	

which takes 4 μsec to execute and requires an additional memory cell for the integer constant 3. When programmers wrote in assembly language, they were free to choose the first of these sequences rather than the second, knowing that it is faster and more compact. However, in a high-level language like FORTRAN, a programmer can only write $x = x + 3$ and hope that the compiler is "smart enough" to select the faster of the two implementations.

Because efficiency was so important to programmers of the 1950s and 1960s, these early first- and second-generation compilers spent a great deal of time doing **code optimization**. In fact Backus himself said that ". . . we did not regard language design as a difficult problem, but merely a prelude to the real problem: designing a compiler which could produce efficient programs." These compiler pioneers were quite successful in solving many of the problems of optimization, and early FORTRAN compilers produced object programs that ran nearly as fast as highly optimized assembly language code produced by top-notch programmers. After seeing these startling results, programmers of the 1950s and 1960s were eventually won over. They could gain the benefits of high-level languages—a powerful virtual environment—without loss of efficiency. The code optimization techniques developed by Backus and others were one of the most important reasons for the rapid acceptance of high-level programming languages during the early years of computer science.

However, conditions have changed dramatically since the 1950s. Because of dramatic reductions in hardware costs, code optimization no longer plays the central role it did 30 or 40 years ago. Programmers rarely worry about saving a few memory cells when even the tiniest PC has 16 Mbytes, and 32 to 128 Mbytes of memory is quite common. Similarly, as processor speeds increase to 30 to 50 MIPS (million instructions per second) for small machines and to 300 MIPS for bigger ones, removing a few instructions becomes much less important. For example, eliminating the execution of 1,000 unnecessary instructions saves only 0.00001 second on a 100-MIPS machine. Therefore, compilers are no longer judged solely on whether they produce highly optimized code.

At the same time that hardware costs are coming down, programmer costs are rising dramatically. A powerful high-speed graphics workstation can be purchased for about $5,000, but the programmers developing software for that system may earn 10 to 20 times that amount in annual salary. The operational phrase of the 1990s is the exact opposite of what was true in the 1950s: "Hardware is cheap, programmers are expensive!"

The goal in compiler design today is to include a wide array of **compiler tools** to simplify the programmer's task and increase his or her productivity. This includes such tools as **visual development environments** that use graphics and video to let the programmer see what is happening, sophisticated **on-line debuggers** to help programmers locate and correct errors, and **reusable code libraries**, which contain a large collection of already-written program units. When a compiler is embedded within a collection of supporting routines such as debuggers, editors, and libraries, it is called an **integrated development environment**. It is these types of *programmer optimizations*, rather than code optimizations, that have taken center stage in language and compiler design in the 1990s.

However, this does not mean that code optimization is no longer important or that programmers will tolerate extreme inefficiency. A little bit of effort by a compiler can frequently pay large dividends in reduced memory space and lower running time. Thus optimization algorithms are still part of most compilers. Let's briefly survey what they do and how they help improve the finished product.

There are two types of optimization: local optimization and global optimization. The former is relatively easy and is included as part of most compilers. The latter is much more difficult, and it is usually omitted from all but the most sophisticated and expensive production-level **optimizing compilers**.

In **local optimization**, the compiler looks at a very small block of instructions, typically from one to five. It tries to determine how it can improve the efficiency of this local code block without regard for what instructions come before or after. It is as though the compiler has placed a tiny "window" over the code, and it optimizes only the instructions inside this optimization window:

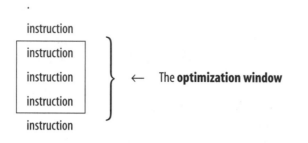

Here is a list of some possible local optimizations:

1. **Constant evaluation.** If an arithmetic expression can be fully evaluated at compile time, it should be, rather than evaluating it at execution time.

   High-Level Statement: `x = 1 + 1;`

Nonoptimized code:		*Optimized code:*	
LOAD	ONE	LOAD	TWO
ADD	ONE	STORE	X
STORE	X		

2. **Strength reduction.** The compiler replaces a slow arithmetic operation by a faster one. For example, on most computers increment is faster than addition, and addition is faster than multiplication, which in turn is faster than division. Whenever possible, the compiler replaces an operation with one that is equivalent but executes more quickly.

   High-Level Statement: `x = x * 2; // x times 2 is equivalent to x + x`

Nonoptimized code:		*Optimized code:*	
LOAD	X	LOAD	X
MULTIPLY	TWO	ADD	X
STORE	X	STORE	X

3. **Eliminating unnecessary operations.** It is possible that the compiler will produce instructions that are not incorrect, just unnecessary. For example, because of the nondestructive read principle, when a value is stored from a

register into memory, its value is still in the register, and it does not need to be reloaded. However, because the code generation phase translates each statement individually, there may be some unnecessary LOAD and STORE operations.

High-Level Statement: $x = y;$

$z = x;$

Nonoptimized code:	LOAD	Y	-- This is $x = y$	*Optimized code:*	LOAD	Y
	STORE	X			STORE	X
	LOAD	X	-- This is $z = x$		STORE	Z
	STORE	Z				

Looking at the code in Figure 9.11, we can see two local optimizations:

- There are unnecessary LOAD and STORE operations. For example, the first four instructions in Figure 9.11 read

    ```
    LOAD    X
    ADD     Y
    STORE   TEMP
    LOAD    TEMP
    ```

    The STORE and LOAD operations on lines 3 and 4 are both unnecessary because the sum (X + Y) is still in register R.
- The code uses two memory cells called TEMP and TEMP2 to hold temporary values. Neither of these variables is needed.

Locally optimized code for the assignment statement $x = x + y + z$ is shown in Figure 9.12. It uses only 7 instructions and data generation pseudo-ops rather than the 13 of Figure 9.11, a savings of about 45%.

FIGURE 9.12

Optimized Code for the Assignment Statement
$x = x + y + z$

```
LOAD    X
ADD     Y
ADD     Z
STORE   X        -- X now holds the correct result
    .
    .              -- The remainder of the program goes here
    .
X:  .DATA   0
Y:  .DATA   0
Z:  .DATA   0
```

The second type of optimization is **global optimization**, and it is much more difficult. In global optimization the compiler looks at large segments of the program, not just small pieces, to decide how to improve performance. The compiler examines large blocks of code such as loops, if statements, and procedures to determine how to speed up execution. This is a much harder problem, both for a compiler and for a human programmer, but it can produce enormous savings in time and space. For example, earlier in the chapter we showed a loop that looked like this:

```
sum = 0.0;
i = 0;
while (i <= 50000)
{
  sum = sum + (2.0 * x[i]);
  i = i + 1;
}
```

By moving the multiplication outside the loop, it is possible to eliminate 50,000 time-consuming operations. An optimizing compiler would analyze the entire loop and restructure it in the following way:

```
sum = 0.0;
i = 0;
while (i <= 50000)
{
  sum = sum + x[i];
  i = i + 1;
};
sum = sum * 2.0;
```

Such restructuring requires the ability to look at more than a few instructions at a time. The compiler cannot look at only a small "optimization window" but must be able to examine and analyze large segments of code. It requires a compiler that can see the "big picture," not just a small scene. Seeing this big picture is difficult, and many compilers are unable to do the type of global optimizations just discussed.

There is one final comment about code optimization that is extremely important: Optimization *cannot* make an inefficient algorithm efficient. As we learned in Chapter 3, the efficiency of an algorithm is an inherent characteristic of its structure. It is not something programmed in by a programmer or optimized in by a compiler. A sequential search program written by a team of world-class programmers and optimized by the best compiler available will still not run as fast as a nonoptimized binary search program written by first-year computer science students. Code optimization should not be seen as a way to create fast, efficient programs. That goal is achieved when we decide which algorithm to use to solve a problem. Optimization is more like the "frosting on the cake," whereby we take a good algorithm and make it just a little bit better.

"I Do Not Understand," Said the Machine

Chapter 6 showed that translating assembly language into machine language is quite easy. This chapter demonstrated that translating high-level programming languages into machine language is more difficult, but it can be done. What about the next step—the translation of natural languages such as English? If a computer could understand our own spoken language, then we could use it, rather than the artificial languages studied in Chapters 7 and 8, to communicate.

Unfortunately, getting computers to understand and use natural language is nowhere near a reality. In fact, **natural language understanding** may be the single most difficult research problem in computer science. Success in this area may be dozens of years away, or it may never be achieved. After all, millions of years of evolution have left virtually every animal except humans without sophisticated language capabilities.

What makes natural languages so much more difficult to understand than formal languages? Why is this problem of such immense magnitude? There are far too many reasons to discuss in these brief paragraphs, but most have to do with the immense richness and complexity of natural languages. The number of rules in an English language grammar would probably number in the tens of millions, far beyond the ability of any modern computer. Furthermore, most words in English have many meanings, and we must determine by the context what is meant. This type of sophisticated linguistic discrimination is very difficult, and a complete, unambiguous semantic analysis of English sentences is beyond the ability of computer systems.

It actually gets much worse, because meaning may be extracted from a sentence using not just context but also our own human experiences. Computers do not have human experiences, so it is enormously difficult for them to determine the full meaning of many sentences.

This is a rather pessimistic outlook. Is there any hope at all for getting computers to understand natural languages? In two special areas, the answer is a qualified yes. First, limited success can be achieved when a computer works with a small vocabulary and grammar within a very limited problem domain. This has been demonstrated, for example, in the flying of planes by voice. The pilot speaks commands in English that are interpreted by a computer and translated into the proper actions on the airplane. In this very specialized problem domain, the computer has only to understand a few hundred words (*up*, *down*, *turn*, and so on) and some simple sentence structures. It does not have to discuss global politics or existential philosophy.

A second area where some successes have been demonstrated is using a computer to do initial "rough" translations from one natural language to another. A human would complete the translation, smoothing out choppy phrases and filling in areas where the computer was unable to determine the correct meaning.

No matter how it is done, there is no doubt that having a computer understand natural language is a task whose solution is not on the immediate horizon. In fact, just as the use of sophisticated language distinguishes humans from animals, it may also distinguish humans from computers.

9.3 CONCLUSION

This chapter has merely touched on some of the many issues involved in compiler design. Topics such as syntax, grammars, parsing, semantics, and optimization are rich and complex, each worthy of an entire book rather than one brief chapter. In addition, there are topics not even mentioned here that play an important role in compiler design:

- Development environments and support tools
- Compilers for alternative languages, such as functional, object-oriented, or parallel languages
- Language standards
- Top-down versus bottom-up parsing algorithms
- Error detection and recovery

The key point is that, unlike building the assemblers of Chapter 6, building a compiler is hard, and compilers for languages like Pascal, Scheme, and C++ are large, complicated pieces of software. John Backus reported that the construction of the first FORTRAN compiler in 1957 required about 18 person-years of effort to design, code, and test. Even though we know much more today about how to build compilers, and numerous support tools are available to assist in this effort, it still requires a team of programmers working months or years to build a correct and efficient compiler for a modern high-level programming language.

The previous three chapters looked at the implementation phase of software development. They focused on the languages used to write programs and the methods used to translate programs into instructions that can be executed by the hardware. However, there are limits to computing. The next chapter will show that no matter how powerful your hardware capabilities and no matter how sophisticated and expressive your programming language, there are some problems that simply cannot be solved algorithmically.

EXERCISES

1. Identify the tokens in each of the following statements. (You do not need to classify them; just identify them.)

   a. **if** $(a == b1)$ cin >> x >> y;

   b. $delta = epsilon + 1.23 -$ sqrt(zz);

   c. cout << Q;

2. Assume that we are working in a programming language that allows underscores (_) to appear in variable names. When a scanner sees a character string such as AB_CD, would it be more likely to be classify this string as the single token AB_CD or as three separate tokens: AB, _, CD? Explain your answer.

3. In the Pascal language a comment can be enclosed either in braces { } or in the symbols (* *). How do you think a scanner would group the four symbols {, }, (*, *) for purposes of classification? That is,

would each symbol be given its own classification number or would some share classifications?

4. Using the token types and classification values given in Figure 9.3, show the output of a scanner when it is presented with each of the following statements:

   a. limit = begin + end

   b. $a = b - 1$;

   c. **if** $(c == 50)$ $x = 1$; **else** $y = x + 44$;

   d. thenelse == error --

5. a. Write a BNF grammar that describes the structure of a nonterminal called <number>. Assume that <number> contains an optional + sign followed by exactly 2 decimal digits, the first of which cannot be a 0. Thus 23, +91, and +40 are legal, but 9, +01, and 123 are not.

b. Using your grammar from part (a), show a parse tree for the value +90.

6. a. Write a BNF grammar that describes the structure of U.S. telephone numbers, which can be either (*xxx*)*xxx-xxxx* or *xxx-xxxx*, where *x* can be any digit from 0 to 9.

   b. Modify your grammar from part (a) to recognize that (1) the middle digit of an area code must be either a 0 or a 1, (2) the first digit of an area code cannot be a 0 or a 1, and (3) the first digit of the 7-digit phone number cannot be a 0 or a 1.

   c. Using your grammar from either part (a) or part (b), show a parse tree for the phone number (612)555-1212.

7. a. Write a BNF grammar for identifiers that consist of an arbitrarily long string of letters and digits, the first one of which must be a letter.

   b. Using your grammar from part (a), show a parse tree for the identifier AB5C8.

8. Assume that we represent dollar amounts in the following way:

   $number.numberCR

   The dollar sign and the dollar value must be present. The cents part (including both the decimal point and the number) and the CR (which stands for CRedit and is how businesspeople represent negative numbers) are both optional. "number" is a variable-length sequence of one or more decimal digits. Examples of legal dollar amounts include $995, $99CR, $199.95, and $500.000CR.

   a. Write a BNF grammar for the dollar amount just described.

   b. Modify your grammar so that the cents part is no longer an arbitrarily long sequence of digits but is exactly two digits, no more and no less.

   c. Using your grammar from either part (a) or part (b), show a parse tree for $19.95CR.

9. Describe the language defined by the following grammar:

<goal>	::=	<letter> | <letter> <next>
<next>	::=	, <letter>
<letter>	::=	A

10. How does the language defined by the following grammar differ from the language defined by the grammar in Exercise 9?

<goal>	::=	<letter> | <letter> <next>
<next>	::=	, <letter> | <letter> <next>
<letter>	::=	A

11. a. Create a BNF grammar that describes simple Boolean expressions of the form

   var AND var   var OR var

   where var is one of the symbols *w*, *x*, *y*, and *z*.

   b. Modify your grammar from part (a) so that the Boolean expressions can be of the form

   expr AND expr   expr OR expr

   where expr is either a simple variable (*w*, *x*, *y*, or *z*) or an expression of the form

   (var == var)   (var < var)   (var > var)

   c. Modify your grammar one more time to allow a Boolean expression to have an *arbitrary* number of terms connected by either AND or OR. That is, your expressions can be of the form

   expr AND expr OR expr OR expr AND expr. . . .

12. Using the grammar of Figure 9.8, show a parse tree for the statement

   $$y = x + y + y + z$$

   Is your parse tree unique? If not, how many other parse trees exist for this statement? What does the existence of these different trees imply about the meaning of this assignment statement?

13. What is the language defined by the following pair of BNF rules?

<number>	::=	<digit> | <digit> <number>
<digit>	::=	0 | 1

   Where have you seen this language before?

14. Write a BNF grammar that describes an arbitrarily long string of the characters *a*, *b*, and *c*. The string can contain any number of occurrences of these three letters (including none) in any order. The strings "empty", *a*, *accaa*, *abcabccba*, and *bbbbb* are all valid members of this language.

15. What are the different interpretations of the English language sentence

   I bought a shirt in the new store that was too large.

16. Write a BNF grammar to describe the following simplified C++ input statement:

```
cin >> var >> var >> ... >> var;
```

The statement begins with the word "cin" followed by one or more sequences of the operator >> followed by a variable. The entire statement ends with a semicolon. Variable names are arbitrarily long strings of digits and letters, the first of which must be a letter.

17. Discuss what other information, in addition to name and data type, might be kept in a semantic record. Where would this other information come from?

18. How do you think a compiler would translate into machine language a branch in the parse tree that looked like the figure at the bottom of this page? Show the code that could be generated from this production and the semantic record created for the new nonterminal symbol <Boolean expression>.

19. Referring to the parse tree in Figure 9.11, why is the production

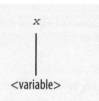

appearing to the left of the = not labeled with an A? Does this production generate any code?

20. Assume that our language specifically permits you to assign an integer value to a real variable. The compiler handles this **mixed mode** by generating code to perform data conversion from an integer to a real representation. Consider the following declarations:

```
int x;
double y;
```

The assignment statement $y = x$ is legal in this language. Explain how a compiler would handle the assignment statement above. You do not have to show the exact code that would be generated. Just describe how a compiler would deal with the statement, and show at what point in the code generation process the compiler would discover that it needs to produce the data conversion instructions.

21. Explain how the concept of **algebraic identities** could be exploited during the code optimization phase of compilation. An identity is a relationship that is true for all values of the unknowns. For example,

$x + 0 = x$ for all values of x.

Describe other identities and explain how they could become part of the optimization phase. Would this be considered local or global optimization?

22. Assume that we wrote the following pairs of assignment statements:

```
Delta = 2.9 + (a + b + c * 3) /
  (x - 5.7);
Epsilon = (a + b + c * 3) +
  sqrt(3.1 * y);
```

How could a compiler optimize the execution of these two statements? Would this be considered local or global optimization?

23. If we assume that all mathematical operations take 1 μsec to execute (a typical value), how much time did your optimization from Exercise 22 actually save? What does this value say about the importance of compiler optimizations?

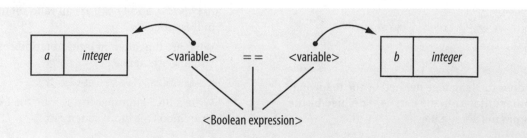

CHALLENGE WORK

1. Our discussion on lexical analysis in Section 9.2.1 may lead you to believe that every lexical analyzer is unique and built "from scratch." That is absolutely not true. In fact, it is quite rare to write a scanner when building a compiler for a new language. The reason is that there exists a special program called a **scanner generator** that can, with the appropriate input, act as a "universal scanner" for any language. To use a scanner generator, we need only provide a formal linguistic description of the tokens in our language and their classification. Next this description is input to the scanner generator, which then locates and classifies tokens according to the description provided. Thus, instead of writing a program called a scanner, you provide data to an already-written program called a scanner generator.

    One of the most widely used scanner generators is a program called **lex**, and it has been used to build dozens of compilers, assemblers, and other linguistic interfaces. Read about scanner generators in general and lex in particular. Find out how they work and the techniques for describing the structure and classification of tokens. Then show how you would formally describe in lex the following token types:

    a. C++ identifiers
    b. Signed integers
    c. Signed real numbers

   If your installation has lex available, enter your formal descriptions and have lex locate tokens of each of these types.

2. The techniques described in Challenge Exercise 1 also work for the parsing phase of the compilation process. That is, instead of writing a parsing program, we can provide data to an already-written program that will do the job for us. A special program called a **parser generator**, also called a **compiler-compiler**, can act as a universal parser for any language that can be described using the BNF notation given in this chapter. To use a parser generator, you simply input the productions of the grammar of your language and the sequence of tokens to be parsed. The output of the parser generator is a parse tree, if the sequence of tokens is legal according to your productions, or an error message if it is not.

    The most widely used parser generator is a program called **yacc**, an acronym for "Yet Another Compiler-Compiler." Yacc, like lex, has been used to build a great number of compilers for such languages as Pascal and C++. Read about parser generators and yacc, and write a report describing how yacc works and how you formally represent BNF productions. If you have yacc available at your installation, enter the BNF rules for <assignment statement> and let yacc parse the statement

    $x = y + z;$

FOR FURTHER READING

The classic book on compiling is the "Dragon Book," so called because of the design on its cover:

Aho, A.; Sethi, R.; and Ullman, J. *Compilers: Principles, Techniques, Tools.* Reading, MA: Addison-Wesley, 1986.

There are also a large number of good reference books on languages, BNF, and compilers. Here is a sampling of these books:

Appel, A. *Modern Compilers: An Introduction.* New York: Cambridge University Press, 1997.

Fisher, C. and LeBlanc, R. *Crafting a Compiler with C.* Chicago: Benjamin Cummings, 1991.

Gries, D. *Compiler Construction for Digital Computers.* New York: Wiley, 1971.

Holmes, J. *Building Your Own Compiler with C++.* Englewood Cliffs, NJ: Prentice-Hall, 1995.

Louden, K. *Compiler Construction: Principles and Practice.* Boston: PWS, 1997.

Pittman, T. and Peters, J. *The Art of Compiler Design.* Englewood Cliffs, NJ: Prentice-Hall, 1992.

MODELS OF COMPUTATION

10.1   INTRODUCTION

Our whole theme throughout the book to this point has been, in one way or another, algorithmic problem solving. We've discussed the concept of an algorithm, how to represent algorithms, the importance of their correctness and efficiency in solving problems, the hardware world that executes algorithms, various levels of abstraction in which the programmer deals with algorithms, and the system software that translates from these abstractions back to the elementary hardware level. It seems as though algorithms, and problems that are solvable by algorithms, represent the entire scope of the computer science universe.

But we are about to bump up against the limits of that universe. *There are problems that do not have any algorithmic solution.* Be sure you understand what a powerful statement this is. Of course, there are many problems for which, although no algorithmic solution has yet been found, we might find one if we were only clever enough to discover it. Indeed, such new discoveries are made all the time. But here we are saying that there are also problems for which *no* algorithmic solution exists; it does not matter how inventive we may be in the future, or how remarkable our hardware or software; *there are no algorithms to solve these problems.*

We will prove this statement in this chapter by actually finding such a problem. Here we've set ourselves a rather difficult task. If we pose a candidate for such a problem, and then search for an algorithmic solution and fail to find one, that does not prove that such an algorithm does not exist. It might only mean that the algorithm is a difficult one and we have not yet been able to figure it out. Instead, we must show that no one can ever find such an algorithm—that one does not exist.

Algorithms, as we noted in Chapter 1, are carried out by computing agents (people, robots, computers). Throughout most of this book, we've assumed that the computing agent is a real computer. Ordinarily, we would choose to execute an algorithm on the most modern, high-speed computer available, with all the bells and whistles we could find. But to show that something cannot be done by *any* computer, we want the bells and whistles out of the way so we can concentrate on the fundamental nature of "computerhood." What we need is a simple "ideal" computer—something that will be easy to work with yet that is theoretically as powerful as the real thing. We need a model of a computer; indeed, to consider algorithms in general, we need a model of a computing agent.

10.2   WHAT IS A MODEL?

Many toys for children (and some toys for grownups) are models. Model cars, model trucks, model airplanes, and dolls (model people) are forever popular with children. Children use these toys to "play" at being grown up—

at being drivers, pilots, and parents—because the toys capture the spirit of the objects they model. A model car, for example, looks like a car. The more expensive the model, the more features it has that make it look more realistic. The model is never a real car, however. Though it captures the essence of a car, so that any child recognizes it as a "car," it is (usually) smaller in scale, suppresses many of the details of a real car, and does not have the full functionality of a real car.

Models are a very important way of studying many physical and social phenomena. Weather systems, creation of stars, movement of land masses, natural resource utilization, water pollution, agricultural cycles, spread of epidemics, the economy, population demographics, chemical molecules—all are phenomena that have been studied via modeling. Like a model car, a model of such a phenomenon

1. Captures the essence—the important properties—of the real thing
2. Probably differs in scale from the real thing
3. Suppresses details of the real thing
4. Lacks the full functionality of the real thing

The model might be a physical model or a pencil-and-paper mathematical model. For example, a physical model of a chemical molecule might use Velcro-covered balls stuck together in a certain way to represent the molecular structure. This model illustrates certain important properties: how many atoms of each element are present and where they are located in relation to one another. It is much larger than the real molecule, does not display the details of the chemical bonding, and is certainly not a real molecule.

A simple example of a mathematical model is the equation that gives the distance d that a moving vehicle travels as the product of rate r and time t:

$$d = r \times t$$

Although this equation can give approximate information, it ignores the details of variations in the speed of the vehicle by assuming that the rate is a constant. Because this is not a physical model, it does not have a size as such, but there is a difference in the time scale from the actual moving vehicle. A calculation that a vehicle traveling at (approximately) a constant rate of 60 miles per hour for 2 hours will cover (approximately) a distance of 120 miles can be done in an instant by simply plugging values into the equation. A system of equations representing a weather system is an example of a more complex mathematical model. This model would include equations that represent the various major factors influencing weather—wind, humidity, barometric pressure, and so on—and how they work together, but the many minor influences that also affect the weather would have to be ignored. Again, a difference in time scale exists: calculations using the model equations will complete in a few minutes the equivalent of actions that take days or weeks in the real weather system. Of course, the system of equations is not the weather system itself, any more than the distance equation is really the moving vehicle.

What can be gained by studying models if they are not the real thing? They can enhance our understanding of the real phenomena being modeled. By changing some aspect within the model (attaching a new atom to the chemical molecule, changing the rate in the distance equation, or varying the humidity value in the weather equations), we can see the effects of the change. These changes might be very costly, difficult, or dangerous to make in the real phenomena. It would be impossible, for example, to change humidity in a real weather system, and even if we were able to do so just to see what happens, the consequences could be disastrous. The real phenomena might also operate at a time scale—either too fast or too slow—that would make the results of a change difficult to observe. The effects of changing the molecular structure of a compound used in a chemical reaction might be hard to observe if the reaction takes place quickly; the effects on water pollution of changes in land use might be hard to observe because they take place too slowly.

Models therefore give us a safe and controlled environment to play with "what ifs"—what might be the effect if this or that factor in some real phenomenon were changed? The answers can be used to guide future decisions. What change would lowering interest rates have on the economy? Consult our economic forecasting models. How best to regulate industrial runoff? Consult our water pollution models.

Models can also provide environments for learning and practicing interactions with various phenomena. An aircraft flight simulator, for example, can give the trainee pilot realistic experience in a danger-free setting.

Not only can models give us information about existing phenomena, they can also be used as design tools. Let's say that a new automobile or a new airplane is being designed. A model of the new design may reveal its capabilities and its limitations with considerably less time, expense, and potential danger than building a design prototype only to find that the design contains a major flaw.

Whether the model is used to predict behavior of existing phenomena, as a simulator for training purposes, or as a testbed for proposed designs, the information gained is only as good as the model used. If the model does not incorporate the major aspects of the system being modeled, if relationships are represented incorrectly, or if so much detail has been omitted as to make the model a totally inaccurate representation, then little faith can be placed in what the model tells us. We'll talk more in Chapter 14 about the social implications of relying on computer-generated models.

PRACTICE PROBLEMS

1. Describe some situation (besides aircraft pilot training) where a simulator would be useful as a training device.

2. What factors might a model of groundwater pollution need to include? What would be the advantages of a good model? Are there potential disadvantages to using such a model?

10.3 A MODEL OF A COMPUTING AGENT

We want to construct a model for the "computing agent" entity. If it is a good model, it will capture the fundamental properties of what it means to be a computing agent and thus will enable us to explore the capabilities and limitations of computation in the most general sense.

10.3.1 PROPERTIES OF A COMPUTING AGENT

Our job in constructing a model is to abstract the important properties of the phenomenon being modeled while suppressing lower-level details. This means we must decide which features are central to a computing agent and which are relatively incidental and can be ignored. For example, a computing agent must be able to follow the instructions in an algorithm. The instructions must be presented in some form that makes sense to the computing agent, but we don't want to worry about whether the instructions are presented in English as opposed to Japanese, or in words as opposed to a series of pictures.

However the instructions are presented, the computing agent must be able to read them, listen to them, scan them, or absorb them in some way. Likewise, the computing agent must be able to take in any data pertinent to the task. When we dealt with real computers, we described this as an input task, but the ability to accept input is central to any computing agent—from a human being following instructions to a programmable VCR. The instructions and data must be stored somewhere during the period of time when the algorithm is being executed, and they must be retrievable as needed, whether it be in a computer's memory, the VCR microprocessor memory, a human being's memory, or written on a sheet of paper that the human being refers to.

The computing agent must be able to take action in accordance with algorithm instructions. These instructions may take into account the present situation or state of the computing agent, as well as the particular input item being processed. In a real computer, a conditional operation may say "if condition A then do B else do C." Condition A may involve the value of some variable or variables that have already been read into memory; we may think of the contents of memory (that is, how the various bits are set) as the present state of the computer. The VCR microprocessor may have an instruction that says "if the time is 7 P.M. and I have been programmed to record at 7 P.M., then turn on." Here the action of the VCR depends on both the input of the current time from its clock and the "state" of its programming. The human being carrying out the algorithm of ordering lunch from a menu reacts both to the "input" (what items are on the menu) and to his or her present state of hunger.

Finally, the computing agent is expected to produce output because we required that the outcome of an algorithm be an observable result. The computer displays results on a screen, prints them on a sheet of paper, or writes them to a file; the VCR puts signals on a magnetic tape; the human being speaks or writes.

To summarize, we shall require that any computing agent

1. Can accept input
2. Can store information in and retrieve it from memory
3. Can take actions according to algorithm instructions, and that the choice of what action to take may depend on the present state of the computing agent as well as on the input item presently being processed
4. Can produce output

Of course, a real computer has all of these capabilities and is an example of a computing agent, as are a human being and a programmable VCR. The VCR, however, has a very limited set of primitive operations it can perform, so it can react only to a very limited algorithm. The computer, though it has a limited set of simple primitives, is a general-purpose computing agent because, as we have seen in the previous chapters, those primitives can be combined and organized to accomplish complex tasks. The "primitive operations" available for human beings to draw on haven't been fully explored, but in many ways they seem to exceed those of a computer, and we would certainly classify a human being as a general-purpose computing agent.

In the next section, we will discuss one particular model for a computing agent. It will have the four required properties just specified, and it will represent a general-purpose computing agent able to follow the instructions of many different algorithms.

10.3.2 THE TURING MACHINE

We think of "computing" as a modern activity—something done by electronic computers. But interest in the theoretical nature of computation far predated the advent of modern computers. By the end of the nineteenth century, mathematicians were interested in formalizing the nature of proof, with two goals in mind. First, a formal basis for mathematical proofs would guarantee the correctness of a proof because the proof would contain no intuitive statements such as "It is clear that . . ." or "We can now see that . . . ." Second, a formal basis for proofs might allow for mechanical theorem proving, where correct proofs could be generated simply by following rules. In 1931, an Austrian logician named Kurt Gödel looked at formal systems to describe the ordinary arithmetic of numbers. He demonstrated that in any reasonable system, there will be true statements about arithmetic that cannot be proved using that system. This led to interest in finding a way to recognize which statements are indeed unprovable in a formal system—that is, in finding a computational procedure (what we have called an algorithm) to recognize such statements. This in turn led to an investigation of the nature of computational procedure itself, and a number of mathematicians in the mid-1930s proposed various models of computational procedures, along with models of computing agents to carry out those procedures. We will look at the model proposed by Alan Turing.

Alan Turing, Brilliant Eccentric

The Turing machine was proposed as a model for a computing agent by the brilliant British mathematician Alan Turing in 1936. Turing began by thinking of how to generalize the typewriter as an "automatic device." But despite its name, the Turing machine is not a machine at all. It is a model of the pencil-and-paper type that captures the essential features of a computing agent.

Alan Turing (1912–1954) was a colorful individual and a brilliant thinker. Stories abound about his "absent-minded professor" demeanor, his interest in running (through the streets of London with an alarm clock flopping about, tied to his belt by a piece of twine), and his fascination with a children's radio show whose characters he would discuss daily with his mother. Convicted of homosexual acts in 1952, he chose drug treatment over prison, primarily because he feared a prison term would impede his intellectual work. There was even a Broadway play (*Breaking the Code*) written about him, years after his death by suicide.

Turing made three distinct and remarkable contributions to computer science. First, he devised what is now known as the Turing machine, using it—as we will see in this chapter—to model computation and to discover that some problems have no general computable solution. Second, during World War II, his team at the British Foreign Office built the Colossus machine, which used cryptanalysis, the science of code breaking, to break the secret code used on the German Enigma machine. The details of this work, carried on in a Victorian country mansion called Bletchley Park, were kept secret until many years later. Breaking the code allowed the British to gain access to intelligence about German submarine movements that contributed significantly toward winning the war. Third, after the war Turing investigated what it means for machines to "think." We'll discuss his early contribution to *artificial intelligence* in Chapter 13.

A **Turing machine** includes a (conceptual) tape that extends infinitely in both directions. The tape is divided into cells, each of which contains one symbol. The symbols must come from a finite set of symbols called the **alphabet**. The alphabet for a given Turing machine always contains a special symbol b (for "blank"), usually both of the symbols 0 and 1 (zero and one), and sometimes a limited number of other symbols, let's say X and Y, used as placeholders or markers of some kind. At any point in time, only a finite number of the cells contain nonblank symbols. Figure 10.1 shows a typical tape configuration, with three nonblank cells containing the alphabet symbols 0, 1, 1, respectively.

The tape will be used to hold the input to the Turing machine. We know that input must be presented to a computing agent in a form it can understand; for a Turing machine, this means that the input must be expressed as a finite string of

.	.	.	b	b	0	1	1	b	b	.	.	.

FIGURE 10.1
A Turing Machine Tape

nonblank symbols from the alphabet. The Turing machine will write its output on the tape, again using the same alphabet of symbols. The tape will also serve as memory.

The rest of the Turing machine consists of a unit that reads one cell of the tape at a time and writes a symbol in that cell. There is a finite number k of "states" of the machine, labeled $1, 2, \ldots, k$, and at any moment the unit is in one of these states. A state can be thought of as a certain condition; the Turing machine may reach this condition partly on the basis of its history of events, much as your "hungry state" is a condition reached because of the meals you have skipped recently.

Figure 10.2 shows a particular Turing machine configuration. Using the tape of Figure 10.1, the machine is currently in state 1 and is reading the cell containing the symbol 0, so the 0 is what the machine is seeing as the current input symbol.

The Turing machine is designed to carry out only one type of primitive operation. Each time such an operation is done, three actions take place:

- Write a symbol in the cell (replacing the symbol already there).
- Go into a new state (it might be the same as the current state).
- Move one cell left or right.

The details of the actions (what to write, what the new state is, and which direction to move) depend on the current state of the machine and on the contents of the tape cell currently being read (the input). Turing machines follow instructions that describe these details. Each instruction tells what to do for a specific current state and current input symbol. Each instruction therefore says something like

> if you are in state i

and

> you are reading symbol j

then

> write symbol k onto the tape
>
> go into state s
>
> move in direction d

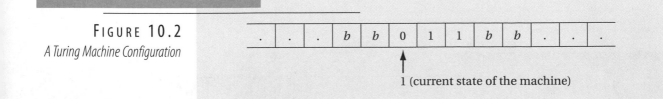

FIGURE 10.2
A Turing Machine Configuration

| . | . | . | b | b | 0 | 1 | 1 | b | b | . | . | . |

1 (current state of the machine)

The single primitive operation the Turing machine does is to check its current state and the current input symbol being read, look for an instruction that tells what to do under these circumstances, and then carry out the three actions specified by that instruction.

For example, one Turing machine instruction might say

> if you are in state 1

and

> you are reading symbol 0

then

> write symbol 1 onto the tape
>
> go into state 2
>
> move right

If a Turing machine is in the configuration shown in Figure 10.2 (where the current state is 1 and the current input symbol is 0), then this instruction applies. After the machine executes this instruction, its next configuration will be that shown in Figure 10.3, where the previous 0 symbol has been overwritten with a 1, the state has changed to state 2, and the "read head" has moved one cell to the right on the tape.

Let's develop a shorthand notation for Turing machine instructions. There are five components:

Current state

Current symbol

Next symbol

Next state

Direction of move

We'll give these five things in order and enclosed in parentheses.

(current state, current symbol, next symbol, next state, direction of move)

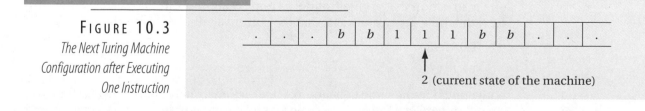

FIGURE 10.3
The Next Turing Machine Configuration after Executing One Instruction

| . | . | . | b | b | 1 | 1 | 1 | b | b | . | . | . |

2 (current state of the machine)

The instruction that we talked about earlier,

> if you are in state 1

and

> you are reading symbol 0

then

> write symbol 1 onto the tape
>
> go into state 2
>
> move right

is therefore represented by

$$(1,0,1,2,R)$$

Similarly, the Turing machine instruction

$$(2,1,1,2,L)$$

stands for

> if you are in state 2

and

> you are reading symbol 1

then

> write symbol 1 onto the tape
>
> go into state 2
>
> move left

Note that in following this instruction, the machine writes in the current cell the same symbol (1) as was already there and remains in the same state (state 2) as before.

A Turing machine can execute a whole sequence of instructions. A clock governs the action of the machine. Whenever the clock ticks, the Turing machine performs its primitive operation; that is, it looks for an instruction that applies to its current state and the symbol currently being read and then follows that instruction. Instructions may be used more than once.

There are a couple of details we've glossed over. What if there is more than one instruction that applies to the current configuration? Suppose, as in Figure 10.2, that the current state is 1, that the current symbol is 0, and that

$$(1,0,1,2,R)$$

$$(1,0,0,3,L)$$

both appear in the same collection of instructions. Then the Turing machine has a conflict between the actions to be taken. Should it write a 1, go to state 2, and move right, or should it write a 0, go to state 3, and move left? We'll avoid this ambiguity by requiring that a set of instructions for a Turing machine can never contain two different instructions of the form

$(i, j, \text{-}, \text{-}, \text{-})$

$(i, j, \text{-}, \text{-}, \text{-})$

On the other hand, what if there is no instruction that applies to the current state–current symbol for the machine? In this case, we specify that the machine halts, doing nothing further.

We impose two additional conventions on the Turing machine regarding its initial configuration when the clock begins. The start-up state will always be state 1, and the machine will always be reading the leftmost nonblank cell on the tape. This ensures that the Turing machine has a fixed and definite starting point.

Now let's do a sample Turing machine computation. Suppose the instructions available to a Turing machine are

1. $(1,0,1,2,R)$
2. $(1,1,1,2,R)$
3. $(2,0,1,2,R)$
4. $(2,1,0,2,R)$
5. $(2,b,b,3,L)$

Also suppose the Turing machine's initial configuration is again that of Figure 10.2:

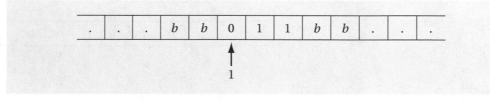

This satisfies our convention about starting in state 1 at the leftmost nonblank cell on the tape. The Turing machine looks for an appropriate instruction for its current state, 1, and its current input symbol, 0, which means it looks for an instruction of the form $(1,0,\text{-},\text{-},\text{-})$. Instruction 1 applies; this was our example instruction earlier, and the resulting configuration agrees with Figure 10.3:

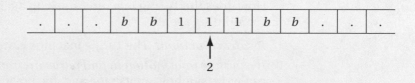

Now let's continue. At the next clock tick, with current state 2 and current symbol 1, the Turing machine looks for an instruction of the form (2, 1, -,-,-). Instruction 4 applies, and after the appropriate actions are performed, the resulting configuration is

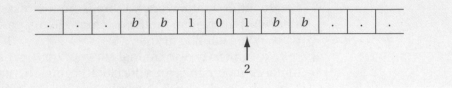

Instruction 4 applies again and results in

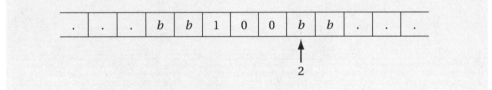

Instruction 5 now applies, leading to

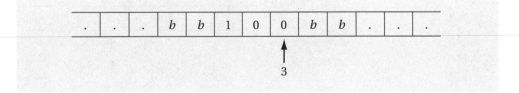

At this point the machine is in state 3 reading the symbol 0. Because there are no instructions of the form (3,0,-,-,-), the machine halts. The Turing machine computation is complete.

Although we numbered this collection of instructions for reference, we saw that the Turing machine does not necessarily execute instructions in the order of this numbering. We also saw that some instructions may not be executed at all, and some more than once. The sequence of instructions used depends on the input written on the tape.

How does the Turing machine stack up against our list of required features for a computing agent?

1. *It can accept input.* The Turing machine can read symbols on its tape.

2. *It can store information in and retrieve it from memory.* The Turing machine can write symbols on its tape and, by moving around over the tape, can

go back and read those symbols at a later time, so the tape has stored that information.

3. *It can take actions according to algorithm instructions, and the choice of action to take may depend on the present state of the computing agent and on the input item presently being processed.* Certainly the Turing machine satisfies this requirement insofar as Turing machine instructions are concerned; the present state and present symbol being processed determine the appropriate instruction, and that instruction specifies the actions to be taken.

4. *It can produce output.* The Turing machine writes symbols on its tape in the course of its normal operation. If (when?) the Turing machine halts, what is written on the tape at that time can be considered output.

In the Turing machine computation that we just finished, the input was the string of symbols 011 (ignoring the surrounding blanks) and the output was the string of symbols 100. Starting with the same input tape but with a different set of instructions could result in different output. Given the benefit of hindsight, we could say that we wrote this particular set of instructions to carry out the task of transforming the string 011 into the string 100. Writing a set of Turing machine instructions to allow a Turing machine to carry out a certain task is similar to writing a computer program to allow a computer to carry out a certain task. We can call such a collection of instructions a **Turing machine program**.

Thus it seems that a Turing machine does capture those properties we identified as essential for a computing agent, which qualifies it as a model of a computing agent. Furthermore, it represents a general computing agent in the sense that, like a real computer, it can follow many different sets of instructions (programs) and thus do many different things (unlike the one-job-only VCR). By its very simplicity of operation, it has eliminated many real-world details, such as exactly how symbols are read from or written to the tape, exactly how input data are to be encoded into a string of symbols from the alphabet in order to be written on the tape, how a string of symbols on the tape is to be interpreted as meaningful output, and exactly how the machine carries out the activities of "changing state." In fact, the Turing machine is such a simple concept that we may wonder how good a model it really is. Did we eliminate too many details? We'll answer the question of how good a model the Turing machine is later in the chapter.

A Turing machine is different in scale from any real computing agent in one respect. A Turing machine can, given the appropriate instructions, move right or left to the blank portion of the tape and write a nonblank symbol. When this happens, the machine has gobbled up an extra cell to use for information storage purposes—that is, as memory. Depending on the instructions, this could happen over and over, which means that there is *no limit* to the amount of memory available to the machine. Any real computing agent has a limit on the memory available to it. In particular, a real computer, although it has a certain amount of internal memory and has access to external memory in the form of disks or tapes on which data can be stored, still has such a limit. There are only so many disks or tapes in the world available for any particular computer to use.

This difference in scale means that a Turing machine (elementary device though it may seem to be) actually has more capability in one respect than any real computer that exists or ever will exist. In this sense, we must be careful about the use of the Turing machine model and the conclusions we draw from it about "real" computing (that is, computing on a real computer). If we find some task that a Turing machine can perform (because of its limitless memory), it *may* not be a task that a real computer could perform.

PRACTICE PROBLEMS

1. A Turing machine has the following instructions:

$(1,0,0,2,R)$

$(2,1,1,2,L)$

$(2,0,1,2,R)$

$(1,b,1,1,L)$

For each of the following configurations of this Turing machine, draw the next configuration.

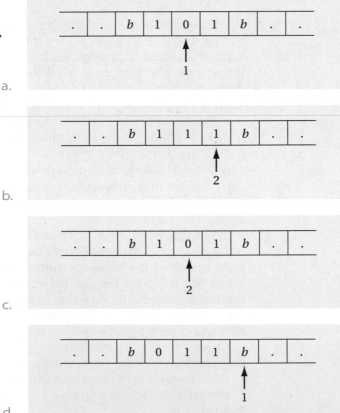

a.

b.

c.

d.

2.   Consider a Turing machine that has the instructions

(1,1,0,2,*R*)

(2,1,1,1,*R*)

Find the output when it is run on the following tape. (Remember that a Turing machine starts in state 1, reading the leftmost non-blank cell.)

| . | . | *b* | 1 | 1 | 1 | *b* | . | . |

10.4 A MODEL OF AN ALGORITHM

An algorithm is a collection of instructions intended for a computing agent to follow. If we accept the Turing machine as a model of a computing agent, then it would seem that the instructions for a Turing machine should be a model of an algorithm. Remember from Chapter 1 that an algorithm must

1. Be a well-ordered collection
2. Consist of unambiguous and effectively computable operations
3. Halt in a finite amount of time
4. Produce a result

Let's consider an arbitrary collection of Turing machine instructions and see whether it exhibits these properties of an algorithm.

1. *Be a well-ordered collection.* The Turing machine must know which operation to carry out first and which to do next at any step. We have already specified the initial conditions for a Turing machine computation: that the Turing machine must begin in state 1 reading the leftmost nonblank cell on the tape. We have also insisted that in any collection of Turing machine instructions, there cannot be two different instructions that both begin with the same current state and current symbol. Given this requirement, there is never any confusion about what operation to do next. There is *at most* one instruction that matches the current state and current symbol of the Turing machine. If there is one instruction, the Turing machine executes the operation that instruction describes. If there is no instruction, the Turing machine halts.

2. *Consist of unambiguous and effectively computable operations.* No problem here. Recall that this property is *relative to the computing agent;* that is, operations must be understandable and doable by the computing agent. Each individual Turing machine instruction describes an operation that (to the Turing

machine) is unambiguous, requiring no additional explanation, and any Turing machine is able to carry out the operation described. After all, Turing machine instructions were designed for Turing machines to be able to execute.

3. *Halt in a finite amount of time.* In order for a Turing machine to halt when executing a collection of instructions, it must reach a configuration where no appropriate instruction exists. This depends on the input given to the Turing machine—that is, the contents initially written on the tape. Consider the following set of Turing machine instructions:

$(1,0,0,1,R)$

$(1,b,b,1,R)$

and suppose the tape initially contains, as its nonblank portion, the single symbol 1. The initial configuration is

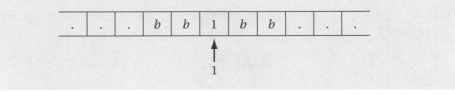

and the machine halts immediately because there is no applicable instruction. On the other hand, suppose the same set of instructions is used with a starting tape that contains the single symbol 0. The Turing machine computation is then

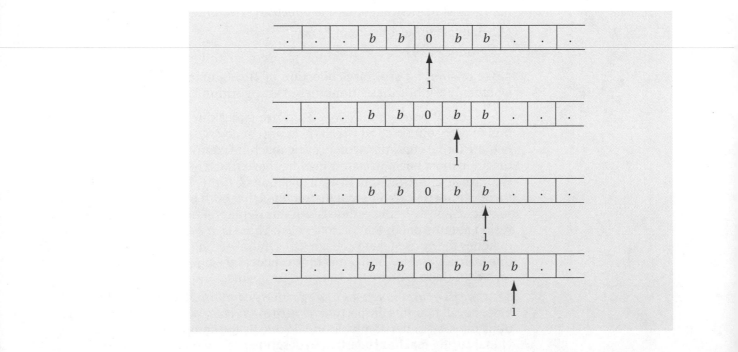

We can see that the second instruction will continue to apply indefinitely and that this Turing machine will never halt.

Typically, an algorithm is designed to carry out a certain type of task. Let us agree that *for input appropriate to that task*, the instructions must be such that the Turing machine does indeed eventually halt. If the Turing machine is run on a tape containing data that are not appropriate input for the task of interest, it need not halt.

This may seem to be a change in our definition of an algorithm, but it simply confirms that there is always a "universe of discourse" connected with the problem we are trying to solve. As an example, we can use a simple algorithm for dividing one positive integer by another using repeated subtraction until the result is negative. Thus $7 \div 3$ can be computed using this algorithm as follows:

$$7 - 3 = 4$$
$$4 - 3 = 1$$
$$1 - 3 < 0$$

The quotient is 2 because two subtractions could be done before the result became negative. However, if we attempt to use this same approach to compute $7 \div (-3)$, we get

$$7 - (-3) = 10$$
$$10 - (-3) = 13$$
$$13 - (-3) = 16$$
$$16 - (-3) = 19$$

and so on

The process would never halt because the result would never become negative. Yet this approach is still an algorithm *for the problem of dividing two positive numbers*, because it does produce the correct result and then halt when given input suitable for this problem.

4. *Produce a result.* We have already imposed the requirement that the Turing machine instructions must lead to a halting configuration when executed on input appropriate to the problem being solved. Whatever is written on the tape when the machine halts is the result.

A collection of Turing machine instructions that obeys these restrictions satisfies the properties required of an algorithm. Yet it is not a "real" algorithm because it is not designed to be executed by a "real" computing agent. It is a model of an algorithm, designed to be executed by the model computing agent called a Turing machine.

Most of the time, no distinction is made between a Turing machine as a computing agent and the instructions (algorithm) it carries out, and a machine together with a set of instructions is called "a Turing machine" and is thought of as an algorithm. Thus we say we are going to write a Turing machine to do a particular task, when we really mean that we are going to write a set of instructions—a Turing machine program, an algorithm—to do that task.

10.5   TURING MACHINE EXAMPLES

Because the Turing machine is such a simple device, it may seem nearly impossible to write a Turing machine to carry out any significant task. In this section, we'll look at a few Turing machines that, although they do not accomplish anything earth-shaking, should convince you that Turing machines can do some rather worthwhile things.

10.5.1 A BIT INVERTER

Let's assume that the only nonblank portion of the input tape for a particular Turing machine consists of a string of bits (0s and 1s). Our first Turing machine will move along its tape inverting all of the bits—that is, changing 0s to 1s and 1s to 0s. (Recall that our sample Turing machine computation inverted the bits in the string 011, resulting in the string 100. Do you think that machine is a bit inverter? What if the leftmost nonblank symbol on the input tape is a 1?)

The Turing machine must begin in state 1 on the leftmost nonblank cell. Whatever the current symbol that is read, the machine must invert it by printing its opposite. Machine state 1 must therefore be a state in which 0s are changed to 1s and 1s to 0s. This is exactly what we want all along the tape, so the machine never needs to go to another state; it can simply move right while remaining in state 1. When we come to the final blank, we want to halt. This can be accomplished by putting in no instruction of the form

$(1,b,-,-,-)$

This describes the Turing machine algorithm in words, but let's represent it more precisely. In the past, we've used pseudocode to describe algorithms. Here we'll use an alternative form of representation that corresponds more closely to Turing machine instructions. A **state diagram** is a visual representation of a Turing machine algorithm where circles represent states, and arrows represent transitions from one state to another. Along each transition arrow, we show three things: the input symbol that caused the transition, the corresponding output symbol to be printed, and the direction of move.

For the bit inverter Turing machine, we have only one state and hence one circle in the state diagram, Figure 10.4. The arrow originating in state 1, marked $0/1/R$, and returning to state 1 says that when in state 1 (the only state) reading an input symbol of 0, the machine should print the symbol 1, move right, and remain in state 1. Be sure you understand what the second arrow means.

The complete Turing machine program for the bit inverter is

1. $(1,0,1,1,R)$ Change the symbol 0 to 1.
2. $(1,1,0,1,R)$ Change the symbol 1 to 0.

FIGURE 10.4

State Diagram for the Bit Inverter Machine

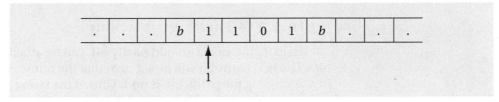

(We've added a comment to each instruction to explain its purpose.) Here's a sample computation using this machine, beginning with the string 1101 on the tape:

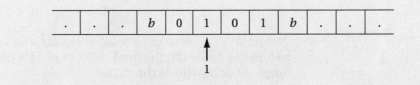

Using instruction 2,

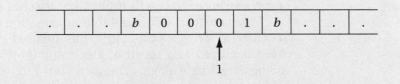

Using instruction 2 again,

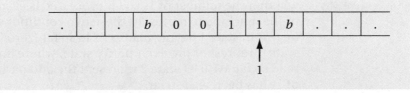

Using instruction 1,

Using instruction 2,

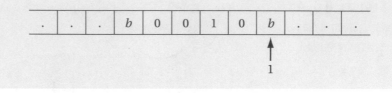

and the machine halts with the inverted string 0010 as output on the tape.

Bit inversion may seem like a trivial task, but recall that in Chapter 4 we saw an electronic device called a NOT gate that is essentially a bit inverter and is one of the components of a real computer.

10.5.2 A PARITY BIT MACHINE

An extra bit, called an **odd parity bit**, can be attached to the end of a string of bits. The odd parity bit will be set such that the number of 1s in the whole string of bits, including the parity bit, is odd. Thus, if the string preceding the parity bit has an odd number of 1s, the parity bit is set to 0 so that there is still an odd number of 1s in the whole string. If the string preceding the parity bit has an even number of 1s, the parity bit is set to 1 so that the number of 1s in the whole string is odd. As an example, the following string of bits includes as its rightmost bit an odd parity bit.

1 1 0 0 0 1 0 1 0 1

The parity bit is set to 1 because there are four 1s (an even number) in the string before the parity bit; the total number of 1s is five (an odd number). Another example of odd parity is the string

1 0 1 1 0 0

where the parity bit (the rightmost bit) is a 0 because three 1s (an odd number) appear in the preceding string. Our job here is to write a Turing machine that, given a string of bits on its input tape, attaches an odd parity bit at the right end.

We know from Chapter 4 that information in electronic form is always represented as strings of bits. Parity bits are used as a way to detect errors that may have occurred as a result of electronic interference when transmitting such strings. If a single bit gets changed from 1 to 0 or from 0 to 1, then the parity bit will be incorrect and the error can be detected. The information can then be retransmitted. Again, we are devising a Turing machine for a significant real-world task.

Our Turing machine must somehow "remember" one of two conditions: whether the number of 1s so far processed is even or odd. We can use two states of the machine to represent these two conditions. Because the Turing machine begins in state 1 having read zero 1s so far (zero is an even number), we can let state 1 represent the even parity state, where an even number of 1s has been read so far. We'll let state 2 represent the odd parity state, where an odd number of 1s has been read so far.

FIGURE 10.5

State Diagram for the
Parity Bit Machine

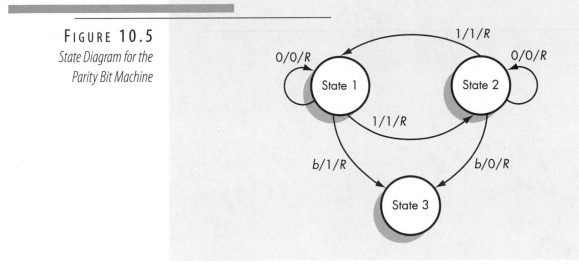

We can read the input string from left to right. Until we get to the end of the bit string, the symbol printed should always be the same as the symbol read, because the input string is not changed. But every time a 1 bit is read, the parity should change, from even to odd or odd to even. In other words, the state should change from 1 to 2 or from 2 to 1. Reading a 0 bit does not affect the parity and therefore should not change the state. Thus if we are in state 1 reading a 1, we want to go to state 2; if we are in state 1 reading a 0, we want to stay in state 1. If we are in state 2 reading a 1, we want to go to state 1; if we are in state 2 reading a 0, we want to stay in state 2.

When we come to the end of the input string (when we first read a blank cell), we write the parity bit, which will be 1 if the machine is in state 1, the even parity state, or will be 0 if the machine is in state 2, the odd parity state. Then we want to halt, which can be accomplished by going into state 3, for which there are no instructions.

The state diagram appears in Figure 10.5. The Turing machine is

1. $(1,1,1,2,R)$ Even parity state reading 1, change state.
2. $(1,0,0,1,R)$ Even parity state reading 0, don't change state.
3. $(2,1,1,1,R)$ Odd parity state reading 1, change state.
4. $(2,0,0,2,R)$ Odd parity state reading 0, don't change state.
5. $(1,b,1,3,R)$ End of string in even parity state, write 1 and go to state 3.
6. $(2,b,0,3,R)$ End of string in odd parity state, write 0 and go to state 3.

Let's do an example. The initial string is 101, which contains an even number of 1s, so we want to add a parity bit of 1 and have the final output be the string 1011. Here's the initial configuration:

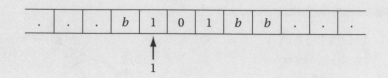

Using instruction 1,

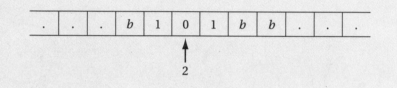

Using instruction 4,

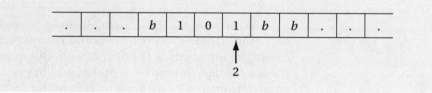

Using instruction 3,

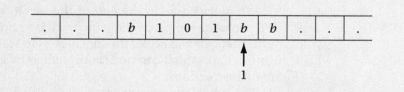

and finally using instruction 5 to write the parity bit, we get

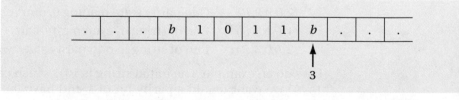

whereupon the machine halts.

10.5.3 MACHINES FOR UNARY INCREMENTING

Turing machines can be written to accomplish arithmetic using the non-negative numbers 0, 1, 2, and so on. Working with these numbers poses a problem we did not face with the bit inverter or the parity bit machine. In those examples, we were manipulating only bits, 0s and 1s, already part of the Turing machine alphabet of symbols. We can't put numbers like 2, 6, or 754 in cells of the Turing machine tape because these symbols are not part of the alphabet. Therefore, our first task is to find a way to encode such numbers using 0s and 1s. We could use binary representation, as a real computer does. Instead, let us agree on a simpler **unary** representation of numbers (*unary* means that we will use only *one* symbol, namely 1). In unary representation, any number n will be encoded by a sequence of $n + 1$ 1s. Thus

Number	Turing Machine Tape Representation
0	1
1	11
2	111
.	.
.	.
.	.

[You may wonder why we don't simply use 1 to represent 1, 11 to represent 2, etc. Such a representational scheme would mean using no 1s to represent 0, and then the machine could not distinguish a single 0 on the tape from nothing (all blanks) on the tape.]

Using this unary representation of numbers, let's write Turing machines to accomplish some basic arithmetic operations. We can write a Turing machine to add 1 to any number, which is often called **incrementing** the number. Using the unary representation of numbers just described, we need only stay in state 1 and travel over the string of 1s to the righthand end. When we encounter the first blank cell, we write a 1 in it and go to state 2, which has no instructions, in order to halt. Figure 10.6 shows the state diagram.

FIGURE 10.6

State Diagram for Incrementer

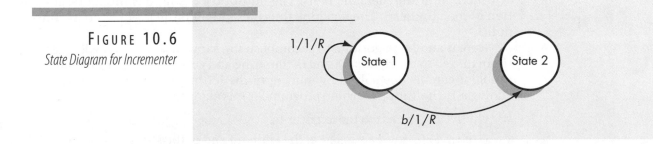

1/1/R   State 1   State 2

b/1/R

The Turing machine is

(1,1,1,1,R)   Pass to the right over 1s.

(1,b,1,2,R)   Add a single 1 at the righthand end of the string.

Here's a quick sample computation:

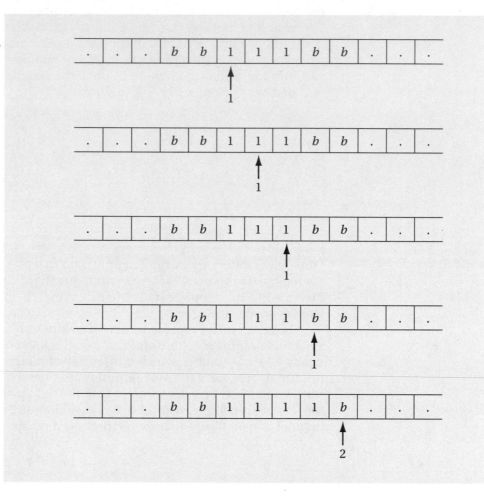

at which point the machine halts. The output on the tape is the representation of the number 3. The machine thus incremented the input, 2, to the output, 3.

Here is another algorithm to accomplish the same task. The preceding algorithm moved to the righthand end of the string and added a 1. But the increment problem can also be solved by moving to the lefthand end of the string and adding a 1. The Turing machine program for this algorithm is

(1,1,1,1,L)   Pass to the left over 1s.

(1,b,1,2,L)   Add a single 1 at the lefthand end of the string.

If we apply this algorithm to the same input tape, the computation is

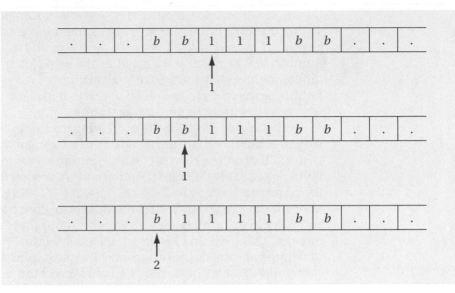

Once again, 2 has been incremented to 3. But whereas the first computation took four operations—that is, four applications of Turing machine instructions—the second computation took only two.

Let's compare these two algorithms further in terms of their time and space efficiency. We'll take the execution of a single Turing machine instruction as a unit of work, so we measure the time used by a Turing machine algorithm by the number of instructions executed. The "space" a Turing machine algorithm takes on any given input will be the number of nonblank cells on the tape that are used during the course of running the program. The input itself occupies some nonblank cells, so the interesting question is how many additional cells the algorithm uses in the course of its execution.

Suppose that the number 5 is to be incremented using algorithm 1. The initial input tape will contain six 1s (the unary representation for 5). The machine moves to the right, over all the 1s on the tape, until it encounters the first blank cell. It writes a 1 into the blank cell and then halts. An instruction is executed for each move to the right. By the time the blank cell is reached, six instruction executions have been done; actually, the first instruction has been executed six times. One final execution, this time of the second instruction, completes the task. Altogether, seven steps were required, two more than the number 5 we were incrementing. One "extra" step comes because of the unary representation, with its additional 1, and a second "extra" step is used to write over the blank cell. Therefore, it is easy to see that if the problem is to increment the number n, then $n + 2$ steps would be required using algorithm 1. Algorithm 2 does a constant number of steps (two) no matter what the size of n. Both algorithms use $n + 2$ cells on the tape: $n + 1$ for the initial input and one more for incrementing. The algorithms are equivalent in space efficiency, but algorithm 2 is more time efficient.

Looking at an input such as 5, our example here, the difference in time efficiency between the two algorithms does not seem great. Figure 10.7 shows the steps required by algorithms 1 and 2 for larger input sizes. As the input gets larger, the difference in efficiency becomes more obvious. If our hypothetical Turing machine actually existed and could do, say, one step per second, then algorithm 1 would take 2 hours, 46 minutes, and 42 seconds to increment the number 10,000. Algorithm 2 could do the same job in 2 seconds! This significant difference gives a definite edge to algorithm 2 as the preferable solution method for this problem. In the notation of Chapter 3, algorithm 1 is an $\Theta(n)$ algorithm, whereas algorithm 2 is an $\Theta(2)$ algorithm.

Although we can compare two Turing machine algorithms for the same task, we can't really compare the efficiency of a Turing machine algorithm with an algorithm that will be run on a "real" computer. For one thing, the data representation is probably different (numbers aren't written in unary form). But more to the point, the basic unit of work is different. It takes many Turing machine operations to do a trivial task, because the entire concept of a Turing machine is so simplistic. Turing machines, as we saw in our few examples, work by carefully moving, changing, and keeping track of individual 0s and 1s. Given such a limited range of activities, a Turing machine must exert a lot of effort to accomplish even mildly interesting tasks. The Turing machine simply plods along, doing its little thing over and over until—eventually—the job is done.

10.5.4 A Unary Addition Machine

A Turing machine can be written to perform the addition of two numbers. Again using unary representation, let's agree to start with the two numbers on the tape separated by a single blank cell. When the Turing machine halts, the tape should contain the unary representation of the sum of the two numbers. The separating blank should be gone. We can think of sliding the entire first number one cell to the right on the tape if we erase the leftmost 1 and then fill in the blank with a 1. Also, both numbers are originally written on the tape using unary representation, which means that there is an extra 1 for each number. When we are finished, we want to have only one extra 1, for the unary representation of the sum. Therefore a second 1 should be removed from the tape. Our plan will be to erase the two leftmost 1s on the tape, proceed rightward to the separating blank, and replace the blank with a 1.

FIGURE 10.7 *Time Efficiency for Two Turing Machine Algorithms for Incrementing*	The Number to Be Incremented, n	Number of Steps Required	
		Algorithm 1	Algorithm 2
	10	12	2
	100	102	2
	1,000	1,002	2
	10,000	10,002	2

As an example, suppose we wish to add 2 + 3. The original tape representation (we're tired of drawing the individual cells, so we'll just show the tape contents) is

$$...b b \underline{1 1 1} b \underline{1 1 1 1} b b...$$
$$\quad\quad 2 \quad\quad 3$$

and the final representation—somewhere on the tape—should be the unary representation for the number 5,

$$...b b \underline{1 1 1 1 1 1} b b b b...$$
$$\quad\quad 5$$

Our algorithm will accomplish this transformation in stages. Erase the leftmost 1:

$$...b b b 1 1 b 1 1 1 1 b b...$$

Erase a second 1 from the left end (see Exercise 22 for the case when there is no "second 1"):

$$...b b b b 1 b 1 1 1 1 b b...$$

and then move to the right and fill in the blank:

$$...b b b b \underline{1 1 1 1 1 1} b...$$
$$\quad\quad\quad 5$$

The Turing machine begins in state 1, so we'll use that state to erase the leftmost 1 and move right, changing to state 2. The job of state 2 is to erase the second 1 and move right, changing to state 3. State 3 must move across any remaining 1s until it encounters the blank, which it changes to a 1 and then goes into a "halting state," state 4. (State 4 will be a halting state because we'll make no instructions for that state.) A state diagram (Figure 10.8) illustrates the desired transitions to next states.

Here is the Turing machine program:

$(1,1,b,2,R)$	Erase the leftmost 1 and move right.
$(2,1,b,3,R)$	Erase the second 1 and move right.
$(3,1,1,3,R)$	Pass over any 1s until a blank is found.
$(3,b,1,4,R)$	Write a 1 over the blank and halt.

Try "running" this machine on the preceding 2 + 3 problem.

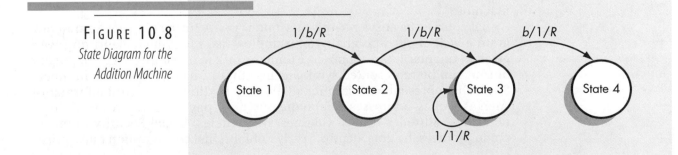

FIGURE 10.8

State Diagram for the Addition Machine

PRACTICE PROBLEMS

1. a. Decide what you think the output will be when the parity bit Turing machine is run on the tape

   $\ldots b\,1\,1\,0\,1\,b \ldots$

   b. Run the parity bit Turing machine on this tape and see whether you get the answer you expect.

2. Set up the input and run the Turing machine to compute 3 + 4.

3. Write a Turing machine that, when run on the tape

   $\ldots b\,1\,1\,1\,0\,b \ldots$

   will produce an output tape of

   $\ldots b\,1\,1\,1\,0\,1\,b \ldots$

Laboratory Experience 16

This laboratory experience will allow you to run simulations of Turing machines using Turing machine algorithms that we have developed in the text. You will see each Turing machine execute a sequence of its basic operations, moving along the tape, possibly modifying the input string, and then halting.

10.6   THE CHURCH–TURING THESIS

Just how good is the Turing machine as a model of the concept of algorithm? We've already seen that any Turing machine exhibits the properties of an algorithm, and we've even produced Turing machine algorithms for important tasks. But perhaps we were judicious in our choice of tasks and happened to use those for which Turing machine instructions could be devised. We should ask whether there are other tasks that are "doable" by algorithm but not "doable" by Turing machine.

Of course, the answer to this question is yes. A Turing machine cannot program a VCR or shampoo hair, for example—tasks for which algorithms were given in Chapter 1. But suppose we limit the task to one for which the input and output can be represented symbolically—that is, using letters and numbers. Symbolic representation is, after all, how we traditionally record information such as names, addresses, telephone numbers, pay rates, yearly profits, temperatures, altitudes, times, volumes, frequencies, Social Security numbers, grade averages, heights, depths, yearly rainfalls, fuel consumption rates, prices,

The Turing Award

The most prestigious technical award given by the Association for Computing Machinery is the annual Turing Award, named in honor of Alan Turing. It is given to an individual selected for "contributions of lasting and major technical importance to the computer field." Some of the individuals we've mentioned in this book have been recipients of the Turing Award, which was first given in 1966.

1971: John McCarthy (Chapter 8)

1972: E. W. Dijkstra (Chapter 8)

1977: John Backus (Chapters 8 and 9)

1983: Dennis Ritchie (Chapter 8)

1984: Niklaus Wirth (Chapter 8)

Other recipients of the award have made contributions in areas we have discussed or will discuss in later chapters.

1975: Allen Newell as one of the founding fathers of artificial intelligence, beginning his work in this area in 1954

1981: Edgar F. Codd for fundamental contributions to database management systems

1982: Stephen A. Cook for exploring the class of problems that in Chapter 3 we called "suspected intractable"

1986: John Hopcroft and Robert Tarjan for early work on analysis of algorithms

1990: Fernando J. Corbato for pioneering work in the 1960s on general-purpose, time-shared mainframe operating systems

1991: Robin Milner, in part for the development of the functional language ML

1992: Butler Lampson for work in the 1970s and early 1980s on hardware and software that demonstrated solutions to problems of distributed computing done on personal workstations linked by a local area network

1993: Juris Hartmanis and R. E. Stearns for their work in 1965 on the computational complexity of algorithms

1996: Manuel Blum for his work on computational complexity theory and how it can be used in cryptography and program checking

---

growth rates, and so on. Taking symbolic representation of information and manipulating it to produce symbolic representation of other information covers a very wide range of tasks, including everything done by "traditional" computing. Now let's ask a modified version of our previous question: Are there symbol manipulation tasks that are "doable" by algorithm but not "doable" by Turing machine?

The answer to this question is generally considered to be no, as stated by the Church–Turing thesis, named for Turing and another famous mathematician, Alonzo Church.

Church–Turing Thesis: *If there is an algorithm to do a symbol manipulation task, then there is a Turing machine to do that task.*

This is quite an extraordinary claim. It says that any symbol manipulation task that has an algorithmic solution can also be carried out by a Turing machine executing some set of Turing machine instructions. Processing the 1997 Internal

Revenue Service records, for example, or directing the guidance and navigation systems on the space shuttle, can be done (according to this claim) using Turing machines. The thought of writing a Turing machine program to process IRS records is mind-boggling, but our examples may have convinced you that it is possible. Given that such a program could be written, one can hardly imagine how many centuries it would take to execute, even with a very rapid "system clock." But the Church–Turing thesis says nothing about how efficiently the task will be done, only that it *can* be done by some Turing machine.

There are really two parts to writing a Turing machine for a symbol manipulation task. One part involves encoding symbolic information as strings of 0s and 1s so that it can appear on Turing machine tapes. This is not difficult, and we know that real computers store all information, including graphical information, in binary form. The other part is the heart of the challenge: Given that we get the input information encoded on a Turing machine tape, can we write the Turing machine instructions that will produce the encoded form of the correct output? Figure 10.9 illustrates the problem. The bottom arrow is the algorithmic solution to the symbol manipulation task we wish to emulate. To perform this emulation, we must encode the symbolic input into a bit string on a Turing machine tape (left arrow), write the Turing machine that solves the problem (top arrow), and decode the resulting bit string into symbolic output (right arrow). The Church–Turing thesis asserts that this can always be done.

What exactly is a thesis? According to the dictionary, it is "a statement advanced for consideration and maintained by argument." That sounds less than convincing—hasn't the Church–Turing thesis been proved? No, and that's why it is called a thesis, not a theorem. Theorems are ideas that can be proved in a formal, mathematical way, such as "the sum of the interior angles of a triangle equals 180°." The Church–Turing thesis can never be proved, because, despite all our talk about algorithms and their properties, the definition of an algorithm is still descriptive, not mathematical. It would be like trying to "prove" that an

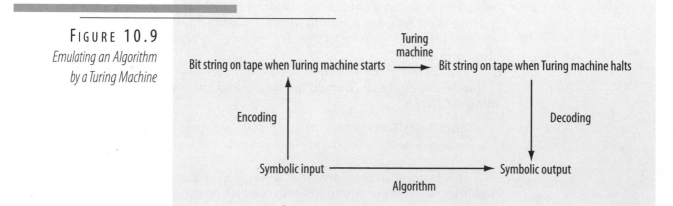

FIGURE 10.9

Emulating an Algorithm by a Turing Machine

ideal day at the beach is sunny and 85°F. We might all agree on this, but we'll never be able to "prove" it. Well, then, the Church–Turing thesis makes a remarkable claim and can never be proved! Sounds pretty suspicious—what are the arguments on its behalf? There are two.

One argument on behalf of the Church–Turing thesis is that early on, when the thesis was first put forward, whenever computer science researchers described algorithmic solutions for tasks, they also tried to find Turing machines for those tasks. They were always successful; no one was ever able to put forth an algorithm for a task for which a Turing machine was not eventually found. This does not mean that no such task exists, but it lends weight to a body of evidence in support of the thesis.

A second argument on behalf of the thesis is the fact that a number of other mathematicians attempted to find models for computing agents and algorithms. All of these were proved to be equivalent to Turing machines and Turing machine programs in the following sense: Whatever could be done by these other computing agents running their algorithms could also be done by a Turing machine running a Turing machine program, and vice versa. This suggests that the Turing machine captures all of these other ideas about "algorithm."

The Church–Turing thesis is now widely accepted by computer scientists. They no longer feel it necessary to write a Turing machine when they talk about an algorithmic computation. After describing an algorithm to carry out some task, they simply say, "Now let T be the Turing machine that does this task." You may make your own decision about the Church–Turing thesis, but in this book we will go along with convention and accept it as true. We are then accepting the Turing machine as an ultimate model of a computing agent, and a Turing machine program as an ultimate model of an algorithm. We are saying that Turing machines define the limits of **computability**—that which can be done by symbol manipulation algorithms. What can be done by an algorithm is doable by a Turing machine, and what is not doable by a Turing machine cannot be done by an algorithm. In particular, if we find a symbol manipulation task that no Turing machine can perform (in its elementary way of moving around over a tape of 0s and 1s), then there is no algorithm for this task, and no real computer, no matter how sophisticated, will be able to do it either. That's why the Turing machine is important. You can now see where this is all leading in terms of our search for a problem that has no algorithmic solution. Suppose we can find a (symbol manipulation) problem for which we can prove that no Turing machine exists to solve it. Then, because of the Church–Turing thesis, no algorithm exists to solve it either. The problem is an **uncomputable** or **unsolvable** problem.

Note again that if we pose a problem and try to construct a Turing machine to solve it but are not successful, that alone does not prove that no Turing machine exists. What we must do is actually prove that no one can ever find such a Turing machine—that it is not possible for a Turing machine to exist that solves this problem. It may appear that the introduction of Turing machines hasn't helped at all and that we are confronted by the same dilemma we faced at the beginning of this chapter. Ah, but Alan Turing, in the late 1930s, found such a problem and proved its unsolvability.

10.7   UNSOLVABLE PROBLEMS

The problem Turing found is an ingenious one that itself involves Turing machine computations. A Turing machine that is executing an algorithm (a collection of Turing machine instructions) to solve some task must halt when begun on a tape containing input appropriate to that task. On other kinds of input, the Turing machine may not halt. It is easy enough for us to decide whether any specific configuration of a given Turing machine is a halting configuration. If a Turing machine program consists of the instructions

$(1,0,1,2,R)$

$(1,1,0,2,R)$

$(2,0,0,2,R)$

$(2,b,b,2,L)$

then the configuration

$$\ldots b\,1\,1\,b\,b\,b\ldots$$
$$\uparrow$$
$$2$$

is a halting configuration because there is no instruction of the form $(2,1,\text{-},\text{-},\text{-})$. It is also easy to see that this configuration will arise if the Turing machine is begun on the tape

$$\ldots b\,0\,1\,b\,b\,b\ldots$$

Similarly, we can see that if the Turing machine is begun on the tape

$$\ldots b\,1\,b\,b\,b\ldots$$

then it will never halt. Instead, after the first step (clock tick), the machine will cycle forever between the two configurations

$$\ldots b\,0\,b\,b\,b\ldots \qquad \ldots b\,0\,b\,b\,b\ldots$$
$$\uparrow \qquad\qquad\qquad \uparrow$$
$$2 \qquad\qquad\qquad 2$$

In a more complicated case, however, if we know the Turing machine program and we know the initial contents of the tape, then it may not be so easy to decide whether the Turing machine will eventually halt when begun on that tape. Of course, we could always simply execute the Turing machine—that is, carry out the instructions. We don't have all day to wait for the answer, so we'll set a time-out for our Turing machine system clock. Let's say we are willing to wait for 1,000 clock ticks. If we come to a halting configuration within the first 1,000 steps, then we know the answer: This Turing machine, running on this input tape, halts. But suppose we have not come to a halting configuration within the first 1,000 clock ticks. Can we say that the machine will never halt? Should we wait another 1,000 clock ticks? 10,000 clock ticks? Just running the Turing machine doesn't necessarily enable us to decide about halting.

Here is the problem we propose to investigate:

Decide, given any collection of Turing machine instructions together with any initial tape contents, whether that Turing machine will ever halt if started on that tape.

This is a clear and unambiguous problem known as the **halting problem**. Does it have a Turing machine solution? Can we find one Turing machine that will solve every instance of this problem—that is, that will give us the answer "Yes, halts" or "No, never halts" for every (Turing machine, initial tape) pair?

This is an uncomputable problem; we will show that no Turing machine exists to solve this problem. Remember that we said it was not sufficient to look for such a machine and fail; we actually have to prove that no such machine can exist. The way to do this is to assume that such a Turing machine does exist and then show that this assumption leads to an impossible situation, so such a machine could not exist after all. This approach is called a **proof by contradiction**.

We'll assume, then, that P is a Turing machine that solves the halting problem. On the initial tape for P we will have to put a description—using the binary digits 0 and 1—of a collection T of Turing machine instructions, as well as the initial tape content t on which those instructions run. This is the encoding part of Figure 10.9. Translating Turing machine instructions into binary form is tedious but not difficult. For example, we could use unary notation for machine states and tape symbols, designate the direction in which the read unit moves by 1 for R (right) and 11 for L (left), and separate the parts of a Turing machine instruction by 0s. Let's use T^* to symbolize the binary form of the collection T of Turing machine instructions. P is then run on a tape containing both T^* and t, so the initial tape for P looks like the following, where T^* and t may occupy many cells of the tape.

$$\ldots b\,b\,T^*\,b\,t\,b\,b \ldots$$

Our assumption is that P will always give us an answer ("Yes, halts" or "No, never halts"). P's yes–no answer would be its output—what is written on the tape when P halts; therefore P itself must always halt. Again, because the output is written on P's tape, it also has to be in binary form, so let's say that a single 1 and all the rest blanks represents "yes," and a single 0 and all the rest blanks represents "no." This is the decoding part of Figure 10.9. To summarize:

When begun on a tape containing T^* and t

P halts with 1 on its tape exactly when T eventually halts when begun on t

P halts with 0 on its tape exactly when T never halts when begun on t

Figure 10.10 is a pictorial representation of the actions of P when started on a tape containing T^* and t.

When P halts with a single 1 on its tape, it does so because there are no instructions allowing P to proceed in its current state when reading 1. For example, P might be in state 9, and there is no

$$(9,1,\text{-},\text{-},\text{-})$$

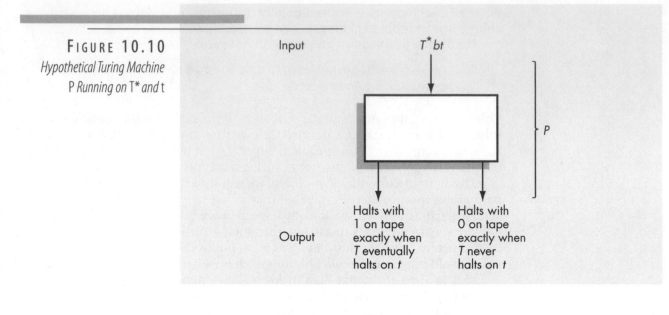

FIGURE 10.10

Hypothetical Turing Machine P Running on T* and t

Input T^*bt

Output

Halts with
1 on tape
exactly when
T eventually
halts on *t*

Halts with
0 on tape
exactly when
T never
halts on *t*

P

instruction in *P.* Let's imagine adding more instructions to *P* to create a new machine *Q* that behaves just like *P* except that when it reaches this same configuration, it moves forever to the right on the tape instead of halting. To do this, pick some state not in *P*, say 52, and add the following two new instructions to *P*:

(9,1,1,52,*R*)

(52,*b*,*b*,52,*R*)

Figure 10.11 represents *Q*'s behavior when started on a tape containing T^* and *t*.

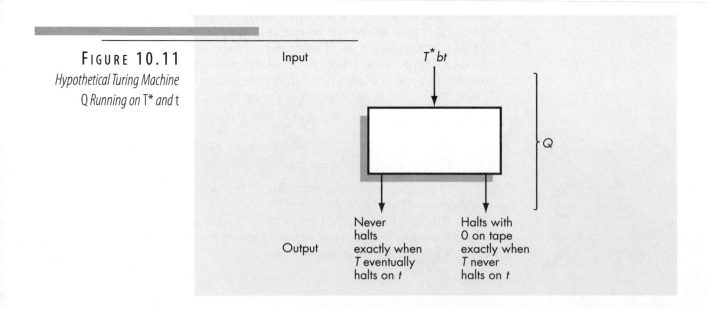

FIGURE 10.11

Hypothetical Turing Machine Q Running on T* and t

Input T^*bt

Output

Never
halts
exactly when
T eventually
halts on *t*

Halts with
0 on tape
exactly when
T never
halts on *t*

Q

Finally, we'll create a new machine S. This machine first makes a copy of what appears on its input tape. (This is a doable if tedious task. The machine must "pick up" a 0 or 1 by going to a particular state, move to another part of the tape, and write a 0 or 1, depending on the state. It travels back and repeats the process; however, each time it picks up a 0 or 1, it must mark the tape with some marker symbol, say X for 0 and Y for 1, so that it doesn't try to pick them up again. At the end of the copying, the markers must be changed back to 0s and 1s.) After S is finished with its copying job, it uses the same instructions as machine Q.

Now what happens when machine S is run on a tape that contains S^*, the binary representation of S's own instructions? S first makes a copy of S^* and then turns the computation over to Q, which is now running on a tape containing S^* and S^*. Figure 10.12 shows the result; this figure follows from Figure 10.11 where T^* and t are both S^*. Figure 10.12 represents the behavior of S running on input S^*. The final outcome is either (left output)

> S running on input S^* never halts
> exactly when S halts running on S^*—this is a contradiction

or (right output)

> S running on input S^* halts with 0 on the tape
> exactly when S never halts running on S^*—also a contradiction

(Perhaps you'll need to read this several times while looking at Figure 10.12 to convince yourself of what we have said.) We have backed ourselves into a real corner here, but that's good. This is the impossible situation we were hoping to find.

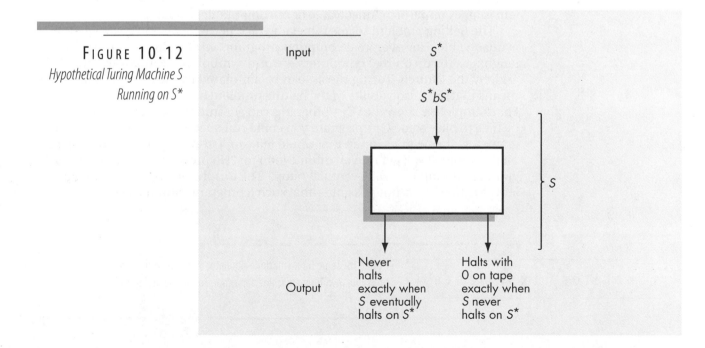

FIGURE 10.12

Hypothetical Turing Machine S Running on S*

Input S^*

$S^* b S^*$

S

Output

Never halts exactly when S eventually halts on S^*

Halts with 0 on tape exactly when S never halts on S^*

Couldn't Do, Can't Do, Never Will Be Able to . . . .

Unsolvable problems are not confined to problems about running programs (C++ programs or Turing machines).

In Chapter 9 we talked about grammars that can be described in Backus-Naur Form (BNF) and about how a compiler parses a programming language statement by applying the rules of its grammar. We noted that ambiguous grammars are not suitable for programming languages because they can allow multiple interpretations of a statement. It would be nice to have a test (an algorithm) to decide whether any BNF grammar is ambiguous. This is an unsolvable problem—no such algorithm can exist. Deciding whether any two such grammars produce the same language is also unsolvable.

One of the earliest "decision problems" was posed by the British mathematician David Hilbert in 1900. Consider quadratic equations of the form

$$ax^2 + bx + c = 0$$

where a, b, and c are integers. We can easily decide whether any one such equation has integer solutions by applying the quadratic formula to solve the equation. But consider more general polynomial equations in several unknowns, such as

$$ax^4 + by^2 + cz^6 + dw^4 + e = 0$$

where the unknowns are x, y, z, and w and the coefficients (a, b, c, d, and e) are integers. Is there an algorithm to decide whether any such equation has integer solutions? In 1970 this problem was finally shown to be unsolvable.

We assumed that there was a Turing machine that could solve the halting problem, and this assumption led to an impossible situation. The assumption is therefore incorrect, and no Turing machine can exist to solve the halting problem. Therefore, no algorithm can exist to solve this problem. The halting problem is an example of an unsolvable or uncomputable problem.

The halting problem seems rather abstract; perhaps we don't care whether it is unsolvable. However, real computer programs written in real programming languages to run on real computers are also symbol manipulation algorithms and, by the Church–Turing thesis, can be simulated by Turing machines. This means that the unsolvability of the halting problem has practical consequences. For example, we know that C++ programs can get stuck in infinite loops. It would be nice to have some C++ program you could run ahead of time on any C++ program, together with its input, that would tell you "Oh-oh, if you run this program on this input, it will get into an infinite loop" or "No problem, if you run this program on this input, it will eventually stop." The unsolvability of the halting problem says that this is not possible—that such a program cannot exist.

Laboratory Experience 17

Using the same Turing machine simulator as before, you can now design and run your own Turing machine algorithms for simple problems.

PRACTICE PROBLEMS

1. Explain how a proof by contradiction is done.

2. a. Write in your own words a statement of the halting problem.
   b. Write a paragraph that describes the proof of the unsolvability of the halting problem.

Other unsolvability problems, related to the halting problem, have the following practical consequences:

- No C++ program can be written to decide whether any given C++ program always stops eventually, no matter what the input.
- No C++ program can be written to decide whether any two C++ programs are equivalent (will produce the same output for all inputs).
- No C++ program can be written to decide whether any given C++ program on any given input will ever produce some specific output.

This last case means it is impossible to write a general automatic program tester—one that can check for any program whether, given input A, it produces correct output B. That is why program testing plays such an important role in the software development life cycle described in Chapter 7.

It is important to note, however, that these problems are unsolvable because of their generality. We are asking for *one* program that will decide something about *any* given program. It may be very easy to write a program *A* that can make a decision only about a specific program *B* by utilizing specialized properties of *B*. (*Analogy:* if I ask you to be ready to write "I love you" in English, you can do it; if I ask you to be ready to write "I love you" in any language I might later specify, you can't do it.)

10.8   CONCLUSION

We began this chapter by proposing that there are unsolvable problems—problems for which no solution algorithm exists. To prove such a statement, we looked for appropriate models of "computing agent" and "algorithm" that would enable us to concentrate on the fundamental nature of computation. We discussed the nature of models in general and their importance in helping us understand real phenomena. After developing a list of properties inherent in any computing agent, we defined the Turing machine, noted that it incorporates these properties, and accepted it as a model of a computing agent. A Turing machine program incorporates the properties of an algorithm described in Chapter 1, so we accepted it as a model of an algorithm. Are these good models? Do they capture everything that is fundamental about computing and algorithms? After looking at a few Turing machines devised to do some simple tasks, we stated our position with a resounding *yes* in the form of the Church–Turing thesis: Not only is a Turing machine program an example of an algorithm, but every symbolic manipulation algorithm can be done by a Turing machine (we believe). This leap of faith—putting total confidence in Turing machine programs as models of algorithms—allows us to define the boundaries of computability. If it can't be done by a Turing machine, then it is not computable. Thus the real value of Turing machines as models of computability is in exposing problems that are uncomputable—problems for which no algorithmic solution exists no matter how intelligent we are or how long we keep looking. As a practical matter, recognizing uncomputable problems certainly saves time; we are less likely to devote our lives to searching for algorithms that can never be. As a philosophical matter, it is important to know that computability has its limits, beyond which lies the great abyss of the uncomputable!

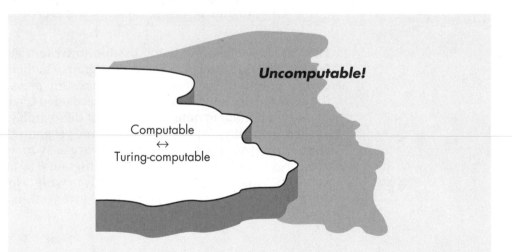

EXERCISES

In this set of exercises, when writing Turing machine algorithms, include comments for each instruction or related group of instructions. The comments should convey information in terms of the algorithm the Turing machine is accomplishing. Thus the instruction

$$(1,0,0,1,R)$$

might have a comment like "Pass to the right over all the 0s," not a comment like "In state 1 looking at a 0, write a 0, stay in state 1, and move right," which gives no additional information.

1. Describe what factors might be included in a model for the spread of an epidemic.

2. Say an automobile manufacturer designs a new car using a sophisticated and detailed computer simulation, but no prototype vehicles, and the automobile is later found to have a defect. Do you think the manufacturer is accountable? Is the manufacturer accountable if it builds prototypes that do not reveal the defect, but does not do a simulation?

3. Give an example of a potential use of computerized models in
   a. The pharmaceutical industry
   b. The food processing industry
   c. The insurance industry

4. Which of the following could be considered computing agents and why?
   a. A clock radio
   b. A thermostat
   c. A video camera
   d. A programmable calculator

5. Given the Turing machine instruction
   $(1,1,0,2,L)$
   and the configuration
   $\ldots b\,1\,0\,b\ldots$
   $\uparrow$
   1
   draw the next configuration.

6. Find the output for the Turing machine
   $(1,1,1,2,R)$
   $(1,0,0,2,R)$
   $(1,b,1,2,R)$
   $(2,0,0,2,R)$
   $(2,1,0,1,R)$
   when run on the tape
   $\ldots b\,1\,0\,0\,1\,b\ldots$

7. Find the output for the Turing machine
   $(1,1,1,2,L)$
   $(2,b,0,3,L)$
   $(3,b,1,4,R)$
   $(4,0,1,4,R)$
   when run on the tape
   $\ldots b\,1\,b\ldots$

8. Describe the behavior of the Turing machine
   $(1,1,1,1,R)$
   $(1,0,0,2,L)$
   $(2,1,0,2,L)$
   $(2,b,1,3,L)$
   $(3,b,b,1,R)$
   when run on the tape
   $\ldots b\,1\,0\,1\,b\ldots$

9. Describe the behavior of the following Turing machine on any input tape containing a binary string.
   $(1,1,1,1,R)$
   $(1,0,0,1,R)$
   $(1,b,1,1,R)$

10. Write a Turing machine that, when run on the tape
    $\ldots b\,1\,1\,1\,1\,1\,b\ldots$
    produces an output tape of
    $\ldots b\,0\,1\,1\,1\,1\,b\ldots$
    You should be able to use only one instruction.

11. Say a Turing machine is supposed to change any string of 1s to a string of 0s. For example,
    $\ldots b\,1\,1\,1\,b\ldots$
    should become
    $\ldots b\,0\,0\,0\,b\ldots$
    Will the following Turing machine do the job? Why or why not?
    $(1,1,0,2,R)$
    $(2,1,0,3,R)$
    $(3,1,0,4,R)$

12. a. Write a Turing machine that, when run on the tape
    $\ldots b\,1\,1\,1\,1\,1\,b\ldots$

produces an output tape of

$...b11110b...$

b. Write a Turing machine that, when run on any tape containing a unary string, changes the rightmost 1 to 0 and then halts. (If your solution to part (a) was sufficiently general, you will not have to change it here.)

13. Write a Turing machine to perform a unary **decrement** (the opposite of an increment). Assume that $n > 0$.

14. Write a Turing machine to perform a unary decrement. Assume that n may be 0, in which case a single 0 should be output on the tape to signify that the operation would result in a negative number.

15. Write a Turing machine that operates on any binary string and changes it to a string of the same length with all 1s. It should, for example, change the tape

$...b011010b...$

to

$...b111111b...$

However, you must write instructions that allow your Turing machine to work on *any* binary string, not just the one shown here.

16. Write a Turing machine that operates on any string of 1s and changes it to a string of alternating 1s and 0s.

17. Write a Turing machine that begins on a tape containing a single 1 and never halts but successively displays the strings

$...b1b...$
$...b010b...$
$...b00100b...$

and so on.

18. Write a Turing machine that operates on the unary representation of any number and decides whether the number is 0; your machine should produce an output tape containing the unary representation of 1 if the number was 0 and the unary representation of 2 if the number was not 0.

19. A **palindrome** is a string of characters that reads the same forward and backward, such as radar or IUPUI. Write a Turing machine to decide whether any binary string is a palindrome by halting with a blank tape if the string is a palindrome and halting with a nonblank tape if the string is not a palindrome.

> *Note:* The world's longest single-word palindrome is the Finnish word for "lye dealer":
>
> *Saippuakivikauppias*
>
> Other palindromes include
>
> *Slap a ham on Omaha pals*
> *Do geese see god*
> *A man a plan a canal Panama*

20. Write a Turing machine that takes any unary string of an even number of 1s and halts with the first half of the string changed to 0s. (*Hint:* You may need to use a "marker" symbol such as X or Y to replace temporarily any input symbols you have already processed and do not want to process again; at the end, your program must "clean up" any marker symbols.)

21. Write a Turing machine that takes as input the unary representation of any two different numbers, separated by a blank, and halts with the representation of the larger of the two numbers on the tape. (*Hint:* You may need to use a "marker" symbol such as X or Y to replace temporarily any input symbols you have already processed and do not want to process again; at the end, your program must "clean up" any marker symbols.)

22. The Turing machine described in Section 10.5.4 to add two unary numbers was designed to erase the two leftmost 1s on the tape, move to the right to the blank separating the two numbers, and replace the blank with a 1. If the first of the two numbers being added is 0, then there are not two 1s before the separating blank. Does the algorithm still work in this case?

23. Draw a state diagram for a Turing machine that takes any string of 1s and changes every third 1 to a 0. Thus, for example,

$...b111111b...$

would become

$...b110110b...$

24. Draw a state diagram for a Turing machine that increments a binary number. Thus if the binary representation of 4 is initially on the tape,

    $...b100...$

    then the output should be the binary representation of 5,

    $...b101...$

    or if the initial tape contains the binary representation of 7,

    $...b111b...$

    then the output should be the binary representation of 8,

    $...b1000b...$

25. Analyze the time and space efficiency of the following Turing machine operating on a unary string of length n.

    $(1,1,1,1,R)$

    $(1,b,b,2,L)$

    $(2,1,0,2,L)$

    $(2,b,b,3,R)$

    $(3,0,1,3,R)$

26. Suppose we already have Turing machine instructions to copy a unary string; we also know how to add two unary numbers. Describe (in words only) the design of a Turing machine to multiply two unary numbers.

27. Two other Turing machine unary addition algorithms follow.

    Fill in the separating blank with a 1, go to the far right end and erase two 1s

    Erase a 1 on the left end, fill in the separating blank with a 1, erase a 1 on the right end

    a. Do both of these algorithms work correctly?
    b. Write the Turing machine for each of these algorithms.

c. Informally, which of the three addition algorithms (the one given in the chapter and these two) seems most time efficient?
d. Suppose that the numbers to be added are n and m. The original tape contains the unary representation of n, followed by a blank, followed by the unary representation of m. Write exact expressions in terms of n, m, or both for the time efficiency of each of the three algorithms. Does this confirm your answer from part (c)?
e. Again assuming that the numbers to be added are n and m, write an exact expression for the space efficiency of each of the three algorithms.

28. Your boss gives you a C++ computer program and a set of input data and asks you to determine whether the program will get into an infinite loop running on these data. You report that you cannot do this job, citing the Church–Turing thesis. Should your boss fire you? Explain.

29. What is the significance of the unsolvability of the halting problem?

30. The **uniform halting problem** is to decide, given any collection of Turing machine instructions, whether that Turing machine will halt for every input tape. This is an unsolvable problem. Which of the three practical consequences of unsolvability problems described in this section (page 509) follows from the uniform halting problem?

31. The **10-step halting problem** is to decide, given any collection of Turing machine instructions, together with any initial tape contents, whether that Turing machine will halt within 10 steps when started on that tape. Explain why the 10-step halting problem is computable.

CHALLENGE WORK

1. Several alternative definitions of Turing machines exist, all of which produce machines that are equivalent in computational ability to the Turing machine as defined in this chapter. One of these alternative definitions is the **multitrack Turing machine**. In a multitrack Turing machine, there

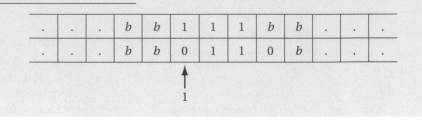

FIGURE 10.13

A Two-Track Turing Machine

are multiple tapes. The machine reads a cell from each of the tapes and, on the basis of what it reads, it writes a symbol on each tape, changes state, and moves left or right. Figure 10.13 shows a two-track Turing machine currently in state 1 reading a 1 on the first tape and a 0 on the second tape.

An instruction for this Turing machine would have the following form:

(current state, current first tape symbol, next first tape symbol, current second tape symbol, next second tape symbol, next state, direction of move)

An instruction of the form

$(1,1,0,0,0,2,R)$

applied to the machine configuration of Figure 10.13 would result in the configuration of Figure 10.14.

As in the original Turing machine definition, some conventions apply. Each tape can contain only a finite number of nonblank symbols, and the leftmost nonblank symbols must initially "line up" on the two tapes. The read head begins in this leftmost nonblank position in state 1. At any time, if no instruction applies to the current machine configuration, the machine halts.

a. Design a two-track Turing machine that compares two binary strings and decides whether they are equal. If the strings are equal, the machine halts in some fixed state; if they are not equal, the machine halts in some other fixed state.

b. Solve this same problem using the regular Turing machine from this chapter.

c. Prove the following statement: Any computation that can be carried out using a regular Turing machine can be done using a two-track Turing machine.

d. On the basis of parts (a) and (b), make an argument for the following statement: Any computation that can be carried out using a two-track Turing machine can be done using a regular Turing machine.

2. Read some biographical information on Alan Turing and write a report on his life, concentrating particularly on his contributions in computability theory, cryptology, and artificial intelligence.

FIGURE 10.14

New Configuration for the Two-Track Machine

| . | . | . | b | b | 0 | 1 | 1 | b | b | . | . | . |
| . | . | . | b | b | 0 | 1 | 1 | 0 | b | . | . | . |

↑
2

FOR FURTHER READING

A classic explanation of Gödel's work on the limitations of formal systems describing arithmetic can be found in

Nagel, E., and Newman, J. R. "Gödel's Proof." *Scientific American*, June 1956.

The foundational textbook in the area of models for various sorts of computation tasks, including Turing machines, is

Hopcroft, J. E., and Ullman, J. D. *Introduction to Automata Theory, Languages, and Computation.* Reading, MA: Addison-Wesley, 1979.

Other books that cover much the same ground, but perhaps in less detail, include

Linz, P. *An Introduction to Formal Languages and Automata*, 2nd ed. Sudbury, MA: Jones and Bartlett, 1996.
Sipser, M. *Introduction to the Theory of Computation.* Boston: PWS, 1997.

For a stimulating experience in "thinking about thinking," try the Pulitzer-prize-winning book

Hofstadter, D. R. *Gödel, Escher, Bach: An Eternal Golden Braid.* New York: Basic Books, 1979.

10.9 SUMMARY OF LEVEL 4

In Level 4, "The Software World," we examined one procedural programming language, C++, as an example of a means for expressing algorithms at a high level of abstraction. Other high-level languages exist, including other procedural languages, special-purpose languages, and those that follow other philosophies, such as functional languages and logic-based languages. Because algorithms written in high-level languages ultimately run on low-level hardware, program translators must convert from one level of algorithmic expression to another. We've looked at the series of tasks that a language compiler must be able to perform in order to carry out this conversion. This final chapter of Level 4 proved that there are limits to computability—that there exist problems that can never be solved algorithmically.

With all of the hardware and software machinery in place to implement algorithmic problem solutions, we are ready to proceed to the next level—the level of applications—to see some of the ways in which computers (and algorithms) are being put to use.

APPLICATIONS

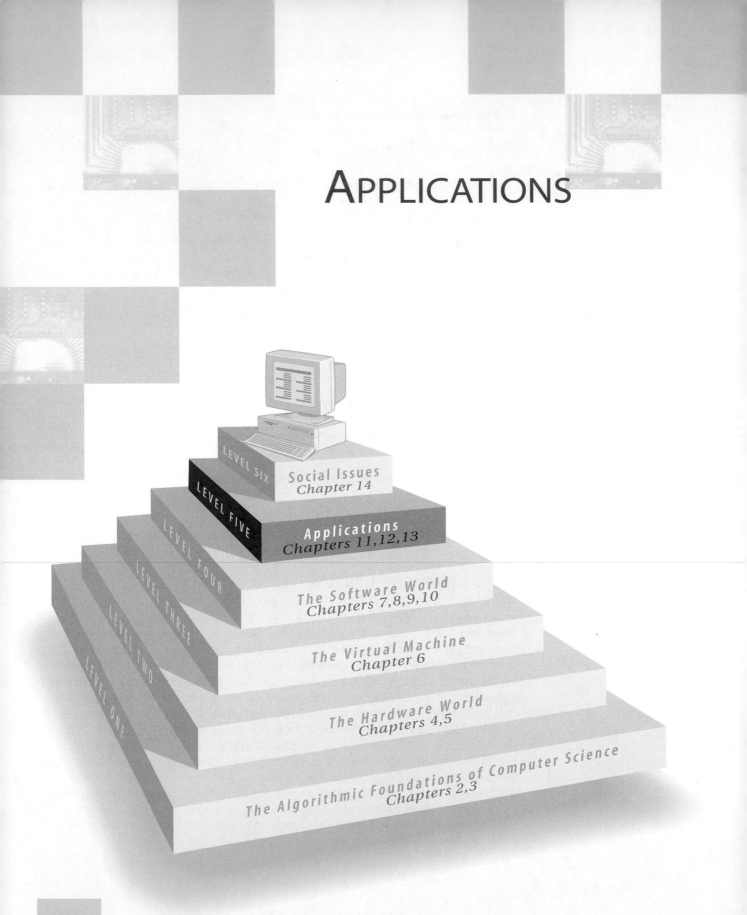

LEVEL SIX

Social Issues
Chapter 14

LEVEL FIVE

Applications
Chapters 11,12,13

LEVEL FOUR

The Software World
Chapters 7,8,9,10

LEVEL THREE

The Virtual Machine
Chapter 6

LEVEL TWO

The Hardware World
Chapters 4,5

LEVEL ONE

The Algorithmic Foundations of Computer Science
Chapters 2,3

5

At this point, we can review our progress upward through the various levels of abstraction. We began with the study of algorithms as the foundation of computer science, showed how to build a machine to execute those algorithms, described languages in which we can express our solutions, showed how those languages are understood by the machine, and explored the limitations of algorithmic problem solving.

Now, what can be done with these ideas? How are they used to support the many and various applications that exist today? There is hardly any area of daily life or any field of study that has not been greatly affected by the use of computer technology. We cannot hope to cover even a small fraction of the many applications of computers that you may encounter in your everyday life or your professional career at the present time, much less what may await us all in years to come. We can only give a sampling of some of the important developments.

In the next three chapters, we will discuss applications for using and managing data (spreadsheets, database software, and symbolic computation software), computer networks, and artificial intelligence. The list of applications we don't discuss is practically boundless; it includes word processing, presentation software, CAD/CAM (computer-aided design/computer-aided manufacturing), GIS (geographic information systems), scientific visualization, sophisticated graphics for the entertainment industry, project scheduling and management software, computer-generated music, robotics, virtual reality, and much more. We urge you to explore on your own some of these areas that interest you.

Computer applications are near the peak of the pyramid of levels of abstraction. Looking downward along that pyramid, we're not going to study in detail the algorithms or the actual programming language code used to write the applications, nor are we going to worry about how program instructions are translated into machine language. We are certainly not going to trace how various logic gates within the machine are activated while one of these applications runs. But because we've had a peek behind the scenes, our view will be more technical than that of a user of the application who is unaware that all of these things go on. Although these applications are highly complex and sophisticated, there is nothing mysterious or magical about them. We want to show how they build on foundations covered earlier in this book. Certainly, the people who created these applications had to understand the ideas we have already discussed.

USING AND MANAGING DATA: A CASE STUDY IN THREE SCENES

11.1   INTRODUCTION

In this chapter we examine three different applications, all concerned with using and managing data, that might be of interest to a hypothetical small business, the Huli Huli Pineapple and Papaya Company. These applications are

- Spreadsheets
- Databases
- Symbolic and numeric computation

Each application is possible because of advances that have taken place in computer hardware and software. Although we use a small business context to present these applications, they are equally useful, in various forms, for individuals and for multinational corporations.

11.2   SPREADSHEETS

An **electronic spreadsheet** combines elements of a calculator, a word processor, a database manager, a graphing tool, a modeling and forecasting tool, and an accountant's ledger. The first spreadsheet software, VisiCalc, developed in 1979, was modeled after the traditional accountant's ledgerbook or spreadsheet. But the advantages of an *electronic* spreadsheet soon became apparent, and this single software package was a principal motivater in the growth of microcomputer use. Today, spreadsheets are one of the most widely used software packages, and they continue to incorporate increasing capabilities. Spreadsheets are of value to individual homeowners and investors, business planners, scientists, economists, teachers, and anyone who has text and numeric information to organize, manipulate, or display.

11.2.1 BASIC SPREADSHEET OPERATION

An empty spreadsheet contains a two-dimensional grid of cells. The rows are labeled by numbers 1, 2, 3, . . . , and the columns are labeled by letters A through Z, then AA, AB, and so on. Giving a column letter and a row number identifies a particular cell in the grid. On some systems, cells, or blocks of cells, can also be named and referred to by name. The dimensions of the grid are defined by the software package but are usually in the range of thousands of rows and a few hundred columns. Only a portion of the grid, called a **window**, is visible at any one time on the screen. The user may **scroll** (move) the window through the grid to make different parts visible. The user can also adjust the width of any column in the grid.

FIGURE 11.1

Part of a Spreadsheet

	A	B	C	D	E	F	G
1							
2				//////////////			
3							
4							
5							
6							
7							

Initially, the window is always located in the upper left corner of the grid, at the beginning of the letter-number cell identification system (cell A1). Figure 11.1 shows a window in an empty spreadsheet, with cell D2 shaded. The user generally selects a certain cell to be "active" by using a mouse, the tab key, or the arrow keys to move a **cursor** (marker) to the desired cell.

Three kinds of information can be stored in a spreadsheet cell. A cell can contain **text information**, also called a **label**, which appears on the screen in that cell. Text information is used at the top of a column to label the data appearing in that column, or at the left of a row to label data in that row. Text can also be used to label any single cell. Text information may be longer than the standard-sized cell, so the column size is frequently expanded to accommodate text information. The user can use formatting commands to direct how the text will be displayed, including whether it is to be centered or right- or left-justified within the cell; what the type font and size are to be; and whether certain words should be boldface or italic. In Figure 11.2, cells A1, B1, and C1 contain labels.

The second kind of information that a cell can contain is a **numeric value**. Numeric values also appear on the screen, and, as with text, the user can choose the format in which the number will be displayed. For example, the user might choose to display decimal data rounded to two decimal places (the usual convention for dollars and cents) and to display negative numbers in parentheses

FIGURE 11.2

A Simple Spreadsheet Calculation

	A	B	C	D	E	F	G
1	Item 1	Item 2	Total				
2	3.25	5.75	9.00				
3							
4							
5							
6							
7							

(a standard accounting notation). Numeric values have been entered in cells A2 and B2 of Figure 11.2. (Although cell C2 displays a numeric value, this is not a value we entered but one that the spreadsheet computed for us, as explained in the next paragraph.)

The third kind of information a cell can hold is a **mathematical formula**. To enter a formula into a cell usually requires that some extra keystroke be done first to denote that what comes next is a formula, rather than a label or a numeric value. The formula does not appear on the screen; it is associated with the given cell in a "hidden" fashion. The formula is a mathematical expression that almost always includes references to other cell locations. In Figure 11.2, the formula

A2 + B2

was entered for cell C2. At that point the current values in cells A2 and B2 were added together, and the results were immediately displayed in cell C2. (If A2 and B2 had contained text information or had been blank, then an error message would have resulted.)

Huli Huli Pineapple and Papaya (HHP&P) uses a spreadsheet to compute information about its current employee payroll for a given work period. Figure 11.3 shows the spreadsheet with the initial text and numeric values entered. The columns are labeled, so we know that column A contains each employee's ID number, column B contains the employee name, and so on. Each row from 2 through 6 represents data about one employee. Columns B and D have been widened to accommodate text information (the employee name in column B and the column header for column D). The values for *Pay*, column F, have not been entered; we'll use formulas to compute these values.

To compute the value of Janet Kay's pay to date, cell F2, we want to multiply Janet's pay rate per hour (cell D2) by her hours worked to date (cell E2). This may seem to suggest using the formula

16.60*94

in cell F2. Using a formula with specific values, however, defeats the whole purpose of a spreadsheet, which has the ability to do instant recalculations. Suppose we use the preceding formula and then discover that we need to change the data;

	A	B	C	D	E	F	G
1	ID	Name	Age	PayRate	Hours	Pay	
2	86	Janet Kay	51	16.60	94		
3	123	Francine Perreira	18	8.50	185		
4	149	Fred Takasano	43	12.35	250		
5	71	John Kay	53	17.80	245		
6	165	Butch Honou	17	6.70	53		
7							

FIGURE 11.3

Data for HHP&P Employees

perhaps an error was made and Janet's pay rate is really 16.70. We can change the entry in cell D2, but then the result in cell F2 is incorrect; we must also remember to change the hidden formula for cell F2.

Instead of using a formula with the specific values from cells D2 and E2, we use a formula that references the cell locations. Hence we enter the formula

D2*E2

in cell F2. The spreadsheet does the calculation and displays the result on the screen in cell F2. If the numeric entry in cell D2 (or E2) is changed, the formula automatically recomputes the new result and displays it instantly in cell F2.

A similar formula would serve for all the other rows in column F; cell F3 would use data from row 3, so its formula should be

D3*E3

Instead of having to enter the appropriate formula in each cell of the F column, however, we can simply copy the formula used for cell F2. The spreadsheet automatically adjusts the formula to include references to cells in the appropriate row. Figure 11.4(a) shows what has been entered in each cell (including the hidden formulas in column F). Figure 11.4(b) shows what actually appears on the screen, where the values in column F have been computed using the hidden formulas.

11.2.2 BELLS AND WHISTLES

Over and above its basic functions, every spreadsheet package provides its own versions of extra features (extra goodies in a software package are often called **bells and whistles**). We'll mention some of these features, but not the details of how to use them.

A spreadsheet provides a number of built-in functions for common tasks, such as averaging a group of values or finding a maximum value. The user simply selects the desired function and the cell or group of cells to which the function should be applied. The spreadsheet software can also present the information from selected cells in **graphical form** as a bar chart, a line graph, a pie chart, or the like. Figure 11.5 shows a pie chart of the pay to date by employee ID for HHP&P employees (column F of the spreadsheet of Figure 11.4). Various areas of the spreadsheet grid can be printed in a report format, which can also include graphical information.

Multiple sheets can be handled at one time. If the sheets are similar in structure, then a formula entered in the "active" sheet propagates to all the other sheets as well, creating a three-dimensional spreadsheet. For example, we might keep a sheet in the form of Figure 11.4 for each month. Data from these multiple sheets could then be gathered into a yearly summary sheet.

The spreadsheet user can write a **macro**, which is a series of instructions bundled together and given a name—essentially a computer program. When the macro is invoked, these instructions are executed exactly as though they had just been entered. Thus a single name can serve as a shortcut notation to commence a series of tasks. If this series of tasks is frequently done, then the macro is a time saver. As an example, a macro could be written that would cause a chart to be made using the current data in the spreadsheet, the chart to be inserted in a report, and the report to be printed. Then each time the user updates the data, a new report with a chart based on the new data can be printed simply by giving

	A	B	C	D	E	F	G
1	ID	Name	Age	PayRate	Hours	Pay	
2	86	Janet Kay	51	16.60	94	D2*E2	
3	123	Francine Perreira	18	8.50	185	D3*E3	
4	149	Fred Takasano	43	12.35	250	D4*E4	
5	71	John Kay	53	17.80	245	D5*E5	
6	165	Butch Honou	17	6.70	53	D6*E6	
7							

(a) What We Entered

	A	B	C	D	E	F	G
1	ID	Name	Age	PayRate	Hours	Pay	
2	86	Janet Kay	51	16.60	94	1560.40	
3	123	Francine Perreira	18	8.50	185	1572.50	
4	149	Fred Takasano	43	12.35	250	3087.50	
5	71	John Kay	53	17.80	245	4361.00	
6	165	Butch Honou	17	6.70	53	355.10	
7							

(b) What We See

FIGURE 11.4
*Pay-to-Date Has Been
Computed for HHP&P
Employees*

FIGURE 11.5
*Pie Chart of Pay to Date for
HHP&P Employees*

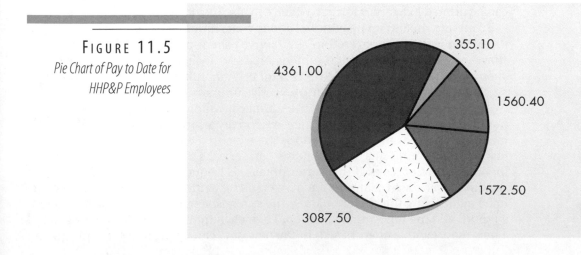

the single macro name. Many spreadsheets also have the capability of simple database management software, which we discuss in Section 11.3.

11.2.3 SPREADSHEETS AS MODELING TOOLS

So far we know that the spreadsheet has the basic form of an accountant's ledger, can contain text and generate reports like a word processor, can create graphical presentations of data, can perform computations much as a calculator does, and can function as a database management system. Remarkable as all this is, if a spreadsheet could do nothing more, it would not have become the indispensable tool it is. A spreadsheet's power lies in its ability to provide a fluid medium for varying data and immediately obtaining corresponding results. Suppose, for example, that the end of the next week comes along, HHP&P's employees have worked more hours, and we want to compute the new pay to date. Only the entries in the hours column, column E, need to be changed. The pay, column F, is recomputed automatically.

This ability to vary data entries and immediately view the results does not have to be confined to actual data that *are*; it can also be applied to data that *might be*. After all, these are only bits, not real dollars or hours or employees. Why not use the spreadsheet to examine some possibilities?

As a simple case, suppose that the owners of HHP&P have had an especially good year and would like to give their employees a raise. How much of a raise, they wonder, can they afford? As a start, suppose the owners investigate the cost of a fixed, across-the-board pay raise of 2% by recomputing the pay at the new rate. Another cell can be created in the spreadsheet to hold the fixed increase, and another column can be created to contain the resulting pay. Figure 11.6 shows one possibility. The formula for new pay in cell G2 is

D2*(1 + $C$8/100)*E2

	A	B	C	D	E	F	G
1	ID	Name	Age	PayRate	Hours	Pay	NewPay
2	86	Janet Kay	51	16.60	94	1560.40	1591.61
3	123	Francine Perreira	18	8.50	185	1572.50	1603.95
4	149	Fred Takasano	43	12.35	250	3087.50	3149.25
5	71	John Kay	53	17.80	245	4361.00	4448.22
6	165	Butch Honou	17	6.70	53	355.10	362.20
7							
8		Base % Increase	2				
9						Totals	$10936.50	$11155.23
10							

FIGURE 11.6

A 2% Increase in Pay Rate for HHP&P Employees

Here Janet's pay rate, contained in cell D2, is multiplied by 1.02 (1 plus the content of cell C8 divided by 100) to take into account a 2% raise, and the result is then multiplied by the number of hours Janet worked, contained in cell E2. The $ signs in the formula indicate that C8 is to be treated as a *fixed cell reference*. As a consequence, when we copy this formula into the rest of column G, cell C8 will still be cell C8, but the other cell references will change to suit the row. Cell G3, for example, will contain the formula

D3*(1 + $C$8/100)*E3

which is exactly what we want.

We've also created new cells to hold the total salaries under the existing pay rate and the proposed pay rate. These are computed by using the built-in SUM function applied to a range of cells. The formula entered in cell F9 is

SUM(F2:F6)

which indicates that the cells between and including F2 and F6 are to be added together. When this formula is copied to cell G9, it becomes SUM(G2:G6), which also gives the correct total for the new pay.

The owners can repeatedly change the percent raise in cell C8 to see what the effect is. Figure 11.7 shows the result of increasing the percent raise to 3%; note that only the contents of cell C8 had to be changed to get the new values.

Instead of a uniform raise, the owners can give each individual worker some "merit" percentage over the fixed across-the-board increase. Figure 11.8 shows what the results might look like in this case. Here a new column has been inserted for the merit percentage. The formula in cell H2 (previously in G2) has been changed to

D2*(1 + ($C$8 + G2)/100)*E2

	A	B	C	D	E	F	G
1	ID	Name	Age	PayRate	Hours	Pay	NewPay
2	86	Janet Kay	51	16.60	94	1560.40	1607.21
3	123	Francine Perreira	18	8.50	185	1572.50	1619.68
4	149	Fred Takasano	43	12.35	250	3087.50	3180.13
5	71	John Kay	53	17.80	245	4361.00	4491.83
6	165	Butch Honou	17	6.70	53	355.10	365.75
7							
8		Base % Increase	3				
9					Totals	$10936.50	$11264.60
10							

FIGURE 11.7

A 3% Increase in Pay Rate for HHP&P Employees

	A	B	C	D	E	F	G	H
1	ID	Name	Age	PayRate	Hours	Pay	Merit	NewPay
2	86	Janet Kay	51	16.60	94	1560.40	3	1638.42
3	123	Francine Perreira	18	8.50	185	1572.50	2	1635.40
4	149	Fred Takasano	43	12.35	250	3087.50	3	3241.88
5	71	John Kay	53	17.80	245	4361.00	2	4535.44
6	165	Butch Honou	17	6.70	53	355.10	1	365.75
7								
8		Base % Increase	2					
9					Totals	$10936.50		$11416.80
10								

FIGURE 11.8

Base Pay Increase Plus Merit Pay Increase

The ($C$8 + G2)/100 adds the fixed base increase of 2% in cell C8 to Janet's merit increase of 3% in cell G2, giving 5%, and then changes this to a decimal by dividing by 100. Hence the pay rate, cell D2, is multiplied by 1.05 and the result multiplied by the hours worked, cell E2. Rows 3 to 6 in column H are adjusted accordingly by copying the formula from cell H2. The formula for the total was moved from cell G9 to cell H9 when the new column was inserted, and it automatically adjusted to sum up the values in column H.

The owners of HHP&P believe they can spend $12,000 in salary money for this pay period. In a process called **goal seeking**, some spreadsheets can automatically vary one quantity (in this case, the base percent increase) until another quantity (in this case, the new total in cell H9) achieves a target value. Thus the owners could set a target value of $12,000.00 and have the spreadsheet determine the base percent increase that would achieve this target value. From the results in Figure 11.9, the owners are happy to find that they can give everyone a base pay increase of 7.33%.

Imagine the power of this "what-iffing" in more complex business situations. A user can vary the price of a product, the cost of supplies, or the cost of wages or fringe benefits and see immediately the effect on profit. An instructor, keeping grades in a spreadsheet, can vary the weight given to various exams and assignments in the course and see the effect on final grades. A biologist can forecast growth of a species of aquatic plant life by varying the nutrient mix in the water, a chemical engineer can "experiment" via spreadsheet with the amount of additive necessary to obtain a smooth flow of liquid in a pipe assembly, an economist can track the effects of a proposed tax increase on revenue, and so on. The spreadsheet has become a modeling and forecasting tool.

We discussed the concept of models in Chapter 10, as preparation for studying the Turing machine and its instructions as a model for a computing agent and the algorithms it carries out. There we noted that an effective model should capture the essence of the real thing and provide a safe and controlled environment to play with "what-ifs." We also noted that the model is reliable only if we can

	A	B	C	D	E	F	G	H
1	ID	Name	Age	PayRate	Hours	Pay	Merit	NewPay
2	86	Janet Kay	51	16.60	94	1560.40	3	1721.62
3	123	Francine Perreira	18	8.50	185	1572.50	2	1719.24
4	149	Fred Takasano	43	12.35	250	3087.50	3	3406.49
5	71	John Kay	53	17.80	245	4361.00	2	4767.96
6	165	Butch Honou	17	6.70	53	355.10	1	384.69
7								
8		Base % Increase	7.33					
9					Totals	$10936.50		$12000.00
10								

FIGURE 11.9

Base Pay Increase to Achieve Target Total Pay Value

include enough detail to represent accurately the system we are modeling and if we can represent correctly the relationships among the elements involved. In a spreadsheet, we are constrained to representing elements numerically and to representing relationships by mathematical formulas. In Section 11.4, we'll see how to model systems whose elements are represented only symbolically.

A spreadsheet also does not conveniently incorporate the element of time; it gives us a static picture of certain quantities. We can do one of two things to see how something will change over the course of time. We can repeatedly run the spreadsheet program, using new data values representing different points in time. This gives us a series of sheets, each of which is a static snapshot of some point in time. Alternatively, we can make time one of the columns in the spreadsheet and insert down this column (or have the spreadsheet compute) various values for time and, on the basis of those values, compute corresponding values for other time-dependent quantities. Then each row in the spreadsheet is a static snapshot of some point in time. We are simulating a time-dependent system by using a **discrete simulation**—looking at the system at separate moments in time—rather than a **continuous simulation**, where we could see outcomes as time varies continuously. The difference is a bit like watching time go by on a digital clock (one that displays numbers) as opposed to an analog clock (one where hands go around).

11.2.4 COMPUTER SCIENCE ISSUES

Let's investigate a bit of what goes on technically during the operation of a spreadsheet. There are actually three levels of "programming" that can take place. At the highest level, the user can write macros to carry out tasks involving spreadsheets. The language used to write macros is a true programming language that allows for sequential, conditional, and looping instructions. (Remember that sequential, conditional, and looping are the only control mechanisms needed in a programming language, no matter how complex the task.)

At the intermediate level, any user of a spreadsheet is immersed in a programming environment. This environment is based on a graphical user interface.

The spreadsheet itself is laid out in a visual fashion, and users may use mouse control, pull-down menus, scrolling windows, and so on. The grid can be thought of as a representation of memory, one value being stored per cell. There is a correlation between a cell in the spreadsheet and an actual memory location, but more information is connected with a cell than just what appears on the screen. For example, a number on the screen may be computed from a formula entered for that cell. Then the cell location, the name given to that cell (if any), the formula, the computed result of applying the formula, and the designated format for displaying this result are all associated with this one cell. (In compiler theory terms—Chapter 9—we could call this the semantic record for the cell.)

The spreadsheet itself contains both data and programming instructions (formulas), all somewhat arbitrarily laid out within the grid. A spreadsheet has aspects of machine language programming in that the user must keep track of the "address"—the grid location, say D3, of each and every item of data. Of course, the user can see the "address" right on the screen, so this is not such a difficult task. It can be avoided by naming cells or sections of the spreadsheet, which is analogous to naming variables or arrays in C++. The programming instructions available in the spreadsheet are essentially all assignment statements, assigning the value of some expression (given by a formula) to the active cell. Alternatively, we could think of the spreadsheet "programming language" as a functional language (see Chapter 8), because all tasks involve evaluating functions defined by formulas. At any rate, it is an **interpreted language**, rather than a compiled language. A compiler translates an entire program and stores the resulting object code (machine language instructions) in a file. The object code can then be loaded and executed. Recompilation is required only when changes are made in the program. In an interpreted language, each instruction (formula) is translated and then executed one at a time as it is entered. No permanent object code is created, and the translation is redone whenever changes are made.

Each formula is evaluated or re-evaluated as soon as the values it uses are available or have been changed. Thus the order in which instructions are executed is not, as in a procedural language, determined entirely by the program itself. Rather, it is determined by the order in which the user of the spreadsheet performs certain actions, such as entering formulas or changing data values. The "program" as a whole waits for the user to generate events to which it reacts. A spreadsheet is thus an example of **event-driven programming**.

There is often a built-in "IF" function that can be used as the formula in a given cell. The IF function evaluates some condition, which can depend on the current contents of other cells, to determine whether it is true or false. If it is true, then one formula will be used in the current cell; if it is false, then another formula will be used. The formula

IF(A3 > B3, A3 − B3, B3 − A3)

entered in cell C3 will cause the value of A3 − B3 to be entered in that cell if the current value in A3 is larger than the current value in B3. If not, then the value of B3 − A3 will be entered in C3. The effect is to provide a conditional control structure in that a decision is made as to which program instruction (formula) is computed next.

A looping control structure is also present. Suppose the spreadsheet is used to compute the value needed in one cell to achieve a target value in another cell, as in finding the base increase needed for the target value of $12,000 total pay. This is done by an iterative (looping) mechanism. The value of the independent cell is changed, and the corresponding value of the dependent cell is compared to the target value. If the target value has not been obtained, then the process is repeated: adjusting the value of the independent cell, comparing the new value of the dependent cell against the target value, and so on. The adjustments are made in some intelligent way so as to minimize the number of recalculations required. In our example, if a positive change in the base increase results in too large a total pay, then on the next iteration, a smaller value of the base increase is used. There are a number of algorithms for "converging" on the desired value in a small number of steps.

Thus at the intermediate level, programming instructions (functions) are computed on the basis of a sequence controlled by the user, possibly based on conditions entered by the user, and possibly involving looping.

At the lowest level, the software carries out the computations indicated in a formula. If the formula in cell D1 is

A1*B1*C1

the multiplication operations are carried out sequentially left to right, and the result is stored in cell D1. If the formula in cell D1 is

ABS(A1)

(the absolute value function), the software evaluates whether the current value of cell A1 is negative or not and, on the basis of this decision, stores either the value of A1 or its negative in cell D1. And if the formula in D1 is SUM(B2:B10), the software loops through a series of additions. Thus sequential, conditional, and looping control structures are buried in the rules for how various individual formulas are evaluated.

Laboratory Experience 18

If you have a commercial spreadsheet package available to use, you can work through the exercises in this laboratory experience. You'll become familiar with some of the types of calculations that can be carried out on a spreadsheet.

PRACTICE PROBLEMS

1. In the spreadsheet shown in Figure 11.7, if the value of cell C8 is changed to 4, what will the resulting value be in cell G2?

2. In the spreadsheet shown in Figure 11.8, what is the formula in cell H5?

3. a. In Figure 11.2, show what would be entered in cells D1 and D2 to label and compute the amount of tax at a fixed rate of 5% on the total shown in cell C2.

   b. In Figure 11.2, show what would be entered in cells D1 and D2 to display the tax rate (currently 5%) and what would be entered in cells E1 and E2 to label and compute the tax amount at this rate on the total shown in cell C2.

11.3   FILE MANAGEMENT AND DATABASES

The management and organization of data have always been important problems. It is likely that a strong impetus for the development of written language was the need to record commercial transactions ("On this day Procrastinus traded Consensius 4 sheep for 7 barrels of oil.") From there it is a short step to recording inventories ("Procrastinus has 27 sheep"), wages paid, profits gained, and so on. As the volume of data grows, it becomes more difficult to keep track of all the facts, harder to extract useful information from a large collection of facts, and more difficult to relate one fact to another.

With the 1890 census (Chapter 5), Herman Hollerith demonstrated the advantages of mechanizing the storage and processing of large amounts of data. From this beginning, **data processing** has been a term synonymous with business uses of computing, but how businesses manage data has changed as more powerful applications packages have been developed. This same power, coupled with increasing ease of use, has put data management capabilities on the desktop of the individual as well. Today it is not uncommon for people to use powerful database packages and file management software to keep track of their personal investments, household goods, bibliographic information, medical histories, and so forth.

11.3.1   BASIC FILE MANAGEMENT

Related items of information are stored in **files** on secondary storage devices such as floppy disks, hard disks, and magnetic tape. A file can be a data file—that is, a file containing data that some computer program could use. But that computer program—a collection of instructions written in some programming language—is also stored in a file. The object code produced when that program is compiled is stored in a file. The compiler itself is stored in a file, as is other system software. A file can store a text document, produced by a word processor or text editor, or graphical information, produced by a paint program. In other words, the computer may need access to a variety of files that are stored in secondary storage, and it must be able to locate those files as needed. A **file manager** gives the user, and the computer, the ability to work with files. Although our primary interest in this section will be with data files, let's first consider the basic file management capabilities that apply to any type of file.

A computer's operating system, as we learned in Chapter 6, functions as a basic file manager. In its capacity as a file manager, the operating system provides certain elementary capabilities that we will describe shortly. The operating system also provides commands (which really invoke other programs supplied with the operating system) that use these elementary capabilities to allow the user to perform a variety of file-related tasks.

The file manager must know where each file is stored. It maintains a mapping that says, "The file with such-and-such a name is located in a section of storage that begins at such-and-such an address." This information is kept in a **directory structure** along with associated information, such as the size of the file and the date and time the file was stored. An empty directory structure is created on a floppy disk when that disk is formatted. It is the file manager's job to maintain the directory structure. When the user's application program requests the operating system to store file TEST.CPP on that disk, the file manager secures the necessary space on the disk and makes an appropriate entry in the directory structure (see Figure 11.10). When the user's application program later requests the operating system to load TEST.CPP, the file manager consults the directory structure and provides the location of the beginning of that file. The file manager must also be able to modify entries in the directory structure, such as changing the date and time if the file is modified, and it must be able to delete entries in the directory structure. The file manager thus has four elementary capabilities:

- Create an entry in the directory structure.
- Read the information in a directory structure entry.
- Update the information in a directory structure entry.
- Delete an entry in the directory structure.

Operating system commands (issued by typing text, clicking on an icon, or picking from a menu) available to the user for file-related tasks will use these elementary capabilities. For example, a common command would ask for a list of all the files present on a disk. The program that carries out this command starts at the top of the directory structure and repeatedly uses the file manager's capability to read the information in a directory structure entry in order to display the name of the file, the file size, the date of last modification, and so on. Another command may request that all the files on a disk be deleted. This command also steps through the entire directory structure, repeatedly using the file manager's capability to delete an entry.

Note that the operating system does not allow the user to create files directly; files must be created within some other application—a word processor, a C++ program, or the like. This is because the task of creating a file involves low-level details that must be done carefully in order for the file manager to be able to store the file properly. The user is not entrusted (or burdened) with these details.

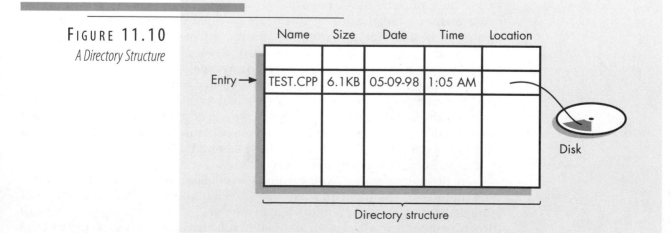

FIGURE 11.10

A Directory Structure

The file management tasks that we have described here require no knowledge of the internal structure of the files. A file named TEST.CPP may suggest to us, the user, that the file contains a C++ program, and we may be able to instruct the file manager to associate certain file names with certain applications, but the file manager itself is unable to distinguish program files from graphics files from data files. It treats files as indivisible units and can never see the "parts" inside any file. Clearly, in order to make use of files, it's going to be necessary at some point to "see inside them."

11.3.2 Data Organization

What are the parts of a file? Because we are concerned in this section with management or manipulation of the user's data, we'll confine our description to data files. As we learned in Chapters 4 and 5, the most basic unit of data is a single **bit**, a value of 0 or 1. A single bit rarely conveys any meaningful information. Bits are combined into groups of eight called **bytes**; each byte can store the binary representation of a single character or of a small integer number. A byte is a single unit of addressable memory. A single byte is often too small to store meaningful information, so a group of bytes is used to represent a string of characters—say, the name of an employee in a company or a larger numerical value. Such a group of bytes is called a **field**. A collection of related fields—say, all the information about a single employee—is called a **record**, a term inherited from the pencil-and-paper concept of "keeping records." Related records—say, the records of all the employees in a single company—are kept in a **data file**. (*File* is another term inherited from the familiar *filing cabinet*.) And finally, related files, such as all the files (employee data, inventory data, sales data, and so on) for a single company make up a **database**. Thus

Bits combine to form bytes.

Bytes combine to form fields.

Fields combine to form records.

Records combine to form files.

Files combine to form databases.

Figure 11.11 shows this hierarchical organization of data elements. (This figure was drawn to look neat, but files in a database are almost never all the same size or "shape.")

Bits and bytes are too fine a level of detail for what we will discuss in this section. Also, for the moment, let's simplify the situation to the case where the database consists of only a single file. Figure 11.12 illustrates a single file made up of five records (the rows), each record composed of three fields (the columns).

Figure 11.12 looks somewhat like the array data structure we described in Chapter 7. In an array, however, each array entry must be of the same data type, so that a given array could store only character data or only integer data. The various fields in a record can hold different types of data. One field in each record might hold character strings; another field in each record might hold integer data.

Each record in a file contains information about an item in the "universe of discourse" that the file describes. In our example, we are assuming that the "universe of discourse" is the set of employees at HHP&P and that each record corresponds

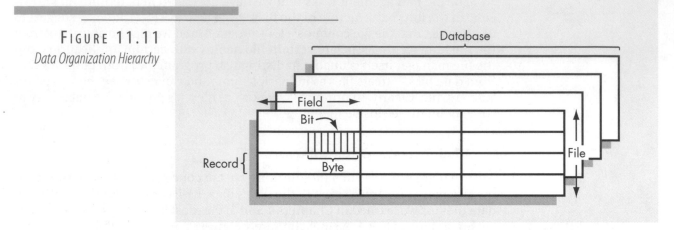

to a single employee. An individual employee record, with six different fields, is shown in Figure 11.13. Here it is clear that the *Name* field holds character strings and that the *PayRate* and *Pay* fields are for real numbers. The type of data being stored in the *Age* field is not clear to us as humans from looking at the record; it could be either integer data or character strings. However, the data type would have been specified when the file was created.

11.3.3 DATABASE MANAGEMENT SYSTEMS

A **database management system (DBMS)** manages the files in a database. We know that such files actually consist of collections of individual records. However, Edgar F. Codd (mentioned in Chapter 10 as a Turing Award winner for his work in database management systems) proposed the conceptual model of a file as simply a two-dimensional table. In this **relational database model**, the *Employee* file at HHP&P would be represented by the *Employee* table of Figure 11.14, which looks a great deal like the spreadsheet of Figure 11.4(b).

With the change from actual records in a file to a table representing data come some changes in terminology. The table represents information about an **entity**, a fundamental distinguishable object, in the HHP&P business—namely,

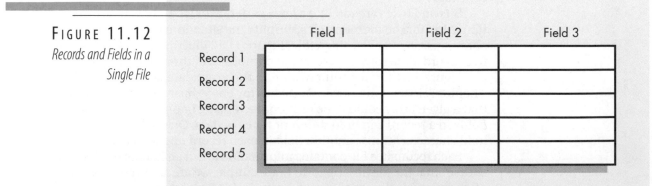

FIGURE 11.13
One Record in the HHP&P
Employee File

ID	Name	Age	PayRate	Hours	Pay
149	Fred Takasano	43	12.35	250	3087.50

FIGURE 11.13
One Record in the HHP&P
Employee File

its employees. A row of the table contains data about one instance of this entity—that is, one employee—and the row is called a **tuple** (in Figure 11.14, each row is a 6-tuple, containing six pieces of information). How the tuples (rows) are ordered within the table is not important. Each category of information (*ID*, *Name*, *Age*, and so on, in our example) is called an **attribute**. The heading above each column identifies an attribute. The table thus consists of tuples of attribute values. (In other words, in the relational model, files are thought of as tables, records as tuples, and fields as attributes.) A **primary key** is an attribute or combination of attributes that uniquely identifies a tuple. In our example, we are assuming that *ID* is a primary key; *ID* is underlined in the heading in Figure 11.14 to indicate that it is the primary key for this table. The Social Security number is often used as a primary key to identify uniquely tuples that involve people.

A database management system, unlike a simple file manager, works at the level of individual fields in the individual records of the file; in more appropriate terminology, we should say that it works at the level of individual attribute values of individual tuples in the relation table. Given the *Employee* table of Figure 11.14, a database management system could be directed to

```
SELECT ID, NAME, AGE, PAYRATE, HOURS, PAY

FROM EMPLOYEE

WHERE ID = 123;
```

This would get all the information about the employee with ID 123. Because *ID* is the primary key, this may appear to be an easy task. But the following request to locate all the information about an employee with a given name,

```
SELECT ID, NAME, AGE, PAYRATE, HOURS, PAY

FROM EMPLOYEE

WHERE NAME = 'John Kay';
```

FIGURE 11.14
Employee Table for HHP&P

Employee

ID	Name	Age	PayRate	Hours	Pay
86	Janet Kay	51	16.60	94	1560.40
123	Francine Perreira	18	8.50	185	1572.50
149	Fred Takasano	43	12.35	250	3087.50
71	John Kay	53	17.80	245	4361.00
165	Butch Honou	17	6.70	53	355.10

is done just as easily even though the *Name* attribute may not uniquely identify the tuple. If multiple employees in the table have the same name, all of the relevant entries are produced.

If only some of the attributes are wanted, an instruction such as

```
SELECT NAME, PAY

FROM EMPLOYEE

WHERE NAME = 'John Kay';
```

produces just the name and pay for the employee(s) with the given name.

Database management systems usually require the use of specialized **query languages** to enable the user or another application program to **query** (ask questions of) the database in order to retrieve information. The three preceding SELECT examples are written in **SQL**, *Structured Query Language*. We briefly discussed SQL in Chapter 8.

To appreciate the power of SQL, consider the following simple SQL queries for more complicated tasks.

```
SELECT *

FROM EMPLOYEE

ORDER BY ID;
```

says to get all of the attribute values (the asterisk is shorthand for listing all the attributes) for all the tuples (because there is no further qualification) in the *Employee* table in order by *ID*. Thus we have effectively sorted the tuples in the relational table by a single command. This is a significant gain in productivity over the step-by-step process of comparing items and moving them around that was required when we wrote a sorting algorithm in Chapter 3. (Of course, SQL has invoked its own sorting algorithm, but the user is shielded from the details of this algorithm and is allowed to work at a more abstract level.) The query

```
SELECT *

FROM EMPLOYEE

WHERE AGE > 21;
```

gets all the tuples for employees older than 21. Here we've effectively done a search of all the tuples on a particular attribute, again without having to engineer the details as we had to do when writing the sequential search or binary search algorithms of Chapter 3.

Managing a relational table involves more than just making queries about the existing table. One must be able to add new tuples to the table (which is how the existing tuples got into the table in the first place), delete tuples from a table, or change information in an existing tuple. These tasks are easily handled by the INSERT, DELETE, and UPDATE commands available in SQL.

In order to explore further the power of a DBMS, let's expand our HHP&P database to include a second relational table. The *Insurance* table, shown in Figure 11.15, gives information on the insurance plan type and the date of issue of the policy for an employee with a given ID.

FIGURE 11.15

Insurance *Table for HHP&P*

Insurance

ID	PlanType	DateIssued
86	A4	02/23/78
123	B2	12/03/91
149	A1	06/11/85
71	A4	10/01/72
149	B2	04/23/90

In the *Insurance* table, there is a composite primary key in that both *ID* and *PlanType* are needed to identify a tuple uniquely. The *ID* attribute is a primary key in another relational table, the *Employee* table, and each value of *ID* in the *Insurance* table exists as an *ID* value in a tuple of the *Employee* table. Because of these properties, the *ID* attribute is called a **foreign key** into the *Employee* table. This foreign key establishes the relationship that employeees may have insurance plans. Because *ID* is only part of the primary key for *Insurance*, a given employee may have more than one plan, as is the case with ID 149 in Figure 11.15. It is also true that an employee may have no plan; in Figure 11.15, there is no tuple with ID 165, although there is an employee with ID 165.

The database management system can relate information between various tables through the key values—in our example, the linkage between the foreign key *ID* in the *Insurance* table and the primary key *ID* in the *Employee* table. Thus the following query will give us information about Fred Takasano's insurance plan even though Fred's name is not in the *Insurance* table:

```
SELECT EMPLOYEE.NAME, INSURANCE.PLANTYPE

FROM EMPLOYEE, INSURANCE

WHERE EMPLOYEE.NAME = 'Fred Takasano' AND

EMPLOYEE.ID = INSURANCE.ID;
```

The query is an instruction to retrieve the *Name* attribute from the *Employee* table and the *PlanType* attribute from the *Insurance* table by looking for the tuple with *Name* attribute value Fred Takasano in the *Employee* table and then finding the tuple(s) with the matching *ID* value in the *Insurance* table. (Here is the Boolean AND operation we encountered in Chapter 4 in our discussion on Boolean logic.) It is the last term in the WHERE clause of the query (the last line) that causes the two tables to be joined together by the match between primary key and foreign key. The result of the query will be

```
Fred Takasano      A1
Fred Takasano      B2
```

The correspondence between primary keys and foreign keys is what establishes the relationships among various entities in a database. The SQL command to create a table requires specification of the various attributes by name and data type, identification of the primary key, identification of any foreign keys, and identification of the tables into which these are foreign keys. This information is pertinent to building the actual file that stores the data in the tuples.

We've now done a fairly complex query involving two different tables. It is easy to see how these ideas can be expanded to multiple tables, linked together by relationships represented by foreign keys and their corresponding primary keys. Figure 11.16 shows an expansion of the HHP&P database to include a table called *Policy* that contains, for each type of insurance plan, a description of its coverage and its monthly cost. *PlanType* is the primary key for this table. This makes *PlanType* in the *Insurance* table a foreign key into the *Policy* table, as shown in Figure 11.16. This linkage would allow us to write a query to find, for example, the monthly cost of Fred Takasano's insurance (see Practice Problem 2 at the end of this section).

Using multiple tables in a single database reduces the amount of redundant information that must be stored. For example, a stand-alone insurance file for HHP&P employees would probably have to include employee names as well as IDs. It also minimizes the amount of work required to maintain consistency in the data (if Francine Perreira gets married and changes her name, the name change need only be entered in one place). But most important of all, the database gives the user, or the user's application software, the ability to combine and manipulate data easily in ways that would be very difficult if the data were kept in separate files.

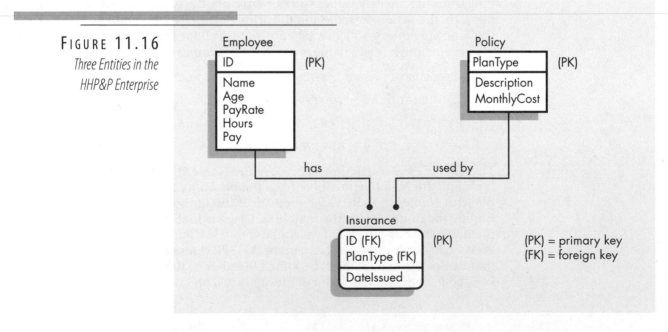

FIGURE 11.16

Three Entities in the HHP&P Enterprise

11.3.4 ODDS AND ENDS

Our file system and database example utilized a business setting, but databases are not confined to business uses. Microcomputer database software, and specialized software packages that incorporate database management capabilities, are available to the individual for purposes of money management, tax preparation, mailing lists, nutritional planning, and countless other applications. Through the power of telecommunications (the subject of Chapter 12), personal computer users can access, from many remote sources, database information on sports, investment, travel, consumer information, and much more.

A **hypermedia system** is a form of database management. Here information is kept in a variety of forms, including audio clips, photographic images, video clips, graphics, text, and so on. A hypermedia application allows the user to navigate these various sources of information in relatively unstructured ways by choosing what to access next. This mimics how we might learn about a topic, given various resources at our disposal; we might stop to look up the meaning of a word in a dictionary or, finding some interesting reference in a paragraph, look up a photograph that illustrates the topic. The "links" that are traversed between sources of information are similar to the links between relational tables in a database.

In the section on spreadsheets earlier in this chapter, we mentioned that a spreadsheet may have simple DBMS capabilities. A section of a sheet, or a separate sheet, can be used as a relational table. Each row is treated as a tuple or record, each column as an attribute or field. Indeed, we already noted the similarities between the spreadsheet layout of Figure 11.4 and the relational table of Figure 11.14. The spreadsheet can locate records whose fields have certain values. The effect, though not the details of how it is done, is much like the SQL SELECT operation.

If a database management system can easily make connections between different files of data, and even—as we'll see shortly—data stored at different locations, how difficult would it be to link information in the IRS database with information in the FBI database, the Social Security database, credit card databases, banking databases, and so on? What are the safeguards, if any, against a super government database through which authorized (or unauthorized?) users could access information about every facet of your life? Suddenly, a business aid or a personal convenience has become a tool with potential social, ethical, and legal implications. We discuss this important issue in Chapter 14.

11.3.5 COMPUTER SCIENCE ISSUES

As we have seen by looking at some queries, SQL is a very high-level language where a single instruction is quite powerful. In terms of the language classifications of Chapter 8, it is also a nonprocedural language. An SQL "program" merely asks for something to be done (sort all tuples in some order, search all tuples to match some condition) but does not have to issue the specific sequence of instructions on *how* it is to be done.

Performance issues definitely affect the user's satisfaction with a database management system; a slow response to a query is at best annoying and at worst unacceptable. Large files are maintained on disk in secondary storage rather than being brought in total into main memory. Accessing a record in the file involves at least one disk input/output operation, which is a much slower process than accessing information stored in main memory. In Chapter 5 we talked about the three components that contribute to reading an individual disk sector into memory or writing from memory to a disk sector: seek time (time to position the read/write head over the correct track on the disk), latency (time for the correct sector to rotate under the read/write head), and transfer time (time to read from or write to the entire sector). Organizing the way records are stored on the disk can help minimize the time to access a particular record by reducing the number of disk I/O operations that must be done before finding the sector that contains the desired record. Also, creating additional records to be stored along with the file, while using up extra storage, may significantly reduce access time. The idea here is much like that of a library catalog system. The user who wants to "access" a book first consults a smaller structure that is organized in a useful way (alphabetically) and that then directs the user to the point in the library where the desired book can be found. The smaller structure stored with the file may even be organized in a tree-like manner that is a generalization of the tree structure we used in Chapter 3 to visualize the binary search. Following the branches of the tree can quickly lead to information about the location in the file of the record with a particular primary key value. The DBMS will incorporate the services of a sophisticated file manager to organize the disk files in an optimal way.

Distributed databases allow the physical data to reside at various locations that are electronically networked together. The user at site A makes a database query that needs access to data physically stored at site B. The database management system and the underlying network make the necessary links and connections. To the user, it still appears that everything is at his or her fingertips. This convenience is making distributed databases increasingly common, although they introduce additional technical problems. For example, access time is increased across a network, and a computer failure or network failure at one site can make data unavailable to all other sites.

Job Hunting the Modern Way

Job openings across the country are now maintained on-line by America's Job Bank database, which works with state Departments of Labor. The interesting part is that this database can be accessed from job kiosks that feature something like a bank's automated teller machine. Kiosks have been set up in shopping malls, convenience stores, and other public sites. Access to the database is free, and job seekers can request information on specific types of jobs, jobs in particular geographic areas, or data on employment trends. Go to

http://www.ajb.dni.us/index.html.

PRACTICE PROBLEMS

1. Using the *Employee* table of Figure 11.14, what will be the result of the following SQL query?

   ```
   SELECT ID, PAYRATE

   FROM EMPLOYEE

   WHERE NAME = 'Fred Takasano';
   ```

2. Complete the following SQL query to find the monthly cost of Fred Takasano's insurance.

   ```
   SELECT EMPLOYEE.NAME, _____

   FROM EMPLOYEE, INSURANCE, _____

   WHERE _____ AND

   EMPLOYEE.ID = INSURANCE.ID AND

   _____;
   ```

3. Using the *Insurance* table of Figure 11.15, write an SQL query to find all the employee IDs for employees who have insurance plan type A4.

11.4 NUMERIC AND SYMBOLIC COMPUTATION

11.4.1 THE IMPORTANCE OF NUMERIC APPLICATIONS

Historically, the earliest and most important application of computers was for **numeric computation**—what is jokingly referred to as "number crunching." Charles Babbage's Analytic Engine of the early nineteenth century was a machine meant to do one thing: solve mathematical equations. The motive behind Herman Hollerith's development work at the end of the nineteenth century was the enormous volume of statistical work done by the U.S. Census Bureau. Virtually all the computer pioneers of the 1940s were motivated by the need to solve huge military-based mathematical problems (such as the generation of ballistics tables) too large for people and mechanical calculators.

Today, numeric computation is still one of the largest and most important applications of computers. Our universities, corporations, and research centers are working on massive problems that require the evaluation of billions (10^9), trillions (10^{12}), or even quadrillions (10^{15}) of mathematical operations. These problems are in such diverse areas as weather forecasting, econometric modeling, molecular analysis, real-time imaging, high-energy physics, space flight simulation, and natural language understanding, and they are all characterized by the unbelievably large number of computations that must be completed in a flickering instant of time. These huge numeric problems were the major reason for the development of the **supercomputers** and **parallel processors** first described in Section 5.3.4. These superfast machines currently execute on the order of 100 Gflops, or 10^{11} (100 billion) floating-point operations per second, which is fast enough to attack many of these huge problems. Some problems need still more computational speed, and that is the motivation driving the creation of the "teraflop machine" mentioned at the end of Chapter 5. A teraflop machine can execute 10^{12} floating-point operations per second. This number is so large that it is hard to grasp. For example, in the time it takes a 2,000 mph F-18 jet fighter to fly *1 inch*, a teraflop computer could add 28 million numbers.

As one example of these new, computationally intensive problems, let's analyze the application known as **real-time imaging**, an important component of the new field called **virtual reality**. With virtual reality, a computer generates simulated visual images in the same time frame and with the same orientation that would occur if these scenes were being viewed in real life. These images are displayed on glasses or a headset to give the feeling that you, the viewer, are actually inside that environment. For example, as you are moving your arms, legs, and eyes, the computer might be generating and displaying simulated images of what you would see during a leisurely stroll through a forest. To give the illusion that you are really in a forest rather than in the computer laboratory, these images must be produced fast enough to match what you would actually see if you were walking and moving your head at that rate of speed. The display must "keep up" with the user; otherwise, there will not be a true sense of reality.

To create high-quality animation, a computer must generate about 24 frames, or images, per second. Each frame is made up of a large number of distinct points, called **pixels**, or **picture elements**, just as a newspaper photograph is composed of thousands of distinct dots. As we mentioned in Section 7.8, a typical high-resolution color image contains about $1,000 \times 1,000$ pixels, for a total of 1,000,000 picture elements per frame. For each new image, the computer must compute the color and intensity values of every one of the million pixels in that image. This can be a very difficult computation requiring the execution of hundreds or even thousands of mathematical operations. The computer must determine how far you have moved since the last image was produced, how your eyes and head are positioned, and what is and what is not visible from this new perspective. Using this information, along with the rules of geometry, trigonometry, and algebra, the computer builds the new image point by point and displays it for you to see.

Thus, good quality real-time imaging requires 24 new frames per second, 1,000,000 pixels per frame, and perhaps as many as 1,000 computations per pixel—a total of 24 billion mathematical operations per second. This is well beyond the capacity of ordinary computers and requires either a supercomputer or a parallel processor of the type described in Chapter 5. Problems in weather forecasting, molecular analysis, and high-energy physics can be even larger and thus require computers with even more "horsepower." For example, in the rather esoteric field called *quantum chromodynamics*, a branch of particle physics, there are problems that require the evaluation of one hundred trillion (10^{14}) mathematical operations to produce a single result. A regular Von Neumann computer operating at 50 million floating-point operations per second (50 Mflops) would need about 1 month to generate the answer. A supercomputer working at 50 billion operations per second (50 Gflops) would need only about 45 minutes. A teraflop machine would need about 2 minutes.

Thus the historical importance of number crunching persists in modern times, and a significant percentage of computing time is still dedicated to solving the same kind of numeric problems that intrigued Leibnitz, Pascal, Babbage, Hollerith, and Von Neumann hundreds or dozens of years ago, only on a much, much larger scale. In spite of the growing importance of non-numeric applications such as word processing, database systems, and electronic mail, scientific and numeric computing is still the "meat and potatoes" work of many installations.

However, in addition to traditional number crunching, there is just now beginning to appear a new and very different use of computers in mathematics, science, and engineering, and it is quite unlike anything our computational ancestors could have imagined. This new application, termed **symbolic computing**, has the potential to enhance significantly the types of problems solved and even to change the way that people do mathematics. We will discuss symbolic computing in the remainder of this section.

11.4.2 SYMBOLIC COMPUTING

The examples in the previous section are problems in which the computer is working with and manipulating actual numbers. The problems may be big and "ugly-looking," but they are always numeric—for example:

$$Z = \sqrt[3]{\frac{13.1842}{1.976}} \times \sin(2.1 \times \pi) + 4.06893 \times 10^{-2}$$

$$= 1.31346$$

Similarly, the spreadsheet example of Figure 11.3 involved a numeric computation, the computation of pay from the values of pay rate and hours worked:

$$\text{Pay} = 94 \text{ hours} \times \$16.60/\text{hour}$$

$$= \$1,560.40$$

Here the values may have been expressed as the contents of cell locations, but they were still specific numeric values.

However, we know from our high school algebra classes that we do not always manipulate numbers directly but often use symbols such as x and y that *represent* nonspecific numbers. Problems are expressed not in terms of explicit numeric quantities such as -4.32 but in terms of symbols, called **unknowns** or **variables**, and are solved in this form. For example, when the algebraic addition problem

$$x^2 + 2x - 7$$
$$+ 2x^2 - 5x + 3$$

is solved to get the result $3x^2 - 3x - 4$, the symbol x does not represent one specific numeric value. Instead, it represents any numeric quantity, and the solution is true for all values of x. Solving problems expressed in terms of variables like x and y rather than numeric values like -3.7 and 8.6×10^7 is called **symbolic computing**. Here are some other examples of symbolic problems:

- Simplify: $3x^2 - 2x + x^2 - 7 + 9x + 2 - 2x^2$
- Solve: $x^3 + 2x^2 - 5x + 13 = 0$
- Factor: $x^3 + x^2 - 3x - 3$
- Plot: $Sin(3x)$ for all values $0 \le x \le 2\pi$

Symbolic problem solving is becoming an important tool in a number of fields, including mathematics, the physical and natural sciences, engineering, medicine, and economics. No longer must computers be viewed as only glorified arithmetic devices, capable of simple operations such as addition, multiplication, and square roots. Instead, they can be powerful "mathematical assistants" capable of carrying out high-level operations from algebra, geometry, trigonometry, statistics, and calculus. Just as it is no longer necessary to remember such arcane arithmetic techniques as taking square roots by hand, it may no longer be necessary to carry out manually such laborious and mind-numbing algebraic tasks as expanding $(1 + x + 3y)^4$ or factoring $(x^{10} - 1)$. Letting computers do these difficult symbolic manipulations frees up people to do what they do best: creative problem solving.

Let's take a look at the capabilities of symbolic computation systems. To illustrate our discussion, we will show the commands that you would enter to use one particular package currently available in the marketplace, *Mathematica* by Wolfram Research Inc. (Their Mathematica home page is located at http://www.wolfram.com/mathematica/.) This program was first developed in 1988 and is currently used by hundreds of thousands of students, scientists, businesspeople, and researchers. However, there are many other symbolic computation systems available, and they run on many different computer systems. The following examples may look advanced, but they can be done on virtually any personal computer or desktop workstation with the appropriate software.

Most symbolic computation programs are interactive. The user enters a request via the keyboard or mouse, and the program immediately computes the answer and displays the result. (In all our examples, the user request is displayed in this **boldfaced type font** and the output of the program is shown in this `monospaced type font` immediately following.)

Although these packages are primarily for symbolic work, they are certainly capable of doing all the numeric computations we would expect of any computer or calculator. For example, to evaluate an expression *expr*, we might enter the command **N[expr, i]**, and the answer would be computed and displayed to *i* significant digits. That "ugly-looking" computation shown earlier would be no problem for most symbolic programs. (*Note:* The symbol ^ means exponentiation.)

N[(((13.1842 / 1.976) Sin[2.1 Pi])^ (1.0 / 3.0) + 0.0406893, 6]

```
1.31346
```

It is interesting that most symbolic systems treat each separate digit of the result as a character, rather than viewing the entire result as a single number. In Section 4.2 we learned how to represent integers using the binary numbering system. Using *b* binary digits, the largest unsigned integer that can be represented is $2^b - 1$. (This is the binary pattern 1111 . . . 111.) Even for large values of *b*, this is not a particularly huge number. For example, if $b = 32$, then the largest integer is $2^{32} - 1$, about 4 billion. When $b = 64$, the largest value is about 10^{19}. However, instead of considering the entire number as one integer, we could treat it as a sequence of characters, with each character stored using the ASCII character code (Figure 4.3) and occupying one byte of memory. For example, using this representation, the integer 41 would not be stored as the binary value 101001 (32 + 8 + 1 = 41) but as the 8-bit ASCII representation for the character '4' followed by the 8-bit ASCII representation for the character '1'. Now, the only limit to the accuracy that can be achieved is the number of characters that can be stored in memory. We learned in Chapter 5 that most systems today have millions of bytes of storage, so it is possible (at least theoretically) to generate answers with millions of digits. This representational technique is called **infinite precision arithmetic**, and it is used in many symbolic packages to work with monstrously large numbers. For example, in most symbolic systems it would not be a problem to compute π to 250 decimal places:

N[Pi, 250]

```
3.1415926535897932384626433832795028841971693993751105
  8209749445923078164062862089986280348253421170679821
  4808651328230664709384460955058223172535940812848111
  7450284102701938521105559644622948954930381964428
  8109756659334461284756482337867831652712019091
```

It is also quite easy to display the value 200!, which is $200 \times 199 \times 198 \times \ldots \times 2 \times 1$ and is called *200 factorial*. This evaluation would "choke" any regular computer or calculator because the answer contains 375 digits.

200!

```
7886578673647905035523632139321850622951359776871732639
2947425332443594499634033429203042840119846239041772
1213891963883025764279024263710506192622495282993111
3462857270763317237396988943922445621451664240254033
2918641312274282948532775242424075739032403212574055
7856866022603190417032406235170085879617892222278962
3703897374720000000000000000000000000000000000000000000
000000000
```

However, it is in the area of symbolic, not numeric, manipulation where symbolic computation packages really stand out. They can perform a wide range of standard algebraic manipulations. For example, we can simplify the expression

$$(x - 1)^2 + (x + 2) + (2x - 3)^2 + x$$

by using the command **Simplify[expr]**. This command attempts to reduce *expr* to the least number of terms using the rules of algebra.

Simplify[(x − 1)^2 + (x + 2) + (2x − 3)^2 + x]

```
12  − 12x  + 5x²
```

Factoring polynomials like $x^{10} - 1$ is an important operation in cryptography. It is an easy operation using the command **Factor[polynomial]**. This command displays all the factors of the specified polynomial.

Factor [x^10 − 1]

$$(-1 + x)(1 + x)(1 - x + x^2 - x^3 + x^4)(1 + x + x^2 + x^3 + x^4)$$

Doing this factoring operation by hand would be enormously difficult and time-consuming.

We can expand the formula $(1 + x + 3y)^4$ using the **Expand[expr]** command, which performs all the algebraic operations contained in the expression

Expand [(1 + x + 3y) ^ 4]

$$1 + 4x + 6x^2 + 4x^3 + x^4 + 12y + 36xy + 36x^2y + 12x^3y + 54y^2$$

$$+ 108xy^2 + 54x^2y^2 + 108y^3 + 108xy^3 + 81y^4$$

Looking at this result, it might be interesting to think about (1) how long it would take you to do this expansion by hand and (2) the likelihood that you would do it correctly. People are quite good at setting up a problem—that is, at getting the problem into the form $(1 + x + 3y)^4$—but they have difficulty with the tedious algebra needed to solve it. Boredom and frustration quickly lead to sloppiness and errors. Computers do not get bored, so they are much better at this arduous task.

Symbolic packages are also very good at solving equations, a task that can be painfully difficult by hand. For instance, we can use the command **Solve[equation, unknown]** to solve a quadratic equation such as $x^2 - 5x + 4 = 0$ whose two answers are $+4$ and $+1$: (*Note:* In the following examples, the operation $==$ means equality.)

Solve[x^2 − 5x + 4 == 0,x]

```
{{x -> 4}{x -> 1}}
```

It might be interesting to look back at Chapter 7 and think about how much effort it would take to design, code, debug, and test a C++ program to solve quadratic equations like the one shown above. Using a symbolic computation package, that effort is reduced to a single command: **Solve.** That is quite an improvement in productivity.

We are not limited to solving polynomials but can also solve a class of equations called **transcendental equations**. These involve not just powers of x, such as x^2 and x^3, but also more complicated functions of x such as $1/x$, $\sin(x)$, and e^x. For example, to solve the transcendental equation

$$e^x - 1.5 = 0$$

we can use the **Solve** command just described. (*Note:* **Exp[x]** is the exponential function e^x.)

Solve[Exp[x] − 1.5 == 0,x]

```
{x -> 0.405465}
```

We can use symbolic systems to tackle not just individual equations but also **systems of linear equations**, such as

$$2x + y = 11$$
$$6x - 2y = 8$$

This is called a 2×2 system of equations because there are two equations and two unknowns (x, y). Systems of linear equations occur in many disciplines, except that they are much larger, sometimes consisting of hundreds of equations and unknowns. Systems of this size are impossible to deal with by hand, but they become relatively easy using symbolic computational systems:

Solve[{2x + y == 11, 6x − 2y == 8}, {x,y}]

```
{{x -> 3, y -> 5}}
```

You probably spent days or weeks in high school and college mathematics classes learning how to solve systems of linear equations by hand. Symbolic computation systems give a different perspective on how this task should be done. They say to the student, "You set up the problem to be solved (the creative part), and then let the computer crank out the solution (the boring part)." Unfortunately, many mathematics classes spend the bulk of their time teaching the boring part—carrying out by hand the long and tedious algebraic manipulations needed to solve problems like the one just given. Symbolic computation packages may begin to change that emphasis and enable us to spend more time on the creative aspects of problem solving.

So far, all our examples have represented traditional algebraic manipulations. However, symbolic mathematical systems are capable of much, much more. They can handle complex problems in such advanced areas as geometry, trigonometry, calculus, statistics, probability, and topology. We will give a few brief examples of these capabilities. If you are not familiar with either these branches of mathematics or the operations that are shown, it is not important. Our purpose here is simply to demonstrate a few of the advanced features of these systems.

All symbolic packages are capable of carrying out the two fundamental operations of calculus, **differentiation** and **integration**. For example, using the command **D[expr, x]**, a symbolic package can determine the derivative with respect to x of the cubic equation $(x^3 + 6x - 7)$, written in most calculus textbooks as $\dfrac{d}{dx}(x^3 + 6x - 7)$.

D[x^3 + 6x − 7, x]

```
6  +  3 x²
```

Using the command **Integrate[expr, x]** we can evaluate the indefinite integral

$$\int \left(\frac{1}{x^4} - \frac{1}{x^3} \right) dx$$

Integrate[1/x^4 − 1/x^3, x]

```
−1/3 x³  +  1/2 x²
```

These packages can even do summation of infinite series. For example, it is possible to evaluate

$$\frac{1}{2} + \frac{1}{4} + \frac{1}{8} + \frac{1}{16} + \frac{1}{32} + \ldots = \sum_{i=1}^{\infty} \frac{1}{2^i}$$

even though there are an infinite number of terms. This is because the series $\frac{1}{2} + \frac{1}{4} + \frac{1}{8} + \ldots$ *converges* to the value $+1$.

N[Sum [1/2^*i*, {*i*, 1, Infinity}]]

```
1.0
```

It is also possible to determine when a series *diverges*—that is, when it does not converge to a finite value. For example, the series $\frac{1}{2} + \frac{1}{3} + \frac{1}{4} + \frac{1}{5} + \frac{1}{6} + \ldots$ is a diverging sum that grows bigger than any finite number.

N[Sum [1 / *k*, {*k*, 2, Infinity}]]

```
Sum diverges
```

One of the most impressive and useful capabilities of symbolic computation systems is their ability to do high-quality **graphics**—to make mathematics a *visual* as well as a numeric discipline. We are all familiar with the Chinese phrase "One picture is worth a thousand words." This is particularly true in mathematics, and we stressed this issue when discussing the concept of graphical programming in Section 7.8. For example, a formula such as $x^2 + x - 2$ is simply a string of abstract symbols with little intuitive meaning. But when viewed graphically:

Plot[*x*^2 + *x* − 2, {*x*, −3, +2}]

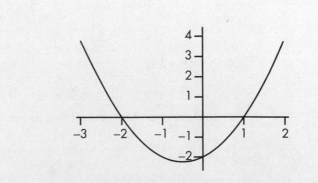

its behavior is much clearer. Similarly, the periodic behavior of a function like $y = 5 \sin(3x)$ is more easily understood when visualized.

Plot[5 Sin[3x], {x, 0, 2 Pi}]

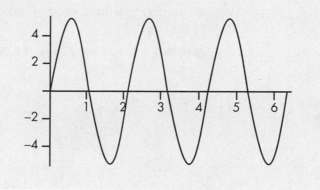

Not only can we plot functions like x^3 and $\sin(x)$; we can also determine the best possible line or curve to fit a collection of experimental data points. This is an important statistical operation called **curve fitting**. For example, assume we have the following set of 20 experimental data points:

points = {{1,2},{2,3},{3,5},{4,7},{5,11},{6,13},{7,17},{8,19},

{9,23},{10,29},{11,31},{12,37},{13,41},{14,43},

{15,47},{16,53},{17,59},{18,61},{19,67},{20,71}}

Instead of working with these points as a list of numbers, we can plot them using the **ListPlot[points]** command and examine the output visually.

ListPlot[points]

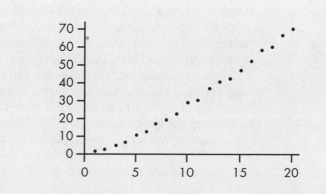

We can now use the **Fit** command to determine the straight line that best fits these 20 data points.

Fit [points, {1, x}, x]

```
-7.67368 + 3.77368x
```

We can display this function overlaid on the 20 experimental points to see how closely they match:

Show[Plot[−7.67368 + 3.77368 x, {x, 0, 20}], ListPlot[points]]

The equation $y = 3.77368x - 7.67368$ represents the best linear approximation describing the relationship between the variables x and y. A scan of the preceding diagram shows that it is a close fit to our experimental observations.

These plotting and curve-fitting capabilities are especially important to researchers in the social sciences who analyze large volumes of demographic, economic, and political data to determine relationships between measures. In our previous example, x could be family income and y the percentage of people in that income group graduating from college; alternatively, x could be age and y could be heart disease rate. The equation produced describes the relationship between these two measures and helps researchers better understand their interdependence. Humans collect the data and formulate the problem. A computer assists by carrying out a statistical analysis of that data. Finally, people take those statistical values and attempt to give them meaning and significance. This is the way computers and humans cooperate to solve problems.

Most symbolic systems are not limited to "flat" two-dimensional (2-D) graphs. They are capable of producing highly complex, and quite elegant, three-dimensional (3-D) graphs as well. These 3-D plots can be even more important than 2-D graphics, because people have a particularly difficult time visualizing 3-D surfaces. Symbolic systems can ease this burden by displaying the shapes and enabling users to study them visually. For example, the function $Z = \sin(x*y)$ has a complex behavior that is probably best understood as a three-dimensional graph.

Plot3D[Sin($x\,y$), {x, 0, 3}, {y, 0, 3}]

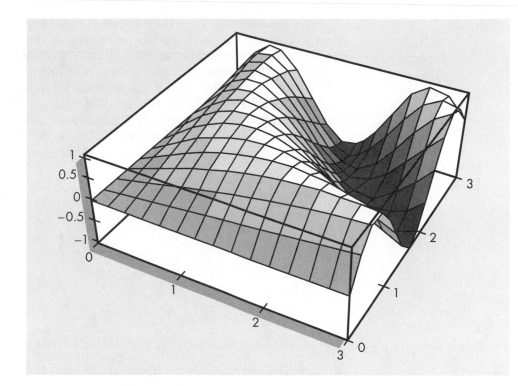

It is certainly easier to understand and deal with this complicated shape visually than as a mathematical equation. **Scientific visualization** is becoming an important part of symbolic and numeric problem solving.

The examples presented here barely hint at the capabilities of this type of software. Symbolic computation programs can do hundreds of different types of mathematical and numeric computations that have applications to virtually all fields of study. Just as calculators revolutionized the way people did arithmetic, these symbolic packages will someday revolutionize how people deal with algebra, geometry, calculus, and statistics. Computers will take on much of the drudgery of large computational problems, allowing the businessperson, scientist, educator, or researcher to concentrate on higher-level conceptual issues. Most people would agree that this is the proper division of labor between people and machines.

11.4.3 THE CASE STUDY

This section will show how a symbolic mathematical software package can be used to solve real-world problems of the type that you may encounter in your classes, your work, and your research activities. We have intentionally chosen this case study from an area that you might not have expected: business and management. Too often, people have the mistaken belief that mathematical problem-solving skills are only for the physicist, engineer, chemist, or computer scientist, not the social scientist, businessperson, or artist. This is absolutely untrue, and nearly every field of study has important quantitative problems that can benefit from the capabilities demonstrated in the previous section.

Let's assume that Huli Huli Pineapple and Papaya (HHP&P) has grown rapidly, thanks to the intelligent use of the spreadsheet and database programs described earlier in the chapter. The company has recently hired a fruit and vegetable marketing specialist, Leile Kahuala, to help it price its products and maximize both income and profit. Fortunately for HHP&P, the new marketing specialist has extensive experience in mathematics, statistics, and computer science, and she is familiar with modern mathematical software systems.

Ms. Kahuala has been collecting data on the price charged by HHP&P for a box of pineapples and the total number of boxes sold per day. Here are those data:

Price ($ per box)	Boxes Sold Each Day
40.00	160
50.00	138
60.00	104
70.00	89
80.00	72
100.00	46

(In "real life" there would be hundreds or even thousands of pieces of data, not six. We have kept the example small to enable us to focus on important concepts.) The marketing specialist sees that as HHP&P raises the price of pineapples, the amount sold goes down. (This phenomenon has been known to merchants and shopkeepers for thousands of years.) However, just looking at the raw numbers, it is hard to get a handle on the nature of the relationship between these two quantities. It would be easier to analyze the data if they were displayed visually rather than listed as numbers in a table. Leile knows that if she enters the data into a mathematical software package, she can get a display using the **ListPlot** command, which plots a set of discrete points.

HHPpoints = {{40,160},{50,138},{60,104},{70,89},{80,72},{100,46}}

ListPlot[HHPpoints]

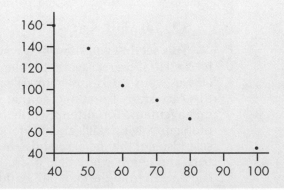

This visualization shows that the relationship between pineapple prices and the amount sold appears to be a straight line, though it has a few wiggles. To confirm this hypothesis, the marketing specialist asks the software package to try fitting a straight line to the observed data and see how close it fits.

Fit[HHPpoints, {1, x}, x]

```
229.214 - 1.91571x
```

The computer has determined that the best linear (straight-line) relationship between pineapple price in dollars (x) and number of boxes of pineapples sold is

Boxes sold = $229.214 - 1.91571x$

To see how well this fits our observations, she asks to see a graph of the preceding formula and a plot of the six experimental data values on the same set of axes so that she can compare the two.

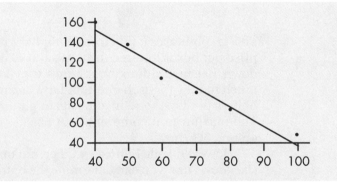

It looks like a good fit, and our marketing specialist decides to use this linear equation as the basis for determining the optimal price of pineapples. If it were not a good fit, then she could have used the software to try different curves, such as quadratic or cubic, and see whether one of these curves was a better description of the experimental data. Again, this is a good example of the way a computer and a person cooperate to solve a problem: The computer carries out the mathematical manipulations, while the person does the data analysis and decides what operations to try next.

The computer has estimated that if the price of a box of pineapples is called x, then the number of boxes sold at that price, y, is given by the formula $y = 229.214 - 1.91571x$. Now the income earned by HHP&P from the sale of pineapples is the price per box times the number of boxes sold at that price:

Income = price per box × number of boxes sold at that price

= $x(229.214 - 1.91571x)$

= $229.214x - 1.91571x^2$

Again, it is hard to gain an understanding of what is going on by just looking at this formula. It would be much easier to understand if we could visualize it.

Therefore, Leile graphs this quadratic equation using the **Plot** command shown in the previous section.

Plot[229.214x − 1.91571 x^2, {x, 0, 120}]

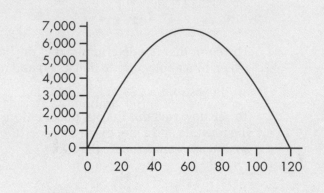

This graph makes it much easier for her to see exactly what is happening. As the price per box is lowered to 40, 30, and 20 dollars per box, the total income goes down, because although they are selling lots of boxes, they are not getting very much money for each one. Similarly, as the price is increased to 80, 90, and 100 dollars per box, total income again plummets because they sell so few boxes. The maximum income of about $6856 occurs when the price is somewhere around $60/box.

However, Leile Kahuala studied not only statistics but calculus as well, and she knows that you can determine the optimal selling price exactly. She remembers from her calculus class that if she takes the derivative with respect to x of the formula $229.214x − 1.91571x^2$, sets it equal to 0, and solves the resulting equation, she will determine the exact value of x where the curve reaches its maximum value. Instead of doing this tedious operation herself, she asks the computer to crank it out for her:

Income = 229.214x − 1.91571x^2

Solve[D[Income, x] == 0]

```
{ x -> 59.8248 }
```

The optimal price per box is $59.82, the price at which the income of HHP&P will be maximized.

This case study has shown that the use of a symbolic computation package is not limited to the nuclear physicist or civil engineer. The ability to examine, analyze, and interpret graphs, tables, and statistics is important in virtually all fields of study—whether in analyzing voting patterns, tracking epidemics, producing economic forecasts, or selling pineapples. (By the way, HHP&P made such huge profits from the proper pricing of its products that the owners sold the company for $100 million and moved to Minnesota to get away from all that sun, sand, and surf!)

11.4.4 COMPUTER SCIENCE ISSUES

The part of the symbolic computation software demonstrated in the previous section is not the "guts" of the system but rather the "front-end" section called the **user interface**. The notion of a user interface was first discussed in Chapter 6. The user interface for this particular system functions as an intermediary between users and a huge collection of programs for solving well-known numeric problems such as root finding, plotting, curve fitting, and integration. These mathematical algorithms and programs are the "heart and soul" of any symbolic computation program. This user interface component has three important responsibilities:

- Accept a user command entered from the keyboard.
- Examine the command to determine exactly what the user wishes to do.
- Invoke the correct program to solve that particular problem.

Looking over this list of responsibilities, we see that the user interface is performing something very similar to the *scheduling* and *dispatching* responsibilities of an operating system that we discussed in Chapter 6. A diagram of the general structure of a typical symbolic computation system is shown in Figure 11.17.

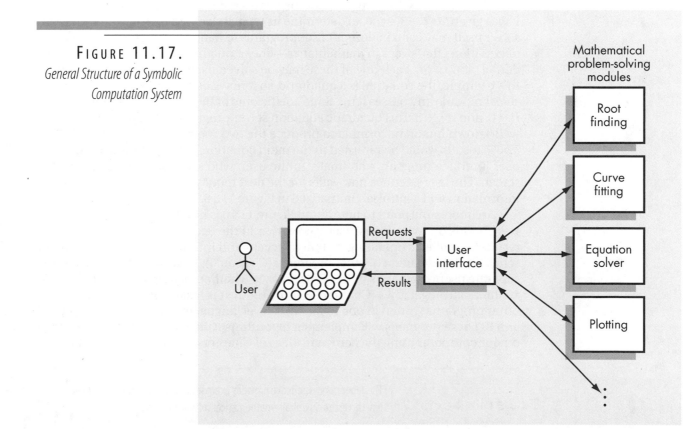

FIGURE 11.17.
General Structure of a Symbolic Computation System

The user interface component sits and waits for the user to enter a command, such as

Solve[x^2 − 3 == 0]

It then must *parse* and *analyze* this command—that is, examine its structure to determine whether it is legal and, if so, analyze its semantics to determine what the user is asking. To do this, it uses many of the same ideas found in the design of high-level language compilers discussed in Chapter 9. For example, the user interface might take this command and separate it into the following four *tokens*:

Solve

[

x^2 − 3 == 0

]

The first token, **Solve**, tells the interface which of the hundreds of numeric programs it will need to activate—in this case, the program that solves mathematical equations. The two tokens [and] delimit the actual equation to be solved: **x^2 − 3 == 0.** The user interface can activate the *equation solver program* and send it the equation the user entered.

The equation solver program now begins execution. It first looks at the equation it was given, x^2 − 3 == 0, to determine its type. It does that because the equation solver itself may contain dozens of subprograms to handle the many different types of equations that occur in mathematics—linear, quadratic, polynomial, transcendental, and so on. Each one of these may be solved using a different algorithm. In this example, the equation is a quadratic, so it now activates a *quadratic equation solver* module and passes it the three coefficients of the quadratic equation: $a = 1$, $b = 0$, and $c = -3$. This quadratic equation solver program would probably use the well-known quadratic formula to produce the two roots $+1.73205$ and -1.73205. These results would be returned to the main equation solver program, then to the user interface program, and finally to the user, who sees them displayed on the screen. The user interface now waits for the next request from the user. This flow of information and control is summarized in Figure 11.18.

An interesting point to note about Figure 11.18 is how the structure of the software builds on many ideas discussed earlier in the text. For example, the user interface acts like an operating system to accept and interpret user requests and to schedule the execution of other programs (Chapter 6). To carry out its task, it must separate user commands into tokens and see whether these tokens fit together in syntactically legal ways (Chapter 9). If the request is legal, it will be passed on to other programs written in one of the high-level languages discussed in Chapters 7 and 8. These programs will implement algorithms (Chapters 2 and 3) and execute on our computer using the hardware ideas of Chapters 4 and 5.

| Laboratory Experience 19 | This laboratory experience provides exercises you can work through if you have access to a symbolic mathematical software package. |

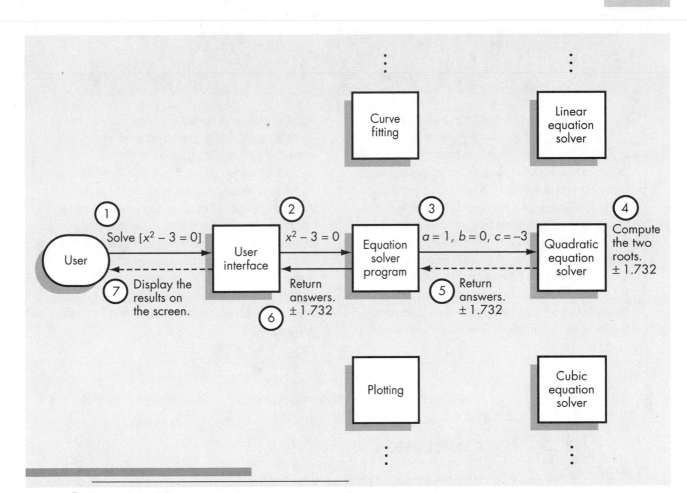

FIGURE 11.18

The Overall Flow of Information and Control in a Typical Symbolic Computation System

PRACTICE PROBLEMS

Use a symbolic computation package such as Mathematica or Maple, if available, for the following problems.

1. Print out the value of 4π to 100 decimal places.

2. Plot the function $x^3 - 6x^2 + 11x - 6$ as x goes from -5 to $+10$. How many times does this function cross the x-axis? These crossings are the roots of the equation $x^3 - 6x^2 + 11x - 6 = 0$. Use the **Solve** operation to find these three roots.

3. Integrate $\int \dfrac{4}{x^4} + \dfrac{3}{x^3}\, dx$.

Beneath the Briny Deep . . .

The oil industry is constantly looking for new sources of oil and natural gas. Many experts believe that oil and gas reservoirs exist under about 60% of the Gulf of Mexico but that many of these deposits are buried beneath large horizontal sheets of salt that may be thousands of feet thick. Geologists explore beneath the ocean floor by firing sound signals down into the water along some path. The compressional waves produced reflect off various rock layers back to the surface and are recorded as a series of seismic events. A composite of all these reflected signals is used to map the geologic structure below the ocean floor at that point. All these data together yield a cross section through the ocean floor along the chosen path. However, salt transmits sound at

about twice the speed of other sedimentary material. This distorts the "picture" of what is beneath it, so this analysis technique is not very accurate above salt sheets.

Scientists are now doing 3-D exploration by repeating this technique along many closely spaced paths. The amount of data that is generated is enormous. One "ping" can generate up to a few thousand seismic events. A few years ago, existing computers could not have analyzed this massive amount of data in months, but today's powerful workstations can generate a complete survey of a given area in about a week of processing time. Improved mapping of the geologic structure has increased the rate of successful drilling from 1 in 10 tries to about 1 in 2.

11.5   CONCLUSION

We have looked at three application areas in this chapter—the use of spreadsheet, database, and symbolic computing packages. Our case study, Huli Huli Pineapple and Papaya Company, has benefitted from all of these.

Our purpose in this chapter has not been to make you an expert user of, say, a database or a spreadsheet. Instead, we have tried to show how these applications build on the computer science concepts discussed in previous chapters. Today's sophisticated systems are intended to shield the user from the technical details of how tasks are accomplished, but behind the helpful user interface, there are significant computer science problems that have been addressed and solved.

EXERCISES

1. In the spreadsheet of Figure 11.4, write a formula to compute the total hours worked by all employees.

2. Assume that an "averaging" function in a spreadsheet works like the SUM function—that is, by

giving the name of the function (AVERAGE) followed by the range of cells to which the function is to be applied. In the spreadsheet of Figure 11.6, put appropriate entries in cells E10, F10, and G10 to label and display the average pay and average new pay.

3. A gradebook spreadsheet contains student names in column A and the results of three equally weighted quizzes in columns B, C, and D. Write the formula to be entered in cell E1 (and copied to other rows in the E column) to compute the average quiz grade.

4. In Exercise 3, assume that quiz 3 counts twice as much as each of the other two quizzes. What is the appropriate formula now?

5. Explain how a spreadhseet could be used to estimate profit on a new product on the basis of cost, quantity sold, and sale price. Assume that cost is a fixed quantity.

6. Try to find someone who uses a spreadsheet in her or his business. Ask to see what the various formulas are. Is the spreadsheet being used as a database? For generating reports? As a forecasting tool?

7. Using the *Employee* table of Figure 11.14, what will be the result of the following SQL query?

```
SELECT  *

FROM EMPLOYEE

WHERE HOURS <100;
```

8. Write an SQL query that retrieves names and ages, ordered by age, from the *Employee* table of Figure 11.14.

9. Using the *Employee* table of Figure 11.14 and the *Insurance* table of Figure 11.15, what will be the result of the following SQL query?

```
SELECT EMPLOYEE.ID,
    INSURANCE.DATEISSUED

FROM EMPLOYEE, INSURANCE

WHERE EMPLOYEE.AGE > 50 AND

EMPLOYEE.ID = INSURANCE.ID;
```

10. Using the *Employee* table of Figure 11.14 and the *Insurance* table of Figure 11.15, write an SQL query that retrieves names, hours, and insurance plan types for all employees who have worked less than 100 hours.

11. Figure 11.16 describes the attributes in a *Policy* table. Write some possible tuples for this table.

12. Assuming the existence of a *Policy* table as described in Figure 11.16, write an SQL query that retrieves the employee name, insurance plan type, and monthly cost for Francine Perreira's insurance.

For Exercises 13–17, use a symbolic computation package such as Mathematica or Maple if available.

13. Print out the value of 3^{500}. How many digits are in the answer? How many bytes of memory are needed to store this value using the infinite precision technique discussed in this chapter?

14. Plot the function $1/\sin(x)$ as x goes from 0 to 10. What does this plot tell you about where this function is undefined—that is, where it tends toward infinity, either positive or negative? Is it easier to understand the behavior of this function as a formula or as a graph?

15. Expand the formula $(x + y + z)^5$. How many terms are in the expansion? How difficult would it be for you to carry out this operation manually?

16. Solve the following system of linear equations:

$$x + 2y + 2z = 16$$
$$4x - y - z = -17$$
$$5x + 3y + z = 7$$

17. Determine the optimal price to charge for a box of pineapples if the data collected by the marketing specialist were as follows:

Price ($ per Box)	Number of Boxes Sold
40	160
50	148
60	132
70	118
80	100
90	84
100	64
110	50
120	34

At that optimal price, what would be the total income earned by HHP&P from the sale of pineapples?

CHALLENGE WORK

1. If you have the use of a commercial database software package designed for a personal computer—for example, Microsoft Access—study the user's manual or the on-line Help system. Work through any tutorial examples.

   a. Create a new database with the *Employee* table of Figure 11.14. Formulate some queries involving just the *Employee* table, such as

      ```
      SELECT ID, NAME, AGE, PAYRATE,
       HOURS, PAY
      FROM EMPLOYEE
      WHERE ID = 123;
      ```

      Your software may have a simpler way to express such a query than the SQL code just given, but chances are that SQL lurks somewhere in the background.

   b. Create the *Insurance* table of Figure 11.15 and relate it to the *Employee* table. Carry out queries involving both tables, such as

   ```
   SELECT EMPLOYEE.NAME,
     INSURANCE.PLANTYPE
   FROM EMPLOYEE, INSURANCE
   WHERE EMPLOYEE.NAME =
     'Fred Takasano' AND
   EMPLOYEE.ID = INSURANCE.ID;
   ```

2. Make a list of all the databases (county, state, federal, school, credit card, bank, and so forth) that you think currently contain information about you. Investigate what laws or restrictions, if any, exist to protect your privacy. Then write a short paper on what additional legislation at the county, state, or federal level you believe is needed to protect consumer privacy, or write a newspaper editorial explaining why no further laws need to be passed.

FOR FURTHER READING

There are many books available on how to use specific application software products such as spreadsheet and database tools. These tools are now extremely powerful, and books range from those that offer a surface overview of the most common features to those that give in-depth information on the fine points.

Detailed information on two Microsoft Office products, a spreadsheet tool and a database tool, respectively, can be found in

Walkenbach, J. *Excel 97 Bible.* Foster City, CA: IDG Books Worldwide, 1997.

Prague, C. N., and Irwin, M. R. *Access 97 Bible.* Foster City, CA: IDG Books Worldwide, 1997.

The following reference gives a complete grounding in the theory of databases:

Date, C. J. *An Introduction to Database Systems*, 6th ed. Reading, MA: Addison-Wesley, 1995.

Information on Mathematica, a popular symbolic computing software package, can be found in the following guidebook by the principal developer of the system:

Wolfram, S. *Mathematica Reference Guide.* Reading, MA: Addison-Wesley, 1993.

The following Web site houses a tutorial on Mathematica:

http://saaz.lanl.gov/math/Math_Home.html

A list of other books on Mathematica, as well as a list of other Mathematica-related Web sites, can be found at

http://saaz.lanl.gov/math/math_pagelast.html#web

12

COMPUTER NETWORKS

12.1 INTRODUCTION

Every once in a while there occurs a technological innovation of such importance that it forever changes society and the way people live, work, and communicate. The invention of the printing press and movable type by Johannes Gutenberg in the mid-fifteenth century was one such development. The books and manuscripts it produced helped fuel the renewed interest in science, art, and literature that came to be called the Renaissance, an era that influenced Western civilization for the next 500 years. The Industrial Revolution of the eighteenth and early nineteenth centuries was the result of a number of technical innovations, including the steam engine, the automated weaving machine, and new steel-making techniques. These advances made consumer goods such as clothing, furniture, and cooking utensils affordable to the middle class and changed European and American societies from rural to urban and from agricultural to industrial. In our own century, we are certainly aware of the massive social changes, both good and bad, wrought by inventions like the telephone, automobile, television, and computer.

Many people feel that we are now poised on the brink of yet another breakthrough, one with the potential to make as great a change in our lives as those mentioned in the preceding paragraph. This innovation is the *computer network*—computers connected for the purpose of exchanging information. During the early stages of network development, the only information exchanged was text such as e-mail, database records, and technical papers. However, the material sent across a network today can be just about anything—TV sound and images, voice, graphics, handwriting, photographs, and movies, to name just a few. If information can be encoded into the 0s and 1s of the binary numbering system, it can be transmitted electronically across a computer network.

The possibilities created by this free flow of data are enormous. Computer networks have the potential to equalize access to information and eliminate the concept of "information haves" and "information have-nots." Geography would no longer play a role in accessing knowledge and ideas. Students in a small, poorly funded rural school would not be handicapped by an out-of-date library collection. On-line access to books, journals, and current reference materials put such students on an equal footing with those at large urban schools and wealthy private institutions. A physician practicing in an emerging economy will be able to transmit medical records, test results, and X-ray images to specialists anywhere in the world and have immediate access to the on-line databases and reference works of major medical research centers. All researchers will have the same ability to communicate with and interact with experts in their discipline, whether they are in New York, New Delhi, or New South Wales. A small business owner will use the network to locate suppliers and reach potential customers. Consumers can browse the network to compare the quality and price of goods from different companies, much as we do today with catalogs and newspaper advertisements but on a massive, international scale.

In addition, networking offers the potential to foster the growth of democracy and global understanding by providing unrestricted access to newspapers, magazines, and radio and TV broadcasts, as well as supporting the unfettered exchange of diverse and competing thoughts, ideas, and opinions. It is no surprise that during recent uprisings, political leaders who wished to prevent the dissemination of opposing ideas moved quickly to restrict Internet access.

In summary, computer networks can deliver huge amounts of information anywhere in the world cheaply, quickly, and virtually error-free. Because we live in an increasingly "information-oriented" society, network technology contains the seeds of massive social and economic change. In this chapter we take a look at this new technology—what it is, how it works, and the benefits it can bring to education, commerce, research, politics, and entertainment. We also examine the single most important computer network now in use, the Internet.

12.2   BASIC CONCEPTS IN COMPUTER NETWORKING

A **computer network** is a set of independent computer systems connected by telecommunication links that together are called the **interconnection network**. The individual computers in the network are frequently referred to as **nodes** or **hosts**, and they can range from small laptops to the massively parallel supercomputers discussed in Chapter 5. In this section we describe some of the basic technical characteristics of a computer network.

12.2.1 COMMUNICATION LINKS

The communication links used to build the interconnection network vary widely in their physical characteristics, error rate, and transmission speed, and in the two dozen or so years that networks have existed, telecommunications facilities have undergone enormous changes.

In the early days of networking, the most common way to send data across a network was via **switched dial-up telephone lines**, the same telephone lines used to talk with friends and family. The term "switched" means that when we dial a telephone number, a **circuit** (a path) is temporarily established between caller and callee. This circuit lasts for the duration of the call, and when we hang up, it is terminated.

The voice-oriented dial-up telephone network is (at least in part) an **analog** transmission medium. This means that the physical quantity used to represent information, usually voltage level, can take on any value. This representation is shown in Figure 12.1(a). Whereas analog is fine for transmitting the human voice, which varies continuously in pitch and volume, a computer produces **digital** information—specifically, a sequence of binary 0s and 1s, as shown in Figure 12.1(b).

In order for the binary signals of Figure 12.1(b) to be transmitted on a switched dial-up telephone line, the signal must be restructured into the analog

FIGURE 12.1

Two Forms of Information Representation

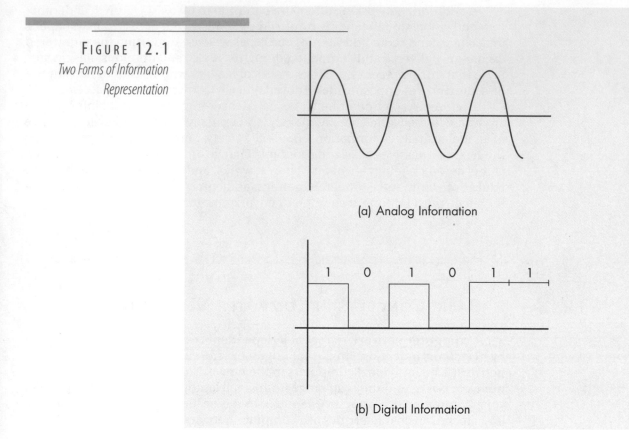

(a) Analog Information

(b) Digital Information

representation of Figure 12.1(a). The device that accomplishes this is a **modem**, because it modulates, or alters, a standard analog signal called a **carrier** so that it encodes binary information. The modem modifies the physical characteristics of the carrier wave, such as amplitude or frequency, so that it is in one of two distinct states, one state representing 0 and the other state representing 1. Figure 12.2 shows how a modem could modulate the amplitude (height) of a carrier wave to encode the binary signal 1010.

At the other end of the transmission line, a modem performs the inverse operation, which is called demodulation. (Modem is a contraction of the two terms *mo*dulation and *dem*odulation.) It takes the received waveform, separates the carrier from the encoded digital signal, and passes only the digital data on to the computer.

Initially, these analog encoding and decoding operations could not be done very fast because of the high error rate and low capacity, or **bandwidth**, of a switched telephone line. In the early days of telecommunications, the rate at which information could be sent and received was limited to 1,200, 2,400, or 4,800 bits per second (bps). Recent advances in modem design have produced devices that transmit at 28,800, 33,600, and 56,000 bps—an order-of-magnitude increase. However, these speeds are nearing the absolute physical limits of the

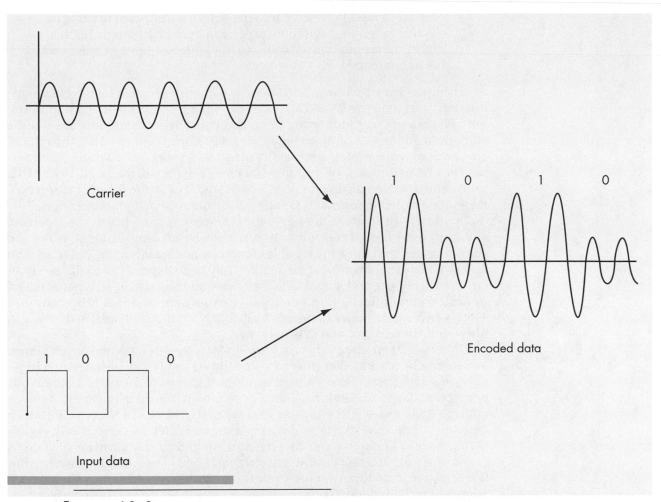

Carrier

1   0   1   0

Encoded data

1   0   1   0

Input data

FIGURE 12.2

Modulation of a Carrier to Encode Binary Information

current dial-up phone system, and further order-of-magnitude increases may not be possible.

The dial-up telephone system is still widely used for remote access to computer networks, especially commercial networks such as America OnLine, and most personal computers sold today include a modem. Unfortunately, their limited transmission speed makes dial-up phone links inconvenient for applications where speed is vital or there are massive amounts of data.

To achieve higher rates, we need to use **dedicated**, rather than switched, communications links—permanent, high-quality lines directly connecting two computers. Two of the most widely used dedicated transmission media are

- *Twisted-pair copper wire.* This is the same type of wiring used for telephone communications except that the circuit is permanent, not established when we dial a phone number. Copper wire is inexpensive, but it has a limited data rate, and signal quality deteriorates at distances greater than about 10 kilometers.

- *Coaxial cable.* This is similar to the type of wiring used to bring cable TV into your home. It is more expensive than twisted-pair, but it has a higher maximum transmission rate and is less subject to noise and signal interference.

Using dedicated transmission lines, we can achieve much higher data transmission rates than the 33,600 bps or so possible with the switched phone system. For example, the following three dedicated services are available in the communications marketplace today: (1) a 128 Kbps (1 Kbps = 1,000 bps) ISDN line, an acronym for Integrated Services Digital Network, (2) a T1 line that transmits at 1.544 Mbps (1 Mbps = 1,000,000 bps), and (3) a high-speed T3 line that sends and receives at the rate of 44.736 Mbps. This latter speed is 3 orders of magnitude higher than what is possible using the switched phone network.

In the late 1980s and early 1990s, the phone companies began the expensive and long-term task of replacing their copper-based long-distance wires and coaxial cables with **fiber-optic cables** that transmit signals using reflected light waves. Fiber can transmit data at significantly higher speeds and with far fewer errors than copper, and it is an ideal transmission medium for all types of digital information. On fiber-optic lines, data can be sent at 155.5 Mbps and 622 Mbps—two international standards (called OC-3 and OC-12) adopted for use in fiber-optic–based voice and data networks.

However, even these rates may not be fast enough for some applications, and researchers are actively investigating the concept of **gigabit networking**—networks with transmission lines that support speeds in excess of 1 billion bits per second (Gbps). In 1991 the federal government funded a long-term research effort in high-speed telecommunications called NREN, the National Research and Education Network. Its goal is to investigate issues associated with gigabit data networks and to have such a network up and running within 10 years. A number of experimental gigabit networks have been implemented and are now being tested. In addition, a fiber-optic transmission standard, OC-48, has been adopted that will support data communication at the rate of 2.488 Gbps.

One might wonder why anyone would possibly need to transmit information at rates of hundreds of millions or billions of bits per second. Do there exist applications that truly need this type of performance? To answer that question, let's determine the time it takes to transmit a high-resolution color image, such as a single movie frame, CAT scan, or page of a product catalog. As we first described in Section 7.8, a high-resolution image contains approximately 1 million distinct picture elements called *pixels*, and each pixel is encoded using 8 to 24 bits. If we assume 16 bits per pixel, then to send a single uncompressed image we would need to transmit 16,000,000 bits of data. Figure 12.3 shows the time needed to send this information at the different speeds discussed.

Figure 12.3 clearly demonstrates the need for high-speed communications to support emerging visual applications such as video on demand, medical imaging, and virtual reality. Sending a single 16 Mb image across a network using a 33.6 Kbps modem takes almost 8 minutes, an agonizingly long time. (I am sure many of you have waited for what seems like forever as a large, graphical Web page s..l..o..w..l..y unrolls across the screen.) That same 16 Mb image can be sent in only 10 seconds using a dedicated T1 line and in 1/10 of a second

FIGURE 12.3

Transmission Time of an Image at Different Transmission Speeds

LINE TYPE	SPEED	TIME TO TRANSMIT 16 MILLION BITS (ONE IMAGE)
Dial-up phone line	33.6 Kbps	7.9 minutes
Dedicated ISDN line	128 Kbps	2.1 minutes
Dedicated T1 line	1.544 Mbps	10.4 seconds
Dedicated T3 line	44.736 Mbps	0.36 second
Fiber-optic OC-3 line	155.5 Mbps	0.10 second
Fiber-optic OC-12 line	622 Mbps	0.026 second
OC-48 gigabit line	2.488 Gbps	0.006 second

using a 155 Mb fiber-optic link. However, even that enormous speed may not be adequate for transmitting multiple images. For example, to view a movie across the network, you need to transmit 24 frames every second, which requires a minimum capacity of $16,000,000 \times 24 = 384$ Mbps.

Encoding graphical information requires a great deal more space than encoding text because of the amount of detail present in an image—such as color, intensity, and lighting. To appreciate the huge difference in scale between text and graphics, let's examine the problem of transmitting an entire 250-page novel across a network, what initially appears to be a monstrously large task. Imagine that each page of the novel contains 500 words and that each word contains 5 characters plus a blank space to separate words from each other. (*Note:* Assume we are transmitting only text, not any font or layout information.) Using these approximations, our novel contains $250 \times 500 \times 6 = 750,000$ characters. We learned in Section 4.2.1 that it takes 8 bits to represent one character, so the number of bits needed to encode the entire 250-page novel is $750,000 \times 8 = 6.0$ million. This is less than 40% of the number of bits (16 million) required to represent a single high-resolution color image. Modern, graphics-oriented applications would not be feasible without the enormous improvements that have occurred in the telecommunications industry. As visually oriented software becomes more widespread, gigabit networking will become a necessity, not a luxury.

A relatively recent development in the telecommunications field is the growth of **wireless data communications** using radio, microwave, and infrared signals. In the wireless world, users no longer need to be physically adjacent to a wired network connection to access data, just as cellular phones have liberated users with regard to voice communications. Using wireless, one can be in a car, at the beach, or walking the factory floor and still send and receive e-mail, access corporate databases, or surf the World Wide Web. The ability to deliver data to users regardless of where they are located is called **mobile computing**, and there are many researchers who believe that in the not-too-distant future, there will be only two types of communication links: fiber-optic cables to support high-speed, error-free wired connections and radio- and microwave-based wireless links for places that fiber does not or cannot reach.

Ubiquitous Computing

The rapid growth of wireless communications, along with the wide availability of extremely cheap microprocessors, has led to a new and exciting area of computer science research called **ubiquitous computing**. In the early days of computing, a single large mainframe served many users. Then, in the PC and workstation era, a single desktop machine served a single user. In the ubiquitous computing model, many computers work together to serve a single user, and rather than being perched on a desktop, they become nearly invisible. The idea is that computers will become so commonplace that they will blend into the background and disappear from our consciousness, much as electricity has today. (Do you actually think about the mass of wires, circuits, and switches inside the walls of your home and office? Probably not.)

Computers will be (and in some cases, already are) placed inside phones, automobiles, appliances, lights, clocks, and even books in order to provide a range of useful services in a totally transparent fashion. For example, when you pulled into the driveway, the computer in your car could signal the computer controlling the home environment to turn on the lights and crank up the heat. And, the "smart badge" on your chest could transmit your current location to the computer inside the central telephone switch so that calls could automatically be routed to the nearest phone. As described by Mark Weiser of Xerox Corp., "ubiquitous computing is invisible, everywhere computing that does not lie on the desktop but in the woodwork."

Although wireless data communication is an exciting prospect, it is not without problems that must be addressed and solved. For example, some forms of wireless, such as microwaves, are line-of-sight, traveling only in a straight line. Because of the curvature of the earth, transmitters must be placed on top of hills or tall buildings and must not be more than 50 to 100 miles apart. Other types of wireless media suffer from environmental problems; they are strongly affected by rain and fog, cannot pass through obstacles such as buildings or large trees, and have a higher error rate than wired communication. In addition, wireless is quite a lot slower than wired communications, which makes it inappropriate for the transfer of large amounts of data.

However, these and other issues are being addressed by the computer science research community, and it is likely that mobile computing will become more widely used. Seeing a laptop with its antenna raised may soon become as common as seeing a person talking on a cellular phone.

12.2.2 LOCAL AREA NETWORKS (LANS)

There are two different types of computer networks. A **local area network**, abbreviated **LAN**, connects hardware devices such as computers, printers, and mass storage devices that are all in close physical proximity. Examples of LANs include the interconnection of machines in one room, in the same office building, and on a single campus. An important characteristic of a LAN is that the owner of the computers is also the owner of the means of communications. Because a LAN is located entirely on private property, the owner is free to install whatever communications medium he or she wants without having to purchase services from a third-party provider, such as the phone company. A LAN is truly

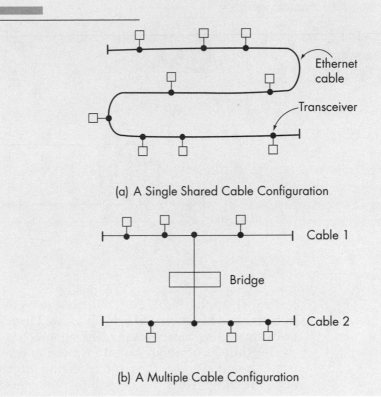

FIGURE 12.4
An Ethernet LAN Implemented Using Cables

(a) A Single Shared Cable Configuration

(b) A Multiple Cable Configuration

a private network, built and managed by its local user community. There are many different types of LANs, but the most widely used model is called the **Ethernet**. With all the LANs that are based on the Ethernet, there are about 60 million users worldwide, and it is the example we will use to describe the general characteristics of a LAN.

The Ethernet was developed in the mid-1970s by computer scientists at the Xerox PARC research center in Palo Alto, California. It was originally designed to operate at 10 Mbps using coaxial cable. However, as we noted earlier, 10 million bits per second is too slow for many applications, so researchers designed a "new, improved" version called **Fast Ethernet,** which is able to transmit at 100 Mbps across coaxial cable, fiber-optic cable, or twisted-pair copper wire.

There are two ways to construct an Ethernet LAN. In the first method, called the **shared cable**, a single wire (such as copper or coaxial cable) is stretched around and through a building or campus. Users tap into the cable at its nearest point using a device called a **transceiver**, as shown in Figure 12.4(a). Because of technical constraints, an Ethernet cable has a maximum allowable length. For a particularly large building or campus, it may be necessary to install two or more separate cables and connect them via a hardware device called a **bridge**. This configuration is shown in Figure 12.4(b).

In the second approach, there is no shared cable strung throughout the building. Rather, there is a box, called a **hub**, located near the center of the building.

FIGURE 12.5

*An Ethernet LAN Implemented
Using a Hub*

FIGURE 12.5

*An Ethernet LAN Implemented
Using a Hub*

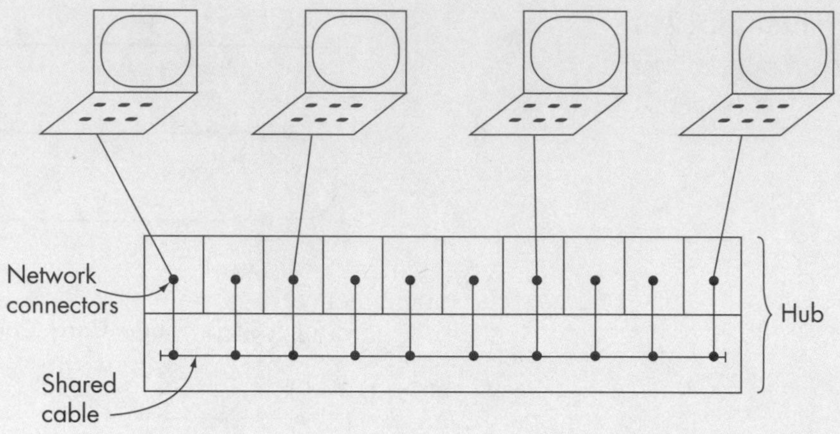

Instead of tapping into the cable, a node joins the network by connecting to the hub. In a sense, the shared cable is located inside the hub instead of inside the walls and ceiling of the building. This approach is diagrammed in Figure 12.5.

Regardless of which data transmission rate or construction technique is used, the rules for sending and receiving information on an Ethernet are exactly the same. The rules describing how messages are transmitted between network nodes are called **communication protocols**, and only nodes using the same protocol can talk directly to each other. Protocols are the "algorithms of communication." They describe the step-by-step procedures required to guarantee an orderly exchange of information across a network. We use protocols for all our communications, although we may not think of them in quite so formal a way. For example, normal "telephone protocols" require the person answering the phone to initiate a conversation by saying "Hello?" and then to remain silent to allow the caller to speak next. Imagine that you violate this protocol by picking up the phone but remaining totally silent. The person on the other end of the line will be confused and will not know what to do. The same is true with networks. When both sides use the same protocol, communication takes place in a logical and orderly fashion. When two nodes use different protocols, they cannot understand each other, and communication is impossible.

The Ethernet protocols use a **contention-based** transmission technique. Users compete for access to a single shared communications line in much the same way that people did for the old-fashioned telephone party line. When a node wants to send a message, it first listens to the line to see whether it is currently in use. If it is not busy, then the node transmits immediately. The message is **broadcast** across the cable, which means that it is received by every node on the net. There is an **address field** attached to the front of the message that identifies the message destination. Every node reads the address field and, if it is not its own, politely discards the remainder of the message without reading it; the node to whom it is addressed, however, accepts and stores it.

If the line is currently busy, then the node wishing to send continually monitors the status of the line and, as soon as it detects that the line has become idle, it transmits. This is shown in Figure 12.6(a). In that diagram, B wants to send but notices that A is using the line. B listens and waits until A is finished, and as soon as that occurs, B is free to transmit.

However, there is a problem. Say two or more users want to send a message and both are monitoring line status. As soon as the line becomes idle, *both* will transmit at exactly the same time. In such a **collision**, all messages become garbled. This is identical to the situation where two people on a party line talk at the same time, and neither can be understood. An example of a collision is shown in Figure 12.6(b). According to the Ethernet protocols, when a collision occurs, the colliding nodes must immediately stop sending, wait a random amount of time, and then attempt to retransmit. Because it is unlikely that both nodes will choose the exact same random time period, one of them will be able to acquire the line and transmit while the other must wait a little longer. This approach is shown in Figure 12.6(c).

One reason why the Ethernet protocol is so popular is that control of the network is *distributed*. That is, responsibility for network operations is shared equally by all nodes in the network rather than centralized into a single "master control center." In an Ethernet, when a computer wants to send a message, it makes its own decisions about what actions to take—when to listen, when to send, when to back off. Therefore, the failure of any one node in the network will not bring down the entire system. In a centralized network, a single control node makes all decisions regarding who may send and who must wait. With this type of protocol, the proper functioning of the control node is critical, and if it fails, the entire network will fail. A centralized network is inherently more unreliable than a distributed one such as the Ethernet.

12.2.3 WIDE AREA NETWORKS (WANS)

A **wide area network**, abbreviated **WAN**, connects devices that may be across town, across the country, or across the ocean. Because WANs cross public property, users cannot go out and string wire between their computers but rather must purchase telecommunications services, like those described in Section 12.2.1, from an external provider. Typically, these are **point-to-point** communication lines that directly connect two machines rather than the shared contention channels commonly found on a LAN. The typical structure of a wide area network is shown in Figure 12.7.

Most WANs use a **store-and-forward, packet-switching** communications protocol. Unlike LAN protocols in which a message is broadcast and received simultaneously by all nodes, in a WAN a message "hops" from one node to another as it makes it way in steps from source to destination. The unit of transmission in a WAN is not a message but a **packet**. A packet is an information block with a fixed maximum size that is transmitted through the network as a unit. If you are sending a small message, then it will be transmitted as a single packet. However, if you are sending a long message, the source will first "chop" it

FIGURE 12.6

*Sending Messages Across
an Ethernet*

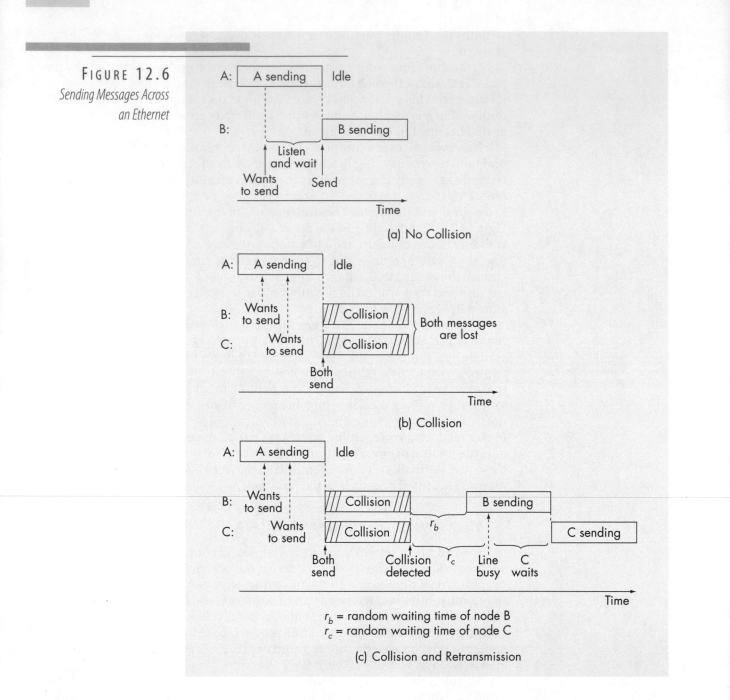

(a) No Collision

(b) Collision

r_b = random waiting time of node B
r_c = random waiting time of node C

(c) Collision and Retransmission

into *N* separate packets (such as the first 1,000 characters, the next 1,000 characters, and so on) and then send each packet independently through the network. When the destination node has received all *N* packets, it reassembles them into a single logical message. This disassembly/assembly process guarantees that no one message, regardless of its size, can monopolize the network's communications resources.

FIGURE 12.7
*General Structure of a
Wide Area Network*

Nodes

Point-to-point links

When a packet is to be transmitted, it is first prefaced with the address of its intended destination and then sent across a point-to-point line to a physically adjacent node, as shown in Figure 12.8. In this figure message M, located at node A, is ultimately destined for node C (not shown). The destination address C is appended to the message (step 1). Then M is sent across the point-to-point line that directly links node A to node B, while a copy of the message is kept at A (step 2). If node B correctly receives message M, it acknowledges that by returning to node A a special **acknowledgment message**, abbreviated ACK (step 3). This allows A to discard the copy of M that it has retained (step 4). The message is now at node B, and the network can repeat this process to move M to the next node on the path to its destination node C.

If, however, B does not correctly receive message M (perhaps there was interference on the line and the message was garbled), A will not receive an ACK. After waiting a reasonable amount of time, node A resends message M to node B, using the copy that it has stored in its memory.

To see how this works in an overall sense, let's use the following diagram and assume that node A wishes to send a message to node D:

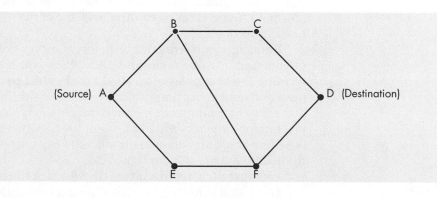

FIGURE 12.8
*Store-and-Forward
Packet Switching*

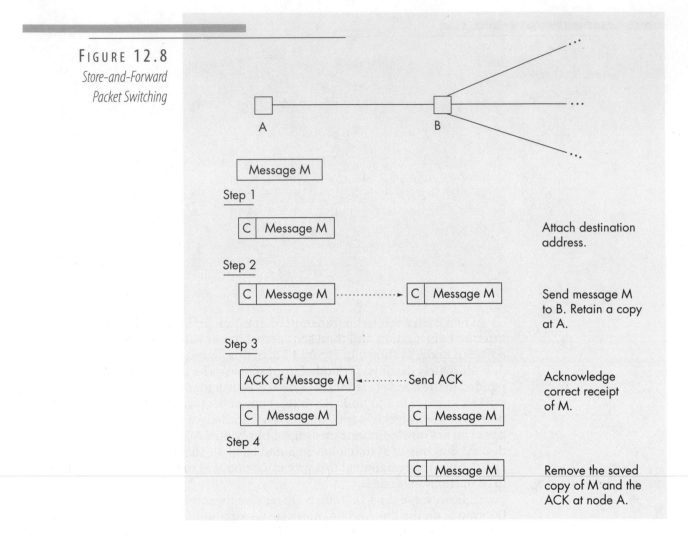

Step 1

Message M

Step 2

| C | Message M |

Attach destination address.

Step 3

| C | Message M | ┈┈┈▶ | C | Message M |

Send message M to B. Retain a copy at A.

| ACK of Message M | ◀┈┈┈ Send ACK

Acknowledge correct receipt of M.

| C | Message M | | C | Message M |

Step 4

| C | Message M |

Remove the saved copy of M and the ACK at node A.

There is no direct connection from A to D, so the message has to be sent along a path that reaches from A to D. In our example network there are four possibilities—ABCD, AEFD, ABFD, and AEFBCD—and the process of selecting the specific path to use is called **routing**. It is one of the most important components of a WAN protocol.

Routing algorithms can be highly complex because of the massive amount of data that must be maintained and the amount of processing required to determine the optimal route, called the **shortest path**. To determine the shortest path between every pair of nodes, we need timing information on every node and every communication line in the network. For small networks this is feasible, but for networks with tens or hundreds of thousands of nodes and links, this is a huge amount of data to obtain and keep current. And even if we can collect these data, we are still not finished.

We must then determine exactly which of the paths should be selected. One way to do that is to calculate the time it takes to transmit a message along every possible path from a source to all possible destinations and pick the one with the lowest delay. However, in Section 3.6 we showed that this type of brute force algorithm is exponential in nature (see Figures 3.24 and 3.25), and it is totally infeasible for any but the tiniest networks. There do exist clever algorithms that can reduce this to $O(N^2)$, where N is the number of nodes. For large networks, where $N = 10^6$ or 10^7, it will take on the order of 10^{12} to 10^{14} calculations—an extremely large amount of work. Therefore, routing is usually done with a quicker but suboptimal approach in which the network attempts to determine not the best route but any reasonably good one.

There are additional problems that make routing difficult. One complication is *topological change:* Most networks are not static but highly dynamic, with new links and new nodes added regularly. Furthermore, network traffic patterns—amounts, destinations—can fluctuate wildly. Therefore, a route that is optimal now may not be optimal a couple of days or even a couple of hours later. For example, the optimal route from A to B in our diagram may currently be A→B →C→D. However, if a new line is added connecting nodes E and D, this could change the shortest path to A→E→D. Because of frequent change, routing tables must be recomputed often, which further magnifies the amount of work.

There is also the question of *network failures.* It may be that when everything is working properly, the optimal route from A to D *is* A→B→C→D. But what if node B fails? What if that system crashes because of a major hardware malfunction or simply because someone accidentally tripped over the power cord? Rather than have all communications between A and D suspended, it would be far preferable for the network automatically to discover this failure, perhaps by having A notice that B has not acknowledged the receipt of *any* message for the last 15 minutes. In that case, A would automatically switch to an alternative route that does not pass through node B, such as A→E→F→D. This ability to dynamically reroute messages would enhance reliability and allow a WAN to continue operating even in the presence of node and link failures.

We have described two different classes of networks, called LANs and WANs, but in reality they are not separate and independent. Virtually all "real-world" computer networks are a mixture of both. A company or a college would typically have one or more LANs interconnecting its local systems. These LAN users also need to access people and information outside their local environment. Thus they need a connection to a national or global WAN, and this is done via a special device called a **router**. A router transmits messages between two distinct networks, including networks that use different protocols—much as an interpreter is placed between two people who speak different languages. For example, a router could be used to send messages from an Ethernet LAN to a packet-switched WAN. A typical mixed LAN/WAN configuration is diagrammed in Figure 12.9.

In Figure 12.9, if node A on LAN1 wants to communicate with node B on LAN2, the three networks will have to carry out the following six steps:

1. Node A on LAN1 broadcasts a message containing the destination address "Node B, LAN2."

2. Every node on LAN1 receives this message, but only router R1 accepts it, because R1 has the explicit responsibility to accept and handle all messages destined for nodes outside LAN1.

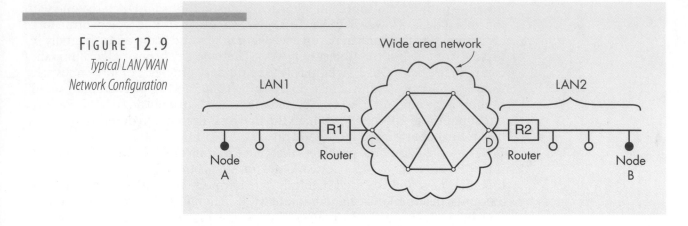

FIGURE 12.9
*Typical LAN/WAN
Network Configuration*

3. Router R1 reconfigures the message so that it is consistent with the protocols and formats of messages sent through the WAN. R1 then passes the message into the WAN via node C.

4. The message is routed from node C to node D using the store-and-forward packet-switching protocols just described. When the message arrives at node D, it is passed on to router R2.

5. R2 again reformats the message, this time to be consistent with the protocols and formats of LAN2, which need not be the same protocols used by LAN1. Then it broadcasts the message on LAN2, where it is received by all nodes.

6. Node B, the node whose address is contained in the destination address field, accepts the message. All other nodes on LAN2 disregard it. The message has correctly arrived at its destination.

12.3   NETWORK SERVICES

At the beginning of this chapter we stated that computer networks have the potential to create enormous social change. Now that we have seen how they are designed and built, let's step back and take a look at the services they offer and their potential impact on society.

One of the most important services of networking is **resource sharing**, the ability of a group of users to share *physical resources*, such as a printer or disk, as well as *logical resources*, such as a data file or piece of software.

The prices of computers and peripherals have been dropping rapidly for the last 10 years, so it is easy to think that everyone can go out and buy whatever I/O or storage devices they need for themselves. However, that is not a very cost-effective way to configure computer systems. For example, a high-quality color laser printer is an expensive output device that is used infrequently. Most users

FIGURE 12.10
The Client-Server Model of Network Computing

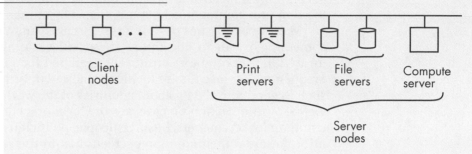

work at their keyboards and screens for long periods of time with only an occasional printout of their work. Buying everyone his or her own color printer would leave most of these devices idle for long periods, wasting valuable equipment funds. If a LAN is available, it is far more efficient to have a few shared printers, called **print servers**, that can be accessed when needed. Similarly, if a group of users require access to a data file or piece of software, it makes sense to keep a single copy on a shared network disk, called a **file server**. Then, when people need the file, they can either access it across the network or copy it from the file server to their own local machine.

The style of computing wherein some network nodes provide services and the remaining nodes are users (or clients) of those services is called, naturally enough, **client-server computing**. We have already seen two examples—print servers and file servers—but there are many others. For example, a **compute server** is a high-speed computer that sits on a local area network and runs jobs that are too big for the client's own system. The philosophy behind the client-server model is that we should use a LAN to share those resources that are too expensive, are too large, or are used too infrequently to warrant replication at every node. A diagram of the client-server model of computing is shown in Figure 12.10.

A WAN provides similar resource-sharing benefits, although users of a WAN may share resources of a different type than users of a LAN. For example, a user probably would not want to output to a printer a thousand miles away, but he or she might need access to a supercomputer that has computational capabilities that are not available locally. (In fact, one of the first applications of the Internet was to give scientific researchers access to the six supercomputer centers operated by the National Science Foundation.)

Information sharing is another important WAN service, and a network is an excellent way to access scientific, medical, legal, and commercial data files stored on systems all over the world. For example, information can be shared among the geographically dispersed sites of a multinational corporation. Files can be transmitted anywhere in the world, and on-line corporate databases can be accessed by anyone in the company regardless of location. Information sharing between different companies is also possible. For example, an inventory program running at company X might notice that the stock of part P is low. The program could use the WAN to ask suppliers about the availability and cost of part P and automatically place an order with the ordering and shipping program of company Y. **Electronic data interchange** is the term for this type of computer-to-computer communications, untouched by human hands.

Many network sites provide a service called an **information utility**, which is something like an on-line library. These nodes contains massive amounts of information that can be electronically searched for specific facts or documents. Frequently the site contains highly specialized information about a single topic, such as geopolitical data about countries of the world, current stock prices and yields, or information on case law and legal precedents. Nowadays, it is more common for researchers, businesspeople, politicians, and citizens to search for information at their computer screen than in the stacks of the public library. Other network sites may provide general news and information to anyone who accesses it. This sounds exactly like the old-fashioned newspaper delivered to our front door, but we must remember that not every country in the world has a free press, and not every person has access to the range of uncensored political opinions that a global computer network can provide. Currently, hundreds of daily newspapers around the world put their news and editorial content on-line, and more are being added all the time.

Another service provided by a network is the ability to support group efforts in producing a shared document such as a user's manual, grant application, or design specification. Workers on a project can communicate via the network, electronic calendars can be checked and meetings scheduled automatically, and documents in progress can be shared, discussed on-line, and jointly reviewed and edited. A rapidly growing area of research in computer science is the design and development of **groupware**—software that facilitates simultaneous joint efforts in preparing a single document.

Electronic mail (**e-mail**) has been the single most popular application of networks for the last 20 years or so. When the Internet was first developed, its designers thought that it would be an ideal way to access advanced, high-performance hardware and software. Instead, what they found was that it was a wonderfully effective way to reach other people.

E-mail is *convenient*. You can send a message whenever you want (3 A.M. Sunday is no problem), and it will wait for the recipient to log on and read it at his or her convenience. No more irritating "telephone tag" trying to reach someone whose schedule or time zone is quite different from yours. E-mail is *fast*. A message from the United States to Australia typically arrives in less than a minute, even though it may have to pass through a dozen or so nodes along the way (using the packet-switching protocols described in the previous section). E-mail can be *cheap* when compared to other forms of communication because transmission costs are *distance-independent*. The cost of sending e-mail is a function of how much you say, not to whom you are saying it. It costs the same to send the same electronic letter from New York to Brooklyn, Boston, or Bombay.

The contents of your electronic messages are not limited to the characters typed at the keyboard. They can also include a wide range of *attachments*—pieces of other documents, records from a data file, or portions of earlier e-mail messages. These attachments can be added to the letter and sent along with your own words. This makes it easy to exchange things like data files, book chapters, or even pictures of your new baby. It is also simple to send an electronic letter to *multiple destinations*. A computer can send a letter to a thousand recipients as easily as it can send it to one. (Be careful when using this feature. The receivers of "electronic junk mail" may not appreciate it.)

However, a major problem associated with using e-mail for person-to-person communications is the issue of *privacy*. Currently, electronic mail does not have the same expectation of privacy accorded to first-class surface mail. The courts and our legislative bodies are wrestling with the issue of the degree of privacy that we should expect when using this new form of communication. We will have more to say about this important issue in Chapter 14.

Another interesting use of networks is **bulletin boards** and **news groups**. A bulletin board is a shared public file where anyone can post notes and messages and everyone is free to browse and read the postings of others. It is an electronic version of the bulletin boards commonly seen in grocery stores, cafes, and public libraries. Most bulletin boards are associated with a particular topic or special area of interest, such as people learning to sail, studying Japanese, or interested in debating Middle East politics. These specialized bulletin boards, called **news groups**, are a wonderful way to create a community of individuals who share a common interest and want to exchange ideas and opinions with others.

One of the most popular collections of news groups is **UseNet**, a global collection of literally thousands of news groups spanning virtually every imaginable topic, from the serious (sci.astro.hubble, a news group devoted to astronomical research conducted using the Hubble Space Telescope) to the humorous (rec.arts.startrek.klingon, a news group discussing Klingon language grammar) to the highly controversial (news groups dedicated to unusual sexual practices). Some news groups support the idea of **chat rooms**—the real-time exchange of messages. That is, rather than posting a message to a data file that would be read at a later time, what the sender types appears immediately on the screen of one or more other individuals. This allows for the direct and immediate exchange of thoughts and ideas.

Electronic commerce (EC) is a general term applied to any use of computers and networking to support the paperless exchange of goods, information, and services in the commercial sector. The idea of using computers and networks to do business has been around for some time; the early applications of EC include (1) the automatic deposit of paychecks, (2) automatic teller machines (ATMs) for handling financial transactions from remote sites, and (3) the use of scanning devices at check-out counters to capture sales and inventory information in machine-readable form.

More recently, EC interest has focused on the use of the Internet and the World Wide Web to advertise and sell goods and services. Initially, the Internet was used mostly by scientists, engineers, students, and teachers. However, the business world is coming to appreciate more and more the potential of a communications medium that can quickly, cheaply, and reliably reach millions of people around the world. In the last few years, traffic on the Internet has changed from primarily academic and professional to include a significant number of commercial applications. For example, at the beginning of 1994, about 4% of sites on the World Wide Web were commercial. By January 1997, that portion had grown to 62%. As of 1997, there were over 650,000 sites contained in the ".com" (commercial) domain of the World Wide Web, and this number is expected to increase dramatically in the coming years.

However, with the rapid growth of business transactions on the Net comes the need to increase security significantly. If a hacker breaks in to a university computer system and looks at grade files or steals software, it is a serious crime, but it generally does not lead to financial ruin. However, if someone steals credit card numbers or gains on-line access to banking records, these crimes may very well lead to a truly catastrophic monetary loss.

One of the major areas of computer science research today is **network security**—ensuring the confidentiality and safety of information transmitted across a network. Network security involves a number of issues, including ensuring that the people who initiate the remote transactions are really who they say they are (the *authentication* problem), providing for the security of information during transmission (the *encryption/decryption* problem) and guaranteeing that even in the presence of a hardware or software failure, information remains safe, and business can continue in a normal, uninterrupted fashion (the *fault tolerance* problem).

As electronic commerce increases in importance, there will be greater and greater pressures on the computer science research community to solve these critical problems. We will have more to say about these issues in Chapter 14.

12.4 A BRIEF HISTORY OF THE INTERNET AND THE WORLD WIDE WEB

In the preceding sections we have been discussing the technical characteristics and benefits of networks in general. However, to most people, the phrase *computer network* isn't a generalized term but a highly specific one—the global Internet and its most popular component, the World Wide Web. This is the worldwide telecommunications network with roughly 29,600,000 host computers and hundreds of millions of users in over 150 countries. (However, the Internet and the Web are growing so fast that these numbers will be out of date when you read them.)

In the words of its designers, "The Internet has revolutionized the computer and communications world like nothing before. It is at once a world-wide broadcasting capability, a mechanism for information dissemination, and a medium for collaboration and interaction between individuals and their computers without regard for geographic location." This very strong statement is quite accurate; the Internet has changed the way people learn and study, search for information, and exchange thoughts and ideas. In the coming years it will have an even greater impact—on the way we shop, get our news, are entertained, conduct financial affairs, and talk with friends and family. There is no doubt that the Internet has had and will continue to have a profound effect on society, and in this section we highlight the development and growth of both the Internet and the World Wide Web. (Much of the information in the following pages is taken from the 1997 article "A Brief History of the Internet," written by its original designers and available on the World Wide Web.[1])

12.4.1 THE INTERNET

Surprisingly, the Internet is not a recent development but an idea that has been around for more than 30 years. The concept took shape during the early and mid-1960s and was based on the work of computer scientists at M.I.T. and the RAND Corporation in the United States and the NPL Research Laboratory in Great Britain. The first proposal for building a computer network was made by J. C. R. Licklider of M.I.T. in August 1962. He wrote his colleagues a memo entitled (somewhat optimistically) "The Galactic Network," in which he described a globally interconnected set of computers through which everyone could access data and software. He convinced other researchers at M.I.T. of the validity of his ideas, including Larry Roberts and Leonard Kleinrock. From 1962 to 1967 they and others investigated the theoretical foundations of wide area networking, especially such fundamental concepts as protocols, packet switching, and routing.

In 1966 Roberts moved to the Advanced Research Projects Agency (ARPA), a small research office of the Department of Defense charged with developing technology that could be of use to the U.S. military. ARPA was interested in packet-switched networking because it seemed to be a more secure form of communications during wartime. (Traditional dial-up telephones were considered too vulnerable, because the failure of the central phone switch would completely cut all voice communications. As we saw earlier, a WAN can automatically route around a failed line or node in order to maintain communications.)

ARPA funded a number of network-related research projects, and in 1967 Roberts presented the first research paper describing ARPA's plans to build a wide area packet-switched computer network. For the next two years, work proceeded on designing the required network hardware and software. The first two nodes of this new network, called the ARPANET, were constructed at UCLA and the Stanford Research Institute (SRI), and in October 1969, the first computer-to-computer network message was successfully sent. (Unfortunately, unlike Neil Armstrong's famous "A small step for a man . . ." statement, the contents of that first Internet message have been lost to history.) Later that year, two more nodes were added (UC-Santa Barbara and the University of Utah), and by the end of 1969, the budding four-node network was well off the ground.

The ARPANET grew quickly during the early 1970s, and it was formally demonstrated to the scientific community at an international conference in 1972. It was also in late 1972 that the first "killer app" (critically important application) was developed—electronic mail. It was an immediate success and caused an explosion of growth in people-to-people traffic rather than the people-to-machine traffic that had dominated the first 3 years of network usage.

The success of the ARPANET in the 1970s led other researchers to develop similar types of computer networks to support information exchange in their specific scientific area: HEPNet (High Energy Physics Network), CSNET (Computer

---

[1] B. Leinter, V. Cerf, D. Clark, R. E. Kahn, L. Kleinrock, D. Lynch, J. Postel, L. Roberts, and S. Wolff, "A Brief History of the Internet," http://www.isoc.org/internet-history/, February 20, 1997.

Science Network), MFENet (Magnetic Fusion Energy Network), and SPAN (Space Physics Access Network). Furthermore, corporations had started to notice the success of the ARPANET and began developing proprietary networks that they planned to market to their customers: SNA (Systems Network Architecture) at the IBM Corp. and DECNet from the Digital Equipment Corporation. The 1970s were a time of rapid expansion of networks in the academic and commercial communities.

Farsighted researchers at ARPA, especially Robert Kahn, realized that this rapid and unplanned proliferation of independent networks would lead to incompatibilities and prevent users on different networks from communicating with each other, a situation that recalls the problems that national railway systems have sharing rail cars because of their use of different gauge track. Kahn knew that to achieve the maximum benefits of this new technology, all computer networks would need to communicate in a simple, transparent fashion. He developed a concept called **internetworking,** which stated that any WAN is free to do whatever it wants *internally*. However, at the point where two different networks meet, both must use a common addressing scheme and identical protocols—that is, they must speak the same language. Essentially Kahn wanted to create a "network of networks."

This is the same concept that governs the design of the international telephone system. Every country is free to build its own internal phone system in whatever way it wants, but all must agree to use a standardized worldwide telephone numbering system (country code, city code, phone number), and each must agree to send and receive telephone calls outside its borders in a universally recognized format that has been standardized by the worldwide telephone regulatory agency. Thus any telephone subscriber in the world can call any other without worrying about the internal differences in telephone service in different countries.

Figure 12.11 is a diagram of this "network of networks" concept. It shows four wide area networks called A, B, C, and D interconnected by a special hardware device called a **gateway** that makes the actual internetwork connection and provides routing services between different WANs.

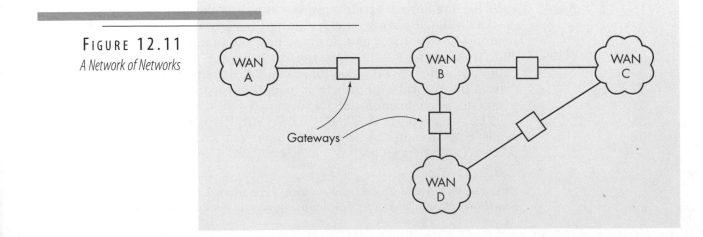

FIGURE 12.11
A Network of Networks

To allow the four WANs of Figure 12.11 to communicate, Kahn and his colleagues needed to create (1) a standardized way for a node in one WAN to identify a node located in a different WAN and (2) a universally recognized format for passing information across WAN boundaries so that each network could send and receive messages from any other network. Kahn, along with Dr. Vinton Cerf of Stanford, began working on these problems in 1973, and together they designed the solutions that were to become the framework for the Internet—the global network of interconnected networks:

- *Addressing.* Cerf and Kahn created a global, hierarchical addressing scheme that uniquely identifies a computer user located anywhere in the world. Most of us have seen these addresses, which look like the following:

    ABSmith@MyComp.CSci.UoT.edu

    This identifies a user, called "ABSmith," with an account on a computer whose network address is represented by everything to the right of the @ character. The computer is MyComp, and it is a machine in Computer Science (CSci), which is a department of the University of Technology (UoT), which is part of the higher educational system of the United States (edu). Thus we can see that the addresses proceed from the specific to the general. This local-to-global hierarchical addressing scheme is called the **Domain Name System** (DNS), and it is similar to the hierarchical addresses used for surface mail:

    Name

    Building, Street

    City, State

    Country

    (Actually, Internet addresses are 32-bit binary numbers, but these numbers are hard to remember and hard to work with, so machines rarely refer to other computers by these numeric codes. Instead, they use the symbolic addresses just described, which are then converted to the proper 32-bit number before transmission.)

- *Protocols.* Cerf and Kahn also designed a standardized set of communications protocols called **TCP/IP**, an acronym for *Transmission Control Protocol/Internet Protocol.* These protocols described the rules and procedures that networks would use for addressing, message formats, routing, and error control, and they are the "glue" that allows different networks to communicate with each other. TCP/IP was to become the "common language" spoken by networks around the world.

During the late 1970s and early 1980s, work proceeded on implementing and installing TCP/IP on the new hardware devices that were beginning to appear in the marketplace, such as personal computers connected to LANs. It is a real tribute to the power and flexibility of the TCP/IP protocols that they were able to adapt to a computing environment very different from the one that existed when they were first created. Originally designed to work with time-shared mainframe computers of the 1970s, they were successfully implemented on PCs and workstations connected by LANs, the computing environment of the 1980s and 1990s.

How This Book Was Written

An excellent example of the use of the Internet is this very textbook. It was written by three individuals located in Minnesota, Hawaii, California, and (part of the time) Indiana. The laboratory software and manual were created by two professors in Virginia, and the project's editor was located in Boston, Massachusetts. Without the ability of all these folks to communicate quickly and easily with everyone else via e-mail, FTP, and the Web, this type of group effort, its contributors separated by thousands of miles and five time zones, would have been much more difficult and would have taken much more time. Electronic mail and other types of network software have become an indispensable way to keep in touch.

By the early 1980s, TCP/IP was in widespread use around the world. Even networks that internally used other communication protocols implemented TCP/IP to exchange information with nodes outside their own network community. At the same time, exciting new applications appeared that were designed to meet the needs of researchers around the world. For example, **Telnet** is a software package that allows users to log on remotely to any other computer on the network and use it exactly as though they were local, without having to pay for an expensive long-distance telephone call. **FTP**, an acronym for **file transfer protocol**, is a way to move files around the network quickly and easily. Along with e-mail (still wildly popular), these and other new applications added more fuel to the superheated growth of computer networks.

With TCP/IP becoming a de facto network standard, a global addressing scheme, and a useful set of applications, the infrastructure was now in place for the creation of a truly international network. The Internet, in its modern form, had begun to emerge.

However, although many of the technical problems had been addressed and solved, the Internet had not yet had a significant impact on the general population for one very important reason: In order to use the original ARPANET, you needed to obtain a research grant from the U.S. Department of Defense (DoD)—not something most people have. Thousands of people were using the Internet by the early 1980s, but they were almost exclusively physicists, engineers, computer scientists, and other academic researchers.

There was one last step needed, and it was taken by the National Science Foundation (NSF) in 1984. In that year the NSF initiated a project whose goal was to bring the advantages of Internet technology to the *entire* academic and professional community, regardless of discipline or relationship with the DoD. NSF planned and built a national network called **NSFNet**, which used TCP/IP technology identical to that developed for the ARPANET. This new network interconnected six NSF supercomputer centers with dozens of new regional networks set up by the NSF. (Actually, NSFNet itself was only the **backbone network**—the transcontinental links that interconnected the regional networks.) These new regional networks included thousands of users at universities, government agencies, libraries, museums, and medical centers. NSFNet also included a direct link to the ARPANET. Thus, by the mid-1980s, the emerg-

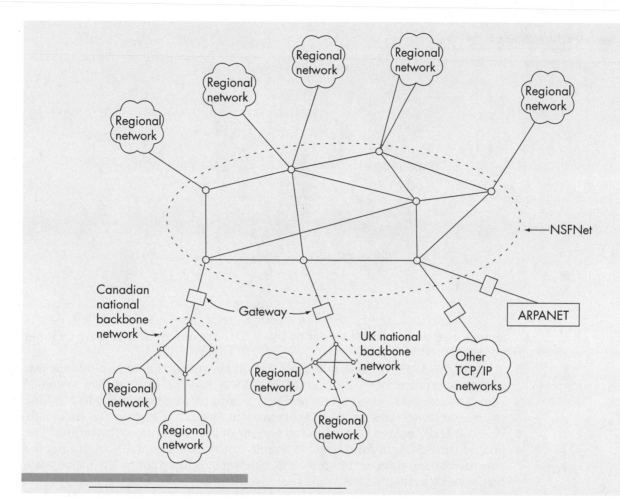

FIGURE 12.12

State of Networking in the Late 1980s

ing "network of networks" had grown to include many new sites and, even more important, a huge group of new first-time users, such as students, university administrators, librarians, museum staff, politicians, and urban planners.

At about the same time, other countries began developing wide area TCP/IP backbone networks like NSFNet to interconnect their own libraries, schools, research centers, and government agencies. As these national networks were created, they were also linked to the growing internetwork, and its user population continued to expand. For the first time since the development of networks, the technology had begun to have an impact on the wider community. A diagram of the state of internetworking in the late 1980s is shown in Figure 12.12.

Some time in the late 1980s, the term ARPANET ceased to be used because, as Figure 12.12 shows, the ARPANET was now only one of many networks belonging to a larger collection. (By 1990 this collection had grown to 3,000 separate networks and a quarter of a million computers.) People began referring to the entire interconnection of computer networks shown in Figure 12.12 as "the Internet," though this name was not officially adopted for many years. The formal

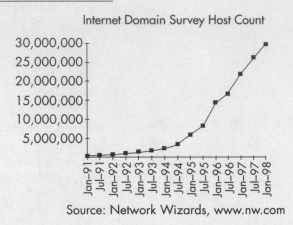

Internet Domain Survey Host Count

Source: Network Wizards, www.nw.com

acceptance of the term **Internet** by the U.S. Government occurred on October 24, 1995.

Like the ARPANET before it, the Internet became an instantaneous success and grew exponentially. By the middle of 1993, it had already grown to 20,000 separate networks, about 1.3 million host computers, and roughly 5 to 7 million users, and its size was doubling every year. In fact, it had become so successful that the NSF decided it was time to get out of the "networking business." The goal of the NSF is to fund basic research, not to become involved in ongoing commercial enterprises. In April 1995, NSFNet closed up shop. The money that was saved was distributed to the regional networks so they could buy Internet connectivity from private vendors such as America OnLine. The exit of the U.S. government from the networking business created a new business opportunity for firms called **Internet service providers**, companies that offer the Internet access capabilities once provided by networks such as the ARPANET and NSFNet.

From a humble beginning of four universities in 1969, by the middle of 1998 the Internet had grown to more than 29,000,000 computers located in just about every country in the world. (The Domain Name System includes extensions for 239 countries, territories, and possessions, including the continent of Antarctica (.aq), Brunei Darussalam (.bn), the Cocos Islands (.cc), Guinea-Bissau (.gw), Kiribati (.ki), Mauritius (.mu), Niue (.nu), Pitcairn Island (.pn), and Tuvalu (.tv).) The exponential growth of the Internet continues to this day. Figure 12.13 shows a graph of the number of host computers connected to the Internet.

The Internet has been one of the biggest success stories in moving research out of the laboratory and into the wider community. What began as the wild idea of a few dedicated researchers has, in only 30 years, grown into a global communications infrastructure moving countless trillions of bits of data among millions of people. It has adapted time and time again—to changes in usage (from research and academic to commercial), changes in hardware environment (from mainframes to PCs and networks), and changes in scale (from thousands of nodes to tens of millions).

Amazingly enough, however, the Internet is still undergoing massive growth and change, this time from the most important new application to be developed for the Internet since e-mail: the World Wide Web.

12.4.2 THE WORLD WIDE WEB

Tim Berners-Lee, a researcher at CERN, the European High Energy Physics Laboratory, first came up with the idea for the World Wide Web in 1989. Because physics research is usually done by teams of people from different universities, he wanted to find a way to allow scientists throughout Europe and North America to exchange quickly and easily information such as research articles, journals, and experimental data. Although they could use the Internet and services such as FTP and e-mail, Berners-Lee wanted to make sharing easier and more intuitive for people not familiar with or comfortable with computer networks. To accomplish this, he designed and built an information-sharing system using a concept called **hypertext**, a collection of documents connected by pointers, called **links**, as shown in Figure 12.14. Berners-Lee's system eventually came to be called the **World Wide Web.**

Most documents are read linearly from beginning to end, but users of hypertext documents (which are called **pages** in Web parlance) are free to navigate the collection in whatever order they want by traversing the links to move from page to page. Berners-Lee reasoned that the idea of hypertext matched up quite well with the concept of networking and the Internet. Hypertext documents could be files stored on the millions of machines of the Internet, and a link would be the name of a page and the Internet address of the machine where that page is stored.

FIGURE 12.14
Hypertext Documents

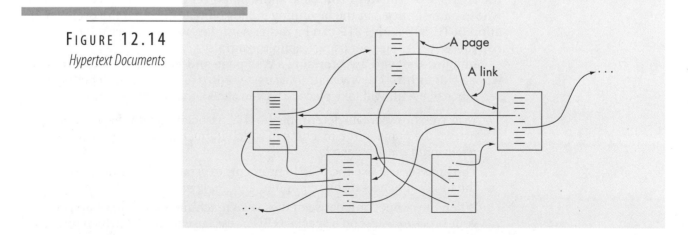

A hypertext link refers to a **URL**, an acronym for **Uniform Resource Locator**, and it is the worldwide identification of one specific Web page. URLs generally look like the following:

protocol://Internet address/page

They have three parts. The first part, "protocol," indicates the nature of the information contained in this page. The most common protocol is "http," which means that it is hypertext information exactly as described. However, the Web has been designed to grow and adapt, so it can accept and display a wide range of other types of information, such as "news" for information from bulletin boards and news groups and "mailto," which allows one to send and receive e-mail documents via the Web. The second part of the URL is the "Internet address" of the machine where the page is stored. This is the global DNS Internet address discussed earlier. The third part is the page identification, which is usually a file stored on the specified machine. Thus a typical URL might be

http://www.math.macalester.edu/welcome.html

which identifies a hypertext (http) document called "welcome.html" that is stored on the file server of the Mathematics and Computer Science Department at Macalester College, whose DNS Internet address is "www.math.macalester.edu".

When a user "clicks" on a link, the network uses the TCP/IP protocols to establish a connection between the user's machine and the remote machine whose Internet address is pointed at by the URL. When the connection is established, the requested page is transferred to the user's machine and displayed on the screen, all of which happens automatically. The package that handles the identification and fetching of pages and their display on the screen is called a **Web browser**; Netscape and Microsoft Internet Explorer are two of the best known. The first graphical browser (Mosaic) was developed in 1993, the year that many people consider to mark the real beginning of the Web.

The TCP/IP protocols are used to establish connections between machines, but Berners-Lee also had to develop a set of procedures for identifying the page being requested and returning that page to the user. These procedures are called the **Hypertext Transfer Protocols**, abbreviated **HTTP**, and this is the protocol whose name appears at the beginning of most URLs. Although the overall operation of TCP/IP and HTTP can be rather complex, we will illustrate how these two pieces work together using a simple example.

Imagine that you are browsing a Web page and have just clicked on a link whose URL is http://www.math.macalester.edu/welcome.html. The following sequence of events will take place to let you access that page:

1. Your Web browser will determine the URL associated with the link and will extract the name of the machine to which it must connect—in this case, *www.math.macalester.edu.*

2. The browser will use the TCP/IP protocols to establish a connection across the Internet between your computer and *www.math.macalester.edu.*

3. When the connection between these two machines has been established, your browser will send a special HTTP message called GET, which indicates

FIGURE 12.15

Operation of the Web

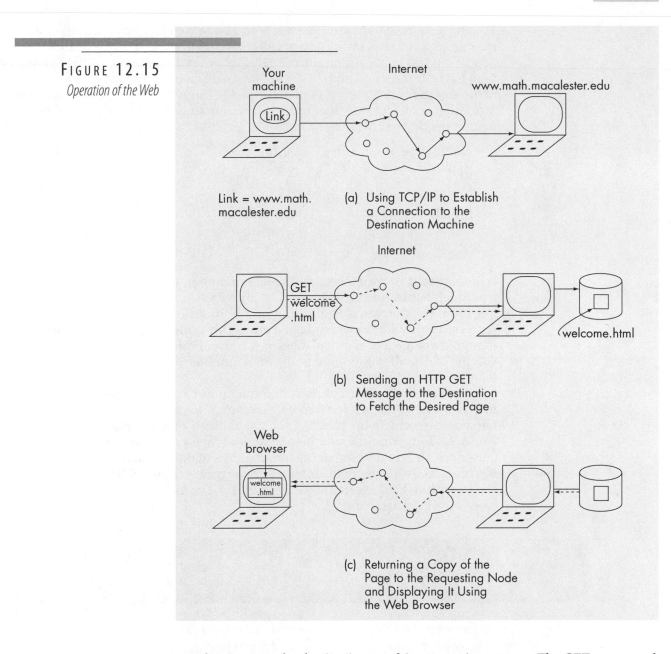

Your machine

Internet

www.math.macalester.edu

Link

Link = www.math.
macalester.edu

(a) Using TCP/IP to Establish a Connection to the Destination Machine

Internet

GET
welcome
.html

welcome.html

(b) Sending an HTTP GET Message to the Destination to Fetch the Desired Page

Web browser

welcome
.html

(c) Returning a Copy of the Page to the Requesting Node and Displaying It Using the Web Browser

that it wants the destination machine to retrieve a page. The GET command contains the name of the desired page, in this case "welcome.html".

4. The remote machine *www.math.macalester.edu* locates the file named in the GET message, reads it, copies it, and returns the copy to your browser, again using TCP/IP and the Internet.

5. Your browser receives the page and displays its contents on your screen.

This sequence of events is diagrammed in Figure 12.15.

From about 100 sites in 1993, the World Wide Web has grown exponentially, reaching 10,000 sites by the end of 1994, 100,000 at the beginning of 1996, and nearly 700,000 by the beginning of 1997. It is by far the fastest-growing component of the Internet. In mid-1995, the National Science Foundation did a study of the volume of different types of traffic on the Internet as a percentage of all information sent. Here are their results. (The remaining traffic is overhead information needed to run the network.)

Traffic Type	Percentage (June 1993)	Percentage (March 1995)
FTP	42.9	24.2
News	9.3	8.3
E-mail	6.4	4.9
Telnet	5.6	2.9
Web	0.5	23.9

If more recent statistics were available (remember, the NSF got out of the networking business in 1995), it would surely show that today the Web is, without question, the dominant application on the Internet. (The reason why e-mail represents only 4.9%, even though it is a highly popular application, is that although there are lots of e-mail messages, most of them are *short*. Thus the total volume of e-mail traffic—that is, the total number of bits sent and received—is relatively small.)

The Web's colorful graphics and simple "point and click" method of getting information has made it the Internet "killer app" of the 1990s and beyond. It has become the vehicle for bringing the capabilities of networking to the entire world. No longer must a user be a student or faculty member at a university, a curator of an art museum, or the librarian of a major research library. The Web has brought the power of the Internet to everyone—from toddlers to senior citizens and from kindergarten students to Ph.D.s. For most people, the World Wide Web *is* the Internet.

Internet Factoids (as of July 1, 1998)

Percentage of adults in the United States and Canada over 16 who use the Internet: 23%
Number of Americans who use the Web: 57,037,000
Number of host computers on the Internet: 29,600,000
Number of domains (subnetworks): 1,301,000
Number of countries and territories with unique Internet DNS identifiers: 239
Percentage of Internet host computers located in the United States: 58%

Amount spent on all Internet services and products: $19,000,000,000 (1996)
Total number of e-mail messages sent on the Internet in 1997: 2.7 trillion (estimated)
Estimated number of Web pages (April, 1998): 320 million

[Data courtesy of Network Wizards Inc. (their home page contains a great number of other interesting network facts, and it can be referenced at http://www.nw.com) and the Internet Index (located at http://www.openmarket.com/intindex).]

Laboratory Experience 20

In this section you read about the history of the World Wide Web, the algorithms and protocols that make the Internet and the Web work, and some of the social implications of the Web. In this laboratory exercise you will learn how to construct your own Web home page using the special language called HTML, an acronym for Hypertext Markup Language. (This language was first introduced in Chapter 8.) Learning how to program in HTML will open the door for you to become a contributor to the Web instead of just a user. You will also learn how to use your Web browser to perform simple file transfers from special computers called ftp servers. This will enable you to access a wealth of software and data files in the public domain.

12.5 CONCLUSION

Computer networking has changed enormously in the 25 to 30 years that it has been around. From a specialized communication system devoted to academic research, it has blossomed into a worldwide information network. What was once the esoteric domain of a few thousand scientists is now used by tens of millions, the vast majority of whom have no formal training in computer science. From providing access to corporate databases and research journals, it has become a way for the average citizen to shop, chat, be informed, and be entertained.

There is every reason to believe that the Internet will grow and evolve as much in the coming years as it has in the past, but it is hard to predict what the future may hold. In 1980, when almost all traffic on the Internet was research oriented, who could have imagined the volume of commercial work or entertainment that would exist just a few years later. In 1993, when there were just a hundred Web sites, who could have envisioned a million Web pages being accessed by tens of millions of people every day?

The next few years may see such innovations as **Internet telephone**, which will support the real-time transmission of voice, and **Internet television**, the real-time transmission of high-quality video. It may also see the creation of a universal "information appliance" that combines the features of TV, radio, stereo, telephone, FAX, and computer in a single digital processing device. This appliance would be hooked up to a high-speed megabit (gigabit?) telecommunications link that will replace the agonizingly slow modems now in use. As network security procedures improve, more financial transactions will be done electronically, making a trip to the bank a quaint anachronism.

However, the most pressing issue facing the Internet is not technology and new applications. Those issues have been and will continue to be addressed and solved by the computer science community. The biggest concern with the Internet today is how the growth and direction of networking will be managed. In the early days, the Internet was run by a core group of specialists without a financial stake in its future, and its management was relatively simple. Currently, the Internet is managed by the *Internet Society*, a worldwide nongovernmental agency dedicated to the orderly growth and utilization of Internet technology. Its home page is at http://www.isoc.org.

However, now that it is a global phenomenon that affects millions of people and generates billions of dollars in revenue, the Internet is being pulled and tugged by many new constituencies and stake holders, such as businesspeople, politicians, lawyers, standards groups, advertisers, government agencies, and computer manufacturers. The question now is who will speak for the Internet in the future and who will help shape its destiny. As the designers of the Internet warned at the end of their paper on the history of networking,

If the Internet stumbles, it will not be because we lack for technology, vision, or motivation. It will be because we cannot set a direction and march collectively into the future.

EXERCISES

1. Show how a modem would encode the binary sequence 11001 onto an analog carrier by:

   a. Modifying its amplitude (the height of the carrier wave)

   b. Modifying its frequency (the number of waves per second)

2. Determine the total time it would take to transmit a complete gray-scale image (with 8 bits/pixel) from a screen with a resolution of $1,000 \times 800$ pixels using each of the following media:

   a. A 28.8 Kbps modem
   b. An ISDN line
   c. A dedicated T1 phone line
   d. A fiber-optic cable using the OC-3 standard

3. a. Find out how many books are stored in your campus library. Then approximate (to the nearest order of magnitude) how many bytes of data there would be if all these books were stored on-line in machine-readable form and were accessible across a computer network.

   b. How long would it take to transfer the entire collection of books if the data rate of the transmission media were 2 Gbps? (This would be the time needed to download your entire campus library.)

4. Why is the address field needed in an Ethernet LAN protocol? Can you think of a useful situation where you might want either to omit the address field entirely or to use some "special" address value in the address field?

5. After reviewing the description of the Ethernet protocol in Section 12.2.2, how do you think these protocols would behave in a *heavily loaded* network—that is, a network environment where there are lots of nodes attempting to send messages? Explain what behavior you would expect to see and why.

6. The Ethernet is a distributed LAN protocol, which means that there is no centralized control node and that the failure of a single node can never bring down the entire network. However, can you think of any advantage to the creation of a centralized LAN in which one node would be in charge of the entire network and would make all decisions about who can send a message and who must wait?

7. a. Assume that we have a wide area network with N nodes, where $N \geq 2$. What is the *smallest* number of point-to-point communication links such that every node in the network is able to talk to every other node? (*Note:* A network in which some nodes are unable to exchange messages with other nodes because there is no path between them is called **disconnected**.)

   b. If you are worried about having a disconnected network, what type of interconnection structure should you use when configuring your network?

8. What happens in the store-and-forward protocol of Figure 12.8 if a message M being sent from node A to node B does correctly arrive at B, but the acknowledgment message ACK from B back to A is

garbled and never arrives? Are there any modifications that we may wish to make to these protocols to handle this particular situation?

9. How would we broadcast a message in a store-and-forward packet-switching protocol like the one shown in Figure 12.8? That is, how could we send the same message to 100 different nodes?

10. Given the following diagram, where the numbers represent the time delays across a link:

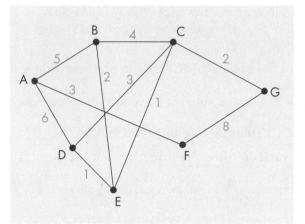

a. How many simple paths (those that do not repeat a node) are there from node A to node G?

b. What is the shortest path from node A to node G? What is the overall delay?

c. If node E fails, would that change the shortest path? If so, what would be the new shortest path?

11. What would be some of the specific responsibilities performed by the device called a gateway (diagrammed in Figure 12.11) that is placed between two different types of networks to allow them to communicate?

12. Look at the home page of the Internet Society (http://www.isoc.org) and discover some interesting facts about the Internet, including its history, its growth, its size, and how it is managed. Compare the current size of the Internet with the numbers given in the box entitled "Internet Factoids." See whether they have changed significantly since this book was published. The home page of the Internet Society has links to many other places that provide a wealth of fascinating information about networks in general and the Internet and the Web in particular.

Challenge Work

The TCP/IP protocols represent the "heart and soul" of the Internet; they are the fundamental rules that govern all communications across the Net. IP (Internet Protocol) is the building block, and it provides the most elementary and low-level of services—the routing of a single message from a source node S to a destination node D. IP does not guarantee that every message sent will correctly arrive at its destination, any more than the Post Office guarantees the correct delivery of every letter. What IP does is make a "good faith" attempt to determine the location of the node to whom the message is addressed and deliver the message to that address without error.

TCP (Transmission Control Protocol) is a higher-level protocol that builds on the low-level services pro-

vided by IP. It provides a higher quality of service than is available from IP alone. TCP provides services such as creating a virtual circuit between source and destination, error-free delivery along that channel (using retransmissions if necessary), guarantee of delivery within a maximum time, and adjustment of sending/receiving rates to avoid congestion and message loss.

Read about the TCP/IP protocols (the Comer book in the list that follows is a good starting point) and write a report describing their basic characteristics and giving a simple overview of the way that they work. (However, avoid the "gory details"—the formal specifications of TCP/IP can run to hundreds of pages.)

FOR FURTHER READING

A number of texts provide good overviews of computer networking. For example, see

Stallings, W. *Data and Computer Communications*, 5th ed. Englewood Cliffs, NJ: Prentice-Hall, 1997.

Tanenbaum, A. S. *Computer Networks*, 3rd ed. Englewood Cliffs, NJ: Prentice-Hall, 1996.

In the following paper, its original creator describes the World Wide Web.

Berners-Lee, T., et al., "The World Wide Web." *Communications of the ACM* 37 (August 1994).

Here are a couple of excellent discussions of TCP/IP, the protocols that form the basis for Internet communications:

Comer, D. E. *Internetworking with TCP/IP*, 3rd ed. Vol. 1. Englewood Cliffs, NJ: Prentice-Hall, 1995.

Stevens, W. R. *TCP/IP Illustrated*. Vol. 1. Reading, MA: Addison-Wesley, 1994.

Here are other books on various topics within the field of computer networks:

Garg, V., and Wilkes, J. E. *Wireless Communications and Personal Computing Systems*. Englewood Cliffs, NJ: Prentice-Hall, 1996.

Huitema, C. *Routing in the Internet*. Englewood Cliffs, NJ: Prentice-Hall, 1995.

Partridge, C. *Gigabit Networking*. Reading, MA: Addison-Wesley, 1994.

CHAPTER 13

ARTIFICIAL
INTELLIGENCE

13.1   INTRODUCTION

Artificial intelligence (AI) is the part of computer science that attempts to make computers act like human beings. Alan Turing, whose investigations into the fundamental nature of computation led to the Turing machine (Chapter 10), was also interested in artificial intelligence. In 1950, before the term *artificial intelligence* was coined, he proposed a test for intelligent behavior of machines.

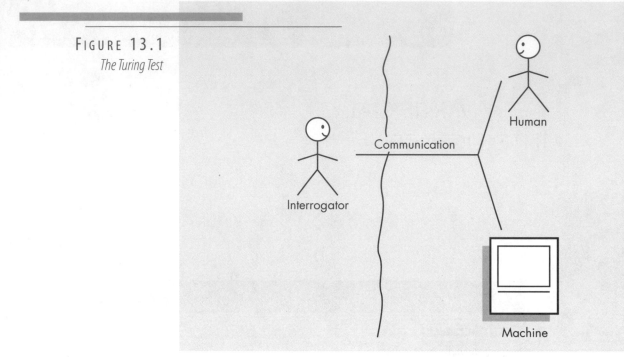

FIGURE 13.1
The Turing Test

The **Turing test** allows a human to interrogate two entities, both hidden from the interrogator (Figure 13.1). One entity is a human and the other a machine (a computer). The interrogator can ask the entities questions and can receive their responses. The communication is carried on in some form that does not by itself give away which entity is the computer; for example, the interrogator's questions could be typed on a keyboard and the responses printed out. If, as a result of this questioning, the interrogator is unable to determine which entity is the human and which the computer, then the computer has exhibited sufficiently human intelligence to pass the Turing test. This test does not explore the nature of human intelligence in some deep philosophical way; it merely says that if a machine exhibits behavior indistinguishable from that of a human, then what's the difference? Carrying this to extremes, one is led to science fiction scenarios where aliens cannot be distinguished from human beings. Do we really know *for sure* that the other people we interact with daily are human beings, or do they only act like humans?

It is probably this science fiction slant that has led to the public fascination with artificial intelligence. From HAL, the chillingly threatening mainframe of the movie *2001: A Space Odyssey* (according to the script, manufactured on January 12, 1997), to the endearing C-3PO of the *Star Wars* series movies, to Lieutenant Commander Data of television's *Star Trek—The Next Generation*, human-like machines have entertained and captivated. Outside of the entertainment field, visions have flourished of a society in which, on the one hand, human-like robots will result in thousands of displaced workers and a new level of social unrest or, on the brighter side, a society in which machines do all the dangerous or uninteresting work, leaving humans free to lead more creative and fulfilling lives.

Initially, the field of artificial intelligence seemed to hold out promises on which it did not deliver. After a period of great expectations came a period of disenchantment. But now, with more realistic expectations, the field of artificial intelligence has produced deliverable results. One of the benefits of artificial intelligence research has been that, in the attempt to make computers "think" more like humans, much has been learned about human thinking itself.

13.2   A DIVISION OF LABOR

In order to understand better what artificial intelligence is all about, let's consider a division of task types. Humans can perform a great variety of tasks, but we'll divide them into three categories, representative but by no means exhaustive:

- *Computational tasks*
    Adding columns of numbers
    Sorting a list of numbers into numerical order
    Searching for a given name in a list of names
    Managing the payroll
    Calculating trajectory adjustments for the space shuttle

- *Recognition tasks*
    Recognizing your best friend
    Understanding the spoken word
    Finding the tennis ball in the grass in your backyard

- *Reasoning tasks*
    Planning what to wear today
    Deciding on the strategic direction a company should follow for the next 5 years
    Running the triage center in the hospital emergency room after an earthquake

Humans can perform computational tasks. These are tasks for which algorithmic solutions exist (we devised algorithms for sorting and searching in the early chapters of this book). As humans, we can, in principle at least, follow the step-by-step instructions. Computational tasks are also tasks for which accurate answers must be found—sometimes very quickly—and that's where we as humans fall down. We make mistakes, we get bored, we aren't very speedy. Computers are better (faster and more accurate) at performing computational tasks, provided they are given programs that correctly embody the algorithms. Throughout most of this book, with its emphasis on algorithms, we've been talking about procedures to solve computational tasks, how to write those procedures, how to get the computer to execute them, and so on.

Humans are better at recognition tasks. We should perhaps expand the name of this task type to sensory/recognition/motor-skills tasks, because we receive information through our senses, primarily seeing and hearing, we recognize or "make sense of" the information we receive, and we often respond to the information with some sort of physical response that involves controlled movement. Although we wait until the second grade to learn how to add, an infant a few weeks old, on seeing its mother's face, recognizes that face and smiles; soon that infant will understand the spoken word. You spot the tennis ball in the yard even though it is green and nestled in among other green things (grass, dandelions). You register whether the tennis ball is close or farther away, and you manipulate your legs and feet to propel you in the right direction.

How do we as humans do these things? Traditional step-by-step procedural algorithms don't seem to apply, or if they do, we don't know what those algorithms are. Rather, it seems that we as humans succeed at these tasks by processing a huge amount of data and then matching the results against an even larger storehouse of data based on our past experiences. Consider the task of recognizing your best friend. You have, in effect, been shown a number of "pictures" of your friend's face that seem to be "burned into" your memory, along with pictures of the faces of everyone else you know well. When you see your friend, you sort through your mental picture file until you come to a match. It is a bit more complicated than that, however, because if you encounter your friend's sister, you may know who it is even though you have never met her before. You find, not an exact match to one of the images in your mental picture file, but a close approximation. Approximation, unlike the exactness required in computational tasks, is good enough. These complex recognition tasks that we as humans find so easy are difficult for computers to perform.

When humans perform reasoning tasks, they are also using a large storehouse of experience. This experience involves not just images but also cause-and-effect situations. You know that you should wear a coat when it's going to be cold because you've experienced being uncomfortable when the weather is cold and you don't wear a coat. You may reason as follows:

1. I don't want to be uncomfortable.
2. If the weather is cold and I don't wear a coat, then I will be uncomfortable.
3. The weather will be cold.

Conclusion: I will wear a coat.

This could be considered "mere" common-sense reasoning, but getting a computer to mimic "mere" common sense, to say nothing of higher-order conceptual, planning, or reasoning tasks, is extremely challenging. There may be no "right" answer to such tasks, and the way humans arrive at their respective answers sometimes seems ambiguous or based at least in part on "intuition," which may be just another name for knowledge or reasoning that we don't yet understand.

Figure 13.2 summarizes what we've outlined as the relative capabilities of humans and computers in these three types of tasks. Again, where computers fall below humans is where procedural algorithms either don't work or aren't known, and there seems to be a high level of complexity and perhaps approximation or ambiguity. Artificial intelligence seeks ways to improve the computer's capabilities in recognition and reasoning tasks, and we'll look at artificial intelligence ap-

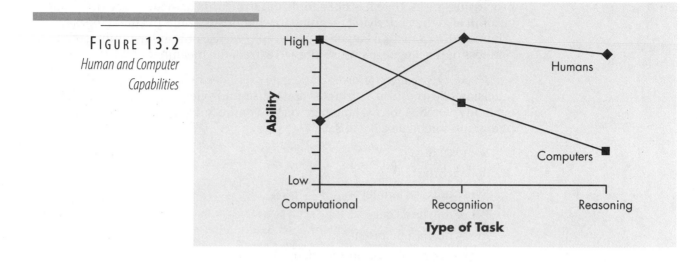

FIGURE 13.2

Human and Computer Capabilities

proaches in these two areas in the rest of this chapter. As mentioned earlier, however, both types of tasks seem to require a storehouse of information—images, past experiences, and so on—for which we'll use the general term *knowledge*. Therefore, we'll first look at various approaches to representing knowledge.

13.3 KNOWLEDGE REPRESENTATION

We can consider **knowledge** about some topic as a body of facts or truths. In order for the computer to make use of that knowledge, there must be some representational form in which the knowledge is stored within the computer. (At the lowest level, of course, only 0s and 1s are stored within the computer, but strings of 0s and 1s are organized and interpreted at a higher level of abstraction—as integers or characters, for example.) For computational tasks, the relevant knowledge is often isolated numeric or textual items. This is the usual data (such as integers and characters) that we've manipulated with procedural programs. What about more complex knowledge?

There are many workable representation schemes; let's consider four possibilities.

1. *Natural Language.* A paragraph or a page of text written in English, French, or some other natural language that contains all the knowledge we are trying to capture. Here is an example:

> *Spot is a brown dog and, like any dog, has four legs and a tail. Also like any dog, Spot is a mammal, which means Spot is warm-blooded.*

Note that although this representational form is text, it is text in a different sense from the character strings that are used in computational (or word processing) tasks. Here it is not simply the strings of characters that are important but also the underlying meaning in what those strings of characters say. When reading a natural language paragraph, we use our understanding of the richness of the language's vocabulary to extract the meaning.

2. *Formal Language.* A formal language sacrifices richness of expression for precision of expression. Attributes and cause-and-effect relationships are more explicitly stated. A formal language version of the foregoing natural language paragraph might look like this:

Spot is a dog.

Spot is brown.

Every dog has four legs.

Every dog has a tail.

Every dog is a mammal.

Every mammal is warm-blooded.

The term *language* was used in Chapter 9 to mean the set of statements derivable by using the rules of a grammar. But here the term **formal language** means the language of formal logic, usually expressed more symbolically than we have done in our example. In the usual notation of formal logic, we might use $D(x)$ to symbolize that the symbolic entity x has the attribute of being a dog. $B(x)$ would be interpreted as meaning that x has the attribute of being brown. Similarly $F(x)$, $T(x)$, $M(x)$, and $W(x)$ could symbolize the four-legged, tail, mammal, and warm-blooded attributes, respectively. The specific entity Spot could be represented by S. Then $D(S)$ would mean that Spot has the attribute of being a dog. Cause-and-effect relationships are translated into "if-then" statements. Thus "Every dog has four legs" is equivalent to "For every x, if x is a dog, then x has four legs." An arrow symbolizes cause-and-effect (if-then); "If x is a dog, then x has four legs" would be written symbolically as

$$D(x) \rightarrow L(x)$$

To show that every x that has the dog property also has the four-legged property, we would use a *universal quantifier*, $(\forall x)$, which stands for "for every x." Therefore,

$$(\forall x)(D(x) \rightarrow L(x))$$

means "For every x, if x is a dog, then x has four legs" or "Every dog has four legs." Symbolically, the preceding six formal language statements become

Statement	Symbolic Representation
Spot is a dog.	$D(S)$
Spot is brown.	$B(S)$
Every dog has four legs.	$(\forall x)(D(x) \rightarrow F(x))$
Every dog has a tail.	$(\forall x)(D(x) \rightarrow T(x))$
Every dog is a mammal.	$(\forall x)(D(x) \rightarrow M(x))$
Every mammal is warm-blooded.	$(\forall x)(M(x) \rightarrow W(x))$

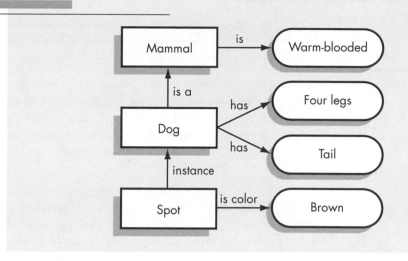

FIGURE 13.3
A Semantic Net Representation

3. *Pictorial.* Information is stored in pictorial form as an image—a grid of pixels that have attributes of shading and color. In this representation we would have a picture of Spot, showing that he is brown and has four legs and a tail. We might have some additional labeling that says something like "Spot, the dog." This visual representation would contain additional knowledge about Spot's appearance that is not embodied in the natural language paragraph or the formal language statements, but it would also fail to capture the knowledge that Spot is a mammal and that mammals are warm-blooded. It also wouldn't tell us that all dogs have four legs and a tail. (After all, a photo of a three-legged dog does not tell us that all dogs have three legs.)

4. *Graphical.* Here we are using the term *graphical* not in the sense of "visual" (we have already talked about pictorial representation) but in the mathematical sense of a graph with nodes and connecting arcs. Figure 13.3 is such a graph, also called a **semantic net**, for our dog example. In the terminology of object orientation that we used in Chapter 8, the rectangular nodes represent classes or objects, the oval nodes represent properties, and the arcs represent relationships. The "is a" relationship represents a subclass of a class that will inherit properties from the parent class; "dog" is a subclass of "mammal," and any dog object inherits all the properties of mammals in general, such as being warm-blooded. The "instance" relationship shows that something is an object of a class; Spot is a particular object from the dog class. Note that in our formal language, almost everything is an attribute (property) of a symbolic entity x, so $M(x) \rightarrow W(x)$ means that if x has the mammal attribute, then x also has the warm-blooded attribute. In graphical representation, we can more carefully distinguish between objects or classes and their properties.

Any knowledge representation scheme should have the following four characteristics:

1. *Adequacy.* The representation method must be adequate to capture all of the relevant knowledge. Because of its rich expressive powers, a natural

Write a natural language paragraph that describes a hamburger. Draw a semantic net that incorporates the same knowledge.

language will surely capture a lot of knowledge. However, it may be difficult to extract exactly what that knowledge is. One may have to wade through a lot of unnecessary verbiage, and one must also understand the nuances of meaning within the natural language. A formal language representation has the advantage of extracting the essentials.

2. *Efficiency.* We want the representational form to be minimalist. This means avoiding redundant information wherever possible. It also means allowing some knowledge that is not explicitly represented to be inferred from the knowledge that is explicitly represented. In the preceding example, it is easy to infer from the natural language, the formal language, or the semantic net that because Spot is a dog, he has four legs and a tail and also is a mammal and therefore warm-blooded. This knowledge, as we have said, is not captured in the pictorial format. On the other hand, it would take a much longer English paragraph to describe all the additional knowledge about Spot that is captured in the picture.

3. *Extendability.* It should be relatively easy to extend the representation to include new knowledge. For example, the semantic net can easily be extended to tack on another "dog" instance. It would also be easy to capture the fact that dogs have two eyes or that mammals do not lay eggs; these properties can simply be plugged in as new ovals connected into the network.

4. *Appropriateness.* The representation scheme used should be appropriate for the knowledge domain being represented. For example, a pictorial representation scheme would appear to be the most appropriate way to represent the knowledge base for a problem dealing with recognition of visual images. We saw before that a pictorial representation is probably not appropriate for the kind of knowledge about Spot that is difficult to display visually.

The choice of representational form for knowledge therefore depends on the knowledge to be captured and on the type of task for which the knowledge is to be put to use.

13.4   RECOGNITION TASKS

If artificial intelligence aims to make computers "think" like humans, then it is natural to investigate and perhaps attempt to mimic the way the human brain functions. It is estimated that the human brain contains about 10^{11} to 10^{12} neu-

FIGURE 13.4

A Neuron

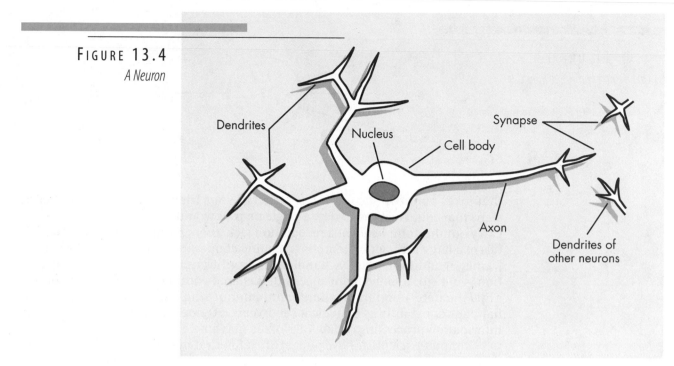

FIGURE 13.4

A Neuron

rons. Each **neuron** is a cell capable of receiving stimuli, in the form of electro-chemical signals, from other neurons through its many **dendrites** (see Figure 13.4). In turn, it can send stimuli to other neurons through its single **axon**. The axon of a neuron does not directly connect with the dendrites of other neurons; rather, it sends signals over small gaps called **synapses**. Some of the synapses appear to send the neuron activating stimuli, whereas others seem to send inhibiting stimuli. A single neuron collects all the stimuli passing through all the synapses around its dendrites. The neuron sums the activating (positive) and inhibiting (negative) stimuli it receives and compares the result with an internal "threshold" value. If the sum equals or exceeds the threshold value, then the neuron "fires," sending its own signal down its axon to affect other neurons.

Each neuron can be thought of as an extremely simple computational device with a single on-off output. The power of the human brain lies in the vast number of neurons, the many interconnections between them, and the activating/inhibiting nature of those connections. To borrow a term from computer science, the human brain uses a **connectionist architecture**, characterized by a large number of simple "processors" with multiple interconnections. In some areas of the brain, an individual neuron may collect signals from as many as 100,000 other neurons and send signals to an equally large number of other neurons. This extensive parallelism is evidently required because of the relatively slow time frame within which a neuron fires. In the human brain, neurons operate on a time scale of milliseconds (thousandths of a second), as opposed to the nanoseconds (billionths of a second) in which computer operations are measured, a difference of 6 orders of magnitude. In a human processing task

FIGURE 13.5

One Neuron with Three Inputs

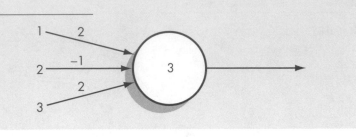

that takes about ¹⁄₁₀ second (recognition of your friend's face), the number of steps that could be executed by a single neuron would be on the order of 100. To carry out the complexity of a recognition task, then, requires the parallel activities of a large number of neurons executing cooperatively within this short time frame. In addition, massive parallelism supplies redundancy so that information is not stored only in one place but is shared within the network of neurons. Thus the deterioration of a limited number of single neurons (a process that happens constantly as biological cells wear out) does not cause a failure of the information processing capabilities of the network.

Computer scientists have built **artificial neural networks**, usually just called **neural networks**, to simulate the connectionist architecture of the human brain and have applied those networks to recognition tasks. Individual neurons in a neural network may be simulated in hardware, resulting in a massively parallel network of simple devices that act somewhat like biological neurons. (Recall our discussion in Chapter 5 of parallel processing and non-Von Neumann architectures). Alternatively, the effect of a neural network may be simulated in software on an ordinary sequential-processing computer. In either case, each neuron has a threshold value, and its incoming lines carry weights that represent stimuli. The neuron fires when the sum of the incoming weights equals or exceeds the threshold value. The input lines are activated as a result of the firing of other neurons. A single neuron could be represented as shown in Figure 13.5.

The neuron in Figure 13.5 has a threshold value of 3, and it has three input lines with weights of 2, –1, and 2, respectively. If all three input lines are activated, the sum of the incoming signals is $2 + (-1) + 2 = 3$ and the neuron will fire. It will also fire if only lines 1 and 3 are activated, because the sum of the incoming signals is then $2 + 2 = 4 > 3$. Any other combination of activated input lines will not carry sufficient stimulation to fire the neuron.

As a simple example of a neural network that has mastered a recognition task, consider Figure 13.6. There are four neurons. N1 and N2 both have a threshold value of 1, N3 has a threshold value of 3, and N4 has a threshold value of –3. The weights of the various connections are shown. The input connection from each of the A or Y symbols carries a weight of 2, the connection from N2 to N4 carries a weight of –2, and so on. The purpose of this network is to be able to recognize that all of the three different forms of the letter A are equivalent, as are all of the three forms of the letter Y, and that no form of A is equivalent to any form of Y. Such a capability could be part of a character recognition system.

FIGURE 13.6

A Neural Network for Comparing
Two Characters

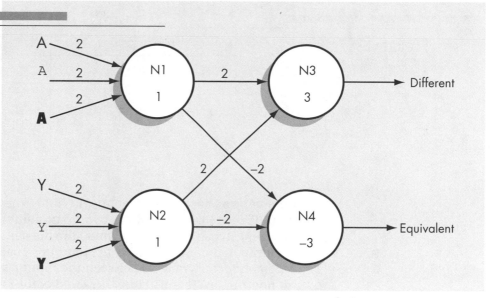

In Figure 13.6, exactly two characters are presented to the neural net—two As, two Ys, or one of each—by sending a signal of the correct weight along the appropriate input lines. If two As are presented, the signal reaching N1 has a total value of 4, which will cause N1 to fire. This sends a signal of weight 2 to N3—not enough to meet N3's threshold value of 3, so N3 does not fire. A signal of weight –2 reaches N4, which exceeds N4's threshold value of –3, so N4 fires, indicating that the two As were equivalent. A similar thing happens if two Ys are presented to the network. However, if one A and one Y are presented, then a signal of 2 reaches both N1 and N2—sufficient to cause each of them to fire. A combined signal of –4 reaches N4; this is below its threshold value of –3, so N4 does not fire. A combined signal of 4 reaches N3, causing it to fire, thus indicating that the two symbols presented to the network were not equivalent.

The neural net of Figure 13.6 contains two layers of neurons. The "input layer" consists of those neurons, N1 and N2, that receive input signals. The "output layer" consists of those neurons, N3 and N4, that generate output signals. The network must make a decision about the input that is presented to it in one time step, going directly from the input layer to the output layer. Such networks are called **perceptrons**. Most recognition tasks are too complex for a perceptron to do the job; an inner, or hidden, layer of neurons is required, whose interconnections and weights enable the network to store enough information about the desired pattern to allow recognition to take place.

For example, suppose the neural net is supposed to respond to two binary signals and determine whether they are the same or different. A truth table representing the behavior of the net is shown in Figure 13.7. The Boolean operation represented by this truth table is called exclusive OR, or XOR, because the output is true (1) when one or the other input is true, but not when both are true.

FIGURE 13.7

The Truth Table for XOR

Inputs		Output
x_1	x_2	
0	0	0
1	0	1
0	1	1
1	1	0

A perceptron for this operation (no hidden layer) would have the form shown in Figure 13.8. Each of the two input neurons, representing x_1 and x_2, would accept signals of 1 or 0; a 1 would fire the neuron, and a 0 would not. The single output neuron would either fire (output signal 1) or not (output signal 0). The interconnection weights between the input layer neurons and the single output neuron, together with the threshold of the output neuron, are yet to be determined. But in fact, no combination of interconnection weights and threshold value will succeed in making the network behave as we wish. If exactly one input of signal 1 is enough to fire the output neuron, which is the desired behavior, then two inputs of signal 1 can only increase the tendency for the output neuron to fire. Another way to express the problem is to say that the output neuron must behave in the same way for input patterns that are quite different from each other (two 1s or two 0s). The network of Figure 13.8 is not able to keep track of this much information.

Figure 13.9 shows a neural net with a hidden layer that implements the XOR truth table. When both input signals are 0, nothing fires. When only one input

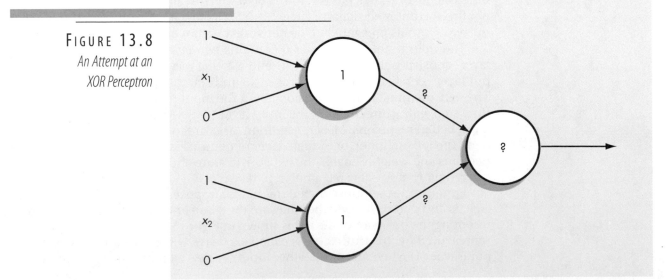

FIGURE 13.8

*An Attempt at an
XOR Perceptron*

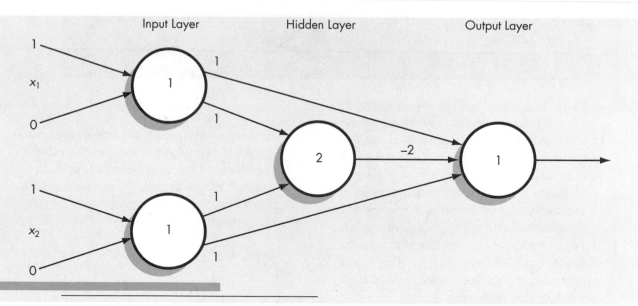

<comment>Figure labels: Input Layer, Hidden Layer, Output Layer</comment>

FIGURE 13.9

Neural Net for XOR

signal is 1, one input neuron fires, but the hidden neuron does not fire, so the output neuron is not inhibited and fires as well. But when both input signals are 1, the hidden neuron also fires and damps out the excitation of the output neuron so that it does not fire.

Conventional computer processing can be said to work on a knowledge base where the information is stored as data in specific memory cells that can be accessed by the program as needed. In a neural network, both the knowledge representation and also the "programming" are stored in the network itself as the weights of the connections and the thresholds of the neurons. If you want to build a neural network to perform in a certain way, how do you determine these values? Although the examples we've seen are simple enough that trial and error could produce a solution, such is not the case for a network with thousands of neurons. Fortunately, the right answer doesn't have to be found the first time. Remember that neural networks are modeled on the human brain; you learned to recognize your best friend through repeated "learning experiences" that modified your knowledge base until you came to associate certain features or characteristics with that individual.

Similarly, a neural network can learn from experience by modifying the weights on its connections (even making some connections "disappear" by assigning them 0 weights). A network can be given an initial set of weights and thresholds that is simply a first guess. The network is then presented with **training data**, for which the correct outputs are known. The actual output from the network is compared to the correct output for one set of input values from the training data. For those output neurons that produce correct values, their threshold values and the weights on their inputs will not be changed. Output neurons that produce erroneous values can err in one of two ways. If an output neuron fires when it is not supposed to, then the positive (excitatory) input values coming into it are adjusted downward, and the negative (inhibitory) weights

A C is a **C** is a C

Visual pattern recognition involves establishing classes of patterns by identifying features that are common to each class and are not shared by other classes. When an unknown pattern is presented, its features are analyzed and compared with those of the various classes to find the closest match. Features can be physical characteristics that are concrete and measurable, such as no loops, one concavity, or three corners.

These **feature analysis** techniques are used for identification of cancer cells, optical character recognition, fingerprint identification, and so on. The Federal Bureau of Investigation has over two hundred million fingerprints on file and receives over thirty thousand search requests per day.

The optical character recognition system used by banks requires a special set of characters; you've seen them on the bottom of your checks:

0123456789

These characters allow for exact pattern matching; each character scanned on the check strip will exactly match one of the ten patterns. Machine recognition of handwritten characters is more difficult, of course, because of the many variations. What is the feature analysis process that we humans use to identify each of the following as the letter C?

C C C C C C

coming into it are adjusted upward. If it fails to fire when it is supposed to, the opposite adjustment is made. But before these adjustments take place, information on the errors is passed back from each erroneous output neuron to the neurons in the hidden layer that are connected to it. Each hidden-layer neuron adds these error counts to derive an estimate of its own error. This estimate is used to calculate the adjustments to be made on the weights of the connections coming to it from the input-layer neurons. Finally the weights are all adjusted, and then the process is repeated for the next set of input values from the training data.

This **back propagation algorithm**, so named for the error estimates that are passed back from the output layer, eventually causes the network to settle into a stable state where it can correctly respond, to any desired degree of accuracy, to all inputs in the training set. In effect, the successive changes in weights have reinforced good behavior and discouraged bad behavior, much as we train our pets, until the paths for good behavior are imprinted on the connections (as in Fido's brain). The network has "learned" what its connection weights should be, and its ability to recognize the training data is embedded somehow in the col-

Laboratory Experience 21

In this lab experience, you will train a neural network to recognize certain characters you select. Then you can test the network's ability to identify correctly variations on those characters.

PRACTICE PROBLEM

If input line 1 is stimulated in the following neural network (and line 2 is not stimulated), will the output line fire? Explain.

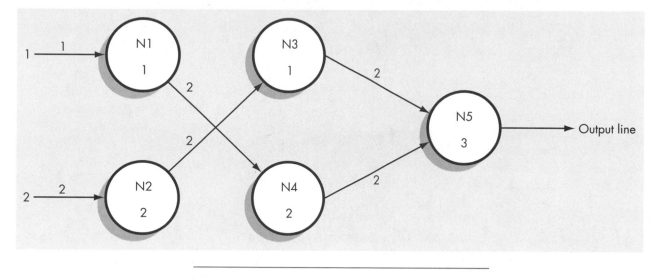

lective values of these weights. At the end of its training, the neural network is ready to go to work on new recognition problems that are similar to, but not the same as, the training data and for which the answers are unknown.

Neural networks have found their way into dozens of real-world applications. A few of these are handwriting recognition, speech recognition, recognizing patterns indicative of credit card fraud, recognizing bad credit risks for loans, predicting the odds of susceptibility to cancer, limited visual recognition systems, segmenting magnetic resonance images in medicine, adapting mirror shapes for astronomical observations, and discovering the best routing algorithm in a large communications network (a problem we mentioned in Chapter 12). With the ever-lower cost of massively parallel networks, it appears that neural networks will continue to find new applications.

13.5   REASONING TASKS

We noted that one of the characteristics of human reasoning seems to be the ability to draw on a large body of facts and past experience to come to a conclusion. In this section we look at several ways in which artificial intelligence specialists try to get computers to emulate this characteristic.

FIGURE 13.10

*Decision Tree for
Sequential Search*

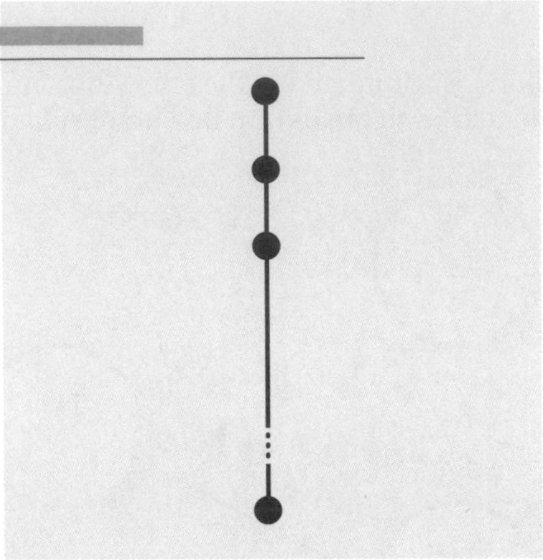

13.5.1 INTELLIGENT SEARCHING

Earlier in this book, we investigated two algorithms for searching—sequential search and binary search. These search algorithms look for a perfect match between a specific target value and an item in a list. The work involved is $\Theta(n)$ for sequential search or $\Theta(\lg n)$ for binary search. A **decision tree** for a search algorithm illustrates the possible next choices of items to search if the current item is not the target. In a sequential search, there is only one item to try next: the next item in the list. The decision tree for sequential search is linear, as shown in Figure 13.10.

A decision tree for a binary search, such as the one shown in Figure 13.11, reflects the fact that if the current item is not the target, there are only two next choices (the midpoint of the sublist before this node or the midpoint of the sublist after this node). Furthermore, the binary search algorithm specifies which of the two nodes to try next.

The classical search problem benefits from two simplifications:

1. The search domain (the set of items being searched) is a linear list. At each point in the search, if the target is not found, the choice of where to look next is highly constrained.

2. We seek a perfect match, so the comparison of the target against the list item results in a binary decision—either they match or they do not.

Suppose, however, that condition 1 does not hold; the search domain is such that after any one node has been searched, there are a huge number of next choices to try. (Figure 13.12 attempts to convey this idea.) Then the search problem does not yield to the classical list-based search algorithms. A brute force approach to solving such a search problem requires tracing all branches of the decision tree so that all possible choices are tested and no test cases are repeated. This becomes a massive bookkeeping task because the number of tree branches grows exponentially.

FIGURE 13.11

Decision Tree for Binary Search

Many types of problems fall into this exponential-growth category. Finding the shortest path through a network, finding the winning strategy in a board game, and finding the most successful investment strategy in the stock market are all examples.

Given that time and computing resources are limited, an intelligent search needs to be employed. An intelligent search narrows the number of tree branches that must be tried and thereby puts a cap on the otherwise exponential growth of the problem. Intelligent searching involves two aspects:

Best-first search: picking a good starting node from which to search. This requires being able to recognize the differences between where you are and the desired destination. (If you are looking for a particular building on the north side of town, you drive to the right neighborhood before you start a detailed search.)

Means-end analysis: making a wise choice of where to go next from the present node. This requires knowing what to do to reduce the differences you recognized in the previous step. (If you're still too far south for the address of the building, you drive north.)

An intelligent chess-playing strategy, for example, is one that makes an appropriate first move and that, at each step, makes a move more likely than others to lead to a winning board configuration. Even a grand master of chess cannot pursue the brute force approach of mentally trying out all the possible next moves, all the possible moves following from each of those moves, and so

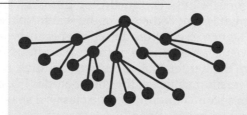

FIGURE 13.12

A Decision Tree with Exponential Growth

Kasparov versus Deep Blue in Chess

In May 1997, international attention was focused on a historic chess match between world champion Garry Kasparov and the IBM chess-playing computer known as Deep Blue. In a 1996 competition between Kasparov and an earlier version of Deep Blue, Kasparov was defeated in the opening game. Somewhat shocked that his aggressive play from a position of weakness failed to intimidate the machine (it had always intimidated his human opponents), Kasparov changed tactics and went on to win the match. IBM scientists returned to the drawing board for a year to beef up Deep Blue's capabilities. In the second face-off, Kasparov and Deep Blue played neck and neck with one win and three draws apiece, but in the sixth game Kasparov lost the match by falling for a well-known trap. Kasparov's error, which was considered a major blunder for a player of his ability, probably reflected his weariness and the emotional strain of competing against an unexpectedly strong, utterly impassive foe. These human frailties, of course, were not shared by Deep Blue.

Photo by E. J. Camp. Courtesy of International Business Machines Corporation. Unauthorized use is not permitted.

Although some hailed the victory of Deep Blue as a triumph of machine over human being, it is worthwhile to look at the differences between how the human (Kasparov was 34 years old at the time and is of Russian birth) and the machine (Deep Blue is based on the IBM RS/6000 massively parallel computer system) play chess.

---

on, for very many steps. Intelligent searching is required. There must be a deep storehouse of experience that can be "consulted" on the basis of the overall present configuration of the board—experience that suggests the best course of action for this configuration. A grand-master-level player may need a mental database of around 50,000 of these board configurations, each with its associated information about the best next move.

Building a machine that could beat a human at chess was long thought to be a supreme test to demonstrate artificial intelligence—machines that "think." Successfully playing chess, it was believed, would surely epitomize logical reasoning, true "intelligence." Chess is difficult for humans. Yet the rules for chess are straightforward; it is simply the size of the search space that is overwhelming. As artificial intelligence researchers delved deeper into supposedly "simpler" problems such as visual recognition—things we humans do easily—it became clear that these were the harder challenges for machines. Nonetheless, the contest of human being versus machine at the chessboard is irresistibly fascinating.

What if the second condition of the classical search problem—that of seeking an exact match with a specified target value—is relaxed? Suppose we no longer want to know whether we've found the exact target value. Instead, we are

KASPAROV	DEEP BLUE
Can evaluate up to 3 chess positions per second, or 540 in the 3 minutes allowed between moves	Can evaluate up to 200,000,000 chess positions per second, or 50 billion in 3 minutes
Selects which few positions to evaluate on the basis of recognition of successful strategies or tactical approaches	Pursues a large number of random positions to determine the optimal move
Uses his brain, including experience and intuition	Uses its 512 communicating processors that act algorithmically, following their C programming
Can assess his opponent's weaknesses and dynamically adjust his playing strategy	Can be modified by its development team between games to change its approach
Is subject to human emotions and weaknesses	Does not tire or allow emotional responses to alter its play
Is cognizant that he is Garry Kasparov playing a world-class chess tournament against a machine	Is unaware of its own existence, the identity of its competitor, or the circumstances of the game.

Both Kasparov and Deep Blue are relying on the respective strengths of their "species," Kasparov utilizing recognition and reasoning, and Deep Blue churning out its high-speed computations (see Figure 13.2). But the biggest difference is the last one shown in the accompanying table; Deep Blue has no idea what it has accomplished by winning this chess match, whereas Kasparov has issued a challenge for a rematch.

Because our definition of artificial intelligence requires only that machines act like humans, not that they have the self-awareness characteristic of humans, we can still ask whether Deep Blue utilizes artificial intelligence. The answer is no, in the sense that although the IBM team has enriched Deep Blue's computational prowess by assigning weights to various features of a given chess position, the machine is still depending on its brute force search capabilities—not on pattern recognition in the neural network sense, not on truly logical reasoning, and on only mildly intelligent searching.

The major lesson to be learned from the human-computer chess competition that has been going on for 40 years is that chess playing—originally thought to be the epitome of "machine intelligence"—is actually easier to program into a machine than the many things that every human can easily accomplish (pattern recognition, intelligent search, higher-order reasoning). In fact, some artificial intelligence researchers feel that it is the last of the "easy" hard problems.

looking for close matches. This requires that we have some way to measure distance from a target value, as well as a definition of the maximum distance beyond which we are no longer "close."

Internet search engines perform this kind of search. On the basis of keywords that are entered, the search engine scans its database for Web documents containing those words. Most search services return a list of possible "hits," usually ordered from closest to farthest away from the keyword targets. A document that contains all (as opposed to some) of the keywords entered, that contains multiple instances of these keywords, and that often contains these keywords together will rank as highly likely. However, this is still unintelligent searching; the search engine knows nothing about the user requesting the search, and it is still relying on a target-comparison model, though a more complex one than simply matching one target item against a list. The Internet search engine that the user chooses does not run out and search the World Wide Web every time the user makes a query. This would be too slow. Instead, the search engine taps its own database of URL addresses to respond to the user's query. This database it-self is built from searches done on behalf of the search engines as a sort of back-ground process. Software that "crawls through the Web" looking for new Web sites to add to the search engine database is called a **spider**.

But what if the user could pose a query about information on the Web and have a search engine that starts with keywords entered by the user but that also acts on a database of its own knowledge about the user's interests, preferences, and lifestyle to perform a really intelligent search? Suppose, for example, that the user requests information about "mustangs," but the search engine "knows" that the user has a collection of classic cars. The search engine therefore as-sumes that the user is referring to information about automobiles rather than wild horses. Imagine that the search engine can even act on its own, somewhat as a good friend might, and notify the user of an upcoming car show in his or her geographic area.

Capabilities such as these get into the realm of what are called **intelligent agents**. An intelligent agent is a software technology designed to interact collab-oratively with a user somewhat in the mode of a personal assistant. Imagine that you have hired your own (human) personal assistant. In the beginning, you will have to tell your assistant what to do and how you would like it done. Over time, however, your assistant comes to know more about you and soon can anticipate what tasks need to be done and how to perform them, what items to bring to your attention, and so forth. Your assistant becomes more valuable as he or she becomes more self-directed, always acting with your best interests in mind. You, in turn, put more and more trust in your assistant.

Like the human personal assistant, an intelligent agent will soon not merely wait for user commands but will initiate communication, take action, and per-form tasks on its own on the basis of its increasing knowledge of your needs and preferences. Although this sounds like the realm of science fiction movies, intel-ligent agents with greater or lesser capabilities are beginning to appear in our lives. Here are some examples that exist today:

- Desktop office software may come with the services of an assistant. This little animated object attempts to display appropriate help messages as you work by assessing the context of the task you are trying to perform. Suppose you are using a word processor to create a document, and you decide to insert a table. If your assistant is active as you begin to insert a table, it may automatically provide you with a "tip" on how to use some feature of the software to make this task easier. Or, again while creating a table, you can click on the assistant image, and it will provide you with a choice of help topics related to working with tables. Finally, you can ask the assistant a specific query, and it will search its database and display a choice of relevant help topics. Here the assistant doesn't learn more about you as you work, but it is aware of the task you are trying to perform.

- A personalized Web search engine allows you to profile items of interest to you and then automatically delivers appropriate information from the Web. For example, you may request updated weather conditions for your geographic area, along with news items related to sports and European trade. At periodic time intervals, this **push technology** downloads your updated, personalized information directly to your screen to be displayed whenever no other task is active.

- A more intelligent version of this personalized Web searcher enables you to "vote" on each article it sends you and then dynamically adjusts what it sends in the future as it learns about your preferences.

- An even more intelligent search agent not only narrows down choices from topics you have chosen but can suggest new, related topics for you to explore. This is accomplished by having your agent run around the Web and communicate with similar agents, even when you are not on-line. If your agent knows of your interest in French cuisine, for example, it will communicate with other agents to find those that represent users with the same interest. It may learn from these agents that many of their users are also interested in Creole cooking. Your agent will then judge whether these suggestions are coming from agents whose recommendations on the whole have been well received by you in the past. If so, it will ask whether you also want information about Creole cooking. If you do not agree to this proposal, your agent will note what agents made that suggestion and, on the next pass, will give less consideration to their ideas. The more agents that participate, the more accurate each one becomes at "understanding" the interests of its user.

- An on-line catalog sales company uses an agent that monitors incoming orders and makes suggestions. For example, a customer who orders a camera may be presented with a list of related accessories for sale, such as tripods and lens filters.

- A manufacturing plant uses an intelligent agent to negotiate with suppliers on the price and scheduling of parts delivery in order to maximize efficiency of production.

Some not-too-distant future applications include

- Buying and selling agents that will negotiate with one another over the Web for the sale and purchase of goods and services, using price/cost parameters set by the sellers and buyers. If negotiations reached a successful conclusion, the transaction would be logged and the terms reported to the buyer and seller.

- Travel agents (electronic, not human) that will book airline flights, rent automobiles, and make hotel reservations for you on the basis of your destination, schedule, price range, and preferences.

- Office manager agents that screen incoming telephone calls and e-mail, putting meetings on their users' schedules and drafting replies.

- Monitoring agents that will help nuclear power plant operators to sift through quantities of data to spot and diagnose potential failures.

Intelligent agent technology has been an area of interest in artificial intelligence for many years, but its applications are just beginning to be seen in everyday life. The First International Conference on Autonomous Agents was held in 1997. Several important aspects of research and development lie ahead. For example, standards and protocols must be established for intelligent agents so that they can more easily work together. In addition, intelligent agents will have to display significant learning capabilities and "common sense" before users will trust them to make autonomous decisions and commit resources of time and money.

13.5.2 EXPERT SYSTEMS

Although intelligent agents incorporate a body of knowledge to "filter" their choices and thereby appear to capture certain aspects of human reasoning, they still perform relatively limited tasks. Consider the more unstructured scenario of managing the triage center in a busy hospital emergency room. The person in charge draws on (1) past experience and training to recognize various medical conditions (which may involve many recognition subtasks), (2) understanding of those conditions and their probable consequences, and (3) knowledge about the hospital's capabilities and resources in general and at the moment. From this knowledge base, a chain of reasoning is followed that leads, for example, to a decision to treat patient A immediately in a particular fashion and to let patient B wait. We consider this to be evidence of quite general "logical reasoning" in humans.

Artificial intelligence simulates this kind of reasoning through the use of **rule-based systems**, which are also called **expert systems** or **knowledge-based systems**. (The latter term is a bit confusing, because all "intelligent activity" rests on some base of knowledge.) A rule-based system attempts to mimic the human ability to engage pertinent facts and string them together in a logical fashion to reach some conclusion. A rule-based system must therefore contain these two components:

- A **knowledge base**—a set of facts about the subject matter
- An **inference engine**—a mechanism for selecting the relevant facts and for reasoning from them in a logical way

Note that the knowledge base contains facts about a *specific* subject domain in order to narrow the scope to some manageable size.

The facts in the knowledge base can consist of certain simple assertions. For example, let's say that the domain of inquiry is U.S. presidents. Three simple assertions are

1. Lincoln was president during the Civil War.
2. Kennedy was president before Nixon.
3. FDR was president before Kennedy.

Another type of fact is a *rule*, a statement of the form *if . . . then . . .*, which says that whenever the clause following "if" is true, so is the clause following "then." For example, here are two rules that, taken together, define what it means for one president to precede another in office. In these rules, *X*, *Y*, and *Z* are variables.

I. If *X* was president before *Y*, then *X* precedes *Y*.
II. If *X* was president before *Z* and *Z* precedes *Y*, then *X* precedes *Y*.

Here we are using a formal language to represent the knowledge base.

What conclusions can be reached from this collection of three assertions and two rules? Assertion 2 says that Kennedy was president before Nixon. This matches the "if" clause of rule I, where *X* is Kennedy and *Y* is Nixon. From this, the "then" clause of rule I yields a new assertion, that Kennedy precedes Nixon, which we'll call assertion 4. Now assertion 3 says that FDR was president before Kennedy, and assertion 4 says that Kennedy precedes Nixon. This matches the "if" clause of rule II, where X is FDR, Z is Kennedy, and Y is Nixon. From this, the "then" clause of rule II yields a new assertion, that FDR precedes Nixon, which we'll call assertion 5. Hence

4. Kennedy precedes Nixon.
5. FDR precedes Nixon.

are two new conclusions or assertions. These assertions were previously unknown and were obtained from what was known through a process of logical reasoning. The knowledge base has been extended. We could also say that the system has *learned* two new pieces of knowledge.

If this example sounds familiar, it is because this is part of the example we used in Chapter 8 to illustrate the logic programming language Prolog. Prolog provides one means of implementing an inference engine for a rule-based system.

The inference engine is basically using the following pattern of reasoning:

Given that the rule

If A then B

and the fact

A

are both in the knowledge base, then the fact

B

can be inferred or concluded.

This reasoning process, as we noted in Chapter 8, goes by the Latin name of **modus ponens**, which means "method of assertion." It gives us a method for making new assertions. We humans use this deductive reasoning process all the time. However, it is also suitable for computerization because it is basically a matching algorithm that can be implemented by brute force trial and error. Systems like Prolog, however, apply some additional guidelines in their search for matches in order to speed up the process; that is, they employ a form of intelligent searching.

Inference engines for rule-based systems can proceed in several ways. **Forward chaining** begins with assertions and tries to match those assertions to the "if" clauses of rules, thereby generating new assertions. These may in turn be matched with "if" clauses, generating still more assertions. This is the process we used in our example. **Backward chaining** begins with a proposed conclusion and tries to match it with the "then" clauses of rules. It then looks at the corresponding "if" clauses and tries to match those with assertions, or with the "then" clauses of other rules. This process continues until all "if" clauses that arise have been successfully matched with assertions, in which case the proposed conclusion is justified, or until no match is possible, in which case the proposed conclusion is rejected. Backward chaining in our example would have said "Here's a hypothesis: FDR precedes Nixon," and the system would have worked backwards to justify this hypothesis.

1. Given the assertion "Frank is bald" and the rule "If *X* is bald, then *X* is tall," what conclusion can be inferred?

2. Given the assertion "Frank is not bald" and the rule "If *X* is bald, then *X* is tall," what conclusion can be inferred?

In addition to the knowledge base and the inference engine, most rule-based systems also have an **explanation facility**. This allows the user to see the assertions and rules used in arriving at a conclusion, as a sort of check on the path of reasoning or for the user's own enlightenment.

Of course, a rule-based system about some particular domain is only as good as the assertions and rules that make up the knowledge base. The builder of such a system acquires the information for the knowledge base by consulting "experts" in the domain and mining their expertise. This process, called **knowledge engineering**, requires a great deal of interaction with the human expert, much of it in the domain environment. If the domain expert is the manager of a chemical processing plant, for example, a decision to "turn down valve A whenever the temperature in pipe P exceeds 235°F and valves B and C are both closed" may be such an ingrained behavior that the expert won't remember it as part of a question-and-answer session on "what you do on your job." It only emerges by on-site observation. For the hospital example, one might need to follow people around in the emergency room, observe their decisions, and later question them on why those decisions were made.

Rule-based systems have been implemented in many domains, including specific forms of medical diagnosis, computer chip design, monitoring of manufacturing processes, financial planning, purchasing decisions for retail stores, and diagnosis of failures in electronic systems. They will no doubt be even more commonplace in the future.

13.6   CONCLUSION

In this chapter we have touched on three basic elements of artificial intelligence: knowledge representation, recognition problems, and reasoning problems. Artificial intelligence applications involve one or more of these elements, and we have mentioned only some of the many application areas of AI today. Others include speech recognition, natural language processing, natural language translation, image analysis, target recognition, robotics, and game playing.

We no longer expect artificial intelligence to manufacture a Lieutenant Commander Data—at least not in the foreseeable future—but it is not unreasonable to expect intelligent X-ray or CAT analysis; a speech recognition system that will handle a limited subset of English and enable us to control our telephones, appliances, and computers by talking to them; an intelligent agent to

A View of the Future

The following excerpt by Donald A. Norman, a fellow at Apple Computer, Inc., is taken from the book *Beyond Calculation: The Next 50 Years of Computing.* This book contains twenty-four essays from pioneers of the computer industry who were asked to reflect on the scientific, social, and economic impact of computers and to project some of the new directions that may emerge in coming decades. The book was commissioned in 1997 on the occasion of the fiftieth anniversary of the founding of the Association for Computing Machinery, the first professional society for people working with computers.

The modern era of information technology has been with us but a short time. Computers are less than a century old. The technology has been constructed deliberately to produce mechanical systems that operate reliably, algorithmically and consistently. Their bases are mathematics, or more precisely arithmetic, in the case of the first computing devices, and logic in the case of the more modern devices. Even analog computers followed similar guidelines. The design was algorithmic and precise; repeatable, understandable operation was the goal.

Contrast this with the human brain. Human beings are the results of millions of years of evolution, where the guiding principle was survival of the species, not efficient, algorithmic computation. Robustness in the face of unexpected circumstances plays a major role in the evolutionary process. Human intelligence has coevolved with social interaction, cooperation and rivalry, and communication. The ability to learn from experience and to communicate and thereby coordinate with others has provided powerful adaptations for changing, complex environmental forces.

...

If we want to empower people, we must translate symbolic problems and data collections into perceptual ones. Human working memory for symbolic information is limited: provide rich external sources of information. Exploit human sensory capabilities, which are extremely powerful and robust.

Rely on people for rapid assessment and analysis. Use people for strategic overviews. Let people interpret and provide meaning to information.

Do not rely on people for accurate or reliable responses or for precise information (e.g., numerical values, names or positioning control). Instead, treat any such information as an approximation. Ideally, machines should take over the requirement for accuracy and reliability, letting people provide high-level guidance and interpretation.

Peter J. Denning and Robert M. Metcalfe, eds., *Beyond Calculation: The Next 50 Years of Computing* (New York: Copernicus (Springer-Verlag), 1997). Reprinted by permission.

manage our appointment schedule; and a robotic system that can handle routine household chores. Advances in massively parallel architectures and new understanding of **cognitive science** (how we as humans think and learn) will bring artificial intelligence to exciting frontiers in the twenty-first century.

EXERCISES

1. Suppose that in a formal logic, $G(x)$ means that x has the attribute of being green, $B(x)$ means that x has the attribute of being a bullfrog, and J stands for the specific entity Jeremiah. Translate the following formal statements into English:

   a. $B(J)$
   b. $(\forall x)(B(x) \rightarrow G(x))$

2. Draw a semantic net that incorporates the knowledge contained in the following paragraph:

If I had to describe what distinguishes a table from other pieces of furniture, I guess I would say it has to have four legs and a flat top. The legs, of course, hold up the top. Nancy's table is made of maple, but mine is bigger and is walnut.

3. a. Use an Englishlike formal language to represent the knowledge explicitly contained in the following semantic net:

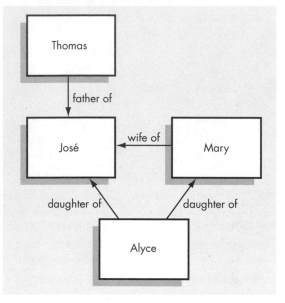

b. Add to your list from part (a) the knowledge that can be inferred from the semantic net.

4. In the following neural network, which event or events will cause node N3 to fire?

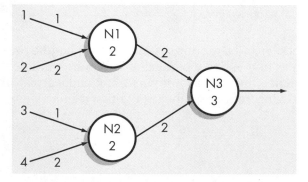

5. Design a neural network with four nodes. N1 and N2 are input nodes; each is fed two input lines representing A and B. N3 and N4 are output nodes. N3 is to fire if and only if two As are input; N4 is to fire if and only if two Bs are input. If one A and one B are input, neither N3 nor N4 should fire.

6. Try to find some literature or product information on a **PDA** (**personal data assistant**) device or palm-held computer that allows pen-based handwritten entries. What sort of scheme does this system use for handwriting recognition? Does the system use a neural network? Does it require initial training on the user's handwriting?

7. You are a knowledge engineer and have been assigned the task of developing a knowledge base for an expert system to advise on mortgage loan applications. What are some sample questions you would ask the loan manager at a bank?

8. We described both forward chaining and backward chaining as techniques used by inference engines in rule-based systems. In Section 9.2.2. we described how a parser might analyze a programming statement to produce a parse tree (see page 440). Does the method described in Chapter 9 correspond more closely to forward chaining or to backward chaining? Explain.

9. A rule-based system for writing the screenplays for mystery movies contains the following assertions and rules:

The hero is a spy.
The heroine is an interpreter.
If the hero is a spy, then one scene should take place in Berlin and one in Paris.
If the heroine is an interpreter, then the heroine must speak English.
If the heroine is an interpreter, then the heroine must speak Russian.
If one scene should take place in Berlin, then there can be no car chase.
If there can be no car chase, then there can be no crash scene.
If one scene should take place in Berlin, then the hero is European.
If one scene should take place in Paris, then the hero must speak French.

Can the following assertion be inferred? Explain.
The hero must speak French and there can be no crash scene.

10. In Exercise 9, is it possible to add the following assertion to the knowledge base? Why or why not?
The hero is American.

11. If you studied Prolog in Chapter 8 and have a Prolog interpreter available, try implementing the rule-based system of Exercise 9 in Prolog.

CHALLENGE WORK

1. A neural network is to be built that behaves according to the table in Figure 13.13, which represents the Boolean AND operation. Input to the network consists of two binary signals; the single output line fires exactly when both input signals are 1.

   a. This looks similar to the XOR problem discussed in Section 13.4, but unlike that problem, this one is solvable with a perceptron of the form shown in Figure 13.8, which is repeated in Figure 13.14. Find values for the weights and the threshold of the output neuron that will cause the network to behave properly.

   b. Because this is a relatively simple problem, it is easy to guess and come up with a combination of two weights and one threshold value that works. The solution is not unique; there are many combinations that will produce the desired result. In a large network with many connections, it is impossible to find a solution by guessing. Instead, the network learns to find its own solution as it is repeatedly exercised on a set of training data. For networks with hidden layers, the back propagation algorithm can be used for training. For a general class of perceptrons of the form shown in Figure 13.15, an easier training algorithm exists, which will be described here. Note that in Figure 13.15, the input signals are binary, and all neurons are assumed to have the same threshold value θ. The table in column 2 sets up the notation needed to describe the algorithm.

   Initially, the network is given arbitrary values between 0 and 1 for the weights $w_1, w_2, \ldots$, and the threshold value θ. A set of input values $x_1, x_2,$

SYMBOL	MEANING
$x_1, x_2, \cdots$	Binary input values from the training set
y	The binary output value from the network
t	The target binary output value from the network for this set of input values
α	The "learning rate" for the network, a small positive value that controls how rapidly the weights change during training
$w_1, w_2, \cdots$	The current set of weights
θ	The current threshold value
$w_1', w_2' \cdots$	The next set of weights
θ'	The next threshold value

. . . from the training data is then applied to the network. Because we are working with training data, the correct result t for this set of input values is known. The actual result from the network, y, is computed and compared to t. The difference between the two values is used to compute the next round of values for the weights and the threshold value, which are then tested on another set of values from the training data. This process is repeated until the weights and threshold value have settled into a combination for which the network behaves correctly on all of the training sets. The network is fully trained at this point.

Each new weight w_i' is computed from the previous weight by the formula

$$w_i' = w_i + \alpha\,(t - y)x_i \tag{A}$$

and the new threshold value θ' is computed from the previous value by the formula

$$\theta' = \theta - \alpha\,(t - y) \tag{B}$$

FIGURE 13.13
The AND Truth Table

Inputs		Output
x_1	x_2	
0	0	0
1	0	0
0	1	0
1	1	1

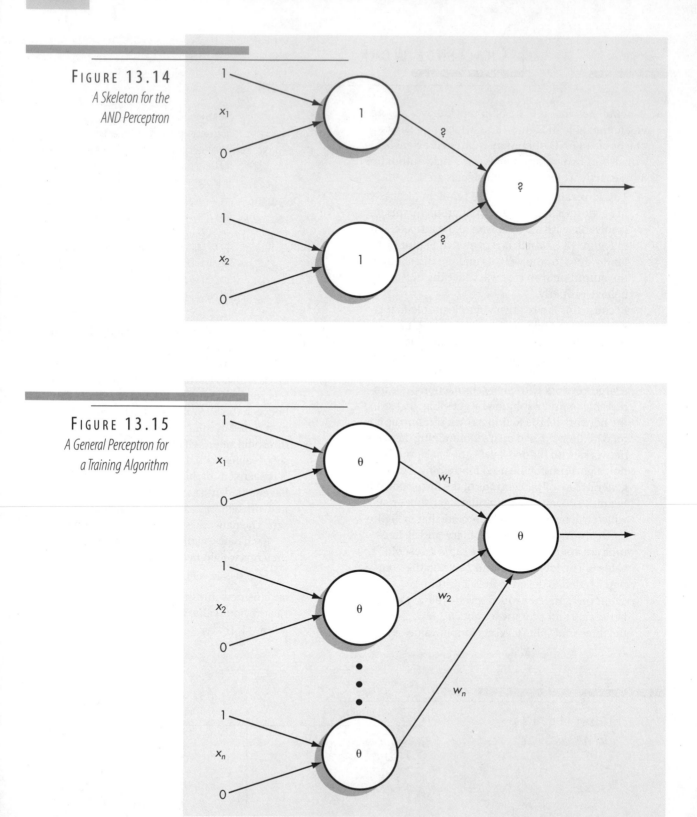

FIGURE 13.14
A Skeleton for the AND Perceptron

FIGURE 13.15
A General Perceptron for a Training Algorithm

There are three cases to consider:

i. If the network behaved correctly for the current set of data—that is, if the computed output y equals the desired output t—then the quantity $\alpha(t - y)$ has the value 0, so when we use formulas (A) and (B), the new weights and threshold value will equal the old ones. The algorithm makes no adjustments for behavior that is already correct.

ii. If the output y is 0 when the target output t is 1, then the quantity $\alpha(t - y)$ has the value α, a small positive value. Each weight corresponding to an input x_i that was active in this computation (i.e., had the value 1) gets increased slightly by formula (A). This is because the output neuron didn't fire when we wanted it to, so we stimulate it with more weight coming into it. At the same time, we lower the threshold value by formula (B), again so as to stimulate the output neuron to fire.

iii. If the output y is 1 when the target output t is 0, then the quantity $\alpha(t - y)$ has the value $-\alpha$, a small negative value. Each weight corresponding to an input x_i that was active (i.e., had the value 1) gets decreased slightly by formula (A). This is because the output neuron fired when we didn't want it to, so we dampen it with less weight coming into it. At the same time, we raise the threshold

value by formula (B), again so as to discourage the output neuron from firing.

We will use the training algorithm to train an AND perceptron. The training set will be the four pairs of binary values shown in the table of Figure 13.13. (Here the training set is the entire set of possible input values; in most cases, a neural net is trained on some input values for which the answers are known and then is used to solve other input cases for which the answers are unknown.) For starting values, we choose (arbitrarily) $w_1 = 0.6$, $w_2 = 0.1$, $\theta = 0.5$, and $\alpha = 0.2$. The value of α stays fixed and should be chosen to be relatively small; otherwise, the corrections are too big and the values don't have a chance to settle into a solution. The initial picture of the perceptron is therefore that of Figure 13.16. Note that with these choices we did not stumble on a solution because input values of $x_1 = 1$ and $x_2 = 0$ do not produce the correct result.

The following table shows the first three training sessions. The current network behaves correctly for the first two cases ($x_1 = 0$ and $x_2 = 0$; $x_1 = 0$ and $x_2 = 1$), so no changes are made. For the third case ($x_1 = 1$ and $x_2 = 0$), an adjustment takes place in the weights and in the threshold value.

w_1	w_2	θ	x_1	x_2	y	t	$\alpha(t-y)$	w_1'	w_2'	θ'
0.6	0.1	0.5	0	0	0	0	0	0.6	0.1	0.5
0.6	0.1	0.5	0	1	0	0	0	0.6	0.1	0.5
0.6	0.1	0.5	1	0	1	0	-0.2	0.4	0.1	0.7

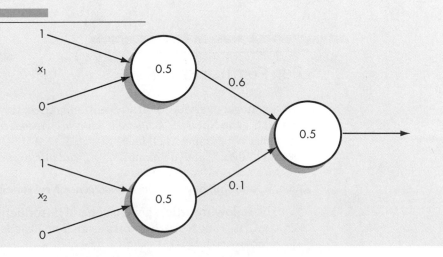

FIGURE 13.16

Initial Configuration of Perceptron to Be Trained

After these changes, the new network configuration is that shown in Figure 13.17.

Continue the table from this point, cycling through the four sets of input pairs until the network produces correct answers for all four cases.

2. Pick one of the three technologies discussed in this chapter (neural networks, intelligent agents, or expert systems) and investigate how it has been applied to a real-world product or problem. Here are some places on the Web to start:

See this page for a lot of general information on neural networks, and then click on "Commercial Applications."

http://www.emsl.pnl.gov:2080/docs/cie/neural/

Eclectic collections of Web links on intelligent agent work can be found at

http://lcs.www.media.mit.edu/cgi-bin/find
http://ai/iit/nrc.ca/subjects/Agents.html

but this is such a rapidly changing field that you will need to search again for current information.

For expert systems in medicine and accounting, respectively, visit

http://amplatz.uokhsc.edu/acc95-expert-systems.html
http://www.bus.orst.edu/faculty/brownc/es_tutor/acc_es.htm

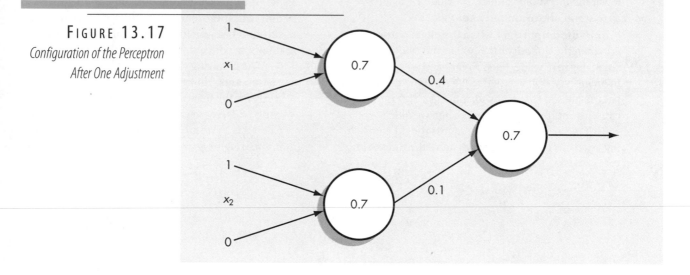

FIGURE 13.17
Configuration of the Perceptron After One Adjustment

FOR FURTHER READING

For a general overview of artificial intelligence, try the following textbooks:

Russell, S., and Norvig, P. *Artificial Intelligence: A Modern Approach*, 2nd ed. Englewood Cliffs, NJ: Prentice-Hall, 1998.

Dean, T.; Allen, J.; and Aloimonos, Y. *Artificial Intelligence: Theory and Practice*. Reading, MA: Addison-Wesley, 1995.

Rich, E., and Knight, K. *Artificial Intelligence*. New York: McGraw-Hill, 1991.

The following article gives a general introduction to neural networks:

Hinton, G. E. "How Neural Networks Learn from Experience." *Scientific American* (September 1992): 144–151.

A more thorough introduction to neural networks can be found in

Haykin, S. *Neural Networks.* Englewood Cliffs, NJ: Prentice Hall/IEEE Press, 1994.

Some of the research issues associated with intelligent agents are presented in the following issue of the major publication of the Association for Computing Machinery, which is a special issue devoted to intelligent agents.

Communications of the ACM (July, 1994).

The following fascinating study of the chess-playing HAL of the film *2001, A Space Odyssey* reveals which of HAL's capabilities have been achieved and which are still beyond the grasp of artificial intelligence at the present time.

Stork, D. G., ed. *HAL's Legacy: 2001's Computer as Dream and Reality.* Cambridge, MA: M.I.T. Press, 1997.

Commentaries on the chess match between Kasparov and Deep Blue can be found in

Communications of the ACM (August 1997): 21–25.
IEEE Computer (October 1997): 29–35.

And, again, the essays cited earlier on the future impact of computing:

Denning, P. J., and Metcalfe, R. M., eds. *Beyond Calculation: The Next 50 Years of Computing.* New York: Copernicus (Springer-Verlag), 1997.

13.7   SUMMARY OF LEVEL 5

At the beginning of Level 5, we noted that we would be able to give only a sampling of the important developments in and applications of computers. We hope two things have been accomplished:

1. We hope your appetite has been whetted to learn more about some application area that interests you.
2. We hope you view computer applications as building upon the foundations of computer science, not as magical tools that come in a box.

At the rate at which technological change is occurring, by the time this book is printed there will be new applications, tools, and software packages to do ever-more-amazing things. You'll be equipped to run in the fast track and incorporate those that you want or need to use.

There is, however, one more level to our story. With all the capabilities that exist today and will be developed tomorrow, what is the larger picture of computer technology within society? What are the ethical, legal, and social consequences of these capabilities? What should we welcome? What should we watch for or regulate? Is there anything we should prohibit? Level 6 raises some of these questions in more detail, though, of course, it provides no definitive answers. Each individual, armed with adequate knowledge, must hammer out his or her own position on many of these complex social issues. This is one of the responsibilities that comes with our unprecedented opportunity to enjoy the benefits of computer technology.

SOCIAL ISSUES

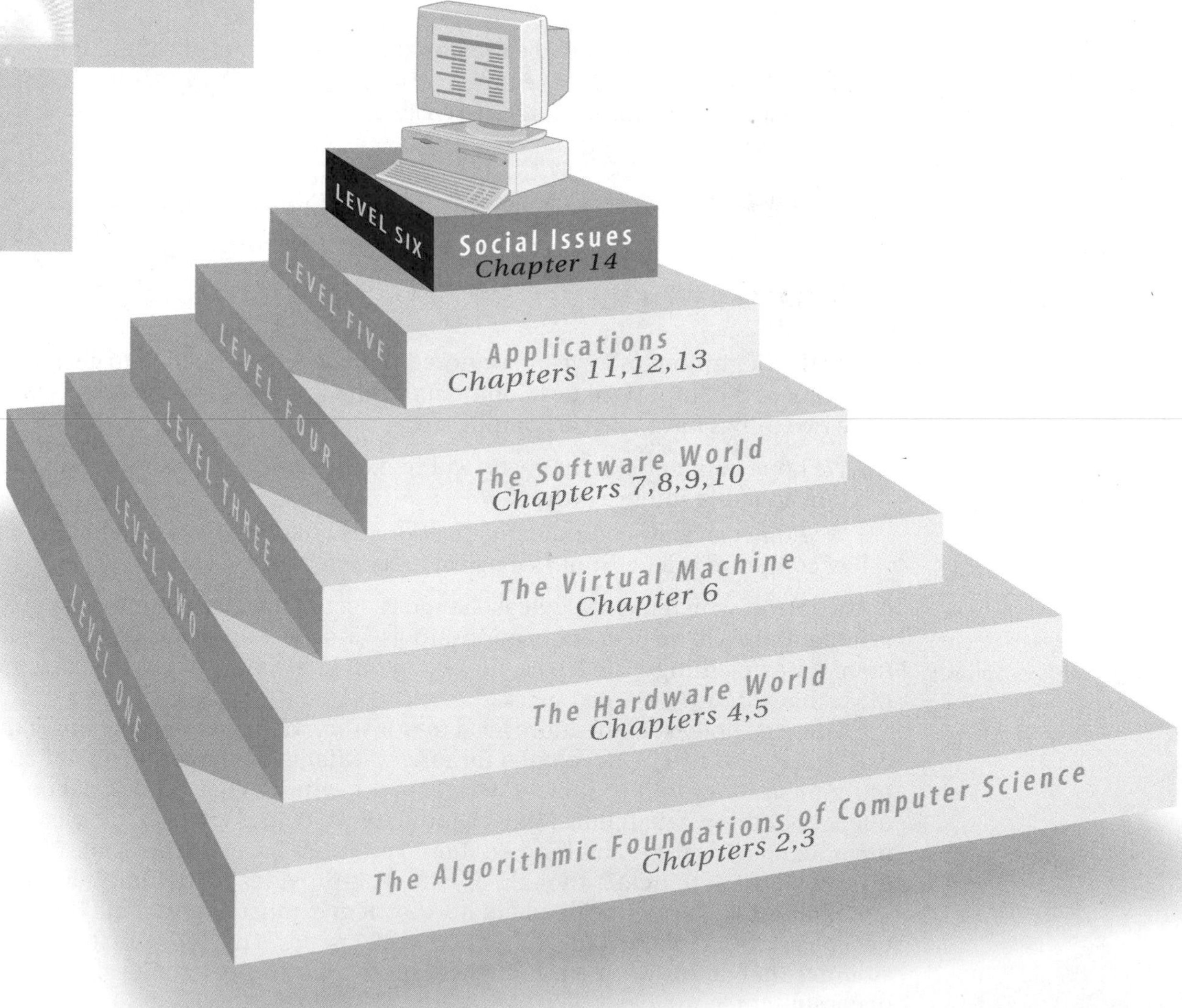

LEVEL SIX

Social Issues
Chapter 14

LEVEL FIVE

Applications
Chapters 11,12,13

LEVEL FOUR

The Software World
Chapters 7,8,9,10

LEVEL THREE

The Virtual Machine
Chapter 6

LEVEL TWO

The Hardware World
Chapters 4,5

LEVEL ONE

The Algorithmic Foundations of Computer Science
Chapters 2,3

6

In Level 6, we leave the technical issues of computer science in the background and begin to examine how the use of computers affects our society and our daily lives. We look at the benefits of computers, the changes they have brought about, and some of the problems they have generated, such as threats to privacy and computer crime. Many complex systems—financial, communications, transportation, medical, and so on—now depend on computers. Here we consider some of the risks involved in such systems.

And we try to put the problems and benefits of computers in perspective. How do they compare with what came before? Which problems are new? And which are old human problems in a new context?

In this chapter we raise many questions. We hope the discussions here will provide the background you will need in the future to analyze new issues related to the use of computers.

CHAPTER

14

SOCIAL
AND LEGAL ISSUES

14.1   A GIFT OF FIRE

Prometheus, according to Greek myth, brought us the gift of fire. It is an awesome gift. It gives us the power to heat our homes, cook our food, and run the machines that make our lives more comfortable, healthy, and enjoyable. It is also awesomely destructive, both by accident and by arson. The Chicago fire in 1871 left 100,000 people homeless. Fires destroyed major parts of San Francisco after the earthquake of 1906. In 1990 the oil fields of Kuwait were intentionally set ablaze. In 1994 wildfires burned a million acres, destroyed homes, and killed people. In spite of the risks, in spite of these disasters, few of us would choose to return the gift of fire and live without it. We have learned, gradually, how to use it productively, how to use it more safely, and how to respond more effectively to disasters, be they natural, accidental, or intentional.

Computer technology, many people agree, is the most significant new technology since the beginning of the Industrial Revolution. It is an awesome technology, with the power to make the completion of routine tasks quick, easy, and accurate, to improve medical technology, to help us explore space, to enhance communications, and to do thousands of other tasks. But like fire, the power of computers has introduced serious problems: multimillion-dollar thefts, potential loss of privacy, and breakdowns of large, complex systems such as communications networks and banking systems.

In this chapter we reach the highest level in our six-level hierarchy. We don't consider details of hardware, software, or algorithms. Rather, we examine some relationships between the use of computers and law, work, public policy, ethics, responsibility, science, freedom of action, and quality of life. The issues here are more abstract, but nonetheless important.

We describe some of the remarkable benefits of computers, some of the problems associated with them, and some of the means for reducing problems and coping with their effects. Our focus is primarily on privacy, reliability of computer systems, computer crime, the application of constitutional principles to electronic media, and encryption issues. Some of the issues we discuss are of special concern to computer professionals; an example is the responsibility for designing systems that will tend to be reliable and secure. Others are of concern to everyone from computer professionals to people who do not know or care how computers work. These include interactions between computers and social policy, personal privacy, and the like.

There are other important legal and social issues that we do not have space to cover here. Copyrighting of software is a subject of much current debate and litigation. (Is it ethical to copy software from a friend? Will copyright survive in a world in which electronic copying is so easy? Should it survive?) Signed documents, contracts, letters, memos, and photographs are frequently used as evidence in court trials. As more written and visual material is stored in computer files—which can be edited—rather than on paper, how can the authenticity of such evidence be ensured? How do computers affect the way we do our work? How do they affect international trade and communication? Whole books have been written on these topics, and we encourage the reader to explore them.

14.2   HERE, THERE, EVERYWHERE

14.2.1 SOME OF THE BENEFITS

Computers have had an immense impact on society, the economy, and our daily lives. Chapters 11 through 13 described some applications, but only a small sampling of them. Discussions of social issues related to computers often focus on problems, and indeed we will discuss some of the problems. But the uses and benefits of computers are an important social issue too. Thus we will mention more applications here to emphasize the variety of uses of computers, some of which are truly wonderful.

Computers are used for information services, consumer services, communications, education, entertainment, medical equipment and research, business planning, resource management, writing (word processing, in modern jargon), robot-controlled processes, scheduling crews for airline flights, improving the routing of garbage trucks to save fuel and time, weather forecasting, scientific research, banking, and the design of buildings, airplanes, automobiles, satellites, space ships, and beer cans. Microprocessor chips are built into microwave ovens, bread-baking machines, automobile ignition systems, VCRs, compact disk players, fax machines, medical instruments, and a large number of other appliances and machines. We now have pocket-size computers that can read handwriting, display video, and send faxes.

Ovid wrote his love poems two thousand years ago without a word processor. For many tasks where we now use computers, they are not a necessity. They are a convenience; they provide more options. Sometimes they enable us to work faster and more accurately than before. For some applications, they reduce the amount of resources, including human effort, required for a task. They let us do old tasks more safely. We had airplanes, and we trained air traffic controllers before we had computers, but now, using graphics and speech recognition systems, an air traffic controller can be trained in a mock-up tower whose windows are projection screens. He or she directs air traffic that is completely simulated by computer. If the trainee directs two airplanes to land on the same runway at the same time, no one is hurt.

Some applications of computers let us do things that were impossible before. For example, MRI (magnetic resonance imaging) machines use computers to process the data generated by reflections from a magnetic field around a human body. They produce pictures of internal body organs, muscle, and other soft tissue that X rays cannot "see." Microprocessors in medical instruments such as intravenous pumps allow patients to use sophisticated equipment at home, eliminating the expense and inconvenience of a hospital visit. People with poor eyesight can direct a computer display to use a large font. Computers equipped with character scanners and voice synthesizers can read a book aloud to a blind person. Where noise is a problem (or for a person both blind and deaf), the voice output can be replaced by a grid of buttons raised and lowered by the computer to form Braille characters. People who cannot use their hands can employ speech recognition systems built into computers to write and do other productive work. (If scanners and voice systems were developed only for handicapped users, each unit would be very expensive, but ordinary business applications have created a mass market for these technologies and driven the prices down.)

Information and consumer services, such as CompuServe, Prodigy, America Online, and Microsoft Network, began to give consumers access to a vast amount and variety of information. *Consumer Reports*, movie reviews, weather reports, and news reports came on-line and became available quickly and easily from our home computers. Then, within just a few years, the World Wide Web, with its easy graphical interface, encouraged businesses, organizations, and individuals to set up Web pages, thus generating another leap in the amount and variety of information available at home. Many tasks that used to require transporting people to libraries or bookstores in motor vehicles can now be done by transporting the information to people through telephone lines and optical fiber—at big savings in time and energy. Encyclopedias and works of art are available on compact disk. Eventually, miles of library book shelves will be replaced by electronic storage, reducing the demand for paper. This process has already begun. In 1993, for example, the law school library at Columbia University canceled plans to build a $20 million building to store new books. Instead, it bought a $1.5 million supercomputer on which to store the contents of tens of thousands of deteriorating old books, freeing shelf space for new ones. Now there are many "digital libraries."

Electronic storage of text, and the ability to edit and update it, are reducing the need for paper in many businesses. A large insurance company reduced its use of paper by one hundred million pages in a nine-month period by keeping its manuals on computers instead of printing them. A department store chain reported saving $1 million worth of paper per year by keeping sales reports on computer instead of paper. Trash, too, can be reduced when, instead of throwing away last month's issue of a magazine, we simply delete it from our disk and download the new issue into the same space. (The electronically distributed newsletter of the Electronic Frontier Foundation ends with the line "This newsletter is printed on 100% recycled electrons.")

Customer service from mail-order companies, banks, credit card companies, and many others has improved because customer service agents can find a person's order or account information instantly, provide up-to-date information, and make changes. Computerized medical records are available to hospital and HMO staffs at all times (unless the system is down). Paper files are unavailable nearly 50% of the time (they may be in another doctor's office or misfiled). One study of a hospital with computerized patient records showed that patients there were released from the hospital almost a day earlier and had bills averaging almost $900 less. Supermarket scanners speed the check-out process, improve accuracy, and update inventory records. Better product management means reduced waste and therefore lower prices.

Chapter 12 described some of the concepts and techniques involved in communications on computer networks. Computers also design telephone networks and handle the switching and routing of calls. In the late 1940s, nearly all routing and switching was done by human operators plugging wires into boards. The volume of telephone calls in the United States has increased so much that if this work were still done manually instead of with computers, half the adult population of the country would have to be employed as telephone operators.

Fax technology provides fast and convenient delivery of documents. Electronic mail, described in Chapter 12, offers the advantages of telephone calls without the disadvantages. The mail arrives at the recipient's computer as quickly as a phone call, but the recipient is not interrupted during important work, dinner, or a shower; the message can be read at any convenient time. The sender need not undergo the frustration of getting busy signals, nor does he or she have to consider differences in time zones when sending messages to other countries. E-mail was first used largely by computer scientists. Now, as more people and businesses are connected to computer networks, their use has expanded to scientific researchers, businesses, and millions of other people. Computer networks span the globe. By the late 1990s, the Internet had approximately 29 million computers connected to it in more than 200 countries on 7 continents. The number of users was estimated at 70 to 100 million and was still growing rapidly. In 1997, the number of e-mail users in the United States alone was estimated at 39 million.

Modems and faxes allow more people to work at home. For many of us this is simply a convenience. For the elderly or disabled, who may find commuting difficult or dangerous, it is a significant benefit. For single parents with young children, the flexible work hours may reduce child care expenses.

Robot arms are used in factories to assemble products faster and more accurately than people can. Robots are also used in environments that are hazardous to humans. For example, robots inspect undersea structures and communication cables. The computer-controlled Sojourner rolled across the surface of Mars—and modern telecommunications allowed millions of people worldwide to watch it on television or on their computer screens.

We could go on. In fact, we could easily write several books just describing the uses of computers. But this brief account and our everyday experience should suffice to suggest the enormous variety of their uses. More than 100 million personal computers have been sold. There are also mainframes, minicomputers, and workstations. And there are hundreds of millions of appliances, devices, and machines that contain microprocessors.

14.2.2 CHANGES

It was not always this way. The microprocessor is now older than most first-year college students, but just barely. New technology replaces older technology. Your university library's catalog system is probably computerized and accessible from a home computer with a modem. Until recently, the library catalog filled a large room with racks of trays containing 3×5 paper index cards. A computerized insurance system for recording insurance claims replaced more than 30 million index cards.

Developments in computer technology happen so fast that *new* and *old* are slippery words. In the mid-1980s, Steve Wozniak, the co-inventor of the Apple computer, gave a talk to a few hundred electrical engineering and computer science students at Berkeley. He described how he invented the Apple a decade earlier, what problems he had to overcome, what constraints he worked under, and what motivated him. To some of the faculty in the audience who had worked with paper tape and punch cards, it was a fascinating account of the ingenuity that went into the development of something new—a major step in bringing computers from the laboratory to the desktop, from specially trained scientists to ordinary people. To the students it was ancient history. When Wozniak mentioned that his first Apple had only 4K of memory, the students burst out laughing. They could barely imagine something so primitive.

Computers have made some jobs and products obsolete. Recall from Chapter 5 that slide rules were invented in the seventeenth century. Engineers used them for many of the computations they performed to design buildings, bridges, and other large projects. Keuffel & Esser, the company whose name was synonymous with the slide rule to generations of American engineers, first sold this innovative computation tool in the United States in 1880 and steadily improved it. In the late 1950s, Keuffel & Esser sold 20,000 slide rules per month. In 1975, when engineers were carrying the new electronic calculators on their belts and the Apple was on its way, Keuffel & Esser produced its last slide rule.

Major industries have moved across continents and oceans because some people saw the potential of the computer and others did not. What country is most noted for making watches? If you are in college today, you probably cannot think of any significant competitor to Japan. But until the 1960s, the phrase *good watch* was virtually equivalent to *Swiss watch*. The Swiss were the greatest watchmakers in the world for a long time. In the 1960s they looked at digital technology but decided to continue making mechanical watches. Japanese companies looked at digital technology and saw the future.

The extraordinary pace of development in computer technology requires people to adapt to the prospect of jobs becoming obsolete, to the necessity of learning new skills. To some this is frightening and disruptive; we noted in Chapter 5 that the Luddites went as far as burning factories that used new technology. But to others the development of computer technology is an inspiring reminder of the potential for human progress.

It is astonishing to realize that in the 1940s many scientists who worked with the first computers believed that only a few—perhaps half a dozen—computers would be needed for the whole United States. In 1976 the *New York Times* published a book called *Science in the Twentieth Century*; it mentions computers only once, indirectly, in an article about calculating the orbits of the planets. The enormous potential of a new technology may not be seen or imagined even by some of the people who work with it or study it. Fortunately for us, there was no central decision maker who could decide whether the technology of computing should be developed. The decision was left to individual engineers, researchers, entrepreneurs, venture capitalists, and customers—and to teenagers who tinkered in their garages.

PRACTICE PROBLEMS

1. List two machines or devices that existed before computers but that now have computers or microprocessors built in. (Give examples that were not mentioned in the text.)

2. Try to think of some product (other than slide rules) that has been in use for approximately 100 years or more but that may become obsolete in the near future because of computer technology.

3. Think up some computerized device or program that does not yet exist but that you would be very proud to help develop.

4. List several jobs that computers have made obsolete. List at least a dozen new jobs that would not exist without computers.

14.3   PRIVACY

14.3.1 INTRODUCTION

After the fall of the communist government in East Germany, the people examined the files of Stasi, the secret police. They found that the government had used spies and informers to build detailed dossiers on the opinions and activities of roughly six million people, a third of the population. The informers were neighbors, coworkers, friends, and even family members of the people they reported on. The paper files filled an estimated 125 miles of shelf space. Computers were not used at all.

Movie and television stars cannot relax in their back yards or walk past an uncurtained window in their home without fearing that someone will take unflattering pictures of them for supermarket tabloids. The tool of the invasion of their privacy is a camera with a telephoto lens, not a computer.

Computers are not necessary for the invasion of privacy. To emphasize that the problems, issues, and solutions do not always depend on a specific technology, we will sometimes use examples and analogies that do not involve computers. But we discuss privacy at length in this chapter because the use of computers has made new threats possible and old threats more potent.

As we saw in the discussions of databases and networks in Chapters 11 and 12, computers make the collection, analysis, storage, and distribution of large amounts of information much easier than before. In Chapter 5 we learned that a sector of data on a disk can be accessed in roughly 10 milliseconds—faster than we can turn a page in a book. Computers have increased both the speed and the anonymity with which a person can do searches. Today there are many databases, both government and private, containing information about us. In this chapter we are not concerned with the details of how a database is organized, such as whether it is centralized or distributed or what query language is used to access the information. In this top level of our hierarchy, we will address increasing concerns about how the information in these databases is collected, how it is protected, how it may be used without our permission or knowledge, and how information from different databases is combined to build a detailed picture of our political, medical, financial, legal, and personal affairs.

Some examples of government databases that contain personal information are listed in Figure 14.1. This is just a small sample, intended to give you an idea of the variety of information that is stored. Examples of private databases are listed in Figure 14.2. Many people do not realize that these records are maintained, that the information provided by a person in one context can be used in another, and that many government databases are open to the public. The risks that arise from the existence of all this information include

- Unauthorized use by insiders, the people who maintain the information
- Inadvertent leakage of information through negligence or carelessness

FIGURE 14.1
Government Databases

- Tax records
- Bankruptcy records
- Arrest records
- Census information
- Marriage license applications
- Filings of lawsuits
- Social Security records
- Records of property ownership
- Motor vehicle files
- Lists of people with permits to carry firearms
- Voter registration lists
- Medical records (for example, those covered by Medicare or the armed forces)
- Welfare records
- Books checked out of public libraries

- Propagation of errors and the harm caused by them
- Intentional uses (marketing or decision making) that some people find objectionable

Philosophical (and legal) questions are implicit in many of the issues to be discussed here. Is privacy a right to be protected by law? Is it a preference that may influence our choices and behavior but that we may not impose on other people? Is it a service that we can purchase to the degree we are willing to pay for it? Is privacy like happiness, in that all that is guaranteed is the right to pursue it?

There are more than eight hundred federal and state laws concerning confidentiality of personal information. We will mention several laws in our discussion. Instead of merely summarizing them to describe what the law is, we will try to bring out the issues and controversies that one should consider when thinking about what the law *should be.*

14.3.2 BIG BROTHER'S FILES

Federal government agencies maintain more than two thousand databases containing personal information. Most of them are computerized. As early as 1982, it was estimated that federal agencies had approximately 3.5 billion personal files, an average of 15 for every person in the country. In addition to name, address, and Social Security number, government file systems contain information about our health, finances, and education and other aspects of our lives. Many of the systems are now accessible by computer networks, and the information is used by other government agencies as well as private organizations.

FIGURE 14.2
Private Databases

- Credit histories
- Medical records
- Charge account records
- Subscription lists
- Membership lists
- Customer lists (including a history of purchases)
- Video rentals
- Bank records
- Telephone records
- Employment files
- Airline travel records
- Records of sites a person visits on the World Wide Web

Many agencies perform **computer matching** and **computer profiling**. Computer matching means combining and comparing information from different databases (generally using a person's Social Security number to match records). Computer profiling means using data in computer files to determine the characteristics of people who are most likely to engage in certain behavior.

The Privacy Act of 1974 is the main legislation regulating the federal government's use of personal data. It was passed in part because of concerns in the 1960s and early 1970s about many abuses by the federal government. These abuses included wiretappings, mail openings, burglaries, harassment of individuals for political purposes, and questionable use of personal records. The provisions of the Privacy Act of 1974 are summarized in Figure 14.3.

Although it was an important step in attempting to protect our privacy from abuse by federal agencies, there are problems with the Privacy Act. It allows

FIGURE 14.3
*Provisions of the Privacy
Act of 1974*

- Restricts the data the government may collect
- Requires agencies to publish a notice of their record systems in the *Federal Register* so that the public may be informed about what databases exist
- Allows people to access their records and correct inaccurate information
- Requires procedures to protect the security of the information in databases
- Prohibits disclosure of information about a person without his or her consent

many exceptions, and government agencies simply do not comply with some of its provisions. A study by the federal government's General Accounting Office (GAO) found that 17% of the record systems reported by federal agencies are exempt from the Privacy Act. Among the larger systems that *are* subject to the act, the GAO found that by 1989, 15 years after the act was passed, 35% were not reported in the *Federal Register* as required. Information in 56% of the largest systems can be accessed by other state and federal agencies and by private organizations. Private organizations that provide information to and get information from federal databases include health-care providers, marketing companies, insurance companies, unions, schools, universities, real estate brokers, banks, and credit bureaus.

Federal agencies are supposed to protect personal privacy. For 8% of their largest systems, however, they did not know the purpose for which their databases were being used by other government and private organizations. Although agencies are supposed to protect the security of their databases, a significant number reported serious security weaknesses and numerous incidents of employees gaining unauthorized access to personal data. A 1986 study found government data vulnerable to theft, sabotage, and employee abuse. In a few cases, employees of the Social Security Administration and other federal agencies have been arrested for selling data from government files on thousands of people. A high-ranking Internal Revenue Service (IRS) official was indicted for selling information from tax files, and at one time the IRS reported that several hundred of its employees were under investigation for unauthorized snooping in people's tax files. It is likely that most of such activity goes undetected. Computer law scholars report widespread lack of compliance with minimum security standards.

Some of the purposes of the record systems are to help government agencies perform their functions efficiently, to determine eligibility for government jobs and benefits programs, to detect fraud, and to recover payments on delinquent debts (both debts to the government such as student loans and private debts such as child support payments). Fraud in programs such as welfare and workers' compensation and defaults on guaranteed student loans cost billions of dollars each year. Restrictions on the government's ability to use computer matching and other techniques would encourage more fraud and waste. However, because of the scope of the government's activities, the mass of data available to it, and its power to require us to provide information whether we wish to or not, the use and misuse of government databases pose serious threats to the liberty and personal privacy of honest people.

For example, a few dozen federal agencies use computer profiling to identify people to watch. Profiles can be developed for kidnappers or terrorists, but they can also be developed for political dissidents, homosexuals, parents likely to educate their children at home, or any other group of people whose opinions and activities are outside the mainstream. Profiling has been used by the IRS to characterize people likely to hide income and by the Drug Enforcement Administration (DEA) to characterize people likely to sell drugs. Both the IRS and the DEA have the legal authority to seize property from people who have not been convicted of a crime. There have been several incidents in which the DEA seized large amounts of cash from people who fit a "drug seller" profile but were completely innocent.

Traditionally, law enforcement officials start with a crime and use a variety of techniques to look for a suspect. Computer matching and profiling reverse the process; law enforcement officials can search through huge volumes of information, seeking people who look suspicious for any reason. Should the government be permitted to use these tools to generate investigations of people who were not previously suspected of any crime?

The IRS collects information from other agencies and private organizations on millions of people each year. For example, it uses boat registrations and professional directories to find people likely to have large incomes and then reviews their tax records to see how much tax they have paid. If someone is not earning as much as the IRS expects, they may be subject to investigation. What if the IRS matches tax returns with credit applications that ask for a person's income? Or with the files of a computerized dating service that solicits information on income? (If the latter example seems frivolous or unlikely, consider that the Selective Service bought the birthday list from a major ice cream parlor chain that gave free sundaes to customers on their birthdays. The list was used to find 18-year-old men who had not registered for the draft.)

14.3.3 FIFTY LITTLE BROTHERS

State and local governments have their own computerized databases containing personal information about us. Many of the issues raised by these databases are the same as those we have already discussed. For example, there is the issue of whether government agencies should have access to files of other government agencies—in this case, state and local agencies. Some years ago, the FBI asked a few dozen libraries to provide lists of people who checked out a particular book and lists of books checked out by people of East European background. Now almost every state has a law against libraries disclosing what books an individual has checked out. Librarians believe very strongly in protecting the privacy of readers.

State and local government agencies have the same problems as the federal government with unauthorized access by employees. For example, the Los Angeles Police Department found that a significant number of employees illegally snooped for criminal records on people they knew or were considering hiring for such jobs as babysitter. State and local government databases are a good source of examples for one new issue: Should the public have access to "public"—that is, government—records?

DEPARTMENT OF MOTOR VEHICLES RECORDS.   Consider the records kept by state departments of motor vehicles. With modern computer technology, it is easy to find the name, address, and phone number (even if it is unlisted) of a driver if her license plate number is known. Given someone's driver's license number, it is easy to find the number of accidents he has been involved in. Many states allowed anyone to obtain this information. More states are digitizing our photographs and storing them in computer files. Access to the files could even be made available over the phone. But should it? Let us consider some of the uses to which the information might be put.

It may seem reasonable to be able to get the name and address of a driver who sideswipes your car and does not stop. On the other hand, a man used motor vehicles records to obtain the home address of actress Rebecca Schaeffer, and he killed her. Battered women could be vulnerable if their ex-spouses or ex-boyfriends could easily get their current addresses. Direct-mail marketers use driver's license and car registration data to compile lists of tall people, people who wear corrective lenses, owners of a particular kind of car, and the like. Car insurance companies and car rental companies may want to check your driving record before doing business with you or before deciding how much to charge. Private detectives use motor vehicle records for a myriad of purposes.

Policies about motor vehicle records vary widely among the states. In Massachusetts the records used to be closed, but a few years ago a new law made them available to anyone. Some states are adding more privacy protections, whereas others are adding more money to state revenues (for example, more than $15 million a year in Florida) by selling driver information.

Responding to Rebecca Schaeffer's death and to the use of motor vehicle records by anti-abortion protestors to get the home addresses of staff and patients of abortion clinics, Congress passed a national law regulating privacy of motor vehicle records. The law, which took effect in 1997, requires states to include on renewal notices a clear place where drivers may indicate that they do not want information about them to be sold for marketing purposes. The law permits the release of personal information from driver records, without driver consent, for a long list of purposes. Deciding who should be exempt from the consent requirement is not simple. Should the news media, for example, have access to the records? Some of the exemptions are reasonable (insurance, safety recalls); others may raise questions (information may be released to private detectives and any government agency). The law prohibits the release of information to individuals unless their request falls in one of the categories listed in the law.

ANOTHER CASE.   Another aspect of the release of government files is illustrated by a dispute in several cities about the list of people granted a permit to carry a gun in public. When the government prohibits people from doing something and then grants permission to a small number of people as a special privilege, do we have the right to know who has been given the privilege? In one case, a large percentage of contributors to the county sheriff's reelection campaign had been given permits by the sheriff. Thus the release of the list served the purpose of informing the public about an abuse: people in power granting favors to friends. On the other hand, a jeweler who often carries a large number of diamonds might fear that the release of his name could make him more vulnerable.

14.3.4 SHOULD GOVERNMENT FILES BE OPEN?

There are some legitimate uses of government databases that contain personal information, and there are some threatening uses. We will review some arguments for and against different approaches to release of information to the public (individuals and businesses). Our discussion is not intended to be complete. Consider the complexities of the issues and try to think of additional arguments. Sometimes rules that at first seem very sensible can have odd effects. Recall that the Privacy Act of 1974 prohibits disclosure of government files about a person without his or her consent. A newsman who was held hostage in the

Middle East for more than a year decided to write a book about his ordeal. His requests for relevant government files were denied by several federal agencies; he was told that to protect the privacy of his captors, he would need their permission to see the files.

Those who favor having government databases open to the public make the following arguments:

- It would discourage fraud and waste.
- It would discourage abuse and corruption.
- We the taxpayers pay to collect the information and maintain the databases; we own them and should have access to them.

Others argue that having government databases closed to the public would

- Protect privacy
- Increase people's safety
- Avoid embarrassment for people who, for example, receive welfare or have been arrested

Perhaps there could be a provision that a person's closed files be released to anyone who had that person's consent. For example, if we wish to buy a service such as car rental or insurance, and the company wants to check our driving record, we can grant them permission to do so. Of course, a consent requirement might sometimes be inconvenient, and it is not obvious how to apply a consent requirement to files that concern more than one person.

The range of government activity is so broad that no one simple policy is appropriate for all types of government data. Here is one possible way of deciding what files should be open. Information about people who get benefits from the government—that is, from the taxpayers—could be open to the public, providing the advantages of open files just described. Some examples of such data are salaries and expense accounts of government employees, recipients of government-guaranteed student loans, welfare recipients, and payments to government contractors. Databases containing information that people are required to provide but for which they don't receive payments or special privileges could be closed to the public (unless permission is obtained for the release of data), thus securing the advantages of privacy. Examples might include tax, motor vehicle, voter registration, and marriage license records.

14.3.5 BUSINESS AND INDIVIDUAL USES OF PERSONAL DATA

Two of the most common uses of personal information are in marketing and decision making.

MARKETING.   Using computer matching, it is easy to combine information from several databases to produce special target lists for sales promotions. Thus a consumer may receive a letter saying, "Because you own a sports car, have no children, buy a lot of rock-and-roll CDs, earn over $35,000, eat at Italian restaurants often, and fly to Chicago once a month, you may be interested in our product." Many people find it disturbing that someone can collect information from a variety of sources to construct a detailed picture of their lives.

In recent years, much attention has focused on the activities of the three major credit bureau companies: TRW (now Experian), Equifax, and Trans Union. They receive and process millions of records daily. The data are supplied by banks, stores, and other businesses. The primary purpose is to provide a central storehouse of credit data to be used to evaluate applicants for credit. In the past, these companies used their credit databases and other sources to produce and sell mailing lists of "elite retail shoppers," "highly affluent consumers," and other specially targeted groups. In fact, they produced catalogs describing and promoting the variety of lists that are available. As a result of public criticism and pressure, Equifax decided in 1991 to terminate its marketing mailing list business. In 1993, the Federal Trade Commission pressured TRW and Trans Union to do the same.

Aside from the "big three" credit bureaus, many businesses and organizations sell, rent, and exchange mailing lists for marketing purposes. If you enter a contest, fill out a warranty questionnaire, or call a 900 telephone number, information about you may be entered into a database and made available to list purchasers. If you buy skis, you may get a solicitation from a magazine about skiing. If you send a donation to a charity, you are likely to get pleas from other charities of a similar nature. If you file a change-of-address notice with the Post Office, your name and new address may be sold to marketers for lists of recent movers. (This last practice may violate the Privacy Act of 1974 and postal regulations. It has been criticized by a congressional committee and may be terminated.) Many people are happy to receive the additional mailings. They purchase enough of the products and services offered to make the mailings worthwhile to the businesses and organizations that send them. People who do direct mailing point out that more finely targeted mailings reduce overhead and, ultimately, the cost to the consumer. Other people refer to such mailings as "junk mail" and find them annoying.

Electronic junk mail ("spam") is increasing rapidly. So far, it seems to be less well targeted than paper mail and is quite an annoyance to most recipients.

DECISION MAKING.   Private and government databases are used for a wide range of decision-making applications. A person's bill-paying history is used in decisions about loan applications. A college transcript may be used in an employment decision. In these cases, the person usually chooses to provide the information in exchange for the opportunity for the loan or job. In other cases, the information may be provided without the applicant's knowledge.

There are organizations like the Medical Information Bureau (MIB) that collect medical information much as credit bureaus collect credit information. MIB's purpose is to detect and deter medical insurance fraud. It exchanges information among insurance companies. There is concern that the release of some kinds of medical information can cause a person to lose a job or to lose insurance or the opportunity to buy it. (Hiding relevant information, however, may be fraud, not a legitimate preservation of privacy.)

A business may compile lists (from government records) of people who have filed malpractice, product liability, or wrongful termination suits; people who have filed for bankruptcy; or people who have been arrested for certain kinds of crimes. A business may collect and sell information about people who rent housing. Do they pay their rent on time? Have they ever been evicted? A student organization at a college may establish a database with the opposite perspective: a list of local apartment owners or managers, with their good and bad points. Do they make repairs and return deposits promptly? Better Business Bureaus and consumer organizations collect information from consumers about the quality of the products and services provided by many businesses. In such cases, the information is provided willingly, but by only one party to a transaction.

The widespread reliance on information provided by credit bureaus, medical information bureaus, and the like raises serious concerns about the accuracy of the information in the databases. We will discuss accuracy problems in Section 14.4.3.

THREE IMPORTANT ISSUES.   When magazine subscription lists and credit card company records are used for mailing magazines and billing customers, there is no privacy problem. It is "secondary use"—the use of information for a purpose other than the one for which it was supplied—that causes concern. Concern increases when information collected by one business or organization is shared with or sold to another without the knowledge or consent of the person who provided the information.

In the situations just mentioned, a person has knowingly provided some personal information for a specific use. Computer technology has made it easy (and now common) for large amounts of data to be collected without a person even knowing about it. Many users of supermarket club cards or check-cashing cards do not know that all of their purchases are recorded, along with their name, when they use the card. People who surf the World Wide Web are not always aware that the sites they visit can record the visitor's, or customer's, activities. On-line services can compile information about what you view, what discussion groups you participate in, and so on. Collecting information as a side effect of an activity, where the person may not be aware the information is being collected, is called **invisible information gathering.**

A third issue is the collection and sale of information about children. There are many Web sites for children, containing games, information, chat rooms for kids, and so on. Some require that a child provide a lot of personal and family information to register to use the site. And some sell the information collected in this manner to direct-marketing companies. A young child, tempted by a game, may not make an informed, responsible decision about what information to provide.

THE INFORMATION UNDERGROUND.   One of the more chilling threats to privacy is the so-called *information underground.* Virtually any information about a person can be bought. Starting with just a name, and sometimes an address and Social Security number, unscrupulous data dealers provide any or all of the following: bank account balances, credit card purchases, unlisted phone numbers, phone numbers recently called, mortgage payments, tax returns, medical history, employer, location of relatives, and a variety of other information. Credit card purchases alone can provide a detailed picture of a person's activities and whereabouts. Private detectives could always get a lot of this information, but now it is so much easier.

14.3.6 WHAT TO DO

It is often said that if you live in a small town, you have no privacy; everyone knows everything about you. In a big city you are more anonymous. But if people know nothing about you, they may be taking a big risk if they rent you a place to live, hire you, lend you money, sell you automobile or medical insurance, cash your checks, accept your credit card, and so forth. We give up some privacy for the benefits of dealing with strangers. How much? And how can we set our own limits?

SOME AIDS TO PRIVACY.   If the owner of a database *wants* to protect privacy, there are some technical and management procedures that can be used to do so. We will describe a few here. It is the responsibility of good computer system designers and managers to be familiar with such techniques. Technological and management solutions do not solve policy problems, though. Later we will consider more high-level policy issues related to ways to control access to information about ourselves that other people want.

A mailing list is a valuable asset. The owner of the list and the people on it have a common interest in preventing unlimited distribution. Usually when a list is rented to another organization or business, the renter never actually receives a copy (electronic or otherwise); the mailing is done by a firm that specializes in doing mailings. The risk of unauthorized copying is thus restricted to a small number of firms whose reputation for honesty is important to their business. This idea of using "trusted" third parties to process confidential data can be invoked in other applications too.

A well-designed database for sensitive information includes several privacy protections. First, as we saw in Chapter 6, each person with authorized access to the system has a unique ID and password that he or she must provide to use the system. Figure 6.17 showed that users may be restricted from performing certain operations, such as writing or deleting, on some files. Passwords may be coded so that they give access only to specific parts of a record. For example, a billing clerk in a hospital does not need access to the results of a patient's lab tests. Second, the computer system keeps track of each access, including the person looking at a record and the particular information viewed or modified. This is called an **audit trail.** It can be used later to trace unauthorized activity. The knowledge that a system contains such provisions discourages many privacy violations.

In this chapter we are focusing largely on how computerized databases threaten privacy. It is worth noting that they can help protect privacy too. Consider, for example, that computerized medical records replace paper records. Studies have shown that when a person is in a hospital, his or her record may be read by approximately 75 to 80 people (doctors, nurses, lab technicians, billing clerks, and so on). In such a paper-based environment, it is easy for unauthorized people to see the record, and it is easy for people to read parts of it that they do not need to see. The techniques described in the previous paragraph can increase a patient's privacy.

Encryption—that is, storing information in a coded form—provides privacy protection, reducing some abuses by unauthorized employees and intruders from the outside. We will say more about encryption in Section 14.7.

Some libraries have a policy of destroying the check-out record when a book is returned—the best protection against disclosure. This technique cannot be

FIGURE 14.4

The Code of Fair Information Practices

1. There should be no systems whose existence is secret.

2. There should be a way for a person to find out what data about him or her are in the system and how they are used.

3. Information obtained for one purpose should not be used for another purpose without the person's consent.

4. There should be a way for a person to correct errors in his or her files.

5. Any organization creating, maintaining, using, or distributing personal data is responsible for the reliability and security of the data.

used for most databases, but it is a good reminder of a goal. There is a tendency among people not to throw anything away, including information. Privacy is protected by a policy of destroying records that are old or are no longer needed.

SOME POLICY GUIDELINES. Several guidelines, or principles, have been suggested for dealing with privacy of personal data. The "Code of Fair Information Practices" was recommended in 1973 by a government Advisory Committee on Automated Personal Data Systems. Its provisions are listed in Figure 14.4. The Code has been adopted as policy by several companies. Some of its provisions appear in the Privacy Act and the Fair Credit Reporting Act. Some states have enacted it into law to govern a variety of databases.

There are always tradeoffs when we try to protect privacy. Implementation of provisions in the Code of Fair Information Practices can be so restrictive that it violates freedom of contract and freedom of speech. An example of the former is a law prohibiting agreements in which a consumer gives a blanket waiver permitting future uses of his or her information. An example of the latter is a legal prohibition on disclosure of certain kinds of facts, even if they are independently and unintrusively discovered or are a matter of public record—for example, the fact that a particular person has a criminal record.

When trying to decide what is an appropriate or ethical policy, or what should be required or prohibited by law, it is helpful to distinguish among the following factors:

- How the data were obtained (such as by voluntary agreement, by theft, or by independent discovery).

- If the data were obtained by agreement, what the agreement said about the use of the data.

- The specific kind of information (say, a customer list versus the specific purchases made).

- The nature of the prospective user of the data (government, business, or individual) and the intended purpose.

Perhaps the most important principle in the collection and use of personal information is **informed consent.** When a person provides information, he or she should be informed about how it is to be used. Other uses are not part of the agreement and are not permitted without a further agreement.

There are many ways to implement an informed consent policy, and there is much disagreement about which method should be used. For example, consider the controversy about opt-in and opt-out policies. Under the opt-in scheme, any form on which you supply information that the information collector wants to use for secondary uses (such as selling to marketing list companies) must solicit your permission and have you check a box to indicate your agreement. If you do not check the box, your information cannot be released. Under the opt-out scheme, the form tells about the secondary uses and provides a box for you to check if you do *not* want your information used in that way. Because many people do not read the details on forms they fill out, the opt-out scheme would allow marketers to use more information.

Who should make decisions about privacy policies, and how should they be made? Businesses and industry organizations can set their policies in response to their own ethical standards and market pressures. Legislators and regulators can write detailed rules. Consumers and businesses can agree to terms in contracts. Consumers and privacy organizations can use publicity and consumer pressure to influence business policies. We will look briefly at each of these approaches.

REGULATION.   Laws can express fairly general principles—for example, that stealing is illegal or that consumers must be informed about how personal information collected by a business will be used. On the other hand, laws can include specific details about activities that are prohibited or required and can specify exactly what notice in what type of font is required.

For example, consider the choice between opt-in and opt-out policies for the secondary use of consumer information. Some people argue that the choice should be up to the individual business; the consumer can (and has the responsibility to) read an agreement that he or she signs. Others advocate laws requiring that all businesses use the opt-in approach. Thus we can see a difference in point of view about how far the law should go in mandating consumer-friendly policies and about how detailed such laws should be.

A flexible, less restrictive approach demands more awareness and responsibility from consumers. With a strict or detailed regulatory approach, it can be very difficult to anticipate all the uses to which information may be put, some of which are quite reasonable. If a law is structured to specify explicitly who will be given or denied access to information, it is very likely that some users will be overlooked or that future uses will be unintentionally stymied or unintentionally permitted. Let's consider a few examples.

France and Sweden prohibit the collection and maintenance of some lists, such as lists of people's religious affiliation or sexual orientation. A business owned by gay people, or by people of a nontraditional religion, may want to send an advertisement targeted to people who share that attribute. In the United States where openly gay people are more affluent than average, some businesses buy lists of subscribers to gay and lesbian publications for marketing purposes. Thus it is not the existence of a list that is sinister or questionable; it is the use to which we suspect antigay people or people with religious prejudices might put it. Should the lists be prohibited?

Some laws are written in response to special-interest lobbying pressure or after highly publicized dramatic events, rather than after careful study and thought about what general principles should be established. The Video Privacy Protection Act prohibits video rental stores from selling the list of movies rented by a customer. The sale of such lists had been rare. Why do video rentals have more federal privacy protection than, say, medical records or lists of members of nontraditional political or religious organizations? In 1987, when Judge Robert Bork was being considered by the Senate for a seat on the U.S. Supreme Court, a news reporter published a list of movies that Judge Bork had rented. The reporter obtained the list from a video store clerk. Members of Congress, perhaps worried about being embarrassed if their own rentals were publicized, quickly passed the video law.

OWNERSHIP OF DATA. Can some privacy issues be resolved using the concept of ownership of information? Do we own personal information about ourselves and our activities? Should laws prohibit the collection and distribution of such information without our permission? The concept of property rights can be very useful even when applied to intangible property (computer programs, for example), but serious problems arise when we try to apply this concept to information. First of all, our activities and transactions involve other people. Who owns the information about a business–customer relationship, the business or the customer? Should either one be prohibited from distributing information about the other's performance, such as the customer bouncing checks or the business failing to honor a guarantee? Do you own your birthday? Or does your mother own it? Can anyone own a fact? Ownership normally implies almost complete control over the use of the owned object. Information is stored on computers, but it is also stored in our minds. Can we own information about ourselves without abridging the freedom of thought and freedom of speech of others?

CONTRACTS. Contracts allow flexible and diverse agreements to be made. To some people that is an important advantage. To others it is a flaw, because it requires that consumers exercise their responsibility to be informed and make tradeoffs, rather than depending on a standard set of rules.

Some privacy advocates argue for prohibitions on certain types of contracts or agreements to disclose data. For example, they would prohibit prospective employers and employees from agreeing that the person seeking a job will provide a copy of his or her police record for the employer. An American Civil Liberties Union (ACLU) spokesperson argued that banks should be prohibited from including in a credit card agreement a provision that customer data may be sold to direct marketers. An argument for this point of view is that the job applicant or credit card applicant is in so much weaker a bargaining position than the employer or bank that he or she cannot make a free decision about the tradeoffs involved. Should people be denied an option in order to protect them?

Sometimes contracts are implicit. In some transactions, confidentiality is expected because of long tradition and professional codes of ethics. We expect our medical records to be kept confidential by the doctors and hospitals we patronize (though we often explicitly waive confidentiality when we fill out insurance claim forms). We expect our financial records at an investment brokerage firm to be private (except for required reporting to the IRS). Most people expect that their specific credit card purchases will be kept confidential by the credit card companies.

If we have not waived confidentiality or explicitly agreed otherwise, we would like the law to recognize an implicit assumption that sensitive private information is to be confidential. The mere fact that we are a customer of a particular firm might not deserve the same assumption. Because different people desire different degrees of privacy, it is not always obvious what should be assumed in an implied contract. Explicit written agreements help avoid confusion.

MARKETS, OPTIONS, AND CONSUMER PRESSURE.   We have already mentioned that public pressure led Equifax to discontinue its sale of credit-based mailing lists to marketers. There are several similar examples. When AOL decided to sell the phone numbers of its subscribers, several privacy organizations publicized and criticized the plan. The resulting customer complaints led AOL to change its plans. Consumer action terminated a very large project: Lotus Development Corporation's "Marketplace: Households." Lotus planned to sell a database including information on nearly half the population of the United States, along with software that would permit the user to generate mailing lists based on a variety of marketing criteria (such as income categories and shopping habits). The intended customers for the low-priced product were thousands of small businesses. Very little detailed information about specific individuals was included; information was provided about neighborhoods. The information in the database was already available to clients of the large credit bureaus, and some of it is available to anyone from a variety of government agencies. Nonetheless, many people were horrified by Lotus's plans. Lotus received more than 30,000 letters, phone calls, and e-mail messages objecting to it. The company dropped the project.

Consider subscription, membership, and customer lists. Many organizations give members and customers the option of opting out from mailing lists. Some organizations have a policy of not releasing their lists at all. Others rent to or exchange with only closely related organizations or businesses. Many businesses offer special discounts or rebates in exchange for collecting and selling consumer information. The policy on mailing list distribution is one of the many factors a person can consider when deciding whether to join an organization or patronize a business. It can be part of the contract between the customer and the business. A business that sells its list may be able to charge lower prices than a competitor that does not. Consumers can choose how much privacy is worth to them. As more customers make it clear that they value privacy or that they expect to be paid for the use of information about them, more businesses and organizations will begin to provide such options.

DISHONEST DATA DEALERS.   What about the data dealers who sell our personal information, such as bank records, credit card purchases, and the telephone numbers we call, to anyone willing to buy? Much of the information sold by the data dealers is obtained in illegal or dishonest ways. Records of our phone calls are obtained by asking (or paying) an employee of the phone company; the employee is violating company policy. Tax records may be obtained from bribed IRS employees. Bank system passwords are sold by dishonest employees (and used both to invade privacy and to steal funds). Credit information may be obtained by setting up a phony business and becoming a client of a credit bureau—or by stealing the identification code of a legitimate client. Some information is obtained from innocent but careless clerks. In all these cases, the problem is not the existence of the records or of computers, although examining records via computer rather than in person cloaks the data dealer in more anonymity.

Solutions to the problem of dishonest data dealers include improvements in law enforcement and data security and the training, screening, and supervision of employees with access to sensitive data. Employers need the ability to fire, sue, and/or prosecute employees who violate laws or company policy concerning the release of data. Companies could be held liable for negligence in protecting data in their care.

We should be careful to distinguish between unscrupulous data dealers and people who provide data obtained legally or honestly. There are businesses—sometimes called **information brokers**—that provide information collected from the many government sources we described earlier. Anyone who knows how to access them may legally do so. The information brokers are simply providing a service: using their knowledge of government systems to collect the information much more quickly and easily than we could ourselves. To the extent that such services raise privacy problems, the problem is not with the broker but with the government's policies about what files should be open.

COMMENT. Flexibility and diversity are valued in the private sector, whereas for policies concerning release of government files, consistency and uniformity may be important to ensure fairness. Why do different criteria characterize the different arenas? Private firms are owned by individuals or groups of individuals who have invested their own resources in the business. In a free society, they may offer a variety of products and services as they choose. In a competitive market, the buying decisions of consumers will reward those who best provide what consumers value. It is impossible to calculate in advance how much money, convenience, or other benefits people will want to trade for more or less privacy. Just as some people buy Chevrolets and others buy Hondas, different levels of privacy can be offered by different companies, satisfying different consumers. Government agencies, by contrast, do not have a market incentive to satisfy the public; they do not go broke if their decisions and actions make no sense or reflect the moods and prejudices of the employee. Further, most government agencies are monopolies, and we are forced to give them information whether we like their policies or not.

PRACTICE PROBLEMS

1. Add two examples to the list in Figure 14.1 and to the list in Figure 14.2.

2. List two government databases that probably contain information about you. For each one, tell what service or benefit, if any, you got in exchange for providing information about yourself. List two private databases that probably contain information about you. For each one, tell what service or benefit, if any, you got in exchange for providing information about yourself.

3. A city government wants to track down people who run small businesses and do not pay the city's $125 business license fee. The city has hired a

private detective to obtain IRS tax records of city residents and determine who has reported small business income to the IRS but not paid for a license. Privacy experts warn of the potential for abuse by city employees with access to sensitive data and point to the risk that some of the IRS information may be released or sold by people who will be working on the project. The city argues that this is simply a new enforcement method that will help reduce its budget deficit and benefit honest businesses. Do you think this kind of "information sharing" between the IRS and a city government should be permitted or prohibited? Give your reasons.

4. A business distributes to stores a list of the names of shoplifters. What are the benefits and risks of doing this? Should distribution of such a list be prohibited by law? Give your reason(s).

5. a. If we did not have computers, is it likely that video stores would maintain lists of the specific videos rented by customers?
   b. If we did not have computers, would we have VCRs?

6. List three features that can be designed into computer systems to protect privacy.

14.4   THE COMPUTER SAID SO

In the early 1950s, computers were called giant brains. For many years, when computers were large, expensive, and used only by specially trained staff, people thought of them as mysterious but brilliant and nearly infallible. Later, the advent of personal computers and the availability of complex software of varying quality taught most computer users to expect bugs. Some of us have received computer-generated bills for $0. We have heard about people getting paychecks with several extra zeros on the end of the amount. The mystique is gone. We know that people design, write, and use computer programs. People make mistakes. Yet many people still think the computer is always right. In this section, we consider how reliable computer programs are. Should we use them in applications where people's safety is at risk? Should we believe something just because a computer said it was so?

14.4.1   "MISTAKES I CANNOT SEA"

Most word processing programs now come with spelling checkers: programs that go through a document and look up each word in a dictionary stored on the disk. If a word is not found in the dictionary, the program alerts the user that it might be spelled incorrectly. A computer can check all the words in less time than we might spend flipping through the pages of a printed dictionary to find the first one. If the spelling checker does not flag any words, does that mean our document will get an A from an English teacher? Consider the following poem, which circulated on a computer network.

I have a spelling checker.
It came with my PC.
It plainly marks four my revue,
Mistakes I cannot sea.
I've run this poem threw it,
I'm sure your pleased too no.
It's letter perfect in it's weigh,
My checker tolled me sew.

Producing a newsletter used to be a long process. The steps included writing, editing, preparing artwork, typesetting, and printing. Because a large investment of time and money was involved, care was taken at each step. Now the ease and speed with which a newsletter or a Web page can be produced on a computer, with nice type fonts and fancy graphics, have led some people to put less time and effort into the writing and editing. Some very good-looking newsletters, Web pages, and student term papers contain very poor writing, numerous grammatical errors, and unchecked "facts." This is one example in which the convenience of using a computer encourages mental laziness. To produce good work and make wise policy decisions, we must understand what computers can do well and reliably, and where humans must exercise good judgment and take responsibility.

14.4.2 MAJOR FAILURES

What are the risks of depending on computers for the operation of communications systems, military systems, and banking systems? Should we trust our lives to computers? Consider these incidents.

A software error directed an F-16 jet fighter to flip upside down when the plane crossed the equator. A software error directed a radiation machine to give large overdoses of radiation to some patients. A program to detect a missile attack by the Soviet Union mistook the rising moon for a barrage of missiles coming over the horizon. An error appeared in software for AT&T's long-distance telephone system. A software error disrupted processing of transactions at a major bank. An arithmetic overflow error (a problem discussed in Section 4.2.1) caused the computers in the French Ariane 5 rocket to shut down. A commercial airline pilot selected the wrong option when giving information to a computerized autopilot system.

Some of these errors were detected in time to avoid disasters; others were not. The F-16 never really flipped over; the problem was detected during a computer simulation of the plane. In this case, one computer program was used successfully to ferret out an error in another. Tragically, the radiation machine killed some patients, and others suffered from the overdoses. The U.S. military did not attack the rising moon. AT&T's long-distance service, for both voice and data communications, was disrupted on several occasions for many hours. The bank's faulty software cost the bank several million dollars. The multimillion-dollar Ariane rocket crashed. The airliner, on autopilot, crashed into a mountain.

When we use sophisticated modern devices, we rely on physics and chemistry, on proper design, on careful manufacturing processes, and on proper maintenance. The same can be said for computer systems, where good programming is another key step. The potential for life-threatening failures in computer systems, as in other fields, should always remind computer professionals of the importance of doing their job responsibly.

Computer system failures can result from ambiguous or incomplete specifications, design errors, programming errors, hardware errors, data entry errors, and errors in interpreting the results. We saw in Chapter 7 that a program's specification and design must be done carefully. Software designers must ponder the unusual circumstances that can occur, not just the normal, expected situations. They must allow for mistakes users will make. Redundant computations can be included to help ensure that crucial values (such as radiation dosages) are correct. Testing should be extensive and well planned. Test data or test cases need to be chosen to exercise all branches of a program (or as many as is feasible in a complex system). Many techniques (and even computer programs) have been developed to help build systems that are more reliable.

But failures like the ones described earlier in this section do occur. So again: How much should we rely on computers? Should certain applications be outlawed because they are too risky? We trust our lives to technology almost every day. We trust older, noncomputer technologies every time we step into an elevator, a car, or an airplane. These inventions were not very safe when they were first developed. If the death rate from commercial airline accidents were the same now as it was 40 years ago, eight thousand people would die in plane crashes each year (instead of fewer than two hundred). We learn how to make improvements; problems are discovered and solved; engineers study disasters and learn how to prevent them. This process occurs with computer systems too.

What kind of legislation might help prevent major failures? A law saying that a radiation machine should not overdose a patient would be silly. We know that it should not do that. No one knew in advance that this particular computer application would cause harm. Should we outlaw the use of computer control devices for applications where an error could be fatal? Is it more or less likely that a computer program will compute the wrong dose than it is that a sleepy, lazy, or poorly trained technician will set a dose control dial incorrectly? Would you feel safe riding a train that had no human operator? The subway shuttle system at the Seattle–Tacoma airport has carried more than 250 million passengers between the airline terminals. It is automated and controlled by a computer; there are no drivers on the trains. If it seems frightening or risky to eliminate the driver, recall that elevators used to have human operators. (Imagine trusting an elevator door to open and close automatically without injuring anyone!) What about cardiac pacemakers? A failure could kill the patient, but without it the patient might have died of heart failure much sooner. When evaluating the risks of computers in a particular application, we should compare those risks with the failure rate of noncomputerized alternatives. On the whole, computers usually save, extend, and improve lives, but they can never be risk-free.

We have made two points: (1) There is a learning curve for new technologies, and (2) risks should be compared with risks of other methods or with benefits obtained. This does not mean that accidents should be excused as part of the learning process, and it does not mean that accidents should be excused because, on balance, the contribution of computers is positive. Knowing that one will be liable for the damages one causes is a strong incentive to find improvements and increase safety. When evaluating a specific instance of a failure, we can look for those responsible and try to ensure that they bear the costs of the damage they caused. It is when evaluating the technology *as a whole* that we look at the balance between risks and benefits.

Laws that try to regulate a new technology directly are likely to restrict innovation and progress. Perhaps most important in the legal realm are well-designed liability laws—not so extreme that they discourage all innovation, but clear and strong enough to provide incentives to produce safe systems.

14.4.3 INCONVENIENCES, ANNOYANCES, AND SOMETIMES WORSE

Far more numerous than catastrophic failures are the smaller errors that cause us inconvenience and headaches and sometimes seriously disrupt our lives. The examples that follow come from the comp.risks news group on Usenet, the "Inside Risks" column of the *Communications of the ACM, Privacy Journal,* the book *Privacy for Sale* by Jeffrey Rothfeder, the author's own experience, and other sources. It is useful to study these sometimes funny, sometimes frustrating incidents, because the same kinds of programming and human errors could have more serious consequences in other applications. By studying them, we can learn to reduce their occurrence.

One woman was billed $6.3 million for electricity; the correct amount was $63. The cause was an input error made by someone using a new computer system. The IRS told a woman she owed $67,714 in back taxes and then sent her a bill for $1 billion, including penalties. The auto insurance rate of a 101-year-old man suddenly tripled. Rates depend on age, but the program was written to handle ages only up to 100; it mistakenly classified the man as a teenager. These problems could have been avoided with better program specifications. The programs should have included tests to determine whether the amount was outside some reasonable range or had changed significantly from previous bills. From your study of high-level languages in Chapters 7 and 8, you can see how easy it would be to include such tests and place a message for a clerk to review this case.

A fifth-grader's computer-graded placement test was given a score of zero, and the child, despite objections, was required to repeat the fifth grade. Weeks later, someone looked at the test and discovered that an extra blank space in the child's name had confused the grading program and caused the zero score. Here is an extreme case of people mindlessly accepting the computer's result. The scoring program had a flaw, but the test should have been examined by someone at the school before such a drastic action was ordered.

We have already discussed privacy issues related to large government and private databases. Reliance on these databases also raises another issue: *accuracy.* Whether or not we consider a particular use of a database an infringement of privacy, if the information is not accurate, people can suffer inconvenience or serious harm. When information is entered automatically by other computer systems, mistakes that might be obvious to a human can be overlooked. Even if an error is corrected, the problems may not be over for the person affected. Computer records are copied easily and often; copies of the incorrect data may remain in many other systems. We will describe some cases.

A county agency used the wrong middle name in a report to a credit bureau about a father who did not make his child support payments. Another man in the same county had the exact name reported; he could not get credit to buy a car or a house. A woman in Canada could not get her tax refund because the tax agency insisted she was dead. Her identification number had been mistakenly reported in place of her mother's when her mother died. These cases illustrate the importance of using more than one piece of information for identification. If both a name and an identification number had been used, the errors might have been detected and corrected sooner. Note that although computerized records were used in these cases, computers did not cause the problem. The errors would have been just as likely to occur with paper files.

Studies of the FBI's National Crime Information Center (NCIC) database have found that a large percentage of the arrest warrants listed in it are inaccurate or no longer valid. People are arrested when a check of the database shows a warrant for them—or for someone with a similar name. One man was arrested five times within 14 months in Los Angeles because of inaccurate information in NCIC. (He eventually sued and won a judgment against the city.)

Thousands of residents in several New England states were listed incorrectly in TRW records as not having paid their local property taxes. The problem was attributed to an input error. People were denied loans before the scope of the problem was identified and it was corrected. (TRW paid damages to many of the people affected.)

The big credit bureaus and medical information bureaus have received heavy criticism for incidents where incorrect information has caused people to lose their homes, cars, jobs, or insurance.

How might we try to improve the accuracy of the information in databases? Some approaches for private databases are regulatory legislation, liability, and market forces. In general, regulatory legislation requires that certain procedures be followed and that various records be kept; sometimes it includes provision for inspection by government employees. Such regulation has been advocated by some people concerned with privacy issues. Unfortunately, the paperwork may be quite expensive, and the goal—be it privacy, accuracy, safety, less pollution, or whatever—tends to get lost in the details of the procedures and records. Regulations that require specific procedures discourage or prevent the use of newer and better procedures that the people who wrote the rules didn't think of. On the other hand, liability and breach of contract are concepts that focus on the goal rather than the procedures. Some people who have suffered serious economic loss have successfully sued negligent providers of false, damaging information. Breach of contract could be an appropriate complaint for a customer of an information service that sells inaccurate information. The power of market forces should not be underestimated. A reputation for accuracy is an asset to an information business.

Achieving and maintaining accuracy in government databases is another problem altogether. Market forces and the concept of contract do not apply. The government often permits itself to do legally what would be illegal for private citizens or businesses to do. The government can refuse to be sued. When someone does win a suit, it is the taxpayers, not the people at fault, who pay the award. Regulatory laws applied to government agencies have many of the same weaknesses mentioned above. Here, however there may be no better alternative.

14.4.4 CASE STUDIES ON EVALUATING COMPUTER MODELS: CRASHING CARS AND GLOBAL WARMING

SOCIAL ISSUES.   Computers are used extensively to model and simulate both physical systems and abstract systems. Chapter 10 mentioned examples such as airplane flight simulators, natural resource utilization, the dispersal of pollution, population demographics, and the design of new cars and airplanes. The very abstract notion of an algorithm was examined via a computerized model in the lab exercises for Chapter 10. In Chapter 11, we used spreadsheets, a modeling tool that can help in making business and investment plans (and has numerous other uses as well).

Models enable us to investigate the possible effects of different designs, scenarios, and policies. They have obvious social and economic benefits, including the ability to consider alternatives and make better decisions and the reduction of waste, cost, and risk.

Let's review the way we described the concept of a model in Section 10.2. A model—whether it is a toy model car or a sophisticated computer program for weather forecasting—has the following properties:

- It includes the "essence," the important properties.
- It is probably different in scale (size or time) from the real thing.
- It suppresses details.
- It lacks the full functionality of the real thing.

As we emphasized in Chapters 10 and 11, a model is reliable only if it accurately represents the system being modeled. We will use two examples, or case studies, to illustrate our discussion of evaluating computer models and simulations: crash analysis models used in the design of cars and climate models used to study potential global warming. These examples will help us consider some of the following issues.

Computer modeling is now widely used in the design and development of new products. How safe are the products? Should computer simulations replace physical tests for crucial decisions such as approving a new car design or certifying a pilot?

Computer models for the effects of new taxes and regulations, for the use of natural resources, for the effects of changes in climate, and so on are sometimes used to justify multibillion-dollar government programs and/or laws and regulations that significantly affect the economy and the lifestyle and standard of living of hundreds of millions of people. Especially in cases in which no physical testing is possible, how can we decide whether the models are reliable enough to use as a basis for government policy or to warrant changes in our personal behavior? We are not naive enough to think that anything must be true just because "the computer said so." It is important for both computer professionals and the general public to have some idea how to evaluate claims or predictions based on these models.

EVALUATING MODELS.   We will use the following three questions to help assess the validity and accuracy of two models.

1. How well do the modelers understand the underlying science or theory (be it physics, chemistry, economics, or whatever) of the system being studied? How well understood are the relevant properties of the materials involved?

2. Computer models necessarily involve simplifications of reality (suppression of details). What are the simplifications in the model?

3. How closely do the results of the computer programs correspond to results from physical experiments?

CAR CRASH ANALYSIS PROGRAMS.   Car crash analysis programs gained wide usage by the late 1980s. One of the major programs, DYNA3D, was developed at Lawrence Livermore National Laboratory for military applications but is now used in product design. This program models the interactions of physical objects on impact. DYNA3D is especially designed for high-speed collisions. It uses a technique called the **finite element method.** A grid is superimposed on the frame of a car, dividing the car into a finite number of small pieces, or elements (see Figure 14.5). The grid is entered into the program, along with data describing the specifications of the materials that make up each element (such as density, strength, and elasticity). Suppose we are studying the effects of a head-on collision on the structure of the car. Data can be initialized to represent a crash into a wall at a specified speed. The program computes the force, acceleration, and displacement at each grid point and the stress and strain within each element. These calculations are repeated to show what happens as time passes in small increments. Using graphics programs, the simulation produces a picture of the car at intervals after impact, as illustrated in Figure 14.5. To simulate 40–100 milliseconds of real time from the impact takes up to 35 hours of time on a supercomputer. Clearly, these programs require intensive computation, or number crunching, as we called it in Chapter 11.

The cost of a real crash test can range from $50,000 to $800,000. The high figure is for building and testing a unique prototype for a new car design. The crash analysis programs allow engineers to vary the thickness of steel used for selected components, or change materials altogether, and find out what the effect would be without building another prototype for each alternative. But how good are the programs?

How well is the physics of car crashes understood? Force and acceleration are basic principles; the physics involved in these programs would be considered fairly easy. The relevant properties of steel, plastics, aluminum, glass, and other materials in a car are well known. There are good data on the density, elasticity, and other characteristics of materials used in the model. However, although the behavior of the materials when force is applied gradually is well known, the behavior of some materials under abrupt acceleration, as in a high-speed impact, and their behavior near or at their breaking point are less well understood.

What simplifications are made in the programs? The grid pattern is the most obvious; a car is smooth, not made up of little blocks. Also, time is continuous; it does not occur in steps. The accuracy of the simulation will depend in part on how fine the grid is and how small the time intervals are. As computer speeds increase, we can do more precise computation. In the early 1990s, crash analysis programs used roughly ten thousand to fifty thousand elements and updated the calculations for time intervals of one-millionth of a second.

How do the computed results compare to actual crash tests on real cars? How are such comparisons performed? The real tests are taped by high-speed cameras. Various kinds of sensors, such as strain gauges, are attached to the car, and reference points are marked on the frame. The tapes can be visually compared with the computer output. The values recorded by the sensors are compared with values computed by the program, and the distortion or displacement of the reference points can be physically measured and compared to the computed positions. From the results of the physical crash, elementary physics can be used to calculate backward and determine the deceleration and other forces

FIGURE 14.5

LS-DYNA3D Simulation of a Frontal Crash at 35 mph Before Impact and at 20 and 70 Milliseconds After (Reproduced by kind permission of Saab Automobile AB, Linkoping University, and Livermore Software Technology Corporation)

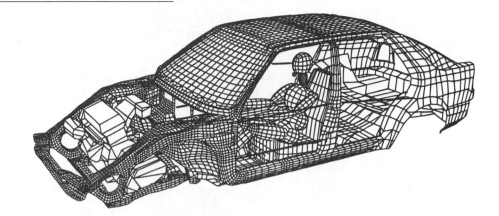

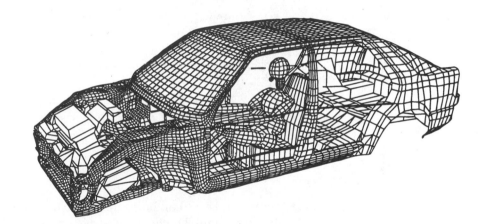

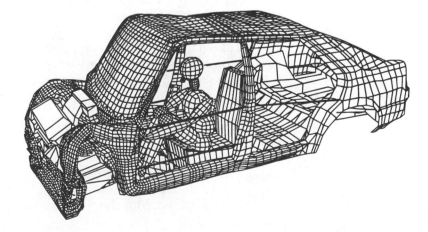

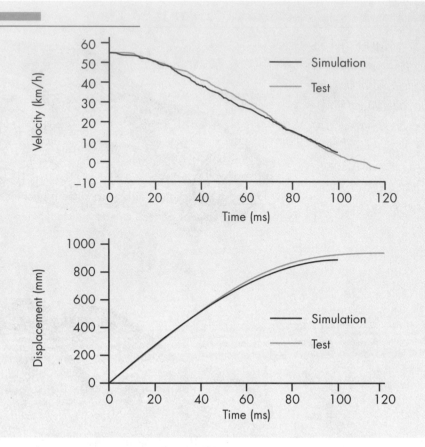

FIGURE 14.6

Comparing Results from Simulations and Real Crashes (Adapted from a figure in "Numerical simulation of frontal impact and frontal offset collisions," by Thomas Frank and Karl Gruber, Cray Channels, Winter 1992)

acting on the car. These can be compared to the values computed in the simulation. The conclusion? The crash analysis programs do an extremely good job. Figure 14.6 shows how results from the program correspond to data collected in actual test crashes.

Once we know that the models are reasonably accurate, we can conclude that the computer programs provide some benefits that we cannot get from physical testing. The computer can provide more data than the sensors, and it can tell us what is happening in areas of the car that the cameras cannot see. The simulation can also provide more information than a real crash if there is unexpected damage in a position where few sensors were placed.

USES OF THE CRASH ANALYSIS MODELS.   Car crash analysis programs are replacing physical crash testing as a design tool for new cars. The crash test is used as confirmation and is required by the federal government. Should the simulation results replace the physical crash? The answer to this question may depend on its context. Suppose the government did not require a physical crash test. Would you buy a car that had been certified crashworthy only by a computer? To decide whether to do physical crash tests, a car manufacturer would probably consider

FIGURE 14.7

Other Uses of Crash Analysis Programs

- To predict damage to a hazardous waste container if dropped
- To predict damage to an airplane windshield or nacelle (engine covering) if hit by a bird
- To determine whether beer cans would get dented if an assembly line were speeded up
- To simulate a medical procedure called balloon angioplasty, in which a balloon is inserted in a blocked artery and inflated to open the artery (The computer program helps researchers determine how to perform the procedure with less damage to the arterial wall.)
- To predict the action of airbags and the proper location for sensors that inflate them
- To design interior parts of cars to reduce injuries during crashes (such as injuries from impact of a steering wheel on a human chest)
- To design bicycle and motorcycle helmets to reduce head injuries
- To design cameras to reduce damage if dropped
- To forecast the effects of earthquakes on bridges and buildings

the accuracy of the models, the costs of physical testing, liability laws, and public relations. A company that provides liability insurance for car manufacturers would consider whether the simulations are reliable enough for them to do accurate risk analysis. A legal scholar or an economist might consider whether the law should specify a specific test or focus on the result by specifying rules for liability—letting the manufacturer decide how best to ensure that its cars are safe. A legislator might consider the reliability of the simulations, public attitudes about computers, and the arguments of lobbyists. In fact, engineers who work with the crash analysis programs do not believe that physical crashes will or should be eliminated. They remind us that the simulation is an implementation of theory. The program may give poor results if it is used by someone who does not understand it well. Results may be poor if something happens that the program simply was not designed to consider. Overall, the crash analysis programs are excellent design tools that make it possible to promote increases in safety with far less development cost. But the real crash is the proof.

Variations of the crash analysis programs are used in a wide variety of other impact applications, some of which are listed in Figure 14.7. One reason for these many uses is the increase in computing power and the declining cost. (In the late 1970s, serious engineering applications of crash analysis programs were run on $10 million computers. In the 1990s, applications are run on workstations in the $20,000–$60,000 range.) Another reason is the confidence that has developed over time in the validity of the results.

CLIMATE MODELS AND GLOBAL WARMING. In this section we will look at the computerized climate models that led to intense publicity and concern about global warming in the late 1980s and early 1990s. First we need a little background.

The earth is warmed by solar radiation. Some of the heat is reflected back; some is trapped by gases in the atmosphere. This phenomenon is known as the **greenhouse effect.** Without it, the earth would be too cold to support life. The main "greenhouse gases" are water vapor, carbon dioxide (CO_2), methane, chlorofluorocarbons (CFCs), and ozone. Among those whose concentration has been increased by human activity, CO_2 is the most important. The problem of concern now is that this increase may enhance the greenhouse effect significantly, increasing temperatures and causing other major changes in climate, including changes in precipitation and sea level. Computerized climate models are used to try to determine what changes will occur and when.

CO_2 currently makes up roughly one-thirtieth of 1% of the atmosphere, or 355 parts per million (ppm) by volume. The concentration of methane is currently about 1,700 parts per billion (ppb). The concentrations of these gases are substantially higher than they were for most of the past 160,000 years.[1] An upward trend in both CO_2 and methane, from near their lowest values, began roughly 16,000 years ago. However, since the beginning of the Industrial Revolution, concentrations have been increasing at a faster rate. Since 1950 the climb has been very steep. The main source of increased CO_2 is the burning of fossil fuels (such as oil and coal). The top three sources of methane are thought to be natural wetlands, animals (such as cattle), and industry (coal, natural gas, and petroleum).

The computer models that are used to study climate are called **general circulation models** (GCMs). GCMs were developed from atmospheric models that have been used for a long time for weather prediction. They are quite complex. They contain information about the sun's energy output; the orbit, inclination, and rotation of the earth; geography (a map of land masses); topography (mountains, etc.); clouds; sea and polar ice; soil and air moisture; and a large number of other factors. Like the crash analysis models, the GCMs use a grid. The grid circles the earth and rises through the atmosphere. The computer programs solve equations for each grid point and element (grid box), for specified time intervals. The equations simulate factors such as atmospheric pressure, temperature, incoming solar energy, outgoing radiant energy, thermal patterns, wind speed and direction, moisture, and precipitation. For global-warming studies, the atmospheric models are combined with models of the oceans that include temperature, currents, salinity, and other factors.

Because of the global importance of potential changes in climate, the Intergovernmental Panel on Climate Change (IPCC), sponsored by the United Nations and the World Meteorological Organization, published two major reports in 1990 and 1992 on the scientific assessment of climate change. The reports were prepared and reviewed by several hundred scientists worldwide. They are considered an authoritative review of the state of scientific knowledge about climate change. They are the main references used for this discussion.[2]

To forecast the effects of increased concentration of greenhouse gases, a model is first run to simulate several decades of real time, starting with some

---

[1] The data for the distant past come from measurements of gases trapped in ice cores drilled in Antarctica and Greenland.

[2] The IPCC published another report in 1995. Although many improvements had been made in the years between the reports, the conclusions did not differ in fundamental ways.

base conditions. Then the model is run again with increased values for the greenhouse gas concentrations. The results are compared to give an estimate of the effect of the increase. Many computer studies focus on computing the effects of increasing CO_2 concentration from 300 ppm to 600 ppm—that is, doubling the CO_2 concentration from its approximate level at the beginning of the twentieth century. (Current trends suggest that CO_2 concentration will reach 600 ppm sometime in the twenty-first century.) More recent studies include other greenhouse gases as well.

To evaluate the climate models, we will consider the same questions we asked about the car crash analysis programs: How well is the underlying science understood? What simplifications are made in the models? How do the calculated results compare to physical experiments?

How well is the science of climate activity understood? The climate system is composed of five subsystems: atmosphere, oceans, cryosphere (ice packs, snow), geosphere (land, soil), and biosphere (vegetation). Effects in the air, such as changes in temperature, wind speed and direction, and so on, can be computed using well-understood principles of physics. The laws of physics are used to compute temperature and other effects in the oceans as well. However, a great deal of scientific uncertainty remains about each component. We will describe some of these sources of uncertainty.

The oceans have a large capacity to absorb heat. The circulation of water in the oceans, due to currents, affects heat absorption. Surface currents are fairly well known; deep currents are less well known. Currents were thought to be constant, but there is now evidence that they shift and that such changes can have a radical and rapid influence on temperature. Not enough is known about the exchange of energy between the oceans and the atmosphere.

Clouds are extremely important to climate. Many processes involved with the formation, effects, and dissipation of clouds are not particularly well understood.

Measurements and estimates of emissions (sources) of greenhouse gases are not precise. (In 1990, the IPCC ranked rice fields as the second highest source of methane. In 1992, revised estimates moved them to fourth place.) We also do not know enough about the *sinks*—that is, the materials and processes that cause the gases to dissipate. Thus the relationship between emissions and concentrations in the atmosphere is not fully understood. Between 1990 and 1992, the IPCC scientists revised their estimates of the indirect effects of many greenhouse gases; they said that the figures published in 1990 were likely to be in substantial error and that they did not yet know enough to give new values.

If temperatures rise, natural wetlands give off more methane, contributing to more warming. This is called positive, or destabilizing, feedback. An output or side effect of the process amplifies the original effect. There are negative, or stabilizing, feedbacks too. When the earth warms, more water evaporates and forms clouds; the clouds reflect some of the sun's heat back up away from the earth. (Clouds have positive-feedback effects also.) Many such feedback mechanisms affect climate, and for some, it is not known whether the feedback is positive or negative. Many uncertainties in the models are attributed to lack of knowledge or lack of full representation of feedback mechanisms.

Another area of uncertainty is natural variation in climate. The earth has experienced ice ages and warm periods. There is also a lot of year-to-year fluctuation.

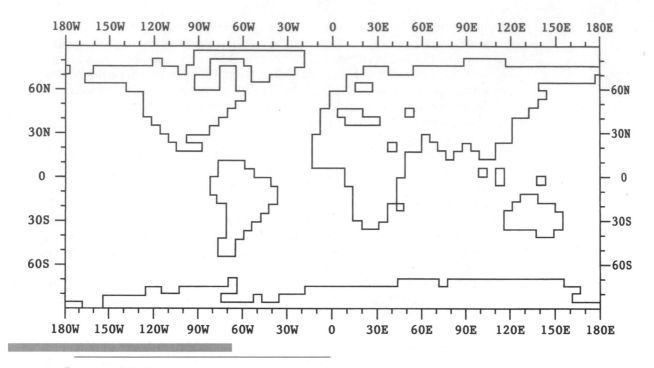

FIGURE 14.8

*The Land Map for a Typical
Climate Model (Courtesy of
Dr. Ulrich Cubasch, Deutsches
Klimarechenzentrum)*

We do not know all the causes of these changes, and we do not know the current natural temperature trend.

What simplifications are made in the models? There are about half a dozen major climate-modeling centers in the world. The models vary in many ways, and they are being modified and improved as time passes. Recall that our focus is on the models used in the late 1980s—those on which fears of catastrophic global warming were based. Some of our comments are generalizations; they may not all be true of all the models at any one time.

The grid points in the models were typically spaced about 500 kilometers (roughly 300 miles) apart. The state of California, for example, would have been represented by roughly half a dozen grid points. Islands as small as Japan and England did not appear on some "maps" at all, because they lay between grid points in an ocean or sea. See Figure 14.8 for a sample map. The grids were coarse because the computing time required to run the programs depends on the number of points. Recall that it takes up to 35 hours of computer time to simulate 40–100 milliseconds of a car crash. To be useful, climate studies must be done faster than real time. A 500-kilometer grid rising ten layers in the atmosphere has roughly 20,000 points. Because of the coarse grid size, the models can describe the development and movement of large weather systems, but small storms and other less extensive phenomena fall between the grid points and either are not fully represented or are expanded to fill a cell of the grid.

Other simplifications include not distinguishing between day and night,[3] doubling CO_2 concentration all at once instead of gradually, and representing only the top layers of the oceans.

Ideally, all of the processes that affect climate would be represented in the GCMs by equations derived from the underlying science (generally, physics and chemistry). This is not possible, however, because it would require too much computation time and because not all the underlying science is known. Many processes are represented by simplified equations, called *parametrizations*, that seem to give realistic results but are not derived from scientific theory. The specific parametrizations used vary among the models, reflecting the skill and art of the modelers. Values for estimated variables are chosen to make the models predict present conditions with reasonable accuracy. The process of modifying the values until the desired result is achieved is called **tuning** the model. Although models can be tuned by balancing the values for several variables so that the model accurately describes present conditions, it is not known whether that choice of values will make the model predict future conditions accurately.

Of the five major climate subsystems, the atmosphere is modeled most extensively. Ocean modeling is less advanced. The interaction and effects of some components, such as vegetation, are represented minimally or not at all.

How closely do the results of the computer programs correspond to results from physical experiments? We cannot do physical experiments for global warming. Thus we need to consider other ways to assess the results of the computer simulations.

First we need to know what the models say. Predictions from the models for average global temperature increase ranged from a little more than 1°C to a little more than 5°C. The increase would not be uniform. It would be greater near the poles and in winter, less at other times and places. Many models predict an increase in precipitation, though the predicted amounts vary substantially.

The wide variation in the predictions of the models, by itself, suggests that we are far from having a clear understanding of climate behavior and the impact of greenhouse gases. For a well-understood phenomenon, the predictions of good models would converge to similar results.

Scientists gain confidence in the models because they predict seasonal variations and other broad-scale phenomena. The general patterns of the predictions generated by different models are similar. For example, they all predict that warming will occur and that more of the warming will take place near the poles and in winter.

Perhaps the most obvious test that could be done to validate the models is to run them for conditions of the past century, including the increase in greenhouse gases that has occurred so far, and see whether they predict current

---

[3]This is significant because temperature records for some areas of the Northern hemisphere show increases in the nighttime winter lows and decreases in the daytime summer highs, which could be a benign or even beneficial form for an average warming to take.

temperature, precipitation, and sea level. Unfortunately, because we do not have sufficient data about past conditions and for other technical reasons, the validity of the experiments that have been done is not clear. We will describe and analyze the results briefly.

As we noted earlier, concentrations of greenhouse gases in the atmosphere have increased very steeply since about 1950. Between the late nineteenth century and 1990, the average temperature rose by 0.3°C to 0.7°C. This rise in temperature was not uniform geographically or over time. Temperatures increased for the first fifty years, and then they declined from the 1940s to the mid-1970s. In the 1970s another rise began. Most of the warming during the past century occurred before 1950. Some of the climate models predicted temperature increases three to five times as high as what actually occurred. Evaluating these results is not a simple task, because so many factors affect temperature. Aerosols (airborne particles) in the atmosphere, from volcanic eruptions and industrial activities, contribute to cooling. Urbanization and other human activities besides the emission of greenhouse gases caused some warming. Still other factors, such as variation in solar output and other natural phenomena, could have affected the temperature in either direction. It is not known what fraction of the net warming over the past century is attributable to greenhouse gases or whether they would have caused even more warming in the absence of other factors that had a cooling effect. The magnitude and rate of the temperature change in the past century may not be unusual; it is possible that all of it is within the range of natural fluctuation. Considering all the uncertainties and the overly high predictions of the models, IPCC scientists estimated that if all the warming that occurred was due to greenhouse gases, then the probable future warming would be 1°C to 2°C—that is, at the lower end of the range predicted by the GCMs.

The 1990 IPCC report predicts a global mean temperature increase of 0.2°C to 0.5°C per decade. Satellite data show an average global temperature rise of only 0.06°C for the decade of the 1980s.

Another way to try to understand the accuracy of GCM predictions is to consider how sensitive they are to modifications and improvements. There is much scientific uncertainty about the behavior of clouds and their feedback properties. One modeling center did an experiment wherein the investigators ran the same model except that clouds were treated differently each time. Their predictions for temperature increase ranged from 1.9°C to 5.2°C. The most detailed and flexible—and hence perhaps the most realistic—treatment of clouds gave the lowest temperature prediction. Some newer models, using more nearly complete representations of the oceans, also show reduced or slower warming.

Conclusions. GCMs have improved dramatically in the few decades that scientists have been developing and working with them. Some features that had been estimated (parametrized) in early models are now represented by equations based on science. Increased computer power has made it possible to run more experiments and has resulted in better calibration and increased resolution (smaller grid size). Increased data collection and basic science research have improved our understanding of the behavior and interactions of climate system components. But given the results so far and the complexity of climate phenomena, it seems fair to conclude, as the IPCC report does, that "climate models are still in an early stage of development." They seem to overestimate the amount of warming that will occur. The IPCC 1992 update says that "Since the 1990 report there has been a greater appreciation of many of the uncertainties which affect our predictions of the timing, magnitude and regional patterns of climate change." The models are a tool for understanding climate change, but they are not yet at a stage where we can have much confidence in the precision of their results. Certainly, they have not achieved the level of reliability of the car crash analysis models.

PRACTICE PROBLEMS

1. Rewrite the spelling checker poem, correcting all the mistakes. (There are more than ten mistakes.)

2. a. Suppose you write a program to add two integers. Assume that both integers and their sum will fit in the standard memory unit used by the computer for integers. How likely do you think it is that the sum will be correct? (If you used the program a million times on different pairs of integers, how many times do you think it would give the correct answer?)

   b. Suppose a telephone company has a million customers and it runs a program to determine whether any customers have overdue bills. How likely do you think it is that the results of the program will be correct?

   c. Probably your answers to parts (a) and (b) were different. (They should be.) Give some reasons why the probable numbers of errors are different in these two examples.

3. If your class has access to Usenet or the World Wide Web, read a few recent postings in comp.risks, the Risks news group.

4. Suppose the government no longer required physical crash tests for new cars. What factors would you consider in deciding whether to buy a car that was crash-tested only by computer simulation? What magazines or technical literature would you consult, if any, in making your decision?

5. An article in the magazine *Audubon* (March/April 1993) states that "Since the 1960s more than 100 separate studies have confirmed that a doubling of the CO_2 concentration would raise average surface temperatures by one to four degrees centigrade." Is this an accurate statement? Explain your answer.

14.5   COMPUTER CRIME

14.5.1 WHAT IS COMPUTER CRIME?

We saw in our discussion of privacy that many of the issues involved are independent of computers. Computers have magnified some problems and increased our vulnerability. They provide a degree of anonymity that makes invasions of privacy easier to commit and harder to detect. Similarly, much of what is called computer crime fits into existing categories of crime: embezzlement, theft (of goods and services), fraud, vandalism, and destruction of property. Computers have provided new ways to commit old crimes, and they provide new challenges for prevention, detection, and prosecution.

The term **computer crime** covers a wide range of activities from hacking to the embezzlement of millions of dollars. Various writers have offered definitions, but they are probably less informative than a discussion of examples. Some distinguish between crimes where computers are the targets and crimes where computers are the tools, but this distinction can often be blurred. We will take a brief look at several kinds of computer crime, including some that might be most tempting to students.

FRAUD, EMBEZZLEMENT, AND THEFT.   Fraud and embezzlement cost society several billions of dollars each year. Dishonest employees with access to company computers can manipulate accounts and payments to steal large amounts of money. Fraudulent billing for nonexistent products and services is made easier when large numbers of transactions are processed by computers.

Criminals have developed many schemes to use computer technology to rob other people. In one such scheme, a new automated teller machine (ATM) was installed in a shopping mall in Connecticut and seemed to work fine for a while. Later, after reading each customer's card and requesting the customer's PIN (personal identification number), it displayed a message telling the customer that the transaction could not be processed. After about two weeks, the machine was removed. The machine was a phony. It was not connected to any banking system. Its purpose was to read the account numbers magnetically recorded on the cards and store the PIN typed in by the customer. It is alleged that the people who installed the machine then created counterfeit cards and used them at real ATMs to steal nearly $100,000 from their victims.

One of the benefits of computer technology is the convenience of getting cash from a machine when the bank is closed. The same technology clearly provides new opportunities for thieves.

It is not easy to get reliable data on the amount of computer fraud and embezzlement, in part because financial institutions and other victims prefer not to publicize their losses and weaken customer confidence. Losses attributed to ATM fraud, credit card fraud, and cell phone fraud are estimated at more than $1 billion each year.

STEALING DATA.   We have already discussed unauthorized access to personal data in a variety of databases. Another target of data theft is trade secrets and other sensitive and valuable information that businesses keep on computers: plans for new products, product and market research, customer lists, pricing policy, and so on.

Industrial espionage is not new, but it used to require physical infiltration of the victim's business, theft of paper documents, or the physical copying of documents by hand or with a camera. Now such spying can be accomplished from a remote location using a computer network. Large quantities of digital information can be copied quickly. More damage may be done while the victim remains unaware. In one incident, a person at a business left a voice mail message for a supplier indicating interest in purchasing a very expensive product. The next day the caller received a packet of advertising material about a similar product—from the supplier's competitor. It appeared that the competitor had cracked the voice mail system and was able to collect information about potential customers.

HACKING OR CRACKING.   Many people think of computer crime as **hacking,** or breaking into computer systems without authorization. Chapter 6 briefly introduced us to the issue of hackers. The targets include school computers where grades or exams are stored, credit bureau databases, communications systems, and military computers. In the early days of computing, a hacker was a creative programmer who wrote very elegant or clever programs. A good hack was an especially clever piece of code. Hackers tended to be outside the social mainstream; they spent many hours at their computers. They learned as much as they could about a computer system—partly from reading about it, but mostly from experimenting. Even if they found ways into systems where they were not invited, the early hackers were interested primarily in learning and in intellectual challenges. Most of them had no intention to disrupt services; they frowned on doing damage. Unfortunately, sensationalized news stories made it easy to confuse the asocial, clever computer programmers with those who broke into systems and did mischief or serious damage. Out of respect for the hackers who produced some excellent software, we will use the terms **cracker** and **intruder** for those who break into computer systems.

What do crackers do once they break into a system? If it is a school system, they may change their grades or the grades of their friends. They may steal solutions to homework problems or delete files that belong to other students. If they have broken into a credit bureau computer, they may just read people's files, or they may copy files and distribute them. (Changing data in such files is quite a lot harder than reading them.) Some have cracked the telephone system and use their knowledge to make calls without paying for them. Others crack computer systems and use services for which users are normally charged. Malicious crackers have destroyed medical records, potentially putting patients at risk. In the case made famous by Clifford Stoll in his book *The Cuckoo's Egg*, a German cracker broke into dozens of U.S. computers, including military systems, looking for information to sell to the Soviet Union.

These examples can have serious consequences, but the damage is limited to a small number of people or companies. Another concern is the vulnerability of the Internet as a whole. Intruders have shut down entire systems by "bomb-ing" them with e-mail or exploiting security holes. Because so much of our fi-nancial, communications, and other activities now depend on the Net, damage by intruders can have much more widespread consequences. The 1986 Com-puter Fraud and Abuse Act provides for a $250,000 fine and up to five years in prison for anyone who intentionally accesses computers[4] without authorization and causes loss to others amounting to $1,000 or more.

VIRUSES AND WORMS. A computer **virus** is a program that is written to "hide" in another program and reproduce itself on many computers. A **worm** is an in-dependent program that duplicates itself on many computers. Some viruses and worms reproduce when an unsuspecting computer user downloads an infected program from the Internet or a bulletin board or loads a program from an in-fected floppy disk. Some spread through computer networks. Computer viruses, like biological viruses, may be harmless or quite destructive. They may do noth-ing more than use up a little space. They may put funny messages on the screen. They may reproduce so rapidly that they clog machines and prevent other pro-grams from running. They may modify or destroy files.

Spreading viruses, worms, and other destructive programs—like cracking systems—does not normally provide any financial gain to the perpetrator. The motive may be to show off, to succeed at a challenging task, or maliciously to cause inconvenience or damage.

14.5.2 IS CRACKING SYSTEMS WRONG?

Many high school and college students who crack computer systems do not think they are doing anything wrong. They may offer the following reasons for this point of view.

- No harm is done. The cracker is just curious to see what is there.
- The crackers are performing a service by exposing security weaknesses in the system.
- If the owners of the system want to keep outsiders out, it is their respon-sibility to provide better security. (This argument is used sometimes when harm is done as well.)

All these arguments can be refuted. Often the analogy of breaking into a house is used; it is a good analogy. Imagine arriving home late at night and finding a man standing in your living room. He says, "Don't worry; I'm not here to steal anything or cause you harm. I was just curious to see what kind of stereo system you have. And you should appreciate my showing you that your security system is vulnera-ble." Even if he leaves immediately, you may not sleep well that night. The prob-lems are numerous. You do not really know whether he stole anything. You do not know whether he made a copy of the spare key you keep in a kitchen drawer. You do not know what he would have stolen or destroyed if you had not arrived when you did. You do not know how he got in; there are no signs of forced entry. You do not know whether he will tell others how he got in and what kind of stereo you

---

[4]Not all unauthorized access is covered, but the act is broad enough to include most network attacks.

have. You do not know when he will be back. You will be uneasy about the safety of your personal documents, your belongings, and your children. The intruder has invaded your space—your property—without your permission. The manager of a jewelry store, a medical office, or virtually any place of business would react similarly to finding someone inside when arriving for work.

All these concerns apply to the on-line intruder as well. Whether or not we choose to put deadbolt locks on our doors, the fact that an intruder is able to enter the house—or the computer system—does not give him or her the right to do so. Breaking into someone else's computer system is ethically equivalent to breaking into someone else's house or business.

14.5.3 CHALLENGES

Computer crime poses challenges for people who have responsibility for computer systems and for those who write laws that define categories of computer crime and specify punishments. A person who is responsible for valuable or sensitive data on a computer system, or for the smooth operation of a system on which many people depend, has a professional and ethical obligation—and in some cases a legal obligation—to take reasonable security precautions to protect the system. System designers and managers must continually develop new techniques for protecting their systems from intrusion and damage by intruders and malicious authorized users. They also must balance the need for security with the need to maintain a reasonably open, accessible system for legitimate users.

A challenge for those who write and administer the laws is how to distinguish between young computer users who crack systems for fun and those who intend to steal or do damage. Just as trespass is a less serious crime than arson, cracking a system to just look around should be a less serious crime than destroying files or disrupting systems.

What is an appropriate penalty for a person who damages files or disrupts a system? Should it depend on whether the disruption was intended or accidental? Should the punishment be designed primarily to compensate for damage done, to punish the intruder, or to "send a signal" to others who might be thinking of trying something similar? These are basic questions about the purpose of inflicting a penalty for any crime or accidental damage.

Although compensating the victims may seem most important to many people, our criminal justice system does not provide for it. Fines imposed in criminal trials go to the government. Victims must sue in civil court to recover for damages. Unfortunately, with or without computers, it is possible for someone to cause far more damage than he or she can pay for. Some of the wildfires that destroyed thousands of acres and hundreds of homes in California in 1993 were set by an arsonist's match. There is no hope that the arsonist, even if found and convicted, could pay for the damage. Thus another challenge is to teach ethics—to make it clear to people that it is wrong to damage the property of others.

What penalties are appropriate for those who unintentionally do damage? Here too, it is possible for someone to cause more damage than he or she can pay for. (One of the California wildfires started accidentally when a campfire got out of control.) The teaching of ethical behavior should include the importance of understanding the dangers and accepting responsibility for being careful.

14.5.4 THE INTERNET WORM

The case of the Internet Worm illustrates some of the issues and problems we are discussing. In 1988 Robert T. Morris, a graduate student at Cornell University, wrote a worm program and released it onto the Internet. The worm spread quickly, jamming computers with so many copies that normal processing could not proceed. It was estimated that as many as 2000–3000 computers on the Internet were affected. It took about a full day for systems programmers to discover and decode the worm and rid their systems of it. Some infected sites were not functioning normally until several days later. It turned out that the worm did not destroy any files or release any passwords. Mostly, it just made multiple copies of itself on systems running a particular version of UNIX that could be reached through the Internet. It also took action to hide itself.

How much damage did the worm do? One estimate would be the cost of computer time on the infected systems for the time they were not functioning productively, plus overtime salary for the programmers and system managers who fought the worm through the night—easily hundreds of thousands of dollars.

What punishment should Morris have received? There are some indications in the worm program itself that Morris did not intend or expect it to cause the degree of disruption that it did. It may have reproduced faster than he intended because of an error he made in the program. When he realized the extent of the problem, he made a feeble effort to distribute information about how to stop it. (The infected systems were bogged down so much that the message did not get through to many of them. He did not use the telephone.) In several ways Morris's actions were like starting a campfire in a dry, brushy canyon, leaving it unattended for a while, and not calling the fire department upon discovering it out of control. (Analogies should not be carried too far; the fire did much more damage.)

Morris was convicted under the Computer Fraud and Abuse Act, sentenced to 3 years of probation, fined $10,000, and required to perform 400 hours of community service. Many observers thought the punishment was reasonable because his intentions were not malicious and the worm was not destructive. Others thought the interpretation of Morris's motives was too generous and the punishment too lenient. Some students and programmers saw Morris as a hero and repeated that old argument that we should be grateful to him for demonstrating the vulnerabilities of the UNIX system. Most computer professionals saw his behavior as utterly irresponsible. He disrupted research and other activities and inconvenienced a large number of people. The investigating commission at Cornell University commented that UNIX users know the system has security flaws. "It is no act of genius or heroism to exploit such weaknesses," says their report. "The act of propagating the worm was fundamentally a juvenile act that ignored the clear potential consequences."

PRACTICE PROBLEMS

1. People have been robbed after withdrawing cash from an ATM at night. In what sense, if any, is this a computer crime?

2. Do you agree with our analogy between cracking computer systems and breaking into a house or business? Give your reasons.

14.6   CONSTITUTIONAL AND CIVIL LIBERTIES ISSUES

14.6.1 THE FIRST AND FOURTH AMENDMENTS TO THE U.S. CONSTITUTION

Constitutional law professor Lawrence Tribe has suggested a new amendment to the U.S. Constitution:

> *This Constitution's protections for the freedoms of speech, press, petition, and assembly, and its protections against unreasonable searches and seizures and the deprivation of life, liberty or property without due process of law, shall be construed as fully applicable without regard to the technological method or medium through which information content is generated, stored, altered, transmitted or controlled.*

Is such an amendment necessary to extend constitutional protection to the electronic frontier? Or should such protection be considered implicit already? No matter how one might think the constitution *should* be interpreted, the government has sometimes been reluctant to extend protection to new technologies that were not explicitly mentioned in it. Although television, for example, is similar to newspapers in its role of providing news and entertainment, the Supreme Court ruled in the 1940s that the First Amendment did not apply and that television is subject to government control and licensing. The Internet and the World Wide Web are now becoming major arenas for the distribution of news, information, and opinion. The First Amendment protects freedom of speech and of the press. The Fourth Amendment protects against unreasonable search and seizure. Several dramatic cases in recent years have focused attention on the issue of how these protections will apply to electronic media. We will discuss three such cases.

CENSORSHIP VERSUS FREEDOM OF SPEECH.   There is a lot of sexually explicit material on the Internet. In the 1970s, the Supreme Court established guidelines for determining what material was "obscene" and not protected by the First Amendment. Most of the sexual material on the Internet is not illegal under this standard, but much is not appropriate for children. Groups who oppose access to sexually explicit material in general and groups concerned about access by children lobbied heavily for a law to restrict such material on the Net. Congress passed the Communications Decency Act (CDA) in 1996. This law established criminal penalties (prison terms and large fines) for transmission of "indecent" material and display of "patently offensive" material. To try to avoid conflict with the First Amendment, some parts of the law pertain specifically to material available to minors or sent to minors. The constitutionality of the CDA was immediately challenged by a group of organizations, including the American Library Association and the American Civil Liberties Union. This case was recognized as a landmark case that will have a major impact on the future of the Internet.

The controversy over the law continued for several years, before and after Congress passed it. In 1997 the Supreme Court ruled that the core provisions of the CDA were unconstitutional. The Court recognized the Internet as an extraordinarily diverse and valuable medium of communication that deserves strong First Amendment protection. Here are some of the reasons for their decision.

- The speech restricted by the CDA is protected by the First Amendment. The definitions of *indecent* and *patently offensive* in the CDA are too broad and vague. The law would probably cover valuable medical, educational, and literary material (such as AIDS information and some great works of literature). Also, the vagueness would probably discourage people from discussing, posting, or sending information on topics that they feared might be interpreted as violating the law. This would "chill" the exercise of legitimate communication protected by the First Amendment.

- Because of the nature of the Internet, it is difficult to determine whether a visitor to a site or a participant in a discussion is a child or an adult. Thus the CDA would have the effect of reducing discussion on the Net to a level suitable for children.

- There are less restrictive measures available to prevent access by children to inappropriate material. For example, parents can install software that blocks access to specific sites.

SEARCH AND SEIZURE AND FREEDOM OF THE ELECTRONIC "PRESS."   In the 1970s, the *New York Times* planned to publish the "Pentagon Papers," documents describing government policies and activities related to the war in Vietnam. The documents were given to the *Times* without authorization. The government tried unsuccessfully to obtain a court order to prevent their publication. What the government did *not* do was raid the *New York Times* offices and seize their copy of the Pentagon Papers, along with reporters' notes and files and the newspaper's printing presses. The First Amendment's guarantee of freedom of the press protected the *Times* from a government raid and from an order not to publish the documents. Seizure of its presses would have been a ludicrously unreasonable seizure.

In 1989, an electronic hacker newsletter called *Phrack* published part of a document about the 911 telephone emergency system. The document had been downloaded by a cracker who accessed a Bell South telephone company computer without authorization. It was of interest mainly for its amusingly dense concentration of bureaucratic language. The results for *Phrack* were not amusing. The Secret Service *did* raid the publisher; it seized computer equipment, software, and the list of subscribers.[5] The publisher of *Phrack* and the cracker who originally obtained the document were charged with several crimes.

What is the difference between the two cases? There are two reasons why *Phrack* was raided and its publisher prosecuted—and why journalists, civil libertarians, and the public did not react with the concern they would normally show for a threat to freedom of the press. One reason is the common view that all hackers are dangerous criminals. The other reason is that *Phrack* was not published on paper; it was distributed electronically. There was no printing "press" to be protected by the First Amendment.

---

[5]In addition to its more well-known role in protecting the President, the Secret Service is responsible for investigating some kinds of computer crime.

In the *Phrack* case, paranoia about the unknown and fear of hackers led to an embarrassment for the government, which argued that the 911 document, alleged to be valued at $79,449, was vital to the security of the 911 system. On the fourth day of the *Phrack* trial, the case was dropped. The defense showed that the document was available in a booklet sold by another telephone company for $13.

The *Phrack* raid was one of a series conducted by the Secret Service in early 1990. In several cases, government agents burst through the doors of homes with guns drawn and held families at gunpoint while gathering up the computer equipment used by their teenage children. The raids had the same style as drug raids. Using warrants that authorized a search for stolen files and other evidence of criminal activity, the government seized computer equipment, diskettes, telephones, telephone-answering machines, audio equipment and tapes, and printers. In most of the cases, charges were never filed against the people whose property was seized, but it was many months or longer before the property was returned. Probably one reason why the Secret Service agents seized everything electronic, even audio equipment, was that they did not know enough about computers to tell where data and files might be stored.

The Secret Service raids raised questions about government behavior in the investigation of possible crimes involving hackers. Some of the issues were resolved in a case brought against the government by one of the victims. Steve Jackson Games is a company that operates a computer bulletin board system (BBS) and publishes role-playing games. It was raided in 1990; the Secret Service seized computers, printers, disks, the manuscript for a book about to be published, a BBS, business records, and paper records. The government claimed that an employee of the company had a copy of the 911 document and that he put it on the company's BBS. The document was not in fact on the system, and no charges were ever filed against the company, its owner, or the employee. However, the seizure and long delay in returning the seized material caused disruption of business, financial loss, and the layoff of some employees. Although many of the raids may have violated the Fourth Amendment, which requires that the material to be seized be described in particularity, the fact that Steve Jackson Games is a publisher and BBS operator provided an especially strong basis for a court challenge. Steve Jackson Games argued that the government violated two major laws intended to implement First and Fourth Amendment protections.

The Privacy Protection Act of 1980 says that law enforcement agencies may not search for or seize materials from newspapers, broadcasters, and publishers (with a few exceptions). A court may issue an order to provide certain material, but the person or business served with such an order has an opportunity to contest it and may supply copies of the information demanded without losing the ability to function. The act was passed after a government raid on a newspaper office. It applies to anyone who is preparing information for public dissemination. The issues in the Steve Jackson Games case were whether this act applied to electronic publishers and to nontraditional kinds of publications. The judge ruled that it did. The search and seizure were illegal.

The Electronic Communications Privacy Act of 1986 (ECPA) is one of the recent laws specifically designed to make it clear that certain privacy and First Amendment protections do not depend on the technology used. Under previously existing law, the government may not read people's mail or tap telephones without court permission, which specifies the particular people whose mail or telephones are to be monitored. The ECPA extends that protection to electronic mail. The Secret Service seized the Steve Jackson Games BBS, which contained private e-mail of more than 100 people who were not suspects. The judge concluded that government agents read and destroyed some of the messages, in violation of the law.

The Steve Jackson Games case is significant for clarifying protection accorded the fast-growing area of computerized news, information, and communications systems. The Fourth Amendment says we have the right to be "secure in [our] persons, houses, papers, and effects." It mentions papers, not disks, but of course it is the content, not the medium, whose protection was intended. There are still cases where equipment (such as bulletin board systems) was not returned after a year, although no charges were filed. However, as some law enforcement officials learn more about computer systems, they are getting better at pinpointing the information they are searching for in a criminal investigation, and they are copying disks rather than carrying off all of a family's or business's electronic equipment.

Law enforcement agencies have the responsibility to investigate crime, and there is plenty of crime committed with computers. Although the case of the 911 document may have been poorly planned, researched, and executed, there are cases where computer bulletin boards are used to assist criminal activities. On some boards, people trade software (in violation of copyright), lists of stolen credit card numbers, passwords for computer systems, and information about how to break into systems; others commit fraud and access credit reports and other files without authorization. How should the need to investigate be balanced with constitutional protections? The purpose of the Bill of Rights is to protect innocent people from intrusions and abuse by the government and to provide a set of rules that will protect the guilty from unreasonable treatment. There will always be a tension between aggressive criminal investigation and protection of the rights of both innocent and guilty people.

14.6.2 MORE FREEDOM-OF-SPEECH ISSUES ON THE INTERNET

There are several interesting issues related to the Internet: how to treat potentially dangerous or offensive material, the degree of responsibility of the business or person who operates a multiuser forum, and the operator's right to control content.

Suppose an Internet discussion group or a computer bulletin board system (BBS) includes discussions of how to access computer systems without authorization. Is discussion of criminal activity itself a criminal activity, or is it protected by the First Amendment? The fundamental issues are not new to computers. Is a detailed memo about the (physical) security system in a bank evidence of a planned crime, or is it part of training for security personnel? Is a description of how to build an ammonium nitrate bomb evidence of terrorism, an example to be studied by physics students, or a useful tool for farmers? Courts usually take the view that discussion of potentially dangerous or criminal topics is protected by freedom of speech and that the government should have evidence that someone has used the information criminally or has imminent plans to do so before confiscating the material or arresting someone. This principle has not been uniformly applied in other areas. For example, in many states, possession of drug paraphernalia (devices for using illegal drugs) is illegal. It is easier to prohibit distribution or possession of certain types of information (or devices) than it is to determine what someone plans to do with them. It is easier to prove that someone has the information than to prove he or she committed a crime. Is it right for the government to take the easy way?

A related issue, though not specifically a constitutional issue, is the degree to which a system operator is responsible for the material posted on the system. If people plan a crime over the phone, telephone equipment is not seized, and a telephone company is not held responsible. If people send mail to plan a crime, Post Office officials are not held responsible, and mail-sorting equipment is not seized. Is the Internet like a telephone or mail system? Suppose a group of people are committing credit card fraud, and they use a BBS to discuss their activities and trade stolen credit card numbers. If they are using a large system like America Online, we might expect the operators of the system not to be prosecuted. On the other hand, if the BBS being used is small and most of its use is related to the credit card fraud, it seems reasonable to consider the operator of the BBS part of the criminal group, much like the driver of a getaway car for a bank robbery. How should laws be written to distinguish between these two kinds of cases? Even large companies like Prodigy and CompuServe were not immune to suits and prosecution because of member activity. Prodigy and AOL have been sued for allegedly libelous postings by members, and CompuServe was sued because members posted copyright-protected material without authorization. In Germany, CompuServe was threatened with prosecution because it allowed access to sites with material that is banned in Germany. It is important that laws be clear enough so that a person or business can tell in advance whether he or she will be subject to prosecution, or to having equipment seized by the government, for engaging in a certain activity. It is also important that such laws be narrow enough not to cause people to refrain, out of fear of prosecution, from legitimate, First Amendment–protected speech.

Does the operator of a BBS or an information service have the right to restrict the material posted on the system, or is this censorship? Usenet has a vast variety of special-interest news groups, a few of which contain material some people consider offensive (racist, sexist, or sexually explicit). Similarly, does a business or university have the right to exclude access to certain Web sites or Usenet news groups from its computers? Some universities have done so. Is this censorship or a legitimate area for private organizations to set their own policy?

The First Amendment is a restriction on the power of government, not individuals. For individuals and organizations, freedom of speech inherently includes freedom *not* to promote ideas we do not agree with. We also have property rights—that is, rights to use our property as we choose. (There are cases where courts have shrunk these rights. For example, owners of shopping centers are required to permit people to circulate petitions in the shopping center even if the owners disagree with the petition.)

Publishers are not required to publish material they consider offensive, poorly written, or unlikely to appeal to their customers for any reason. When they do publish something, there is a contract with the author specifying what editing may be done. Similar policies and contractual arrangements should be appropriate for many areas of electronic publishing. The word *publishing*, however, is changing in meaning. Is an article or a brief comment posted to an on-line discussion group a publication? Can the operator reject or edit it? Telephone companies do not control or edit the content of telephone conversations. Is a BBS or information system more like a publisher or a telephone system?

New difficulties arise where the government is the owner of a communications system or network or if it substantially subsidizes such systems. Will the government control content? When the government pays for something, it sets policy. In the 1980s, for example, federally subsidized family planning clinics were not permitted to discuss abortion. No matter how the policy changes with different presidents, the point is that the government can restrict speech if it chooses. It may be less likely to do so in a general, widely used communication system, but we cannot be sure. In the past, the government has made it illegal to send some things through the mail that were otherwise protected by the First Amendment. More recently, bills have been introduced in Congress to require public schools and libraries to block access to many Internet sites.

Observe that we have considered similarities between computer information and communications systems, on the one hand, and telephone companies, the Post Office, and publishers, on the other. One reason for some of the confusion about constitutional and legal rights and responsibilities related to computer systems is their immense flexibility. They have similarities to many different established institutions and technologies, because they can be used in so many ways. The older institutions are not all treated the same way by the law. Interesting and intricate questions remain to be resolved for some of the issues we have introduced in this section.

PRACTICE PROBLEM

Prodigy screened messages that were posted on some of its computer bulletin boards and eliminated messages that it considered offensive. Is this a violation of freedom of speech or a permissible policy for a private company to adopt? How does the concept of contract apply here?

14.7   COMMUNICATIONS ISSUES: ENCRYPTION AND WIRETAPPING

14.7.1 USES OF ENCRYPTION

For a very long time, the main users of codes, or **encryption,** were governments and their spies. Governments continually seek ways to improve their own codes and to break the codes of other governments. Now, largely as a result of the increased use of computers, there are many private-sector applications of encryption. According to Computer Professionals for Social Responsibility, encryption is "the most important technical safeguard for ensuring the privacy and

FIGURE 14.9

Uses of Encryption

- Bank records and other financial data—to protect privacy and to guard against theft of funds
- Credit card numbers—for electronic commerce
- Passwords and personal identification numbers (PINs) used for electronic funds transfers, automated teller machines, and so on
- Any sensitive data stored in databases, such as medical records
- Research and product development files—to protect trade secrets
- Sensitive business communications
- E-mail and telephone communications—to protect privacy
- Personal files on home computers
- Tests and student grade files kept by teachers

authenticity of all messages that travel along computer networks."[6] Encryption software is now widely available as a commercial product, and encryption capabilities are provided with commonly used applications such as word processors and communications. A few examples of the uses of encryption are listed in Figure 14.9.

The increasing use of encryption and the government's response have implications for privacy, international trade, and civil liberties. Government policy concerning the tapping of telephone and other electronic communications raises similar issues.

14.7.2 GOVERNMENT POLICY ON ENCRYPTION

Because of the history of the military use of encryption, the government has for many decades classified coding machines and encryption software as "munitions" subject to export control. Under these controls, the government has permitted the export of only encryption software that is fairly weak and easy for government agencies to break. Now, when encryption has so many peaceful, privacy- and security-enhancing applications, the export restrictions have become the focus of controversy. Those who oppose these export restrictions make two main arguments. One is that the export restrictions are ineffective at stopping the spread of strong encryption in other countries but are economically harmful to U.S. firms. The other is that the export restrictions have the side effect of reducing the availability of strong encryption to people within the United States. For example, because of the easy international access to the Internet, the government has interpreted publication of encryption software on the Internet

---

[6]Authenticity is protected because encrypted data cannot be easily modified by someone who does not know the encryption key. Also, the technique known as public key cryptography provides verifiable "signatures."

as a violation of the export rules, a position that interferes with development, discussion, and use of such software within the United States.

The export restrictions have significant economic effects. Computer and communications systems, devices, and software sold in the United States with high-quality built-in encryption cannot be sold to customers in other countries. This means that U.S. manufacturers must go to the extra expense of making two versions of each product (one for the domestic market and one for export), or sell the weaker versions in the United States as well, or give up their export business. The better encryption schemes are available in other countries, and the algorithms appear in technical publications available around the world. Thus U.S. products produced for export are less competitive than those of foreign competitors who use the better encryption techniques. (One data security expert reported that a $100 million contract for financial computer terminals went to a European company after U.S. companies were prohibited by the government from exporting a truly secure system.)

Some observers have long suspected that the intent of the export restrictions was not simply to keep unbreakable encryption schemes from enemy governments but also to keep them from U.S. citizens. Recent events support this view. The government has taken explicit steps to try to ensure its access to the files and communications of U.S. citizens and businesses. It tried to restrict publication of research in cryptography. It pressured the industry to adopt as an encryption standard a scheme that experts consider much too easy to break. In 1991 the FBI proposed that all encryption schemes used in electronic communications be designed so that the government can obtain the plain text (decoded version) of any messages and data. (One critic compared this to requiring building contractors to provide the government with master keys for all buildings in the country.) In 1993 the government introduced an encryption scheme for communications systems, developed by the National Security Agency and widely known as the Clipper Chip. The central (and the controversial) aspect of the Clipper Chip was that the government holds the keys for the codes used in the chips and thus would be able to intercept and decode communications. Each of two government "escrow" agencies holds half of every key, so no one agency could use the keys secretly. The escrow agencies are not permitted to release the keys to other government agencies without a court order. The Clipper Chip was heavily criticized by the computer industry, by organizations such as the Electronic Frontier Foundation and Computer Professionals for Social Responsibility, by privacy advocates, and by civil libertarians. Objections included economic and technical arguments as well as issues of privacy, security, and potential abuse by government.

After promotion of the Clipper Chip faded because of technical problems and public and industry opposition, the government continued to restrict the export of strong encryption and has developed several proposals to regulate the use of encryption within the United States. The goal is to ensure that law enforcement agents can obtain the encryption key needed to decode any encrypted communication. (The proposals include the provision that law enforcement agencies must have a court order to obtain someone's encryption keys.) The main argument for these proposals is that the government needs to be able to decode communications of drug dealers, terrorists, and other criminals.

In a more flexible version of "key escrow encryption," the government would allow any encryption scheme to be used, but the keys would be kept by "escrow agents" so that they would be available to law enforcement agencies. This plan also met with heavy opposition because of potential security breaches and potential abuse by government. Currently, the government is proposing "key recovery," rather than key escrow. The idea here is that encryption schemes would provide some mechanism for keys to be recovered, but the keys would not be provided in advance. To encourage software companies to set up key recovery schemes, the government announced that it will allow the export of software with strong encryption if a key recovery mechanism is provided.

Members of Congress have introduced bills to establish encryption policies of each extreme. One bill would severely restrict use of strong encryption in the United States unless the government is provided with access to the keys in advance; another would establish the right to use encryption without providing for government access to one's messages in advance. At this writing, none of the bills has passed. The controversy about the conflict between private and secure communications on the one hand, and access by the government on the other, continues.

14.7.3 THE WIRETAPPING LAW

The government cannot decode a message if it does not have the message in the first place. It uses wiretaps to intercept and record communications. Federal law prohibits wiretapping of voice communications without a court order. The Electronic Communications Privacy Act of 1986 extends similar protection to electronic communication, such as electronic mail. Tapping voice and electronic communication, with a court order, is an important part of some criminal investigations. For many years, the law required that the communications industry cooperate with lawful wiretap requests from law enforcement agencies, and the industry has generally done so. The government used its own sophisticated equipment and generally paid most of the cost of the operation. According to the FBI, advances in communications technology, such as the use of optical fiber, began making it more difficult to intercept communications, thus necessitating a new law.

The Communications Assistance for Law Enforcement Act (CALEA), passed in 1994 after two years of controversy, *requires* that telecommunications equipment be designed so that government agencies can tap it. The government may impose fines of $10,000 a day for communications equipment that does not meet its requirements. CALEA requires that the government be able to tap communications from a remote government location in real time. It also requires the ability to tap mobile users—for example, people using portable phones or portable computers.

The wiretap law, like the encryption controversy, raises issues of economics and security of communications. Estimates of the cost of modifying equipment and software to meet the government requirements range from $500 million to several billion dollars. In the 1990s, federal and state courts authorized a little more than one thousand wiretaps per year (most of them for suspected drug offenses). Critics of CALEA point out that the FBI had several million dollars

PRACTICE PROBLEM

It is legal for someone to encrypt a message and send it through the mail. Do you think the laws concerning encryption should be the same for mail sent through the Post Office and mail sent electronically? What should the laws say?

budgeted for upgrading its equipment. They argue that with continuing cooperation from industry, law enforcement agencies should be able to work out ways to carry out their relatively small number of lawful taps without such extraordinary control of technology and without such high cost. The additional expense and the resulting reduced security and privacy would make U.S. communications products less competitive in other countries. The federal government's General Services Administration emphasized security problems in a report before CALEA passed, saying, "the proposed legislation would assist eavesdropping by law enforcement, but it would make it easier for criminals, terrorists, foreign intelligence (spies) and computer hackers to electronically penetrate the public network and pry into areas previously not open to snooping."

We have mentioned some of the practical (economic and security) issues related to CALEA and have noted proposals for access by law enforcement agencies to keys for encrypted messages. Next we ask more fundamental questions.

14.7.4 THE FUNDAMENTAL QUESTIONS

Aside from the practical arguments, the issues discussed in this section raise questions about the fundamental relationship between the people and the government: How much should the freedom and privacy of honest and peaceful people be weakened to aid the government's law enforcement activities? How far can we trust the government not to abuse its power? Are we obligated to make it easy for the government to spy on us, or do we have a right to use the best technology available to improve the speed, convenience, cost, and privacy of communications (or any other endeavor)? Should the government have the authority to ban or restrict a technology because it makes government surveillance more difficult?

EXERCISES

1. During the next week, keep a list of every time you use a computer or device containing a microprocessor. (Include such things as a microwave oven and the computer scanning system at your supermarket check-out counter.)

2. The federal government gives the Malcolm Baldrige National Quality Award to businesses that make significant efforts to improve quality. A newspaper report disclosed that finalists for the award are subjected to intense investigation without their knowl-

edge. The investigators search files of the police, FBI, IRS, and other government agencies. The purpose is to make sure that the winner selected is a good role model. Do you think this use of government files is proper? Give your reasons.

3. Some IRS employees are authorized to obtain credit reports from credit bureaus (for official use by the agency). The IRS found that its employees were illegally accessing other people's credit reports for their own purposes at a 5% rate. Suggest some procedural measures to reduce this problem. Suggest appropriate penalties for violations.

4. In many states, voter registration records show the political party to which each registrant belongs and the elections in which he or she voted. Should such records be public? Explain your reasoning. Try to identify the principles behind your decision; then think of another example of government records where you can apply the same principles.

5. Find out what policy your university has about releasing the names, addresses, and telephone numbers of students.

6. If you have a credit card and still have the multipage booklet full of small type that describes the credit card agreement, read it and describe the provisions concerning use of the information that the credit card company collects about you.

7. What policy concerning openness or confidentiality do you think is appropriate for motor vehicle records (driver's licenses, vehicle registration, ticket and accident records)? Give your reasons. If you chose a policy where records are not released without the driver's consent, consider the following case. A car sideswipes a parked car and does not stop. The owner of the damaged car has the license plate number of the other driver. She could report the number to the police, but if the damage was small, they might not consider it serious enough to pursue. The owner might be willing to take the driver to Small Claims Court if she could locate him. Is this a good argument for making motor vehicle records open to the public? Is it a weakness in a permission-only policy that you would be willing to accept?

8. Suppose you start a business renting computers to students at your college. In your files you have the following information about each customer: name, address, phone number, credit card number or

bank account number, driver's license number, history of rental payments, and type of communications software package the customer uses. Develop a privacy policy for your business. Consider the different categories of information, and tell under what circumstances you would release each type of information to someone else.

9. When a driver uses valet parking at a theater or restaurant, he or she gives the car keys to the valet. The key ring may contain house keys as well. What is the implicit contract between the driver and the parking company? What may the valet use the keys for? What are some impermissible uses? Describe an example where we provide information for a computerized database that is analogous to the valet parking situation.

10. Be an informed consumer: Write or call the customer service department of a business or organization that has a computerized database containing information about you and ask what their policy is on selling the information to other businesses or organizations. Ask whether it would release information to a government agency that made an informal request or would not release information unless the agency had a subpoena.

11. Current telephone technology makes it possible for the phone number of a person placing a call to be displayed on the telephone of the recipient of the call. This is commonly called Caller ID.

    a. Is this a protection of privacy for the recipient of the call? Or is it a violation of privacy for the caller?

    b. What policy do you think the telephone companies should have concerning Caller ID? Mention any practical problems that this policy might cause.

    c. Different states have passed laws specifying different policies for Caller ID. What do you think the law should say about it? Give your reasons.

12. If you use a check-cashing card or membership card in a supermarket, the store may have a database containing a record of your purchases. Do you think there should be laws about what the store can and what it cannot do with this information? If so, what should the laws say?

13. Suppose you join a nontraditional religious organization. Would you personally mind if it sold its

membership list to other organizations? What policy do you think the organization should have concerning the list? Do you think there should be a law regulating the distribution of the list?

14. A discount department store chain asked customers who used a charge card for their address and phone number. This is now illegal in at least one state. What are some reasons why the store might ask for such information? What do you think is the purpose of the law making it illegal to do so? Do you think there should be such a law? Why?

15. Many cities have companies that help landlords screen potential tenants. Information about pending eviction actions is a matter of public record, available to anyone who wants to look it up. However, one state has a law prohibiting tenant-screening companies from reporting pending eviction actions to landlords. Give some arguments for and against this law. Do you think there should be such a law? Why?

16. In Section 14.3.6 we listed four factors relevant to policies for collection, release, and distribution of personal data: how the data were obtained, the specific kind of information, the nature of the prospective users, and the projected uses of the data. How much weight do you think each factor should have in determining privacy policies within a private company? How much weight do you think each factor should have in determining privacy laws?

17. Find the text of one of the following laws. Read it and write a summary. Also find out whether there have been amendments to it.
    a. The Privacy Protection Act of 1980
    b. The Bank Secrecy Act and the Financial Privacy Act
    c. The Fair Credit Reporting Act (1970)

18. A search warrant is not required, in some cases, to search the home of a person convicted of a crime and currently on probation. The San Francisco police searched a man's apartment without a warrant; their computer indicated that he was on probation. It turned out that the man was on parole, and a search warrant was required. Give several possible causes of the error.

19. Make a list of any computer errors you remember hearing about (of the sort described in the sections on major failures and inconveniences). For each one, explain whether you think the cause was poor specifications, design error, programming error, input error, an error in interpreting the results, or some other factor.

20. During the remainder of this course, keep a newspaper and magazine clipping file in which you collect articles about computer errors. Classify them as in the previous exercise. To keep from getting discouraged, keep another clipping file in which you collect articles about beneficial uses of computers.

21. Many records stored on computers include a date, and many older software systems use two digits to represent the year (such as 78 or 95). Pick any two applications (such as billing for telephones or driver's license renewal) and describe problems that might occur in the year 2000.

22. We suggested that different people and institutions would consider different factors when deciding whether to require physical crash testing of cars. Which group do you think would rely most heavily on technical information about the quality of the computer simulation programs: customers, car manufacturers, companies that insure the manufacturers, legal scholars, or legislators?

23. Many people concerned about global warming advocate extensive and expensive programs to cut greenhouse gas emissions. One of the authors of the report by the Intergovernmental Panel on Climate Change was asked whether the temperature data from the past hundred years, showing little warming so far, would reduce demands for emission-cutting programs. He replied, "The data don't matter. We're not basing our recommendations upon the data; we're basing them upon the GCM climate models." Do you think his confidence in the computer models is justified? Give your reasons.

24. Suppose three companies make a similar product. One does physical tests to check the safety of the product. One uses only computer simulations. The third will not disclose what testing methods it uses. Suppose you are on a jury for a case where someone is suing one of the companies because of an injury received from the product.
    a. Would your decision about awarding money to the plaintiff be affected by the company's policy

about testing? If so, how? If not, what factors are more important to you?

b. Suppose reliable data show that the injury rate for the product is almost identical for all three companies. Given that additional information, would your decision be affected by the company's testing policy?

25. Suppose you have the following data:

The number of tons in the known reserves of an important natural resource like, say, copper

The average amount of the resource used per person (worldwide) per year

The total population of the world

a. Write a program (using any programming language or tool) to determine in how many years the resource will run out. The program's input should be the three data described above.

b. One obvious flaw in the program is that it assumes the population is constant. Include the rate of population increase per year as another input.

c. Suppose your program is correct and the input data are reliable. List all the reasons you can think of why this program is really not a good predictor of when we will run out of the resource.

d. In 1972, a group called the Club of Rome received a lot of attention when it published a study using computer models that implied that the world would run out of several important natural resources in the 1980s. Today, many of those resources are cheaper than they were then, which indicates that they are now *less* scarce. Why do you think so many people accepted the predictions in the study?

26. Which of the following models do you think produce very accurate results? Which do you think are less reliable? What do you think are some reasons for weaknesses in the weaker models?

Models that predict the position of the moon
Models that predict employment in a particular sector of the economy

Models that predict the effects of a housing development on bird population in the area

27. Suppose a newspaper reports that a computer analysis predicts a certain increase (or decrease) in the number of new AIDS cases over the next 10 years. Would you accept the prediction because "a computer said so"? If not, what are some questions you would ask to decide how reliable the prediction is?

28. Suppose someone steals a credit card and uses it to buy $500 worth of goods. The thief is not caught. Who should be liable for the $500: the card owner, the merchant, or the credit card company? Consider the following factors: Did the card owner report the theft? Did the merchant check the signature or call the card company to check whether the card was stolen? What does the contract between the customer and the card company say? What does the contract between the merchant and the card company say? Suppose the thief is caught and convicted. What do you think is an appropriate penalty?

29. Get a copy of the 1986 Computer Fraud and Abuse Act. Write a summary of the provisions about accessing computer systems without authorization.

30. Write up a policy you would like your university to adopt concerning students who crack campus computers and log on to accounts that belong to other students.

31. Survey at least 10 friends or fellow students who have personal computers. Find out how many have ever had a virus on their computer, how much damage it did, and how they removed it.

32. Write out your answers to the questions asked about encryption and wiretapping in Section 14.7.4.

33. Read the ACM Code of Ethics and Professional Conduct, written for computer professionals. Write a summary of its main points. (The code appears in *Communications of the ACM*, February 1993.)

FOR FURTHER READING

This book expands on the topics in this chapter and covers many other topics as well, including the impact of electronic media on copyright, the impact of computers on work and employment, a variety of social issues, and the ethical issues surrounding the design, implementation, and use of computers.

Baase, S. *A Gift of Fire: Social, Legal, and Ethical Issues in Computing.* Englewood Cliffs, NJ: Prentice-Hall, 1997.

Covers many areas of privacy related to personal information.

Branscomb, A.W. *Who Owns Information?* New York: Basic Books, 1994.

A collection of articles on hacker activities and Internet security.

Denning, D. E., and Denning, P. J., eds. *Internet Besieged: Countering Cyberspace Scofflaws.* Reading, MA: Addison-Wesley, 1998.

A fictional scenario in which a robot kills a worker. Examines numerous professional, ethical, and legal issues using (fictional) newspaper articles, trial transcripts, and so forth.

Epstein, R. *The Case of the Killer Robot.* New York: Wiley, 1996.

A collection of articles that includes different points of view on many topics.

Ermann, M. D. ; Williams, M. B.; and Shauf, M. S., eds. *Computers, Ethics, and Society,* 2nd ed. New York: Oxford University Press, 1997.

A collection of articles on many issues in this chapter and more.

Johnson, D. G., and Nissenbaum, H., eds. *Computers, Ethics & Social Values.* Englewood Cliffs, NJ: Prentice-Hall, 1995.

An advanced text on software safety by one of the best people in the field. Includes case studies.

Leveson, N. G. *Safeware: System Safety and the Computer Age.* Reading, MA: Addison-Wesley, 1995.

Neumann is the founder and moderator of the comp.risks forum on Usenet. He has spent many years collecting information on cases of computer failure and studying their causes.

Neumann, P. G. *Computer-Related Risks.* Reading, MA: Addison-Wesley, 1995.

A study of good and bad user interfaces on many everyday devices and appliances. Norman emphasizes that machines should be designed for the human user; people should not have to adapt to the machine's way of doing things. (See also Norman's comments on page 619.)

Norman, D. *The Psychology of Everyday Things.* New York: Basic Books, 1988.

An in-depth report by a committee of government, industry, and academic experts on the importance of encryption, with recommendations for government policy.

National Research Council. *Cryptography's Role in Securing the Information Society.* Washington, DC: National Academy Press, 1996.

14.8   SUMMARY OF LEVEL 6

In this last and highest level of abstraction in our study of computer science, we have looked at some of the important issues that arise from the impact of computers on social institutions. It is virtually impossible now to live a week without using computers, even for a person who knows nothing about them. Computers are in wristwatches, cars, washing machines, radios, and numerous other appliances. Computers let us accomplish our tasks more easily, more accurately, and more efficiently. With them, scientists can do research that was impossible before. We can save lives and make our own lives more enjoyable.

We have seen that problems such as fraud, embezzlement, and invasion of privacy existed before computers, but computer technology makes possible new variations on these old problems. Government and private databases contain numerous details of our personal lives. The ability to collect, analyze, search, store, and distribute huge quantities of data brings us new and improved services. But it also makes new privacy violations possible and old ones easier. Good solutions for privacy abuses will allow for diversity, reflecting the fact that people do not value privacy equally.

Millions of dollars of financial transactions flow through telecommunications lines each day. This means an economy can run more efficiently, but it also means new openings for thieves. Computer "pranks" such as unleashing viruses and cracking systems can cause financial losses and serious disruption of important work. Cracking systems in safety-critical applications, such as medical systems, can endanger people's lives. It is reasonable to treat such behavior as criminal.

Many issues that we discussed—such as privacy, encryption of communications, and law enforcement—raise questions about the relationship between ordinary people and the government. How shall we apply freedom of the press, freedom of speech, and freedom from unreasonable search and seizure to electronic media? More than two hundred years ago, these protections were written into the Bill of Rights because the intellectual leaders of the American Revolution considered it wise to be suspicious of government power. As the capabilities of surveillance tools and the size of government databases grow, how can we protect our freedoms from abuse of that power while preventing high-tech crime and catching criminals?

Complex software often contains errors. Even relatively simple software may be poorly designed, poorly tested, and unreliable. Errors range from the minor and rather humorous to those that inflict major inconvenience or disruption of lives and those that may cause injury and death. Computer professionals must take responsibility for the quality of their work. Legal scholars must hammer out principles of liability to guide decisions when something goes wrong.

We should all try to develop a realistic understanding of the capabilities of computers. They bring us great benefits, but they cannot substitute for good science and good judgment. They cannot make reliable predictions about phenomena that we do not yet understand well. And they cannot answer ethical questions for us.

CHAPTER 2

Section 2.2.2

1.

Step	Operation
1	Get values for x, y, and z
2	Set the value of *average* to $(x + y + z)/3$
3	Print out the value of *average*
4	Stop

2.

Step	Operation
1	Get a value for r, the radius of the circle
2	Set the value of *circumference* to $2 * \pi * r$
3	Set the value of *area* to $\pi * r^2$
4	Print out the values of *circumference* and *area*
5	Stop

3.

Step	Operation
1	Get values for the amount of electricity used and the cost per kilowatt-hour
2	Set the value of *cost* to the amount of electricity used times the cost in kilowatt-hours
3	Set the value of *tax* to $0.08 * cost$
4	Set the total amount of the bill to $cost + tax$
5	Print out the total amount of the bill
6	Stop

Section 2.2.3

1. If $x \geq 0$ then

   Set the value of y to 1

   Else

   Set the value of y to 2

2. Get values for x, y, and z

   If $x > 0$ then

   Set the value of *average* to $(x + y + z)/3$

   Print out the value of *average*

   Else

   Print out the message 'Bad Data'

   Stop

3. Repeat until $x = 999$

   Get a value for x

   Set the value of a to x^2

   Set the value of b to $sin(x)$

   Set the value of c to $1/x$

   Print out the values of a, b, and c

   End of the loop

   Stop

Section 2.3.2

You must change the operation on line 7 from a greater than (>) to a less than (<). That line will now read as follows:

If $A_i < $ *largest so far* then ...

That is the only required change. However, to avoid confusion about what the algorithm is doing, you probably should also change the name of the variable *largest so far* to something like *smallest so far* on lines 3, 7, 8, and 12. Otherwise, a casual reading of the algorithm might lead someone to think incorrectly that it is still an algorithm to find the largest value rather than the smallest.

Section 2.3.3

1.

   a. NAME = Adams

i	operation	Found
1	Compare Adams to N_1, Smith. No match	No
2	Compare Adams to N_2, Jones. No match	No
3	Compare Adams to N_3, Adams. Match	Yes

Output = 921-5281

b. NAME = Schneider

i	operation	Found
1	Compare Schneider to N_1, Smith. No match	No
2	Compare Schneider to N_2, Jones. No match	No
3	Compare Schneider to N_3, Adams. No match	No
4	Compare Schneider to N_4, Doe. No match	No

Output = Sorry, but the name is not in the directory.

2. $n = 7$ $A = 22, 18, 23, 17, 25, 30, 2$

Largest So Far	Location	i	Operation
22	1	2	Computer A_2 and *largest so far*. Is 18 > 22. No
22	1	3	Compare A_3 and *largest so far*. Is 23 > 22. Yes, so reset values
23	3	4	Compare A_4 and *largest so far*. Is 17 > 23. No
23	3	5	Compare A_5 and *largest so far*. Is 25 > 23. Yes, so reset values
25	5	6	Compare A_6 and *largest so far*. Is 30 > 25. Yes, so reset values
30	6	7	Compare A_7 and *largest so far*. Is 2 > 30. No.

Output: Largest = 30. Location = 6.

3. Pattern = an $m = 2$. The pattern has 2 characters.

   Text   = A man and a woman $n = 17$. The text has 17 characters.

k	i	Mismatch	Operation
1	1	No	Compare P_1, the "*a*", to T_1, the "*A*." No match.
		Yes	End of the check for a match at position 1 of the text.
2	1	No	Compare P_1, the "*a*", to T_2, the blank. No match.
		Yes	End of the check for a match at position 2 of the text.
3	1	No	Compare P_1, the "*a*", to T_3, the "*m*." No match.
		Yes	End of the check for a match at position 3 of the text.
4	1	No	Compare P_1, the "*a*", to T_4, the "*a*." Match.

| 4 | 2 | No | Compare P_2, the "n", to T_5, the "n." Match. |
| 4 | 3 | No | i (3) is greater than m (2), so we exit the loop. |

Output: There is a match at position 4

In a similar way, the program will produce the following two additional lines of output:

There is a match at position 7

There is a match at position 16

CHAPTER 3

Section 3.2

The numbers from 1 to n, where n is even, can be grouped into $n/2$ pairs of the form

$1 + n = n + 1$

$2 + (n - 1) = n + 1$

.

.

.

$n/2 + (n/2 + 1) = n + 1$

giving a sum of $(n/2)(n + 1)$. This formula gives the correct sum for all cases shown, whether n is even or odd.

Section 3.3

1. *legit* = 3

2	4	1	1

2.

2	0	4	1

2	4	1

3. *legit* = 3

2	1	4	1

4. For example,

1	2	0	0

Section 3.4

1.

n	Best Case	Worst Case	Average Case
10	1	10	5
50	1	50	25
100	1	100	50
1000	1	1000	500
10,000	1	10,000	5,000
100,000	1	100,000	50,000

2. The basic shape of the curve as n gets large is still n^2 because as n gets large, the n^2 term dominates the other two terms.

Section 3.5

1. a. 4, 8, 2, 6
    4, 6, 2, 8
    4, 2, 6, 8
    2, 4, 6, 8
   b. 12, 3, 6, 8, 2, 5, 7
    7, 3, 6, 8, 2, 5, 12
    7, 3, 6, 5, 2, 8, 12
    2, 3, 6, 5, 7, 8, 12
    2, 3, 5, 6, 7, 8, 12
   c. D, B, G, F, A, C, E
    D, B, E, F, A, C, G
    D, B, E, C, A, F, G
    D, B, A, C, E, F, G
    C, B, A, D, E, F, G
    A, B, C, D, E, F, G

2. Devi, Nathan, Grant

3. Pattern = AAAB; Text = AAAAAAAAA; $m = 4$; $n = 9$; $m \times n = 36$; the exact number of comparisons is $4 \times 6 = 24$.

Section 3.6

1. 38 paths:

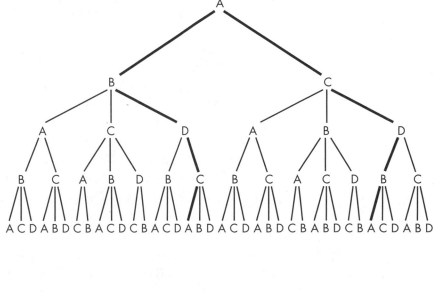

2.

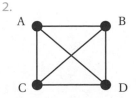

CHAPTER 4

Section 4.2.1

1.

    a. $10101000 = (1 \times 2^3) + (1 \times 2^5) + (1 \times 2^7)$

                      $= 8 + 32 + 128$

                      $= 168$ as an unsigned integer value

    b. $10101000 = (1 \times 2^3) + (1 \times 2^5)$

                      $= 8 + 32$

                      $= 40$

This is the value of the magnitude portion of the number. The leftmost bit represents the sign bit. In this example it is a 1, which is a negative sign.

                $= -40$ as a signed integer value

2. To answer this question, you need to represent the decimal value as a sum of powers of 2 and then convert that representation to binary.

          $99 = 64 + 32 + 2 + 1$

              $= 2^6 + 2^5 + 2^1 + 2^0$

              $= 1100011$

However, this is only 7 bits and we need 8, so we must add one leading 0 to fill out the answer.

              $= 01100011$

3. The 10 bits would be represented as 9 bits for the magnitude and the leftmost bit for the sign. To represent the magnitude, we must rewrite 300 as the sum of powers of 2, as we did in the previous question.

   $300 = 256 + 32 + 8 + 4$

      $= 2^8 + 2^5 + 2^3 + 2^2$

      $= 100101100$ in 9 bits

To make it a negative value, we must add a 1 bit (the negative sign) to the leftmost position of the number.

   $-300 = 1100101100$

     $254 = 128 + 64 + 32 + 16 + 8 + 4 + 2$

        $= 2^7 + 2^6 + 2^5 + 2^4 + 2^3 + 2^2 + 2^1$

        $= 011111110$ to 9 bits of accuracy for the magnitude

To make it a +254, we must add a 0 (the + sign) to the leftmost position of the number.

   $+254 = 0011111110$

4. To see what this value would look like, we first look up the letters "A," "B," and "C" in the ASCII conversion table to see what their internal representation is in decimal.

   "A" $= 65$

   "B" $= 66$

   "C" $= 67$

We then convert these decimal values to unsigned 8-bit binary values.

"A" = 65 = 01000001
"B" = 66 = 01000010
"C" = 67 = 01000011

The internal representation of the three-character string 'ABC' is formed by putting together all three of the preceding values, producing the following 24-bit string:

010000010100001001000011

which is how a computer stores 'ABC'.

5. a. $+0.25 = 0.01$ in binary
$= +0.1 \times 2^{-1}$ in scientific notation

so the mantissa is $+0.1$ and the exponent is -1

$= \underbrace{0\ 100000000}_{\text{mantissa}} \quad \underbrace{1\ 00001}_{\text{exponent}}$

b. $-32\frac{1}{16} = -100000.0001$
$= -0.1000000001 \times 2^6$
$= \underbrace{1\ 100000000}_{\text{mantissa}}\ \underbrace{0\ 00110}_{\text{exponent}}$

Note that the last 1 in the mantissa was not stored because there was not enough room. The loss of accuracy that results from limiting the number of digits available is called *truncation error*.

Section 4.3.1

1.

a. $(x = 1)$ AND $(y = 3)$
True AND False
False.   The final answer is False.

b. $(x < y)$ OR $(x > 1)$
True OR False
True   The final answer is True.

c. NOT $[(x - 1)$ AND $(y = 2)]$
NOT [True AND True]
NOT [True]
False   The final answer is False.

2. $(x = 5)$ AND $(y = 11)$ OR $([x + y] = z)$
True AND False OR True

We now must make an assumption about which of the two logical operations to do first, the AND or the OR. If we assume the AND goes first, then we get

False OR True
True

If we assume that the OR goes first, then the expression would be evaluated as follows:

True AND True
True

In this case the answer is the same, but we arrive at the answer in different ways.

Section 4.4.2

1. The four separate cases are

$$\bar{a} \cdot \bar{b} \cdot \bar{c} \qquad \bar{a} \cdot b \cdot \bar{c} \qquad \bar{a} \cdot b \cdot c \qquad a \cdot b \cdot \bar{c}$$

Combining them by using the OR operator produces the following Boolean expression:

$$\bar{a} \cdot \bar{b} \cdot \bar{c} + \bar{a} \cdot b \cdot \bar{c} + \bar{a} \cdot b \cdot c + a \cdot b \cdot \bar{c}$$

When this Boolean expression is represented as a Boolean diagram, it appears as follows:

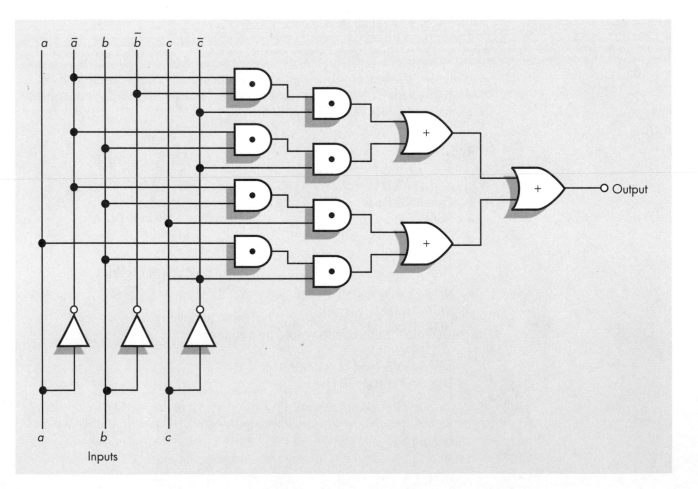

2. The Boolean expressions for the two cases are

$\bar{a} \cdot b$

$a \cdot \bar{b}$

Combining these two by using the OR operator produces

$\bar{a} \cdot b + a \cdot \bar{b}$

Pictorially, the corresponding circuit diagram is

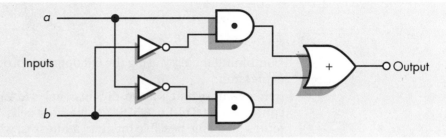

3. The Boolean expression for this is

$\bar{a} \cdot \bar{b} \cdot \bar{c} + a \cdot b \cdot c$

Pictorially, the corresponding circuit diagram is

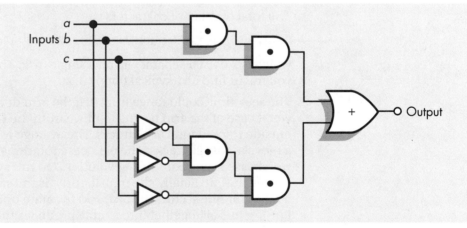

Section 4.4.3

Bit-compare $a > b$, where both a and b are one bit in length. The truth table for this circuit would be as follows:

a	b	Output	
0	0	0	
0	1	0	
1	0	1	(because a is greater than b)
1	1	0	

There is only one case where there is a 1 bit in the output. It is in the third row and corresponds to the following Boolean expression:

$a \cdot \bar{b}$

We can skip step 3 because with only one case, there is no combining of Boolean expressions. Thus the circuit diagram for this circuit is

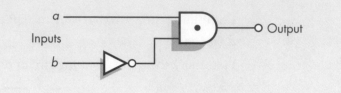

CHAPTER 5

Section 5.2.1

1. If the memory unit is a two-dimensional grid 1,024 (2^{10}) by 1,024 (2^{10}), then it contains a total of 1,048,576 (2^{20}) memory cells. We need a total of 20 bits to represent all the possible memory addresses, which range from 0 to $2^{20} - 1$.

2. Because there are $2^{10} = 1,024$ row and column lines, we would need to send 10 (of the 20) bits in the MAR to the row decoder and 10 bits to the column decoder.

Section 5.2.2

1. The total number of characters is

2 surfaces/disk × 50 tracks/surface × 20 sectors/track × 1,024 ch/sector

which is 2,048,000 characters on a single disk. This is approximately what you might find on a typical floppy disk.

2. The seek time could range from 0, if the arm does not need to move, to a worst case of the arm having to move from the far inside track to the far outside track, a total of 49 tracks. The average as stated in the problem is a move across 20 tracks. The best-case rotational delay is 0, whereas the worst case is one complete revolution. On the average we will wait about ½ a revolution. Finally, the transfer time is the same in all cases, the time it takes for one sector (½₀ of a track) to rotate under the read/write head. Putting this all together into a table produces the following values:

	Best Case	Average Case	Worst Case
Seek time	0.0 msec	20*0.4 = 8.0 msec	49*0.4 = 19.6 msec
Latency	0.0	0.5 rev = 12.5	1 rev = 25.0
Transfer	1.25	1.25	1.25
Total	1.25	21.75	45.85

21.75 milliseconds is a fairly typical access time for a floppy disk.

Section 5.2.4

Assuming that *a* is memory location 100
b is memory location 101
c is memory location 102
d is memory location 103

a.

Memory Location	Op Code	Address Field	Comment
50	LOAD	101	Register R contains the value b
51	ADD	102	R now contains the sum b + c
52	ADD	103	R now contains the sum b + c + d
53	STORE	100	And we store that sum into a

There are many other possible solutions to this and the following problems, depending on which instructions you choose to use. This solution uses the one-address format. The two- and three-address formats will lead to different sequences.

b.

Memory Location	Op Code	Address Field	Comment
50	COMPARE	100, 101	Compare the values of A and B
51	JUMPNEQ	54	If they are not equal go to address 54
52	LOAD	103	Otherwise load R with the value D
53	STORE	102	And store it into C
54			The next instruction begins here

c.

Memory Location	Op Code	Address Field	Comment
50	COMPARE	100, 101	Compare A and B and set condition codes
51	JUMPGT	55	Jump to address 55 if A > B
52	LOAD	103	Load R with the value of D
53	STORE	102	And store it into C
54	JUMP	58	Jump to address 58
55	LOAD	103	Load R with the value D
56	ADD	103	R now contains 2D
57	STORE	102	And store that result into C
58			The next instruction begins here

d.

Memory Location	Op Code	Address Field	Comment
50	LOAD	103	R contains the value D
51	STORE	100	And store it into A
52	LOAD	100	R now contains the value A
53	ADD	101	R now contains the value A + B
54	STORE	100	And store that sum into A
55	COMPARE	100, 102	Compare A and C, set condition codes
56	JUMPLE	52	Jump back and do the loop again if A ≤ C
57			The next instruction begins here

As with part (a), there are many different solutions to parts (b), (c), and (d), depending on which instructions you choose to use.

CHAPTER 6

Section 6.3.1

1. Initial values $R = 20$ memory location $80 = 43$
memory location $81 = 97$

Operation	Final Contents of Register R	Final Contents of Mem Loc 80	Final Contents of Mem Loc 81
a. LOAD 80	43	43	97
b. STORE 81	20	43	20
c. COMPARE 80	20	43	97
		(and the GT indicator goes ON)	
d. ADD 81	117	43	97
e. IN 80	20	Whatever value is entered by the user	97
f. OUT 81	20	43	97

2. Initial value   memory location $50 = 4$

Operation	Final Contents of Register R
a. LOAD 50	4
b. LOAD 4	A copy of the contents of memory cell 4.
c. LOAD L	Because *L* is equivalent to 50, this operation is equivalent to LOAD 50, which is the same as part (a).
d. LOAD L + 1	A copy of the contents of memory cell 51. This operation means LOAD ($L + 1$), which is equivalent to LOAD 51. LOAD $L + 1$ does arithmetic on addresses, not contents.

Section 6.3.2

1.
   a.   INCREMENT X

                     .

                     .

                     .

        X: .DATA   0

   Another way to do the same thing is

                     LOAD   X

```
            ADD       ONE
            STORE     X
            .
            .
            .
ONE:        .DATA     1
X:          .DATA     0
```

However, the first way is much more efficient. It takes two fewer instructions and one fewer DATA pseudo-op.

b.
```
            LOAD      X
            ADD       FIFTY
            STORE     X
            .
            .
            .
FIFTY:      .DATA     50
X:          .DATA     0
```

c.
```
            LOAD      Y          --R holds a copy of contents of mem loc Y
            ADD       Z          --R now holds sum of CON(Y) + CON(Z)
            SUBTRACT  TWO        --R now holds CON(Y) + CON (Z) − 2
            STORE     X
            .
            .
            .
X:          .DATA     0
Y:          .DATA     0
Z:          .DATA     0
TWO:        .DATA     2
```

d.
```
            LOAD      FIFTY      --R holds the constant 50
            COMPARE   X
            JUMPGT    THEN       --if X > 50 go to label THEN
            IN        X          --input a new value
```

		JUMP	DONE	--and jump to done because we are all finished
	THEN:	OUT	X	
	DONE:			--the next statement starts here

.

.

.

| | X: | .DATA | 0 | |
| | FIFTY: | .DATA | 50 | |

2.		.BEGIN		
	LOOP:	IN	NUMBER	
		LOAD	ZERO	
		COMPARE	NUMBER	--see whether number > 0
		JUMPLT	DONE	--the number is negative so go to done
		INCREMENT	COUNT	--It is positive so increment count
		JUMP	LOOP	--and repeat the loop
	DONE:	OUT	COUNT	--print out the final count
		HALT		
	COUNT:	.DATA	0	--count of number of positive values
	ZERO:	.DATA	0	--the constant 0 used for comparison
	NUMBER:	.DATA	0	--place to store the input value
		.END		

Section 6.3.3

1.		.BEGIN		
		CLEAR	NEGCOUNT	--Step 1. Not really necessary because
				--negcount is already set to 0
		LOAD	ONE	--Step 2. Set i to 1. Also not really
		STORE	I	--necessary because I is initialized to 1
	LOOP:	LOAD	FIFTY	--Step 3. Check whether $i > 50$, and if so
				--terminate the loop
		COMPARE	I	
		JUMPGT	ENDLOOP	

```
              IN          N              --Step 4. Read a value

              LOAD        ZERO           --Step 5. Increment negcount if

              COMPARE     N              --N is less than zero

              JUMPGE      SKIP

              INCREMENT   NEGCOUNT

SKIP:         INCREMENT   I              --Step 6. Count one more loop iteration

              JUMP        LOOP           --Step 7. and start the loop over

ENDLOOP:      OUT         NEGCOUNT       --Step 8. Produce the final answer

              HALT                       --Step 9. and halt

NEGCOUNT:     .DATA       0

I:            .DATA       1

N:            .DATA       0

ONE:          .DATA       1

FIFTY:        .DATA       50

ZERO:         .DATA       0

              .END
```

2.

a.

COMPARE = 0111   Y = decimal 10 = 0000 0000 1010
instruction = 0111 0000 0000 1010

b.

JUMPNEQ = 1100   DONE = decimal 7 = 0000 0000 0111
instruction = 1100 0000 0000 0111

c.

DECREMENT = 0110   LOOP = decimal 0 = 0000 0000 0000
instruction = 0110 0000 0000 0000

3. LOOP is the address of an instruction (IN X), but decrement is treating it as though it were a piece of data and subtracting 1 from it. Thus what this instruction is doing is "computing" (IN X) − 1, which is meaningless. However, the computer will be very happy to carry out this meaningless operation.

4. The address values that you come up with will depend entirely on your solution. The symbol table for the program in Question 1 would be as follows: (*Note:* The solution assumes that each instruction occupies one memory location.)

Symbol	Address
LOOP	3

SKIP	11
ENDLOOP	13
NEGCOUNT	15
I	16
N	17
ONE	18
FIFTY	19
ZERO	20

Section 6.4.1

If there is 1 chance in 4 that a program is blocked waiting for input/output, then there is a $(1/4) \times (1/4) = 1$ chance in 16 that both of the two programs in memory are simultaneously blocked waiting for I/O. Therefore, the processor will be busy 15/16, or about 94%, of the time. This is the processor utilization. If we increase the number of programs in memory to 4, then the probability that all 4 of these programs are blocked at the same time waiting for I/O is $(1/4) \times (1/4) \times (1/4) \times (1/4) = 1$ chance in 256. Now the utilization of the processor is 255/256, or about 99.6%. We can see clearly now why in a multiprocessor system it is helpful to have more programs in memory. It increases the likelihood that at least one program will always be ready to run.

CHAPTER 7

Section 7.4

1. the first three
2. **int** Number;
3. 12; 12 * 4 = 48
4. Box[0][0]

Section 7.5.1

1. cout << "Enter a value for Quantity" << endl;
   cin >> Quantity;
2. cout << setw(6) << Height << endl;
3. This isgoodbye

Section 7.5.2

1. Next = NewNumber;
2. 55.00

Section 7.5.3

1. 30
2. 3
   5
   7

> 9
> 11
> 13
> 15
> 17
> 19
> 21

3. Yes

4. **6**

5.
```
if (Night == Day)
    cout << "Equal" << endl;
```

Section 7.6.1

1.
```
//program to read in and write out
//user's initials

#include <iostream.h>
void main()
{
    char First_Initial, Last_Initial;

    cout << "Give your first and last initials."
        << endl;
    cin >> First_Initial >> Last_Initial;
    cout << "Your initials are" << First_Initial
        << Last_Initial << endl;
}
```

2.
```
//program to compute cost based on price per item
//and quantity purchased

#include <iostream.h>
void main()
{
    double price, cost;
    int quantity;

    cout.setf(ios::fixed);
    cout.precision(2);

    cout << "What is the price of the item?" << endl;
    cin >> price;
    cout << "How many of this item are being
        << purchased?" << endl;
    cin >> quantity;
    cost = price * quantity;
    cout << "The total cost for this item is $" << cost
     << endl;
}
```

3.

```cpp
//program to test a number relative to 5
//and write out the number or its double

#include <iostream.h>
void main()
{
    int number;

    cout << "Enter a number:";
    cin >> number;
    if (number < 5)
            cout << number;
    else
            cout << 2*number;
    cout << endl;
}
```

4.

```cpp
//program to collect a number, then write all
//the values from 1 to that number

#include <iostream.h>
void main()
{
    int number;
    int counter;

    cout << "Enter a positive number" << endl;
    cin >> number;
    counter = 1;
    while (counter <= number)
    {
        cout << counter << endl;
        counter = counter + 1;
    }
}
```

Section 7.7

1. 11

2. 7

3.

```cpp
void Get_Input(int &One, int &Two)
{
    cout << "Please enter two integers" << endl;
    cin >> One >> Two;
}
```

4. a. `double Tax(double Subtotal)`

   b. `return Subtotal*Rate;`

   c. `cout << "The tax is " << Tax(Subtotal) << endl;`

CHAPTER 8

Section 8.2.1

```
ITIME .LE. 7
```

Section 8.2.2

```
cout << setw(18) << "This is the output" << endl;
```

Section 8.2.3

no

Section 8.2.4

1. *Rate* refers to the contents of the memory cell called Rate; *&Rate* refers to the address of that cell.

2. 10

Section 8.2.5

Prints the numbers from 1 through 10 on a single line with a blank space between them.

Section 8.3.3

1. ```
The area of a square with side 10 is 100
```

2. Height and Base

*Section 8.4*

1. Results in the names of all vendors from Chicago

2. These are the *times* that try **men's souls**

*Section 8.5.1*

1. a. (2 3 4)

   b. 5

2. ```
(define (threeplus x)
   (+ 3 x))
```

Section 8.5.2

1. ```
No
```

2. ```
X = jefferson
```

3. ```
X = lincoln
X = fdr
X = kennedy
X = nixon
```

*Section 8.5.3*

1. One processor could compute $A + B$ while another computes $C + D$. A third processor could then take the two quantities $A + B$ and $C + D$ and compute their sum.
```

Parallel processing uses a total of two time slots: one to do the two additions $A + B$ and $C + D$ simultaneously and then one to do the addition $(A + B) + (C + D)$. Sequential processing would require a total of three time slots: $(A + B)$, then $(A + B) + C$, then $((A + B) + C) + D$.

CHAPTER 9

Section 9.2.1

1.

Token	Classification
x	1
=	3
x	1
+	4
1	2
;	6

2.

Token	Classification
if	8
(	10
a	1
+	4
b42	1
==	7
0	2
)	11
a	1
=	3
z	1
−	5
12	2
;	6

Section 9.2.2

1. <Boolean operator> :: = AND | OR | NOT

2. <identifier>   :: = <first> <second>

   <first>   :: = i | j

   <second>   :: = <letter> | <digit> | Λ

   <letter>   :: = A | B | C | D | ... | Z

   <digit>   :: = 0 | 1 | 2 | ... | 9

   <identifier> is the goal symbol

3. <expression>   :: = (<var> <op> <var>)

   <var>   :: = x | y | z

   <op>   :: = < | == | >

4.

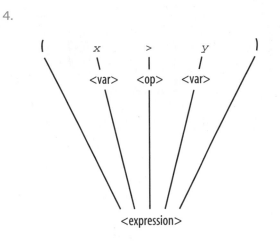

5. You eventually reach the point in the parse where you have the following sequence:

    (<var> <op>)

    which does not match the right-hand side of any rule, and the parse fails.

6. The first rule of Question 3 could be changed to

    <expression> :: = (<var> <op> <var>) | <var> <op> <var>

Section 9.2.2

1.

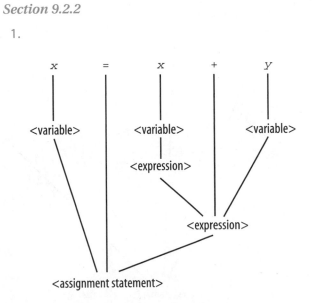

2.

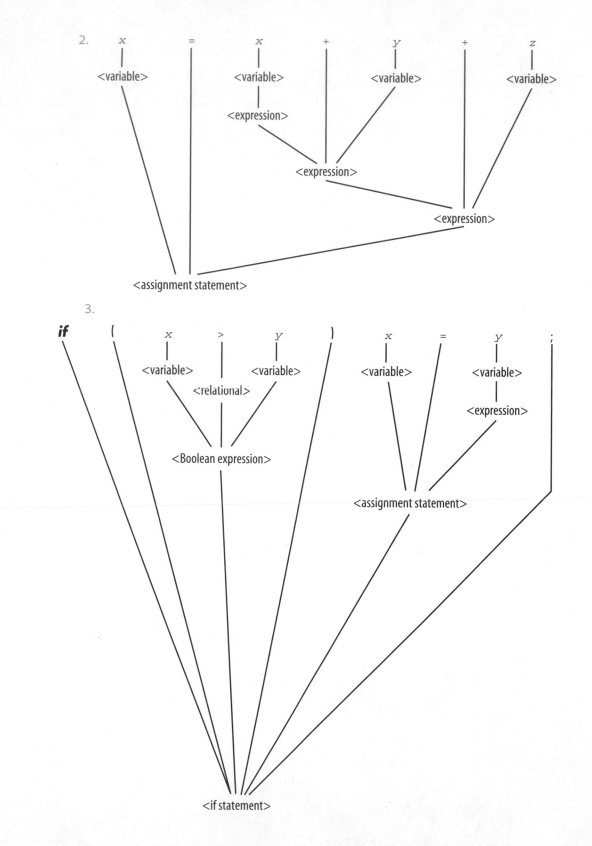

3.

4. The language consists of all strings containing an arbitrary sequence of a and b of length 1 or more.

5. <goal> ::= <pair> | <pair> <goal>

   <pair> ::= AB

Section 9.2.3

The parse tree for this expression is

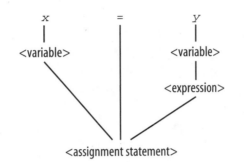

During the construction of this parse tree, you will build four semantic records, two for <variable>, one for <expression>, and one for <assignment statement>.

The code generated is

```
         LOAD      Y
         STORE     TEMP
         LOAD      TEMP
         STORE     X
           .
           .
           .
  X:     .DATA     0
  Y:     .DATA     0
TEMP:    .DATA     0
```

CHAPTER 10

Section 10.2

1. Piloting a boat, performing an operation, fighting a fire.

2. Soil conditions, water supply, types of industrial waste. It could illustrate long-term effects of various waste disposal policies. If it were inaccurate, policies based on the model could be pursued that would result in environmental damage.

Section 10.3

1. a.

$$b\,1\,0\,1\,b$$
$$\uparrow$$
$$2$$

b.

$$b\,1\,1\,1\,b$$
$$\uparrow$$
$$2$$

c.

$$b\,1\,1\,1\,b$$
$$\uparrow$$
$$2$$

d.

$$b\,0\,1\,1\,1\,b$$
$$\uparrow$$
$$1$$

2. $b\,0\,1\,0\,b$

Section 10.5

1. a. $b\,1\,1\,0\,1\,0\,b$

2. $b\,1\,1\,1\,1\,b\,1\,1\,1\,1\,1\,b$ becomes
$b\,b\,b\,1\,1\,1\,1\,1\,1\,1\,1\,b$

3. $(1,1,1,1,R)$
$(1,0,0,1,R)$
$(1,b,1,2,R)$

Section 10.7

1. To prove that something is not true, assume that it is and arrive at a contradiction. The assumption must then be wrong.

CHAPTER 11

Section 11.2

1. 1622.82

2. D5*(1 + ($C$8 + G5)/100)*E5

3. a.
D1: Tax
D2: C2*0.05

b.
D1: Tax Rate
D2: 0.05

E1: Tax
E2: C2*D2

Section 11.3

1. 149   12.35

2.

```
SELECT EMPLOYEE.NAME, POLICY.MONTHLYCOST

FROM EMPLOYEE, INSURANCE, POLICY

WHERE EMPLOYEE.NAME = 'Fred Takasano' AND

EMPLOYEE.ID = INSURANCE.ID AND

INSURANCE.PLANTYPE = POLICY.PLANTYPE
```

3.

```
SELECT ID

FROM INSURANCE

WHERE PLANTYPE = 'A4';
```

Section 11.4

(The following answers were generated using the package **Mathematica**.)

1. **N[4*Pi, 100]**
   12.56637061435917295385057353311801153678867759750042328389977836923126562514483599451213930136846827

2. **Plot[x^3 − 6x^2 + 11x − 6, {x, − 5, +10}]**

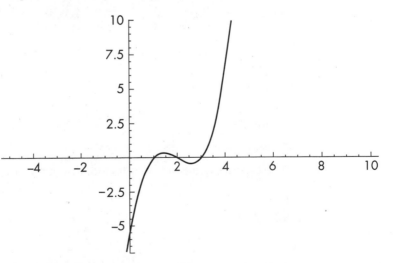

Solve[x^3 − 6x^2 + 11x − 6 = = 0, x]

{ {x → 1}, {x → 2}, {x → 3} }

3. **Integrate[(4/x^4) + (3/x^3), x]**

$$-\frac{4}{3x^3} - \frac{3}{2x^2}$$

CHAPTER 13

Section 13.3

For example, a hamburger is a kind of sandwich. As such, it comes between two pieces of bread, but it is hot. It may have various condiments, such as mustard, ketchup, and pickle.

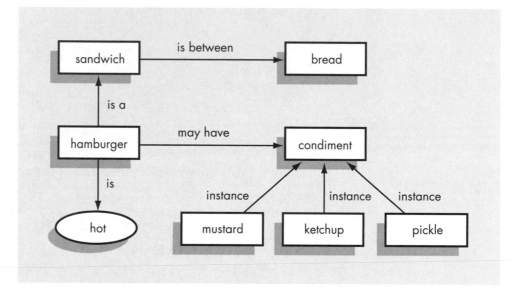

Section 13.4

No. N1 and N4 fire, but N2 and N3 do not, so N5 does not.

Section 13.5

1. Frank is tall.

2. No conclusion can be inferred. Frank may or may not be tall.

CHAPTER 14

Section 14.2.2

1. Watches, microwave ovens, automobiles, burglar alarms, calculators

2. A telegraph

Section 14.3.6

1. a. Hunting licenses
      Records of federal loans and credits
      Passport information
      . . . and many, many others

   b. Magazine subscriptions
      Calls to 1-800 and 1-900 numbers
      Cable TV records
      Insurance information
      . . . and many, many others

Section 14.4

2. a. It would likely be correct every time.

   b. It is quite probable that one or two of the customers will get an incorrect bill.

   c. There is a greater likelihood of error in the telephone billing system because it probably relies on people to enter the raw data—for example, the date when the last payment was received or the amount of money received. There is a significant chance of an error occurring during that manual operation.